# INFORMATION SYSTEMS
# FOR PLANNING
# AND DECISION MAKING

# INFORMATION SYSTEMS
# FOR PLANNING
# AND DECISION MAKING

The Strategic and Operational Management
of Human Resources, Finance, Manufacturing
and Marketing Through Information

## Ernest A. Kallman, Ph.D.
*Professor of Computer Information Systems*
*Bentley College*

## Leon Reinharth, Ph.D.
*Executive Vice President*
*Hoan Products Ltd.*

**VNR** VAN NOSTRAND REINHOLD COMPANY
NEW YORK  CINCINNATI  TORONTO  LONDON  MELBOURNE

Copyright © 1984 by Van Nostrand Reinhold Company Inc.

Library of Congress Catalog Card Number: 83-5817
ISBN: 0-442-25628-0

Manufactured in the United States of America

Published by Van Nostrand Reinhold Company Inc.
135 West 50th Street
New York, New York 10020

Van Nostrand Reinhold Company Limited
Molly Millars Lane
Wokingham, Berkshire RG11 2PY, England

Van Nostrand Reinhold
480 Latrobe Street
Melbourne, Victoria 3000, Australia

Macmillan of Canada
Division of Gage Publishing Limited
164 Commander Boulevard
Agincourt, Ontario M1S 3C7, Canada

15  14  13  12  11  10  9  8  7  6  5  4  3  2  1

**Library of Congress Cataloging in Publication Data**

Kallman, Ernest A.
  Information systems for planning and decision making.

  Includes index.
  1. Management information systems.   I. Reinharth,
Leon.   II. Title.
T58.6.K34      1983        658.4'0388       83-5817
ISBN 0-442-25628-0

To
Sandy Kallman
and
Françoise Reinharth

# Foreword

Sun Tzu, a Chinese general who wrote one of the great books on war about 2500 years ago, stated that victory usually goes to the side with the best information.[1] Sun Tzu wanted good information about the enemy, his own forces, his allies, neutrals, the general political framework of the conflict, terrain, weather, and all the other factors that could affect the outcome of conflict. He was also at pains to deny information to his adversaries or to provide them with inaccurate or misleading information. Sun Tzu was a highly successful general. His work is revered by modern military and intelligence managers. His writing on information (and disinformation) forms one of the basic texts of the Russian KGB.

The information needs of modern corporate organizations are not much different. You must know about your market, your competitors, your capabilities, your suppliers, distribution channels, government activities and intentions, political and social trends, changes in technology, and a host of other factors that affect your success. If you have the information and use it well you and your organization are likely to succeed while competitors fail.

This is a book about information and the information systems used to gather, process and present the information you have. It covers the information you need to do your job, where and how you get it, how you organize it, and what you do with it. It is a practical book, for use by managers and staff at all levels of the organization, and covers the special information needs of each functional area: Human Resources, Finance, Manufacturing and Marketing.

Since most large organizations use computers, the management of information by computers is covered in some detail. At present these systems have intriguing names such as Management Information Systems (MIS) or Decision Support Systems (DSS). These acronyms are labels for the current fads of modern management. New systems with new acronyms are on the way such as Artificial Intelligence (AI) and Videotex. This book tells you about them and what to do about them. Remember that people were running organizations long before there were computers. They also needed information to manage their organizations and they needed information systems—however casual they may have been—to organize their information.

Computers are useful tools if properly used. They are not themselves an answer to your problems. In fact, if your basic systems are not well designed and well managed, computers will only make your problems worse. The basic rule is, *If you cannot do it by hand, you cannot do it with a computer.* Computers are fast. If you incorporate

---

[1] *Ping-fa* "The Art of War"

them into poor systems, your vital information will become a jumbled mess with appalling swiftness.

In practice the main advantage of computers has been to force organizations to improve their systems. Once a company spends the money for computer hardware, then faces the stunning costs of the software, operations, and maintenance, it ceases to be possible to ignore the basic systems. The systems could have been improved without the computer. But without that outlay of cash nothing would have been done. This book guides the functional or general manager through the systems development process to provide an adequate return for this computer expense.

The basic purpose of this book is to insure you get the right information, in a timely manner and at a reasonable cost. The authors, who have extensive business and computer backgrounds, bring a wealth of experience to this guide for management. They know how to write. Their planning book* has been well received, and they are frequent contributors to *Planning Review,* the journal of the North American Society for Corporate Planning.** They have supplemented their own views with those of other experts and with actual examples from real companies such as Prudential Insurance Company of America, Cannon Mills and Ogden Corporation.

Read this book carefully. Think how the material can be applied to your organization. Design your systems. Get them working. Then get your computer to make your systems work faster and—with a little luck—more profitably.

MALCOM W. PENNINGTON
Senior Editor, *Planning Review*
President, The Marketing & Planning Group, Inc.

---

*Leon Reinherth, H. Jack Shapiro, and Ernest Kallman, *The Practice of Planning: Strategic, Administrative, and Operational* (New York: Van Nostrand and Reinhold, 1981).
**For more information on the North American Society for Corporate Planning or *Planning Review* contact the society at P.O. Box 1288, 300 Arcade Square, Dayton, OH 45402 or telephone (513) 223–4948.

# Preface

## WHY SHOULD YOU READ THIS BOOK?

You already know the value of information. You are successful in your trade or profession. You probably have a computer in your organization and may even have a personal computer at home. But you also know that things are changing rapidly and in no place are they changing more rapidly than the area of information management and use. In some areas there is more information than you need, and in others there is not enough. The environment both in and outside the organization is becoming increasingly dynamic and complex. There are so many areas that need automation that you do not have enough resources to serve them all. And it is hard to set the priorities for the resources you do have. If you're not a data processing professional, you really don't understand what the technicians are doing and perhaps don't even trust them! If you are a data processing professional you are sure you are misunderstood and are angry with those it is your job to serve.

## WHY DID WE WRITE THIS BOOK?

We are convinced that knowledge is the key to understanding; and that knowledge of information is the key to allowing a manager to plan better, to make better decisions and to maintain control of the functions he or she is managing. Knowledge of information means understanding the importance of information to the organization, recognizing the relationship of information to organization structure, knowing how to manage information and being able to deal with the information technicians. Specifically it means choosing the right information to support each corporate function. Individual managerial performance and ultimate corporate success require a manager to deal successfully with information. But most managers have not been trained in this essential skill. They need assistance in managing their information resource.

## WHAT DOES THIS BOOK DO?

The books cuts through the jargon and explains to the manager key information systems concepts in clear, understandable terms. The reader will achieve an understanding of how to deal effectively with information as a resource and with the data processing or information systems professional whose responsibility is providing information support to the organization. In addition, the book contains dozens of actual corporate reports to illustrate the kinds of information managers use at both the strategic and operational levels in the areas of finance, human resources, manufacturing and marketing.

## HOW DO YOU USE THIS BOOK?

Chapters are sequenced to build knowledge and confidence in the reader with little prior experience with information systems. More knowledgeable readers can access specific chapters immediately. For example, the knowledgeable information systems specialist can skim chapters 1, 2, 8 and 9, using them for reference and refreshers. On the other hand, this kind of individual will want to examine chapters 3 through 7 carefully as they provide the details of each functional area and its strategic and operational perspective. Likewise, managers familiar with a particular functional area, for instance, personnel, may want to skim the text portion of the human resources chapter but then pay particular attention to the actual reports and outputs from industry. Similarly they will be able to make good use of the information systems (IS) chapters to enable them to deal effectively with IS professionals. Those new to a particular functional area will benefit not only from the outputs provided but from the chapter text which has sections on the description of the function, management information requirements and sources of data.

The information systems chapters are supported by annotated reference lists to encourage further reading in specialized areas. Those four chapters also contain reprints of pertinent articles from the current literature which amplify significant points in the chapter. In addition an appendix contains general articles dealing with areas complementary to the purposes of this book: information systems job descriptions, preparing a request for a hardware or software proposal, dealing with vendors and the pros and cons of a distributed processing system.

The functional chapters have, in addition to the sample outputs, short article reprints, sample procedure manuals, some full article reprints and other documentation to explain fully the areas being discussed.

## HOW IS THIS BOOK ORGANIZED?

There are nine chapters. The first chapter describes the interrelationship between the planning function and the information processing function, and how critical the successful performance of one is to the other. The role of information in the organization is described in detail showing how each organizational level has unique information needs. The kind of planning performed at each level is also reviewed and a connection is made between a level's information needs, the planning performed at that level and the kinds of decisionmaking required. The various kinds of decisions are described (structured, semistructured and unstructured) and the implications of these types for information processing and computers are explained. Finally, the pattern that an organization follows in moving towards a totally computerized information/decisionmaking system is detailed, including the pitfalls and processes common to this evolution.

Chapter 2 describes the steps to be taken in the developing of any information system. The system development plan is then linked to the corporate plan through a discussion of the planning process and the factors than inhibit corporate planning. The need for top management involvement, communication and control in both processes are emphasized. The structure and function of the information systems department is outlined and the role of that department in the organization defined. The concepts of Data Base Management Systems (DBMS), Distributed Data Processing (DDP) and Office Automation (OA) are included as examples of the opportunities that imaginative information systems managers have for servicing the firm. Lastly there is a discussion of the project control and information analysis aids available to the manager of the systems development project. Among the topics discussed are the structured approaches to information analysis, design and control.

The strategic decision perspective is provided in chapter 3. This includes an analysis of the strategic decisionmaking environment and the sources of information external to the organization. Decision Support Systems (DSS) are defined, their functions and components explained and a number of DSS applications described. DSS implementation problems are also discussed. The outputs presented include an IBM ten-year marketing perspective, a Human Resource Model from Prudential Insurance Company of America, a financial model from Management Decision Systems, Inc., and an example of a DSS financial model from Ferox Microsystems Incorporated, as well as some brief articles on the threat of too much information and how to use a computer to create a long-range plan.

A preface to the next four chapters describes the professional and trade associations available to the professional manager and encourages their use as a source of current information. The format of these four chapters is similar in that each describes a functional area, management's information requirements in that area, the sources of this data, sample information system outputs and an evaluation of those outputs. Chapter 4 deals with the Sales-Marketing Information System. The key outputs are actual reports from Cannon Mills Inc. Chapter 5 deals with Manufacturing and describes the opportunities being offered by robotics, computer automated design (CAD) and computer automated manufacturing (CAM). The outputs are primarily those of Standard Motor Products, Inc. Chapter 6 is the Personnel or Human Resources chapter. One objective of this chapter is to describe the expansion of the personnel function to include all aspects of the firm's human resources. The outputs and procedures are primarily from The Prudential Insurance Company. Chapter 7, the final functional chapter, handles the financial area. For this section the Ogden Corporation provided many of the reports and forms shown, as well as outputs from Ferox Microsystems Incorporated and Mini-Computer Systems, Inc.

Chapter 8 picks up the information systems theme by examining the decisions that have to be made in the procurement of computer hardware and the complicated process of deciding whether to make or buy computer software. The different kinds of software are explained and the skills required for a programming staff are described. The steps in the software purchase decision are listed and fully explained. In the hardware area the potential for microcomputers in the business environment is examined and the differences between these and the larger computers are weighed in terms of performance, availability and support.

But the current state of the art is not the final word in computer development. The future is the theme of Chapter 9. Demands for information will increase and the technology to provide it will improve. But there will be problems and challenges that will have to be faced by the manager of the future. The problems/challenges lie in the areas of data communications, home information retrieval systems, software personnel availability, hardware advancements, changes in hardware distribution and service offerings, and the kinds of applications developed. The chapter concludes with some suggestions on how to meet these challenges.

ERNEST A. KALLMAN, Ph.D.
LEON REINHARTH, Ph.D.

# Acknowledgments

To all those who helped in so many ways with this effort we offer our sincere gratitude.

Thanks especially for their ideas and information:

Dick Baldi
Joe Boverman
Don Burnstine
Stan Frankel
Dick Grimley
Steve Haeckel
Jim Hendrickson
Frank Kaepplein
Al Levin
John Patterson
Marijane Whiteman
John Zachman

For their advice and inspiration:

June and Jim Coates
John Gorgone
Jerry and Lorraine Kallman
Frank and Gail Mertz
Gene and Boo Robinson
Paul Schneiderhan
Jack Shapiro
Arthur and Betty Stevens
Andy Taaffe
Sue Wiles

For their aid and perspiration:

Gene Corbo
June DiMattia
Mitch Grossberg
Sharon Hays
Coleen McCarthy

We are particularly grateful to Jim Krok for his assistance with the section on micros and Sandy Kallman for her contribution to the software make or buy discussion. And finally we pay tribute to Malcolm Pennington without whose various kinds of support and worthwhile insights this work would never have come about.

E.K.
L.R.

# LIST OF INFORMATION SYSTEM OUTPUTS

# Contents

# INFORMATION SYSTEMS
# FOR PLANNING
# AND DECISION MAKING

# PART I

# 1
# Information: The Vital Resource

## IS MANAGEMENT DIFFERENT TODAY?

You've seen ads like the ones in Figure 1–1 urging the need to control management information; touting software packages that do almost anything from financial planning, manufacturing control and order processing to supporting high-level management decisionmaking; and suggesting the use of development aids that permit inexperienced users to easily communicate with the computer.

You've also read the headlines and heard the speakers. "We're in the age of information!" "The explosion is happening." "Unless we get our information under control it will bury us." You've seen the catch-phrases and initials such as information resource management (IRM), decision support systems (DSS), distributed data processing (DDP), management information systems (MIS) and the warnings that management must somehow embrace these or suffer the consequences. And you wonder whether this is just alarmist rhetoric or must every manager somehow do something different than he has done for the last twenty years.

After all why should you act differently? You are successul in your trade. You make effective decisions now. You know the value of information and perhaps are even satisfied with the quality and quantity of the information you now receive. You probably have a computer in your organization and may even have a personal computer in your home. So what do all these exhortations mean to the businessman like you? Is there some danger in continuing to deal with the information function as in the past?

The danger lies not only in the expanding volume of information available to management, but also in a corresponding accelerating rate of change in the technology designed to cope with this deluge. And both these phenomena must be addressed if the firm is to gain the greatest value from its information. The information processing approach that is adequate for today will surely not serve management's needs in the future.

As management learns to use the new technology to provide more accurate, timely and complete information, decisions and decisionmaking techniques will improve. If better information is not sought and used, the firm risks losing ground to competitors who have met their information needs. The difference is that successful firms will *manage* their information, not just *process* it.

But how is the information managed? What information is needed? These and other questions are addressed in this and subsequent chapters. But the first question

Figure 1–1A. Ad produced by Schachter, Grambor & Associates, Inc., 16 E 42nd St., New York, NY.

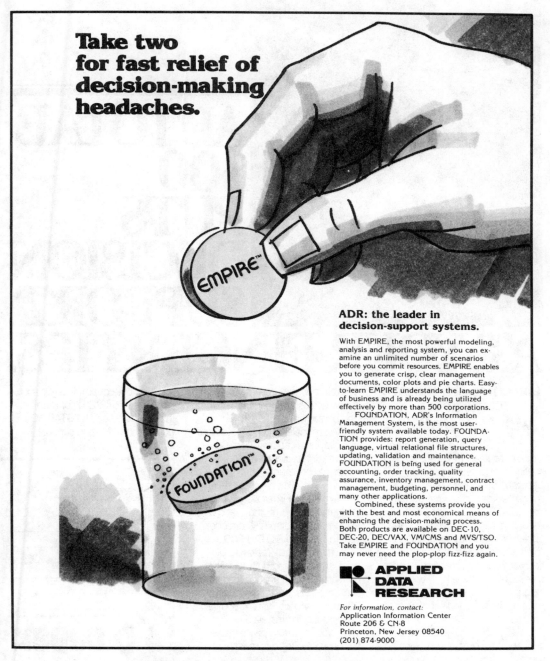

Figure 1–1B. Reprinted with permission from Applied Data Research, Inc.

Figure 1–1C. Reprinted with permission from CAPEX Corporation.

Figure 1–1D. Reproduced courtesy of SPSS Inc.

is who is responsible for information management? The answer is that each manager is ultimately responsible for his own information needs. The organization must be structured in such a way that control of the information resource is shifted from the data processing (DP) technicians to the managers who can best take responsibility for its generation, accuracy and use. The technicians are then left with the task of making that information available where it is needed in a timely and reliable manner. There is still an undeniable need for the DP technician, but the DP responsibility has changed from processing the information to providing a service.

## MANAGE THE INFORMATION AND THE TECHNICIANS

Traditionally, corporate management has allowed DP technicians to acquire the available technology and through control of the technology "rule" the information function. Management was able to get only the information the DP technicians were willing to provide. In many organizations this was not a problem since the information provided was of better quality than that formerly available. But a point is reached in every organization sooner or later when the decision must be made whether this approach should continue or the information itself should be managed, i.e., whether the technology decisions should follow from the information need.

Managing the technology, the old approach, meant leaving the initiative to bring improvements and new applications into the system as technological advances allowed in the hands of the data processing techinicans. Often new technology was acquired simply to upgrade professional DP skills with only minimal residual benefit to the organization in improved information. Managing the information, on the other hand, means establishing the organization's total information needs and building a technical system which fulfills them.

To establish an organization's total information needs, managers must understand what information is, its importance to all levels in the organization, and its relationship to decisionmaking at those levels. In addition, since many organizations have a computer installation and most organizations that do not are candidates for one, it is essential that managers understand the role of the computer in the information function.

The first chapter focuses on information and what it is all about.* Once the implications of information for the organization are clear, it is important to insure that the information resource is being used effectively. Insights into how this is done begin in chapter 2. Subsequent chapters detail the kinds of information real organizations use. And the final chapters review the computer hardware and software options open to management.

---

*It is often useful to distinguish data from information. Such a distinction is usually made on the state of usefulness of the element rather than its form or content. Thus, what is *useful information* in one operation may be *raw data* in another. For example, knowing the exact amount a customer owes is useful information to a credit check, but it is only one of many small pieces of raw data that the controller aggregates into meaningful information in his attempt to forecast cash flows. For purposes of the discussions in this book the distinction between data and information is seen as unimportant and the words are used more or less interchangeably.

## INFORMATION AND ORGANIZATION

Information defines the organization. In other words each business function at any level in the organization is made unique by the content, volume and use of the information it generates, transmits and receives. For instance, in credit checking, the information received to aid in checking credit properly includes the dates and amounts of all outstanding charges, the customer's payment history over a period of time, other orders outstanding, length of time as a customer and the like. The information generated might include totals of outstanding invoices and the flagging and totaling of those over ninety days old. The transmitted information is the final credit determination, i.e., approval or denial. The more we define the information used, the more we define the function. If no credit history exists we have a very shallow credit-checking function. If extensive information exists the function will be elaborate and perhaps the credit check more thorough.

Another way to relate information to the organization is to state that *information follows function*. No organizational function exists without information and there is an ideal set of information which contributes to the optimum output from this function. This ideal information set is what every information system seeks to achieve, one with the qualities of completeness, timeliness, accuracy and appropriateness. Optimum output from a function leads to higher quality management decisions. Better managers result from better decisions. Better decisions result from better information. Better information results from understanding who is responsible for its generation, transmission and accuracy. But most important is knowing precisely what information is required for each function at each organizational level.

Figure 1–2 represents the decisionmaking levels in the organization, the functions at each level and the information flows into and out of the organization. The basic triangular shape represents the classic view of organization structure. Strategic management is at the apex where objectives are set and long-range planning takes place. Moving down toward the middle, administrative management takes over and resources are allocated to specific functional areas. This middle management structure then cascades to the operational level where the day-to-day activities are performed based on a series of goals, budgets and product programs. In most firms this level is supported by an operational data processing system using details of each transaction to generate reports providing operational measurements and controls. The following sections will describe Figure 1–2 in some detail, defining the activities at each management level and the dependency between levels. The kinds of information needed to support each level will be particularly stressed, drawing the conclusion that it is more than just the operational level which needs an information system to make it viable.

### Strategic Level Information

Significant corporate information needs are filled from outside the firm through inputs from five major constituencies: *customers, government, investors, the public and competition.* Likewise, these components of the external environment seek information outputs from the organization. In the customer area, the major inputs

Figure 1-2. Organizational decisionmaking levels and functions.

to the firm are orders for products or services. Often these are requests for new products or variations on old products and thus indicate market trends and new opportunity areas. Outputs to the customer, in addition to the requested products themselves, range from general performance information on which to evaluate the firm as a whole (financial stability, size, geographic locations, etc.) to specific product support information for insuring effective product use such as maintenance aid and user training.

Laws and regulations constitute the major government inputs to the firm. This is true at all governmental levels and the complexity seems to increase as higher levels become involved. The ultimate complexity is probably represented by the multinational situation where many governmental levels in two or more countries are involved. Sometimes it is unclear which body has jurisdiction in some multinational situations, and even more governmental involvement, perhaps a trade treaty, may be required to resolve the dispute. These governmental inputs are signals to industry which seek a specific response from industry.

Antitrust legislation tries to reduce the monopolistic power of a few large concerns. This is a signal to the smaller firm that it can remain in the market and will receive protection from the government. Tax legislation often fosters investments through tax credits or encourages R & D through early write-offs. Then too there are units of government that provide information more directly. Most notable among these organizations are the Bureau of the Census and the U.S. Government Printing Office.

The information the government seeks is not only enormous in volume but results in a significant cost to the firm. Besides "normal" tax reporting there are "Equal Employment Opportunity" reports, "Occupational Safety" reports and "Retirement Fund" reports to name just a few. Specific regulated industries also have their own reports such as those prepared by interstate trucking firms for the Interstate Commerce Commission and those of the pharmaceutical manufacturers which report to the Food and Drug Administration.

Inputs from investors may be more indirect than those of the other constituencies. If company performance, perhaps in terms of profits or dividends, is not "acceptable" the investor may sell his shares and this will affect the stock price which will indicate to management the dropping level of investor confidence. Outputs to investors include formal financial reporting as well as advertising and other forms of public relations activity.

The hardest constituency to define is the public. This is because its membership includes some members of the other groups and also because the nature of the public is such that it is difficult to find its leadership, define its structure or even address its needs. As with customers, government and investors, the public's general input is that it wants the firm to be a good citizen. Perhaps by joining with other groups the public may make demands for product safety or corporate social responsibility. The outputs from the firm to the other groups are also the outputs to the general public but probably most important is the aptly named public relations effort.

And finally, much information is provided among competitors from their own outputs to the external environment and through their actions in the marketplace: product offerings, prices, distribution channels, advertising and the like.

These external information sources impact most heavily the strategic planning level. This level is primarily the concern of corporate (top) management, and the information is essential to formulating corporate goals and objectives.

The strategic planning level is primarily concerned with solving problems and making decisions with long time horizons. The kind of decisions included are those that have to do with analyzing what business area the firm is in now, what areas it would like to be in at some future date, what levels of achievement (profitability, return on investment, etc.) it is capable of under present circumstances and what levels it could attain under various alternative approaches.

Companies have four general alternatives to choose from when considering strategic direction: (1) expansion within their own industry, (2) diversification into a new industry, (3) divestment of existing questionable assets, and (4) a strategy of wait and see.

The process of choosing one or more of these alternatives is the essence of strategic planning. Such planning requires the active participation of key officers in risk-taking and decisionmaking, the ability to analyze data under conditions of uncertainty about the future, and most of all the accumulation of huge amounts of information from both internal and external sources.

## Administrative Level Information

Information accumulated from the strategic planning activity flows down to the administrative or management control level in the form of medium-range goals. This middle level is concerned with the task of structuring the firm's resources in order to create a maximum performance potential. Administrative managers do this by translating the chosen strategic alternatives into medium-range plans that will serve as guidelines for the achievement of the short-range goals of the operating managers.

These lower levels of decisionmaking are quite function-dependent. That is, they are organized around the functional process itself. Therefore, it is necessary to understand the scope of those functions in order to properly treat their information needs. The following sections detail the major administrative functions as displayed in Figure 1–2: *marketing, production, human resources, finance and information.*

**Marketing (The Product-Market Function).** *   In an industrial firm, the product-market function is the key element—it determines the scope of all other functions in the organization. The same principle holds true for service, nonprofit, or governmental organizations, except that a unique service replaces the product concept and a term such as *client* or *public* is used instead of *market*. The importance of this function is evident because the organization exists primarily to supply a product or service to its clients or market. The administrative executive will thus initiate his or her planning task through the product-market function.

During the administrative planning cycle, a certain portion of the total product line or agency service will inevitably reach the end of the life cycle and will have to be replaced by other products or services if market share is to be maintained or enhanced. New product development and introduction are major components of the marketing function, and they present a significant challenge to the ingenuity of the administrative planner. Each new product must fit into the concept of the strategic marketing plan.

If administrative planners are to achieve the goals of the product-market function, product planning must go hand in hand with market analysis. This analysis should include:

1. a demographic profile of current and potential users of the product as well as users of competitive products,
2. a definition of the total market for the product,
3. the major characteristics of the relevant market,
4. current and projected share of the market for the product,
5. strengths and weaknesses of competitors' marketing,
6. quantity and value of market by various channels of distribution.

---

*This section and the three following have been adapted from Leon Reinharth, H. Jack Shapiro and Ernest A. Kallman, *The Practice of Planning: Strategic, Administrative, and Operational* (New York: Van Nostrand Reinhold, 1981).

Depending on their evaluation of these market statistics, administrative planners may then develop various strategies.

In the development of strategy for the product-market function, pricing and promotion must also be considered. A pricing decision takes into account such factors as profitability, competition, the characteristics of the product, market or sales expectations, and consistency with product-line price structure. The options available for the promotion of the product include advertising, public relations, point of sale material, contests, sweepstakes and special offers. The final decision on marketing strategy should thus incorporate product, market, price and promotion factors. A classic example of comprehensive marketing strategy is the campaign conducted each year by automobile manufacturers to introduce their new models.

Once the decision makers at all the affected levels have agreed upon the administrative marketing strategy, the functional planners attached to the operating divisions prepare detailed specifications of which resources and facilities will be needed to insure that these functions coordinate with and help to implement the marketing strategy. Thus, production plans are drawn up to indicate how and at what cost the manufacturing function will contribute to the fulfillment of the marketing strategy. The production planner must take into account plant facilities and locations, technological developments affecting tooling and other manufacturing equipment, and production engineering for more efficient methods, planning, scheduling and control systems, and personnel and organization factors.

**Production (The Inventory and Material Requirements Function).** Planners must decide how much of a product must be produced to fulfill the projected goals. They must also consider (1) maintaining satisfactory inventory levels and (2) stabilizing production.

In a typical manufacturing or trading company, investment in inventories is substantial. The dangers of obsolescence and possible decline in the value of inventories are always present. Even if prevailing market conditions do not jeopardize the value of the inventory, the cost of maintaining excess inventories could severely strain the financial resources of the company. On the other hand, the company must be able to deliver its goods within a reasonable period of time after accepting a sales order. The best inventory level then permits filling all sales orders quickly and yet keeps the dollar investment in inventories at a minimum.

When establishing inventory levels, the planners and production managers must consider stabilizing production. Stable production is desirable because it increases productivity by reducing idle plant capacity and minimizing labor turnover. Such stability of production can be achieved despite sales fluctuations by permitting the level of inventories to fluctuate within established minimum and maximum limits.

A sound management policy should achieve a balance between production and inventory levels after the sales forecast is prepared. A range of permissible inventory levels is set for each item of inventory. Inventory requirements are revised only if there are major changes in the production process or if general business conditions affect the availability of materials and credit.

The next step is to relate the inventory requirements to budgeted sales and production to determine the minimum and maximum inventory levels needed during the year. We can then estimate the annual production budget, which is based upon both the sales forecast for the year and established inventory requirements.

The production budget should not be viewed as an inflexible schedule but as a guide for planning production. It should serve as the foundation for planning material and labor needs, capital additions, and cash requirements, which are integral parts of the plan.

**Human Resources (The Personnel Function).**   Even though chief executives realize that their most important, and most frequent problems are with people, they have often been reluctant to use their personnel departments for solutions. They seem to lack faith in the ability of their personnel managers or the field of personnel management to supply information and assistance in the area of solving personnel problems such as motivation, turnover, career advancement and the like. In part, this is because personnel specialists have not been trained to think in terms of the entire organization. Thus, many executive-development and organizational-development programs have been placed with organization planning units separate from the personnel department. Furthermore, many functional executives have been reluctant to avail themselves of the technical expertise of their colleagues in the personnel department because they regard the staffing function as their own responsibility. However, it has become obvious that effective organizational plans must go beyond simple personnel administration and deal with human resource requirements in the broad sense of the total impact of people on the organization. Failure to employ the specialized knowledge of the personnel executive about human needs and actions may be detrimental to the planning process and costly to the organization.

As the personnel administration function has broadened into human resources management, the manpower planning function emerges as the most critical of all rational personnel activities. The prime objective of manpower planning is to incorporate the planning and control of personnel resources into overall company planning. Another objective is to coordinate all company personnel policies.

These planning areas include salary and wage administration, promotion policies, training and development activities, retirement and layoff systems, dealing with organized labor and the like. Since functional managers in an organization are continually making decisions that affect personnel, the human resource specialists must be responsible for keeping personnel policies consistent throughout the company.

Manpower planning is based upon a systematic analysis of personnel resources currently available within the firm, which are then matched to the company's objectives as transmitted from the corporate level and set forth in the corporate plan. This comparison will reveal whether the personnel required by the plan is available from the present internal personnel supply as well as whether the available personnel need to be moved within the firm.

If it is necessary to recruit from outside the firm, a forecast of external personnel supply is required. Implementation of the personnel plan should include programs for improving the following: the efficient use of personnel; the supply of personnel covering recruitment, promotion, internal mobility, and training of employees to prepare them for the jobs planned; and the personnel policies necessary to recruit and retain staff, including working conditions, remuneration, and industrial relations.

**Finance.**   The value of both the resources and the facilities needed by the functional planners can be expressed in monetary terms. Thus, the financial aspects of each of the functional areas are an integral component of the planning process. There is a very close relationship between the financial plan and the other plans of the organization; nevertheless, the financial manager has a unique role to play in corporate planning.

As mentioned, all corporate strategic plans enunciate a profit objective to be achieved in terms of a percentage of sales or a return on investment. They also outline the capital needed to support the strategy. The administrative planners then allocate the authorized capital investment to the major divisions of the organization and establish profit goals for each. The operational planners are responsible for the day-to-day operations of the subunits of the firm and must be provided with the necessary materials, labor and overhead components including data. The financial planners have to develop a system that translates the needs of these three planning levels into financial terms. This system includes balance sheets, income statements, and other accounting forms expressing the formulated plans in monetary units. Financial management then uses this system to fulfill its two major responsibilities— keeping the business solvent and providing the funds required for planned growth. To maintain financial liquidity, the financial executives must insure the proper balance between working capital and current liabilities, between long-term debt and income to pay principal and interest, and between dividend payments and retained earnings.

On the administrative planning level, the financial planner is primarily concerned with capital expenditure budgeting. In accounting practice, an expenditure that is expected to produce benefits over a period of time, usually longer than a year, is classified as a capital item. Since administrative plans cover a multiyear time period, authorizations for expenditures for physical plant, (computer) equipment and the like fall into this category. The capital expenditures authorized by administrative planners are formally summarized in the capital budget. This budget enables management to evaluate the extent to which proposed capital expenditures tie in with strategic plans, cost and profit objectives, and available funds and personnel. The capital budget also permits management to compare a group of programs simultaneously and to observe the effects of the capital expenditure program upon the total corporate cash flow.

**Data or Information.**   This final function displayed on the administrative level of Figure 1–2 is as much a resource to be planned for and funded as any of the others. It is similar to the financial function in that its plan is a part of the plan of each of the other functions, i.e., each of the functions requires a good information (processing) system to support its efforts. The implications of this required commitment to the information resource is what this book is all about. The details about how this function is managed and how information is developed to aid functional managers at all decisionmaking levels are the substance of the following chapters.

### Operational Level Information

The major functions at the operational planning level reflect those at the administrative level (see Figure 1-2). The operational level is responsible for the efficient day-to-day use of the resources allocated (by the administrative level) to its area of operation. This functional responsibility is commonly carried out through an operating budget. At this level there is usually considerable transaction-oriented data processing which supports the functional activity (see Figure 1-2). The common areas for transaction processing include order processing, inventory management, accounts receivable, market and sales analysis, accounts payable, purchasing, production scheduling and reporting, general ledger, various budgets and other accounting reports and service processing such as payroll and personnel reporting. Often this transaction processing or operational information system is aided by a computer or some other form of mechanization.

Because of the close relationship between the administrative and operational levels, for the purposes of this book we will address these two levels as one which we shall call tactical. The strategic level remains essentially the same although some of the longer-range actions of the administrative level might more properly come under the strategic umbrella rather than be called tactical. Our purpose is to treat the information needs of managers in each of the four major functional areas, *marketing, production, human resources* and *finance,* on both the tactical and strategic levels. Viewing the four areas from the two levels results in an eight-sided approach to managerial information needs. Then for each of the eight needs we will answer the following questions:

1. Where does the information needed by these managers come from?
2. How can that information be organized to serve the manager's needs?
3. How should the information be used for effective decisionmaking?

## INFORMATION AND DECISIONMAKING

Information and decisionmaking are inseparable elements. In the previous sections it has become apparent that each management function has its own information needs, and the extent to which those needs are satisfied has a bearing on how effectively the function is performed. The performance of the function in turn is really a measurement of the quality of the decisions made. Did the firm enter the right markets? Was the product produced in sufficient quantity? Was the right person hired? Such questions and thousands more like them are asked constantly as the firm seeks to evaluate actions.

But all decision situations are not alike. Varying amounts of information are available in different situations, results are known earlier in some situations than in others. A useful way to look at the different kinds of decisions is through the concept of varying degrees of decision structure.

Figure 1-3 is a matrix classifying decisions into three groups: (1) structured, (2) semistructured, and (3) unstructured. These categories appear on the vertical axis

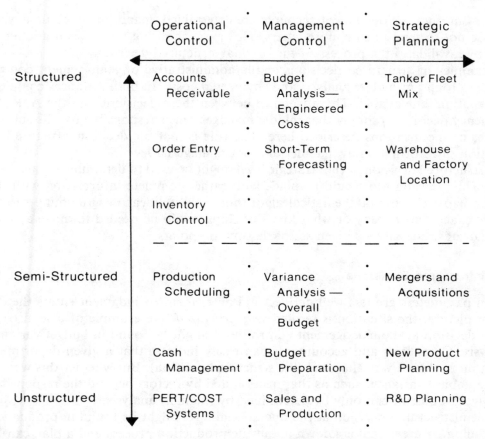

|  | Operational Control | Management Control | Strategic Planning |
|---|---|---|---|
| Structured | Accounts Receivable | Budget Analysis— Engineered Costs | Tanker Fleet Mix |
|  | Order Entry | Short-Term Forecasting | Warehouse and Factory Location |
|  | Inventory Control |  |  |
| Semi-Structured | Production Scheduling | Variance Analysis — Overall Budget | Mergers and Acquisitions |
|  | Cash Management | Budget Preparation | New Product Planning |
| Unstructured | PERT/COST Systems | Sales and Production | R&D Planning |

Figure 1–3. A framework for management information systems. Reprinted from "A Framework for Management Information Systems" by G. Anthony Gorry and Michael S. Scott Morton, *Sloan Management Review,* Vol. 13, No. 1, p. 62, by permission of the publisher. Copyright © 1971 by the Sloan Management Review Association. All rights reserved.

of the figure. The horizontal axis displays the three managerial levels also shown in Figure 1–2, which here are called: (1) operational control, (2) management control, and (3) strategic planning. All degrees of decision structure are found at all managerial levels.

## Structured Decisions

The decision is structured when parameters are known and there can be only one "right" answer. Management can always choose to override a structured decision, but the original decision process will always come up with the same answer. For example, a structured decision at the operational level might be accounts receivable (A/R) delinquency processing. If the A/R delinquency decision rule is to send a dunning letter to anyone with a balance outstanding in excess of ninety days, this structured decision situation will easily isolate all candidates for such letters. No matter who checks the A/R ledger, the same accounts will always be flagged for a letter. But once the delinquent accounts are determined, management could always choose not to send one or more letters. However, choosing not to send a letter in no way invalidates the process of the original structured decision.

Examples of structured decisions at the administrative or management control level are found in budget analysis and engineered costs. In both instances complete information is available. The difference between these decisions and the A/R delinquency decision is simply that middle management is responsible for the subject matter of the decisions described here. The rule is that the decision structure is a function of information availability and not managerial level.

A structured decision at the strategic level might be used to determine tanker fleet mix. This decision too would be made with rather complete information with the aid perhaps of some mathematical algorithm such as linear programming to calculate exactly how many or what kinds of ships would be needed to move a given amount of crude oil to a given set of destination points.

## Semistructured Decisions

When parameters are less well defined and an element of judgment enters the decision picture, the situation is termed *semistructured*. An example of a semistructured decision at the management control level might be found in budget variance analysis. Computers and accountants can easily indicate that a given department spent more than it was allocated (the structured decision). But whether this was an "acceptable" variance, such as that necessitated by factors beyond the responsible manager's control, can only be determined by (human) analysis.

A semistructured decision at the operational level might be found in production scheduling. A great deal is known about the production process and a plan can be made. But not every element of the schedule is quantifiable or accurately predictable. At the time the production run is actually made, anticipated materials may not have been delivered, workers may be absent or output quantities may vary from estimates. Or an "optimal" production schedule might be altered to meet the demands of a preferred customer. These kinds of situations will require ad hoc responses on management's part which could not have been structured into the original schedule.

Semistructured strategic decisions are exemplified by the actions surrounding a merger or acquisition. Certainly financial performance, inventory levels, product lines, personnel skills and much more can be known with certainty. But a significant number of intangibles lessen the structure in such decisions. Some semistructured or not easily predictable areas are the reaction of regulatory bodies to the merger, the actual degree of synergy which can really be achieved among the merging units, the public's reaction to the merger and the like.

## Unstructured Decisions

An unstructured decision is called for when the element of judgment far outweighs the definable parameters as decision inputs. Most creative situations and those involving speculative or forecasted data are unstructured. These are by nature the hardest to pattern and have the most unreliable decision outcomes.

Unstructured decisions at the operational level are exemplified by some PERT (program evaluation and review technique) systems. This method aids in scheduling operational activities and may be heavily based on time or cost estimates. The value of the method is highly correlated to the accuracy of the estimates. If the activities are directed to the initial launching of an experimental rocket such estimates may be extremely unreliable; and the nature of the decisions made, highly unstructured.

At the management control level, sales (and the resultant need for production) are highly dependent on forces outside the control of the firm. Though much information is available to predict sales volume the accuracy of these forecasts is limited and quite subject to influence by thoroughly unpredictable factors such as fads, natural disasters, competitors' actions, etc.

Strategic unstructured decisions include research and development activities which at the extreme of pure research are probably the ultimate unstructured activities. However, even more directed product development activities have sufficient uncertainty as to ultimate operational success or cost/benefit so that they too fall into the unstructured category.

## INFORMATION AND COMPUTERS

By implication and through example we have been referring not only to different decision structures but also to three types of computer processing systems which are related though quite distinct: (1) electronic data processing (EDP) which is most valuable at the structured level, (2) management information systems (MIS) which supports mostly the semistructured area, and (3) decision support systems (DSS) which especially aid in unstructured situations. EDP or transactional processing is a means of paperwork automation which uses operational data and storage capability to produce standard (management) reports. MIS is an attempt to upgrade EDP so that functional (middle) managers can have an integrated system of data files and resulting reports so as to make better decisions about their particular functions. Primary characteristics of the MIS often include inquiry ability, the ability to generate ad hoc reports and access to a database constructed in such a way as to make such processing easy for non-DP trained users. DSS is a further improvement on both MIS and EDP in that it attempts to support all levels of management with operations research and statistical decisionmaking models and the data (often from EDP) to use with those models. There are numerous types of decision support systems and various ways to integrate them into the organization. For more information on DSS structure, performance and potentials, see the article by Ralph Sprague reproduced at the end of this chapter.

In the previous sections we have shown how information needs permeate all levels of the organization, how all levels require information inputs and how all are required to provide information outputs. Finally information was shown to be necessary to meet the decisionmaking requirements of each level whether those decisions were highly structured, not very structured or somewhere in between. Specifically, the computer or other technological aids were not a part of the concepts presented. Though elementary, this distinction is important. The information needs exist independently of the technology. The availability of the technology makes providing the needed information feasible and perhaps cost effective. But the need should lead the computer function, not the other way around. The computer is the tool and should be brought to bear when there is a defined job to do. That job in short is to provide timely, accurate and appropriate information to the decisionmaking process at all levels of management.

Two considerations exist in meeting this criterion: (1) information unavailability and (2) the stages of data processing growth. Information unavailability has two aspects, cost related unavailability and absolute unavailability. Some information is available but is difficult to get and the difficulty can only be overcome through very high dollar expenditures. Such information might be consumer attitudes toward a potential new product which might require a detailed and costly survey. If the cost of the survey could not be offset by the potential revenues of the product, then for all intents and purposes the information is "unavailable." Absolute unavailability deals mainly with information in the external environment. How long will the recession last? Will Congress enact a tax cut? Will our competitor announce a new and cheaper product? Both types of unavailability relate to the degree of structure of the decision being made. Both require *soft* inputs to the decision process, that is, information based on estimates. Managerial judgment, intuition or gut feel must substitute for missing information. When information is determined to be unavailable for either of the above reasons, no computer or other device is going to provide it. Thus, in spite of technology, some decisions will remain unstructured. It is important for management to understand this. Since the computer often structures a great many previously unstructured decisions, management may get the mistaken idea that this ability is unlimited and expect such support in all cases.

The other consideration, the stages of DP growth, is somewhat more complex and yet is the kind of problem which management can solve or at least aid in solving. The six stages of data processing growth are illustrated in Figure 1–4. The figure depicts the development of the data processing function in an organization over time and also reflects the costs associated with that development. The vertical axis shows (from the top) (1) the kinds of applications the DP function performs, (2) the sophistication of the DP organization, (3) the intensity of the planning and control DP management exercises over the DP function and (4) the relationship with the user of the data which is processed. Each of these categories has a different entry depending on the stage in which an organization finds its DP department.

Stage I represents the initial use of the computer in an organization. The applications portfolio typically supports the financial area, and ideally there are some cost savings through better control and more timely information. At this stage also there are few data processing professionals on the staff, and their chief concern is to get the technology to work. The objective is to get the application running. Non-DP people, who are marginally knowledgeable about the field are at the mercy of the DP department. Though there is some "success" it is achieved on the terms set by the DP department.

Stage II is termed *contagion* because it represents rapid growth which springs directly from the successful Stage I accomplishments. The more applications successfully installed, the more influence DP people have in the organization. Beyond the usual accounting applications, DP now enters into operational areas. Applications may include controlling the production process, monitoring labor productivity and others which bear on the nature of the business itself.

Exhibit I
**Six stages of data processing growth**

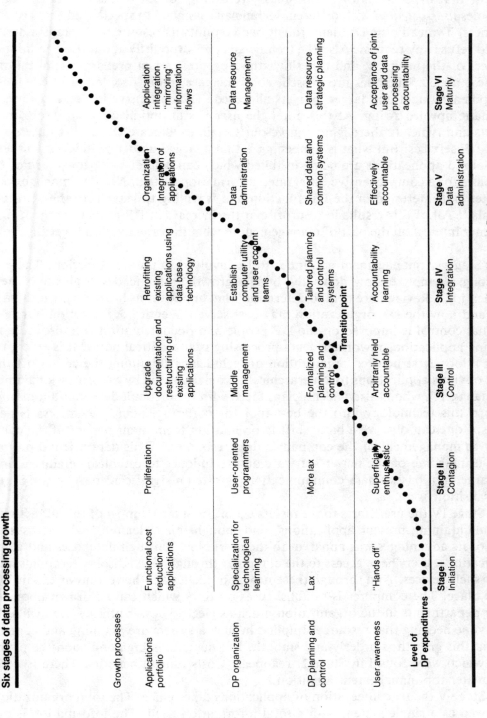

| Growth processes | Stage I<br>Initiation | Stage II<br>Contagion | Stage III<br>Control | Stage IV<br>Integration | Stage V<br>Data administration | Stage VI<br>Maturity |
|---|---|---|---|---|---|---|
| Applications portfolio | Functional cost reduction applications | Proliferation | Upgrade documentation and restructuring of existing applications | Retrofitting existing applications using data base technology | Integration of applications | Application integration "mirroring" information flows |
| DP organization | Specialization for technological learning | User-oriented programmers | Middle management | Establish computer utility and user account teams | Data administration | Data resource Management |
| DP planning and control | Lax | More lax | Formalized planning and control | Tailored planning and control systems | Shared data and common systems | Data resource strategic planning |
| User awareness | "Hands off" | Superficially enthusiastic | Arbitrarily held accountable | Accountability learning | Effectively accountable | Acceptance of joint user and data processing accountability |

**Transition point**

Level of DP expenditures

Figure 1–4. Six stages of data processing growth. Reprinted by permission of the *Harvard Business Review*. Exhibit from "Managing the Crises in Data Processing," by Richard L. Nolan (March/April 1979).
Copyright © 1979 by the President and Fellows of Harvard College; all rights reserved.

Now that other areas of the business are asking for DP support, the DP staff becomes *user-oriented* with different technicians assigned to specialized areas of the business. Typically the DP department overcommits its resources. There is a desire not to refuse any request. Also the technicians know too little about the operational aspects of the business, and this slows their progress when preparing applications in these areas. Schedules are missed, costs increase, more people are hired, more equipment bought and larger budgets allocated. The cost curve in Stage II takes a dramatic upward swing. At this point the user is still optimistic. There are (some) results and typically there is no charge-out system to allocate DP costs to users for their DP services. But what is happening is that a large number of independent and specialized applications are being installed which can neither work together nor be the basis for a comprehensive, integrated information system. Non-DP management is often not interested in the DP function and is willing to leave it to the "professionals." All of this results in a surprise at the increase in DP costs in Stage II and a keener interest on the part of management in what the organization is getting from DP.

In Stage III management continues to be involved in the DP function. There is a strong attempt to slow down the budget growth rate and development of new applications. Reviews are held to determine what applications have the greatest payoffs and how the DP organization may best serve the entire organization. Greater internal control is imposed on the DP people and documentation is improved and existing applications reworked. Data processing is at a critical point. It is emerging from a loosely structured organization of technicians skimming the cream off the most obvious applications to a hierarchical organization led by a "professional middle manager", who is also a technician, faced with the difficult decisions about how to turn this technology into the best tool for corporate management. As Nolan states, "one can observe a basic shift in orientation from management of the computer to management of the company's data resources." This data orientation implies using some of the newer software and techniques to establish, maintain and use large data bases. Data communications is often a significant part of the Stage III transition.

In Stage IV the user starts to see results again. In Stage III most of the DP activity was maintaining present applications, and though this "cleanup" was necessary, little of its advantages was apparent to the user. Now, through databases and communications, users have access to the computer through video display terminals and other such devices. And through these new approaches another round of expansion takes place. The computer is established as a utility which can be drawn upon by other departments in the organization much as electric power utilities are available to anyone needing that resource. Implicit in such a system are planning and control so that this growth is orderly and smooth. But demand is high and soon the problems which were found in Stage II reappear. Costs outrun benefits. There is need for greater top management attention.

In Stage V the true integration of applications takes place. The total organization is viewed as a single system with a total information need. The information is organized and maintained in such a way that each area of the business at any and all levels can access it in support of its (decisionmaking) function. Those areas responsible for the input of data are held accountable for its accuracy, timeliness and completeness. The DP organization does not "own" the data but merely administers it. This leads to Stage VI which reflects a maturing of the process, a system where user and administrator know their functions and responsibilities and where the computer applications mirror the organization information flows. For an insight into such an "information company" from the perspective of the IS professional see the Keen article reprinted at the end of this chapter.

The challenge to managers from the concept of the six stages of DP growth is to determine where their own organization lies. According to Nolan, no firm has yet reached Stages V or VI although some are rapidly putting into place large scale database management systems. And in large organizations with multiple DP facilities, different DP departments can be at different stages in the cycle. But once the stage of a particular department is determined, management will have greater insight with which to evaluate the department and can speedily move it across the problem areas to the next higher level.

To complete our discussion about information in the organization and its needs at the various managerial levels, it is useful to look at an approach proposed by Zachman. His concept as shown in Figure 1–5 is to take Nolan's diagram of the six stages of DP growth (Figure 1–4) and superimpose on it the levels of organizational planning and control (Figure 1–2). But Zachman does this by placing the planning and control triangle on its side so that the base of the triangle representing the operational information system falls in the Stage I area. As the DP organization functions in higher stages it does so in such a manner as to better serve the higher

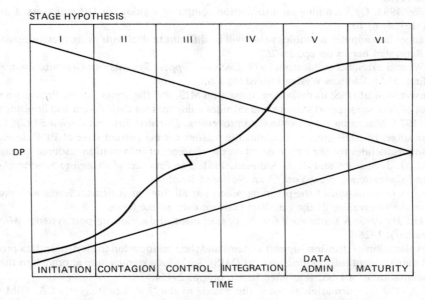

Figure 1–5. Relationship of the managerial hierarchy to the six stages of EDP growth. Reprinted by permission of John A. Zachman. Exhibit from "Information systems: the decade of the '80s" by John A. Zachman, IBM Corporation, Los Angeles, CA (1980).

levels of management. In other words the later stages of DP growth fill strategic information needs; earlier stages, administrative or management control needs; and the very earliest stages, operational needs. The combination diagram shows it all. Every organization should be striving to reach Stage VI. Doing so will mean that all organizational levels are being served by the DP function, and as stated in the first pages of this chapter information will (truly) define the organization.

How does management go about leading the organization to Stage VI? How do you define the organization? How do you define the information needs? Does it matter whether there is already a computer? These and other issues are the basis of chapter 2.

## REFERENCES

Alter, S. 1980. *Decision Support Systems: Current Practices and Continuing Challenges*. Reading, MA: Addison- Wesley Publishing Co.
An in-depth look at decision support systems (DSS) supported by a number of detailed case studies.
Gorry, G. A. and M. S. Scott Morton. 1971. A framework for management information systems. *Sloan Management Review* **13** (Fall): 55–70.
A classic article describing the various kinds of decisionmaking at all management levels. Contains a number of worthwhile illustrations.
Kallman, E. A., L. Reinharth and H. J. Shapiro. 1980. How effective companies manage their information. *Business* (July/August): 35–39.
Reviews the distinction between management levels and the types of information each needs for decisionmaking. Includes an explanation and description of a management information system (MIS) and its use in the decisionmaking process.
Kast, F. E. and J. E. Rosenzweig. 1979. *Organizations and Management*. New York: McGraw-Hill.
A basic explanation of organizations as systems, how they are composed, how they operate and how they are managed.
Keen, P. G. W. 1982. On becoming an information company: a guide for DP managers. *Computerworld* **16** (11a): 5, 6, 10.
Warns of changes in computer technology that will be difficult to deal with using present management methods. Reprinted herein on pp. 25–28.
Keen, P. G. W. and M. S. Scott, Morton. 1978. *Decision Support Systems: An Organizational Perspective*. Reading, MA: Addison-Wesley Publishing Co.
A comprehensive view of DSS: its definition, impact on MIS, and the organization. Provides a number of examples of decision support systems and includes guidelines for their design and implementation.
Nolan, R. L. 1979. Managing the crises in data processing. *Harvard Business Review* **57** (2): 115–126.
Details the six stages of EDP growth. Explains the reasons for the current state of EDP development and sets some guidelines for the future based on the concepts of information resource management.
Reinharth, L., H. J. Shapiro and E. A. Kallman. 1981. *The Practice of Planning: Strategic, Administrative, and Operational*. New York: Van Nostrand Reinhold.
A comprehensive examination of the planning process at all three management levels with particular emphasis on the integration of the activities between each of the levels.
Sprague, R. H., Jr. 1980. A framework for the development of decision support systems. *MIS Quarterly* (December): 1–26.
A thorough explanation of decision support systems and their relationship to electronic data processing (EDP) and management information systems (MIS). Includes a step-by-step approach to the design and implementation of a DSS. Reprinted herein on pp. 29–54.
Zachman, J. A. 1980. Information systems: the decade of the '80s. Los Angeles, CA: IBM Corporation.
An explanation of the information needs in the organization and their relationship to EDP and management.

## ON BECOMING AN INFORMATION COMPANY:
## A GUIDE FOR DP MANAGERS
### By Peter G. W. Keen

We can talk all we want about productivity, teleconferencing, interpretation and so on, but cultural forces and social interests strongly influence the pace at which a new technology is assimilated by individuals and organizations. It is clear that communications technology will change the way business is done, create new markets and alter the nature of work and organizational life. The DP management structure was not designed for a world of communications technology. It reflects a manufacturing focus, a deliberate isolation of computing from the mainstream business and a reactive role for top management. In many instances, DP sets the applications priorities. It is clear that this is changing. In organizations making the most effective use of the new technologies: The DP - or information systems - function reports at a very senior level; steering committees provide the organizational mechanism and authority to set priorities; the job of the systems analyst increasingly emphasizes communication, consulting skills and service; and more and more resources are committed to end-user tools.

Any comprehensive communications-based strategy relies on accelerating the shift from DP as a manufacturing department - in which jobs are based on building systems or on operations - to an "information company."

The head of informations systems has to have the authority, visibility and breadth of focus to coordinate an organizational resource relevant to all business functions and units. User-liaison roles are filled by such key personnel as:

- Business-oriented analysts.
- Office technology specialists.
- Functional support staff for end users (and support for a financial modeling capability).
- Technical support staff (for instance, for a hot line to a DBMS specialist).
- Planners (for network standards and capacity, analysis of user needs and technical options and so on.)
- Educators and trainers.

There is ample reason to expect the current shortage of skilled analysts, technical specialists and, above all, technology managers to grow even worse in the next few years. Backlogs of development projects, already large, will grow as supply creates demand.

## PAPER EXERCISE

It would be an illuminating exercise actually to create the information company on paper by pooling all computer-related costs and assets, including modems, communications lines and terminals. The company's investment in software — if known — should be capitalized and depreciated as the long-term asset it is. (Botched development efforts should be written off.)

The resulting balance sheet may well be among the largest business segments in the organization. Its management structure should reflect this. One may ask how many senior managers it has; how much it spends on research and development, marketing and human resource planning; what the career path is to senior management; and so on. It should have adequate strategic planning mechanisms and sophisticated costing and pricing analyses.

In practice, the information company usually is run by a few overworked, outstanding "hybrids" — people who are fluent about technology and literate about business and applications, or vice versa. There is a virtual absence of middle management talent and no succession planning. Analysts are confronted by new demands of a user-driven environment: communication, awareness of business priorities, service and consultancy skills.

Worse than all this, there is a vast shortage of telecommunications staff to handle technology assessment, network planning, long-term capacity analysis, purchasing, costing of components and services, installation and the traffic to the highways and vice versa.

It will be a waste of time for organizations to get ready to exploit the opportunities communications technology opens up, if those organizations fail to create the roles and to develop the people critical for this new context.

## EDUCATING THE ORGANIZATION

Creating these roles and broadening the management focus is obviously not something information systems can do unilaterally. Communications technology implies a change in authority for planning and setting development priorities, reorganization and major changes in staffing, hiring and promotion. Top management, both at the corporate level and in the user department, needs to be brought into the process.

This means strategic education. In too many companies, DP is gearing up to meet the challenges of the new computing environment but lacks the needed authority and mandates. Management has generally gotten along adequately with limited knowledge of computers. Relatively suddenly, they need to be proactive, not reactive, and to make strategic policy decisions, especially in the following areas:

- Regulating the free market: deciding which aspects of the ideal capability require central direction (and therefore stay within the DP monopoly) and which are local option and can be purchased in the free market.
- Setting the criteria for selective application and establishing priorities. Given even existing backlogs, there is simply no way increased demand for applications can be met.

Unfortunately, management is generally puzzled by computers. The education available to them focuses either on concepts or details and rarely relates them.

It is undesirable either to overwhelm managers with inert details (try explaining X.25 vs. SNA) or to ignore them and rely on simple, general concepts (for example, "A distributed processing system should correspond to the organization's style and structure; it makes no sense to run a fully decentralized system in an organization with a strong central planning and central focus).

Educating top managers is an essential step toward creating the information company and meshing the business and technology plan. This step needs to be supported by a sustained commitment to education at all levels of the organization. For example, implementation skills are imperative for systems personnel; they can no longer just handle technical issues and leave the rest to the user. They have to learn how to design for implementation. Office technology, for instance, involves little systems development, but major organizational changes.

At the same time, users can no longer delegate to technicians decisions that affect every aspect of their businesses. They have to get "involved," but they lack the vocabulary and methods to do so. How do they help develop functional specifications or a testing plan? They need to learn what happens in systems development and what their roles are.

Telecommunications and data management together constitute a new computing environment. There is as urgent a need to get DP people oriented toward that environment as to bring users up to date. In any companies, attention and money is increasingly given to user education, but the busy DP staff gets little of either. They are provided with seminars to update the technical skills they need for current jobs, but not to prepare them for a world of communication and end-user tools where consulting skills and knowledge of business functions are essential.

Strategic computer education is expensive — and vital. If we think of communications technology — and the terminal that is its concrete embodiment — as a culture shock, then education needs to lead rather than follow change.

On the whole, DP has not played an active role in strategic education. In fact, training efforts by

DP have often made the culture gap even wider. Such training programs reinforce users' expectations that computers are boring, complicated, not very useful and, worse, that computer people do not care about helping users. There is a difference between education and training.

## STIMULATE CREATIVE THINKING

The distinction between information highways and information traffic is an important one. With traditional batch-oriented technology, there was relatively little scope for innovative thinking about application. The infrastructure was the traffic. Communications (and, to a lesser extent, the microcomputer) relies on creativity. For example, real estate companies in Boston can now show customers houses in California; mortgage applications can be sent by fax to a bank specializing in home loans; an oil company allows distributors to access a data base on inventory levels in order to smoothe out orders; an insurance salesman carries a briefcase with a modem that allows the creation of custom-tailored plans in the customer's home.

These innovations provide a competitive edge. They are simple, clever ideas that result when an expert in traffic links up with an expert on highways. We simply have no idea of the limits even of existing communications technology on such innovations. Moreover, these innovations tend to be fairly inexpensive because the bulk of the investment has already been made — in the network.

Prestel, the British Post Office's videotext experiment, provides a useful lesson about creative thinking. Prestel was a major technical innovation that was watched carefully in the U.S. It has not become an application innovation. That it would not do so has seemed obvious for several years. Most of the data accessible via Prestel was simply either not worth paying a premium for or better obtained manually: restaurant guides, timetables, price lists or, to the UK government's dismay, guides to Soho pornography stores.

A terminal is just a terminal. A network is just something you take for granted unless it is malfunctioning. Perhaps a key rule for communications technology is: if, in a demonstration, your selling point is the terminal and you need to focus on the network, you are in trouble. The user is excited by functional capability, which for communications means data and/or a business edge. Prestel remains a brilliant infrastructure — with dull traffic.

The people in the organization most likely to come up with creative applications are the ones closest to the business environment: in such areas as marketing, customer service, and corporate planning. The isolation of many DP units from the wider organization means they cannot add to this list. Nor do they have contacts or credibility with marketing.

## IMPROVE DESIGN SKILLS

In a world of communications, the user is a consumer. We all know a lot about consumers — they are ourselves. We buy calculators and cars on the basis of more than just functionality. Such factors as ease of use, aesthetic design, service and packaging differentiate the product.

Some DP units are so used to having a monopoly on computer use that they may not realize that we have moved from supply to demand economics. If a customer or a manager in our organization dislikes our decision support system or teleconferencing capability, that person will not use it.

Quite simply, the quality of many user-system interfaces is horrible. DP professionals' skills have been mainly in the area of data structures and procedures. Lacking clear concepts of users and of the context of use, they too often impose inflexible, uncommunicative systems. This is simply unacceptable to discretionary consumers.

Any analysis of what makes end-user software sell — packages, languages, inquiry systems and so on — will highlight the importance of ease of use, ease of learning, robustness and flexibility. Providing these requires good technical skills, which are hard to learn, and a solid understanding of users and uses, which is easy to learn when the technician recognizes its importance. It mainly requires spending time with users, observing and listening.

The interface is the system.

## GETTING STARTED

It is hard to break away from a technocentric world view. The DP field has not commanded respect for its breadth of focus and its concern for relating its technology to organizational life and business activities. The payoff for telecommunications and business strategy is potentially huge. It involves a joint venture between colleagues — users and systems.

The starting point is the business plan: what are the critical success factors for the organization? What are the opportunities for new products and services? Where can improvements in information access and distribution and in communication improve effectiveness?

If the senior information systems planners do not know where to get answers to these questions, all they can do is build the communications infrastructure and hope. The questions define the criteria for a computing strategy. That strategy cannot in itself answer them.

Given the strategy, management needs to know the strategic choices and trade-offs. The details involve private vs. value-added networks, SNA, X.25, intelligent terminals, capacity and buying bandwidth. The concepts relate to the user — to traffic. Only when management and information systems jointly evaluate what the communications capability should provide, in terms of information creation, access and distribution, can a network architecture be defined. The architecture should not determine the capability and use.

Given the architecture, the final and key issue is delivery. Who leads the planning and implementation process? With what authority? What roles must be filled for effective coordination? What education is needed? What are the design criteria?

The planning horizon for a communications strategy is 1985, not 1982. The technology is still in flux and demand characteristics unclear. We are still a long way from true integration of the technological building blocks underlying the ideal capability. It may well be that the best short-term plan is to try and avoid decisions that commit the organization over the long term.

Information systems needs to get ready for 1985, and that means getting the organization ready. Perhaps the two key components of the 1982 strategy are strategic education and the creation of the new roles communications implies.

Communications technology represents an immense organizational opportunity. It requires an organizational focus.

# A Framework for the Development of Decision Support Systems

By: Ralph H. Sprague, Jr.

## Introduction

We seem to be on the verge of another "era" in the relentless advancement of computer based information systems in organizations. Designated by the term Decision Support Systems (DSS), these systems are receiving reactions ranging from "a major breakthrough" to "just another 'buzz word'."

One view is that the natural evolutionary advancement of information technology and its use in the organizational context has led from EDP to MIS to the current DSS thrust. In this view, the DSS picks up where MIS leaves off. A contrary view portrays DSS as an important subset of what MIS has been and will continue to be. Still another view recognizes a type of system that has been developing for several years and "now we have a name for it." Meanwhile, the skeptics suspect that DSS is just another "buzz word" to justify the next round of visits from the vendors.

The purpose of this article is to briefly examine these alternative views of DSS, and present a framework that proves valuable in reconciling them. The framework articulates and integrates major concerns of several "stakeholders" in the development of DSS: executives and professionals who use them, the MIS managers who manage the process of developing and installing them, the information specialists who build and develop them, the system designers who create and assemble the technology on which they are based, and the researchers who study the DSS subject and process.

## Abstract

This article proposes a framework to explore the nature, scope, and content of the evolving topic of Decision Support Systems (DSS). The first part of the framework considers (a) three levels of technology which have been designated DSS, (b) the developmental approach that is evolving for the creation of a DSS, and (c) the roles of several key types of people in the building and use of a DSS. The second part develops a descriptive model to assess the performance objectives and the capabilities of a DSS as viewed by three of the major participants in their continued development and use. The final section outlines several issues in the future growth and development of a DSS as a potentially valuable type of information system in organizations.

Keywords: Decision Support Systems, development approach, performance objectives, capabilities, issues

ACM Categories: 3.3, 3.5, 3.6

## Definition, Examples, Characteristics

The concepts involved in DSS were first articulated in the early '70's by Michael S. Scott Morton under the term "management decision systems" [32]. A few firms and scholars began to develop and research DSS, which became characterized as *interactive* computer based systems, which *help* decision makers utilize *data* and *models* to solve *unstructured* problems. The unique contribution of DSS resulted from these key words. That definition proved restrictive enough that few actual systems completely satisfied it. Some authors recently extended the definition of DSS to include any system that makes some contribution to decision making; in this way the term can be applied to all but transaction processing. A serious definitional problem is that the words have a certain "intuitive validity;" any system that supports a decision, in any way, is a "Decision Support System."

Unfortunately, neither the restrictive nor the broad definition helps much, because they do not provide guidance for understanding the value, the technical requirements, or the approach for developing a DSS. A complicating factor is that people from different backgrounds and contexts view a DSS quite differently. A manager and computer scientist seldom see things in the same way.

Another way to get a feeling for a complex subject like a DSS is to consider examples. Several specific examples were discussed in The Society for Management Information Systems (SMIS) Workshop on DSS in 1979 [35]. Alter examined fifty-six systems which might have some claim to the DSS label, and used this sample to develop a set of abstractions describing their characteristics [1, 2]. More recently, Keen has designated about thirty examples of what he feels are DSS and compares their characteristics [26].

The "characteristics" approach seems to hold more promise than either definitions or collections of examples in understanding a DSS and its potential. More specifically, a DSS may be defined by its capabilities in several critical areas—capabilities which are required to accomplish the objectives which are pursued by the development and use of a DSS. Observed characteristics of a DSS which have evolved from the work of Alter, Keen, and others include:

- they tend to be aimed at the less well structured, underspecified problems that upper level managers typically face;

- they attempt to combine the use of models or analytic techniques with traditional data access and retrieval functions;

- they specifically focus on features which make them easy to use by noncomputer people in an interactive mode; and

- they emphasize flexibility and adaptability to accommodate changes in the environment and the decision making approach of the user.

A serious question remains. Are the definitions, examples, and characteristics of a DSS sufficiently different to justify the use of a new term and the inference of a new era in information systems for organizations, or are the skeptics right? Is it just another "buzz word" to replace the fading appeal of MIS?

## DSS Versus MIS

Much of the difficulty and controversy with terms like "DSS" and "MIS" can be traced to the difference between an academic or theoretical definition and "connotational" definition. The former is carefully articulated by people who write textbooks and articles in journals. The latter evolves from what actually is developed and used in practice, and is heavily influenced by the personal experiences that the user of the term has had with the subject. It is this connotational definition of EDP/MIS/DSS that is used in justifying the assertion that a DSS is an evolutionary advancement beyond MIS.

This view can be expressed using Figure 1, a simple organizational chart, as a model of an organization. EDP was first applied to the lower operational levels of the organization to automate the paperwork. Its basic characteristics include:

- a focus on data, storage, processing, and flows at the operational level;

- efficient transaction processing;

- scheduled and optimized computer runs;

- integrated files for related jobs; and

- summary reports for management.

In recent years, the EDP level of activity in many firms has become a well-oiled and efficient production facility for transactions processing.

The MIS approach elevated the focus of information systems activities, with additional emphasis on integration and planning of the information

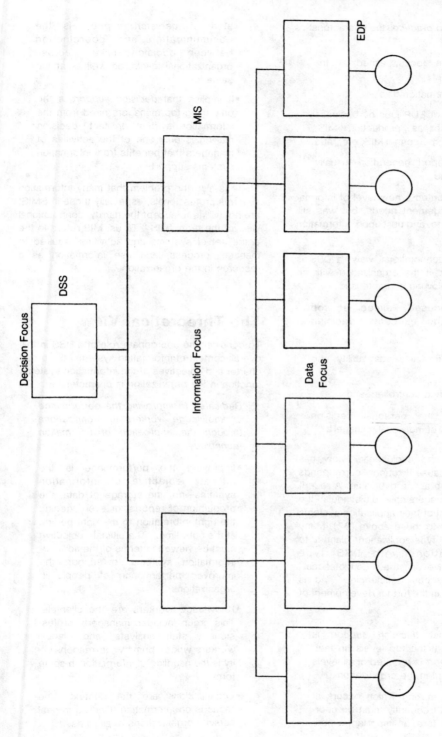

**Figure 1. The Connotational View**

systems function. In *practice*, the characteristics of MIS include:

- an information focus, aimed at the middle managers;
- structured information flow;
- an integration of EDP jobs by business function, such as production MIS, marketing MIS, personnel MIS, *etc.;* and
- inquiry and report generation, usually with a database.

The MIS era contributed a new level of information to serve management needs, but was still very much oriented to, and built upon, information flows and data files.

According to this connotational view, a DSS is focused still higher in the organization with an emphasis on the following characteristics:

- decision focused, aimed at top managers and executive decision makers;
- emphasis on flexibility, adaptability, and quick response;
- user initiated and controlled; and
- support for the personal decision making styles of individual managers.

This connotational and evolutionary view has some credence because it roughly corresponds to developments in practice over time. A recent study found MIS managers able to distinguish the level of advancement of their application systems using criteria similar to those above [27]. Many installations with MIS type applications planned to develop applications with DSS type characteristics. However, the "connotational" view has some serious deficiencies, and is definitely misleading in the further development of a DSS.

- It implies that *decision support* is needed only at the top levels. In fact, *decision support* is required at all levels of management in the organization.
- The decision making which occurs at several levels frequently must be coordinated. Therefore, an important dimension of *decision support* is the communication and coordination between decision makers across organizational levels, as well as at the same level.
- It implies that *decision support* is the only thing top managers need from the information system. In fact, decision making is only one of the activities of managers that benefits from information systems support.

There is also the problem that many information systems professionals, especially those in SMIS, are not willing to accept the narrow connotational view of the term "MIS." To us, MIS refers to the entire set of systems and activities required to manage, process, and use information as a resource in the organization.

# The Threoretical View

To consider the appropriate role of a DSS in this overall context of information systems, the broad charter and objectives of the information systems function in the organization is characterized:

*Dedicated to improving the performance of knowledge workers in organizations through the application of information technology.*

- Improving the performance is the ultimate objective of information systems—not the storage of data, the production of reports, or even "getting the right information to the right person at the right time." The ultimate objective must be viewed in terms of the ability of information systems to support the improved performance of people in organizations.
- Knowledge workers are the clientele. This group includes managers, professionals, staff analysts, and clerical workers whose primary job responsibility is the handling of information in some form.
- Organizations are the context. The focus is on information handling in goal seeking organizations of all kinds.

•The application of information technology is the challenge and opportunity facing the information systems professional for the purposes and in the contexts given above.

A triangle was used by Robert Head in the late '60's as a visual model to characterize MIS in this broad comprehensive sense [22]. It has become a classic way to view the dimensions of an information system. The vertical dimension represented the levels of management, and the horizontal dimension represented the main functional areas of the business organization. Later authors added transactional processing as a base on which the entire system rested. The result was a two dimensional model of an MIS in the broad sense — the total activities which comprise the information system in an organization. Figure 2 is a further extension of the basic triangle to help describe the concept of the potential role of a

DSS. The depth dimension shows the major technology "subsystems" which provide support for the activities of knowledge workers.

Three major thrusts are shown here, but there could be more. The structured reporting system includes the reports required for the management and control of the organization, and for satisfying the information needs of external parties. It has been evolving from efforts in EDP and MIS, in the narrow sense, for several years. Systems to support the communication needs of the organization are evolving rapidly from advances in telecommunications with a strong impetus from office automation and word processing. DSS seems to be evolving from the coalescence of information technology and operations research/management science approaches in the form of interactive modeling.

To summarize this introductory section, a DSS is not merely an evolutionary advancement of EDP

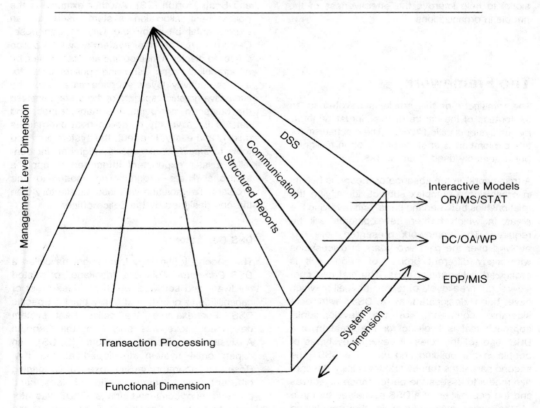

**Figure 2. The Complete View**

and MIS, and it will certainly not replace either. Nor is it merely a type of information system aimed exclusively at top management, where other information systems seem to have failed. A DSS is a class of information system that draws on transaction processing systems and interacts with the other parts of the overall information system to support the decision making activities of managers and other knowledge workers in the organizations. However, there are some subtle but significant differences between a DSS and traditional EDP or so-called MIS approaches. Moreover, these systems require a new combination of information systems technology to satisfy a set of heretofore unmet needs. It is not yet clear exactly how these technologies fit together, or which important problems need to be solved. Indeed, that is a large part of the purpose of this article. It is apparent, however, that a DSS has the potential to become another powerful weapon in the arsenal of the information systems professional to help improve the effectiveness of the people in organizations.

# The Framework

The remainder of this article is devoted to an exploration of the nature of this "thrust" in information systems called "DSS." The mechanism for this exploration is another of the often maligned but repeatedly used "frameworks."

A framework, in the absence of theory, is helpful in organizing a complex subject, identifying the relationships between the parts, and revealing the areas in which further developments will be required. The framework presented here has evolved over the past two years in discussions with many different groups of people.[1] It is organized in two major parts. The first part considers: (a) three levels of technology, all of which have been designated as a DSS, with considerable confusion; (b) the developmental approach that is evolving for the creation of a DSS; and (c) the roles of several key types of people in the building and use of a DSS. The second part of the framework develops a descriptive model to assess the performance objectives and the capabilities of a DSS as viewed by three of the major stakeholders in their continued development and use.

## Three technology levels

It is helpful to identify three levels of hardware/software which have been included in the label "DSS." They are used by people with different levels of technical capability, and vary in the nature and scope of task to which they can be applied.

### Specific DSS

The system which actually accomplishes the work might be called the *Specific DSS*. It is an information systems "application," but with characteristics that make it significantly different from a typical data processing application. It is the hardware/software that allows a specific decision maker or group of decision makers to deal with a specific set of related problems. An early example is the portfolio management system [20] also described in the first major DSS book by Keen and Scott Morton [23]. Another example is the police beat allocation system used on an experimental basis by the City of San Jose, California [9]. The latter system allowed a police officer to display a map outline and call up data by geographical zone, showing police calls for service, activity levels, service time, *etc*. The interactive graphic capability of the system enabled the officer to manipulate the maps, zones, and data to try a variety of police beat alternatives quickly and easily. In effect, the system provided tools to *amplify* a manager's judgment. Incidentally, a later experiment attempted to apply a traditional linear programming model to the problem. The solution was less satisfactory than the one designed by the police officer.

### DSS Generator

The second technology level might be called a *DSS Generator*. This is a "package" of related hardware and software which provides a set of capabilities to quickly and easily build a Specific DSS. For example, the police beat system described above was built from the Geodata Analysis and Display System (GADS), an experimental system developed at the IBM Research Laboratory in San Jose [8]. By loading different maps, data, menu choices, and procedures or command strings, GADS was later used to build a Specific DSS to support the routing of IBM copier repairmen [42]. The development of this new "application" required less than one month.

Another example of a *DSS Generator* is the Executive Information System (EIS) marketed by Boeing Computer Services [6]. EIS is an integrated set of capabilities which includes report preparation, inquiry capability, a modeling language, graphic display commands, and a set of financial and statistical analysis subroutines. These capabilities have all been available individually for some time. The unique contribution of EIS is that these capabilities are available through a common command language which acts on a common set of data. The result is that EIS can be used as a DSS Generator, especially for a Specific DSS to help in financial decision making situations.

Evolutionary growth toward DSS Generators has come from special purpose languages. In fact, most of the software systems that might be used as Generators are evolving from enhanced planning languages or modeling languages, perhaps with report preparation and graphic display capabilities added. The Interactive Financial Planning System (IFPS) marketed by Execucom Systems of Austin, Texas [18], and EXPRESS available from TYMSHARE [44], are good examples.

## DSS Tools

The third and most fundamental level of technology applied to the development of a DSS might be called *DSS Tools*. These are hardware or software elements which facilitate the development of a specific DSS *or* a DSS Generator. This category of technology has seen the greatest amount of recent development, including new special purpose languages, improvements in operating systems to support conversational approaches, color graphics hardware and supporting software, *etc.* For example, the GADS system described above was written in FORTRAN using an experimental graphics subroutine package as the primary dialogue handling software, a laboratory enhanced raster-scan color monitor, and a powerful interactive data extraction/database management system.

## Relationships

The relationships between these three levels of technology and types of DSS are illustrated by

Figure 3. The DSS Tools can be used to develop a Specific DSS application directly as shown on the left half of the diagram. This is the same approach used to develop most traditional applications with tools such as a general purpose language, data access software, subroutine packages, *etc.* The difficulty with this approach for developing DSS applications is the constant change and flexibility which characterize them. A DSS changes character not only in repsonse to changes in the environment, but to changes in the way managers want to approach the problem. Therefore, a serious complicating factor in the use of basic tools is the need to involve the user directly in the change and modification of the Specific DSS.

APL was heavily used in the development of Specific DSS because it proved to be cheap and easy for APL programmers, especially the APL enthusiasts, to produce "throw-away" code which could be easily revised or discarded as the nature of the application changed. However, except for the few users who became members of the APL fan club, that language *did not* help capture the involvement of users in the building and modification of the DSS. The development and use of DSS Generators promises to create a "platform" or staging area from which Specific DSS can be constantly developed and modified with the cooperation of the user, and without heavy consumption of time and effort.

## Evolving roles in DSS

All three levels of technology will probably be used over time in the development and operation of a DSS. Some interesting developments are occurring, however, in the roles that managers and technicians will play.

Figure 4 repeats part of the earlier diagram with a spectrum of five roles spread across the three levels.

- The *manager or user* is the person faced with the problem or decision — the one that must take action and be responsible for the consequences.

- The *intermediary* is the person who helps the user, perhaps merely as a clerical assistant to push the buttons of

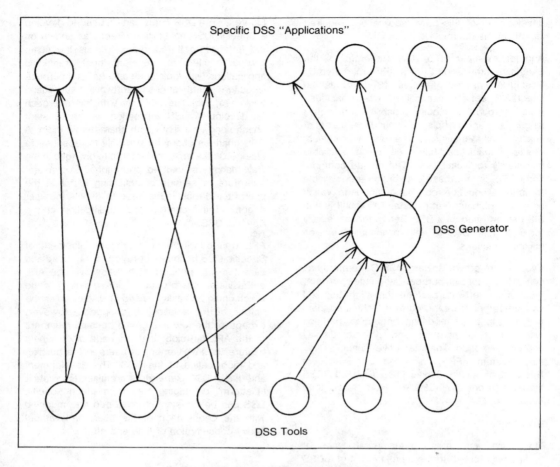

**Figure 3. Three Levels of DSS Technology**

the terminal, or perhaps as a more substantial "staff assistant" to interact and make suggestions.

- The *DSS builder* or facilitator assembles the necessary capabilities from the DSS Generator to "configure" the specific DSS with which the user/intermediary interacts directly. This person must have some familiarity with the problem area and also be comfortable with the information system technology components and capabilities.

- The *technical supporter* develops additional information system capabilities or components when they are needed as part of the Generator. New databases,

new analysis models, and additional data display formats will be developed by the person filling this role. It requires a strong familiarity with technology, and a minor acquaintance with the problem or application area.

- The *toolsmith* develops new technology, new languages, new hardware and software, improves the efficiency of linkages between subsystems, *etc*.

Two observations about this spectrum of roles are appropriate. First, it is clear that they do not necessarily align with individuals on a one-to-one basis. One person may assume several roles, or more than one person may be required to fill a

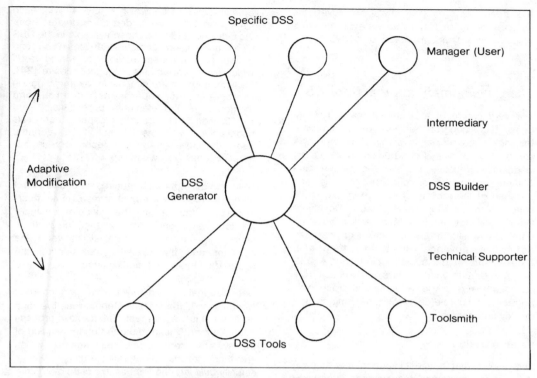

Specific DSS

Manager (User)

Intermediary

Adaptive Modification

DSS Generator

DSS Builder

Technical Supporter

Toolsmith

DSS Tools

**Figure 4. Three levels of DSS with Five Associated Roles for Managers and Technicians**

role. The appropriate role assignment will generally depend on:

- the nature of the problem, particularly how narrow or broad;

- the nature of the person, particularly how comfortable the individual is with the computer equipment, language, and concepts; and

- the strength of the technology, particularly how user oriented it is.

Some managers do not need or want an intermediary. There are even a few chief executives who take the terminal home on weekends to write programs, thereby assuming the upper three or four roles. In fact, a recent survey of the users of IFPS shows that more than one third of them are middle and top level managers [45]. Decisions which require group consensus or systems design (builder) teams are examples of multiple persons per role.

Secondly, these roles appear similar to those present in traditional systems development, but there are subtle differences. The top two are familiar even in name for the development of many interactive or online systems. It is common practice in some systems to combine them into one "virtual" user for convenience. The user of the DSS, however, will play a much more active and controlling role in the design and development of the system than has been true in the past. The builder/technical supporter dichotomy is relatively close to the information specialist/system designer dichotomy discussed in the ACM curriculum recommendations [3]. Increasingly, however, the DSS builder resides in the functional area and not in the MIS department. The toolsmith is similar to a systems programmer, software designer, or computer scientist, but is increasingly employed by a hardware or software vendor, and not by the user's organization. The net result is less direct involvement in the DSS process by the information systems professional in the EDP/MIS department. (Some implications of this trend are discussed later.) Moreover, the interplay between these roles is evolving into a unique development approach for a DSS.

## The development approach for DSS

The very nature of a DSS requires a different design technique from traditional batch, or online, transaction processing systems. The traditional approaches for analysis and design have proven inadequate because there is no single comprehensive theory of decision making, and because of the rapidity of change in the conditions which decision makers face. Designers literally "cannot get to first base" because no one, least of all the decision maker or user, can define in advance what the functional requirements of the system should be. A DSS needs to be built with short, rapid feedback from users to ensure that development is proceeding correctly. It must be developed to permit change quickly and easily.

### Iterative Design

The result is that the most important four steps in the typical systems development process—analysis, design, construction, implementation—are combined into a single step which is iteratively repeated. Several names are evolving to describe this process including breadboarding [31], L'Approache Evolutive [14], and "middle out" [30]. The essence of the approach is that the manager and builder agree on a small but significant subproblem, then design and develop an initial system to support the decision making which it requires. After a short period of use, for instance, a few weeks, the system is evaluated, modified, and incrementally expanded. This cycle is repeated three to six times over the course of a few months until a *relatively* stable system is evolved which supports decision making for a cluster of tasks. The word "relatively" is important, because although the frequency and extent of change will decrease, it will never be stable. The system will always be changing, not as a necessary evil in response to imposed environmental changes, but as a conscious strategy on the part of the user and builder.

In terms of the three level model presented earlier, this process can be viewed as the iterative cycling between the DSS Generator and the Specific DSS as shown in Figure 4. With each cycle, capabilities are added to, or deleted from, the Specific DSS from those available in the DSS Generator. Keen depicts the expansion and growth of the system in terms of adding verbs which represent actions managers require [24]. Carlson adds more dimension by focusing on representations, operations, control, and memories as the elements of expansion and modification [11]. In another paper, Keen deals substantively with the interaction between the user, the builder, and the technology in this iterative, adaptive design process [25].

Note that this approach requires an unusual level of management involvement or management participation in the design. The manager is actually the iterative designer of the system; the systems analyst is merely the catalyst between the manager and the system, implementing the required changes and modifications.

Note also that this is different from the concept of "prototyping"; the initial system is real, live, and usable, not just a pilot test. The iterative process does not *merely* lead to a good understanding of the systems performance requirements, which are then frozen. The iterative changeability is actually *built into* the DSS as it is used over time. In fact, the development approach *becomes the system*. Rather than developing a system which is then "run" as a traditional EDP system, the DSS development approach results in the installation of an adaptive process in which a decision maker and a set of information system "capabilities" interact to confront problems while responding to changes from a variety of sources.

### The Adaptive System

In the broad sense, the DSS is an adaptive system which consists of all three levels of technology in place and operating with the participants (roles), and the technology adapting to changes over time. Thus, the development of a DSS is actually the development and installation of this adaptive system. Simon describes such a system as one that adapts to changes of several kinds over three time horizons [34]. In the short run, the system allows a *seach* for answers within a relatively narrow scope. In the intermediate time horizon, the system *learns* by modifying its capabilities and activities, *i.e.*, the scope or domain changes. In the long run, the system evolves to accommodate much different behavior styles and capabilities.

The three level model of a DSS is analogous to Simon's adaptive system. The Specific DSS gives the manager the capabilities and flexibility to *search*, explore, and experiment with the problem area, within certain boundaries. Over time, as changes occur in a task, the environment, and the user's behavior, the Specific DSS must *learn* to accommodate these changes through the reconfiguration of the elements in the DSS generator, with the aid of the DSS builder. Over a longer period of time, the basic tools evolve to provide the technology for changing the capabilities of the Generators out of which the Specific DSS is constructed, through the efforts of the toolsmith.

The ideas expressed above are not particularly new. Rapid feedback between the systems analyst and the client has been pursued for years. In the long run, most computer systems *are* adaptive systems. They are changed and modified during the normal system life cycle, and they evolve through major enhancements and extensions as the life cycle is repeated. However, when the length of that life cycle is shortened from three to five years to three to five months, or even weeks, there are significant implications. The resulting changes in the development approach and the traditional view of the systems life cycle promises to be one of the important impacts of the growing use of a DSS.

# Performance Objectives and Capabilities

Most of the foregoing discussion has dealt with some aspects of the technological and organizational contexts within which a DSS will be built and operated. The second part of the framework deals with what a DSS must accomplish, and what capabilities or characteristics it must have. The three levels of hardware/software technology and the corresponding three major "stakeholders" or interested parties in the development and use of a DSS can be used to identify the characteristics and attributes of a DSS.

At the top level are the *managers or users* who are primarily concerned with what the Specific DSS can do for them. Their focus is the problem solving or decision making task they face, and the organizational environment in which they operate. They will assess a DSS in terms of the assistance they receive in pursuing these tasks. At the level of the DSS Generator, the *builders* or designers must use the capabilities of the generator to configure a Specific DSS to meet the manager's needs. They will be concerned with the capabilities the Generator offers, and how these capabilities can be assembled to create the specific DSS. At the DSS tool level, the *"toolsmiths"* are concerned with the development of basic technology components, and how they can be integrated to form a DSS Generator which has the necessary capabilities.

The attributes and characteristics of a DSS as viewed from each level must be examined. From the manager's view, six general performance objectives for the Specific DSS can be identified. They are not the only six that could be identified, but as a group they represent the overall performance of a DSS that seems to be expected and desirable from a managerial viewpoint. The characteristics of the DSS Generator from the viewpoint of the builder are described by a conceptual model which identifies performance characteristics in three categories: dialogue handling or the man-machine interface, database and database management capability, and modeling and analytic capability. The same three part model is used to depict the viewpoint of the "toolsmith," but from the aspect of the technology, tactics, and architecture required to produce those capabilities required by the builders.

## Manager's view: performance objectives

The following performance requirements are phrased using the normative word "should." It is likely that no Specific DSS will be required to satisfy all six of the performance requirements given here. In fact, it is important to recall that the performance criteria for any Specific DSS will depend entirely on the task, the organizational environment, and the decision maker(s) involved. Nevertheless, the following objectives collectively represent a set of capabilities which characterize the full value of the DSS concept from the manager/user point of view. The first three pertain to the type of decision making task which managers and professionals face. The latter three relate to the type of support which is needed.

1. *A DSS should provide support for decision making, but with emphasis on semi-structured and unstructured decisions.* These are the types of decisions that have had little or no support from EDP, MIS, or management science/operations research (MS/OR) in the past. It might be better to refer to "hard" or underspecified problems, because the concept of "structure" in decision making is heavily dependent on the cognitive style and approach to problem solving of the decision maker. It is clear from their expressed concerns however, that managers need additional support for certain kinds of problems.

2. *A DSS should provide decision making support for managers at all levels, assisting in integration between the levels whenever appropriate.* This requirement evolves from the realization that managers at *all* organizational levels face "tough" problems as described in the first objective above. Moreover, a major need articulated by managers, is the integration and coordination of decision making by several managers dealing with related parts of a larger problem.

3. *A DSS should support decisions which are* **inter**dependent *as well as those that are* **ind**ependent. Much of the early DSS work inferred that a decision maker would sit at a terminal, use a system, and develop a decision *alone*. DSS development experience has shown that a DSS must accommodate decisions which are made by groups or made in part by several people in sequence. Keen and Hackathorn [24] explore three decision types as:

- *Independent.* A decision maker has full responsibility and authority to make a complete implementable decision.

- *Sequential Interdependent.* A decision maker makes part of a decision which is passed on to someone else.

- *Pooled Interdependent.* The decision must result from negotiation and interaction among decision makers.

Different capabilities will be required to support each type of decision—personal support, organizational support, and group support respectively.

4. *A DSS should support all phases of the decision making process.* A popular model of the decision making process is given in the work of Herbert Simon [33]. He characterized three main steps in the process as follows:

- *Intelligence.* Searching the environment for conditions calling for decisions. Raw data is obtained, processed, and examined for clues that may identify problems.

- *Design.* Inventing, developing, and analyzing possible courses of action. This involves processes to understand the problem, generate solutions, and test solutions for feasibility.

- *Choice.* Selecting a particular course of action from those available. A choice is made and implemented.

Although the third phase includes implementation, many authors feel that it is significant enough to be shown separately. It has been added to Figure 5 to show the relationships between the steps. Simon's model also illustrates the contribution of MIS/EDP and MS/OR to decision making. From the definition of the three stages given above, it is clear that EDP and MIS, in the narrow sense, have made major contributions to the intelligence phase, while MS/OR has been primarily useful at the choice phase. There has been no substantial support for the design

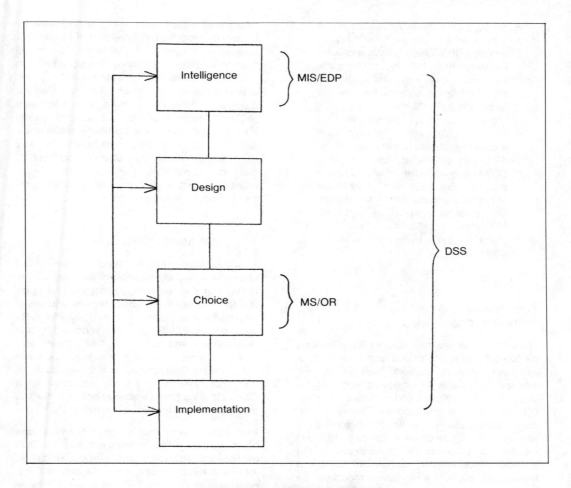

**Figure 5. Phases of Decision Making**

phase, which seems to be one of the primary potential contributions of a DSS. There also has been very little support from traditional systems for the implementation phase, but some early experience has shown that a DSS can make a major contribution here also [42].

5. *A DSS should support a variety of decision making processes, but not be dependent on any one.* Simon's model, though widely accepted, is only one model of how decisions are actually made. In fact, there is no universally accepted model of the decision making process, and there is no promise of such a general theory in the foreseeable future. There are too many variables, too many different types of decisions, and too much variety in the characteristics of decision makers. Consequently, a very important characteristic of a DSS is that it provide the decision maker with a set of capabilities to apply in a sequence and form that fits each individual cognitive style. In short, a DSS should be process independent, and user driven or controlled.

6. *Finally, a DSS should be easy to use.* A variety of terms have been used to describe this characteristic including flexibility, user friendly, nonthreatening, *etc.* The importance of this characteristic is underscored by the discretionary latitude of a DSS's clientele. Although some systems which require · heavy organizational support or group support may limit the discretion somewhat, the user of a DSS has much more latitude to ignore or circumvent the system than the user of a more traditional transaction system or required reporting system. Therefore, a DSS must "earn" its users' allegiance by being valuable and convenient.

## The builder's view: technical capabilities

The DSS Builder has the responsibility of drawing on computer based tools and techniques to provide the decision support required by the manager. DSS Tools can be used directly, but it is generally more efficient and effective to use a DSS Generator for this task. The Generator must have a set of capabilities which facilitate the quick and easy configuration of a Specific DSS and modification in response to changes in the manager's requirements, environment, tasks, and thinking approaches. A conceptual model can be used to organize these capabilities, both for the builders and for the "toolsmith" who will develop the technology to provide these capabilities.

The old "black box" approach is helpful here, starting with the view of the system as a black box, successively "opening" the boxes to understand the subsystems and how they are interconnected. Although the DSS is treated as the black box here, it is important to recall that the overall system is the decision *making* system, consisting of a manager/user who uses a DSS to confront a task in an organizational environment.

Opening the large DSS box reveals a database, a model base, and a complex software system for linking the user to each of them as shown in Figure 6. Opening each of these boxes reveals that the database and model base have some

interrelated components, and that the software system is comprised of three sets of capabilities: database management software (DBMS), model base management software (MBMS), and the software for managing the interface between the user and the system, which might be called the dialogue generation and management software (DGMS). These three major subsystems provide a convenient scheme for identifying the technical capability which a DSS must have. The key aspects in each category that are critical to a DSS from the Builder's point of view, and a list of capabilities which will be required in each category must now be considered.

## The data subsystem

The data subsystem is thought to be a well understood set of capabilities because of the rapidly maturing technology related to databases and their management. The typical advantages of the database approach, and the powerful functions of the DBMS, are also important to the development and use of a DSS. There are, however, some significant differences between the Database/Data Communication approach for traditional systems, and those applicable for a DSS. Opening the Database box summarizes these key characteristics as shown in Figure 7.

First is the importance of a much richer set of data sources than are usually found in typical non-DSS applications. Data must come from external as well as internal sources, since decision making, especially in the upper management levels, is heavily dependent on external data sources. In addition, the typical accounting oriented transaction data must be supplemented with non-transactional, non-accounting data, some of which has not been computerized in the past.

Another significant difference is the importance of the data capture and extraction process from this wider set of data sources. The nature of a DSS requires that the extraction process, and the DBMS which manages it, be flexible enough to allow rapid additions and changes in response to unanticipated user requests. Finally, most successful DSS's have found it necessary to create a DSS database which is logically separate from other operational databases. A partial set of capabilities required in the database area can be summarized by the following:

The DSS

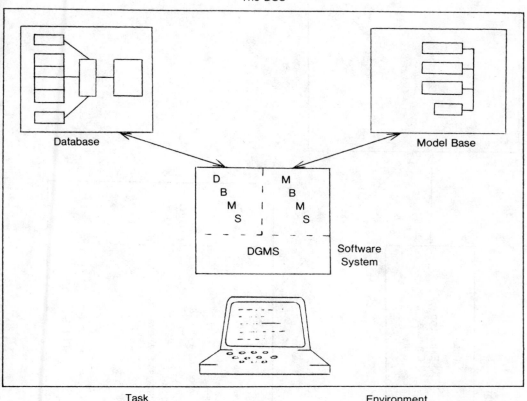

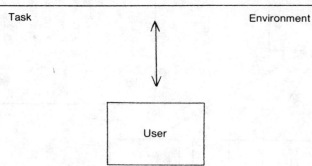

Figure 6. Components of the DSS

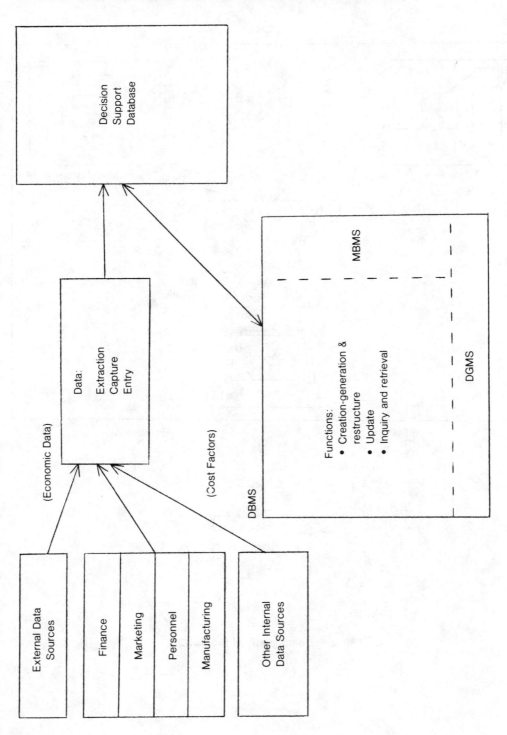

**Figure 7. The Data Subsystem**

●the ability to combine a variety of data sources through a data capture and extraction process;

●the ability to add and delete data sources quickly and easily;

●the ability to portray logical data structures in user terms so the user understands what is available and can specify needed additions and deletions;

●the ability to handle personal and unofficial data so the user can experiment with alternatives based on personal judgment; and

●the ability to manage this wide variety of data with a full range of data management functions.

## The model subsystem

A very promising aspect of a DSS is its ability to integrate data access and decison models. It does so by imbedding the decision models in an information system which uses the database as the integration and communication mechanism between models. This characteristic unifies the strength of data retrieval and reporting from the EDP field and the significant developments in management science in a way the manager can use and trust.

The misuse and disuse of models have been widely discussed [21, 28, 36, 39]. One major problem has been that model builders were frequently preoccupied with the structure of the model. The existence of the correct input data and the proper delivery of the output to the user was assumed. In addition to these heroic assumptions, models tended to suffer from inadequacy because of the difficulty of developing an integrated model to handle a realistic set of interrelated decisions. The solution was a collection of separate models, each of which dealt with a distinct part of the problem. Communication between these related models was left to the decision maker as a manual and intellectual process.

A more enlightened view of models suggests that they be imbedded in an information system with the database as the integration and communica-

tion mechanism between them. Figure 8 summarizes the components of the model base "box." The model creation process must be flexible, with a strong modeling language and a set of building blocks, much like subroutines, which can be assembled to assist the modeling process. In fact, there are a set of model management functions, very much analogous to data management functions. The key capabilities for a DSS in the model subsystems include:

●the ability to create new models quickly and easily;

●the ability to catalog and maintain a wide range of models, supporting all levels of management;

●the ability to interrelate these models with appropriate linkages through the database;

●the ability to access and integrate model "building blocks;" and

●the ability to manage the model base with management functions analogous to database management (*e.g.*, mechanisms for storing, cataloging, linking, and accessing models).

For a more detailed discussion of the model base and its management see [37, 38, 46].

### The User System Interface

Much of the power, flexibility, and usability characteristics of a DSS are derived from capabilities in the user system interface. Bennett identifies the user, terminal, and software system as the components of the interface subsystem [5]. He then divides the dialogue, or interface experience itself into three parts as shown in Figure 9:

1. *The action language* — what the user *can do* in communicating with the system. It includes such options as the availability of a regular keyboard, function keys, touch panels, joy stick, voice command, *etc.*

2. *The display or presentation language* — what the user *sees*. The display language includes options such as character or line printer, display

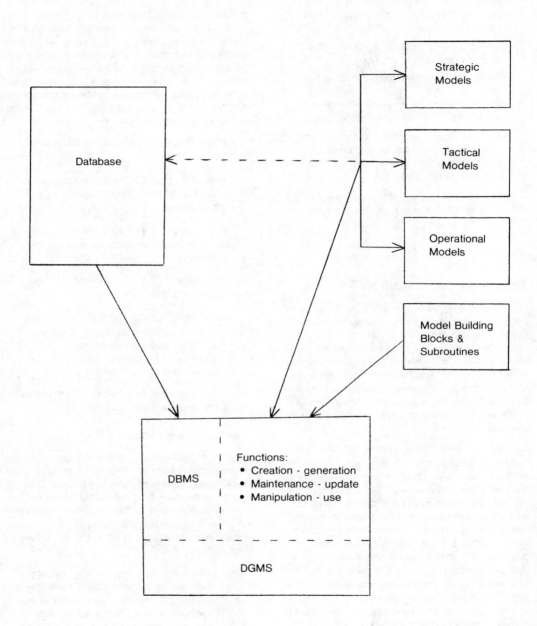

**Figure 8. The Models Subsystem**

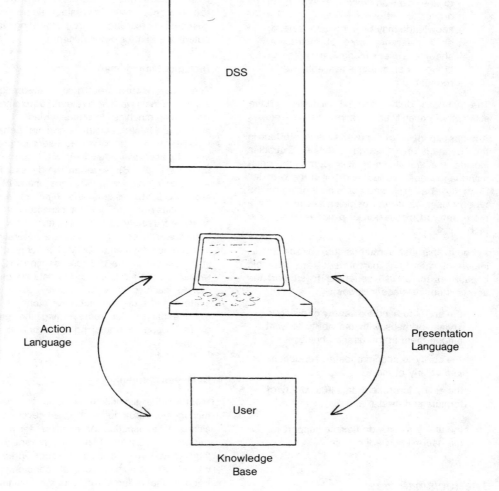

**Figure 9. The User System Interface**

screen, graphics, color, plotters, audio output, *etc.*

3. *The knowledge base* — what the user *must know.* The knowledge base consists of what the user needs to bring to the session with the system in order to effectively use it. The knowledge may be in the user's head, on a reference card or instruction sheet, in a user's manual, in a series of "help" commands available upon request, *etc.*

The "richness" of the interface will depend on the strength of capabilities in each of these areas.

Another dimension of the user system interface is the concept of "dialogue style." Examples include the questions/answer approach, command languages, menus, and "fill in the blanks." Each style has pro's and con's depending on the type of user, task, and decision situation. For a more detailed discussion of dialogue styles see [13].

Although this just scratches the surface in this important area, a partial set of desirable capabilities for a DSS generator to support the user/system interface includes:

- the ability to handle a variety of dialogue styles, perhaps with the ability to shift among them at the user's choice;

- the ability to accommodate user actions in a variety of media;

- the ability to present data in a variety of formats and media; and

- the ability to provide flexible support for the users' knowledge base.

## The toolsmith view: the underlying technology

The toolsmith is concerned with the science involved in creating the information technology to support a DSS, and the architecture of combining the basic tools into a coherent system. The same three part model can be used to describe the toolsmith's concerns because the tools must be designed and combined to provide the three sets of capabilities.

Each of the three areas—dialogue, data handling, and model handling—has received a fair amount of attention from toolsmiths in the past. The topic of DSS and the requirements it imposes has put these efforts in a new perspective revealing how they can be interrelated to increase their collective effectiveness. Moreover, the DSS requirements have revealed some missing elements in existing efforts, indicating valuable potential areas for development.

### Dialogue Management

There has been a great deal of theoretical and some empirical work on systems requirements for good man/machine interface. Many of these studies are based on watching users' behavior in using terminals, or surveying users or programmers to ascertain what they want in interactive systems [10, 16]. A recent study examines a series of interactive applications, many of which are DSS's, to assess the *type* of software capabilities required by the applications [43]. This study led directly to some creative work on the software architecture for dialogue generation and management systems (DGMS) as characterized in the model of the previous section [12]. This research uses a relation as the data structure for storing each picture or "frame" used in the system, and a decision table for storing the control mechanism for representing the potential users' option in branching from one frame to another.

### Data Management

Most of the significant work in the database management area during the past several years is aimed at transaction processing against large databases. Large DBMS's generally have inquiry/retrieval and flexible report preparation capabilities, but their largest contribution has been in the reduction of program maintenance costs through the separation of application programs and data definitions. On the other hand, DBMS work has generally had a rather naive view of the user and the user's requirements. A DSS user will not be satisfied merely with the capability to issue a set of retrieval commands which select items from the database, or even to display those selected items in a report with the flexible definition of format and headings. A DSS user needs to interact repeatedly and creatively with a relatively small set of data. The user may only need 40-100 data variables, but they must be the *right ones;* and what is right may change from day to day and week to week. Required data will probably include time series data which are not handled comprehensively by typical DBMS's. Better ways are needed to handle and coordinate time series data as well as mechanisms for capturing, processing, and tagging judgmental and probabilistic data. Better ways are also needed for extracting data from existing files and capturing data from previously non-computerized sources. The critical area of data extraction with fast response, which allows additions and deletions to the DSS database from the large transaction database was a major contribution of the GADS work [8, 29]. In short, the significant development in database technology needs to be focused and extended in some key areas in order to directly serve the needs of a DSS.

### Model Management

The area of model creation and handling may have the greatest potential contribution to a DSS. So far, the analytic capability provided by systems has evolved from statistical or financial analysis subroutines which can be called from a common command language. More recently, modeling languages provide a way of formulating interrelationships between variables in a way that permits the creation of simulation or "what if" models. As we noted earlier, many of the currently viable DSS Generators have evolved from these efforts. Early forms of "model management" seem to be evolving from enhancements to some modeling languages, which permit a model of this type to be used for sensitivity testing or goal seeking by specifying target and flexibility variables.

The model management area also has the potential for bringing some of the contributions of artificial intelligence (AI) to bear on a DSS. MYCIN, a system to support medical diagnosis, is based on "production rules," in the AI sense, which play the role of models in performing analytic and decision guidance functions [15]. A more general characterization of "knowledge management" as a way of handling models and data has also been tentatively explored [7]. More recent work proposes the use of a version of semantic networks for model representation [17]. Though this latter work is promising, AI research has shown the semantic network approach to be

relatively inefficient with today's technology. Usable capabilities in model management in the near future are more likely to evolve from modeling languages, expanded subroutine approaches, and in some cases, AI production rules.

# Issues for the Future

At this stage in the development of the DSS area, issues, problems, and fruitful directions for further research/development are plentiful. At a "task force" meeting this summer, thirty researchers from twelve countries gathered to discuss the nature of DSS's and to identify issues for the future. Their list, developed in group discussions over several days, was quite long [19]. The issues given here, phrased as difficult questions, seem to be the ones that must be dealt with quickly, lest the promise and potential benefits of DSS's be diluted or seriously delayed.

## *What's a DSS?*

Earlier it was noted that some skeptics regard DSS as "just another buzz word." This article has shown that there is a significant amount of content behind the label. The danger remains, however, that the bandwagon effect will outrun our ability to define and develop potential contributions of a DSS. The market imperatives of the multi-billion dollar information systems industry tend to generate pressures to create simple labels for intuitively good ideas. It happened in many cases, but not all, of course, with MIS. Some companies are still trying to live down the aftereffects of the overpromise/under-undelivery/ disenchantment sequence from the MIS bandwagon of the late '60's. Eventually, a set of minimal capabilities or characteristics which characterize a DSS should evolve. In the short range, a partial solution is education — supplying managers with intellectual ammunition they can use in dealing with vendors. Managers should and must ask sharp, critical questions about the capabilities of any purported DSS, matching them against what is really needed.

## *What is really needed?*

After nearly two decades of advancements in information technology, the real needs of managers from an information system are not well understood. The issue is further complicated by the realization that managers' needs and the needs of other "knowledge workers" with which they interact, are heavily interdependent. The DSS philosophy and approach has already shed some light on this issue by emphasizing "capabilities" — the ability for a manager to do things with an information system — rather than just "information needs" which too often infer data items and totals on a report.

Nevertheless, it is tempting to call for a hesitation in the development of DSS's until decision making and related managerial activities are fully understood. Though logically appealing, such a strategy is not practical. Neither the managers who face increasingly complex tasks, nor the information systems industry which has increasingly strong technology to offer, will be denied. They point out that a truly comprehensive theory of decision making has been pursued for years with minimum success.

A potential resolution of this problem is to develop and use a DSS in a way that reveals what managers can and should receive from an information system. For example, one of Scott Morton's early suggestions was that the system be designed to capture and track the steps taken by managers in the process of making key decisions, both as an aid to the analysis of the process, and as a potential training device for new managers.

The counterpart of the "needs" issue is the extent to which the system meets those needs, and the value of the performance increase that results. Evaluation of a DSS will be just as difficult, and important, as the evaluation of MIS has been. The direct and constant involvement of users, the ones in the best position to evaluate the systems, provides a glimmer of hope on this tough problem. Pursuit of these two tasks together may yield progress on both fronts with the kind of synergistic effect often sought from systems efforts. The iterative design approach and the three levels of technology afford the opportunity, if such a strategy is developed from the beginning.

## Who will do it?

A series of organizational issues will revolve around the roles and organizational placement of the people who will take the principle responsibility for the development of DSS's. Initiative and guidance for DSS development efforts frequently come from the user area, not from the EDP/MIS area. Yet current technology still requires technical support from the information systems professional. The DSS builder may work for the vice president of finance, but the technical support role is still played by someone in the MIS department. To some extent, the demand for a DSS supports the more general trend to distribute systems development efforts out of the MIS department into the user department. The difference is that many DSS software systems, or generators, specifically attempt to directly reach the end user without involvement of the MIS group. The enlightened MIS administrator considers this a healthy trend, and willingly supplies the required technical support and coordination. Less enlightened DP administrators often see it as a threat. Some companies have set up a group specifically charged with developing DSS type applications. This strategy creates a team of "DSS Builders" who can develop the necessary skills in dealing with users, become familiar with the available technology, and define the steps in the developmental approach for DSS's.

## How should it be done?

One of the pillars on which the success of DSS rests, is the iterative development or adaptive design approach. The traditional five to seven stage system development process and the system life cycle concept have been the backbone of systems analysis for years. Most project management systems and approaches are based on it. The adaptive design approach, because it combines all the stages into one quick step which is repeated, will require a redefinition of system development milestones and a major modification of project management mechanisms. Since many traditional systems will not be susceptible to the iterative approach, a way is also needed for deciding when an application should be developed in the new way instead of the traditional way. The outline of the approach described earlier is conceptionally straightforward for applications that require only personal support. It becomes more complicated for group or organizational support when there are multiple users. In short, DSS builders will need to develop a set of milestones, checkpoints, documentation strategies, and project management procedures for DSS applications, and recognize when they should be used.

## How much can be done?

The final issue is a caveat dealing with the limitations of technical solutions to the complexity faced by managers and decision makers. As information systems professionals, we must be careful not to feel, or even allow others to feel, that we can develop or devise a technological solution to all the problems of management. Managers will always "deal with complexity in a state of perplexity" — it is the nature of the job. Information technology can, and is, making a major contribution to improving the effectiveness of people in this situation, but the solution will never be total. With traditional systems, we continually narrow the scope and definition of the system until we know it will do the job it is required to do. If the specification/design/construction/implementation process is done right, the system is a success, measured against its original objectives. With a DSS, the user and his systems capabilities are constantly pursuing the problem, but the underspecified nature of the problem insures that there will never be a complete solution. Systems analysts have always had a little trouble with humility, but the DSS process requires a healthy dose of modesty with respect to the ability of technology to solve all the problems of managers in organizations.

# Conclusion

The "Framework for Development" described above attempts to show the dimensions and scope of DSS in a way that will promote the further *development* of this highly promising type of information system.

1. The relationships between EDP, MIS, and DSS show that DSS is only one of several important technology subsystems for improving organizational performance, and that DSS development efforts must carefully integrate with these other systems.

2. The three levels of technology and the interrelationships between people that use them provide a context for organizing the development effort.

3. The iterative design approach shows that the ultimate goal of the DSS development effort is the installation of an *adaptive system* consisting of all three levels of technology and their users operating and adapting to changes over time.

4. The performance objectives show the types of decision making to be served by, and the types of support which should be built into, a DSS as it is developed.

5. The three technical capabilities illustrate that development efforts must provide the DSS with capabilities in dialogue management, data management, and model management.

6. The issues discussed at the end of the article identify some potential roadblocks that must be recognized and confronted to permit the continued development of DSS.

In closing, it should now be clear that DSS is more than just a "buzz word," but caution must be used in announcing a new "era" in information systems. Perhaps the best term is a "DSS Movement" as user organizations, information systems vendors, and researchers become aware of the field, its potential, and the many unanswered questions. Events and mechanisms in the DSS Movement include systems development experience in organizations, hardware/software developments by vendors, publishing activities to report experience and research, and conferences to provide a forum for the exchange of ideas among interested parties.

It is clear that the momentum of the DSS Movement is building. With appropriate care and reasonable restraint, the coordinated efforts of managers, builders, toolsmiths, and researchers can converge in the development of a significant set of information systems to help improve the effectiveness of organizations and the people who work in them.

# References

[1] Alter, S. "A Taxonomy of Decision Support Systems," *Sloan Management Review*, Volume 19, Number 1, Fall 1977, pp. 39-56.

[2] Alter, S. *Decision Support Systems: Current Practice and Continuing Challenges*, Addison-Wesley Publishing Co., Reading, Massachusetts, 1980.

[3] Ashenhurst, R. L. "Curriculum Recommendations for Graduate Professional Programs in Information Systems," *ACM Communications*, Volume 15, Number 5, May 1972, pp. 363-398.

[4] Barbosa, L. C. and Hirko, R. G. "Integration of Algorithmic Aids into Decision Support Systems," *MIS Quarterly*, Volume 4, Number 1, March 1980, pp. 1-12.

[5] Bennett, J. "User-Oriented Graphics, Systems for Decision Support in Unstructured Tasks," in *User-Oriented Design of Interactive Graphics Systems*, in S. Treu (ed.), Association for Computing Machinery, New York, New York, 1977, pp. 3-11.

[6] Boeing Computer Services, c/o Mr. Park Thoreson, P. O. Box 24346, Seattle, Washington, 98124.

[7] Bonezek, H., Hosapple, C. W., and Whinston, A. "Evolving Roles of Models in Decision Support Systems," *Decision Sciences*, Volume 11, Number 2, April 1980, pp. 337-356.

[8] Carlson, E. D., Bennett, J., Giddings, G., and Mantey, P. "The Design and Evaluation of an Interactive Geo-Data Analysis and Display System," *Information Processing-74*, North Holland Publishing Co., Amsterdam, Holland, 1974.

[9] Carlson, E. D., and Sutton, J. A. "A Case Study of Non-Programmer Interactive Problem Solving, *IBM Research Report RJ1382*, San Jose, California, 1974.

[10] Carlson, E. D., Grace, B. F. and Sutton, J. A. "Case Studies of End User Requirements for Interactive Problem-Solving Systems," *MIS Quarterly*, Volume 1, Number 1, March 1977, pp. 51-63.

[11] Carlson, E. D. "An Approach for Designing Decision Support Systems," *Proceedings*, 11th Hawaii International Conference on Systems Sciences, Western Periodicals Co., North Hollywood, California, 1978, pp. 76-96

[12] Carlson, E. D. and Metz, W. "Integrating Dialog Management and Data Management," *IBM Research Report RJ2738*, February 1, 1980, San Jose, California.

[13] Carlson, E. D. "The User-Interface for Decision Support Systems," unpublished working paper, IBM Research Laboratory, San Jose, California.

[14] Courbon, J., Drageof, J., and Jose, T. "L'Approache Evolutive," *Information Et Gestion No. 103*, Institute d' Administration des Enterprises, Grenoble, France, January-February 1979, pp. 51-59.

[15] Davis, R. "A DSS for Diagnosis and Therapy," *Data Base*, Volume 8, Number 3, Winter 1977, pp. 58-72.

[16] Dzida, W., Herda, S., and Itzfeldt, W. D. "User-Perceived Quality of Software Interactive Systems," *Proceedings*, Third Annual Conference on Engineering (IEEE) Computer Society, Long Beach, California, 1978, pp. 188-195.

[17] Elam, J., Henderson, J., and Miller, L. "Model Management Systems: An Approach to Decision Support in Complex Organizations," *Proceedings*, Conference on Information Systems, The Society for Management Information Systems, Philadelphia, Pennsylvania, December 1980.

[18] Execucom Systems Corporation, P. O. Box 9758, Austin, Texas, 78766.

[19] Fick, G. and Sprague, R. H., Jr., (eds.). *Decision Support Systems: Issues and Challenges*, Pergamon Press, Oxford, England, forthcoming in 1981.

[20] Gerrity, T. P., Jr. "Design of Man-Machine Decision Systems: An Application to Portfolio Management," *Sloan Management Review 12*, Volume 12, Number 2, Winter 1971, pp. 59-75.

[21] Hayes, R. H. and Noland, R. L. "What Kind of Corporate Modeling Functions Best?" *Harvard Business Review*, Volume 52,

May-June 1974, pp. 102-112.

[22] Head, R. "Management Information Systems: A Critical Appraisal," *Datamation*, Volume 13, Number 5, May 1967, pp. 22-28.

[23] Keen, P. G. W. and Scott Morton, M. S. *Decision Support Systems: An Organizational Perspective*, Addison-Wesley Publishing Company, Reading Massachusetts, 1978.

[24] Keen, P. G. W. and Hackathorn, R. D. "Decision Support Systems and Personal Computing," Department of Decision Sciences, The Wharton School, The University of Pennsylvania, Working Paper 79-01-03, Philadelphia, Pennsylvania, April 3, 1979.

[25] Keen, P. G. W. "Adaptive Design for DSS," *Database*, Volume 12, Numbers 1 and 2, Fall 1980, pp. 15-25.

[26] Keen, P. G. W. "Decision Support Systems: A Research Perspective," in *Decision Support Systems: Issues and Challenges*, Pergamon Press, Oxford, England, 1981.

[27] Kroeber, H. W., Watson, H. J., and Sprague, R. H., Jr. "An Empirical Investigation and Analysis of the Current State of Information Systems Evolution," *Journal of Information and Management*, Volume 3, Number 1, February 1980, pp. 35-43.

[28] Little, J. D. C. "Models and Managers: The Concept of a Decision Calculus," *Management Science*, Volume 16, Number 8, April 1970, pp. B466-485.

[29] Mantey, P. E. and Carlson, E. D. "Integrated Geographic Data Bases: The GADS Experience," IBM Research Division, *IBM Research Report RJ2702*, San Jose, California, December 3, 1979.

[30] Ness, D. N. "Decision Support Systems: Theories of Design," presented at the Wharton Office of Naval Research Conference on Decision Support Systems, Philadelphia, Pennsylvania, November 4-7, 1975.

[31] Scott, J. H. "The Management Science Opportunity: A Systems Development Management Viewpoint," *MIS Quarterly*, Volume 2, Number 4, December 1978, pp. 59-61.

[32] Scott Morton, M. S. *Management Decision Systems: Computer Based Support for Decision Making*, Division of Research, Harvard University, Cambridge,. Massachusetts, 1971.

[33] Simon, H. *The New Science of Management Decision*, Harper and Row, New York, New York, 1960.

[34] Simon, H. "Cognitive Science: The Newest Science of the Artificial," *Cognitive Science*, Volume 4, 1980, pp. 33-46.

[35] Society for Management Information Systems, *Proceedings of the Eleventh Annual Conference*, Chicago, Illinois, September 10-13, 1979, pp. 45-56.

[36] Sprague, R. H. and Watson, H. J. "MIS Concepts Part I," *Journal of Systems Management*, Volume 26, Number 1, January 1975, pp. 34-37.

[37] Sprague, R. H. and Watson, H. J. "Model Management in MIS," *Proceedings, 7th National AIDS*, Cincinnati, Ohio, November 5, 1975, pp. 213-215.

[38] Sprague, R. H. and Watson, H. "A Decision Support System for Banks," *Omega - The International Journal of Management Science*, Volume 4, Number 6, 1976, pp. 657-671.

[39] Sprague, R. H. and Watson, H. J. "Bit by Bit: Toward Decision Support Systems," *California Management Review*, Volume XXII, Number 1, Fall 1979, pp. 60-68.

[40] Sprague, R. H. "Decision Support Systems — Implications for the Systems Analysts," *Systems Analysis and Design: A Foundation for the 1980's*, Elsevier-North Holland, New York, New York, 1980, in press.

[41] Sprague, R. H. "A Framework for Research on Decision Support Systems," in *Decision Support Systems: Issues and Challenges*, Fick, G. and Sprague, R. H. (eds.), Pergamon Press, Oxford, England 1981, in press.

[42] Sutton, J. "Evaluation of a Decision Support System: A Case Study with the Office Products Division of IBM," San Jose, California: *IBM Research Report FJ2214* 1978.

[43] Sutton, J. A., and Sprague, R. H. "A Study of Display Generation and Management in Interactive Business Applications," *IBM Research Report No. RJ2392*, IBM Research Division, San Jose, California, November 9, 1978.

[44] TYMSHARE. 20705 Valley Green Driver, Cupertino, California, 95014.

[45] Wagner, G. R. "DSS: Hypotheses and Inferences," Internal Report, EXECUCOM Systems Corporation, Austin, Texas, 1980.

[46] Will, Hart J. "Model Management Systems," in *Information Systems and Organizational Structure*, E. Grochla and H. Szyperski (eds.), Walter de Gruyter, New York, New York, 1975, pp. 467-483.

## About the Author

**Dr. Ralph H. Sprague, Jr.** *is Professor and Chairman of the Decision Sciences Department in the College of Business Administration at the University of Hawaii. His research and consulting specialty is computer based information systems for management, with particular emphasis on Decision Support Systems. He has lectured widely on this and related subjects including a series of seminars this past summer in Kuwait, Vienna, Austria, and Norway. In 1979 he won a national award from The Society for Management Information Systems for his article describing the computer based financial planning system at Louisiana National Bank. He has published articles in* California Management Review, Decision Sciences, Management Accounting, Journal of Bank Research, *and* Journal of Systems Management.

# 2
# Structuring the Information System

## INTRODUCTION

Chapter 1 established a need for the organization to devote time, effort and dollars to management of its information resource. How the organization accomplishes this information resource management is the critical factor in how well the information serves the organization and in turn how well the firm meets its objectives. This is true whether or not a computer is involved. But since computer support of the information system function is the most likely situation, we will proceed as if one were being used. To generalize the example further we will assume the organization is installing one for the first time. However, the same approach applies to upgrading an installed computer to greater capability.

The steps in systems development are rather standard. The variability is in their execution. For the purposes of this book we will explain what the development cycle consists of but will only address the specifics of those areas where critical management issues arise. The purpose is to inform management what it can do to minimize any negative effects and maximize the positive aspects of such an important and pervasive undertaking. This explanation is not meant to be a detailed guide for the IS professional.

## STEPS IN SYSTEMS DEVELOPMENT

Systems development, or the systems development life cycle as it is sometimes called, is divided into three major categories: *the definition phase, the technical phase, and the implementation or operation phase* (see Figure 2-1). The definition phase includes the feasibility study and the systems analysis. The technical tasks are the systems design, program coding and program testing. Implementation includes file conversion, cutover to the new system and a continuing post installation audit which may result in changes or modifications.

The first step however which happens prior to systems development is recognizing the need. This may be an action by one manager who suddenly discovers that his operation is critically hampered by the lack of information, or it may be a general feeling among the management of the organization that something must be done to help them make decisions.

Clues to discovering that there is a need for a new or modified information system often include errors in reports, late arriving information, inaccurate information,

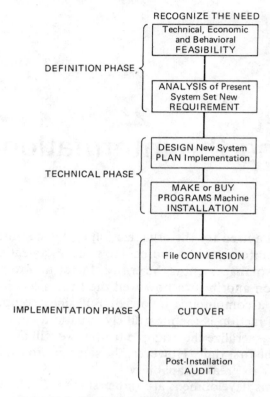

Figure 2-1. Systems development life cycle.

unreconciled data in different departments, interdepartmental conflict, and discovering that competitors have information and decisionmaking tools not available to this organization. Or the need may be expressed in specific terms such as need for reduced labor costs, need for improved operations through better inventory control or customer service, need for better accounting and managerial control, and need for increased productivity and profitability.

Once a need is felt, a preliminary investigation or feasibility study is made to confirm that in fact this need is real and seems to be satisfiable. Such an evaluation is specifically concerned with the technical, economic and behavioral feasibility of the project. Technical concerns have to do with whether the hardware is available and the software expertise exists to perform the task. Economic feasibility focuses on the cost/benefit ratio between the proposed change and its value to the organization. Behavioral feasibility reflects the human element in the use of the system outputs as well as human impact on the inputs. (*Note:* For this step and all the others in this process, any number of text books will provide the detail of how to do them. See reference list at the end of this chapter.) This investigation almost always confirms that there is a need. It results in a written report which formally documents the scope of the need in general terms. The study report includes cost *guesstimates* (since actual costs are not yet known), estimates of cost savings and other tangible and intangible benefits, explanations of alternative approaches to meeting the requirements where such alternatives exist, a plan for developing the recommendations and an estimate of the resources required. Management receives the feasibility study report and, after some lively give-and-take sessions which may alter the plan, approves it. This initiates the systems analysis phase.

The systems analysis is a more detailed study of the problem areas identified in the preliminary investigation. A great deal of effort is spent documenting the present system and defining user needs, i.e., the improvements required to make the system more effective. Specific computers or other machines are usually not chosen until after the analysis phase, but the analysts doing the study certainly have computer knowledge and are asking questions with general computer solutions in mind. In some instances however hardware will already exist or there may be other constraints or requirements limiting the options open to the analyst in the approach to the new system.

In a good systems analysis everything is questioned. The study team crosses any and all departmental lines to gather information. There are no sacred cows. All procedures, deadlines, report forms, coding systems, office arrangements, personnel assignments and management responsibilities are candidates for change. The result of this phase is a set of detailed system requirements.

In the design phase the new approach to each job is defined in detail so that the machines needed to support it are known, the exact functions of the required programs are defined and all the manual subsystems and controls are specified. The final design report includes diagrams of how each system will work, what the inputs will look like, who will prepare them, what processing will take place, what files will be retained, what the outputs will look like and who will get them. Explanations of the timing, accuracy and control of the information will also be included. The implementation plan emerges from this step so that every task to be performed between now and the implementation of the computer system is detailed. Usually this is shown on a chart noting the estimated time for each task versus the actual time expended. This includes not only program development, but also physical site preparation, personnel selection, hiring and training, forms and supplies ordering, file conversions and the like. Also included in the design report may be a more specific cost/benefit analysis. (*Note:* A major part of this phase is the selection of any new equipment or packaged software to meet the needs of the organization as defined in the design. This is a major management task and will be addressed in detail in chapter 8.)

Approval of the design results in program development and testing or in package purchase if that route is chosen (see chapter 8). If another machine is available for doing testing, installation of (and payment for) your own computer may be delayed. If this is impossible, uneconomic or inconvenient, then your equipment will have to be installed at this time. When all individual programs have been successfully tested a parallel or major test operation is run, and finally file conversion and actual cutover to the new system takes place. The cutover period may last many months as individual applications and jobs are phased in. Once implementation is "completed" a review is held to determine how closely original objectives are being met. Usually there is some disparity between what was planned and what took place. This situation arises from a number of factors. One is the desire to meet a "fixed" schedule. This schedule inflexibility results in the elimination or deferral of certain design requirements. For instance, the decision may be to move ahead with the inventory control system except for the economic order quantity calculations. In this instance the inventory accounting portion will work fine, but the management and control portion will work less well.

Another factor contributing to suboptimal information system operation is the incompleteness of the original design. This often results from a lack of knowledge of the business by the designers or from a lack of knowledge of the computer by the users. By implementation time or shortly thereafter both know quite a bit more and are aware of changes in the design which would make the system more useful. But it is too late to change and still meet the deadlines. The solution to this disparity between the desired and the actual is found in the ongoing plan for the information system function. The implementation is never complete. The organization is dynamic and the IS function must change to meet the organization's changing needs. The ongoing IS plan accommodates these changes and includes all the new applications which the organization needs as well as the revision of existing jobs to meet new needs or take advantage of new technologies. These same development steps of analysis, reporting, approval, implementation and review required for the initial installation apply to and are no less important for the development of new applications and revisions to currently operating systems.

But truly none of these studies should be made and no information systems plan produced unless they are within the framework of what the total organization is planning. In chapter 1 the relationship between corporate planning and information was explained. For the purpose of that explanation it was assumed that a planning function existed in the organization either formally or informally. But in reality this is not always the case. Many organizations operate without any structured planning or decisionmaking approach. Since good information systems planning depends on good corporate planning, it is valuable to review here the scope of the planning function, its value, and some of the reasons for resistance to it so that managers responsible for IS planning can better understand the framework within which they should be operating. And, if that framework does not exist, perhaps they will gain some insight into why that is so and what they can do about it.

## THE PLANNING DEFINITION*

In simple terms, the planning function can be defined as making decisions now about the future. This future-oriented decision process involves setting objectives; gathering, organizing and analyzing information; determining feasible courses of action and choosing among them; implementing the actions; and monitoring the results to insure compliance with the objectives. If the objectives are not being met, modified or alternative plans are employed.

Can there be an operational definition of planning that applies to all organizations? We think not. Planning differs among different organizations and among

---

*Adapted from Leon Reinharth, H. Jack Shapiro and Ernest A. Kallman, *The Practice of Planning: Strategic, Administrative, and Operational* (New York: Van Nostrand Reinhold, 1981).

the various levels in an organization. What planning means to one company is not the same for a company of similar size in a different industry. And what planning means for a young company may be different from what it means to a more mature company in the same industry.

Size alone or number of employees or marketplace are not common denominators of the planning function. A young company may be served adequately by a simple survival plan, whereas a more mature company in the same industry will need a formal planning function. A small firm in a high-technology area may have a desperate need for planning, whereas a large firm in a static industry may have less need. The planning needs of any organization are individual and situational. Thus, managers must understand the industry their firm operates in, the size and maturity of the firm relative to others in the industry, and the specific objectives the firm has in the marketplace. Above all they must know whether a particular functional area or the entire firm is the subject of the plan.

If the entire firm is the planning subject, planning takes place on the strategic level. If one of the functional areas such as marketing is being planned for, then planning will take place on the administrative and operational levels but always within the guidelines of the next higher level. To develop the appropriate plan, managers must have this perspective on the fit of their plan to the overall plan.

## The Value of Planning

As mentioned previously, planning means different things to different organizations. The value of planning to a given organization depends on its objectives, needs, and circumstances. Even so, planning has sufficient value so that whatever the situation in an organization it is always beneficial.

One of the benefits of the planning process is that it enables management to make rational decisions. When the planning process is followed, managers are presented with alternatives to choose from which have undergone a thorough analysis reflecting all available facts. This minimizes the use of emotion, intuition and guesswork.

The capability of making rational decisions based on a thoughtful analysis puts management in the enviable position of being able to act when necessary rather then simply react. As a result, management maintains the initiative. When quick response is essential, management will be ready because alternatives have been decided and their priorities have been established. If something should go awry, the contingency plan is in place. Thus, the computer manufacturing firm that wishes to market to small firms in the United States might have as its second alternative to move into overseas markets and as its third to approach larger American firms. If forecasted demand for the first priority is not realized, the firm's management would be prepared to move immediately to the overseas alternative. Thus, the organization is able to capitalize on opportunities and ward off threats more effectively.

In order to have an effective planning process, management must define relationships within and without the organization. This definition alone constitutes one of the major benefits of the planning process. Defining who is responsible for each organizational function insures that each function lies in someone's area of responsibility. In addition, management can determine whether each function is properly placed and whether the responsible individual has the authority to execute the required actions. It also insures that only one area is responsible for a given function.

Defining an organization and its relationships is usually more valuable if the managers themselves—not just top management—participate. In this way, the definitions are not imposed on those who must operate within them, but rather they reflect the understanding and willingness of the managers themselves. Such an approach fosters communication and cooperation. Managers will be more willing to be responsive to the needs of another department when they are sure that the responsibility is theirs, and they will be more willing to seek assistance from other areas if they are confident that such help is properly due them. In summary, defining relationships as part of the planning process opens up the lines of communication in an organization.

Organizations are dynamic. They change. In fact, they must change. When organizational change is random however it is difficult to determine where the firm changed from or whether it is better off for the move. Planning eliminates the dilemma. When the planning process is in place and when management is committed to planning, an organization can change rapidly and from a known position. The new position is rationally chosen, and it can be defined and evaluated relative to the original base. Thus planning provides for the constant change in an organization, but the change is controlled and directional.

A good planning process, which allows all levels of management to participate, builds confidence in an organization for it gives everyone a long-term perspective. It shows that management has a direction, that decisionmaking is under control and that the total organization is working to achieve the same objectives.

Finally, planning provides a standard of performance. The plan states what will be done. At any time, the level of achievement can be compared to this standard. On the operational level, the standards are set through a budget; this is the goal against which expense performance is measured. On the strategic level, corporate objectives such as a certain level of annual gross revenue become the standard by which management can be evaluated. This facet of planning provides an element of control at all levels of management. Management monitors performance and perceives whether changes should be made in order to maintain the standard, or it may indicate that the standard needs to be changed. In either case, the planning process provides the guidelines for rational controlled action.

Planning can be undertaken from many perspectives depending on the needs of an organization. The challenge to management is to discover the kind(s) of planning the organization needs and to invoke the part of the process that will achieve the greatest overall return.

## Fear of Planning

Many business people would prefer to avoid planning, and they offer strong objections when it appears that a planning function will be implemented. Often the form of these objections masks their real meaning and in many cases reflects an underlying fear on the part of the objector. The following is a list of what they often say and parenthetically what they really mean.

- We don't need anything that complex.
  (It's too hard. I might fail to do a good job.)
- There is too much structure.
  (It constrains my actions. I can't act on impulse.)
- It requires too many decisions.
  (When I make decisions I become vulnerable.)
- It takes too much time.
  (I'd rather get involved in day-to-day activities.)
- It is not precise. There are too many estimates.
  (It contains criteria for critique and evaluation, and I might not measure up.)
- There is too much to analyze.
  (Such analysis will set direction and bring organization out of chaos. This removes a very good excuse.)
- Planning brings its own chaos and disruption.
  (It will be hard for me to get rid of my bad habits and adapt to the discipline of the plan.)

Are the consequences of these fears necessarily the ones suspected? Can more positive consequences be achieved? If managers could somehow be induced to embark upon a planning project, they would soon learn that their fears were unfounded. Here is one example: A small but fast growing electronics company was grossing about $10 million per year when it was persuaded by its auditors to institute an elementary budgeting system. This basic planning function would highlight which funds would be spent by each functional area. There were separate budgets for administration, finance, production and marketing. The company had no other formal planning system nor any inclination to plan. The proposal to budget and the required thought process were both severely resisted by all but the financial officer.

Fears were rampant among managers. (Suppose I overspend? Suppose I forget to include something? Should I put in for more than I need to protect myself? What expenses can I dump on another area?) But the auditors prevailed. Historical data were prepared showing expenses in each area over the prior 3 years. Each officer was asked to project expenses for the next 2 years. The historical information had an astounding effect. For the first time, the managers had some idea of the costs for the functions in their operation. Moreover, they could see immediately where their greatest expenses were and where they had the most cost control. Thus, they could concentrate their efforts on those areas with the greatest payoff. The managers recognized that the budget allowed them to see just how well they were performing. Such specific evaluation was much more desirable than a nebulous feeling of doing a good job. Finally, underbudget performance became a source of pride.

### Plan vs. Planning

Although plans are valuable, the planning process itself is more important. An organization gains significant benefits just by moving through the organized, logical and systematic process of developing a plan. Some of the benefits are immediate; for example, weaknesses, strengths, threats and opportunities are discovered during the analysis phase. Even the initial step of defining the purposes and goals of the organization often provides top management with a much needed clarification of where the organization is headed, through which it can evaluate its decision.

Planning is a continuing management function; it is never finished. The planning process includes many stages—from goal-setting to analysis to strategy formulation and evaluation to implementation. Implementation is always followed by feedback and control; that is, the originally developed premises are continually tested against reality, and, as reality changes, the planning process must be reinstituted and the premises (and analyses) reworked. For instance, in some five year plans, every twelve months a formal review is held to measure achievement of objectives. The remaining four years are evaluated and perhaps revised and then a new fifth year added. In other words, the plan—the result of the planning process—is dynamic and constantly adapting to changes in the internal and external environment. That is as it should be, because a static plan would be of no value to a dynamic organization.

As mentioned previously, planning is a mangement function, and it cannot be effective in an organization without the active participation of all levels of management. However, although each level of manager has responsibility for some aspect of planning, the initial support must come from the top (the chief executive), and the commitment must be evident to everyone in the organization. Top management will focus on the strategic long-range aspects of the plan, leaving administrative planning to middle management and the day-to-day operational aspects of the planning cycle to lower levels in the organization. At whatever level planning is being done, it is part of an integrated, company-wide effort. And the chief executive is the chief planner.

## PLANNING THE INFORMATION FUNCTION

Just as in the corporate plan, top management input is vital for the information systems (IS) plan. The chief executive is the top IS person as well as the top planner. In much the same way that the corporate plan provides the decisionmaking umbrella for the functions of the organization, the IS function provides the information umbrella for the organization. And it too must be planned in such a way that its objectives coincide with and support the organization's objective.

The starting point of the IS plan should be the corporate plan. The first step of the feasibility study should be to examine the corporate plan and determine what kinds of information are required to support it and to what extent that information is being provided by the current information system. If the corporate plan is undeveloped, haphazard and incomplete it will be impossible for the feasibility study to come up with a valid information approach for the organization. In other words if the organization doesn't know what it is doing, it doesn't know its information needs and therefore cannot build an information system.

Other aspects of the plan include an assessment of current and future hardware, software, people, facilities and dollar requirements. An evaluation of present processing functions must be performed and detailed recommendations made for upgrading the present system and adding new applications. In addition, priority rankings should be given to all system changes and a tentative implementation schedule prepared. Finally all constraints and assumptions upon which the plan is based should be clearly explained. The IS professionals have the responsibility to produce such a plan. But management has the responsibility to provide input to it, review it and approve it.

## THE COMMUNICATION PROBLEM

The objective of this book and that of every information processing system is to see that the right information gets to the right person at the right time. But there are obstacles to this happening. An organization can have a comprehensive corporate plan, a well-coordinated information systems plan, adequate hardware, software, personnel and other resources, and yet the information needs of that organization may not be met. How can this happen? One way is when the user does not understand what he or she wants or can get from an information system. Another way is when the analyst does not understand what the user wants or needs. When there is any kind of confusion between the user's concept and the analyst's or designer's concept of what is needed, the resulting product will be unsatisfactory.

Where does the fault lie? Actually both are to blame, but using the principle that higher knowledge bears more responsibility, the analyst/designer is the more to blame because he or she should know better. Understanding the user's need is part of that job. The user's primary job is to perform a function (run a factory, make sales, hire qualified people). It is not reasonable to expect a specialist in a particular business area to also be a specialist in designing information systems. However, the user must be willing to give honest and complete information to the analyst.

What can be done? More education about computers and about computer use in their business function may help the users. There are many education programs which attempt to expose the non-IS person to computer capabilities and also numerous sources of information on the "modern" way to manage particular business functions. Professional associations, consulting firms, commercial schools, colleges, high schools and even grade schools have courses to improve the computer literacy of present and future generations, and many of these also teach "new" business techniques.

The ad shown in Figure 2–2 asks, "Do you and your computer programmer speak the same language?" The Univac answer is to give the executive his own language. But this too is only a partial solution, and one suggested simply because designer/ analysts often cannot talk "executive language." The burden to bridge this communication gap must fall most heavily on the IS professional.

Through both IS and interpersonal communication skills the trained systems analyst/designer must seek, understand and translate (valid) user needs into a workable, efficient computer operation which is consistent with overall corporate objectives. Just being technically competent is not sufficient for understanding and evaluating user needs. The perfect combination is an IS professional with years of experience in programming, design and operations, who also has industry functional experience performing tasks similar to those to be implemented. This coupled with the ability to allay user fears and elicit user cooperation almost insures success. An impossible ideal? No. A difficult one to achieve? Quite. But the closer to that ideal one comes, the better the product. The ability of the analyst/designer is the limiting

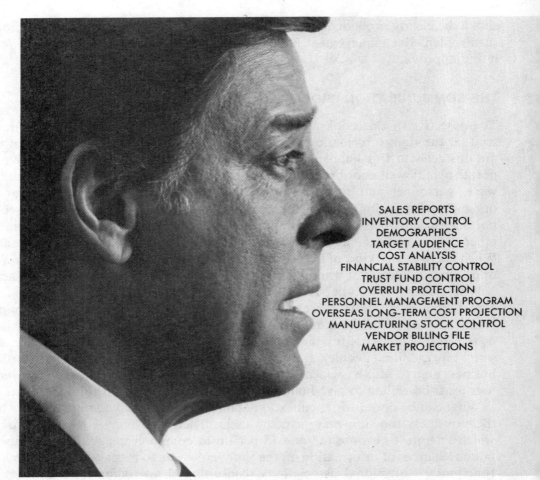

SALES REPORTS
INVENTORY CONTROL
DEMOGRAPHICS
TARGET AUDIENCE
COST ANALYSIS
FINANCIAL STABILITY CONTROL
TRUST FUND CONTROL
OVERRUN PROTECTION
PERSONNEL MANAGEMENT PROGRAM
OVERSEAS LONG-TERM COST PROJECTION
MANUFACTURING STOCK CONTROL
VENDOR BILLING FILE
MARKET PROJECTIONS

# DO YOU AND YOUR COI
# SPEAK THE SA

You need to know something fast. And you figure that your computer ought to be able to give you the answer.

The problem is communicating to your computer programmer exactly what questions you have.

Sperry Univac thinks executives shouldn't have to master a second language to get information from a computer.

That's why we created MAPPER™ software.

MAPPER software lets you talk to th computer. Directly. And in plain Englisl

What's more, MAPPER software means immediate and direct on-line acce to the information that's in your Sperry Univac 1100 series computer. That mea you can get the information you need for

*Sperry Univac is a division and registered trademark of Sperry Corporation.*

Figure 2–2. Ad recognizing user/computer communications gap. Courtesy of Sperry Univac Division of Sperry Corporation.

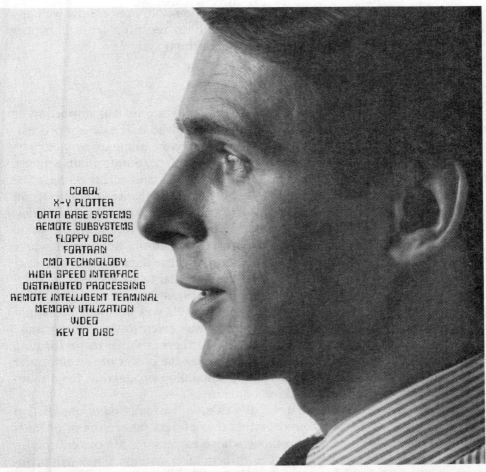
Figure 2–2. (Cont.)

factor in the success of the information processing system. No matter how well any and all the other resources are applied, poor definition resulting from improper understanding of what is needed will lead to a suboptimal system.

## THE DESIGN PROCESS

To better appreciate this dilemma and to be able to mitigate it, it is important to understand the typical background of those who are involved in the design process. The information systems department is headed by a director, manager or vice president who hopefully reports to the very highest levels of corporate management. (See Appendix A for a complete description of IS functions and career paths.) The president or an executive vice president is the best choice because it is important that the IS function report to someone who has broad corporate responsibilities. This is to insure that a given area does not receive the bulk of the information resources to the detriment of the greater corporate good simply because of where the function reports and also insures the cooperation of those departments who may not be benefitting from the computer but who are essential to its success.

In former times most computers were housed in the financial area, and as a result most applications were of a financial nature. This in itself was not bad, but application development in non-financial areas typically was given lower priority and/ or less resources. Today, it is recognized that though there is value to performing financial applications, there is often more value to using the power of the computer to aid in the running of the basic business, e.g., scheduling production for a manufacturer or routing vehicles for a trucking company.

This information systems head, whatever the title, will usually have one of two very different and distinctive backgrounds, either that of data processing or of business operations. The most common are those whose careers are almost entirely in some aspect of data processing, computers or information systems. They will probably not have held positions in the firm outside the IS area. They will most likely have had a number of computer-related jobs with a number of different employers and will have extensive programming, systems and information systems operations experience. They will have some managerial skill and will be quite knowledgeable about current hardware and software trends.

The less common group, those with business operations experience may be termed the *professional managers*. These are management generalists who have developed the managerial skills of planning, organizing, staffing, directing and controlling while doing such things as marketing efforts, building factories, or developing corporate plans, rather than concentrating on the specifics of any one given area. Their strength lies in their ability to bring good business practice to an area irrespective of the technical detail that the area is concerned with. When this type of manager is made head of information systems it is usually in response to his breadth of experience with the particular firm or industry. The hope is that he will appreciate the problems of the people he serves and will be a counterforce to the non-business-knowledgeable technical specialists in the information systems department.

That such professional managers are appearing with increasing frequency in IS may be due to a number of factors some of which are controversial and others of which have not yet been proven. Among them are: (1) good management skills reap a better reward than good technical knowledge at the IS head level; (2) people who know the business are more valuable (and easier to find) than those who know IS; (3) due to college courses and numerous other methods, even the extreme management generalist has a rather good grounding in IS; (4) heading IS with a company-oriented manager allows that manager to move from IS head to other positions in the firm when promoted and thereby provides a career opportunity that did not otherwise exist. (Often the only opportunity for advancement for an IS head is to move to another firm.) There may be other reasons for the increase in general managers, but the question of the value of using a general manager rather than an IS professional to run IS will have to await the test of time to be fully answered. At the moment there is no clear answer which approach is better.

Among those reporting to the IS head will be the designers (system analysts) who prepare the specifications in computer terms for what the user "really wants," programmers who develop the programs using the designer's definitions and the operations people who actually run the computer.

The user is any person who comes in contact with the computer through providing input, or using output either directly or indirectly. Some users are managers, some are staff and some clerical or production employees. Some may receive paper reports; others may communicate with the computer through a device such as a video display terminal. In any case it is the responsibility of the designer to insure that the use of the computer is simple, convenient and pleasant for the users and that the content is accurate, timely and useful. The latter three characteristics are harder to achieve and thus where the most effort is spent not only in design but in actual operation. The former, making the system *user friendly,* though quite achievable, is often ignored by designers, or at best given cursory attention.

To illustrate the impact of different backgrounds upon the design process, let us look at a typical situation from the point where a need is recognized, as described in a previous section. Resources are requested up the managerial hierarchy and finally the approval is given for the information systems department to "automate" a particular function, for instance, finished goods inventory. With management approval of the finished goods inventory feasibility report the designer/analyst will interview everyone connected with finished goods inventory processing to determine how reporting is done now, what is desirable about the present method and what improvements are needed. Here is where the dilemma begins. Does the inventory manager know enough about the inventory function (and developing information systems) to request those things which will really help the inventory control? If the inventory manager does not know what is required, does the analyst know? If the inventory manager merely appears to know, is the analyst astute enough to detect this, and can he (politically) reorient the design. If the analyst knows what a good inventory system requires and the manager admits not knowing, will the manager believe the analyst? If the manager believes the analyst, will the inventory manager really be skilled enough to use the new system properly? This is an almost no-win situation. Again, the burden is on the designer. Even if he does not know the inventory function he must be so skilled in interview and investigative techniques that he can make the user define a worthwhile system through his questions. In such an approach the user will view the system as being of his own design and will be more likely to understand it and use it properly.

## INFORMATION SYSTEMS—A SERVICE FUNCTION

This design dilemma is often impacted by the attitude of IS personnel. Sometimes they see their function as an end in itself rather than as a service function. They fail to see that processing information is not the reason the firm exists but that information services are provided to aid the main business operation. Such a misguided attitude results in the IS department "withholding" information and arbitrarily refusing to service certain users or giving their processing low priorities. Such an attitude is the direct result of top management not having sufficient input to or knowledge about the IS function. The IS department which acts this way has become "independent" of any real control by management. Top management has become "hostage" to the technocrats with the computer.

Such hostage situations, where control of such a vital corporate resource has given a disproportionate power base to the IS department, often result in the organization failing to take full advantage of new technologies and opportunities. Three such technologies are database management systems (DBMS), office automation (OA) and distributed data processing (DDP) and each of these could be lost to the firm through uncooperative attitudes and actions on the part of the IS leadership.

### Database Management Systems (DBMS)

In the DBMS concept, all the information elements needed by an organization are defined in a consistent manner and labeled and stored for easy access for any appropriate application. And each element of information is stored only once. This contrasts to non-DBMS computer installations where various pieces of information are found in more than one data file. For instance, both the marketing file and the accounts receivable file may contain customer names and addresses since both need to correspond with customers. Having the information in more than one place has the disadvantages of (1) taking up extra space, (2) having to update multiple files when changes are made, and (3) running the risk of the common data not being identical in all files, e.g., making an address change to one file and failing to make the identical change to the other files containing that same customer. This situation eventually leads to havoc as more inconsistencies develop and it becomes unclear which file (if any) is the truly accurate one.

The other advantages of DBMS have to do with better data definition and programming ease. Defining information elements consistently requires the cooperation of both the user and the designer and eventually of every subsequent user. The DBMS provides an organized way to state what each element means and what subelements it contains. Agreement on this *data dictionary* goes a long way to fostering communication between user and designer. When new users desire system outputs, they can scan the dictionary to decide what information they want (and are entitled to). Failing to find all that they need initiates a further definition phase and more elements are added to the dictionary.

Programmers benefit too. All files are defined in terms of the elements they contain. The names of all the elements are set and the dictionary describes the sizes and other characteristics. Rather than design and define files the programmer only has to use what has already been set up. Further, programs written by different programmers which use common data elements will have more consistency through the use of the common names and element definitions. This aids both program documentation and future maintenance and modification.

If we accept the value of the unique data or information element, the next logical step is to realize that some person or function is responsible for putting that information into the file and insuring that it stays accurate. Appealing to the management principle of unity of command, we can only have one person or function responsible for any piece of data. In our customer name and address example, it must be decided whether marketing or accounts receivable maintains the customer names and addresses. Which one is chosen is immaterial in this example, but one *must* be chosen. If, for instance, marketing is chosen (perhaps by some joint user/ IS committee), then marketing becomes the "owner" of the customer name and address file. IS actually possesses the file and makes it available on demand to those who properly need its contents. But it belongs to marketing. Others use the file as they need it. This concept of ownership of data elements by responsible functional departments, although fostered by a DBMS, may be invoked with or without one. In either event such an approach flies in the face of old-time IS attitudes. The old approach had the files belonging to the IS department to be controlled as best suited their needs. Changing this attitude is a first step to replacing the hostage, that is, to making IS a service where full benefit can be recevied from a technique like DBMS.

## Office Automation (OA)

Office automation offers another instance of where the IS function may be holding the firm hostage. Office automation means bringing the power of the computer to secretarial/clerical office functions. Such phrases as *word processing, text editing, electronic mail* and the like refer to aspects of office automation. In its simplest form OA may mean using a typewriter that has a memory so that when a letter is typed the text is saved for future use. Such use arises after the author reviews and makes corrections to the letter. The typist plays back the letter, inserts the required changes, and automatically prints a perfect copy with only a minimum of new keying. The largest and most sophisticated office automation systems connect the office directly to the firm's computer. In such systems vast amounts of memory, capable of storing many pages or even books, are available to every typist. Video display screens and keyboards replace typewriters for input. Output is performed on high speed letter-quality printers. Messages can be transmitted from one video display terminal (VDT) to any other in the system whether in the same office or some other office in the building or any other connected through communication facilities. Telephones can be dialed and answered automatically and messages taken when the recipient is out. These are just some aspects of OA and that portion of it called electronic mail. The question is where does office automation end and data processing begin? Or put another way, who is responsible for OA? Is it the IS head? Is it the VP administration? Office manager? Who? Should IS get involved with elementary OA approaches like memory typewriters? If not, at what point is the technology sufficiently complimentary to warrant IS entry?

If the IS people are not involved, at least as consultants at the very beginning, the firm runs the risk of ultimately building two technical staffs with similar capabilities, one for OA and one for IS. The usual problem when OA is put under the IS head initially is that the head views the IS projects as more worthwhile and challenging and resources are diverted from the OA projects. This is where the firm begins to become hostage again to the uncontrolled IS head. The same kind of jurisdictional dispute arises from the availability of personal computers. These small, mobile and powerful machines can be easily installed in office or home and can be of great value to the user. They can operate either independently or as intelligent terminals connected to a larger computer, taking advantage of the vast power of the larger machine. The question again is whether the IS head should be responsible for all computers and automation functions in the organization? Is it too large a job for one person? Will the best interests of the organization be served? There is no one best answer to any of these. But organization decision makers must be aware of the dilemma and seek to avoid its pitfalls.

## Distributed Data Processing (DDP)

A third phenomenon which occasions the same kinds of questions is the increasing popularity of distributed data processing. This simply means that access to the computer (input and output) takes place outside the actual computer room. This could mean a video display terminal in the accounts receivable department to handle credit inquiries, or a printer in the payroll department so that checks and other confidential payroll information are seen only by authorized personnel. Or on a grander scale, distributed DP could mean a series of small computers at other sites of the firm's geographic locations, doing local processing locally while transmitting to the main computer the information required for corporate functions. At either end of the spectrum, distributing the data processing raises the questions of who is responsible for the information. The answer is similar to the DBMS example. When input and output responsibility leaves the computer room, the functional department doing the input and output is responsible for it. This is another instance of the diminishing of the IS head's empire. When there are multiple computers as satellites to the large home office computer, the question of control also arises. Who selects the remote computers? Who designs and programs them? Who decides what jobs will be processed on them? Suppose different locations establish different priorities, how will conflicts between local and corporate operating schedules be resolved? If the control is local, it means duplicating skills of the home office. If the control is from the home office, it means lessening the authority (and perhaps ability to meet objectives) of the local manager. This is another instance of where there is no clear answer. But recognizing the dilemma is part of the solution. The discussion here is really one of management control and setting of priorities. With ample knowledgeable top management involvement, empire-building IS technicians will not be able to ignore the corporate plan and will have to follow priorities set for the corporate good. The alternative is chaos. Appendix D guides management through the DDP decision process and the subsequent development and implementation of a DDP.

## MANAGEMENT AIDS

If an information system is to be developed properly and maximum benefit attained for the organization, management must take charge and insure that the complete job is done. For non-IS management and in many cases for the technically trained manager, this is not an easy task. The magnitude of the task of meeting the organization's total information needs, the abundance and variety of hardware and software available and the dynamics of the environment both inside and outside the firm all contribute to the conclusion that the responsible manager, whatever his or her qualifications, is going to need competent staff and much help from available management techniques.

Throughout this chapter we have alluded to the need for competent staffing through discussion of the organization of the information systems department, the analyst/designer function, and the operations area. The skills and training needed to support information systems are in fact rather well defined. What is more of a problem is managing the functions of the information systems department. There are a number of aids for the manager who is faced with the responsibility for defining and designing an information system.

These management aids are approaches to control, analysis and communication which the manager must understand and where appropriate apply to the project. The following sections examine some management aids and their usefulness. The list is not exhaustive but will indicate the kinds of tools which are available.

### Project Control Aids

No matter who is designated the functional leader of the information systems area, top management must establish a management steering committee to give overall direction to this significant allocation of corporate resources (see Figure 2–3). This is especially true for a first computer or a major overhaul. The president leads this committee and appoints the various functional vice presidents, typically marketing, manufacturing and finance. Any other key executives whose areas will be greatly affected by the information system should also be included. The main objective of establishing such a committee is to convey quite strongly to all levels of the organization and all departments that top management is supportive of this information systems effort.

The functions of the committee are in the areas of planning, review and control. Many of the committee members were prime participants in the establishment of the corporate plan and the resultant information systems plan. Now they are overseeing the execution of what has been planned. This implies that there will be a timetable and a set of financial constraints. The management steering committee must set the deadlines and must provide sufficient funds so that an effective system

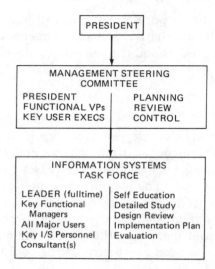

Figure 2-3. Key project control committees.

can be built in the time required. Another reason for having this committee involved in the scheduling and the funding is that both areas seem to be perennially underestimated. This committee therefore is the place where progress is reviewed, cost and time overruns evaluated and additional resources allocated should the circumstances warrant.

Specifically the committee oversees the progress of another group called the *information systems task force*. By showing their support for the project, the committee is endorsing the task force and aiding it in eliciting the cooperation of the various departments. The task force is a study group which has a number of members which reflect the major functions of the organization. All functions planned to be part of the system should be included. The members should be well experienced in the particular organizational functions they represent. Data processing knowledge is not a requirement for membership. They will be supplemented by one or more people with systems analysis and information systems experience. If any skills are unavailable inside the company people may have to be hired or consultants engaged. The use of consultants here and at other points in the project can be very helpful through their expert skills and outside (independent) viewpoint. The leader of the task force should be assigned full time to that project. Other members may serve on a part-time basis. But it must be clear to task force members' managers that the task force is a high priority function and must not be unduly subordinated to other assigned tasks of the member.

Normally the leader has information systems experience, though like the IS head, this is not an absolute requirement. The major quality necessary in the leader is project management ability. The leader should be of high enough rank (vice president is best) so that his voice can be heard in upper management levels and he can deal from strength with lower organization levels. The authority of this leader and of the task force generally must be made known clearly throughout the organization because there is sure to be some resistance to this effort. And finally, to insure task force success, the first task it undertakes should be its own education in both computers and the impact of information systems on the organization. This can be done by in-house seminars as well as through schools and professional associations.

## Information Analysis Aids

With the management committee and task force in place, the next important decision is how to approach the assessment of the organization's information requirements. Often an *ad hoc* investigative approach is used for this. But a more formal and directed assessment is recommended. A number of methods are available. Among those most discussed are IBM's business systems planning (BSP), John Rockart's critical success factors (CSFs) and Donald Burnstine's business information analysis and integration technique (BIAIT). Each of these varies according to popularity, state of development and applicability to a particular information systems situation.

BSP is what IBM calls "a structured approach to assist a business in establishing an information systems plan to satisfy its near and long-term information needs." It is characterized by a business-wide perspective, top-down analysis, bottom-up implementation and systems and data independence. Its total view of the entire business organization is consistent with the ideas we have advocated in this and the previous chapter. We have insisted that there are information needs at all levels of the business and any information system must address all these needs.

In top-down analysis the broad major areas of the business are defined and then refined into their smaller components. Each level or layer is analyzed with respect to the processes it performs and the information it needs. During the design phase the process is reversed and the design begins from the bottom. The detailed data required for the business process are designed into the system and system sections are linked to form the information system. This achieves system and data independence of the organizational structure. If the total business is serviced rather than one department or division, changes in organizational structure will not affect the usefulness of the information system.

Critical success factors (CSFs) is an M.I.T.-developed approach to helping executives define their information needs through a series of interviews. First the executive is asked to define goals and then the discussion moves to the CSFs which underlie those goals. Four specific sources for success factors have been isolated: (1) the nature of the industry, (2) the situation of that company in the industry (strategy, position and geographic location), (3) the external environmental factors such as the state of the economy, and (4) temporal factors which provide for exceptions and extraordinary situations. Further detail on CSFs may be found in Rockhart's article referenced at the end of this chapter.

The approach is to define the CSFs and the reports and information which support them. Then (information) systems are designed to accommodate those information needs. Its focus is on top management (and to some extent middle management) decisionmaking.

BIAIT, the newest of the three approaches, takes an entirely different track. Its purpose is similar to the others, that is, to establish requirements which reflect the information needs of the organization and also to identify issues that must be resolved before the design of the information system can be stabilized. However, a major BIAIT objective is to bridge the gap between the manager and the IS technician to insure that both are solving the same problem. What is different about the BIAIT approach is that the BIAIT system produces a model of the business organization. This model defines both the jobs which must be done in order for that organization to be successful and the information needs for individual job success. The BIAIT process then matches a given organization against the model to discover discrepancies.

These discrepancies can come at any level; jobs may exist in the model which are not a part of the organization and the same kind of inconsistencies may hold true for the presence or absence of information. When these discrepancies are resolved the organization is better structured to meet its objeectives, and the required information is in place to support that structure. In addition to defining the organization and its information needs, BIAIT also defines the information responsibility. Not only is the appropriate information available for each function, but BIAIT indicates who is responsible for its acquisition, timeliness, accuracy and if necessary modification. This avoids multiple information owners and the problem of having information for which no one is responsible. This assignment of information responsibility is a major feature of BIAIT and totally consistent with the concept of *information ownership* which was introduced earlier in the chapter. For a feature-by-feature comparison of BSP and BIAIT see Zachman's article reprinted at the end of this chapter.

## Communication and Design Aids

Though each of the analysis aids described above has a design element, there have been some specific design aids developed recently which not only make the design process more efficient but also enhance the communication between the user and the system designer. These aids fall generally under the heading of *structured techniques*. Much of the credit for both developing and promulgating structured approaches goes to Edward Yourdon and his associates. A number of their works are listed in this chapter's reference list, and one chapter from a recent Yourdon book detailing the structured approach to the project life cycle is reprinted at the end of this chapter.

Although there are many structured techniques and numerous variations of them, the essence of these approaches can be gained through a brief discussion of structured analysis, design, programming and the concept of the structured walkthrough.

Structured analysis still maintains the investigative portion required in any systems analysis but differs in that the documentation of the findings uses some new techniques for graphically displaying data flow and for defining the data to be used and the logic of the process. As a substitute for the standard systems flow chart, structured analysis calls for the use of a charting technique called *data flow diagramming*. Rather than using a series of geometrical shapes representing various data processing functions, data flow diagrams (DFDs) use circles and arrows and explanatory phrases to accomplish the same thing. This has the advantage of not obscuring the process for the user by hiding it in differently shaped boxes and makes the resultant diagram a more usable communication vehicle where the users can see and understand the information flow that affects them and correct or assent to its validity. (For a more detailed explanation of DFDs see the Gane & Sarson book listed in this chapter's reference list.)

In addition to the DFD the structured analyst will also use the data dictionary approach to define the information needed in the processes shown whether or not a database management system is ultimately employed. All data names which appear in the DFD are defined logically in the data dictionary. This means that the major data elements are identified, all the components of that data element are defined and finally at the lowest level the size of the element and some indication as to whether it is alphabetic, numeric or both are shown. Though defining data elements is not a new process of the analysis phase, this approach to it is new and designed in such a way that the analyst and user can both easily understand the composition of the data and insure that it is adequate for the process defined.

Structured English or pseudocode is the third element of structured analysis and is used to define the logic of the business processes which are performed by the department under study. To do this, the analyst uses a selected list of English verbs and nouns to describe the decisions in the process and the alternatives of each condition. For example, pseudocode would be employed by the analyst to describe to the programmer the conditions under which a delinquent customer might receive a dunning letter. Once again, the object is to facilitate communication between the user and the analyst. With an English-like explanation of the process, the user can easily verify the logic, and the approved documentation is in a form which is quite appropriate for the structured programmer.

Before programming however we should discuss the topic of design. Structured design is concerned with organizing a program and all programs related to it into modules or elements to insure that they are complete in themselves and that together they form a complete system meeting the analysis specifications. According to Yourdon structured design is a collection of five related elements: documentation techniques, criteria for distinguishing between good and bad systems at the modular level, heuristics or rules of thumb for evaluating the ''goodness'' of a particular design, design strategies which allow systematic solutions to common types of data processing problems (such as top-down design) and implementation strategies for prioritizing module coding and implementation.

As for documentation techniques besides data flow diagrams and structured English one of those most commonly used for structured design is the *hierarchy, plus input, process, output* chart commonly called the HIPO chart. It shows the overall design of a system beginning at the top with the major modules and then moving down the hierarchy to the more subordinate modules. This modular display is again a communication facilitator between user and analyst as the relationship between modules and the module functions are clearly defined.

Structured programming is not necessarily useful as a communication tool between user and programmer since they rarely interact and the other communication devices described perform the job adequately. But structured programming benefits from the documentation techniques used and from the modular approach to design. Thus, the programmer has through structured English a well-defined logic which uses familiar terms rather than industry jargon. The modular approach allows the programming to be distributed among many programmers and major modules and linkages can be written and tested early, thus detecting any major design flaws when they are easier to correct. Also the structured programmer is using a basic approach to programming which provides for specific ways to express logic in a program and severely discourages a programming linkage technique called the *GO-TO*. Using this logic approach and avoiding the GO-TOs makes the programming much more standard and allows improved understanding of the program by those who did not write it which facilitates maintenance and modification, two of the most costly and cumbersome of the programming tasks.

The last structured technique is termed the *structured walkthrough,* and it, more than any of the others, is a communications device. As in the other structured techniques, much of what takes place in a walkthrough is not new, it is just done in an organized, orderly and controlled manner—and this makes it effective. A walk through is little more than a planned review session. But it is the planning (and the resultant structure) that makes it work. There are many rules about how to conduct walkthroughs and some controversy over them as well, such as whether managers ought to attend or only peers should be present. But all agree some rules are essential for the process to be effective. First, walkthroughs should be held at all stages of systems development, starting before the analysis stage begins and at every stage through and after implementation. A corollary being, if in doubt, hold another walkthrough. Second, the attendees should include all who may be affected by the proceedings. This definitely means inviting the users to those sessions where their input is appropriate. At programming walkthroughs, other programmers working on connecting modules must be included. When in doubt, include more participants. Third, walkthroughs should take as long as necessary. Some last for days. But break them up into smaller productive periods of a few hours. The time spent reviewing every line of programmer code before it gets to the machine saves both machine and programmer time in the long run. When in doubt, lengthen rather than shorten a walkthrough. And last, establish the proper spirit of the walkthrough by insuring that they are conducted by a trained coordinator in a spirit of cooperation rather than criticism, seeking system improvement rather than exposing weaknesses in individuals, trying for a better end product and not the embarrassment of anyone participating in it. Reports of results from walkthroughs should emphasize the improved nature of the design rather than the failure of the initial offering. With such a spirit, confidence in the walkthrough technique is fostered and walkthroughs will be sought rather than resisted.

Now with an understanding of the importance of information to the organization, the role of management in meeting organization needs through technology, and the kinds of techniques that are available to assist management in the process, the next chapters will display the kinds of information that the organization may hope to obtain at each of the decisionmaking levels. The materials are from real managers in real firms.

# REFERENCES

Bowman, B., G. Davis and J. Wetherbe. 1981. Modeling for MIS. *Datamation* (July): 155–164.
A comparison of various modeling and information analysis techniques.

Buchanan, J. and R. F. Linowes. 1980. Understanding distributed data processing. *Harvard Business Review* **58** (4): 143–153.
A primer on the advantages and disadvantages of centratized vs. decentratized computer power. Reprinted herein on pp. 469–479.

Burnstine, D. C. 1979. *The theory behind BIAIT—Business Information Analysis and Integration Technique.* Petersburg, NY: BIAIT International.
Details the information study technique developed by the author and the theory behind it.

*Business Systems Planning—Information Systems Planning Guide.* 1981. White Plains, NY: IBM Corporation.
The IBM recommended approach to information need analysis is described thoroughly.

Carlson, W. M. 1979. Business information analysis and integration technique (BIAIT)—the new horizon. *Database* **10** (4): 3–9.
An explanation and example of this information study technique.

DeMarco, T. 1979. *Structured Analysis and System Specification.* New York: Yourdon Press.
A lucid explanation of these "modern" techniques. One of the original works on this subject.

FitzGerald, J., A. F. FitzGerald and W. D. Stallings, Jr. 1981. *Fundamentals of Systems Analysis.* New York: John Wiley & Sons.
A basic text and reference for the systems analysis and design functions.

Gane, C. and T. Sarson, 1979. *Structured Systems Analysis: Tools and Techniques.* Englewood Cliffs, NJ: Prentice-Hall.
An overview of the new approaches to systems analysis. Particularly good explanation of data flow diagrams.

Kerner, D. C. 1979. Business information characterization study. *DataBase* **10** (4): 10–17.
A detailed explanation of one variation of an information study technique.

Rockart, J. F. 1979. Chief executives define their own data needs. *Harvard Business Review* **57** (2): 81–93.
An explanation of the critical success factor (CSF) approach to information analysis.

Senn, J. 1982. *Information Systems in Management.* 2nd ed./Belmont, CA: Wadsworth Publishing Co.
A comprehensive text and reference for the information function in the organization.

Withington, F. G. 1980. Coping with computer proliferation. *Harvard Business Review* **58** (3): 152–164.
An interesting insight into the problems of distributing computers throughout an organization. Faces the issues of control, priorities, overlapping resources and the like.

Yourdon, E. 1979. *Managing the Structured Techniques.* New York: Yourdon Press.
An overview of the latest approaches to analysis, design and programming.

Yourdon, E. 1982. *Managing the Systems Life Cycle.* New York: Yourdon Press.
A management view of the structured approach to managing systems development. Chapter 3 is reprinted herein on pp. 78–93.

Zachman, J. A. 1982. Business systems planning and business information control study: a comparison. *IBM Systems Journal* **21** (1): 31–53.
A comprehensive comparison of two emerging study techniques. Reprinted herein on pp. 94–116.

# the structured life cycle

# 3

## 3.1 Introduction

With this chapter, we arrive at the main subject of the book: the structured system, or project, life cycle. We begin by discussing the basic concepts of a life cycle and attempt to answer two questions: What is the purpose of the project life cycle? Why do we have one?

Before introducing the structured project life cycle, it is important to examine the classical project life cycle used in many EDP organizations today, primarily to identify its limitations and weaknesses. This examination will be followed by a brief discussion of the so-called *semi-structured* project life cycle: a project life cycle that includes some, but not all, of the elements of structured systems development.

Finally, we introduce the *structured* project life cycle, presenting an overview to show the major activities and how they fit together. In subsequent chapters, we will examine in considerably greater detail each of the major activities — the survey, analysis, design, implementation, test generation, and quality assurance.

In this chapter, we will also explore the concept of *iterative* or *top-down* development in greater detail than in the previous discussions. In particular, we will introduce the notion of radical top-down development and conservative top-down development. Depending on the nature of your project, there may be valid reasons for adopting one approach rather than the other. It is even possible that your situation calls for a combination of the two.

## 3.2 The concept of a project life cycle

As a consultant, I have visited hundreds of EDP organizations during the past dozen or so years — organizations ranging in size from few to thousands of people, with anywhere from one to one thousand projects simultaneously underway. As you might expect, the smaller organizations tend to be relatively informal: EDP projects are begun as the result of a verbal discussion between the user and the project manager (who may also be chief analyst, programmer, computer operator, and janitor!), and the project proceeds from analysis through design and implementation without much fuss.

In the larger organizations, however, things are done on a much more formal basis. The various communications between users, management, and the project team tend to be documented, and everyone understands that the project will go through several phases before it is complete. Even so, I have often been surprised by the major differences between the way two project managers in the same organization will conduct their respective projects. Indeed, it is often left to the discretion of the individual project manager to determine what phases and activities his project will consist of, and how those phases will be conducted.

Recently, however, the approach taken to systems development has begun to change. More and more large *and* small organizations are adopting a single, uniform project life cycle — otherwise known as a project plan or systems development methodology, or simply, "the way we do things." Usually contained in a notebook as ponderous as the standards manual that sits (unread) on every programmer's desk, the documented project life cycle provides a common way for everyone in the EDP organization to go about the business of developing a computer system.

The approach may be home-grown, or alternatively, the EDP organization may decide to purchase a project management package, and then tailor it to company needs.* But regardless of whether the system to develop systems is home-grown or vendor-supplied, the trend is one that merits further examination. It seems apparent that aside from providing employment for the people who create project life cycle manuals (and for those who write textbooks about them!), the project plan is desirable. What then is the purpose of having a project life cycle? The following paragraphs provide an answer.

Three obvious objectives may be discerned from the comments above: One purpose of the project life cycle is to define the activities that must be carried out in an EDP project. A second is to introduce consistency among the many EDP projects in an organization. A third objective is to provide checkpoints for management control and checkpoints for go/no-go decisions.

The first objective is particularly important in a large organization in which new people are constantly entering the ranks of project management. The fledgling project manager may overlook or underestimate the significance of important project phases if he follows only his intuition. Indeed, it can happen that junior programmers and analysts may not understand where and how their efforts fit into the overall project unless they are given a proper description of *all* of the phases of the project.

The second objective is also important in a large organization. For higher levels of management, it can be extremely disconcerting to try to supervise a hundred different projects, each of which is being done in a different way. For example, if project A defines the analysis activities differently than does project B and project B doesn't include a design phase, how is the second-level or third-level manager to know which project is in trouble and which is proceeding on schedule?

The third objective of a standard project life cycle pertains to management's need to control a project. On trivial projects, the sole checkpoint is likely to be the end of the project: Was it finished on time and within the specified budget? But for larger projects, management should have a number of intermediate checkpoints during the

---

*There are at least half a dozen such packages on the market, costing anywhere from less than $10,000 to somewhat more than $100,000. For a variety of reasons, I won't comment in this book on any specific project management package; I will only suggest that you keep the concepts presented in this book in mind if and when you select a vendor-supplied package.

project, which provide it with opportunities to determine whether the project is behind schedule, and whether additional resources need to be procured. In addition, an intelligent user will also want checkpoints at several stages in the project so that he can determine whether he wants to continue funding it!*

Having reported all of this, let me remind you that the project life cycle definitely is not going to run your project for you. It will not relieve you of the difficult responsibility of making decisions, weighing alternatives, fighting political battles, negotiating with recalcitrant users, boosting the morale of dejected programmers, or any of the other trials and tribulations that face a project manager. If you're going to be the project manager, then you still have to *manage,* in every sense of the word. The only help that the project life cycle can provide is that it can *organize* your activities, making it a little more likely that you'll address the right problems at the right time.

### 3.3 The classical project life cycle

Before we examine the structured project life cycle, I'd like to make a distinction. If you've worked in the data processing field for more than a few years, there's a good chance that much of this information about project methodologies is familiar to you. You may already have a project life cycle in your organization, and you probably have a number of opinions about it. But I suspect that the kind of project life cycle that your organization is using right now differs from the one to which we'll be devoting most of our attention in this book.

The classical or conventional project life cycle is shown in Fig. 3.1 below. Most of the phases, or activities, should be fairly familiar to you, and I won't bother discussing them in detail here. Certainly every project, whether structured or not, goes through some kind of analysis, design, and implementation, even if it's not done in exactly the way I show it here. The project life cycle used in your organization, for example, might differ from the one shown in Fig. 3.1 in one or all of the following ways: The survey phase and the analysis phase may be lumped together into a single phase. (This is especially common in organizations in which anything the user wants is deemed at the outset to be feasible.) There may not be a phase called hardware study if it can be taken for granted that any new system can be implemented on an existing computer without causing any major operational impact. The preliminary design and detail design phases may be lumped together in a single phase simply called design, or possibly, several of the testing phases may be grouped together into a single phase; indeed, they may even be included with "coding." Thus, *your* project life cycle may have five phases, or seven phases, or twelve phases — but it is still likely to be of the classical variety.

What is it that really characterizes a project life cycle as being classical? Two features stand out: a strong tendency toward bottom-up implementation of the system, and an insistence on linear, sequential progression from one phase to the next.

---

*In fact, the politics of most EDP projects are such that there is only one checkpoint at which the user has an obvious, clean way of backing out: at the end of the survey, or feasibility study, phase. In theory, though, the user should have the opportunity to cancel an EDP project at the end of *any* phase if he thinks he is wasting his money.

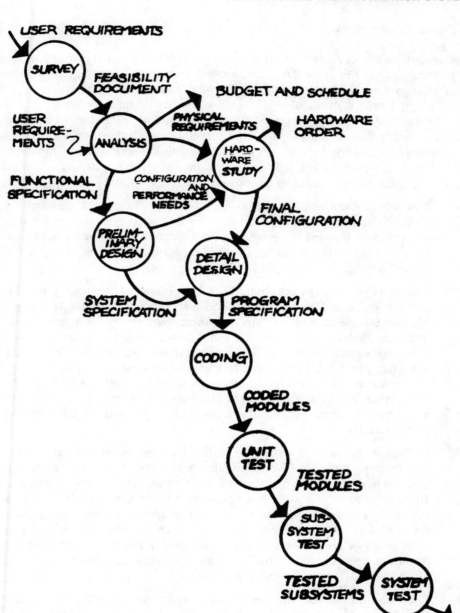

Figure 3.1.   The classical project life cycle.

### 3.3.1 Bottom-up implementation

The use of bottom-up implementation is, in my opinion, one of the major weaknesses in the classical project life cycle. As you can see from Fig. 3.1, the project manager is expected to carry out all of his module testing *first,* then subsystem testing, and finally system testing. I'm not quite sure where this approach originally came from, but I wouldn't be surprised if it was borrowed from assembly-line industries. The bottom-up implementation approach is a good one for assembling automobiles on an assembly line — *but only after the prototype model has been thoroughly debugged!* Unfortunately, most of us in the computer field are still producing one-of-a-kind systems, for which the bottom-up approach has a number of serious difficulties:

- Nothing is done until it's *all* done. Thus, if the project gets behind schedule and the deadline falls right in the middle of system testing, there will be nothing to show the user except an enormous pile of program listings — which, taken in their entirety, do nothing of any value for the user!

- The most trivial bugs are found at the beginning of the testing period, and the most serious bugs are found last. This is almost a tautology: Module testing uncovers relatively simple logic errors inside individual modules; system testing, on the other hand, uncovers major interface errors between subsystems. The point is that major interface errors are *not* what you want to find at the end of a development project; they can mean recoding of large numbers of modules, and can have a serious impact on the schedule, right at a time when everyone is likely to be somewhat tired and cranky from having worked so hard for so many months.

- Debugging tends to be extremely difficult during the final stages of system testing. Note that we distinguish here between *testing* and *debugging:* Debugging is the black art of discovering *where* a bug is located, after the process of testing has determined that there *is* a bug. When a bug is discovered during the system-testing phase of a bottom-up project, it's often extremely difficult to tell which module contains the bug — it could be in any one of the hundreds (or thousands) of modules that have been combined for the first time. Tracking down the bug is often like looking for a needle in a haystack.

- The requirement for test time usually rises exponentially during the final stages of testing. More specifically, the project manager often finds that he needs large chunks of computer time for system testing — perhaps twelve hours of uninterrupted computer time. Since such a large amount of computer time is often difficult to obtain,* the project often falls seriously behind schedule.

---

*I'm convinced that yet another of the Murphy-type laws applies in this regard: The larger and more critical the project, the more likely it is that its deadline will coincide with end-of-year processing and other organizational crises that gobble up all available computer time!

*3.3.2 Sequential progression*

The second major weakness with the classical project life cycle is its insistence that the phases proceed sequentially from one to the next. There is a natural, human tendency to want this to be so: We want to be able to say that we have *finished* the analysis phase and that we'll never have to worry about that phase again. Indeed, many organizations formalize this notion with a ritual known as "freezing the specification" or "freezing the design document."

The only problem with this desire for orderly progression is that it's completely unrealistic! In particular, the sequential approach doesn't allow for real-world phenomena having to do with personnel, company politics, or economics. For example, the person doing the work — such as the analyst or designer — may have made a mistake, and may have produced a flawed product. Indeed, as human beings, we rarely do a complex job right the first time but we are very good at making repeated improvements to an imperfect job. Or, the person reviewing the work, in particular the user who reviews the work of the analyst, may have made a mistake. Or perhaps, the person carrying out the work associated with each phase may not have enough time to finish, but may be unwilling to admit that fact. This is a polite way of saying that, on most complex projects, analysis and design (and system testing, too) finish when you run out of time, not when you *want* them to finish!

Other problems are commonly associated with the sequential, classical project life cycle: During the several months (or years) that it takes to develop the system, the user may change his mind about what he wants the system to do. During the period that it takes to develop the system, certain aspects of the user's environment may change, for example, the economy, the competition, or the government regulations that affect the user's activities.

An additional characteristic of the classical project life cycle is that it relies on outdated techniques. That is, it tends to make no use of structured design, structured programming, walkthroughs, or any of the other modern development techniques. But because the classical project life cycle *ignores* the existence of these techniques, there is nothing to prevent the project manager from using them. Unfortunately, many programmers, analysts, and first-level project leaders feel that the project life cycle is a statement of policy by top-level management — and if management doesn't say anything about the use of structured programming, then they, as mere project members and leaders, are not obliged to use non-classical approaches.

## 3.4 The semi-structured life cycle

The comments I made in the previous section make it seem as if most EDP organizations are still living in the Dark Ages. Indeed, that picture is somewhat unfair: Not *every* organization uses the classical project life cycle. Particularly during the past five years, there has been a growing recognition that techniques like structured design, structured programming, and top-down implementation should be officially recognized in the project life cycle. This recognition has led to the semi-structured project life cycle, shown in Fig. 3.2 below.

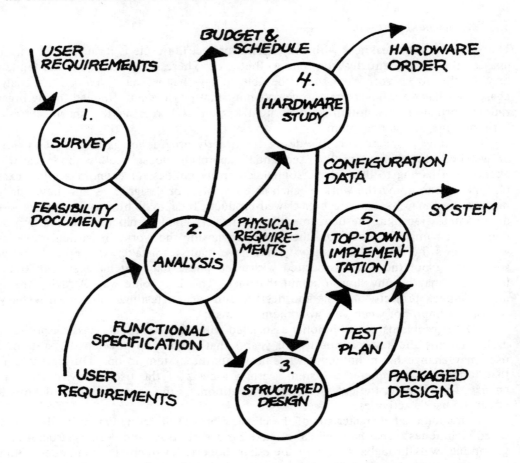

**Figure 3.2. The semi-structured project life cycle.**

As you can see, Fig. 3.2's life cycle shows two obvious features not found in the classical approach:

- The bottom-up sequence of coding, module testing, and system testing is replaced by top-down implementation, as discussed in Chapter 2. There is also a strong indication that structured programming is to be used as the method of actually coding the system.

- Classical design is replaced by structured design, as discussed in Chapter 2.

Aside from these obvious differences, there are some subtle points about this modified life cycle. Consider, for example, that top-down implementation, as described in Chapter 2, means that some coding and testing are taking place in parallel. That certainly represents a major departure from the sequential phases that we saw in the classical life cycle! In particular, it can mean *feedback* between the activity of coding and that of testing and debugging. When he tests the top-level skeleton version of his system, the programmer is likely to be heard to mutter to himself, "Jeez, I had no idea the double-precision FRAMMIS instruction worked *that* way!" Naturally, you can be sure his subsequent use of the double-precision FRAMMIS instruction will be quite different from the use made in the skeleton version.

Perhaps more important, the use of top-down implementation tempts the implementors (and the analysts, if they haven't abandoned the project by this time) to talk to the users *after* the specifications have been ceremoniously frozen. Thus, it is possible that the user will point out errors or misunderstandings in the specification; he may even express a desire to *change* the specification — and if the conversation takes place directly between the user and the implementor, a change may actually be effected before EDP project management knows what is happening. In short, top-down implementation often provides feedback between the implementation process and the analysis process — although this feedback exchange is not specifically shown on Fig. 3.2, and although the user and the EDP project manager might well deny that it is taking place!

There is one final subtle point about the semi-structured life cycle: A significant part of the work that takes place under the heading of structured design is actually an effort to fix up bad specifications. You can see this by looking at Fig. 3.3, a diagram depicting structured design.

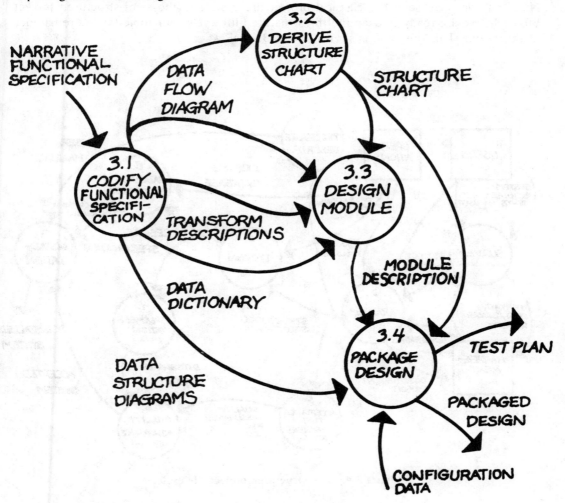

Figure 3.3.  A closer look at structured design.

In Fig. 3.3, Activity 3.1, labeled CODIFY FUNCTIONAL SPECIFICATION, represents a task that designers have long had to do: translate a monolithic, ambiguous, redundant, narrative document into a useful, non-procedural model to serve as the basis for deriving the module hierarchy. In other words, people practicing structured design have traditionally assumed that they would be given a classical specification; consequently, their first job, as they see it, is to transform that specification into a package of data flow diagrams, data dictionaries, and process descriptions. This is a more difficult job than you might imagine: Historically, it was a task carried out in a vacuum. Designers generally had little contact with the analyst who wrote the long narrative specification, and he certainly had *no* contact with the user!

Obviously, such a situation is ripe for change. Introducing structured analysis into the picture, as well as expanding on the idea of feedback between one part of the project and another, creates an entirely different kind of project life cycle. This is the structured project life cycle, which we discuss in the next section.

### 3.5 The structured project life cycle

Now that we have seen the classical project life cycle and the semi-structured project life cycle, we are ready to examine the structured life cycle, our topic for the remainder of this book. This life cycle is shown in Fig. 3.4 below:

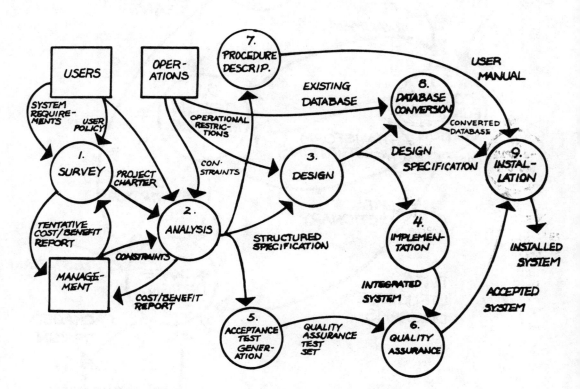

Figure 3.4. The structured project life cycle.

At this point, let us look briefly at the project life cycle's nine activities and three terminators, as shown in Fig. 3.4. Let's begin by defining the outside entities on the diagram — that is, the rectangular boxes labeled *users, management,* and *operations.* These are individuals, or groups of individuals, who provide input to the project team and who are the ultimate recipients of the system. Although the purpose of this book is to concentrate on the task of building an EDP system, we must clarify what *we* mean by the words "user," "management," and "operations."

What do we mean, for example, when we say "user"? Many people suggest that "customer" might be a more apt name, since this is the person who ultimately pays for the system (and thus, indirectly, pays the salaries of the people who build the system!). But by whatever name we choose to call him, there is one crucial property unique to the user: Only he can accept the system when it is finished. Only he can decide whether it is suitable, and whether it will be integrated into his existing business operation. As we will see in subsequent chapters of this book, this has a significant impact upon the business of acceptance testing (Activities 5 and 6).

One other distinction should be made about users: In most cases, there are different *types* of users who come into contact with the EDP system during its formulation, its construction, and its actual operational use. It's useful to identify three different classes of users who interact with the project team that builds an EDP system: the *strategic* user, the *tactical* user, and the *operational* user.

The first of these types of users, the strategic user, is the person primarily concerned with the long-term profitability, or return on investment, that will be generated by the proposed new system. This person is often head of an operational division, for example, the manager of accounting or the vice president of manufacturing, and is primarily concerned with the survey phase (Activity 1) and the early stages of analysis (Activity 2). The tactical user is the person who supervises the day-to-day operation of some piece of the business, and whose performance is usually measured against a budget. This person usually has a good overview of the day-to-day functioning of his part of the business, though he may not be intimately familiar with the lowest-level procedural details. The tactical user usually supervises at least one administrative or clerical worker, and is concerned that the development of a new EDP system not interfere with his subordinates' work; hence, the systems analyst will often hear the tactical user exclaim, "Don't talk to my people — they're far too busy! I'll tell you everything you need to know about their jobs!" The third type of user, the operational user, is the clerical or administrative user in a typical EDP system. This is the person who will have the most contact with the EDP system, once it has become operational. For on-line systems, it is this person for whom such things as man-machine dialogues and error messages are most important.

Just as the term "user" covers a broad spectrum, so too does the term "management," as we have used it to represent an outside entity in Fig. 3.4. In some cases, user and manager are one and the same; indeed, it may well turn out that management is what we described as the strategic user above. In other cases, the term might represent a higher authority — the executive committee or even the board of directors. In the context of this book, we are only interested in identifying a person (or group of people) who approves the funding of the project and provides *organizational* constraints.*

---

*An example of such organizational constraints might be the following message from management to the project team: "We don't care what the users want; we have a company policy that *all* projects will be implemented on Blatzco computers."

The third outside entity shown in Fig 3.4 is simply labeled "operations." Again, this can mean several things: In the case of a small, stand-alone minicomputer system, the *user* may also be the *operator*. In most cases, though, it is meaningful to distinguish between the two, and to identify the person or group responsible for the day-to-day operation of the computer hardware and software that will comprise the system being built. In the vast majority of business EDP projects, the new system will operate, along with dozens of other systems, on computer hardware controlled by a centralized group (even though the hardware itself may be decentralized). Hence, our model of the system for building systems should show this interaction, and the project team should be prepared for comments like, "We don't care what the users want, and we don't care what management says; all we care about is that whatever system you develop doesn't use more than 256K bytes of memory."

These three entities — users, management, and operations — interact with the nine activities that we have shown in Fig. 3.4. Each of the activities is summarized below:

- *Activity 1:  The Survey.* This activity is also known as the feasibility study or initial business study.  Typically, it begins when a user requests that one or more portions of his business be automated.  The major purpose of the survey activity is to identify current deficiencies in the user's environment; to establish new goals; to determine whether it is feasible to automate the business, and if so, to suggest some acceptable scenarios; and finally, to prepare a project charter that will be used to guide the remainder of the project.

- *Activity 2: Analysis.* The primary purpose of the analysis activity is to transform its two major inputs — user policy and project charter — into a structured specification.  This involves modeling the user's present environment with data flow diagrams and the other tools described briefly in Chapter 2.  Using this physical model as a basis, the user's *new* environment is modeled in logical terms.

- *Activity 3: Design.* The activity of design is concerned with identifying the proper hierarchy of modules and interfaces between those modules, to implement the structured specification.  In addition, this activity includes a step known as packaging, in which the design is adjusted or modified to take into account the limitations of the computer hardware being used to implement the system.

- *Activity 4: Implementation.* This activity includes both coding and the integration of modules into a progressively more complete skeleton of the ultimate system.  Thus, Activity 4 includes both structured programming and top-down implementation.

- *Activity 5:  Acceptance Test Generation.* The structured specification should contain all of the information necessary to define an acceptable system, from the user's point of view.  Thus, once the specification has been generated, work can commence on the activity of generating a set of acceptance test cases from the structured specification.

- *Activity 6:  Quality Assurance.* Quality assurance is also known as final testing or acceptance testing.  This activity requires, as its input, acceptance test data generated in Activity 5, and an integrated system produced by Activity 4.

- *Activity 7: Procedure Description.* Throughout this book, we concern ourselves with the development of an *entire* system — not just the automated portion, but also the manual portion. Thus, one of the important activities to be performed is the generation of a formal description of those portions of the new system that will be performed by humans, as well as a description of how the users actually will interact with the automated portion of the new system. The output of Activity 7 is a user's manual.

- *Activity 8: Database Conversion.* In some projects that I have been associated with, database conversion involved more work (and more strategic planning) than did the development of code; in other cases, there might not have been any existing database to convert. In the general case, this activity requires, as input, the user's current database, as well as the design specification produced by Activity 3.

- *Activity 9: Installation.* The final activity, of course, is installation; its inputs are the user's manual produced by Activity 7, the converted database produced by Activity 8, and the accepted system produced by Activity 6. In some cases, however, installation may simply mean an overnight cutover to the new system, with no excitement or fanfare; in other cases, installation may be a gradual process, as one user group after another receives user's manuals, hardware, and training in the use of the new system.

It's important that you view Fig. 3.4 for what it is: a *data flow diagram.* It is *not* a flowchart; there is no implication that all of Activity N must finish before Activity N+1 commences. On the contrary, the networks of data flows connecting activities strongly imply that several activities may be going on in parallel. It is because of this nonsequential aspect that I use the word *activity* in the structured project life cycle, instead of the more conventional word *phase.* Phase has traditionally referred to a particular period of time in a project when one and only one activity was going on.

There is something else that must be emphasized about the use of a data flow diagram to depict the project life cycle (see Fig. 3.4): A data flow diagram does not explicitly show feedback, nor does it show control. Virtually every one of the activities in Fig. 3.4 can, and usually does, produce information that can provide suitable modifications to one or more of the preceding activities. Thus, the activity of design can produce information that may revise some of the cost/benefit decisions that take place in the analysis activity; indeed, knowledge gained in the design activity may even require revising earlier decisions about the basic feasibility of the project.

Indeed, in the most extreme cases, certain events taking place in any activity could cause the entire project to terminate abruptly. The input of management is shown only for the analysis activity, because analysis is the only activity that requires *data* from management; it is assumed, however, that management exerts *control* over all of the activities.

In summary, then, the diagram only tells you the input(s) required by each activity, and the output(s) produced. The sequence of activities can be implied only to the extent that the presence or absence of data makes it possible for an activity to commence.

Clearly, Fig. 3.4 does not provide you with enough information to actually manage a project. In fact, most of the activities have half a dozen or more subactivities, and there is much to say about each of them. The subsequent chapters of this book explore each project management activity in greater detail.

### 3.6  Radical versus conservative top-down implementation

In the previous section, I pointed out that the structured project life cycle allows more than one activity to take place at one time. Let me put it another way: In the most extreme situation, *all* of the activities in the structured project life cycle could be taking place simultaneously. At the other extreme, the project manager could decide to adopt the sequential approach, finishing *all* of one activity before commencing on the next.

I've found that it's useful to have some terminology to help talk about these extremes, as well as about compromises between the two extremes. A *radical* approach to the structured project life cycle is one in which Activities 1 through 9 take place in parallel from the very beginning of the project — that is, coding begins on the first day of the project, and the survey and analysis continue until the last day of the project. By contrast, in a *conservative* approach to the structured project life cycle, all of Activity N is completed before Activity N+1 begins.

Obviously, no manager in his right mind would adopt either one of these two extremes. The key is to recognize that the radical and conservative extremes defined above are the two end-points in a range of choices. This is illustrated in Fig. 3.5 below:

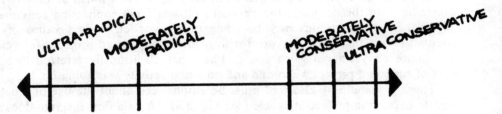

**Figure 3.5.  Radical to conservative range.**

Keep in mind when you begin your next project that there are an infinite number of choices between the radical and conservative extremes. You might decide to finish seventy-five percent of the survey activity, followed by completion of seventy-five percent of analysis, and then seventy-five percent of design, in order to produce a reasonably complete skeleton version of a system whose details could then be refined by a second pass through the entire project life cycle. Or, you might decide to finish *all* of the survey and analysis activities, followed by completion of fifty percent of design and fifty percent of implementation. The possibilities are truly endless, but how should you, as a project manager, decide whether to adopt a radical or a conservative approach on your next project? Basically, there is no right answer. You must base your decision on the following factors:

- How fickle is the user?

- What pressure are you under to produce immediate, tangible results?

- What pressure are you under to produce an accurate schedule, budget, and estimate of manpower and other resources?

- What are the dangers of making a major technical blunder?

As you can appreciate, not one of these questions has a straight black-or-white answer. For example, you can't ask the user of the system, in casual conversation, "By the way, how fickle are you feeling today?" On the other hand, you should be able to assess the situation, based on observation, especially if you're a veteran project manager who has dealt with many users and many upper-level managers before.

If you judge that you're dealing with a fickle user — one whose personality is such that he delays final decisions until he sees how the system is going to work — then you would probably opt for a more radical approach. The same is true if you're dealing with an inexperienced user, who has had very few systems built for him. Why spend years developing an absolutely perfect set of specifications only to discover that the user didn't understand the significance of the specifications?

If, however, you're dealing with a veteran user who is absolutely sure of what he wants — and if he works in a business area that is stable and unlikely to change radically on a month-to-month basis, then you can afford to take a more conservative approach. Of course, there are lots of in-between situations: The user may be sure of *some* of the business functions to be performed, but may be somewhat unsure of the kinds of reports and management information he would like the system to provide. Or, if he is familiar only with batch computer systems, he may be unsure of the impact that an on-line system will have on his business.

Besides fickleness, there's a second factor to consider: the pressure to produce immediate, tangible results. If, due to politics or other external pressures, you simply *must* get a system up and running by a specific date, then a somewhat radical approach is warranted. You still run the risk that your system will only be ninety percent complete when the deadline arrives, but at least it will be a working, ninety-percent-complete skeleton that can be demonstrated and perhaps even put into production. That's generally better than having finished all of the analysis, all of the design, and all of the coding — but none of the testing.

Of course, all projects are under some pressure for tangible results — it's simply a question of degree. And it's an issue that can be rather dynamic: A project which begins in a low-key fashion with a comfortable schedule can suddenly become high-priority, and the deadline may be advanced six months or a year. One of the advantages of doing the analysis, design, coding, and implementation top-down is that one can stop an activity at any point, and leave the remaining details for subsequent consideration; meanwhile, the top-level analysis that has been completed can be used to begin the top-level design — and so forth.

Yet another factor in project management is the ever-present requirement, in most large organizations, to produce schedules, estimates, budgets, and the like. In some organizations, this tends to be done in a fairly informal fashion, typically because the projects are relatively small, and because management feels that any errors in estimating will have an insignificant impact on the whole organization. In such cases, one can adopt a radical approach, even though any attempts at estimating will have to be gut-level guesses. By contrast, most large projects require relatively detailed estimates of manpower, computer resources, and so on; and this can only be done after a fairly detailed survey, analysis, and design have been completed. In other words, the more detailed and accurate your estimates have to be, the more likely you are to follow a conservative approach.

Finally, you should consider the danger of making a major technical blunder. For example, suppose that all of your past experience as a project manager has been with batch-oriented IBM 360/30 computer systems — and now, all of a sudden, you find yourself developing an on-line, real-time, multi-processing database management information system that will process half a million transactions a day from one thousand terminals scattered around the country. In such a situation, one of the dangers of a radical approach is discovering a major design flaw after a large portion of the top-level skeleton system has been implemented. You may discover, for example, that in order for your whizbang system to work, some low-level module has to do its job in nineteen microseconds — but your programmers suddenly tell you there is no way on earth to code the module that efficiently, not even in assembly language. So, you must be alert to the fact that following the radical approach requires that you pick a "top" to your system relatively early in the game, and that there is always the danger of discovering, down toward the bottom, that you picked the wrong top!

However, consider another scenario: You've decided to build an EDP system with new hardware, a new operating system, a new database management system (produced by someone other than the hardware vendor), and a new telecommunications package (produced by yet another vendor). All of the vendors have impressive, glossy manuals describing their products — but the vendors have never interfaced their respective hardware and software products together. Who knows if they'll work together at all? Who knows if the throughput promised by one vendor will be destroyed by the system resources used by one of the other vendors? Certainly, in a case like this, the project manager might elect a radical approach — so that a skeleton version of the system could be used to explore possible interface problems between the vendors' components.

If you're building a very familiar kind of system, such as your ninety-ninth payroll system, then you probably have a very good idea of how realistic your goals are. You probably remember, from your last project, what sort of modules you're going to need at the detailed level, and you probably remember very clearly what the top-level structure looked like. In such a case, you may be willing to accept the risks of making a mistake because of the other benefits that the radical approach will give you.

In summary, the radical approach is most suitable for thinly disguised research and development efforts. It is good in environments in which something *must* be working on a specific date and in situations in which the user's perception of what he wants the system to do is subject to change. The conservative approach, on the other hand, tends to be used on larger projects, in which massive amounts of money are being spent, and for which careful analysis and design are required to prevent subsequent disasters. However, every project is different and requires its own special blend of radical and conservative top-down implementation. In order to deal with the individual nature of any project, you should be prepared to modify your approach midstream, if necessary.

## 3.7  Summary

The major purpose of this chapter has been to provide an overview of project life cycles in general.  If your organization is currently using a formal project life cycle, you should be able to tell whether it falls into the category of classical, semi-structured, or structured — and you may have already gotten some ideas for modifying your own project life cycle to avoid some of the problems discussed in this chapter.

If you are accustomed to managing projects that are working on only one activity at a time, the discussion of radical top-down implementation and conservative top-down implementation in the final section of this chapter may have disturbed you.  This was my intent as the major purpose in this section was to make you think about the *possibility* of overlapping some of the major activities in an EDP project.  Obviously, it's more difficult to manage any project that has several activities taking place in parallel — but to some extent, that always happens in every project.  Even if you, as the project manager, decide that your people will concentrate all of their efforts on one major activity at a time, there will still be a number of subactivities taking place in parallel.  Multiple analysts will be interviewing multiple users simultaneously; various pieces of the final product of systems analysis will be in various stages of progress throughout the analysis phase.  One of your jobs, as a project manager, is to exercise sufficient control over those subactivities to ensure that they coordinate smoothly.  And in virtually every EDP project that I have observed or participated in, this same kind of parallel activity operated at a higher level, too — that is, despite what the organization's formal project life cycle may have recommended, the reality is that many of the major project activities do overlap to some extent.  Nevertheless, if you decide to insist on a strictly sequential progression of project activities, the project life cycle presented in this book will still work.

In the next chapter, we begin examining the first of the major project activities in detail: the survey.  As we will see, the purpose of this activity is to develop a *project charter* — a document that defines the broad scope within which the project team may work.  When you next read about or hear about a major EDP project failure, try to find out whether the project team developed any charter at all; you'll often find that, because of the lack of a charter, members of the project team thought they were engaged in a state-of-the-art research project, while top management thought the project team was building a mundane production system to generate additional revenue for the organization.  The solution: a formal project charter, developed along the lines presented in Chapter 4.

*Business Systems Planning (BSP) and Business Information Control Study (BICS) are two information system planning study methodologies that specifically employ enterprise analysis techniques in the course of their analyses. Underlying the BSP and BICS analyses are the data management problems that result from systems design approaches that optimize the management of technology at the expense of managing the data. In comparing BSP and BICS, five similarities and five differences are selected for discussion, and, finally, the strengths and weaknesses of each methodology are noted. The choice between using one or the other methodology is strongly influenced by the immediate intent of the study sponsor, tempered by the limiting factors currently surrounding the BICS methodology.*

# Business Systems Planning and Business Information Control Study: A comparison

## by J. A. Zachman

Business Systems Planning (BSP)[1] and Business Information Control Study (BICS)[2] are representative of enterprise analysis tools that are growing in importance and are likely to become mandatory for any business that continues to grow and evolve. BSP and BICS have common roots in their attempts to describe a business at the enterprise level in terms of its information characteristics. As our understanding of information systems evolves, it is becoming clear that some enterprise-level description of a business unit is required for several reasons.

First, there is a requirement to select information system resource investment opportunities that hold the greatest relative potential benefit for the business unit as a whole. Therefore, some comprehensive identification of enterprise-wide opportunities for employing information technologies must be made in order to establish a context within which the relative assessment can be made.

Second, because of the necessity to produce short-term results in any given enterprise, there is a requirement to design and build large numbers of small systems. To avoid high costs of redesign for integration purposes, the small systems should be built in such a

(Reprint by permission *IBM Systems Journal.* Copyright 1982 by International Business Machines Corporation.)

fashion that they are compatible and consistent at the outset, or so that they will fit together as they are completed. Therefore, an enterprise-level architecture is required to constrain the design and development activity such that the relationships and dependencies can be identified and protected.

Third, because of resource constraints and/or technology limitations, substantial gaps usually exist between what is desired, what is feasible, and what is implemented. Because of this situation, the management of a business is continually in a position of having to trade off between short-term investments and long-term investments. The short-term investments tend to be results-oriented, cost-effective, quick and dirty, cheap, practical, etc. The long-term investments tend to be quality-oriented, flexible, long-lived, best, optimum, etc. Therefore, an enterprise-level architecture is required to serve as a context within which to make the trade-off decisions between the long-term and short-term options. Furthermore, the architecture is required as a base line to manage the change activity which is inevitable as a result of selecting shorter-term options rather than longer-term options, as well as the change activity resulting from the restructuring of the business which can be expected over time.

These issues are arising because the technology increasingly supports enterprise-wide, top-down systems in design, but the practicalities of resource limitations, development project size manageability, and the requirement to produce short-term results make the bottom-up, piece-by-piece approach to implementations mandatory. Therefore, enterprise-wide "architectures," or structures, through BSP, BICS, or some other methodology can be expected to be increasingly prevalent as the technology continues to evolve.

Although many popular information systems planning methodologies, design approaches, and various tools and techniques do not preclude or are not inconsistent with enterprise-level analysis, few of them explicitly address or attempt to define enterprise architectures. Some examples of such popular offerings include

- *Planning Methodologies*: Stage Assessment,[3] Critical Success Factors,[4] Strategy Set Transformation,[5] etc.
- *Design Approaches*: Structured Analysis,[6] Entity-Relationship Approach,[7] etc.
- *Tools and Techniques*: Problem Statement Language/Problem Statement Analyzer (PSL/PSA),[8] Prototype Development Methodology,[9] Structured Analysis and Design Technique,[10] etc.

From an historical perspective, BSP and BICS likely will be looked back on as primitive attempts to take an explicit, enterprise-level architectural approach to information systems.

BSP is a study methodology that has been offered as a market support program by IBM since 1970. It was developed as a result of some internal IBM experience acquired by the IBM Corporate Information Systems (I/S) Architecture group when I/S was still centralized during the late 1960s.

BICS is also a study methodology currently under development at IBM. Although it is not available for general use, it is evolving from some initial experience acquired during the mid-1970s at the IBM Santa Teresa Laboratory. It draws heavily upon a theory called Business Information Analysis and Integration Technique (BIAIT™),[11,12] as well as upon BSP.

The BIAIT theory proposes that the complete information-handling characteristics of a business can be predefined given an understanding of seven binary variables relating to how the business handles its orders. For example, one variable is, "Does the business bill the customer for his order?" If so, then the information-handling characteristics include some form of credit checking, bill preparation, accounts receivable management, etc. If the business does not bill for the order, then it receives cash and in this case information-handling characteristics are not implied. Similarly, the other six variables reveal additional information-handling characteristics about the business. When this analysis is applied to each type of order the business receives, the result is an identification of all the information-handling characteristics of the business. Since BICS has been successfully used in more than six widely diverse internal IBM business units, there is some good empirical evidence that the BIAIT theory can be employed effectively in enterprise analysis.

BSP and BICS are both study methodologies, and, therefore, it is easy to compare them, identifying their major similarities as well as their major differences.

## BSP and BICS similarities

Five similarities have been selected in discussing the two methodologies. These are labeled A through E.

**study objectives**

In Similarity A, the objectives of both BSP and BICS are to support Information Systems planning at the strategy level. The analysis that is performed establishes the utility of taking architectural approaches to information systems, the implications of managing (or not managing) the data of the business, and the areas of the business holding the greatest relative potential for investing information systems resources. The analyses do not result in design specifications or even cost-benefit determinations. In order to get to that level of detail, additional analysis must be performed over and above that specified for the BSP or BICS studies. Therefore, to reiterate, the BSP and BICS analyses are planning-oriented, not design- or implementation-oriented, and they support the strategy level of I/S planning. The kinds of questions they seek to answer are "What design strategy should I/S employ?" "What should the role of I/S be?" "What areas of the business hold the most potential for investing current I/S resources?" "Which I/S resources should be optimized at the expense of which others?"

In Similarity B, the analytical approach employed by both BSP and BICS is "top down." The implications of the words "top down" are multiple and varied, and all apply to these analyses. For instance:

**analytical approach**

- Top down implies scope—that is, looking at the business as a whole as opposed to looking at pieces or subparts of it.
- Top down implies level of detail—that is, looking at the highest level of summarization and then decomposing hierarchically to lower levels of detail as required.
- Top down implies perspective—that is, the perspective of the highest levels of management as opposed to the operational levels of management.

In all of these senses, both BSP and BICS are top-down analyses.

For Similarity C the analyses are data-oriented. Analyses that are performed for the purpose of defining requirements or of defining design specifications tend to focus on function, information, or data. The analyses that are functionally oriented identify and define the function of the business that requires automation, specify what the system has to *do,* and secondarily define the data required or the information that is a by-product. In the context of "input-process-output," the primary focus is on the "process."

**orientation**

Information-oriented analyses identify and define the information required to make a decision, or the form or report that is required, and then secondarily define the input data and processing required to produce the desired information. In the context of "input-process-output," the primary focus is on the "output."

Data-oriented analyses identify and define the data that is required or being used in the business and secondarily define the processes required to acquire the data and the information that can be derived from the data. In the context of "input-process-output," the primary focus is on the "input."

Although neither BSP nor BICS is employed at a level of detail specific enough to result in requirements definition or design specification, they are both data-oriented in nature. That is, they focus primarily on the data required to manage the business (input) and secondarily on the function (process) or information (output). The reasons for the focus on the data, or "input," side of "input-process-output" is that they are both seeking to address the data problems that exist in applications portfolios where there has been a prevalence of functional (process) orientation and/or information (output) orientation at the expense of the data (input). Furthermore, BSP and BICS focus on the data (input) in lieu of information (output) because they are both seeking to establish architectures, which favor stability. The information (output) that the business demands is variable and unstable over time[13] and is not desirable for use in an architectural sense except that whatever architecture is developed must be able to support the information requirements (output) on demand.

BSP does define function (processes) at a fairly high level of aggregation. However, the processes are defined primarily as a vehicle for identifying the data, gaining some assurance that all the data has been identified, and proving that the same data is being used by multiple processes (thus laying a foundation for determining whether a data problem exists in the application portfolio as a result of an historical focus on function or information).

It must be pointed out that even though BSP and BICS tend to focus on the data, the fact that they attempt to produce an architectural statement suggests that they must ultimately provide for a balance between data (input) and function (process) in support of the highly variable information (output) requirements of the business. The BSP architecture product of the study does portray both data and function. The function element of the BICS architecture is currently under development.

**analytical products**

In Similarity D, both analyses result in two analytical products, including

1. A structure, or architecture, in information terms, which describes the business unit under study.
2. An identification of management's priorities as related to the structure developed.

**data gathering technique**

In Similarity E, both analyses employ management interviewing techniques as the source of data for determining the relative priorities of I/S investment opportunities. Furthermore, the questions asked are basically the same although different in approach. BICS asks, "What are your critical success factors?",[14] which is a very practical way to get at "What are your objectives?" BSP also asks, "What are your objectives?" but finds much more substantive analytical data from the inverse, "What are your problems?" The problem and objective questions are the same in that one is the inverse of the other. That is, a problem is not a problem unless there is an objective it is keeping you from meeting.

Another shade of difference lies in the fact that BICS uses a group interview technique, whereas BSP uses the individual interview tech-

Figure 1  Defining BSP processes, an example

| PRODUCT/SERVICE | SUPPORTING RESOURCES | | | |
|---|---|---|---|---|
| MEN'S APPAREL | RAW MATERIALS | FACILITIES | CASH | PERSONNEL |

REQUIREMENTS

— — — — — — — — — — Business Planning — — — — — — — — — — — —

| | | | | |
|---|---|---|---|---|
| Product P & C Gov Compliance Market Analysis Product Def | Mstr Production Planning | Facilities  P & C | Facilities  P & C | Personnel P & C |

ACQUISITION

| | | | | |
|---|---|---|---|---|
| Buying  Production | Purchasing | design fac  acquire fac | accounts rec | |

STEWARDSHIP

| | | | | |
|---|---|---|---|---|
| F/G Inventory Control | R/M Inventory Control | Facilities Operations | Acq & Disp | |

DISPOSITION

Adver Whs Re C

nique and then analytically integrates the data. The intent and data gathered from the management interviews are, however, basically the same.

## BSP and BICS differences

Five differences between the two methodologies were selected for comparison.

Difference A is a result of BSP and BICS entering into the business analysis through different avenues. BSP enters into the analysis by defining the products (or services, as the case may be) of the business unit. Next, the resources required to produce the products are identified. Then, by using the product and/or resource life cycle, the processes (or functions) that have to be performed to manage the products and resources over their life cycles are identified. From the processes, the data required to manage the processes is defined. Then the relationship between the processes and the data is documented and constitutes a structure (or architecture) that represents the "functional specifications" and the "material (data) specifications" of the information "product" required to support the business unit. Figure 1 is an example of how BSP initiates the analysis by identifying the products and resources of the business and how it then employs the life cycle concept[15] for identifying the processes. This analysis is used ultimately to develop the process/data class structure which is described in Difference B.

*entrance into the analysis*

Figure  2    BICS analysis of order types using BIAIT, an example[2]

| BUSINESS VARIABLES | ORDERS | MACHINES | MES | MES | EQUIPMENT | ... |
|---|---|---|---|---|---|---|
| BILL<br>CASH | 1 | X | X | X | X | |
| FUTURE DELIVERY<br>IMMEDIATE DELIVERY | 2 | X | X | X | X | |
| CUSTOMER PROFILE<br>NO CUSTOMER PROFILE | 4 | X | X | X | X | |
| PRICE NEGOTIATION<br>FIXED PRICE | 8 | X | X | X | X | |
| RENT<br>SELL | 16 | X | X | X | X | |
| TRACK<br>NO TRACK | 32 | X | X | X | X | |
| MADE TO ORDER<br>PROVIDE FROM STOCK | 64 | X | X | X | X | |
| TOTAL | | 99 | 99 | 35 | 67 | |

In contrast, BICS enters into the analysis through the orders the
business receives. After all of the order types have been identified,
each order type is subject to the BIAIT analysis which, through the
seven binary variables as in Figure 2, selects out of a predefined set of
data categories those categories that are required to support the
orders the business receives. Added to these categories of data are
data categories required to support the "common business functions," which are those functions that are independent of the kinds of
orders received, or those functions that are common to every business
unit. (An example of a common business function might be "pay
employees.") The resultant subset of data categories applicable to
the given business unit are related to the organization structure of
the business, and this serves as the structure (or architecture) that
BICS uses for further analysis. Figure 2 is an example of a BIAIT
analysis of the orders of a business. (Note that two types of orders the
business receives in this case have identical information-handling
characteristics.) This analysis is then used to extract the appropriate
data classes out of the total list of all possible data classes.

BSP, then, enters into its analysis through the products/resources of
the business, whereas BICS enters in through the orders of the
business.

**structures
developed**   In Difference B, the structures that BSP and BICS develop are
decidedly different, although they both use a matrix format to
display the relationships that constitute the structure.

Figure 3   Treatment of data under "technology-managed" systems design[4,16]

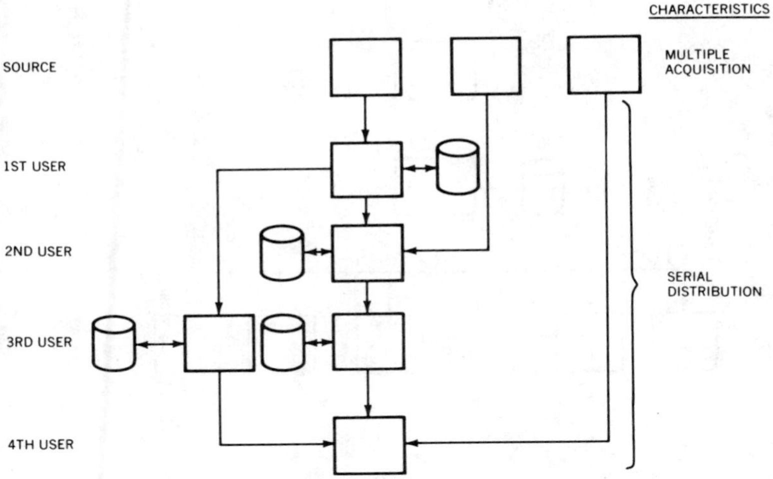

BSP focuses primarily on the process versus data relationship as noted in Difference A. Although there are several other relationships that are developed in the course of the analysis, the others support intermediate and/or secondary conclusions. The process/data relationship is chosen as the primary one because BSP hypothesizes at the outset that the business unit under study has a data problem, and it then sets out to prove (or disprove) the hypothesis. A data problem results when the system design objectives are to optimize the technology resources at the expense of the data—that is, build applications quickly and cheaply in a cost-effective fashion as far as technology is concerned (that is, hardware/software and people), thereby treating the data as a secondary issue. The development methodology in this environment has the following steps:

1.  Identify the functional (or information output) requirements.
2.  Design the systems functions (or information output).
3.  Figure out what data is required and identify the quickest, cheapest source of the data.
4.  Extract the data from an existing file and reproduce it for the new system, recreate it at the source, or use a secondary source.

The repetitive use of this approach results in multiple sourcing and serial distribution of the data[4,16] as in Figure 3. The problem that evolves as applications are added to the applications portfolio is loss of control of the data because the same data begins to reside in multiple systems, is inconsistent, unreconcilable, unavailable, and frustrating to management. If the problem is bad enough, management potentially loses visibility into the data and, therefore, into the operations and resource utilization of the business, and the business develops a control problem.

Figure 4 Treatment of data under "data-managed" systems design[4,16]

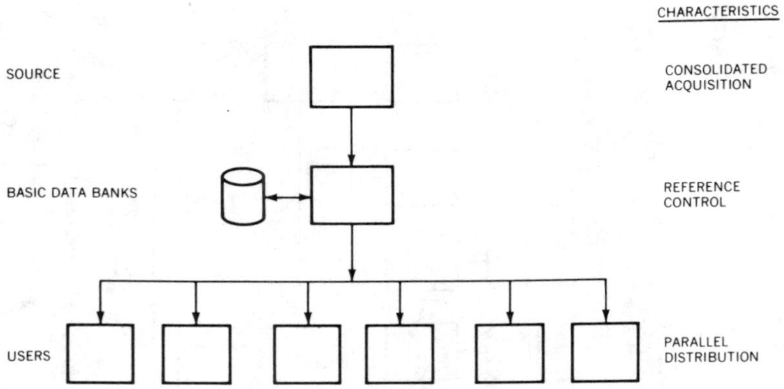

CHARACTERISTICS

SOURCE

CONSOLIDATED
ACQUISITION

BASIC DATA BANKS

REFERENCE
CONTROL

USERS

PARALLEL
DISTRIBUTION

If, in contrast, the systems design objective is to optimize the management of the data at the expense of the technology, the steps in the development methodology would be

1. Identify a single source for every kind of data in the business.
2. Establish a reference control for managing the data.
3. Design the functions required to acquire the data at its source and control the integrity of the data at the source.
4. Design the information output systems on demand using the reference control facility.

This approach results in single-source, parallel distribution of the data[4,16] as represented in Figure 4. The potential problem in this environment is extravagant use of the technology, designing and managing data for which there is no requirement.

Because only around half of the large businesses in the United States in 1979 had evolved to late Stage III or early Stage IV with regard to the Stage Hypothesis,[3] their focus was on managing the technology as opposed to managing the data. The former problem of multiple-source, serial distribution of the data is far more prevalent than the latter problem potentially associated with the data-managed environment.

Therefore, BSP uses the process/data relationship to expose the data problem because by so doing, it can be shown that a single process "creates" some kind of data and that other processes "use" the same data. Hence, a single source with parallel distribution of data naturally exists within the business under study. Figure 5 is an example of a process versus data class matrix in which the "create" points are differentiated from the "use" points. By contrasting the current data processing systems, they can be shown to have multiple

Figure 5 BSP process versus data class matrix, an example

**PROCESS** (columns)

1. DETER FD PLAN
2. ESTABLISH AND APPROVE GOALS AND OBJECTIVES
3. ESTABLISH, EVALUATE, MAINTAIN POLICIES AND PROCEDURES
4. MEASURE AND CONTROL
5. SUPERVISE PERSONNEL
6. EVALUATE FIRE TRENDS DEVELOP FIRE CODE
7. DEVELOP AND MAINTAIN OPERATING PROCEDURES
8. COORDINATE WITH OTHER AGENCIES
9. RESPOND TO INQUIRIES
10. REVIEW LEGISLATION
11. PREPARE REPORTS
12. PRODUCE & CONTROL FORMS
13. ESTABLISH ACCOUNTS
14. DEVELOP OPERATING BUDGET
15. TRANSFER FUNDS
16. ACCOUNT FOR FUNDS
17. MAINTAIN PETTY CASH
18. DEVELOP CAPITAL IMP PLAN
19. DEVELOP A & I PLAN
20. PREPARE FINANCIAL REPORTS
21. ISSUE & MAINTAIN REPORTS
22. BILL FOR SERVICES
23. PREPARE AND MANAGE PURCHASE ORDERS
24. AUTHORIZE PAYMENT
25. COMPENSATE
26. RECORD TIME WORKED AND ACTIVITY
27. FORECAST PERSONNEL REQUIREMENTS
28. SCHEDULE PERSONNEL
29. ESTABLISH STANDARDS
30. CONDUCT EMPLOYEE RELATIONS
31. MONITOR PHYSICAL CONDITION
32. MAINTAIN PERSONNEL RECORDS
33. RECRUIT PERSONNEL
34. ASSIGN PERSONNEL
35. ... PERSONNEL
36–39. ... OPERATIONS
40–42. ... N LABS

**DATA CLASS** (rows)

1. ECONOMY/ENVIRONMENT
2. OPERATING PROCEDURES
3. CODES & REQS
4. COMMUNITY
5. ACCOUNTS
6. PERMITS
7. AMBULANCE BILLS
8. PURCHASE ORDERS
9. VENDORS
10. EMPLOYEE STATUS
11. ACTIVITY
12. EMPLOYEE STAFFING
13. EMPLOYEE DESCRIPTION
14. INCIDENT DESC
15. AMS INCIDENT DESC
16. INCIDENT STATUS
17. APPARATUS STATUS
18. COMPANY STATUS
19. OCCUPANCY DESC
20. OCCUPANCY FIRE PREV
21. NOTICES
22. HYDRANTS
23. ARSON CASE

LEGEND: U = USES
C = CREATES

Matrix entries (U = Uses, C = Creates), by data-class row and process-column number:

| Data Class | 1 | 2 | 3 | 4 | 5 | 6 | 7 | 8 | 9 | 10 | 11 | 12 | 13 | 14 | 15 | 16 | 17 | 18 | 19 | 20 | 21 | 22 | 23 | 24 | 25 | 26 | 27 | 28 | 29 | 30 | 31 | 32 | 33 | 34 | 35 |
|---|---|---|---|---|---|---|---|---|---|---|---|---|---|---|---|---|---|---|---|---|---|---|---|---|---|---|---|---|---|---|---|---|---|---|---|
| 1 ECONOMY/ENVIRONMENT | C | U | | | U | | | | | U | | | | | U | | | | | U | U | | | | | | | | | | | | | | U |
| 2 OPERATING PROCEDURES | | C | U | | U | C | C | U | U | U | U | C | | | U | | U | U | U | U | | U | U | U | | U | U | U | | U | U | U | U | U | U |
| 3 CODES & REQS | U | U | C | | U | C | U | U | U | C | U | | | | U | | U | U | U | U | | U | U | U | | U | U | U | | U | U | U | U | U | U |
| 4 COMMUNITY | U | U | | | U | | C | | U | | | | | | | | | | | U | U | | | | | | | | | | | | | | |
| 5 ACCOUNTS | U | U | | U | | | | | | U | | | | | C | C | C | C | C | U | | U | | U | | U | U | U | U | U | | U | | U | |
| 6 PERMITS | | U | | U | | U | | | | U | U | | | | U | | | | | U | | | U | C | U | | | | | | | | | | |
| 7 AMBULANCE BILLS | U | U | | | | | | | | U | | U | | | U | | | | | U | | | U | C | | | | | | | | | | | |
| 8 PURCHASE ORDERS | | | | | | | | | | | | | | | | | | | | U | | | | | | | | | | C | U | | | | |
| 9 VENDORS | | | | | | | | | | | | | | | | | | | | U | | | | | | | | | | | U | | | | |
| 10 EMPLOYEE STATUS | U | U | | U | U | | | | | | | | | | | U | U | U | | U | | | U | | | U | | U | | U | C | U | U | U | U |
| 11 ACTIVITY | U | U | | | U | | | | | U | U | U | | | | U | | | | U | | U | | | | U | | | | U | C | U | U | C | |
| 12 EMPLOYEE STAFFING | C | U | | | | | | | | U | U | | | | U | U | U | | | U | U | U | | | | U | U | U | | | U | C | C | | |
| 13 EMPLOYEE DESCRIPTION | U | | | | U | | U | | | U | | | | | | | | | | | | | | | | | | | | U | | U | | | |
| 14 INCIDENT DESC | U | | | | U | | U | U | U | U | | | | | | | | | | U | U | | U | U | | | | | | | | | | | |
| 15 AMS INCIDENT DESC | U | U | | | | | U | | | | | | | | | | | | | | | | | | | | | | | | | | | | |

sources of the same data with serial distribution. The hypothesis that there is a data problem is thereby proved because under these conditions, redundancies and inconsistencies and the integrity of the data cannot be controlled.

Furthermore, BSP chooses the process/data relationship because of its stability over time and because it serves to highlight the long-term versus short-term trade-off decisions that must be made regarding information systems investments. The stability derives from the fact that substantial effort is invested to extract the variable aspect from both the processes and the data as they are represented in the structure. Stability is found in the "what," whereas variability is found in the "how." In the case of processes, "what processes (functions) have to be performed" is stable over time, whereas "how the processes are performed" varies considerably. By the same token, in the case of data, "what things the business needs to know about" is fairly stable, but "how the data about the things is used" varies considerably. Therefore, the process/data relationship can be stated in such a way that it is stable by focusing on the "what" rather than the "how."

With regard to the long-term versus short-term trade-off, the long-term option is represented by the data rows of the matrix, whereas the short-term option is represented by the process columns of the matrix. The long-term strategy is to take a data-driven approach to information systems design, identifying the single data source and providing data design for multiple usages of the same data, some of which may not materialize until some time later. The short-term strategy is to take a process-driven approach, building application systems to support processes, serially supplying data (that is, ignoring the data problem), which is the more prevalent approach being used by the data processing community at this stage of its evolution.

In summary, BSP chooses the process/data class structure because it is trying to identify the data problem, it is seeking to develop a stable foundation for architectural use, and last, it is attempting to highlight the long-term, short-term trade-off decisions that must be made by the management of the business.

**Figure 6** BICS organization versus data class matrix, an example[2]

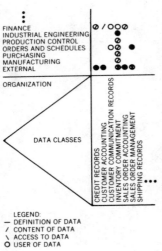

LEGEND:
— DEFINITION OF DATA
/ CONTENT OF DATA
\ ACCESS TO DATA
O USER OF DATA

In contrast, BICS focuses on the data/organization relationship (see Figure 6) primarily because its thrust is toward quick implementations. BICS does not seek to use the data/organization structure in an architectural sense. That is, it does not use the structure to identify system dependencies, interfaces, or boundaries, nor to identify the long-term or short-term trade-off alternatives, nor to use it in the future as a foundation upon which to develop hardware, software, or geographic (distribution) architectures. Neither is BICS attempting to use the structure explicitly to expose the data problem, that is, the multiple-source, serial distribution of data versus single-source, parallel distribution.

BICS is, however, using the data/organization structure as an analytical tool to identify a specific data problem and suggest a specific data solution. Therefore, it examines organizational responsibilities with regard to the data in order to identify conflicts in authority which cause data control problems. Further, when superimposing some business problem analysis on the data/organization structure, it seeks to identify a specific organization in which to localize a data problem solution. As an implementation, BICS suggests finding the best available copy of some specific data, wherever it can be found, in whatever state of integrity it exists, dumping that data into a relational data base management system, establishing administrative controls at the point it enters the relational system, and making it available to users. BICS does not suggest going to the source for control or dealing with the transaction processing apparatus at all. It, in effect, treats the acquisition of the data by the relational system as the single source.

BICS can take this short-term (quick and cheap) approach to implementation, without addressing the transaction processing or data source issue, and still be considered a data-oriented, longer-term perspective on several counts. First, since it does not attempt to deal with transaction processing, the relational data base environment is an appropriate implementation. Second, the relational data base environment is very forgiving when unforeseen data relationships require support as new data views are identified by management. Third, because BICS is employing predefined data classes at the enterprise level (see Difference C), it is reasonable to predict that at some point in the future it will have predefined the data "elements" and predefined the reasonably anticipated data relationships. Therefore, BICS will have simplified resolving the enterprise-level data problem through predesign.

Observe that BICS does not ignore the longer-term issues, that is, controlling the integrity of the data at its source and establishing an architecture for managing the data resources. The study strategy is to establish an environment conducive to addressing the longer-term issues by quickly relieving some current management frustration with the data and introducing tools (Data Base Management Systems, Dictionary, Data Administration, etc.) and the data-oriented mentality which are foundational for the long-term solution. Subsequently, as some of the frustration with the data processing organization of a business is alleviated, and as skills develop and value is perceived with regard to managing the data, the environment is prepared for addressing the transaction processing and data source control issues.

Time favors this study strategy. Not only does the price-performance trend of the technology make the longer-term approaches to solving the data problem more feasible and desirable, but also, development work continues on the BICS methodology. Work is now being done on BICS to incorporate processes (functions) into the data/organization structure. This work will allow predefined processes to be selected from a generalized model on the basis of the BIAIT variables just as the data classes are currently selected. With a process/data/ organization "model," it would be possible to raise the longer-term data issues during the initial study even though the BICS strategy may continue to emphasize the shorter-term implementation options.

At this point, the observation must be made that BSP does not ignore the requirement for quick, short-term implementations, just as BICS does not ignore the longer-term, data management issues. A BSP study could well recommend short-term implementations or classic functional (process) or informational (output) systems (see Similarity C) either because a study team did not have a clear understanding of BSP's analytical strategy or because the business was not yet ready to deal with the data problem. As a matter of fact, since the preponderance of businesses in the United States are still in Stage I, II, or III,[3] BSP studies typically have been done in businesses that were not ready to explicitly address the long-term, data issues.

Furthermore, there is nothing about BSP that precludes recommending a BICS-like implementation. In this regard, BSP recommends developing a data class/organization relationship as a desirable option subsequent to the initial BSP analysis and precisely aimed at getting to a quick fix. However, the BSP analysis clearly is designed to confront management with the long-term issue, "Do you want to change your I/S strategy from optimizing the technology to optimizing the data?" and, secondarily, somewhat in answer to this question, to address the short-term implementation options.

To summarize this point concerning the differences between the structures developed by BSP and BICS, we can say the time constraints imposed on enterprise analysis methodologies force them to adopt expedient strategies. BSP chooses to identify the long-term data issue up front and then develop an implementation to relieve current management frustrations. This procedure leads to the use of the process/data class structure during the BSP study. BICS chooses to relieve short-term frustrations up front and deal with the long-term data problem later. This procedure leads to using the data/organization structure during the BICS study. Both methodologies would develop both structures and present both the long- and short-term options if time during the study was available to do so.

**data classification**

Difference C is a result of BSP and BICS using different approaches to data classification. Because BSP and BICS are basically planning-oriented methodologies employing top-down approaches to analysis, they both deal with classes of data rather than data entities and attributes (or "data elements") in a specific sense. Such a level of detail is not necessary for planning, nor is there sufficient time during a study to collect and manipulate the detail that is necessary for design level analysis. Although BSP and BICS classify the data very differently, they both use the same two criteria for classification, namely (1) uniqueness of data by class and (2) uniqueness of source of data by class.

Uniqueness of data by class means that the classification scheme is structured such that no specific "data element" can be assigned to more than one data class at one time. That is, all the specific data elements in a given data class are unique to the class, or there is no redundancy of data between classes. This classification criterion must be met if data redundancy and consistency are to be controlled as a resultant information systems strategy.

Both BSP and BICS attempt to meet this criterion by taking entity-oriented approaches to defining data classes. If every data element is expressed as an attribute of an entity, there is good assurance that all the attributes of an entity are unique to that entity, and, therefore, the "data elements" can be classified uniquely by entity. For example, all the attributes of an entity "Employee" are unique to employee and are not attributes of "Part," "Customer," "Vendor," etc. (There may be generic redundancy but no specific redundancy; for example, "address" is generically attributable to both customer and vendor, but specifically attributable to one or the other.)

Additionally, BSP and BICS deal with classes of entities that are high-level, with aggregations of entities being referred to in data administration vernacular as Business Subject Entities. That level of detail and that designation are appropriate and necessary because of the planning orientation of the studies and the limited time available for analysis.

The difference between the two methodologies (as far as uniqueness of data by class is concerned) lies in the specification of the Business Subject Entities. BICS specifies 12 Business Subject Entities (called Data Inventories) into which all of the entities of the business must be classified. BSP allows the identification of however many Business Subject Entities (called Business Entities) the study team deems necessary to describe the business in terms of the data it must manage. Both approaches, however, are attempting to get at a classification scheme that provides for nonredundancy between classes, or uniqueness of data by class.

The second criterion, uniqueness of source of data by class, is intended to group the attributes of the Business Subject Entities such that all the attributes in the group come from the same source or enter into the business "system" at the same point. This criterion is a subclassification of the entity attributes of the initial classification of Business Subject Entity. It is necessary if the integrity of the data is to be controlled as a resultant information systems strategy because data integrity must be controlled at the point where the data enters the business.

BICS specifies four subgroupings of attributes, namely plan-value attributes, plan-descriptive attributes, actual-value attributes, and actual-descriptive attributes. Then, within each of the four groupings of attributes, a further classification is specified which is unique by source based upon empirical observation and experience acquired employing the BICS model. There may be one or more such subclasses for each grouping. The BICS data classification scheme is illustrated in Figure 7.

In contrast, BSP attempts to satisfy the second criterion, uniqueness of source of attributes by class, by suggesting that there are four

Figure 7 BICS data classification structure

| TAXONOMY | | | | | BICS TERMS |

| BUSINESS SUBJECT ENTITY | | | | DATA INVENTORY (12 SPECIFIED) |
|---|---|---|---|---|
| PLAN | | ACTUAL | | DATA GROUPS |
| VALUE | DESCRIPTIVE | VALUE | DESCRIPTIVE | |
| a, b .......... | d ............ | h ...... | ............ n | DATA CLASSES (UNIQUE BY SOURCE) |

Figure 8 BSP data classification structure

| TAXONOMY | | | | BSP TERMS |

| BUSINESS SUBJECT ENTITY | | | | BUSINESS ENTITY (OPEN ENDED) |
|---|---|---|---|---|
| PLAN | STATISTICAL | INVENTORY | TRANSACTION | DATA TYPE |
| a, b ......... | d ............. | h............. | ...............n | DATA CLASSES (UNIQUE BY SOURCE) |

types of attributes of entities: planning attributes, statistical/ summary attributes, inventory attributes, and transactions. The study team examines each of the processes that have been identified and defines classes of data within the attribute types that are either "used" or "created" by each process. In this fashion, the process/ data relationship illustrated in Figure 5 is created. There may be none, one, or more data classes by type of attribute. The BSP data classification structure is pictured in Figure 8.

The question is, "Which of the two classification schemes is the best?" Actually, any classification scheme that meets the two criteria on uniqueness is adequate. It is highly likely that at the lowest level of detail, the data classes of BSP and BICS are very similar even though they were arrived at very differently. The BICS approach is probably a little bit cleaner because it has had the benefit of about five years' more experience in data-oriented research.

In the current BSP documentation, the material on data classes was conceived and documented around 1975, long before the entity-relationship-attribute[7] material became generally available and the criteria for classifying the data could be clearly articulated. However, even at that time, it was felt that there were some general

Table 1   BSP data class types compared to BICS data groups

| BSP | | BICS |
| --- | --- | --- |
| Plans/models | is roughly equivalent to: | Plan-value Plan-descriptive |
| Statistical/summaries | is roughly equivalent to: | Actual-value |
| Inventory | is roughly equivalent to: | Actual-descriptive |
| Transactions | *have no equivalent.* | |

categories or types of data within the broader business entity classification. The BSP data class types can be generally compared to the BICS data groups as in Table 1.

With regard to the transaction data type of BSP, which has no direct equivalent in BICS, the BSP thinking was that transaction data had to be accounted for in the classification scheme. What was not clear was what was meant by "transaction."

If "transaction" refers to a change in the state of a Business Subject Entity, then it is equivalent to or included as part of the Actual-Descriptive data group of BICS. But if "transaction" refers to a document that records a relationship between two Business Subject Entities, one of which is changed in state (or status) and the other of which is the agent (or recipient) of the change, then the business treats that document, or "transaction," usually called some kind of "order," as a resource in its own right.[15] The business plans for it, inventories it, keeps statistical data about it, in short, treats it like another business entity. An "order" has data attributes in its own right, including serial number, date, status, etc., over and above the attributes of the other two Business Subject Entities whose relationship the order records. Therefore, if "transaction" refers to "order," it is not a type of data but another Business Subject Entity and should appear on the Business Entity axis and not the Data Type axis of the Business Entity/Data Type Matrix used by BSP. (See Figure 9.)

The confusion arises concerning what is meant by transaction in the BSP classification scheme because the examples in the BSP documentation use transactions interchangeably to mean change of status in some instances and orders in others. As a matter of fact, many of the examples of the other data class types in the BSP documentation (Figure 9) are not pure with regard to the classification criteria primarily because the criteria had not been clearly articulated at the time the document was published.

Figure 9   BSP data classification, an example[1]

| BUSINESS ENTITIES / DATA CLASS TYPES | Product | Customer | Facilities | Material | Vend |
|---|---|---|---|---|---|
| Plans/ Models | Product plans | Sales territory<br><br>Market plans | Facility plans<br><br>Capacity plans | Material requirements<br><br>Production schedule | |
| Statistical/ Summary | Product demand | Sales history | Work in process<br><br>Equipment utilization | Open requirements | |
| Inventory | Product<br><br>Finished goods<br><br>Parts master | Customer | Facilities<br><br>Machine load<br><br>Re | Raw Mater | |
| Transaction | Order | Shipment | | | |

In any case, the key to data classification lies in abiding by the criteria, and given that qualification, the BICS approach meets the criteria by definition. The BSP approach may meet the criteria depending upon the skills and understanding of the analysts.

**data responsibilities**

In Difference D, BSP uses two levels of differentiation of responsibility concerning the data classes, whereas BICS uses four levels of differentiation. Because BSP attempts to expose the issue of data integrity analytically, it must prove that there are single sources for the various data classes and also that there is a requirement for parallel distribution of the data to multiple users. Therefore, BSP specifies which business processes serve as the single source of each data class as differentiated from those processes that merely use the data. The single source is called the "create" point and means that a specific business process is processing the events (or transactions) that originate the data or insert it into the business system as a whole. Processes that merely use the data after it has been acquired by the business are called "usage" points. The "create" and "usage" points imply a natural sequencing for development or implementation which is required if the business is to manage data integrity through controlling the data at its source.

Because BICS focuses upon the data/organization relationship, the issues of authority and accountability are also introduced and added to the concept of create versus use. Different organizations are held accountable for different aspects of the same data. One organization may be responsible for defining the data, a different organization for the content of the data base, a third for authorizing access to the data, and others for using the data. Therefore, BICS uses four levels of differentiation because of its use of organization as a component of its primary structure. The relationships between the BSP and BICS levels are shown in Table 2.

BSP does not need the two additional levels of differentiation because it does not develop the data/organization relationship. That is, authority or accountability is assigned to people (organization), not to process (function). However, BSP's "Create" is roughly equivalent to "Data Content" and "Use" to "Data Usage."

Difference E relates to the manner in which BSP and BICS derive the structures such that they are uniquely tailored to the business unit under study.

**derivation of structure**

In BSP, each structure for each business is uniquely created by the study team such that it describes the business to their own satisfaction. The BSP structure is created from scratch every time and is expressly tailored to fit the business. Its validity is quite dependent upon the skills and understanding of the study team. However, as a result, the BSP structure is very flexible and can describe any business to anyone's satisfaction.

In BICS, the structure is extracted from a superset of predefined categories and relationships which are contained in a generalized model. Those categories and relationships that are pertinent to a specific business are assembled to represent the business under study. Since the BICS structure is predefined, it is quickly generated, reproducible, and somewhat less dependent upon the skills and understanding of the analysts. However, because of its predefinition, some constraints must be accepted in terms of how things are categorized and related.

Table 2  Relationships between BSP and BICS levels

| | BSP | BICS |
|---|---|---|
| 1. | Create | Data content |
| 2. | Use | Data usage |
| 3. | — | Data definition |
| 4. | — | Data access |

## BSP strengths and weaknesses

Several weaknesses can be noted in BSP. First, because BSP is a creative analysis in which the study team manually classifies, defines, relates, analyzes, concludes, etc., its quality is very dependent upon the team's understanding of what they are looking for and their ability to find it. Second, because the structure developed is created from scratch, it is highly customized to the business studied and therefore has little transferability to or comparability with other study structures. Third, it is very difficult to bridge between the planning activity of the study and the implementation. No design falls out of the BSP analysis, and implementations must revert to classic application development techniques. In short, no magic and no design and development shortcuts are inherent in BSP.

Nonetheless, BSP strengths are considerable. It is a very good, structured approach to deal with a very complex problem. Properly applied, it effectively exposes the data issue fully and confronts management with the fact that decisions of the data processing organization are clearly trade-offs between long-term options and short-term options. It helps establish communications among data processing, the user community, and top management. It develops an enterprise-level architecture (albeit rather rudimentary) and objectively deals with the priority issue, identifying areas in which the information system resource can best be invested for the overall interest of the business at a given point in time.

BSP's greatest strength lies in the fact that it is well-documented, supported by IBM education, widely used, well-understood, and available *now*. Actually, in 1981, as far as the general customer environment is concerned, it is almost "the only game in town." As a matter of fact, many of the consulting firms that offer information systems planning-type services explicitly sell BSP or a BSP derivative as a product. (This statement is not meant to exclude or minimize other I/S planning methodologies such as those referred to in the introduction of this paper. Rather, it is meant to emphasize the widespread use of BSP as a tool for *enterprise analysis*.)

In the future, the documentation aspects of BSP could easily be automated, making the process considerably easier. A BSP model has already been described for the Information Management System (IMS) Data Dictionary using the extensibility features.[17] Study teams are beginning to use the Dictionary as a repository for the BSP data. Furthermore, BSP is an excellent study methodology that could be adapted relatively easily for use with other analytical tools. (For example, other analytical tools might include BIAIT,[11] PSL/PSA,[8] SADT,[10] etc.)

## BICS strengths and weaknesses

BICS has several weaknesses to be considered. First, BICS is not supported with an adequate theoretical foundation. The BIAIT theory,[11] though apparently on the right track, needs quite a bit more research and development before it can be considered something of a science. The structures and classifications are based on empirical evidence rather than theoretical foundation. It is only fair to say that this is no more the case for BICS than for BSP; however, BSP does not produce predefined structures that connote theoretical substantiation as does BICS.

Second, although BICS has some good empirical validation, it is by no means extensive at this time. Its use has been largely limited to IBM internal business units, although they have been quite diverse in nature and have therefore served as reasonable test cases.

Third, there is some inflexibility inherent in the BICS model because it is predefined. This inflexibility means that in order to use it, a study team may have to "force-fit" some of the structure.

Fourth, at the present time, BICS is not well-documented, and very few people are trained in the methodology. Therefore, its availability is severely limited.

BICS does have considerable strengths. Because of its predefined structure, the tailored model of the business unit under study is generated rather than created from scratch. At worst it would have to be validated and altered, if considered necessary, to represent the business. Therefore, it is quick, it requires minimal labor, and the resultant structure is reproducible. Any analyst, regardless of skill, should come up with the same structure for the same business. Furthermore, BICS leads to quick solutions, relieving current management frustrations even though the longer-term fixes are deferred until the environment is stabilized.

The greatest strength of BICS lies in its future potential. Given sufficient time, good theoretical substantiation could develop. Even if the theory did not evolve, sufficient empirical evidence would give substantial credence to and/or confidence in the model to make it a valuable tool. Also, additional time will allow other classes of things pertaining to the business to be predefined and added into the data classes in the current model. Other classes of things which would be of interest would be processes (which is nearly complete), objectives, measurements, reports and forms, job classifications, critical success factors, etc. As these additional pieces of work are completed, the resultant structure begins to look like an holistic model of the business which could be used for business planning purposes, not merely information planning purposes.

Further along, since BICS is dealing with predefined classes of things, it is reasonable to suspect that the specific content of the classes could also be predefined. Then, with predefined, specific data entities and attributes, processes (function), objectives, etc., along with predefined relationships between the elements of the model, it is reasonable to suspect that BICS could produce predefined data design and predefined functional code. Therefore, with a limited set of variables describing the business, a structure (or model) could be quickly generated with minimal labor. From the structure, predefined systems design could be generated (both function and data), thus establishing a solid bridge between the planning activity and the implementation. Even if this goal is not practical in the reasonably near future, the preponderant demand for increased productivity in application development makes this BICS potential an exciting consideration.

## Conclusions

The area of enterprise analysis is in its formative stages. As the technology continues to mature and as industry evolves to later stages of learning with regard to managing data,[18] the demand for greater levels of sophistication in enterprise analysis will increase. Enterprise-level dependencies will have to be identified and protected to provide for systems and data integration. Limited information systems resources will have to be effectively allocated. Short-term and long-term trade-offs will have to be made in determining the information system resource investment strategies. Holistic models of the business will be required to support the management planning and control apparatus. These issues will become more pressing over time and will precipitate substantial increases in the body of knowledge concerning enterprise analysis.

It is likely that a science will evolve which will enable the description of the generic structure of a business. With such a science, theoretical definitions could be established for such items as business processes, data classes, objectives, measurements, critical success factors, and so on. Logical boundaries and interfaces or relationships between the various elements of the business could be identified. Structural aspects of tools like BSP and BICS, which are now dependent upon empirical observations, could be theoretically substantiated. With good, theoretically substantiated structures, it would be possible to move with confidence into the realm of automatic code generation and automated data design. These procedures open the door to very sophisticated study methodologies which, in practice, could automatically generate information systems from a very few variables describing the business. It would truly open the door to managing data as a resource.

Business Modeling Technology[19] potentially is the beginning of such a science. The ultimate implications of theoretical frameworks such as Business Modeling Technology reach far beyond merely automating systems design or managing data. They reach into the realms of strategic business planning and management science in general. The business environment of the 1980s likely will contain very strong forces which will demand investment in such science-like research and development projects.

With regard to BSP and BICS, although the future may reveal that they are rather primitive, in the present they are substantive representations of enterprise analysis-oriented planning tools. Their considerable similarity makes them mutually exclusive. That is, a choice has to be made as to which is more appropriate in a given situation. The single difference that is most likely to influence the choice is the difference in study strategy. If the study is intended to get the data issue out in the open and force an overt change in the design approach to information systems, then BSP is the most appropriate choice. If the study strategy is intended to relieve some current management frustrations with specific, data-oriented solutions, then BICS is the most appropriate choice.

The current limited availability, limited depth of empirical validation, and affinity for relational data base implementations of BICS are the tempering factors for selecting BICS at present. Time will mitigate some of these limitations as it will also amplify the strengths of BICS in rapid generation of predefined structures and reproducibility. Ultimately, with continued research and development, the BICS potential of drawing closer to requirements definition and design specification is likely to become very attractive.

Either of these study methodologies may be employed by study teams that are completely oblivious to the more esoteric issues of enterprise architectures, to data-driven systems design, to long-term and short-term investment strategies, to serial versus parallel distribution of data, to data classification criteria, and so on. In this case, it does not really matter which methodology is employed. In fact, many studies have been done by merely following the methodology as a "cook book." By doing so, substantial success may even be achieved, but the results are usually limited to identifying a set of applications projects to work on, establishing increased management involvement in data processing planning, and facilitating communications with the users. Unfortunately, these studies do not get at the heart of management's frustration with the current application portfolio which centers around the data problem and these more complex issues. It then takes a second (or third, or fourth, etc.) iteration. Each iteration considerably increases the learning process of the business with regard to managing its data. Therefore, every iteration is valuable, independent of the methodology; however, the methodology becomes more important as the level of learning increases.

The issues that have to be learned are complex, and the learning can be long and arduous. BSP and BICS (and other enterprise analysis techniques) are catalysts to the learning process as much as they are short cuts. They precipitate learning as well as providing well-thought-through analyses based upon a substantial body of knowledge.

Every business that continues to grow and evolve is likely to have to employ some form of enterprise analysis. BSP and BICS are important representatives of what is available today.

CITED REFERENCES

1. *Business Systems Planning—Information Systems Planning Guide,* Application Manual, GE20-0527, IBM Corporation (July 1981); available through IBM branch offices.
2. D. V. Kerner, "Introduction to Business Information Control Study Methodology (BICS)," *Symposium on the Economics of Information Processing,* December 15–19, 1980, IBM Systems Research Institute, New York; also in *The Economics*

*of Information Processing,* Vol. 1, *Management Perspectives,* John Wiley & Sons, Inc., New York (1981).

3. R. L. Nolan, "Managing the crises in data processing," *Harvard Business Review* **57,** No. 2, 115–126 (March–April 1979).

4. P. D. Walker, "Next in MIS: 'Data managed' system design," *Computer Decisions* **1,** No. 12 (December 1969).

5. W. R. King, "Strategic planning for management information systems," *MIS Quarterly* **2,** No. 1, 27–37 (March 1978).

6. C. Gane and T. Sarson, *Structured Systems Analysis: Tools and Techniques,* Prentice-Hall, Inc., Englewood Cliffs, NJ (1979).

7. P. P. Chen, *Entity-Relationship Approach to Systems Analysis and Design,* UCLA, Los Angeles, CA (December 1979).

8. D. Tiechroew and E. A. Hershey III, "PSL/PSA: Computer-aided technique for structured documentation and analysis of information processing systems," *IEEE Transactions on Software Engineering* SE-3, No. 1, 41–48 (January 1977).

9. D. S. Appleton, "Implementing data management," *AFIPS Conference Proceedings* **49,** 307–316 (1980).

10. *An Introduction to SADT—Structured Analysis and Design Technique,* 9022-78R, Softech, Inc., Boston (November 1976).

11. D. C. Burnstine, *The Theory Behind BIAIT—Business Information Analysis and Integration Technique,* BIAIT International, Inc., Fox Hollow, Petersburg, NY (1979).

12. W. M. Carlson, "Business Information Analysis and Integration Technique (BIAIT)—The new horizon," *Data Base* **10,** No. 4, 3–9 (Spring 1979).

13. D. S. Appleton, "DDP management strategies: Keys to success or failure," *Data Base* **10,** No. 1, 3–8 (Summer 1978).

14. J. F. Rockart, "Chief executives define their own data needs," *Harvard Business Review* **57,** No. 2, 81–93 (March–April 1979).

15. J. W. Forrester, *Industrial Dynamics,* MIT Press, Cambridge, MA (1961).

16. P. D. Walker, "Where do we go from here with MIS?," *Computer Decisions* **1,** No. 11 (November 1969).

17. J. G. Sakamoto, *Use of DB/DC Dictionary to Support Business Systems Planning Studies: An Approach,* G320-2705, IBM Corporation, Los Angeles Scientific Center (July 1980); available through IBM branch offices.

18. R. L. Nolan, "Restructuring the data processing organization for data resource management," *Information Processing 77,* North-Holland Publishing Co., Amsterdam, The Netherlands (1977), pp. 261–265.

19. A. D. Pendleton, "BMT: A Business Modeling Technology," *Symposium on the Economics of Information Processing,* December 15–19, 1980, IBM Systems Research Institute, New York; also in *The Economics of Information Processing,* Vol. 1, *Management Perspectives,* John Wiley & Sons, Inc., New York (1981).

*The author is with the IBM Data Processing Division Western Region, 3424 Wilshire Boulevard, Los Angeles, CA 90010.*

# 3
# Information for Strategic Decisions

It cannot be stressed too strongly or too often that information is universally recognized to be a vital resource of a modern society. No better proof can be offered of the recognition by our business leaders of the importance of information than the flood of advertisements that fill our business periodicals and journals, three typical examples of which are presented here (see Figure 3–1).

The rapid emergence of information as an area of significant concern to business executives may also be seen by the treatment given to information by *Business Week,* one of our leading journals. In its issue of March 29, 1982, *Business Week* published a special advertising section on information resource management. The narrative portion of this supplement is reproduced at the end of this chapter. This was followed on July 12, 1982 by the announcement of the creation of a new information management department. The rationale given by the publisher for setting up this new department is presented in Figure 3–2. These events typify what has been happening throughout all the media targeted at the business community.

With all this emphasis being placed on information, the thoughtful executive will ask:

1. What kinds of information do I need to help me do my job better?
2. Where do I find this information?
3. Having found the information, how do I use it?

We hope to provide clues to the answers to these questions in this and succeeding chapters. It is by now a truism, but nonetheless valid, to assert that we are in the midst of a burgeoning information explosion. To avoid information overload, the business manager must have a clear idea of what information he needs and the skill to search for and select the required information from a large and growing mass of available information. A simple classification scheme facilitates the winnowing down process. Information may be obtained either from within the organization or from the outside environment. Knowledge about which of these two sources to access is the first requirement for reducing information search to manageable proportions. Secondly, we know that the information required to support strategic-level decisions comes for the most part from the outside environment, while much tactical-level decisionmaking is based on information generated within the organization. We are thus provided with a framework for coping with the three questions raised above. This chapter will be devoted to strategic-level decisions and will therefore examine sources of information in the outside environment. Subsequent chapters will deal

# We help decision makers see around corners.

Of course, no one can tell you for certain what the future holds. But McGraw-Hill can help.

In fact, one of our subsidiaries, Data Resources, Inc., is the most sophisticated economic forecasting service in the world.

We can help you forecast your share of market in 1985. Plug you into data banks targeted to specific industries. Or help you anticipate the impact of political and economic shifts on world markets.

We'll give you access to invaluable econometric models and an array of ongoing consulting services.

And provide training programs to insure that your executives and staff make the most of everything we offer. All to help you plan more efficiently—for the next quarter, the next year or the next decade.

DRI's projections and systems have proved so effective over the past twelve years that most Federal agencies and over 300 of the nation's largest industrial corporations now make regular use of them.

DRI has the largest commercially available economic data base in the world, developed and maintained by 400 economists and consultants.

But DRI is only one approach that McGraw-Hill uses in supplying essential information for business, government, science and education. We provide books, magazines, films, television, newswires and audiovisual programs. Our 258 offices worldwide specialize in information of the most important kind: Information that leads to action.

For more details regarding DRI, write: "Data Resources," McGraw-Hill, Inc., 1221 Avenue of the Americas, New York, New York 10020.

## McGraw-Hill Information that leads to action.

Figue 3–1A. Copyright © 1982 by McGraw-Hill, Inc.

# Plugging into the Information Universe.

The vast universe of business information, like electrical energy, has always been out there. But it took a company called TRW to make it more useful and productive for American business.

## Credit where credit is due.

Many important business decisions concern granting credit and, because these decisions usually must be made quickly, reliable up-to-date information about a company is essential. To help keep the wheels of commerce turning, TRW's efficient business credit service gathers, stores and

transmits credit information on business electronically

to thousands of companies nationwide.

## We deliver. In seconds.

When TRW business credit subscribers make a request for information, they receive a print-out in their own office in seconds. Among other data, this report shows a potential buyer's payment pattern.

It's all there...in a TRW Business Profile˜. And with this data, fast, intelligent business decisions can be made with more confidence.

The information

universe is now the information business at TRW. We've plugged into that universe to help make American business more productive... and profitable.

*Tomorrow is taking shape at*

**A COMPANY CALLED**

**TRW**

Figure 3–1B. Courtesy of TRW Inc.

# "INFORMANIA"
# It's having numbers when you need words.

You earn your living by making decisions.

Business decisions.

Big, expensive, tough ones where the margin for error is wafer thin.

So when you need a list of customer names by region and all you've got is a page full of accounts receivable dollars, it's no wonder your stomach churns.

*That's* "Informania."

The solution is information. The right information. In the right form. For the right people in the right place and time.

Burroughs can help. Because we know how to manage information. We've put 95 years of thought and experience into it. We offer a comprehensive solution to the problem of "Informania."

Our computers and office automation systems can help you collect, compose, analyze, store, recall, reformulate and distribute information.

So that you will know. And have numbers when you need numbers, words when you need words.

When "Informania" strikes, the answer is Burroughs. Write for our brochure: Burroughs Corporation, Dept. BW-20, Burroughs Place, Detroit, Michigan 48232.

# Burroughs
## Building on strength

Figure 3–1C. Courtesy of Burroughs Corporation.

**Publisher's memo**

Most of us by now are comfortable with information processing, and most businesses today could not be run without a computer. The question now is not how to process information but what information to process. And once this information is computerized, what do you do with it? How can companies avoid building huge data bases of unorganized information that is, in fact, of little practical use? How, indeed, can computer technology be better used to synthesize information into knowledge that can help executives and business planners and strategists do their jobs better?

**Editor Grossman:** Companies must learn to use information as a competitive tool.

Finding the answers becomes increasingly important as the computer moves ever more deeply into the planning pro-

cess of most companies. And providing those answers is the primary mission of Information management, BUSINESS WEEK's newest department, which makes its debut in this issue on page 56. For its opening article, the department takes a look at the swift spread of personal computers through the nation's executive suites and the headaches their unfettered use is giving some companies—and what can be done about them.

Supervising the new department is Associate Editor Robin Grossman, who, with Senior Editor Robert W. Henkel, has directed the magazine's Information processing coverage for the past four years. "The Information management department," she says, "will concern itself with how,

for instance, information can be used as a competitive weapon. How do companies avoid letting computers become giant number crunchers that do little to provide useful information?" She adds: "Companies need help in understanding how the information industry is changing in order to better reexamine their own corporate missions. We're going to give them that help."

The new department, of course, will get its own information through the thorough, on-the-spot reporting for which the bureau correspondents as well as the editors of BUSINESS WEEK are known. Contributing to this week's opener, for instance, were James R. Norman of the Minneapolis-St. Paul bureau, Amy Borrus in Boston, Larry Armstrong in Chicago, Taylor Moore in San Francisco, Zachary Schiller in Cleveland, and Patrick Houston in Pittsburgh.

*James R. Crane*

with operation-level decisions and will concentrate on information sources within the organization.

## ENVIRONMENTAL SCANNING

F. J. Aguilar has defined environmental scanning as "the activity by which an organization collects information about the opportunities and threats it faces. It is a continuous process because the requirements for such information are endless. Scanning involves collecting information about the state of the current environment as well as about future trends. It involves making decisions about the parts of the environment to be examined, the frequency of examination, and the communication channels within the organization through which this information should be transmitted."[1] Information that is sought for the purpose of strategic decisionmaking involves "scanning for information about events and relationships in a company's outside environment, the knowledge of which would assist top management in its task of charting the company's future course of actions."[2]

The nature of the environment in which an organization operates dictates the frequency and the scope of its scanning efforts. Stable environments, for example, require less scanning than unstable ones. Organizations in stable environments can thus rely on established policies and procedures over longer periods of time. When on the other hand an organization finds itself in a heterogeneous rather than a

[1] F. J. Aguilar, *Scanning the Business Environment* (New York: The Macmillan Company, 1967).
[2] Ibid.

homogeneous environment, in a complex rather than a simple environment, or in an unpredictable rather than a certain environment, more resources must be devoted to scanning the environment, evaluating trends, determining and searching out alternatives, and adapting to change in general.

Once the amount and type of scanning appropriate for a given organization is determined, the categories of useful information must be identified. Despite the diversity of both environments and organizations, most firms find themselves searching for relevant information in the following areas:

1. economic environment
2. government policies
3. demographic conditions
4. technological environment
5. markets and competition
6. social, cultural, and political changes

Before proceeding with a discussion about the sources of such information, it should be recognized that when the relevant information has been acquired, it must be applied to the circumstances of the specific organization. This involves a clear understanding of the strengths and weaknesses of the organization and its ability to achieve objectives formulated as a result of the environmental scanning studies. The mechanism used to study the organization is known as a resources and capability evaluation. The determination as to whether the organization is geared to meet anticipated environmental demands and, if not, what may be needed in the way of additional resources to make it capable of so doing depends upon an analysis of the following organizational areas:

1. market positions
2. technological superiority
3. physical facilities
4. supply position
5. financial strength
6. human resources
7. specialized experience

To sum up, environmental scanning enables the executive to formulate realistic objectives of what and where the organization should be at some given point in the future. The difference between where the organization is today and where it should be at that future time if the objectives are met is known as the *gap*. The capability evaluation will reveal to the executive the degree to which the organization has the potential to close the gap.

## SOURCES OF EXTERNAL INFORMATION

The rapid accretion of information has also led to the proliferation of sources of information. We shall list some of the major sources of information that are available and give some concrete examples of the kinds of information obtainable from each source. There is no implication that the examples cited are the only or best sources available; they are presented only for illustrative purposes.

## A. Economic environment and demographic conditions

1. Subscription services such as:
    a. Economic and Demographic Projections to 2000, a series of volumes and data tapes offered by the Center for Economic Projections of the National Planning Association.
    b. *The World Economy in the 1980's,* a joint publication of Wharton Econometric Forecasting Associates and The Economist Intelligence Unit Ltd.
2. Conferences and seminars such as:
    a. "Conference on the Economic Outlook," sponsored by the University of Michigan Department of Economics in cooperation with the Institute for Social Research and The University of Michigan Extension Service.
    b. "Economic Outlook," presented by Blue Chip Economic Indicators.
    c. "Energy Investments in the 1980's," sponsored jointly by the Department of Engineering-Economic Systems and the Energy Modeling Forum of Stanford University.

## B. Technological environment

1. Conferences and seminars such as:
    a. "The Strategic Management of Technology," offered by the Division of Management Education, Graduate School of Business Administration, The University of Michigan.
2. Publications such as:
    a. *Patterns of Technological Innovation,* by D. Sahal, published by Addison-Wesley Publishing Co., Reading, Mass., 1969.

## C. Markets and competition

1. Information services, directories, and reference works such as:
    a. *The Information Catalog*, containing industry, market and company studies, published by Find/SVP.
    b. *Findex,* a directory of market research reports, studies and surveys, published by Find/SVP.
    c. Public company business and financial information on magnetic tape offered by Disclosure Incorporated.
    d. Acquisitions search services, a series of reports offered by Mergex, Inc., a company of Dun and Bradstreet Corporation.
    e. Directions Intelligence series analyzing specific industries and discussing the strategic directions and diversification policies of major corporations published by International Resource Development Inc.

    f. *How to Find Information About Companies,* published by Washington Researchers.

    g. Strategic Planning Service offered by Futuremics International.

    h. Industry Profiles offered by McGraw-Hill Research.

2. Publications such as:

    a. *Yearbook on Corporate Mergers Joint Ventures and Corporate Policy,* published by Cambridge Books.

    b. *Developing Competitive Strategies Worldwide,* published by Business International Worldwide.

3. Conferences and seminars such as:

    a. "Corporate Strategy: Planning for Diversification/Consolidation," sponsored by Business Week Executive Programs.

    b. AMA's Course in Mergers and Acquisitions, sponsored by American Management Associations.

    c. "Strategic Planning for Energy Companies," sponsored by Executive Enterprises, Inc.

4. International business, such as the following conferences sponsored by the World Trade Institute:

    a. "Australia: New Horizon for Investment."

    b. "Brazil in the 1980's: Opportunities and Challenges."

    c. "Strategic Planning for Multinationals in the Developing Countries."

    d. "International Joint Ventures: Key Considerations for Decision Makers."

    e. "Country Risk Analysis: Developing the Essential Elements for the Financial and Market Planning Process."

## D. Social, cultural, and political environment

1. Conferences and seminars such as:

    a. "Through the 80s—Thinking Globally, Acting Locally" sponsored by the World Future Society.

    b. "Profit/Political Risk—Strategic Planning in an Uncertain World," sponsored by National Credit Office, A Division of Dun & Bradstreet Corporation.

    c. "The Coming Boom: Economic, Political and Social," sponsored by The National Chamber Foundation and The Hudson Institute.

    d. "Planning for Global Interdependence," sponsored by the International Affiliation of Planning Societies.

    e. International Seminar for Senior Executives, sponsored jointly by the International Management Institute,Geneva, and the College of Management, Georgia Institute of Technology.

The listings presented thus far have been grouped into the subject areas of major interest to business executives. In order to use this information effectively within the organization, the manager must be aware of various techniques, organizational functions, and resources. The following listings illustrate external sources of information which cater to these needs.

## E. Planning—General

1. Conferences and seminars such as:
   a. "Strategic Planning in the 1980's: Issues and Options," sponsored by the Wharton School of the University of Pennsylvania.
   b. "Strategy Formulation and Implementation: Long Range Planning," sponsored by the Division of Management Education, Graduate School of Business Administration, The University of Michigan.
   c. "Effective Strategic Planning for Your Enterprise," sponsored by the North American Society for Corporate Planning.
   d. "Strategic Planning Systems," sponsored by The Naylor Group
   e. "International Seminar on Corporate Planning," sponsored by the Center for Education in International Management, Geneva.
   f. "Strategy and the Management Matrix," sponsored by Business Week Executive Programs.
   g. "Strategies for Growth in the 1980's," sponsored by Business Week Executive Programs.
   h. "Strategies for the Eighties," sponsored by The Strategic Planning Institute.
   i. "A Participating Approach to Corporate Planning," sponsored by Roy W. Walters & Associates Inc.
   j. "Recharging the Planner's Batteries," sponsored by The Conference Board.
2. Publications such as:
   a. *Contingency Planning*, published by American Management Associations.
   b. *The Practice of Planning*, by L. Reinharth, H. J. Shapiro, E. A. Kallman, published by Van Nostrand Reinhold Company.

## F. Functional Issues

1. Conferences and seminars such as:
   a. "Human Resource Planning," sponsored by Business Week Executive Programs.
   b. "Strategic Planning of Corporate Research and Development," sponsored by American Management Associations.
2. Publications such as:
   a. "Employment Issues of the 80's," published by the Equal Employment Advisory Council.

## G. Techniques

1. Conferences and seminars, such as:
   a. "Decision and Risk Analysis," sponsored by SRI International.
   b. "Forecasting Corporate Opportunities and Risks," sponsored jointly by Forecasting International, Ltd. and the Business Planning Institute
2. Publications such as:
   a. *Corporate Planning, Techniques and Applications,* by R. J. Allio and M. W. Pennington, published by Amacom.

In order to keep up with the continuing developments in these various fields, attendance at a conference or reading a book is not adequate. Many external sources offer subscriptions to periodicals appearing on a weekly, monthly, quarterly or annual basis. The next category presents a small sampling of such services.

## H. Periodicals

1. Economic environment such as:
   a. *Economics Today.*
   b. *World Economic Service,* published by Wharton Economic Forecasting Services.
   c. *Update, The American States,* a newsletter published by Frost & Sullivan, Inc.
   d. *The Econoclast.*
   e. *Blue Chip Economic Worldscan.*
2. Markets and competition such as:
   a. *Mergers and Corporate Policy,* published by Cambridge Corporation Publishers.
   b. *World Technical and Business Opportunities,* published by Prestwich Publications, Inc.
3. Technological environment such as:
   a. *Technology Forecasts and Technology Surveys.*
   b. *Technology Growth Markets and Opportunities,* published by Creative Strategies International.
   c. *Telegen Reporter,* a monthly on genetic technology data.
4. Social, political, and cultural environment such as:
   a. *World Political Risk Forecasts.*
   b. *Congressional Insight,* published by Congressional Quarterly, Inc.
5. Techniques and functional areas such as:
   a. *Managing Tomorrow,* published by the Global Management Bureau.
   b. *Journal of Forecasting,* published by John Wiley & Sons.
   c. *Strategic Management Journal,* published by John Wiley & Sons.
   d. *The Journal of Business Strategy,* published by Warren, Gorham & Lamont, Inc.
   e. *Planning Review,* published by Robert J. Allio & Associates, Inc. for the North American Society for Corporate Planning, Inc.

Considering the amount of information needed for proper managerial performance and the mass of available information, it should not be surprising that modern managers have to learn how to manage information. The final listing presented herewith provides a sample of external sources of information on information.

## I. Information

1. Conferences and seminars such as:
   a. "The International Information Management Exposition and Conference,' presented each fall at the New York Coliseum.

b. "Managing Information Resources," sponsored by the Executive Development Center, Graduate School of Business Administration, University of Minnesota.

c. "Interface," cosponsored by The Interface Group, Business Week, and Data Communications.

d. "Conference on Information Systems," sponsored by the Society for Management Information Systems.

e. "Decision Support Seminars," sponsored by Execucom.

f. "Strategic Planning for Information Systems," sponsored by the Datamation Institute.

g. "Strategic Information for Management: Key Databases for Decision Makers," sponsored by Information Marketing Group.

h. "Information Utilities," sponsored by Online Inc.

i. "Use of Economic and Financial Models in the Corporate Planning Process," sponsored by the North American Society for Corporate Planning, Inc.

j. "Fundamentals of Data Processing for the Non-Data Processing Executive," sponsored by American Management Associations.

k. "Decision Support Systems for Corporate Planners," sponsored by the North American Society for Corporate Planning, Inc.

l. "The Future of Corporate Planning and Modeling Software Systems," sponsored by Duke University.

2. Periodicals such as:

a. *Datamation*
b. *MIS Week*
c. *MIS Quarterly*
d. *Computerworld*
e. *Computer Decisions*
f. *Infosystems*

The above examples should give the reader an idea of the tremendous range of information available in the outside environment. When a knowledgeable manager needs a certain kind of information, he knows that it's rarely the problem that the information does not exist, but rather that it must be ferreted out from a mass of information, somewhat like searching for a needle in a haystack. Familiarity with the major sources of information will facilitate the search.

## DECISION SUPPORT SYSTEMS

Once the needed information has been obtained, it is analyzed in terms of the problem being studied. The results of the analysis appear in some form of output. Before proceeding with a discussion of information system outputs, it is necessary to review a technique known as the decision support system (DSS) that, over the past half decade, has become the dominant information tool for middle-level and higher-level executives.

## What is a DSS?

Information systems may be classified as a four-level hierarchy.[3]

1. *Basic data processing systems* perform only single data processing tasks. Each task is a self-contained job, like payroll. The outputs are scheduled reports summarizing the transaction data that have been processed. These reports are available to all managerial levels but are of limited value to middle and top management.

2. *Integrated data processing systems*. Almost all of the data processing activities still involve the processing of transaction data and the generation of reports that primarily support lower management decisionmaking. Simple decision models such as those for inventory control are included in the information system at this level.

3. *Management information systems* involve a partially integrated database partitioned by major business functions like marketing, production and personnel. Scheduled reports are available on demand and serve the information needs of middle and top management. Attempts are made to structure appropriate information flows to upper management.

4. *Decision support system* is an integrated system composed of decision models, a database, and a decision maker to support decisionmaking. To support such systems, an enhanced database, one which retains external data and other internal data as well as transaction data, must be maintained. With such data available, it is possible to feed the decision models embedded in the information system.

## Functions of DSS

Blanning[4] has summarized the six functions that may be performed by a DSS as follows:

1. *Selection* of data from a database. This function is not as widely used as the others, primarily because the requirements for a DSS are most frequently accomplished not by retrieving data but by performing analysis of the data. Where used, this function may be facilitated by a database management system.

2. *Aggregation* of data into totals, averages, frequency distributions, etc. A DSS performing with such a function is of limited use in solving unstructured problems, but it can help to identify problem areas (such as cost overruns and low service levels) for further investigation.

3. *Estimation* of the parameters in a probability distribution. This is accomplished by performing statistical analyses of data to determine relationships between important variables. A DSS performing this function is often used when relationships between important variables are difficult to determine but data resulting from processes governed by these relationships are available. Examples are statistical analyses of marketing data and economic data.

4. *Simulation* to calculate the anticipated consequence of proposed decisions or of possible changes in the corporate environment. This technique has been widely

---

[3]Adapted from R. H. Sprague and H. J. Watson, Bit by bit: toward decision support systems, *California Management Review* 22 (Fall 1979): p. 61.

[4]R. W. Blanning, The functions of a decision support system, *Information and Management* 2 (September 1979), p. 88.

used at the lower levels of corporations and increasingly it is being used to address problems at the corporate levels.

5. *Equalization* to calculate decisions whose consequences will meet certain consistency conditions, e.g., interindustry economic models that balance the supply and demand in each of several industries.

6. *Optimization* to determine decisions that will maximize or minimize a single measure of performance or cost without violating constraints on other such measures.

**Components of a DSS**

**1. The Database Subsystem.**   This subsystem consists of the database and the software system for managing it. In most cases, communication linkages are also required from the database to its ultimate destination, the decision maker. A comprehensive database for decision support derives data from several sources:

a. The traditional source is the basic data processing activities of the organization that provide a summary of the organization's performance at the operational level.
b. An additional source of internal data consists of subjective estimates from managers and engineering-related data, generally unavailable from normal data processing activities.
c. External data sources.

Finally, the database must have a variety of logical structures that support multi-attribute retrieval.

**2. The Modelbase Subsystem.**   This subsystem consists of:

a. *Strategic Models.* These are broad in scope with many variables expressed in compressed, aggregated form. Much of the data used to feed the models is external and subjective rather than the familiar and readily available transaction data.
b. *Tactical Models.* These models are commonly employed by middle management to assist in allocating and controlling the use of the organization's resources. Some subjective and external data are needed but the major requirement is for internal data.
c. *Operational Models.* These models are employed to support the short-term decisions generally made at lower organizational levels. They normally use internal, objective data as input.

The modelbase may contain model-building blocks, standard management science and financial models (such as linear programming or capital budgeting), and/or statistical routines (such as time series, multiple regression, etc.). These packaged models may be used separately or combined to form more comprehensive models.

**3. The Decision Maker.** If the DSS is to be a useful tool, it must accommodate the tasks, the cognitive preferences, the abilities, and the decisionmaking style of the user, who is the decision maker. The command language must be flexible enough to service both top managers who may lack the knowledge to deal with computer language and staff analysts who work in finer detail.

## Typical DSS Applications

Decision support systems have been used to cope with a wide variety of organizational problems and requirements. The following applications were developed for some major corporations and indicate the broad range of organizational activities amenable to the DSS approach.[5]

1. *AAIMS:* An analytic information management system. Designed for budget consolidation, revenue yield analysis, corporate performance reporting, and ad hoc reporting.
2. *BIS:* Budget information system. Designed to aid the manager in planning, budgeting and control.
3. *BRANDAID:* Marketing brand management. Designed to support the manager in making decisions on the "marketing mix" (pricing, advertising, salesforce activities, etc.)
4. *CAUSE:* Computer-assisted underwriting system at Equitable. Designed to help Equitable's underwriters calculate renewal rates on group insurance policies.
5. *CIS:* Capacity information system. Designed to assess the impact of changes in product plans on the company's manufacturing operations.
6. *GADS:* Geodata analysis display system. Designed for (1) planning for urban growth, (2) designing police beats, and (3) redefining school district boundries.
7. *IMS:* Interactive marketing system. Designed to assist the marketing manager in identifying potential consumers and analyzing their habits in order to determine the overall strategy of an advertising campaign.
8. *PMS:* Portfolio management system. Designed to support the portfolio or investment manager in a bank's trust department in making decisions to buy or sell securities.
9. *PROJECTOR:* Strategic financial planning system. Designed to integrate a range of advanced tools for financial planning into a "user-oriented" system.

## Problems in Implementing a DSS

Alter has identified several sources of difficulty that arise when implementing a DSS:[6]

---

[5]These examples were chosen from S. L. Alter, *Decision Support Systems: Current Practice and Continuing Challenges,* (Reading, Mass.: Addison-Wesley Publishing Company, 1980); E. D. Carlson, ed., Proceedings of a conference on decision suport systems, *Data Base* **8** (3), Winter 1977; and P. G. W. Keen and M. S. S. Morton, *Decision Support Systems: An Organizational Perspective,* (Reading, Mass.: Addison-Wesley Publishing Company, 1978).

[6]Alter, *Decision Support Systems,* p. 134.

*1. Technical problems.* Existing technology is powerful enough to drive a decision support system effectively. Thus, when "technical problems" are cited, reference is generally to a limited budget that constrains the systems builder from acquiring a larger computer, redundant terminals, better software or more highly skilled programmers.

*2. Data problems.* Data problems in DSS applications are the same as those with any other computer-related project, namely, the data were not correct, the data were not timely, or the data were not measured or indexed properly.

*3. Conceptual design problems.* These problems fall into two categories. The system may have been designed inflexibly so that when conditions change, as when a structural reorganization takes place, the system is no longer applicable. Alternatively, the system may have been designed to attack the wrong problem. Then, when the real problem is addressed, the system cannot handle it. Avoidance of these problems requires meaningful communication between the system builder and the system user during the design phase.

*4. People problems.* Many DSS applications call for the input of projections, forecasts, or *guesstimates* into the system. The basic problem is to get managers to submit realistic estimates of what can be achieved with a reasonably ambitious but attainable level of effort. The system designer must learn to motivate user-managers to set aside their routine tasks and think seriously about their future plans. An additional people problem relates to a general unwillingness or inability of some (usually older) managers to use computers.

*5. Cost/benefit problem.* Modern managers have been trained not to undertake any activity where the benefit derived cannot be shown to exceed the cost. This creates a problem in terms of justifying expenditures to develop a decision support system. A DSS is designed to help improve the manager's effectiveness. At higher managerial levels, it is very difficult to measure effectiveness in general, much less the contribution to effectiveness of any component such as DSS. A DSS will not replace staff nor will it save money directly. The best judgment that can be made is that if we assume rationality and intelligence on the part of most American managers, the rapid expansion in the use of DSS applications demonstrates a strongly held belief and faith in their validity. Fortunately, some DSS applications do have measurable payoffs. Some examples are cited in the *Business Week* article entitled "'What if' help for management" reproduced in this chapter (see Figure 3–3).

## Future Trends

Despite the problems associated with DSS, software firms envisage an exploding market for new DSS products and are allocating research funds in large amounts to develop such products. Recent efforts have focused on developing methodologies for measuring the impact of graphics on problem solving, the use of the microcomputer for personal support systems, and strategies for implementing DSS.

## INFORMATION SYSTEMS OUTPUTS

All human beings including business managers are uncomfortable with uncertainty and therefore continually seek to increase the level of certainty in their lives and

# Information processing

## DATA PROCESSING

# 'What if' help for management

Management at a rapidly growing number of companies is taking advice from a new source to curb soaring business costs. The help is coming from computers, and even in these days of runaway inflation, the payoff can be handsome. At Florida Power & Light Co., the computer showed that centralizing the inventory distribution system would bring clear-cut efficiencies. Result: The Miami-based utility saved $13.5 million last year in inventory carrying costs. Shaklee Corp. expects that by taking its computer's advice it will be able to cut delivery time to customers by one-third and save $850,000 in operating costs this year. And National Airlines Inc.'s computer has shown it how to save as much as $500,000 a month in fuel costs.

All three companies are taking advantage of so-called management support or decision support systems. These are not to be confused with the more conventional applications where a computer collects data, tracks devices, or keeps an account of inventory or unit costs. Generally, computer systems are developed to cope with a specific business problem, and, frequently, the solutions they generate are implemented without regard to the impact—possibly detrimental—they could have on other operations of the company.

**Strategic planning.** With a decision support system, executives in a matter of minutes can sift through the trade-offs among a number of operating plans to find the optimum, or least costly, solutions to manufacturing, distribution, and marketing problems. The primary use is in operational planning, such as in helping to develop complex production schedules. And some companies are using the systems for strategic planning, guiding such decisions as whether to enter a new market.

Stimulating the boom, according to industry experts, is the growing complexity of planning due to such things as government regulations, shortages of raw materials, the lure of big savings, and the declining costs of computers. "Ten years ago consultants were just getting calls from the top 50 companies in the country," says Gerald Brown, a Monterey (Calif.) consultant who designs such systems. "Now we hear from the top 7,000."

At the heart of any management sup-

port system is a computer model in software that describes the process to be managed—a delivery or pricing system, for example, a data base for storing up-to-the-minute details of the company's operations, and the market factors. The computer can then sort through hundreds of "what if" scenarios.

**The right data.** But such a system is not something management can plug in and start running right away. Designing and setting one up not only can be time-

Sloane's Schmitt: A decision support system lifted operating profits $500,000 in a year.

consuming and costly, but also, if the model is not accurate and the operating data are incomplete, can result in a phenomenon well-known to computer users called GI-GO—garbage in, garbage out. Collecting appropriate and accurate data, in fact, is the "biggest obstacle" in developing a sound management support system, believes James C. Spira, director of Cleveland Consulting Associates.

Because sloppy inventory data were entered into its system, R&G Sloane Mfg. Co. had to delay for six months its plans to use its computer model as a master

scheduling tool. "We found that the data we needed just weren't there," says Ralph G. Schmitt, vice-president of operations for the Los Angeles-based manufacturer of plastic pipe fittings. But once the right data were fed to the system, Sloane increased its inventory turns from fewer than three to 3.7 and raised its on-time deliveries by 10% to 94% of total shipments. And by using the system to determine the most profitable product mix for turning out 3,700 different pipe fittings, the company added $500,000 to its total operating profits during 1978.

The lack of relevant data, in fact, was one of the reasons that Shaklee decided to install a management support system. "We convinced [top] management that the condition of our data base was so poor that we ran the risk of making lousy decisions," says Charles D. Fry, manager of materials analysis and planning. At the same time, the Emeryville (Calif.) producer of food supplements, cosmetics, and household cleaners was growing so fast—from $10 million in annual sales 10 years ago to $350 million in 1979—that management was making decisions on a subjective and political basis, he says.

To build its data base, Shaklee has fed in data on plant locations, products made, cost per unit, and production capacity for its three facilities and 20 contract manufacturers. It also has stored details on more than 500 line items, 360 customers, and its 100 distribution centers. The first task was finding the best way to reduce delivery times to customers without increasing production or distribution costs. The system calculated the impact that various delivery requirements would have on transportation costs, the cost of operating distribution centers, and the cost of carrying inventories.

"For the first time," Fry says, "management is able to understand the financial impact associated with various service-level decisions." Without the computer model, he says, "there is no quantifiable way to determine the cost. And decisions become political issues between the sales side of the company, which would like a warehouse in any town where there is a reasonable demand, and

# Information

# processing / CONTINUED

the distribution side, which wants to minimize costs."

Besides finding a way to speed up deliveries to customers and save money, too, Shaklee believes that setting up the new system forced the company to develop its comprehensive data base, which it can use to analyze other operating problems. But it was a big step. All told, it took six months and $250,000 to develop the data base and model. It can often take up to two years to get such a system running. And annual maintenance costs run about 20% of the initial expenditure.

**The payback.** But the payback period on a management support system can be very short. For every dollar spent developing such a system, a company will recover $100 over a five-year period, estimates Paul S. Bender, director of resource allocation systems at International Paper Co. At IP, he figures, the support system usually increases profits by 10%. "This kind of technique," he says, "is one of the best investment opportunities for a company."

National Airlines certainly found this to be true with its new fuel management and allocation system. "In the first month of operation," says D. Wayne Darnell, National's manager of systems and data services, "we cut our fuel costs by 2¢ a gal. Since we used 25 million gal. that month, we saved $500,000." At that rate, National is saving several million dollars annually.

National also kept its flights on schedule during the recent fuel shortages, while compensating for fluctuating supplies and rising costs, thanks to the speed at which its computer model can mirror changing business conditions. The airline stores data on fuel prices and availability, along with storage costs and fuel capacity at each of the 30 cities it serves. The performance and tentative monthly itinerary are also included for each of its 56 aircraft. In just 15 minutes the computer produces a list of the best fueling stations and vendors for each flight, something that used to take a month to do manually. "We used to make up a schedule once a month," Darnell says, "but now we can run it two or three times a week."

**Savings.** Speed also encourages managers to play "what if" games, sometimes with surprising results. The manufacturing department at American Can Co. recently planned to install a $50 million production system at one of its

plants in the Pacific Northwest. But management used its computer to investigate 32 alternative locations and decided instead to locate the new system in a Southeastern plant. If manufacturing had had its way, it would have cost American Can an additional $7 million a year in distribution costs.

Sometimes, however, an idea from middle management can trigger "what-if" games that result in substantial savings. When one of Florida Power & Light's five geographical divisions wanted to build a central warehouse to serve its distribution centers, the utility had 53 distribution centers, each ordering 20,000 different items directly from suppliers. The company asked the computer what would happen if the central warehouse idea was applied across the company. The rest is history, according to Jay W. Spechler, director of management services.

Since 1975, Florida Power & Light has increased its inventory turns to 1.72 from 0.86 and has reduced the dollar value of its inventory (unadjusted for inflation) by nearly 9% to $41 million. Inventory value would be 48% greater had the utility not revamped its distribution system.

Another company enjoying big savings from its management support system is Chevron USA, a division of Standard Oil Co. of California, in San Francisco. But it did not start out that way. Chevron is a good example of what happens to many companies that try to set up a system without the right model and data base—nothing happens. When the company decided that it wanted to make better use of its 340 fuel trucks and 90 supply sites, it tried to use an in-house linear program. But once the program was started, it became clear that the computer would run "for 8 to 10 months without finding a solution," says Richard A. Lambeck, manager of Chevron's order entry and dispatch center.

But Chevron was not about to give up. It hired an outside consultant to develop a program that would cope with the complex variables of the company dispatch system. And now the computer has provided some answers that Chevron says will save it about $800,000 a year in operating its fuel trucks. Says Arthur M. Geoffrion, a professor at UCLA's graduate school of management: "It is this kind of faith and success that is making management-support systems the way of the future." ∎

INFORMATION PROCESSING

Figure 3–3. (Cont.)

their environment. Unfortunately in this century we have had to learn to accept the principle of uncertainty, first enunciated in 1924 by the German physicist Werner Heisenberg, as a universal rule of life. In the business sphere, strategic management deals with events that are likely to take place many years in the future. Since we human beings have not been blessed (or cursed) with the ability to foretell the future, all future projections are shrouded in uncertainty.

One characteristic of certainty is routine or repetitiveness. When a procedure has been performed the same way hundreds or thousands of times, there is no doubt as to exactly what has to be done when the procedure has to be performed again. On the biological level, repetition of the same activity is called a habit. Most human behavior is based upon habits acquired in the past. When we are called upon to perform a habitual act, we do it instinctively, without thinking. Our habits instill a sense of certainty and make us feel comfortable.

Strategic decisionmaking takes place in an environment of uncertainty. Not only are we dealing with an unpredictable future, but we are involved with a unique organism, our own firm. Every one of the millions of business entities in the country differs from every other firm. Each is staffed by a different set of employees; each has a past different from any other and therefore most likely a different future. This does not mean that there are not similarities among companies, nor that one company cannot learn from the experiences of others, but in mapping out a strategic plan for the future, each organization must devise a plan tailor-made for its management philosophy, customs, traditions, unique personnel, and unique position in the economy.

If a strategic plan is unique to an organization, it follows that a strategic information system must also be unique. This is a far cry from an operational information system. Probably 99% of all firms use one of two or three types of accounts receivable information systems, one of perhaps half a dozen production planning information systems or human resource information systems. A company wishing to install a new operational-level information system can in effect pick one off the shelf and implement it as is. This situation does not pertain to strategic information systems.

How then does one explain a strategic information system? The emphasis is placed primarily on the process by which the system is developed and on a demonstration of how the process is applied through the use of illustrative examples. This is one reason why the case study method has become so popular in graduate schools of business. The student is assigned to study the case history of a unique organization, real or fictitious, and to work through the process whereby policy decisions are made. After the student has gone through a sufficient number of cases, he should be able, in theory, to apply the methodology he has acquired to the unique requirements of his own firm. A similar approach is adopted in this chapter. The process for developing a strategic information system involves environmental scanning, knowledge of the sources of external information, ability to perform a capability evaluation, and familiarity with information management techniques, especially decision support systems. Each of these steps in the procedure has been discussed in some detail. We now proceed to illustrate the results of the implementation of the process by presenting three strategic information reports.

**Strategic Marketing Information Report**

When a company looks into the future, it has to select that segment of the future of which it wishes to be a part. The IBM Corporation, for example, identifies itself with the information industry. Thus, when it embarks upon a strategic planning study, it seeks to discern as a starting point what the information industry will be like many years down the road. Once it has a fix on the future of the industry it can decide what share of which segments of the industry it wishes to target as a corporate goal.

As a high technology firm, IBM looks to potential technological advances as the key to the development of new products and new services. These innovations will affect the structure of organizations and change the nature of offices, jobs, and indeed of work itself. In the study presented below, (Figure 3-4), S. H. Haeckel,

THE NEXT TEN YEARS
A MARKETING PERSPECTIVE

S. H. Haeckel
Corporate Marketing
IBM Corporation

| | |
|---|---|
| SATELLITES | OPTICAL FIBERS |
| VLSI | VIDEOTEX |
| MICROPROCESSORS | PERSONAL COMPUTERS |
| "THE SOURCE" | VALUE ADDED NETWORKS |
| SPEECH RECOGNITION | IMAGE PROCESSING |
| ELECTRONIC PUBLISHING | ENCRYPTION |
| THE SMART CARD | DIGITAL FAX, VOICE, TEXT |
| BANKING AT HOME | INTELLIGENT COPIERS |

THE INFORMATION INDUSTRY –
TRENDS AND IMPLICATIONS

| | |
|---|---|
| OFFICE OF THE FUTURE | ELECTRONIC FUNDS TRANSFER |
| CABLE TV | SHOPPING AT HOME |
| VIDEODISKS | ARTIFICIAL INTELLIGENCE |
| HOME INFORMATION SYSTEMS | RELATIONAL DATA BASES |
| COMPUTER ASSISTED LEARNING | ESTABLISHMENT COMMUNICATIONS |
| EXPERT SYSTEMS | COMPUTER STORES |

*(Cont.)*

Figure 3-4. Courtesy of Stephen H. Haeckel, IBM Corporation, 1982.

.   THE DIGITIZATION OF TEXT, IMAGE AND VOICE IS MAKING POSSIBLE NEW OFFERINGS, NEW USERS, AND NEW USAGES OF INFORMATION PROCESSING, E.G.

   -   data and text = word processing equipment (Displaywriter).

   -   text and image = intelligent copiers (6670).

   -   image and voice = video conferencing

   -   voice and data = digital PABX's, voice store and forward

THE OFFICE WILL BE MOST IMPACTED BY THIS TREND TOWARD DIGITIZATION.

.   THE ELEMENTS AND POTENTIAL OF THE "OFFICE OF THE FUTURE" ARE WELL UNDERSTOOD.   THE USE OF IT BY PROFESSIONALS AND MANAGERS IS NOT.

.   ENHANCED ACCESS TO INFORMATION/KNOWLEDGE WILL CHANGE THE NATURE OF THE PROFESSIONAL/MANAGER'S JOB.

   -   we will do better by putting non-optimal workstations in the hands of these professionals, studying the information of highest utility for them, and observing how their jobs change

   -   than we will by trying to develop applications which permit them to do their current jobs more efficiently

.   THE RESISTANCE OF MANAGER/EXECUTIVES TO USING TERMINALS IS A RED HERRING.

   -   "Literacy" and ease of use problems can be overcome if the utility is high enough

   -   there is already widespread literacy in the operation of tv sets - and widespread occupancy - Videotex makes the tv set an intelligent terminal

.   VIDEOTEX IS A PRIME CANDIDATE FOR RAPID DEVELOPMENT OF ON LINE ACCESS TO INFORMATION BY INDIVIDUALS.

   -   it is happening faster, and more importantly, outside the U.S.

.   THE GROWTH OF END USERS WILL SUPPORT GROWTH IN LARGE SYSTEMS FOR NETWORK AND DATA BASE MANAGEMENT AT CLOSE TO RATES OF THE 1970'S.

A SCENARIO FOR THE 1980s:

SEVEN STRATEGIC TRANSITIONS

|  | 1970's | 1990's |
|---|---|---|
| COMPONENT OF PRIMARY ECONOMIC VALUE | -HARDWARE | -INFORMATION |

Figure 3-4. (*Cont.*)

|  | 1970's | 1990's |
|---|---|---|
| PRIMARY ACQUIRER | -DP EXEC | -END-USER |
| PRIMARY SOURCE OF INDUSTRY GROWTH | -EQUIPMENT | -SERVICES |
|  | -INSTITUTIONS | -INDIVIDUAL (BUSINESS & CONSUMER) |
| STRATEGIC ARCHITECTURE | -DP HARDWARE | -NETWORK, DATA BASE |
| PRIMARY DISTINCTION AMONG VENDORS | -PRODUCT | -OFFERINGS |
| PRIMARY INHIBITORS TO GROWTH | -COST OF EQUIPMENT | -USEABILITY |
|  | -COST OF COMMUNICATIONS | -REGULATION |
|  |  | -STANDARDS |
|  | -COMPLEXITY | -INFRASTRUCTURE CHANGES |
|  |  | -COMPLEXITY |
| PRIMARY SOURCE OF "FUTURE" DEMAND FOR CAPACITY | -ON-LINE DATA BASE APPLICATIONS | -NON-CODED INFORMATION APPLICATIONS |

## CONCEPTS

- THE EMERGENCE OF THE KNOWLEDGE-BASED POST INDUSTRIAL ERA

- THE GENERALIZATION OF THE DATA PROCESSING MODEL TO KNOWLEDGE SUPPORT SYSTEMS

- THE OPPORTUNITY FOR "RE-PERSONALIZING" SOCIETY

- THE INDUSTRIALIZATION OF SERVICE

- VALUING INFORMATION IN TERMS OF RESOURCES CONSERVED

- THE EVENTUAL PRE-EMINENCE OF INDIVIDUAL AND DISCRETIONARY ACQUISITION, ENABLED BY THE FALLING COST OF TECHNOLOGY AND COMMUNICATIONS

- THE INTEGRATION OF NEW FORMS OF INFORMATION MEDIA INTO DIGITAL SYSTEMS

Figure 3-4. (*Cont.*)

- THE TRANSITION FROM APPLICATION BY INDUSTRY TO INFORMATION BY OCCUPATION

- THE INTELLIGENT TV (VIDEOTEX) AND ITS POTENTIAL FOR PROVIDING THE INFORMATION INFRASTRUCTURE OF OUR SOCIETY

- THE REPLACEMENT OF HARDWARE AND SOFTWARE COSTS BY SOCIAL, LEGAL AND POLITICAL CONSIDERATIONS AS THE PRIMARY INHIBITORS TO DEMAND

- THE END USER, WHO WAS NOT A SIGNIFICANT FACTOR IN DEMAND FOR OUR INDUSTRY'S PRODUCTS AND SERVICES IN THE 1960'S, IS PROJECTED BY INDUSTRY SOURCES TO BE THE PREDOMINANT FACTOR IN THE 1990'S.

- THE MOTIVATION BEHIND END-USER DEMAND IS THE UTILITY OF THE INFORMATION/KNOWLEDGE TO WHICH THESE OFFERINGS CAN PROVIDE ACCESS.

  - emergence of "post industrial, knowledge-based society"
  - distribution of U.S. work force; productivity implications: leverage via capital investment for the white-collar worker

- THE RAPID IMPROVEMENTS IN PRICE PERFORMANCE OF HARDWARE AND COMMUNICATIONS MAKE ACQUISITION INCREASINGLY FEASIBLE.

  - discretionary vs investment decisions
  - new classes of applications justifiable

- THE COST OF HARDWARE AND COMMUNICATIONS WILL BE GREATLY DIMINISHED AS INHIBITORS TO DEMAND BY 1990.

  - cost of programmer/year greater than current cost of 360/50 level computer
  - reaction of data servicers; integrated hardware, software, data network, offerings

- INFORMATION IS REPLACING HARDWARE AS THE OFFERING ELEMENT OF PRIMARY ECONOMIC VALUE.

Figure 3-4. (Cont.)

. THE PRIMARY OPPORTUNITY AREAS ARE:

- traditional <u>business</u>: small systems, terminals, peripherals

- complementary <u>business</u>: program products, remote computing services, maintenance

- <u>new</u> <u>business</u>: communications, consumer

. TO PROPERLY EXPLOIT THESE, WE MUST DEFINE "THE BUSINESS" OF OUR INDUSTRY TO INCLUDE THE ENTIRE SPECTRUM OF CREATING, PROCESSING, STORING, RETRIEVING AND COMMUNICATING INFORMATION. "PRODUCTS" SHOULD BE INFORMATION-CENTERED OFFERINGS WHICH PACKAGE HARDWARE, SOFTWARE, SERVICE, ACCESS, AND TERMS AND CONDITIONS FOR USE BY INDIVIDUALS AS WELL AS INSTITUTIONS

. THE INDUSTRY IS PROJECTED BY SEVERAL SOURCES TO GROW AT AROUND 16% PER YEAR.

. THIS GROWTH RATE OF 16% IS ESTIMATED TO BE 9% INFLATION AND 7% REAL.

. RECONCILING THE EXCITING AND EXPLOSIVE NATURE OF THE OPPORTUNITY WITH A 7% REAL GROWTH REQUIRES AN UNDERSTANDING OF THE DIFFERENT, AND MORE INTRACTABLE, INHIBITORS WHICH WILL EMERGE AS DETERMINANT IN THE NEXT DECADE:

- complexity

- demonstrating productivity payoffs

- regulation

- standardization

- ease of use, acquisition

- security, reliability, privacy issues

- impacts of change on social infrastructure

THESE WILL REPLACE THE COST OF HARDWARE AND COMMUNICATIONS AS THE PRIMARY INHIBITORS OF DEMAND.

. THE IMPLICATIONS OF THESE DEVELOPMENTS FOR MARKETING ARE PROFOUND.

- As a direct effect of the price performance curve, more and more <u>customers</u> will be individuals - both professional and consumer users. New channels of distribution must be found to cover the acquisition decisions. The focus will be less and less on developing common applications by industry; more and more on discovering the information of highest utility by occupation.

Figure 3-4. (*Cont.*)

- Because knowledge is the primary commodity of the post-industrial society, potential competitors include every firm whose product or service is information- based. In addition to data processing and word processing vendors, this includes banks, newspapers, communication companies, publishers and broadcasters. Competitive advantage will be directly related to the utility and completeness of the offering.

- As a result of the trend toward digitization, offerings will be built around combinations of information media; data, text, voice, and image. These carry implications in terms of more specialized sales forces. Inexpensive ($6-10) chips will be incorporated into a host of "things." We already have the "intelligent carburator," and the "intelligent oven," we will shortly see intelligent lathes, doors, credit cards, telephones, etc. This will permit a degree of specialized, tailorable functions which have significant implications for "repersonalizing" our society.

The mode of marketing for these offerings will change: New products through new channels providing access to new customers.

Figure 3-4. (Cont.)

Director of Advanced Market Development at IBM, takes a look at the next ten years from a marketing perspective. Based on his study of external sources of information, he presents a scenario of how he thinks the information industry will develop over the next decade. We may assme that Mr. Haeckel's report served to trigger additional studies designed to lay the groundwork for IBM's strategic planning effort.

## Strategic Human Resources Information Report

Manpower planning is the strategic element of the human resource function. Management has come to recognize that the best laid plans in the marketing, production and financial areas will come to nought if the right people are not available at the right time to implement these plans. In recent years much effort has been devoted to developing an effective manpower planning function. At The Prudential Insurance Company of America, this effort has included the development of a computerized flow model for management personnel. In the report presented below (Figure 3-5), the model has been applied to estimate the future representation of minorities and women at various managerial and executive levels. If the assumptions used in the model are correct, the results of running the model will reveal to management the degree to which it is likely to be in compliance with Equal Employment Opportunity regulations, thus indicating whether any changes in corporate policies and procedures are called for.

## Strategic Financial Information Outputs

In the financial area there is a very close relationship between operational-level and strategic-level reporting. Implementation of the strategic plan involves the development of operating budgets, and evaluation of the strategic plan entails the analysis of monthly, quarterly and annual operating reports. The interactivity of the

HUMAN RESOURCE MODEL

*TABLE OF CONTENTS*

PREFACE

PREFACE

This report describes a computerized flow model for the management staff at Prudential. The major advantage of these models for personnel planning does not lie in any single projection, but rather, in the ability of planners to run the model repeatedly in order to estimate the future consequences of various assumptions about employee movements. This report, then, should be viewed primarily as a description of a powerful tool for personnel planning rather than as an "answer" to a specific question.

The computerized model "works" in the sense that it correctly simulates personnel movements under a variety of assumptions. However, a model is only as good as its assumptions. Before complete confidence can be placed in projections provided by the model, we should carefully examine the validity of all assumptions and gain an understanding, through repeated-model runs, of the extent to which changes in assumption affect the model's projections. An important early step is to "validate" the model by comparing the model's projections for year-end 1980 with the actual staff at year-end 1980. (The model starts with year-end 1979 data.) As we gain experience in using the model, we may find that additional assumptions should be included.

A final cautionary note—modeling is most effective when the number of employees in various categories is sufficiently large to minimize the influence of rounding errors.

CHAPTER I

MODEL CHARACTERISTICS AND FIXED ASSUMPTIONS

MODEL CHARACTERISTICS

1. *General.* The overall purpose of this model is to estimate the future representation of minorities and women at various Managerial and Executive ranks under a variety of assumptions about terminations, Company growth, and affirmative action policy. The basic unit of analysis is the "employee group" defined by rank, time in rank, sex, and ethnic group (minority or other), e.g., minority male General Managers with three or more years in rank.

*(Cont.)*

Figure 3–5.

2. *Method*. The model was developed and programmed using the BASIC-Plus language on the PDP-11 in-house time sharing system. Historical assumptions for the model were developed using the Special Personnel Analysis file as a data base. The model assumes four sex/ethnic groups but can handle any number of ranks, and up to ten "time in rank" groups.

3. *Coverage*. Each rank, from Level 08 through Departmental Vice President, is covered. Levels 08–09, 11–12–45–31, and Departmental Vice President and above are considered as single ranks. All movement into Level 08–09 is considered as outside hiring in the model. The entire Home Office staff is considered as a whole—transfers between areas are not considered.

4. *Model Output*. Each model run produces a voluminous output which includes the complete staff distributions, by month, year, rank, time in rank group, sex, and ethnic group, and the values taken on by selected variables as the program moves people through the model. This information is printed primarily to verify that the program is operating properly but can also be used to examine questions not covered in the summary tables described below. Summary tables, which appear in Chapter III, display the following information for each of three model years—1979, 1985, and 1990.

    a. *Total staff*. Changes in this number reflect the annual growth assumptions.

    b. *Representation*. The representation of the following groups, expressed as a percentage of total staff.

        (1) All Minority—minority males and females.

        (2) Other Female—non-minority females only. This was done to avoid counting minority females twice.

    c. *Selection rates*. Displayed separately by race and by sex. These reflect the adverse impact of policies embodied in the model. Unusually high selection rates for a group should receive particular attention because the model considers everyone with a specified time at rank to be promotable. However, this is obviously untrue and high selection rates suggest that some individuals who may not be fully qualified are being promoted in order to meet the promotion mix.

    If the promotion mix is determined by the availabilities, (see section F4), all selection rates should be approximately equal.

## FIXED ASSUMPTIONS FOR PERSONNEL MOVEMENT

*General*. The model starts with the actual year-end 1979 staff distribution by rank, time at rank, sex, and ethnic group. Proportions of these employee groups are then terminated, promoted, and hired according to *Variable Assumptions* described in the next chapter. The model is called a "pull model" because movement is controlled by the number of vacancies at the next higher level rather than by assumptions about "readiness for promotion" or advancement rates. The model cycle is one year, from January 1 to December 31.

F1. *"Aging" the staff*. Because the unit of analysis in the model is groups of employees rather than individuals, "aging" is accomplished by establishing time in rank groups in yearly increments. The number of time in rank groups is determined by the number of years in rank necessary to be considered eligible for promotion (see Assumption F4B). All individuals eligible for promotion are considered as a single time in rank group. The first step in a model year is to move all employees into the next higher time in grade group.

F2. *Terminations*. Include all resignations (both voluntary and involuntary), retirements, and transfers to the field. Termination rates are specified in the variable assumptions for each sex/ethnic group within each rank, regardless of years in grade. These rates are assumed to remain constant over the years covered by the model.

The number of people terminating is computed by applying the termination rates to the staff on hand at the end of the previous year. If this number for a particular sex/ethnic group is less than one,

Figure 3-5. (*Cont.*)

the number is accumulated over the years until it reaches one. The effect of this rule is that, in groups with low representation at a particular rank, there may only be one termination every two or three years.

F3. *Vacancies.* The total number of vacancies at each rank is the sum of all terminations, plus all promotions out (see Assumption F4), plus new positions. The number of new positions at a rank is determined by the growth assumptions described in the next chapter (Assumption V1). The proportion of these vacancies that will be filled by outside hiring by Variable Assumption 3.

F4. *Promotions.*

F4A. *Promotion mix.* This term is defined as the proportion of promotions to each rank that should go to members of each of the four sex/ethnic groups. The actual number of employees from each of the four sex/ethnic groups to be promoted is determined by applying these proportions to the total number of vacancies to be filled by promotion. The promotion mix for each rank can either be specified directly (Assumption V2A) or be determined by the availabilities, that is, the number of each group eligible for promotion (see Assumption V2B). When application of promotion mixes results in fractional numbers of employees promoted, rounding is done in favor of minorities and women.

F4B. *Promotion eligibility.* All employees are considered eligible for promotion to the next higher rank if they have been in their present rank for a minimum number of years. These minimums are listed under Assumption V5.

It is important to remember that promotions will generally not occur as rapidly as inspection of the list of minimums might lead one to believe. This is because actual promotions occur only as demanded by the number of vacancies and the promotion mix.

F4C. *Exhausting the pool of eligibles.* This occurs when the number of people from a sex/ethnic group that should be promoted according to the promotion mix exceeds the number of eligibles at the next lower rank. (It cannot occur when the promotion mix is determined by availabilities.) In this case, the "shortage" is made up by hiring an additional number of that particular sex/ethnic group from the outside.

F4D. *Movement of promotees.* Obviously, all promotees (and outside hires) to a rank are assumed to start with less than one year in rank. The number of promotees from a rank is added to the number of vacancies caused by terminations and new positions to compute the total number of vacancies for that rank. The model starts at the highest rank and works its way down.

F5. *Outside hiring.* The "hiring mix" (Assumption V4) is defined as the proportion of outside hires that should belong to each sex/ethnic group. The actual number of each group to be hired is determined by applying the hiring mix proportions to the total number of vacancies to be filled by outside hiring.

One exception to this rule is that if a pool of eligibles for a sex/ethnic group is exhausted (see Assumption F4C), an additional number of people from that group are hired.

# CHAPTER II

## VARIABLE ASSUMPTIONS

V1. *Growth rates.*

V1A. *Historical Growth Rates.*

*Population:* all full-time Home Office employees (excluding CDNO) active at each year-end period from 1974 to 1979.

*Method:* by calculating the yearly percentage increase for each rank, and then averaging these percentages over the six-year period, the following rates were found:

Figure 3–5. (*Cont.*)

| Rank | Average Growth |
|---|---|
| Levs. 08–09 | 5% |
| Levs. 11, 12, 45, 31 | 5% |
| Associate Manager | 7% |
| Manager | 7% |
| Director | 6% |
| Functional VP | 6% |
| Departmental VP | 5% |

V1B. *No Growth Rates.* Assume no growth in staff for all ranks.

V1C. *Conservative Growth Rates.* Assume the following rates:

| Rank | Growth |
|---|---|
| Levs. 08–09 | 2% |
| Levs. 11, 12, 45, 31 | 5% |
| Associate Manager | 5% |
| Manager | 3% |
| Director | 3% |
| Functional VP | 3% |
| Departmental VP | 3% |

V2. *Promotion Mix.*

   V2A. *Promotion Mix Specified Directly.*

      V2A1. *Historical Promotion Mixes.*

         *Population:* all full-time Home Office employees promoted each year from 1974 to 1979 (excluding CDNO).

         *Method:* each year, the proportion of promotions going to each sex/ethnic group and the weighted averages of these proportions over the six-year period were calculated. The promotion mix below gives the greater weight to the years 1978 and 1979. (NOTE: promotions were determined by comparing an employee's rank between successive year-end segments; multiple promotions during any one-year period were counted as a single promotion.)

| Rank | NMM | NMF | MM | MF |
|---|---|---|---|---|
| To Lev. 11, 12, 31 | | | | |
| To Assoc. Mgr. | | | | |
| To Manager | | | | |
| To Director | | | | |
| To Functional VP | | | | |
| To Departmental VP | | | | |

      V2A2. *Affirmative Action Goals Mix.* Promotion mix specified by affirmative Action Plan goals, e.g., To Departmental Vice President rank— % non-minority female, % minorities.

   V2B. *Promotion Mix Determined by Availabilities.*

      V2B1. *Equal Opportunity Promotion Mixes.* Assume the promotion mix is determined by the availabilities of each sex/ethnic group eligible for promotion. For example, if the proportion of eligible candidates for promotion is represented as: 40% non-minority males; 35% non-minority females; 15% minority males; and 10% minority females— the promotion mix would be, respectively, 40%; 35%; 15%; and 10%. This assures that all groups have equal proportions of qualified candidates.

Figure 3–5. (*Cont.*)

V2B2. *Equal Opportunity Promotion Mix Considering Education.* The number of vacancies at each rank to be filled by promotion rather than outside hiring (see V3 below) is split into the number of vacancies to be filled by college graduates and the number of vacancies to be filled by non-college graduates. This split is determined by Assumption V8.

The number of each sex/ethnic group that will be promoted to these vacancies is proportional to their representation among college graduates and non-college graduates at the next lower rank. For example, if it were assumed that vacancies to a particular level would be filled only by college graduates, the promotion mix would be determined entirely by the representation of sex/ethnic groups among college graduates at the next lower rank.

V2B3. *Affirmative Action Promotion Mix.* For specified sex/ethnic groups, assume a promotion mix in excess of the availabilities of eligibles, e.g., minority proportion = 1½ times the availability.

V3. *Proportion of Vacancies Filled by Outside Hiring.*

V3A. *Historical Outside Hiring Rate.*

*Population:* all full-time Home Office employees promoted each year from 1974 to 1979 (excluding CDNO).

*Method:* each year, the total number of people hired at each rank and the weighted averages of these rates were calculated to yield the following hiring rates: (NOTE: assume all entrants to Levels 08–09 are college hires.)

| Rank | Hiring Rate |
|------|-------------|
| Levs. 08–09 | 100% |
| Levs. 11, 12, 31, 45 | 5% |
| Associate Manager | 5% |
| Manager | 3% |
| Director | 2% |
| Functional VP | 1% |
| Departmental VP | 1% |

V3B. *Increased Outside Hiring Rate.*

Assume hiring is increased to the following rates: (NOTE: This amounts to doubling the outside hire rates for ranks up to General Manager.)

| Rank | Hiring Rate |
|------|-------------|
| Levs. 08–09 | 100% |
| Levs. 11, 12, 31, 45 | 10% |
| Associate Manager | 10% |
| Manager | 6% |
| Director | 4% |
| Functional VP | 1% |
| Departmental VP | 1% |

V3C. *Extreme Outside Hiring Rates.*

Assume the outside hiring rate is further increased to the following:

Figure 3–5. (*Cont.*)

| Rank | Hiring Rate |
|---|---|
| Levs. 08–09 | 100% |
| Levs. 11, 12, 31, 45 | 20% |
| Associate Manager | 20% |
| Manager | 15% |
| Director | 10% |
| Functional VP | 5% |
| Departmental VP | 5% |

V4. *Outside Hiring Mix.*

V4A. *Historical Outside Hiring Mix.*

*Population:* all full-time Home Office employees hired each year from 1974 to 1979 (excluding CDNO).

*Method:* each year, the proportion of outside hires going to each sex/ethnic group was calculated. The weighted averages of these proportions over the six-year period, were calculated. The mix below gives the greater weight to the years 1978 and 1979. (NOTE: employees were counted as a hire at each rank by inquiring "Appointment Rank" and "Appointment Year". If "Appointment Rank" is not valued, the employee is not counted.)

| Rank | NMM | NMF | MM | MF |
|---|---|---|---|---|
| Entry Level | | | | |
| Levs. 11, 12, 45, 31 | | | | |
| Associate Manager | | | | |
| Manager | | | | |
| Director | | | | |
| Functional VP | | | | |
| Departmental VP | | | | |

V4B. *Affirmative Action Outside Hiring Mix.*

Assume that the outside hiring rate at Level 11 through Director rank is doubled and that the additional hires are distributed as follows:

| | |
|---|---|
| Minority Male | 25% |
| Minority Female | 25% |
| Non-Minority Male | 20% |
| Non-Minority Female | 30% |

This results in the following outside hire mix:

| Rank | NMM | NMF | MM | MF |
|---|---|---|---|---|
| Levs. 08–09 | | | | |
| Levs. 11, 12, 45, 31 | | | | |
| Associate Manager | | | | |
| Manager | | | | |
| Director | | | | |
| Functional VP | | | | |
| Departmental VP | | | | |

V5. *Termination Rates.*

V5A. *Historical Termination Rates.*

*Population:* all employees who terminated (retired or resigned) as full-time Home Office employees each year from 1974 to 1979.

Figure 3–5. (*Cont.*)

*Method:* each year, for each sex/ethnic group, the number of employees who terminated by year-end out of the number active as of the beginning of the year was claculated. Weighted averages over the six-year period yield the following: (NOTE: employees were countd as terminated by inquiring "Termination Code" and "Termination Year" in the basic segment of the 4Q79 SPA file. If an employee terminated and subsequently was reappointed, the employee is not counted.)

| Rank | NMM | NMF | MM | MF |
|------|-----|-----|-----|-----|
| Levs. 08–09 | | | | |
| Levs. 11, 12, 45, 31 | | | | |
| Associate Manager | | | | |
| Manager | | | | |
| Director | | | | |
| Functional VP | | | | |

V6. *Promotion Eligibility.*

| Current Rank | Minimum Number of Years |
|--------------|-------------------------|
| Levs. 08–09 | |
| Levs. 11, 12, 45, 31 | |
| Associate Manager | |
| Manager | |
| Director | |
| Functional VP | |

V7. *Promotion Rate* (proportion of staff promoted out of rank).
*Population:* all full-time Home Office employees promoted each year from 1974 to 1979 (excluding CDNO).
*Method:* each year, the proportion of staff promoted out of rank was calculated. The weighted averages over the six-year period yields the following:

| Rank | % Promoted Out |
|------|----------------|
| Levs. 08–09 | 10% |
| Levs. 11, 12, 45, 31 | 16% |
| Associate Manager | 8% |
| Manager | 9% |
| Director | 6% |
| Functional VP | 6% |

V8. *Percentage of Promotions to College Graduates vs. Non-College Graduates.*

V8A. *Based on Historical Promotions to Each Rank.* Six-year averages of promotions to each rank were calculated. The percentages below give somewhat greater weight to more recent experience.

| Promotions To | Percent College Graduates |
|---------------|---------------------------|
| Levs. 11, 12, 31 | |
| Associate Manager | |
| Manager and above | |

Figure 3-5. (*Cont.*)

CHAPTER III

MODEL OUTPUT

MODEL  7

ASSUMPTIONS:

- Equal Selection Rates Considering Educational Levels (V2 )
- Conservative Growth (VlC)
- Increased Outside Hiring Rate (V3B)
- Affirmative Action Outside Hiring Mix (V4A)
- Education Mix For Promotions Based on Historical Promotions (V8A)
- Terminations Assumed at all Ranks, for All Sex/Ethnic Groups

| RANK | ANNUAL GROWTH | % OUTSIDE HIRES | % PROMOTIONS TO COLLEGE GRADS | MINIMUM YEARS |
|---|---|---|---|---|
| 08-09 | | | | 1 |
| 11-12 | | | | 2 |
| A.M. | | | | 3 |
| MGR | | | | 3 |
| GM | | | | 4 |
| FVP | | | | 4 |
| DVP+ | | | | 1 |

TERMINATION RATES

| | NON-MINORITY | | MINORITY | |
| RANK | MALE | FEMALE | MALE | FEMALE |
|---|---|---|---|---|
| 08-09 | | | | |
| 11-12 | | | | |
| A.M. | | | | |
| MGR | | | | |
| GM | | | | |
| FVP | | | | |
| DVP+ | | | | |

| OUTSIDE HIRING MIX | | | | PROMOTION MIX* | | | |
| | NON-MINORITY | | MINORITY | | NON-MINORITY | | MINORITY | |
| RANK | MALE | FEMALE | MALE | FEMALE | MALE | FEMALE | MALE | FEMALE |
|---|---|---|---|---|---|---|---|---|
| 08-09 | | | | | | | | |
| 11-12 | | | | | | | | |
| A.M. | | | | | | | | |
| MGR | | | | | | | | |
| GM | | | | | | | | |
| FVP | | | | | | | | |
| DVP+ | | | | | | | | |

*PROMOTION MIX NOT SPECIFIED, DETERMINED BY AVAILABILITIES
AVAILABILITIES ARE ADJUSTED FOR EDUCATIONAL LEVELS

25-Sep-80

Figure 3-5. (Cont.)

MODEL 7

| RANK | YEAR (12/31) | TOTAL STAFF | REPRESENTATION | | | | SELECTION RATES | | | |
|---|---|---|---|---|---|---|---|---|---|---|
| | | | ALL MINORITY | | OTHER FEMALE | | BY RACE | | BY SEX | |
| | | | N | % | N | % | MIN | OTHER | MALE | FEMALE |
| 08-09 | 1979 | | | | | | | | | |
| | 1985 | | | | | | | | | |
| | 1990 | | | | | | | | | |
| 11-12 | 1979 | | | | | | | | | |
| | 1985 | | | | | | | | | |
| | 1990 | | | | | | | | | |
| A.M. | 1979 | | | | | | | | | |
| | 1985 | | | | | | | | | |
| | 1990 | | | | | | | | | |
| MGR | 1979 | | | | | | | | | |
| | 1985 | | | | | | | | | |
| | 1990 | | | | | | | | | |
| GM | 1979 | | | | | | | | | |
| | 1985 | | | | | | | | | |
| | 1990 | | | | | | | | | |
| FVP | 1979 | | | | | | | | | |
| | 1985 | | | | | | | | | |
| | 1990 | | | | | | | | | |
| DVP+ | 1979 | | | | | | | | | |
| | 1985 | | | | | | | | | |
| | 1990 | | | | | | | | | |

Comments: Adjusting the equal selection rate assumption to account for differences in education has virtually no effect on minority representation and only a minimal effect on female representation. Apparently differences between sex/ethnic groups in educational levels are not large enough to significantly affect growth in minority and female representation.

This model was prepared in September 1980 by Philip J. Manhardt, Ph.D. Personnel Research, Corporate Office, Prudential Insurance Co.

Figure 3–5. (*Cont.*)

strategic and operating levels is clearly shown in the diagram of an integrated financial system developed by Management Decision Systems, Inc. and presented in Figure 3–6. Thomas H. Naylor, in an article in *Business Week* herein reproduced (see Figure 3–7), highlights some of the organizational problems created by the overlap between the strategic and operational levels. He points out that while the detailed language of accounting is quite appropriate for the needs and responsibilities of operating managers, it is not as well suited to the lean summary formats that should be presented to top management. When accounting executives are asked to prepare reports for higher-level management, the documents tend to be too detailed to be of use to the executives. He therefore recommends the transfer of responsibilities

# EXPRESS
# The most complete and integrated financial system available today.

EXPRESS Supports This Complex Financial Planning and Control Environment

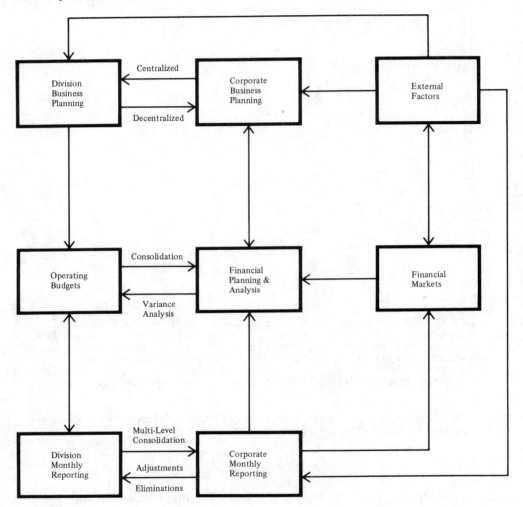

Figure 3–6. EXPRESS is a product of Management Decision Systems, Waltham, Mass. Figure reprinted by permission.

# Management is drowning in numbers

A widely held view among senior executives is that the federal government is the principal culprit in generating ever-increasing paperwork in the executive suite. There is evidence, however, that the reason senior executives pay too much attention to details is not the government but their own accounting and budget directors. This information overload leads to a preoccupation with next year's financial performance, insufficient attention to long-term strategic planning, and inability to cope with change.

At least in theory, a corporation's annual budget should be formulated only after the long-term strategic plan has been developed, and goals and strategies have been defined. The budget should be consistent with the financial plan of the first year of the strategic plan. It does not seem to work this way in all too many organizations.

With pressure on line managers to achieve short-term financial results, the budget takes on a character of its own. It drives the long-term plan, not the other way around.

The major danger in budget-driven planning is that, to meet short-term financial targets, zealous managers will give inadequate attention to research, replacement of plant, and investments in new products to replace aging cash cows. To achieve short-term financial goals, management may be selling the company down the river.

**Snowballing of detail.** Neglect of strategic planning is not the only shortcoming associated with planning systems dominated by the budget. In most companies, the budget director as well as the controller reports to the chief financial officer. If accountants control the budget, as in most companies, inordinate detail will be included in budgets at all levels.

To ensure control, the budgets of operating units may require considerable detail. But as one moves from the unit (say a factory) to a division, to a group of divisions, and finally to the executive offices, the degree of accounting detail required diminishes. If the CEO is reviewing budgets for 8 or 10 major divisions, the number of line items should be small—only major categories of revenue and expenditures. Yet the budgets reviewed by the CEO often contain an incredible amount of detail.

The accountants argue that the long-term financial plan must have sufficient detail to tie back to the general ledger. Controllers and budget directors are likely to challenge highly summarized long-term plans on the ground that their results seem to differ from those indicated by the company's accounting system.

Although accounting may be a useful language for evaluating historical performance, it may not be the most effective for planning and budgeting. They are forward-looking. Accounting looks backward. One language is not suitable for two such dissimilar needs.

In most companies that use the process, formal strategic planning is headed by a director or vice-president, who reports to the CEO. The budget is controlled by the chief financial officer. The potential for conflict between planning and budget directors is enormous. The budget director is concerned with next year's operating results, the planning official with the long run. If the budget director has more political clout, as in most companies, it is not surprising where the emphasis is placed. Further, the CEO is the obvious referee in disputes over long- and short-term results. His easy way out may be to opt for short-run results.

**The big picture.** The detail required by senior management for strategic planning and budgeting is minimal. Strategic planning should be lean and simple. Negotiations between corporate and division managements should concern financial targets and strategic assumptions. Once agreement is reached on them, operating details are the problem of division managers, not the CEO.

Part of the macho self-image of some CEOs is the conviction that a good manager must know in detail the results of divisions and units. But if the CEO trusts the division managers, why is all this detail necessary? Plans and budgets are based on assumptions; if the CEO does not believe in the assumptions, all the detail in the world will not improve his confidence in the division or its manager. Further, if the balance sheet of a financial plan of a muiltibillion-dollar company balances to the nearest cent, that in no way assures the validity of the plan. Plans and budgets are based on such assumptions as the amount and timing of the next increase in oil prices by OPEC and whether there will be peace in the Mideast. These events cannot be forecast.

Northwest Industries has for 10 years been one of the best managed and most successful of the decentralized conglomerates in the U. S. Years ago I was discussing Northwest's sophisticated, computer-based planning system with CEO Ben Heineman. During my visits to his office, the phone never rang. This seemed odd, and I asked Mr. Heineman why. He said he was "employed by the directors of Northwest Industries to do three things—plan, forecast, and think. While I am engaged in these activities, I do not wish to be disturbed by the telephone."

Chief executives should worry more about goals and strategies and less about whether the cafeteria should use plastic or steel spoons. Unfortunately, decisions on such issues are easier than those on the direction of the company.

If properly used, strategic planning and budgeting can be powerful offensive tools. Insecure corporate executives are often put on the defense by aggressive line managers who use plans and budgets to protect their domains. The tendency for senior executives to fall back on excessive

*(Cont.)*

accounting detail in such cases does not strengthen their position. To be effective, senior management must learn to ask the right questions about strategic plans and budgets. And the right questions do not necessarily require vast amounts of data.

Accounting is no substitute for good management. Nor is it an effective language for forward-looking strategic planning and budgeting. Perhaps it is appropriate to consider replacing accounting with economics as the relevant language of strategic planning and budgeting. Economics tends to be more forward-looking than accounting, and it focuses on goals and the decisions necessary to achieve them. The emphasis should be on the economic consequences of alternative strategies, based on different assumptions about the company's external environment. The detail of strategic plans and budgets at corporate level should be highly aggregative—commensurate with the information requirements for managing a decentralized company.

**Reforms.** In summary, there appears to be a major organizational flaw in many corporations. The budget director should not report to the financial officer but to the vice-president of planning. There are two advantages:

First, long-term strategic planning and budgeting are easier to coordinate and integrate if they are under one umbrella rather than two. The corporate planning staff can do some of the long-term versus short-term analyses that the CEO has no time to do under the old structure. The trade-offs between long- and short-term profits can be clearly delineated for the CEO and the executive committee.

Second, placing strategic planning and budgeting under the planning department rather than the accountants should reduce the detail included in plans and budgets reviewed by senior executives. (It should also reduce the size and number of corporate reports and perhaps even the number of accountants.)

Coordinating the strategic planning and budgeting is not likely to be easy. It will require someone' with line management experience who can help the CEO ask the right questions.

But strategic planning and budgeting are not a problem of too little data but of too much. By making economics the language of planning and budgeting, and by moving the budgeting into corporate planning, we will take a giant step toward improving the effectiveness of planning and budgeting in large decentralized companies.

Just as the Office of Management & Budget can be expected to resist any attempt to create an Office of Strategic Planning in the government, corporate budget directors will find countless reasons that budgeting should not be a part of corporate planning. They understand that the officer who controls planning and budgeting controls the company. But the CEO should control the company. The proposal outlined here is designed to transfer control from the accountants to the chief executive, where it belongs. ■

**Strategic planning and budgeting are not a problem of too little data but too much**

Figure 3-7. (Cont.)

for the strategic information system from the accounting function to the executive in charge of planning.

One of the reasons for the growing popularity of decision support systems in the financial area may be that they represent an alternative solution to this problem. Financial executives have created such a demand for DSS applications that fierce competition has erupted among software firms to meet this demand. We have selected some random advertisements from business journals to illustrate this competition. (See Figure 3-8.)

The research efforts expended by these software firms have resulted in the development of a large number of DSS financial applications. Among these commonly found in most systems are:

- budgetary planning and control
- financial reporting and projecting
- balance sheets
- income statements
- cash flow statements
- sources and uses of funds
- ratio analysis
- merger and acquisition analysis
- lease versus buy analysis
- cash flow forecasting
- inflation and interest rate analysis
- business graphics presentations
- consolidations
- investment analysis
- profit planning
- marketing forecasts
- corporate modeling
- what if analysis
- capital budgeting
- strategic planning
- bidding analysis
- real estate analysis
- personal financial planning

As an example of a DSS financial model, we present below a five-year plan offered by Ferox Microsystems Incorporated. This plan is an integrated financial system which has among its outputs an income statement, a balance sheet, a cash flow statement and a ratio analysis. Also illustrated are some of the graphs and plots available from the system (see Figure 3-9).

## EVALUATION OF SYSTEM OUTPUTS

Evaluation of strategic plans is a chancy activity at best. Since by definition a strategic plan covers an extended period of years, the total plan cannot be evaluated

# "THAT'S IT!"

There's nothing like the feeling you get when you've got the solution.

And nothing else will help you solve problems better, smarter, faster than the Visi™ programs for your personal computer.

For example, our VisiCalc® program: It's #1 in the business because it takes the work out of working with business numbers. The VisiCalc program is the powerful "electronic worksheet" that speeds planning and budgeting. It lets you ask "what if?" and see the answers immediately. So you can analyze the impact of decisions before you make them.

Our VisiTrend/Plot™ program combines graphics with forecasting and statistics. It automatically performs complex calculations and produces charts and graphs. So you can analyze the past, forecast the future and plot your results in an easy-to-understand visual form.

© 1982 VisiCorp

In addition, our series includes the VisiFile™, VisiDex™, VisiSchedule™, VisiPlot™, VisiTerm™ and Desktop/PLAN™ programs.

But the Visi programs are far more than individual problem-solvers. They're all inter-related, just like your needs and tasks, to give you a fully integrated solution.

All of the Visi programs work in much the same way, and they automatically interchange data, too. So it's easy to learn and use any of them, work in many different ways with all of them.

They're brought to you by VisiCorp™. The one company whose only business is helping you make the most of the personal computer in your business.

Ask your retail computer store salesperson for a demonstration of the Visi series. They'll help you and your computer do all the things you're intent on doing.

## THE VISISERIES FROM VISICORP
PERSONAL SOFTWARE

Figure 3–8A. VisiSeries advertisement courtesy of VisiCorp.

Figure 3–8B. Courtesy of EPS. Robert M. Peak, Vice President of Sales.

Figure 3–8C. EXPRESS is a product of Management Decision Systems, Waltham, Mass. Figure reprinted by permission.

# Funny what some companies try to pass off as Decision Support Systems.

The phrase Decision Support System is so new and so misunderstood that most managers don't know when to laugh at a poor imitation.

Before you buy, ask if the system includes all of the following...

- Relational data management
- Multi-dimensional analysis
- Time series forecasting
- Non-procedural business modeling
- Color graphics executive display and hard copy
- Delivery via large-scale remote processing network **and** personal computers

If you'd like to know what all these buzzwords mean, catch a Comshare. They can be found in 40 cities throughout North America and Europe. Comshares are DSS specialists. And their Commander® DSS is the first **real** Decision Support System.

To find out more about increasing productivity in business planning, marketing analysis and human resource management, read this no-nonsense brochure. It'll help you have the last laugh!

For your free copy, write Comshare at 3001 S. State Street, Ann Arbor, Michigan 48104, or call Comshare Marketing at 313-994-4800, ext. 599.

HOW TO CATCH A COMSHARE

## COMSHARE®

Figure 3–8D. Courtesy of Comshare.

© 1982 Comshare, Inc.

# FINANCIAL PLANNING SOFTWARE SHOULD BE INVITING.

# NOT INTIMIDATING.

The whole idea behind financial planning and modeling software was to come up with a package simple enough to be used by a financial planner, analyst or manager. Instead of a programmer.

Unfortunately, somewhere along the line, that idea got lost. By everyone except Capex.

Our Autotab package is so simple to operate that instead of intimidating financial people, it actually invites them to use it.

It's the only financial modeling system on the market that offers true "push button, fill in the blanks" simplicity.

But don't be misled. Even though Autotab is incredibly simple to operate, what it can do is simply incredible.

Its consolidation capabilities are unlimited.

And it's the only package that offers a complete graphics system.

A regression analysis becomes a simple task on Autotab. So does a revenue projection. A monthly management report. A variance analysis. Or a capital expenditure analysis.

Autotab even has the power to go far beyond your current planning needs.

To do more continuous planning. More strategic planning. More "What if" analysis.

And you can take advantage of Autotab's power and simplicity on IBM equipment, Hewlett-Packard or time-sharing systems.

For more information, call us or send us the coupon below.

We think you'll find that the only thing Autotab doesn't offer your financial people is the one thing they don't need.

A chance to bone up on computerese.

## BETTER SOFTWARE.

Please send me more information on the Autotab family.

Name _____

Title _____

Company _____

Address _____

City _____ State _____ Zip _____

Mail to: Capex Corporation, 4125 North 14th Street, Phoenix, Arizona 85014. Tel: (602) 264-7241.

Phoenix (602) 244-0101 • Chicago (312) 986-8618 • New Jersey (201) 797-2900

FIGURE 3–8E

FEROX
MICROSYSTEMS
Incorporated

1701 N. FT. MYER DRIVE
SUITE 611
ARLINGTON, VIRGINIA  22209
(703) 841-0800

---

DSS/F  EXAMPLE  MODEL

FIVE  YEAR  PLAN
FINANCIAL  STATEMENTS

Description:

The FIVE YEAR PLAN is an integrated financial statement
model which produces the following pro forma reports:

      1.   INCOME STATEMENT
      2.   BALANCE SHEET
      3.   CASH FLOW STATEMENT
      4.   RATIO ANALYSIS

The model automatically balances the balance sheet with
either short term debt or short term investment and calculates the necessary interest adjustment for the income
statement.  The user can specify minimum and maximum cash
levels that must be maintained and how sales, assets, etc.
are growing.  The user can perform a 'what if' scenario
and the  model will be recalculated with the changes to
income, balance sheet, cash flow and ratios.  Included is
the data input worksheet that DSS/F creates automatically
from the model and some of the graphs and plots.  The
command file FIN.JOB can be run to give the DSS/F commands
automatically.

      COMMAND: <u>JOB</u>

      FILE CONTAINING COMMANDS:  <u>FIN.JOB</u>

*(Cont.)*

Figure 3-9. Copyright © 1982 Ferox Microsystems Inc., Arlington, Virginia.

DSS/F FINANCIAL MODEL EXAMPLE

INCOME STATEMENT

FIVE YEAR PROJECTION

| | 1982 | 1983 | 1984 | 1985 | 1986 |
|---|---|---|---|---|---|
| REVENUES | | | | | |
| GROSS SALES | $ 30,800 | $ 37,946 | $ 46,749 | $ 57,595 | $ 70,957 |
| LESS: ALLOWANCES | 616 | 759 | 935 | 1,152 | 1,419 |
| NET SALES | 30,184 | 37,187 | 45,814 | 56,443 | 69,538 |
| COST OF SALES | 12,236 | 15,760 | 20,299 | 26,145 | 33,675 |
| GROSS PROFIT | 17,948 | 21,427 | 25,515 | 30,298 | 35,863 |
| EXPENSES | | | | | |
| ADMINISTRATIVE | 2,725 | 2,970 | 3,238 | 3,529 | 3,847 |
| R & D | 616 | 759 | 935 | 1,152 | 1,419 |
| MARKETING | 3,080 | 3,795 | 4,675 | 5,759 | 7,096 |
| OTHER OVERHEAD | 924 | 1,138 | 1,402 | 1,728 | 2,129 |
| TOTAL DEPRECIATION | 1,892 | 2,014 | 2,111 | 2,189 | 2,251 |
| PROFIT BEFORE INT & TAXES | 8,711 | 10,751 | 13,154 | 15,941 | 19,122 |
| TOTAL INTEREST EXP/REV | (1,140) | (862) | (720) | (780) | (840) |
| PROFIT | | | | | |
| NET PROFIT BEFORE TAX | 7,571 | 9,889 | 12,434 | 15,161 | 18,282 |
| INCOME TAXES | 3,331 | 4,351 | 5,471 | 6,671 | 8,044 |
| NET PROFIT AFTER TAXES | $ 4,240 | $ 5,538 | $ 6,963 | $ 8,490 | $ 10,238 |

Figure 3-9. (*Cont.*)

DSS/F FINANCIAL MODEL EXAMPLE

BALANCE SHEET

FIVE YEAR PROJECTION

| | 1982 | 1983 | 1984 | 1985 | 1986 |
|---|---|---|---|---|---|
| **ASSETS:** | | | | | |
| CASH | $ 1,000 | $ 1,451 | $ 2,000 | $ 2,000 | $ 2,000 |
| S/T INVESTMENT | - | - | 1,698 | 4,527 | 7,930 |
| ACCOUNTS RECEIVABLE | 3,308 | 4,075 | 5,021 | 6,186 | 7,621 |
| INVENTORIES | 4,894 | 6,304 | 8,120 | 10,458 | 13,470 |
| OTHER CURRENT ASSETS | 1,800 | 2,160 | 2,592 | 3,110 | 3,732 |
| TOTAL CURRENT ASSETS | 11,002 | 13,990 | 19,430 | 26,280 | 34,753 |
| PROPERTY PLANT & EQUIPMENT | 10,000 | 12,000 | 14,000 | 16,000 | 18,000 |
| LESS: ACCUM DEPRECIATION | 2,492 | 4,506 | 6,616 | 8,805 | 11,056 |
| NET PROPERTY PLANT & EQUIPMENT | 7,508 | 7,494 | 7,384 | 7,195 | 6,944 |
| TOTAL ASSETS | $ 18,510 | $ 21,485 | $ 26,814 | $ 33,475 | $ 41,696 |
| **LIABILITIES:** | | | | | |
| ACCOUNTS PAYABLE | $ 2,447 | $ 3,152 | $ 4,060 | $ 5,229 | $ 6,735 |
| ACCRUED EXPENSES | 2,500 | 2,500 | 2,500 | 2,500 | 2,500 |
| CURRENT PORTION OF LTD | 1,000 | 1,000 | 1,000 | 1,000 | 1,000 |
| S/T DEBT | 1,123 | - | - | - | - |
| CURRENT LIABILITIES | 7,070 | 6,652 | 7,560 | 8,729 | 10,235 |
| LONG TERM DEBT | 5,500 | 6,000 | 6,500 | 7,000 | 7,500 |
| TOTAL LIABILITIES | 12,570 | 12,652 | 14,060 | 15,729 | 17,735 |
| PAID IN CAPITAL | 2,500 | 2,500 | 2,500 | 2,500 | 2,500 |
| RETAINED EARNINGS | 3,440 | 6,333 | 10,254 | 15,246 | 21,461 |
| STOCKHOLDERS EQUITY | 5,940 | 8,833 | 12,754 | 17,746 | 23,961 |
| TOTAL LIABILITIES & ST EQUITY | $ 18,510 | $ 21,485 | $ 26,814 | $ 33,475 | $ 41,696 |

Figure 3-9. (*Cont.*)

DSS/F FINANCIAL MODEL EXAMPLE
---
STATEMENT OF CHANGES IN CASH
---
FIVE YEAR PROJECTION
---

| | 1982 | 1983 | 1984 | 1985 | 1986 |
|---|---|---|---|---|---|
| **SOURCES OF CASH** | | | | | |
| | | | | | |
| NET INCOME | $ 4,240 | $ 5,538 | $ 6,963 | $ 8,490 | $ 10,238 |
| DEPRECIATION | 1,892 | 2,014 | 2,111 | 2,189 | 2,251 |
| FROM OPERATIONS | 6,132 | 7,551 | 9,074 | 10,679 | 12,489 |
| CHANGE IN A/P | 2,447 | 705 | 908 | 1,169 | 1,506 |
| CHANGE IN ACCRUALS | – | – | – | – | – |
| CHANGE IN S/T DEBT | (1,877) | (1,123) | – | – | – |
| CHANGE IN CURRENT L/T DEBT | – | – | – | – | – |
| CHANGE IN L/T DEBT | 500 | 500 | 500 | 500 | 500 |
| CHANGE IN PAID IN CAPITAL | – | – | – | – | – |
| | | | | | |
| TOTAL SOURCES | $ 7,202 | $ 7,633 | $ 10,482 | $ 12,348 | $ 14,495 |
| | | | | | |
| **APPLICATIONS OF CASH** | | | | | |
| | | | | | |
| CHANGE IN S/T INVESTMENT | $ – | $ – | $ 1,698 | $ 2,829 | $ 3,403 |
| CHANGE IN A/R | 308 | 767 | 945 | 1,165 | 1,435 |
| CHANGE IN INVENTORIES | 894 | 1,410 | 1,816 | 2,338 | 3,012 |
| CHANGE IN OTHER CURRENT | 300 | 360 | 432 | 518 | 622 |
| CHANGE IN PROPERTY PLANT & EQUIP | 2,000 | 2,000 | 2,000 | 2,000 | 2,000 |
| | | | | | |
| TOTAL APPLICATIONS | $ 5,802 | $ 7,182 | $ 9,933 | $ 12,348 | $ 14,495 |
| | | | | | |
| CHANGE IN CASH | $ 1,400 | $ 451 | $ 549 | $ | $ |

Figure 3-9. (*Cont.*)

DSS/F FINANCIAL MODEL EXAMPLE
_____

RATIO ANALYSIS
_____

FIVE YEAR PROJECTION
_____

|                          | 1982  | 1983  | 1984  | 1985  | 1986  |
|--------------------------|-------|-------|-------|-------|-------|
| **LIQUIDITY RATIOS**     |       |       |       |       |       |
|                          |       |       |       |       |       |
| CURRENT RATIO            | 1.56  | 2.10  | 2.57  | 3.01  | 3.40  |
| QUICK RATIO              | .86   | 1.16  | 1.50  | 1.81  | 2.08  |
| **LEVERAGE RATIOS**      |       |       |       |       |       |
|                          |       |       |       |       |       |
| DEBT TO TOTAL ASSETS     | .68   | .59   | .52   | .47   | .43   |
| TIMES INTEREST EARNED    | 7.64  | 12.47 | 18.27 | 20.44 | 22.76 |
| DEBT : EQUITY RATIO      | .68   | .59   | .52   | .47   | .43   |
| **ACTIVITY RATIOS**      |       |       |       |       |       |
|                          |       |       |       |       |       |
| INVENTORY TURNOVER       | 6.29  | 6.02  | 5.76  | 5.51  | 5.27  |
| AVERAGE COLLECTION PERIOD| 39.20 | 39.20 | 39.20 | 39.20 | 39.20 |
| FIXED ASSET TURNOVER     | 4.10  | 5.06  | 6.33  | 8.01  | 10.22 |
| TOTAL ASSET TURNOVER     | 1.66  | 1.77  | 1.74  | 1.72  | 1.70  |
| **PROFITABILITY RATIOS** |       |       |       |       |       |
|                          |       |       |       |       |       |
| RETURN ON SALES          | .25   | .26   | .27   | .26   | .26   |
| GROSS PROFIT MARGIN      | .58   | .56   | .55   | .53   | .51   |
| RETURN ON ASSETS         | .23   | .26   | .26   | .25   | .25   |
| RETURN ON EQUITY         | .71   | .63   | .55   | .48   | .43   |

Figure 3-9. (*Cont.*)

```
LOOPCOL FOR 2 TO 6
C********************* DSS/F MODEL EXAMPLE ***************************
C
C*************** FINANCIAL STATEMENT AND ANALYSIS FORECAST ***********
C
C ---REVENUES---        ------ INCOME STATEMENT ------
2 'VOLUMNE'
3 'PRICE'
4 'GROSS SALES' = 2 * 3
5 'ALLOWANCES ETC' = 0.02 * 4
6 'NET SALES' = 4 - 5
7 'UNIT COST'
8 'COST OF SALES' = 7 * 2
9 'GROSS PROFIT' = 6 - 8
C ---EXPENSES---
10 'ADMINISTRATIVE'
11 'R & D' = 0.02 * 4
12 'MARKETING' = 0.10 * 4
13 'OTHER OVERHEAD' = 0.03 * 4
14 'CASH EXPENSES' = 10 SUM 13
15 'OTHER DEPRECIATION'
16 'NEW BUILDING'
17 'DEPR DATA'
18 'DEPR BUILDING' = 16 DEPR 17
19 'TOTAL DEPRECIATION' = 15 + 18
20 'TOTAL EXPENSES' = 14 + 19
21 'NET INCOME BEFORE INTEREST AND TAXES' = 9 - 20
C --- INTEREST REV/EXP ---
22 'INTEREST RATE S/T INVEST'
23 'INTEREST RATE S/T DEBT'
24 'INTEREST RATE L/T DEBT'
25 'INTEREST INCOME' = 22 * 31 LAG 1 FOR 2 TO 5
26 'INTEREST EXPENSE S/T DEBT' = 23 * 49 LAG 1 FOR 2 TO 6
27 'INTEREST EXPENSE L/T DEBT' = 24 * 52 LAG 1 FOR 2 TO 6
28 'TOTAL INTEREST EXP/REV' = 25 - 26 - 27
C --- PROFIT ---
29 'NET PROFIT BEFORE TAX' = 21 + 28
30 'TAXABLE PROFIT' = 29 MAX 0.0
31 'TAX RATE'
32 'INCOME TAXES' = 31 * 30
33 'NET PROFIT AFTER TAXES' = 30 - 32
34 'DIVIDENDS PAID'
35 'CHANGE TO RETAINED EARNINGS' = 33 - 34
C
C                      ------ BALANCE SHEET ------
C
38 'A/R --- DAYS OF SALES'
39 'ACCOUNTS RECEIVABLE' = 38 * 6 / 365.0
40 'INVENTORIES %'
41 'INVENTORIES' = 40 * 8
42 'OTHER CURRENT ASSETS'
43 'PROPERTY PLANT & EQUIPMENT' = 43 LAG 1 + 16 FOR 2 TO 6
44 'ACCUMULATED DEPRECIATION' = 44 LAG 1 + 19 FOR 2 TO 6
98 'NET PROPERTY PLANT & EQUIPMENT' = 43 - 44
45 'A/P %'
46 'ACCOUNTS PAYABLE' = 45 * 8
47 'ACCRUED EXPENSES'
48 'CURRENT PORTION OF LTD'
50 'BEGINNING LTD' = 52 LAG 1 FOR 2 TO 6
51 'NEW LTD'
52 'LONG TERM DEBT' = 50 + 51 - 48 FOR 2 TO 6
53 'PAID IN CAPITAL'
54 'RETAINED EARNINGS' = 54 LAG 1 + 35 FOR 2 TO 6
55 'TOTAL STOCKHOLDERS EQUITY' = 53 + 54
C CALCULATE FUNDS TO BALANCE
```

Figure 3-9. (*Cont.*)

```
56 'TRIAL ASSETS' = 39+41+42+43-44
57 'TRIAL LIAB & S/E' = 46+47+48+52+55
58 'PRELIMINARY CASH' = 57 - 56
59 'MINIMUM CASH'
60 'MAXIMUM CASH'
37 'S/T INVESTMENT' = (58 GT 60) * (58 - 60)
49 'S/T DEBT' = (58 LT 59) * (59 - 58)
36 'CASH' = 58 - 37 + 49
C
C CALCULATE TOTALS
62 'TOTAL CURRENT ASSETS' = 36+37+39+41+42
63 'TOTAL ASSETS' = 56+36+37
64 'TOTAL CURRENT LIABILITIES' = 46 SUM 49
65 'TOTAL LIABILITIES' = 64 + 52
66 'TOTAL LIABILITIES & STOCKHOLDERS EQUITY' = 65 + 55
ENDLOOP
C
C                  ----- SOURCES AND APPLICATIONS OF FUNDS -----
C
C   SOURCES
67 'NET INCOME' = 33
68 'DEPRECIATION' = 19
69 'FROM OPERATIONS' = 67+68
70 'CHANGE IN A/P' = 46 - 46 LAG 1
71 'CHANGE IN ACCRUALS' = 47 - 47 LAG 1
72 'CHANGE IN S/T DEBT' = 49 - 49 LAG 1
73 'CHANGE IN CURRENT L/T DEBT' = 48 - 48 LAG 1
74 'CHANGE IN L/T DEBT' = 52 - 52 LAG 1
75 'CHANGE IN PAID IN CAPITAL' = 53 - 53 LAG 1
C
C   APPLICATIONS
76 'CHANGE IN S/T INVESTMENT' = 37 - 37 LAG 1
77 'CHANGE IN A/R' = 39 - 39 LAG 1
78 'CHANGE IN INVENTORIES' = 41 - 41 LAG 1
79 'CHANGE IN OTHER CURRENT ASSETS' = 42 - 42 LAG 1
80 'CHANGE IN PROP PLANT & EQUIP' = 43 - 43 LAG 1
81 'DIVIDENDS PAID' = 34
82 'TOTAL SOURCES' = 69 SUM 75
83 'TOTAL APPLICATIONS' = 76 SUM 81
84 'CHANGE IN CASH' = 82 - 83
C
C                  ----- RATIOS -----
C
C LIQUIDITY
85 'CURRENT RATIO' = 62 / 64
86 'QUICK RATIO' = (62-41) / 64
C
C LEVERAGE
87 'DEBT TO TOTAL ASSETS' = 65 / 63
88 'TIMES INTEREST EARNED' = 21 / (26+27)
89 'DEBT : EQUITY RATIO' = 65 / 66
C
C ACTIVITY
90 'INVENTORY TURNOVER' = 4 / 41
91 'AVERAGE COLLECTION PERIOD' = 39*365.0 / 4
92 'FIXED ASSET TURNOVER' = 4 / (63-62)
93 'TOTAL ASSET TURNOVER' = 4 / 63
C
C PROFITABILITY
94 'RETURN ON SALES' = 29 / 4
95 'GROSS PROFIT MARGIN' = 9 / 4
96 'RETURN ON ASSETS' = 33 / 63
97 'RETURN ON EQUITY' = 33 / 55
C
C COPYRIGHT (C) 1982 FEROX MICROSYSTEMS INC.
```

Figure 3-9. (Cont.)

DATA INPUT WORKSHEET FORM
FOR FIVE YEAR PROJECTION
AUTOMATICALLY GENERATED BY DSS/F

```
VOLUMNE................. 2=  ____  ____  ____  ____  ____  ____
PRICE................... 3=  ____  ____  ____  ____  ____  ____
UNIT COST............... 7=  ____  ____  ____  ____  ____  ____
ADMINISTRATIVE.......... 10=  ____  ____  ____  ____  ____  ____
OTHER DEPRECIATION...... 15=  ____  ____  ____  ____  ____  ____
NEW BUILDING............ 16=  ____  ____  ____  ____  ____  ____
DEPR DATA............... 17=  ____  ____  ____  ____  ____  ____
     COLUMN 1: LIFE (YRS)
     COLUMN 2: METHOD — 100: STRAIGHT LINE (SL)
                       150,200: DECLINING BALANCE
     COLUMN 3: RESIDUAL VALUE AS %
     COLUMN 4: 1/2 YEAR CONVENTION — 0: FULL YR DEPR IN 1ST YR
                                     1: 1/2 YEAR DEPR IN 1ST YR
     COLUMN 5: SWITCHOVER — 0: SWITCHES OVER TO SL
                            1: NO SWITCHOVER
                            2: SWITCHES OVER TO SYD


INTEREST RATE S/T INVEST 22=  ____  ____  ____  ____  ____  ____
INTEREST RATE S/T DEBT.. 23=  ____  ____  ____  ____  ____  ____
INTEREST RATE L/T DEBT.. 24=  ____  ____  ____  ____  ____  ____
*** INTEREST INCOME..... 25=  ____
*** INTEREST EXPENSE S/T 26=  ____
*** INTEREST EXPENSE L/T 27=  ____
TAX RATE................ 31=  ____  ____  ____  ____
DIVIDENDS PAID.......... 34=  ____  ____  ____  ____
A/R — DAYS OF SALES.... 38=  ____  ____  ____  ____
INVENTORIES %........... 40=  ____  ____  ____  ____
OTHER CURRENT ASSETS.... 42=  ____  ____  ____  ____
*** PROPERTY PLANT & EQU 43=  ____
*** ACCUMULATED DEPRECIA 44=  ____
A/P %................... 45=  ____  ____  ____  ____
ACCRUED EXPENSES........ 47=  ____  ____  ____  ____
CURRENT PORTION OF LTD.. 48=  ____  ____  ____  ____
*** BEGINNING LTD....... 50=  ____
NEW LTD................. 51=  ____  ____  ____  ____
*** LONG TERM DEBT...... 52=  ____
PAID IN CAPITAL......... 53=  ____  ____  ____  ____
*** RETAINED EARNINGS... 54=  ____
MINIMUM CASH............ 59=  ____  ____  ____  ____
MAXIMUM CASH............ 60=  ____  ____  ____  ____
```

Figure 3-9. (Cont.)

#11:FIN.RPT

```
 1: COLUMNS 2-6
 2: DECIMAL 0
 3: PAGELENGTH 66
 4: SDATA 35
 5: SNAME 3
 6: WIDTH 10
 7: BRACKETS
 8: COMMAS
 9: CENTER 80,'DSS/F FINANCIAL MODEL EXAMPLE'
10: UTEXT
11: CENTER 80,'INCOME STATEMENT'
12: UTEXT
13: CENTER 80,'FIVE YEAR PROJECTION'
14: UTEXT
15: SKIP 2
16: TEXT C1,'1982',C2,'1983',C3,'1984',C4,'1985',C5,'1986'
17: UTEXT
18: SKIP
19: TEXT 1,'REVENUES'
20: BEFORE '$ '
21: ROWS 4
22: BEFORE ' '
23: NAME 5,'LESS: ALLOWANCES'
24: UDATA
25: ROWS 6
26: SKIP
27: ROWS 8
28: UDATA
29: ROWS 9
30: SKIP
31: TEXT 1,'EXPENSES'
32: ROWS 10-13,19
33: UDATA
34: NAME 21,'PROFIT BEFORE INT & TAXES'
35: ROWS 28
36: UDATA
37: SKIP
38: TEXT 1,'PROFIT'
39: ROWS 29,32
40: UDATA
41: BEFORE '$ '
42: ROWS 33
43: UDATA '='
44: SKIP 2
45: TEXT 0,'COPYRIGHT (C) 1982 FEROX MICROSYSTEMS INC.'
46: NEWPAGE
47: CENTER 80,'DSS/F FINANCIAL MODEL EXAMPLE'
48: UTEXT
49: CENTER 80,'BALANCE SHEET'
50: UTEXT
51: CENTER 80,'FIVE YEAR PROJECTION'
52: UTEXT
53: SKIP 2
54: TEXT C1,'1982',C2,'1983',C3,'1984',C4,'1985',C5,'1986'
55: UTEXT
56: SKIP
57: TEXT 7,'ASSETS:'
58: UTEXT
59: SKIP
60: BEFORE '$ '
61: ROWS 36
```

Figure 3-9. (*Cont.*)

```
2=1000,12%
3=25,10%
7=9.50,15%
10=2500,9%
15=*600
16=6000,*2000
17=10,200,5,0,0
22=*.12
23=*.18
24=*.12
25=1000
26=1000
27=1000
31=*.44
34=2000,15%
38=*40
40=*.40
42=1500,20%
43=8000
44=600
45=*.20
47=*2500
48=*1000
49=3000
51=*1500
52=5000
53=*2500
54=1500
59=*1000
60=*2000
39=3000
41=4000
```

Figure 3-9. (*Cont.*)

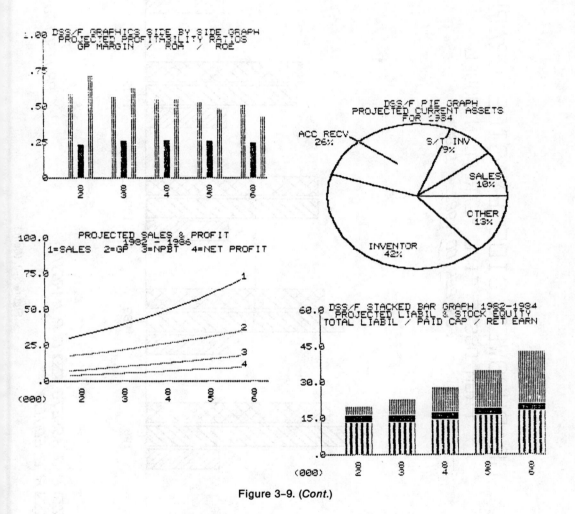

Figure 3-9. (*Cont.*)

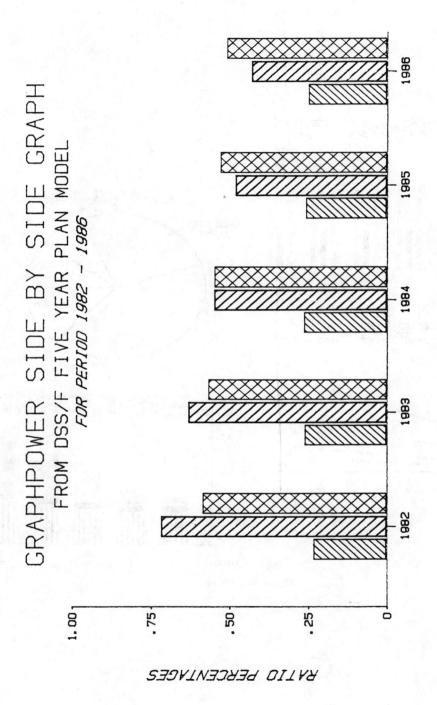

Figure 3-9. (Cont.)

until many years after its formulation and inception. By that time, the attention of top management is focused on the future and on the current strategic plan designed to shape that future. It is also quite likely that the executives who authorized the original plan are no longer holding the same positions of authority to receive credit or accept blame for the result of the plan. About the best that can be done in this area is to review performance annually and determine to what extent progress has been made towards achieving the long-range goals of the plan.

However, this difficulty of evaluating strategic plans does not necessarily eliminate the value of planning. Serious students of planning have pointed out that the true value of planning lies in the process rather than in the plan itself. When management makes a commitment to formal planning, it accepts the responsibility of defining objectives and considering all feasible alternative approaches to achieving those objectives. A well-formulated plan should give some assurance that a rational and objective study was conducted and that the plan that was adopted represents a consensus among top management as to the best direction to take in order to further the interests of the company. In addition, the existence of the plan provides guidelines which coordinate the decisionmaking efforts of all managerial levels towards the achievement of the plan's goals. Thus, according to this school of thought, even if no evaluation were made of a strategic plan, the expenditures involved in the formulation of the plan would be justified by the value derived from the planning process.

If we were to assume that a strategic plan could be easily evaluated, let us look at the possible outcomes of such an evaluation. A favorable evaluation would undoubtedly be interpreted as confirming the high level of managerial proficiency in the firm. It would also indicate the existence of an effective strategic information system. On the other hand, a negative evaluation may be attributed to any one of the following factors:

*1. Unforeseen events.* History has a way of confounding the most accurate forecasts. Few could have predicted the Arab oil embargo of 1973. No one could have predicted the banning of DDT or cyclamates by the Food and Drug Administration in past years. There is no way of designing a strategic information system which can forecast such events.

*2. Poor implementation of the strategic plan.* Since it is difficult to envisage a management blaming itself for poor performance, it would require an outside source such as auditors, consultants, dissident stockholders or an investment firm to form this conclusion. Such an explanation may accept the validity of the strategic information system, but conclude that management did not make proper use of the available information.

*3. Poor intelligence.* The evaluation may reveal that certain information was available at the time of the formulation of the plan, but the information was not brought to the attention of the planners. In this situation, a reorganization of the strategic information function may be called for.

The development of the DSS technique may ease some of the difficulties involved in evaluating strategic plans. The article presented below discusses a management model that was developed to test market assumptions against financial performance (Figure 3–10). Further advances may be anticipated to ease the evaluation problem.

Many Fortune 500 companies are overcoming the uncertainties of business with strategic plans focused on the long-range profitability of the company. For greater flexibility in preparing these plans, planning staffs are investigating several management tools—simulation models among them—that help analyze decisions required for long-range business strategy.

Since acquiring the Lufkin Rule Co. in 1967, the Cooper Group (Raleigh, NC) has grown to be the largest manufacturer of nonpowered hand tools in the world. During the following eleven-year period, revenues of the hand-tool group grew from $18 million to $275 million and operating earnings from $1.9 million to over $61 million. As the Group expanded, it implemented planning systems under the direction of Cooper Industries' corporate management, which provided a sound foundation for guiding future growth. Today, the Group's planning efforts encompass seven national brand-name product lines sold all over the world.

**Tests market assumptions**

The Cooper Group's management model was developed to give management the capability to test market assumptions against the Group's financial performance. The ability to perform sensitivity analysis (the development of alternative scenarios to determine how sensitive your operation is to changes caused by external conditions) on a division-by-division, product-group basis allows the Group to measure the impact of various internal decisions, given cer-

# Creating a five-year plan by computer

A management model tests market assumptions against financial performance and produces over 100 reports related to a five-year strategic plan.

by Harold Brown

tain external events. The basic modeling system provides data computations for over 100 reports related to the annual operating budget and the five-year plan.

The system generates full financial statements for both the operating budget and strategic plan. A mechanism has been built in to allow the first year of the strategic plan to be used in comparison with the budget; also, the current budget year can be used as the base year for the next strategic plan. The data base is cycled through the development of the strategic plan and operating budget and back to the strategic plan again in a way that naturally integrates the plan and the budget.

The primary difference between the development of the strategic plan and operating budget is the specification of one time period instead of five and the addition of a few special reports. The same sales and other financial-statement computational

models used to create the five-year plan are used for the annual budget. This allows the operating budget to then be broken down into quarterly segments. An annual profit reconciliation model and report are a primary feature of the operating budget, which provides price-volume-mix explanations. A special set of reports has been written to show variances between the first year of the strategic plan and the operating-budget year for all the financial statements. Finally, backup reports are available for development of the model; these show the ratios used for each variable input to the model's data base.

**A make-or-buy-decision**

Several options were open to the Group's planning staff in developing its model. The first decision concerned whether the project would become a proprietary system of the Cooper Group. Internal programming resources weren't available for

Figure 3–10. Reprinted from *Computer Decisions,* January, 1982, pages 106–107, copyright 1981, Hayden Publishing Company.

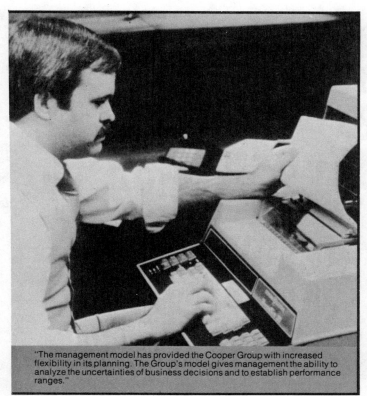

"The management model has provided the Cooper Group with increased flexibility in its planning. The Group's model gives management the ability to analyze the uncertainties of business decisions and to establish performance ranges."

workload over a six-month period: three months of systems specification and evaluation and three months of implementation work, which included needed modifications and the preparation of the documentation.

**Adding up the costs**

Operational costs are the most prominent outlays for a simulation model. Regardless of whether the system is processed internally or through an external timeshare vendor, the model will require computer processing time, terminal connection and transmission charges, and data storage costs. The model's calculations are actually a small part of a sensitivity-analysis run, so expensive timeshare charges are minimized. Storage costs are also low since we limited the number of variables the model had to encompass. The opportunity costs (the return on capital that might have resulted if the capital had been used otherwise) associated with operating the model involve the additional time needed for the planning staff to develop a scenario, run the model, and analyze the results. It should be emphasized that sensitivity analysis with this type of system will probably add to the workload of the planning staff because it expands the depth of analysis.

The hidden costs of a management model are usually uncovered when the degree of difficulty with which the model can be used is established. More important, learning to use the Group's management model has been complicated. Beginners are given one week of classroom instruction, then three weeks of hands-on training. It is hoped that the documentation that has been prepared will decrease the inherent difficulties involved when new people use the model for sensitivity analysis.

The management model has provided the Group with increased flexibility in its planning. The Group's model gives management the ability to analyze the uncertainties of business decisions and to establish performance ranges. Our management model has met its primary objective as a decision-making tool for strategic planning. □

*The author is sales analysis manager for the Cooper Group in Raleigh, NC.*

a project of this magnitude, so we started looking at commercial packages. After considerable analysis, a high-level utility language was selected over available canned modeling programs. The Simplan language offered the Group's planning staff the ability to design, develop, and control its own planning and modeling systems quickly, with minimal dependence on programmers and computer systems analysts.

After the software was developed, a decision was made to utilize the model on an outside timeshare vendor's service because Simplan is written in PL/1, a language that is not supported on the Group's mainframe (a Burroughs 4800). Avco Computer Service, Wilmington, MA, was judged to be the most efficient in a benchmark test of several vendors. The model can be run either in batch or interactive mode. The more expedient and expensive interactive mode is used for most

runs, although large data input should generally be processed in batch. We started by paying for Simplan through a 50 percent surcharge on the timesharing cost.

In the early stages of implementing strategic planning throughout all levels of a corporation, the time and effort needed for preparing and using such a tool would seem to be premature. Even in a mature planning environment, a management model may not fit the objectives of the long-range planners.

Next, the more visible expenses related to programming and developing the model were weighed. The Group's planning function was established enough to warrant the additional resources required to develop its model. An outside consultant, Lisa Post of Social Systems, Inc., Chapel Hill, NC, was retained to develop the model at a very reasonable cost. The model was a major portion of the project manager's

Figure 3–10. (*Cont.*)

Information
Resource
Management
Information
Resource
Management
Information
Resource
Management
Information
Resource
Management

March 29, 1982

BusinessWeek

McGraw-Hill

**Special Advertising Section**

# Information Resource Management

by John J. Connell

Information is everybody's business and, paradoxically, it is nobody's business. Managers and professionals in corporate life are keenly aware that the quality of their performance depends upon the timely availability of pertinent, comprehensive information. They find themselves frustrated, however, that their information needs are not being met.

The problem is not the lack of information; in fact, just the opposite. Thanks to high-speed printers, convenience copiers and bulk mailing rates, today's managers and professionals suffer from an overload of information, most of which is irrelevant. Trying to wade through the morass to find key answers is next to impossible. As a result, professionals analyzing alternative courses of action and managers faced with making operating decisions are being stymied by a dearth of good information.

We are moving from an industrial age to an information age, one where most people will be working on jobs that involve the production or the use of information. Having the right information at the right time can be the competitive edge.

**The right information can provide the competitive edge, but managers are overloaded with irrelevant information.**

One would assume that special management efforts are employed to assure that every manager and every professional is supplied with all the information necessary to do his job. This is not true. Senior management pays little attention to the problem of meeting information needs. Instead, the assignment is turned over to staff specialists, and the results are mixed, at best.

Information may be vital to everybody's business but, when it comes to management, it is nobody's business.

Two developments, occurring almost simultaneously, now offer senior management a unique opportunity to come to grips with the information problem. The first is the need to improve productivity in the office. The second is the concept of information resource management.

## Productivity Improvement

Historically, senior management has ignored office operations. At last, this attitude is changing. The catalyst is the growing recognition that office costs are rising precipitously, faster than in any other sector of business operations.

Senior managers, concerned about the potentially adverse impact of office costs on company profits, are instituting formal programs to improve office productivity. These programs are not being aimed at clericals. The target is the managerial and professional work force which accounts for almost 75% of all office costs.

The programs have three strategy steps: to establish productivity improvement as a corporate goal and set in motion those programs and policies necessary to build that philosophy into every facet of corporate life; to get everyone personally involved in the productivity improvement effort through quality circles, incentive programs and similar activities; and to take full advantage of the potential of new office technologies.

While directing these productivity improvement efforts, senior managers have discovered that nobody

**Senior managers are instituting productivity improvement programs because of rising office costs.**

manages today's office. Managerial assignments relate to departments, to systems and to functions, but no entity or individual short of the chief executive officer is responsible for managing office operations. As a result, the management practices which work so successfully in line operations are employed haphazardly in the office, if at all.

The key question to be asked in any effort to improve the productivity of a given operation is whether the operation should be performed in the first place. When that question is asked in the office, however, no clear answer is forthcoming.

The full benefits of productivity improvement programs are seldom attained because the office is task-oriented rather than goal-oriented.

**John J. Connell is the founder and executive director of the Office Technology Research Group, Pasadena, CA, and a well-known author and speaker in the Office of the Future field.**

## Information Resource Management

The need to improve productivity is one development affecting the office. The other is information resource management, the concept that information should be looked at as a corporate resource, and managed accordingly.

However, the concept has been slow in gaining acceptance, because it has not been widely publicized. It developed in the information-processing community and has been advanced primarily in terms of its impact on that field and on the career aspirations of information processing personnel.

Efforts to explain the concept to senior management have not been successful. Visualizing an intangible, such as information, as a resource with bottom-line implications is very difficult. Considered by itself, the concept appears to be too theoretical, a dubious justification for making substantive changes in business operations.

Some of its advocates cloud the picture further by equating information resource management to information control. They contend that the only way to reduce information overload is to set up an individual or an entity to determine who gets what information and when. The Big Brother implications of such an approach are anathemas to most managers.

**Conceptually, information can be looked at as a corporate resource and managed like other resources.**

Yet the concept does have merit, at least as a means for addressing the information problem. Information is an important corporate resource. In fact, one could argue that it is the premier corporate resource because it is used in the management of all other resources.

## Managing the Office

Any effort to improve office productivity must concern itself with information. By melding the information resource management concept into the office productivity improvement program, senior managers can introduce into the office the expertise they have used so successfully in the line side of the business. Not all of that expertise is directly transferable, but much of it is.

If information is looked on as the product of the office, then cost/benefit analyses can be made of activities involved in acquiring,

**Melding information resource management into office productivity programs will improve performance.**

processing and moving the product. Goals can be established based on product requirements and alternative courses of action evaluated in terms of those goals. Organization structure can be designed to reflect the requirements of producing the product. Capital investment proposals can be compared with those coming from line units using common return on investment criteria. In short, perhaps for the first time, the office can be managed.

The task is not simple. Information is hard to define, not easily valued, and far different from the products ordinarily dealt with in the

## Information Resource Management Information

plant or in the marketplace. Introducing value analysis and return on investment philosophies into an area that traditionally has been oriented to full service is a formidable assignment. The bureaucracy of the office, with its independent fiefdoms, adds to the problem.

But the opportunity is there. Never has the office been confronted with so much change—the growing sophistication in information demands, the extraordinary explosion in new office technologies, the changing nature of the office work force and the desire, in fact, the pressing need to improve office productivity. The way these changes are managed will determine the economic viability of the office in the years to come and the caliber of its contribution to the success of the enterprise.

## Management Responsibility

Experience with productivity improvement programs has validated the thesis that such efforts should be led by senior management. The top-down approach ensures that the programs receive proper visibility, that everyone is encouraged to become involved and that present organizational structures do not become stumbling blocks.

In exploring how best to combine the information resource management concept with office productivity improvement programs, the same philosophy applies. The effort should be led by senior management, and its mission should be to develop a philosophical underpinning for introducing better management into office operations.

**Senior managers should lead and every manager should participate in managing the information resource.**

That managers and professionals are responsible for identifying their own information requirements and deciding how information should be used sounds simplistic—a rudimentary expression of a management principle.

In practice, however, many managers and professionals have limited skills in defining their information needs. In fact, the criticism that computers produce reams of largely irrelevant reports should not be laid exclusively at the feet of computer systems designers. In most cases, the root cause is the inability of managers and professionals to specify their own information requirements, to decide what information they need and what they do not need. As a result, computer-generated reports represent what systems designers think managers need.

In an information age, however, knowledge workers who cannot identify their information needs and use information correctly will fail. As will be shown later, new information technologies help managers obtain operating information directly from machines. Current literature cites cases where chief executive officers

**Knowledge workers must identify their needs and use information correctly, or fail.**

are using terminals to access computer-stored performance information. The emphasis is on interfacing directly with the information base rather than relying on the services of staff specialists.

A strategy for introducing the information resource management concept should insist that every manager and professional participate in the management process. It should also support that participation with education and hands-on experience. By stressing that direct role, senior management can reduce the chance of knowledge workers failing in their assignments and enhance the opportunities for superior performance. Information specialists make their greatest contribution by using sophisticated machines to acquire, process, move and store information. But managing the acquisition, processing, movement and storage of information should not be equated to managing the information resource. The talents of information specialists from many disciplines combined with the capabilties of modern machines are key determinants in meeting the information needs of managers and professionals. In the final analysis, however, corporate success will depend on how well information requirements are specified and how well the information is used.

## Information Technologies

The level of understanding required of managers and professionals about what is happening in information technologies should be deep enough to appreciate the implications of new developments as they are introduced.

These developments have two objectives: to find more cost-effective ways to acquire, process, move and store information, and to provide tools to help make better use of machine-stored information.

Understanding these developments, at least conceptually, is vital to effective management of the information resource, because one can envision no greater change in the years ahead than will occur in the world of information technology and all that it affects.

The traditional way of looking at information technologies is to track their historical development. Data processing grew from punched card equipment in the 1950s to electronic computers in the 1960s to the large datacenters we know today.

**Micrographics has been allied with computers to become one of the most modern technologies.**

Word processing came on the scene in the 1960s in the form of typewriters with magnetic tape storage and grew to the almost overwhelming array of text-editing equipment on today's market.

Micrographics, one of the oldest technologies still extant, has been allied with computers to become one of the most modern technologies.

In fact, the historical approach is reflected in the way the information industry is organized and in the organizational strategy of most corporations. We have organized ourselves around technologies as they have developed historically, and the separateness of technologies has been institutionalized.

**Information technologies are changing and the distinctions among them are blurring.**

All that is about to change. Two developments, operating in concert, will revolutionize the whole world of information technology. The first is the changing of traditional definitions of specific technologies and the blurring of distinctions among them. The second is the interconnection of previously separate technologies through integrated telecommunications networks. These two developments will eventually lead us to one information technology, the integrated network. The machines we know today, or their successors, will be components of the network.

**Computer applications are more sophisticated and complicated than in the past.**

*Informa*

## Data Processing

Data processing is a good example of this process of change. In the 1960s and 1970s, computers were installed in centralized datacenters which provided computer services and processed data in accordance with the instructions programmed into various systems. Orderliness, structure and tight control were the key elements of the approach. Most of the standard accounting systems, payroll, billing and the like, were converted to computers in this environment, and those applications are handled in centralized datacenters to this day.

The appearance of minicomputers in the 1970s introduced some new options. The centralized approach to computing was augmented by the introduction of local computers. Machines began to lose their mystique, and computers became tools for use in the workplace rather than exclusively in the datacenter.

As the use of minicomputers proliferated, a new term was coined—distributed processing—to describe the movement of computing power out of the hands of the information specialists in the datacenter and into the office. The movement was resisted by the data processing community at first, but the approach has proven successful. The more astute data processors are now strong supporters of a multi-tiered machine strategy involving central computers, minicomputers and systems which use telecommunications networks to move computer power to the end user's site.

Distributed processing turned out to be a harbinger of things to come. The basic trend in computing today is to devise better ways to make the technology available to non-technologists. This trend has been accelerated by the introduction of personal computers which are appearing in homes and offices.

# Resource Management

**Distributed processing turned out to be a harbinger of things to come.**

Data processing personnel have had to cope with these changes over the years, and it has not been easy. Computer applications are far more sophisticated and complicated than in the past. Payroll, billing and similar applications, which were transferred to computers years ago, now look like child's play compared to today's applications, which cross departmental lines, require on-line access, and use complex algorithms in the manipulation of information.

Of greater concern today, however, is the limited flexibility of most data processing departments in their ability to respond to new technological opportunities, especially those which apply to the people-intensive world of the office.

Many of the systems in place on today's computers were designed when machine limitations and systems design philosophies combined to make systems changes very difficult. However, systems must change because of new business requirements, governmental regulations and other external fac-

tors. Industry surveys show that making changes in old systems, which is called systems maintenance, accounts for more than 60% of the systems design workload.

Most computer systems design organizations have a three-year backlog of work. The pressure of such a backlog coupled with continuing changes in technology has led to high turnover and job burnout, thus inhibiting even further the ability to respond to the demand

**Most computer systems design organizations have a three-year backlog of work.**

arising from the introduction of new office technologies.

In looking to data processing to play a key role in introduction of the information resource management concept, senior management must recognize the changes which face that technology and the heavy workload and backlog it carries. Both may operate to limit the flexibility of data processing in responding to new technological challenges.

## Word Processing

Computers process data which has been logically defined, according to a set of logical instructions programmed beforehand. Thus, the logical definitions of gross pay as hours times rate and net pay as gross pay less deductions are programmed into a set of instructions to produce paychecks. When one moves from data to text, however, to words, sentences and paragraphs, logical definitions do not work. Instead, text editing requires a human being to interpret the text and then to decide how it should be manipulated.

**Word processing requires a direct, ongoing interface between a human and a machine.**

This distinction is what makes word processing different from data processing. Data processing operates under control of a set of programmed instructions, with the human interaction one of monitoring. Word processing requires a direct, ongoing interface between a human being and a machine. The data processing and word processing machines may look alike, but because one operates on data and the other on text, they have developed separately as two independent technologies and industries.

Word processing has progressed from the stormy period when its installation was justified by taking away the manager's secretary, to instances where it is used to make the team of manager and secretary more productive. In that setting, the secretarial time saved by transferring work to a word processor is filled with work transferred from the manager. The value of the additional work which the manager can take on justifies investment in the equipment.

**Word processing can make the manager and secretary team more productive.**

Latest developments on the low end of word processing equipment provide machines with full text-editing and spelling correction capabilities, at a price which often permits justification of the machine as a direct replacement for a secretary's typewriter.

Developments at the higher end signal the blurring of technologies, for word processing machines now come with data processing capabilities. They also act as computer terminals in providing access to the central computer over telecommunications lines.

Conversely, central computers and minicomputers are being equipped with software packages which give them full word-processing capabilities. Thus, the separateness of the two technologies, so staunchly defended in the past, no longer has a valid technological basis. The machines are what the user wants them to be, and the implementing mechanism is the telecommunications network.

# Information
# Resource
# Management
# Information
# Resource

## Networks

The second change taking place in information technologies adds to this uncertainty and, in fact, charts an entirely new course. That change is the trend toward interconnecting machines through telecommunications. In the final analysis, telecommunications is the basic underlying technology in the future office.

To complicate matters further, telecommunications is changing more rapidly and on many more fronts than any other technology. The literature is filled with news about telecommunications—the settlement of the AT&T anti-trust suit and what it means; the competition among suppliers of satellite-based transmission services; the advantages of digital versus today's analog long-distance network; the debate between broadband and baseband as the technique to be used in local data networks; computerized PBX's; "smart" telephones; the integration of voice and data; control over international data flows; and a host of others. Technological issues, political issues, regulatory issues and, of late, competitive issues mark the world of telecommunications.

**In the future, all information-related machines will be interconnected through telecommunications.**

The importance of telecommunications in the future office cannot be overstressed. Ultimately, every machine in an office which works with information will have built into it the ability to interconnect with a telecommunications network.

**The network makes all the powers of modern technology available to the entire work force.**

Once connected, the machine will be able to share its capabilities with all other machines tied to the network.

From a user's point of view, tying into the network will provide access to information stored in the form of data on computers, text on word processors, images on microfilm and voice on the network itself. The network is the vehicle through which all the powers of modern technology are made available to the entire work force.

Consider this example of how the capabilities of machines can be enhanced and in some cases greatly multiplied by tying them to a network. Word-processing machines are used to produce letters which are then mailed. However, if the machines are tied to a telecommunications network and communicate with other word-processing machines, then letters typed in one location can be printed in another, thereby avoiding the time delays of mailing. Further, if a computer is connected to the network, it can make copies of letters, distribute them to addressees and retain file copies, all electronically. Finally, if microfilm equipment is attached to the network, the file copies can be converted to microfilm for archival storage. Access to a network, then, and to other machines tied to the network, upgrades the capabilities of the word-processing machines from letter production to a full-scale electronic mail system.

Electronic mail is a good example of the impact of networks on infor-mation technologies. It integrates four previously separate technologies—word processing, telecommunications, data processing and micrographics—into a single use, and it would be difficult to define where one starts and the other stops. An electronic mail system can be accessed at work, or at home, or while traveling—in fact, anywhere one can tie into the network with the proper terminal. Its usage is voluntary, based on perception of value.

Information specialists may view it as a word-processing application,

**Electronic mail exemplifies the impact of networks on information technologies.**

or a data-processing application or a micrographics application, depending upon their bias. To the user, however, the manager or the professional, it is a capability available from the network. The future of information technology is summed up in that view, that the network provides an array of capabilities for managers and professionals to use to improve their performance.

Informat
Resourc
Manage

## An Array of Capabilities

The array of capabilities which networks will provide to managers and professionals is growing at an extraordinary pace. This growth stems from the synergism that occurs when one interconnects previously separate technologies and takes advantage of the powerful characteristics of each. Of even greater importance, the capabilities pour forth from the creative minds of designers in the software industry, the fastest growing sector in the information field.

**Networks will provide managers and professionals with an array of capabilities to help improve performance.**

The following is a description of some of the capabilities that are available to managers and professionals. They represent the first steps; additional work is needed to make them more universally available and easier to use. Nevertheless, the existence of these capabilites is a clear indication of forward directions, the move to introduce the powers of modern information technologies into the offices of every manager and professional:

**Electronic mail** is the capability of receiving one's mail over a network, reading it on the screen of a terminal and using the terminal's keyboard to respond.

The distribution of copies to addressees, the maintenance of file copies and the ultimate disposal of the files are all handled by machine. Electronic mail is used for internal correspondence in a number of companies and some efforts are under way to use it for external correspondence to a select user community. Experience shows that casual users tend to send cryptic messages rather than formal letters, so the capability might more properly be called electronic messaging.

**Voice messaging** is a capability similar in principle to electronic messaging, except the terminal is a telephone and the message is spoken and played back rather than typed and read on a screen.

Telephone answering machines offer an entry-level form of voice messaging. More sophisticated machines have voice message distribution, filing and retrieval characteristics that are almost identical to those of electronic messaging. The use of voice message systems is growing rapidly because the terminal device, the telephone, is already in place and well-accepted. Also, the training necessary to use these systems is minimal.

**Internal data base access** is the ability to access information stored on the company's central computer, retrieve it selectively, structure and manipulate it as desired and produce personalized reports.

This capability has extraordinary potential and could have far-reaching impact on the managerial skills required for the future. For the most part, information stored on computers is not easily accessible to managers. To get selected information, one must describe one's requirements to a computer specialist who translates the request into a series of programs steps to access the computer file and produce the desired result. The process is

**For the most part, information stored on computers is not easily accessible to managers.**

cumbersome, time-consuming and frustrating.

The prospect for the future is that managers will use a terminal to access computer-based files directly, quickly find the information they want and use it as they see fit, thus operating in a totally self-sufficient way. This new capability will change the traditional reliance of managers on staff specialists to obtain and analyze data. Some managers will choose to do their own research, and if superior results are obtained, others will also. Thus, the ability to define one's information requirements and make effective use of the information obtained becomes an increasingly important management skill.

**External data base access** is the ability to access information available from external sources. A growing number of firms now offer data base services, consisting of terminal access to a variety of files. Airline guides and stock quotations are obvious examples, but others include industry statistics, abstracts of published literature, current events and a host of others. Thus, the manager developing future plans can supplement company information obtained from internal data bases with information of the world outside.

The provision of computer-based information services will be augmented shortly by videotex, which provides similar services using television screens. The ultimate role of videotex in the information services field is still unknown. Current efforts to exploit its potential support the thesis that a growing body of information will be available externally, in various forms, all accessible by machine.

**Access to text** is the ability to access correspondence and reports which are stored in electronic form. The use of word-processing equipment to produce textual material is creating a growing repository of information in the form of text, which will be available for retrieval in similar fashion to data.

**Information manipulation** is the ability to manipulate information electronically in any way desired. If the information is in the form of data, a program can be written to manipulate it. If text, it can be manipulated directly on a screen by keyboard command. If a permanent record is required, the manipulated information can be printed out or transferred to microfilm. Thus, terminal-based access systems are not merely a mechanism for finding machine-stored information and displaying it on a screen. They offer a full range of capabilities for editing, structuring and manipulating the information in any way one desires.

**Decision support systems** provide the ability to simulate business decisions mathematically and predict the results that will occur from pursuing one course of action versus another.

The effectiveness of decision support systems depends upon whether the variables attendant upon alternative courses of action can be defined and quantified. Great success has been achieved in such areas as cash management and simulation of manufacturing plant operations where the variables are well-known.

Of late, significant results have been achieved in using decision

## Decision support systems will become an increasingly important management tool.

support systems in financial planning, portfolio analysis, tax planning, market analysis and a number of other areas. As decision support systems can be made to interact with company data bases, they will become an increasingly important management tool.

**Graphics** is the ability to take information retrieved from machine storage and convert it to a graphic presentation mode—bar charts, pie charts, curves and other visual displays. The adage that a picture is worth a thousand words is demonstrated no more effectively than when columns of data extracted from a computer file are converted on a screen to a multi-dimensional color display. Graphics can expose the hidden relationships that exist in the data and at the same time present an overview from a new perspective.

## Graphics expose hidden relationships in data while presenting an overview from a new perspective.

**Microfilm access** is the ability to retrieve images which have been stored on microfilm. The key characteristic of microfilm is that once information is recorded on it, the information cannot be manipulated. That, plus its low cost, makes it the ideal storage medium for incoming correspondence, contracts and related legal material, printed matter and other documents which one may wish to access but not change. Computer-aided retrieval capabilities facilitate access to information stored on microfilm.

**Local administrative support** describes the ability to use the storage, manipulation and retrieval capabilities of terminals tied to a network to aid in handling administrative tasks. Keeping track of one's calendar, maintaining local files of information, scheduling, controlling tickler files and a variety of other activities which consume valuable managerial time can be handled more easily and effectively by machine.

**Computer conferencing** is the ability to conduct an ongoing meeting with personnel in different geographic locations. An electronic message system is used to record communications among meeting participants. Each person involved in the meeting can access, read and respond to these communications, regardless of whether other participants are communicating simultaneously or not. The system thus provides a log of the meeting, and the asynchronous method of participation offers extraordinary flexibility, especially if meeting members travel frequently or are in different time zones. The technique has proven to be highly effective for managing the ongoing activities of large projects.

**Teleconferencing** is the ability to conduct meetings in a synchronous mode, where the participants are in different geographic locations. Here, the mediums used are video, audio or some combination of the two, operating over a network, and perhaps augmented by graphics transmission devices.

Experience with teleconferencing thus far shows that the technique reduces travel and speeds up information communication and decision-making. It is ideal for planning, progress reporting and general discussions where meeting participants know each other. Conversely, it is less effective in unstructured meetings, those where emotions play a role and those where one is attempting to sell an idea or a proposal.

The future office, then, is a world in which networks provide an array of capabilities to help managers and professionals do a better job. To reach that world requires not only a technology strategy but a strategy for organizing information to take advantage of machine capabilities. The extraordinary burden that will be placed on information specialists in developing those strategies are factors to be considered by senior management in the planning process.

**Teleconferencing reduces travel and speeds up communication and decision-making.**

# Information Organization

If generalized access to machine-stored information is to be provided to managers and professionals over a network, the information must be organized to facilitate such access. Research is now underway in the information industry to determine how to meet that objective. To implement the information resource management concept, some knowledge of the principles of information organization are essential.

**Systems are needed to manage information and the records in which information is stored.**

Any time one imparts knowledge, a record is created. The record may be transitory, the brief recording of one's words in the brain of another, or more permanent when information is recorded on paper, on film, in the memory of a computer or in some other storage medium. As a result, the strategy for introducing the information resource management concept must consider not only the management of information but also the management of the records in which the information is stored.

When records have some characteristics in common, they are grouped in files. Since paper has been the most common medium for storing recorded information in an office, methods and procedures have been developed for organizing and controlling paper records in paper files. Those methods and procedures have been formalized in a discipline called records management. Over the years, a comprehensive body of knowledge has been

**Several data base management systems have gained acceptance in the data-processing community.**

developed by practitioners in records management governing the creation, use, storage and ultimate disposition of paper records.

When computers came on the scene, little or no thought was given to the idea that a magnetic storage medium might call for a different records management approach than paper. As a result, computer files were set up in exactly the same way as paper files in virtually every computer-based system developed throughout the 1960s.

The proliferation of machine-based files led to file control problems and excessive machine usage. Late in that decade, experimentation began with different approaches to file organization which led to the creation of a new discipline called data base management. It is a form of records management that attempts to organize the storage of information and files on a computer in a manner which makes optimal use of the characteristics of the storage medium used. A number of data base management systems have been developed, and they have gained strong acceptance in the data-processing community.

The approach taken to the storage of textual information in word processing followed the same route as data processing—it copied traditional paper systems. For example, paper correspondence is filed in cabinets according to some classification scheme designed to help

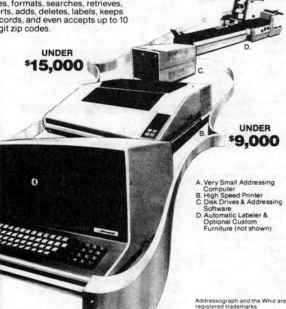
Special Advertising Section

find a particular piece of correspondence at a later date. Correspondence files on word processing magnetic disks have been set up in the same way.

However, machines can scan magnetically stored information and retrieve correspondence based on a name, a date, a particular combination of words or similar criteria. Elaborate prior classification is not necessary.

Thus, the idea of text management is emerging—the development of records management approaches to the storage of text which take advantage of the capabilities of the magnetic medium in which the text is stored. Ultimately, text management systems will join data base management systems as support elements in organizing machine-stored information to facilitate retrieval and use.

Records management principles were applied to microfilm images from the outset, in an ongoing effort to improve access to microfilmed records. The most modern of these is used in computer-aided retrieval. The closer we get to implementation of the network concept, the greater the pressure will be to ensure that those techniques integrate well with the records management systems for data and text. Ultimately, integrated records management systems will be required for records stored in the form of data, text, image and voice.

## Information Resource Management

If productivity improvement efforts in the office are to succeed, this orientation must change. Technology must be looked on not as an end but as a means, a tool to help improve performance. A major educational effort is needed to convince information specialists that the objectives of the business rather than the characteristics of the technology are the bases for developing plans and assigning priorities.

In spite of these problems of education, workload and career concerns, information specialists are eager to get on with the job. Their trade journals are filled with articles about the office of the future, networks, the need to improve office productivity and information resource management. They are looking for leadership from senior management to provide a program to pursue these new developments.

The challenge to management is to make optimal use of the talents of information specialists in combining the information resource management concept into office productivity improvement programs.

# Organizational Strategy

To be successful, office productivity improvement efforts must be organized as an ongoing, long-term activity. When one is trying to improve the productivity of managers and professionals, behavioral changes are needed, changes in the way people think about and handle their jobs. Such changes take time, and the productivity gains occur gradually.

If the information resource management concept is to be melded into the office productivity improvement effort and the whole process used to upgrade the management of office operations, then the same ongoing, long-term approach is needed.

Organizational units in place today should not necessarily be merged together. For the most part,

## Organizational changes should be deferred until an operating strategy is developed.

they were organized around technologies rather than functional responsibilities. The fact that technologies are converging is not sufficient basis for organizational convergence. Rather, it is a signal that today's organizational strategy stems from a philosophy of technological separateness that is no longer valid. New organizational strategies should be based on business operating requirements rather than the idiosyncracies of information technologies.

Many proponents of information resource management see it leading to a new senior management position, the chief information officer. They argue that such a position exists to manage the people resource and the money resource, and similar treatment should be given to the information resource. A position along those lines may be created in the future by some companies, but speculation about it now is premature.

Information resource management is a concept, untested and unproven. It appears to have merit, but it does not have the strength to stand on its own. Melding it with office productivity improvement programs gives it an arena in which

## Office productivity improvement efforts must be an ongoing, long-term activity.

it can be examined and tested. However, if that effort is seen as an excuse for creating a new senior management position, it will probably founder in the morass of political infighting and power struggles.

A better approach is to defer organizational changes until an operating strategy is developed. The strategy should have several components. The first component is the recognition that the goal is to manage the office more effectively—the people, the machines, the facilities and the resource for which the office is most specifically responsible, information. We are trying to make the office a more effective contributor to the success of the enterprise.

## The goal is to manage the office more effectively—people, machines, facilities and information.

The second component is education. Office personnel must be educated in the use of sophisticated management practices in office operations. Managers and professionals must learn about their roles in managing the information resource. Information specialists must know what is happening to information technologies. All must learn about those factors that will have an impact on office operations—the need to improve productivity, the explosion in information technologies, the changing nature of the office work force and similar developments.

The third component is converting the office from task orientation to goal orientation. Critical success factors must be identified, specific performance goals established, and performance measures developed.

The fourth component is the development of plans. One plan is needed to orchestrate the effort to introduce better business practices into the office. A second plan is needed to direct the productivity improvement effort, to establish a framework within which new approaches can be funded and tested, to incorporate productivity improvement into every facet of office operations and to institute appropriate reward systems. A third plan is needed to get managers and professionals directly involved in the process of managing the information resource to fit their specific needs. A fourth plan is needed to manage the introduction of the network concept and to maximize the potential offered by developments in information technologies.

## Managers from many disciplines must participate in strategy development.

Analysis of this strategy indicates that representatives of a number of disciplines must participate in its development. Personnel managers must concern themselves with the educational requirements of the strategy. Corporate planning must participate in the development of goals for the office to ensure that those goals fit with business plans.

## Overall, the strategy development effort must be led by senior management.

Information specialists must participate in planning for the network. Overall, the strategy development effort must be led by senior management because the breadth of the activity, the number of disciplines involved and the ultimate impact on the bottom line demand that level of leadership.

Some companies may have in place a senior executive whose assigned organizational responsibilities encompass large portions of office operations; leadership of the strategy development effort might logically be vested in that individual. Ordinarily, however, responsibility for the management of office operations is fragmented and no one individual is the obvious choice to lead the effort. In that event, the strategy development effort should be carried out by an ad hoc task force led by a member of senior management who has been selected based on proven performance in improving the management effectiveness of operating units.

No one from the outside can specify what strategy a given company should follow to improve of e productivity and implement the formation resource managem concept. Corporate culture, th gree of concern with rising off costs and unfulfilled informati mands, current levels of mana ment sophistication in office o tions, the status of information technologies and the exigencies of the business environment are factors that will affect strategy content and the speed of implementation. Each of these can only be evaluated in the proper perspective from the inside.

However, there are three additional factors that should be incorporated in every strategy: the changing nature of the office work force; the cost of information; and information security.

**Resource Management Information Resource Management**

## The Office Work Force

The office is a people place and will continue to be, regardless of the inroads made by information technologies. The office will never be automated, in the full meaning of the word, nor is office automation a valid corporate objective. Routine office operations may be mechanized, but, beyond that, the value of information technologies lies in their ability to augment the intellectual capacities and capabilities of office personnel.

**The changing nature of the office work force must be recognized in the strategy.**

Given that fact, one must look at the office work force to see if it is willing to use the new tools being offered. Such an examination will reveal that the office work force is changing rapidly and has attitudes and aspirations that are different from its predecessors. The first difference is that the educational level of office personnel is rising. People who work in offices crave intellectual challenge and are openly critical of routine and drudgery. Since the capabilities of information technologies tend to support intellectual activities and minimize routine, the chances of their being used are very good.

Second, office personnel want to see the job through, to be responsible for an activity from its inception to its completion. They resist the old approach where activities were broken into components and responsibility was limited to completion of specific components. Today's office personnel want to see jobs through

**People who work in offices crave intellectual challenge and are openly critical of routine and drudgery.**

from beginning to end and be given wide latitude in determining how the job is to be done. Here again, advanced information technologies support the pursuit of alternative courses of action.

Third, the concept of participative management, of getting more people involved in the decision-making process, is gaining greater acceptance. So are quality circles and other techniques, all aimed at improving operating performance as a team effort. The cogs-in-a-wheel approach where someone else is driving the wagon is passé. The trend now is toward personal participation in determining the best way to get a job done. Again, this greater sense of involvement is supported by the new tools offered by advanced information technologies.

Fourth, the world outside the office is exploding with new technologies. Video games, home video systems, personal computers and a host of other innovations are becoming commonplace. The mystique of electronic technology is disappearing in this new wave of consumer products. People are more comfortable with machines, and that comfort level is flowing over into the office.

## Information Costs

Little consideration has been given in the past to the cost of acquiring information in the office and only

slightly more to the true cost of processing, moving and storing information. If a manager or professional wants a piece of information, office personnel, with their orientation toward full service, will attempt to get the information and pay scant attention to the costs involved. In fact, the higher the rank of the individual making the request, the slimmer the chance that anyone will challenge the reasonableness of the inquiry versus the cost of providing an answer.

Information is unique in that it has no value in itself. Its value is determined by those who use it, and it can vary with time. Such is not the case with other corporate resources. People have intrinsic value. Money's value and the value of materials and facilities are determined by the marketplace. But the value of information is in the minds of its users.

**The cost of acquiring discretionary information must be justified in terms of job performance.**

Information does have a cost, though, a substantial cost when one considers the number of people, the facilities and the machines devoted to handling information. Some information in the office is required by the nature of the business or to meet regulatory requirements. But much of it is discretionary and therefore subject to a test of its value versus cost.

Unfortunately, however, there are no mechanisms now in place to help establish the true cost of information, because information has never been looked at as a resource or even as a separate entity. Managers concerned about the number

of paper files scattered throughout the office may institute records disposal programs. But the concern is much more about the physical space taken up by file cabinets than about the time people spend maintaining information in the files and retrieving it on demand.

Information stored on computers has been structured to produce regularly scheduled reports, and reasonable estimates can be developed as to what those reports cost. However, when someone asks for a special report, no valid technique is available to determine what it costs. Perhaps the best example of the lack of good management in the office is the inability to assign costs to the discretionary acquisition, processing, movement and storage of information.

Melding the information resource management concept into office productivity improvement programs offers an unparalleled opportunity to correct this problem. Part of the education of managers and professionals in their roles in managing the information resource should include the concept that information has a cost just like every other resource.

Incurring that cost must be justified by relating the value of the information obtained to the performance of one's job. Part of the education of information specialists should concentrate on the thesis that every machine use should have built into it the means of determining the true cost of that use. Part of the role of senior management should be to ensure that discretionary information costs are justified according to a value system and a set of priorities that are in consonance with the business plan.

In that way, the management practices developed in the line side of the business concerning discretionary cost justification are applied to the office in the management of the information resource.

## Information Security

As more and more information is transferred from paper to machines, serious consideration must be given to information security. It is not that machine-based systems are less secure than paper systems. In themselves, they are probably more secure. However, they concentrate information in one place and facilitate access, authorized or not, to a vast store of information. The difficulty in finding information in paper files, which frustrates all of us, at least offers the consolation that those not entitled to the information will encounter the same difficulties. Not so with machine-based systems, however; if one can access the files, all the information in them is easily available.

**Security measures should control access to information and assure its authenticity, integrity and validity.**

As a result, systems which provide direct access to machine-stored information must have provisions built into them to prevent unauthorized access. Fraud is one type of unauthorized access; invasion of privacy associated with access to personnel and other records is another.

There are a variety of ways to make machine-based systems secure. Ultimately, however, security depends on people and their willingness to observe the security ground rules. A substantial portion of the education of managers and professionals about their roles in the management of the information resource should be concerned with information security.

**Systems which provide direct access to machine-stored information must have provisions built into them to prevent unauthorized access.**

The use of machine-based systems introduces additional security concerns besides unauthorized access—concerns about the authenticity, the integrity and the validity of the information retrieved from a machine-based system. For example, in an electronic mail system, letters are typed on a terminal and distributed electronically. When an addressee reads a letter on a screen, several security considerations arise, stemming from the ease of manipulating machine-stored information. The first is authenticity. Since the letter is not personally signed, did it actually come from the person to whom it is attributed? The second is integrity. Is the letter complete or were portions deleted from it? The third is validity. Were the contents of the letter changed in any way during transmission, storage and receipt? Control techniques are available to provide answers to all of these questions. The approach to managing information as a resource should include provisions that these techniques are built in to all machine-based systems.

We are presented, then, with an opportunity and a challenge. Effective management of the information resource will provide managers and professionals with the tools necessary to compete in the years ahead. Improving the productivity of the office will change that sector of the enterprise from a drain on the bottom line to a contributor to corporate success. Combining the two activities will facilitate introduction of proven management practices into office operations and assure that the future office will be managed.

In such an atmosphere, all those who work in offices will find themselves challenged to improve their performance and expand their potential. The organizational and operating constraints of the past will be minimized. Networks of tech-

**Ultimately, better management of the office will improve corporate performance and expand human potential.**

nologies will provide an array of capabilities for broadening one's intellectual talents and operating skills. The goal will be to improve corporate performance and, at the same time, to foster personal growth. For it is in the expansion of our potential as human beings that all of our institutions will prosper.

# PART II

# Introduction to Information for Operational Decisions

Historically, operating managers were able to carry out their tasks with decision-making based solely upon internal sources of information. Even when growing technological complexity demanded increasing knowledge and skills, it was possible for the operating manager to perform successfully throughout his career using knowledge acquired in college, professional or vocational school. Over the past twenty years however the rate of change in the technological, economic and social spheres has accelerated to such an extent that managers on the operational level are subject to professional obsolescence if they fail to maintain contact with external sources of information in their fields of specialization.

Professional societies represent one of the most common sources of information for the operating manager. Through membership in his society, the manager has access to journals, periodicals, seminars and conferences, all designed to update him on the latest developments in his field. Many of these professional societies now offer refresher courses to members who wish or are required to keep abreast with their field. In certain states, for example, physicians are required by law to prove attendance at refresher courses if they are to remain eligible for reimbursement from governmental sources. Table 1 presents a representative list of these professional societies.

Another commonly used external source of information for the operating manager is the trade organization. Most industries in the United States have formed associations to represent them in relevant governmental agencies, to represent management in certain cases in industry-wide labor negotiations, and to disseminate information of interest to companies in the industry. This sharing of information has not been found to violate the provisions of the antitrust laws which require an arms-length relationship among competitors in an industry. On the other hand, the extent of the information made available is circumscribed by confidentiality requirements of internal company operations. Nevertheless, between the extremes of collusion and secrecy, enough information is published to give the operating manager a comprehensive picture of developments in his industry. A cross section of these trade associations is listed in Table 2.

The thirst for new knowledge has become so unquenchable that conferences and seminars are now being offered as well by corporations that wish to explain their new products and services; by varied disciplines at many universities that offer the latest in the state of their art; and by associations such as the American Management

### Table 1. Sample List of Professional Associations.

American Bar Association
American Medical Association
American Institute of Certified Public Accountants
National Association of Accountants
American Marketing Association Inc.
North American Society for Corporate Planning
Academy of Management
The Institute of Management Science
American Association of Industrial Management
American Society of Personnel Administrators
American Industrial Science Association
American Production and Inventory Control Society
American Institute of Industrial Engineers
Public Relations Society of America
Chartered Life Underwriters Inc.
Industrial Relations Society
National Association of Purchasing Management Inc.

Associations, U.S. Professional Development Institute, and The Conference Board, Inc. that specialize in upgrading the knowledge and skills of managers.

The growing need for and availability of external sources of information for the operating manager has by no means diminished his dependence upon internal sources of information for most of his day-to-day decisionmaking. Succeeding chapters will describe each of the major managerial functions, define the management requirements of each functional system, explain the sources of data for the system, describe the system function and evaluate the management information utilized by the system. While the average operating manager will undoubtedly be familiar with many of the functional tasks and historical events which will be reviewed in the following chapters, their presentation within the framework of information requirements will hopefully shed new light on the relationship between technology and information.

### Table 2. Sample List of Trade Associations.

The Iron and Steel Institute
Rubber Manufacturers Association
American Electronics Association
Association of Data Processing Service Organizations
National Air Transport Association
National Railroad Intermodal Association
National Retail Merchants Association
National Association of Real Estate Agents
Association of American Publishers Inc.
American Apparel Manufacturers Association
American Bankers Association
National Construction Industry Council
American Nuclear Energy Council
Institute of Nuclear Materials Management
American Association of Advertising Agencies
American Gas Association
American Trucking Associations
American Council of Life Insurance Inc.

# 4
# Sales-Marketing Information System

## DESCRIPTION OF FUNCTION

The primary responsibility of the sales-marketing manager at the operating level is to contribute to the achievement of the corporate marketing goal. Among the major tasks may be listed:

1. to hire, train and supervise a group of sales representatives to operate in the assigned sales territory;
2. to plan and work to achieve targeted volumes for each customer in the territory;
3. to monitor the backlog of bookings, where there is a significant time lag between the receipt of the customer's order and its shipment;
4. to stimulate the sale of products which the company may desire to push for various reasons such as profitability, inventory status or competition;
5. to minimize customer returns;
6. to maximize customer profitability;
7. to extract the maximum return from the expenditure of sales budget dollars in the forms of salary, commisssion and travelling expenses for sales representatives, territorial shows, advertising, sales aids, point-of-sale displays, pricing flexibility and allowances;
8. to educate the customer in the proper use of the product or service;
9. to handle major customers personally.

## MANAGEMENT INFORMATION REQUIREMENTS

The information system should be designed to assist the operational sales-marketing manager to monitor the accomplishment of the goals listed in the previous section. The system will record, measure and report on actual performance which in turn is compared to some predetermined standard.

The establishment of appropriate and realistic standards is crucial to the effectiveness of the information system. The two basic variables of concern to the manager are the customer and the product, and the objectives formulated for each customer and each product form the foundation of the system. By summing the target amounts for each customer or each product assigned to a sales representative, it is possible to arrive at a standard for each sales representative.

Building on the basic information about the customer and the product, the system should be provided with a series of subsidiary standards which deal with each element of the sales-marketing operation. For example, the formulation of standard gross profit figures permits comparison to actual gross profit and the highlighting of variations from the standard. Such measurement may be made by customer, by product and by sales representative. A preselected allowable percentage of returns and allowances to gross shipments enables comparison to actual returns. Similar standards may be established for advertising expenses, travel expenses, and other sales expenses. These comparisons of actual to standard performance in each area enable the operational sales-marketing manager to pinpoint problem areas and to take immediate remedial steps. This information also serves to develop and implement objective reward and punishment systems.

All organizations operate in terms of time periods. On the operational level, the periods used may be day, week, month, quarter and year. A typical weekly report may show the week, month-to-date, and last year. Results for each period may be expressed in units, dollars, or percentages of actual to some standard.

## SOURCES OF DATA

Sales forecasts are usually derived from a variety of sources. Despite the development of sophisticated statistical forecasting techniques, it is probable that old-fashioned executive judgment is still the most widely used technique. The experienced manager, who is thoroughly familiar with his customers, products and sales representatives, and who has developed a "feel" for the market, can probably come up with as accurate a forecast as any other method. However, the key element in relying upon executive judgment is consistency. One consumer product company which introduced a new product line twice a year compiled records of the forecasts of its sales managers. In reviewing these records over several seasons, it was discovered that the most successful field manager was consistently wrong in his forecasts. In other words, those new products for which he displayed enthusiasm invariably failed in the market, whereas the products on which he turned thumbs down became winners. The company decided to base its new product projections on the opposite of this manager's forecasts and the results were most successful.

A second commonly found forecasting technique is that of extrapolation. It is assumed that there is a certain momentum in business activity, and, if past history indicates a certain rate of change (either up or down), it may be projected that the rate of change will continue through the forecast period. The weakness of this assumption is that it does not take into account sudden changes in the trend line. The automobile industry, for example, was completely unprepared when the oil shortages and price increases during the 1970s caused consumer preferences to shift from large, gas-guzzling models to fuel-efficient compact cars.

The life-cycle theory is a widely accepted technique for product forecasting. According to this theory, every product goes through the stages of gestation, youth, maturation and obsolescence. The volume projection for each product thus depends on where it happens to lie along the life cycle at the time of the forecast. This method is effective for the mid-range of products, but does not accommodate the extremes of strong winners or early losers.

Test marketing in limited areas is one technique for coping with these extreme situations. The firm selects a small number of representative markets into which to introduce its new products. If the results are negative, the product can be withdrawn from the market with a minimum loss to the company. If the new product is accepted, the rate of sale in the test market areas provides a clue as to the degree of success and permits the calculation of a realistic forecast on a national level. The value of test marketing was illustrated recently when Anheuser-Busch attempted to introduce a new soft drink aimed at the teenage market. In order to differentiate its product, it mixed a small amount of alcohol into the drink. When the product was test marketed in Virginia, the parents of the teenagers raised strong protests upon learning of the presence of alcohol in the drink. The product was then withdrawn from the market.

Performance targets are frequently derived from econometric data or demographic statistics. Many firms have discovered that their volume has varied in the past proportionately to a specific economic indicator. If, for example, the fortunes of a firm have correlated closely to the gross national product, then a forecast of a 10% increase in the GNP for the following year would probably induce the firm to project a similar 10% increase for its own volume. Similarly, a company whose volume has in the past varied fairly consistently with the change in population or change in the birth rate might forecast its own future performance in terms of population or birth rate projections.

In the consumer product or service field, the use of a *buying power index* has become an important standard of measurement of the geographic distribution of sales. The underlying assumption of this approach is that consumers in each marketing area of the country should purchase the company's products or services in the same proportion as the purchasing power of that area bears to the rest of the country. Thus if a certain marketing area accounts for 2% of the purchasing power of the total American economy, a firm should expect to achieve 2% of its volume in that area. If the information system reveals that only one percent of the company's sales is obtained from that area, the manager is alerted to the fact that there is a marketing management problem in that area and should arrange to take corrective steps. If, on the other hand, the reporting system indicates that 3% of the firm's volume comes from that marketing area, the manager, knowing that the total volume will always add to 100%, recognizes that some other area is being undersold, thus resulting in a higher percentage in this marketing area. He will then take steps to identify and strengthen the selling effort in the undersold area.

The sophisticated American market offers products and services at various price levels. Consumers at various income levels will patronize sellers of products and services appropriate to their income level. Thus a different buying power index has been developed for luxury products and services as compared to popular priced products and services. The potential purchaser of a Cadillac is in all likelihood not a potential purchaser of a Chevrolet. Thus it is important that the marketing manager who wishes to avail himself of the buying power index technique identify the proper index for his firm's products or services. The geographic distribution of higher-income consumers is significantly different from that of lower-income and middle-income consumers.

Standards of sales performance are of course essential but not sufficient for a management information system. Just as the shipment of finished products may be considered the output of the organizational system, purchases of raw materials, utilization of manpower, the production process, and support services are considered as the input and transformation elements of the system. These elements are so important that separate chapters are devoted to the manufacturing, human resource and financial information systems. They are mentioned here however because profitability reporting, which is of vital interest to the sales-marketing manager, draws not only upon sales performance, but also includes all items of expense. The information system can produce gross profit reports by product, customer, sales representative and sales region.

The sales-marketing manager is directly responsible for certain expense items and standards for these items should be incorporated in the information system. Some of these standards may be derived from industry practice. Terms of sale, for example, are usually quite similar across an entire industry. The percentage of sales allocated to advertising expenses is also often determined by industry practice. Standards for other items of expense on the other hand may be formulated by the firm's history and traditions. This may hold true in the areas of permissible returns and allowances and various sales expenses.

With the increasing popularity of matrix or project management, a final approach may be mentioned for the establishment of standards. Managements which operate with planned programs will allocate a certain sum for investment in the program. A certain return is required from the investment. In order to achieve the desired return, a certain volume is required and the volume may be obtained by certain preplanned costs.

Thus, the level of investment in a planned program will automatically predetermine volume and cost standards which are entered into the information system.

## INFORMATION SYSTEM OUTPUTS

Information may be presented at various levels of detail and a key to a successful information system is the provision of information to a manager at the level appropriate to his decisionmaking responsibility. To illustrate this principle, let us look at several of the output reports used by a divisional marketing manager of Cannon Mills Inc. This is one of the leading firms in the manufacture and distribution of towels, sheets and bedspreads in the United States. Cannon Mills has segmented its outlets into some thirty-five trade classes, each headed by a divisional manager. Our manager is responsible for Trade Class 43, the Minimum Mark-Up Division.

The top management of Cannon Mills is responsible for overall company profits and receives summary reports about the performance of each of the 35 trade classes. Below the divisional level, each territorial sales manager receives detailed reports about the performance of each sales representative in his territory. The information system provides reports to the divisional manager dealing with the performance of the territorial sales managers, sales representatives, customers and products in his division.

As indicated above, the starting point for the information system is to translate the goals of the division into an operational marketing plan. Figure 4–1 presents the 1981 Marketing Plan for the sheets product line. Using one of the forecasting methods described above, a monthly and year-to-date quota has been established for each category of sheets. In addition, based on projected monthly shipments, the monthly backlog has been forecast by subtracting the projected shipments from the expected bookings. Thus, on a one-page report each month our divisional manager may obtain a cumulative view of his division's performance in this major product category throughout the year. The year-to-date position of the sheet category and the backlog tells the manager exactly how far ahead or behind his division is at the end of each month. In order to take action on the result indicated by this summary statistic, our manager must now have access to more detailed information which permits him to analyze the summary position figure.

A major factor affecting the bookings and backlog position is customer performance. Several outputs are provided to assist our divisional manager in this area. On a daily basis, the manager receives a listing of the value of each order from each customer processed by the mill. Figure 4–2 presents the last page of the "Sheet Sales Summary" report for December 3, 1981. It may be seen that the division has a 1981 quota of $12,716,000 and has booked $12,515,461 as of December 3, 1981. The quota for the period is $1,246,000, but as a result of order cancellations, the actual booked-to-date for the period is a negative $65,818. The manager can review the source of orders and order cancellations and by referring also to the following reports is in a position to take corrective action.

Another analysis by customer is presented in Figure 4–3. Here we have a list of unshipped orders sold ahead by customer. Since the marketing plan calls for a planned backlog, it is vital that advance orders be written. This report shows that as of October 29, 1981, advance orders for November exceeded the quota by some $875,000. On the other hand, advance orders for December were behind by almost the same amount. The report also shows shippable orders amounting to almost $464,000 which had not yet been shipped. This situation calls for action by our manager in the area of sales-production coordination which is dealt with below.

Our illustrations thus far have dealt with the sale of the sheet product line to Cannon's customers. Our manager however is also responsible for the sale of towels to the customers in his division. In Figure 4–4, we have a report of both towels and sheet orders booked by customers. The manager sees not only the dollar volume of orders by product category by customer, but also the percentage of each category within both towels and sheets. The sales representative for each customer is listed so that the division manager knows whom to address for information or action.

While customer orders are the lifeblood of every business and deservedly merit the time and attention of the sales-marketing manger, the successful businessman is well aware that the order transaction is not complete until the ordered items have been shipped and invoiced. Thus an effective information system also provides billings summaries to our manager for follow-up and control.

On a summary basis, Figure 4–5 provides overall year-to-date sales figures by

PRODUCT: SHEETS  MARKETING PLAN 1981  TRADE CLASS: 43 (MINIMUM MARK-UP DIV.)

| | BEGIN. BACKLOG | JAN. | FEB. | MAR. | APR. | MAY | JUNE | JULY | AUG. | SEPT. | OCT. | NOV. | DEC. |
|---|---|---|---|---|---|---|---|---|---|---|---|---|---|
| Monthly Quota - Bookings | | 1,564 | 1,526 | 2,480 | 483 | 534 | 649 | 343 | 547 | 1,500 | 992 | 852 | 1,246 |
| Actual Monthly Bookings | | 669 | | | | | | | | | | | |
| Bookings Quota (YTD) | | 1,564 | 3,090 | 5,570 | 6,053 | 6,587 | 7,236 | 7,579 | 8,126 | 9,626 | 10,618 | 11,470 | 12,716 |
| Actual Bookings (YTD) | | 669 | | | | | | | | | | | |
| Position (YTD) | | (895) | | | | | | | | | | | |
| Monthly Quota - Billings | | 725 | 1,175 | 1,463 | 888 | 1,113 | 1,750 | 1,100 | 375 | 688 | 713 | 1,225 | 1,285 |
| Actual Monthly Billings | | 594 | | | | | | | | | | | |
| Billings Quota (YTD) | | 725 | 1,900 | 3,363 | 4,251 | 5,364 | 7,114 | 8,214 | 8,589 | 9,277 | 9,990 | 11,215 | 12,500 |
| Actual Billings (YTD) | | 594 | | | | | | | | | | | |
| Position (YTD) | | (131) | | | | | | | | | | | |
| Planned Backlog (YTD) | | 1,843 | 2,194 | 3,211 | 2,806 | 2,227 | 1,126 | 369 | 541 | 1,353 | 1,632 | 1,259 | 1,220 |
| Actual Backlog (YTD) | 1004 | 1,054 | | | | | | | | | | | |
| Position (YTD) | | (789) | | | | | | | | | | | |

Figure 4–1. Reprinted by permission. Richard A. Grimley, Vice President, Consumer Product Sales, Cannon Mills Co.

```
1                         SHEET        SALES  SUMMARY        12-03-81

     MILL     DEPT - GRADE -CUSTOMER    <- - - -  VALUE OF ORDERS - - - ->
     ORDER                              TODAY        P-T-D        Y-T-D


              MINIMUM MARK-UP
     334082   CALDOR INC                    88-
     334098   CALDOR INC                  1063-
     334102   CALDOR INC                   323
     334123   CALDOR INC                   102
     334127   CALDOR INC                   102
     334131   CALDOR INC                    51
     334133   CALDOR INC                   102
     334136   CALDOR INC                   102
     334142   CALDOR INC                   102
     309976   FAMILY DOLLAR STRS INC      9559-
     297394   HART STORES INC             6706-
     297395   HART STORES INC            27684-
     324802   HOWARD BROS DISCOUNT ST    18408-
     329876   JEFFERSON/WARD             30539-
     329887   JEFFERSON/WARD             25107-
     328987   MONTGOMERY RUG & SHADE       149-
     330870   NEW ENGLAND TRADING COR    10124-
     330871   NEW ENGLAND TRADING COR     7228-
     330872   NEW ENGLAND TRADING COR     7364-
     310992   THRIFTY DRUG STORES INC    17480
                                        125655-        65818-    12515461

              MINIMUM MARK-UP QUOTA                    1246000    12716000


              FOOD
     335190   MEYER FRED INC              5898          4.15
                                          5898          5895       222405


              FOOD QUOTA


              DRUG
                                                                  110383


              DRUG QUOTA                                1000       717000
```

Figure 4-2. Reprinted by permission. Richard A. Grimley, Vice President, Consumer Product Sales, Cannon Mills Co.

major product category and by division. Thus it may be seen that as of April 30, 1981, sales of towels in the Minimum Mark-Up Division were 11.24% ahead of the previous year, but sheet sales in the same division were 38.83% behind the same period of the previous year. To obtain the details behind this performance, the manager has access to the monthly "Billings" report, a sample of which is illustrated in Figure 4-6. This report presents the same information as the previous output, but provides detail by customer. The department code identifies the product category, e.g., Code 4 represents towels; and Code 14, sheets. The report highlights the customers who have performed better or worse than the previous year, and thus furnishes the knowledge needed by our manager to plan corrective marketing action.

REPORT 1676

REPORT 1676    PERIOD ENDED 10-29-81
SHEET UNSHIPPED ORDERS SOLD AHEAD
BY TRADE CLASS AND GRADE
MR.R.A.GRIMLEY                     TC 43
C.M.INC.    NEW YORK OFFICE                C

UNSHIPPED ORDERS SOLD AHEAD BY TRADE CLASS AND GRADE

SHEETS SOLD AHEAD BY TRADE CLASS AND GRADE 10/29/81

MINIMUM MARKUP DIV. – 43

| | PAST DUE | NOVEMBER | DECEMBER | JANUARY | FEBRUARY | MARCH | AFTER | TOTAL |
|---|---|---|---|---|---|---|---|---|
| ALBRECHT FRED W GROCERY | $11,521 | $10,855 | | | | | | $22,376 |
| BONANZA STORES INC | $7,108 | | $2,941 | | | | | $10,049 |
| CENTURY 21 INC | $5,855 | | | | | | | $5,855 |
| CLOVER DIV STRAWBRIDGE | | $15,345 | | | | | | $15,345 |
| COOK UNITED INC MAPLE | $64,868 | $3,610 | $1,130 | | | | | $69,608 |
| D & K STORES INC | | $109,289 | | | | | | $109,289 |
| DAYTON-HUDSON FRIDLEY | | $102,933 | | | | | | $102,933 |
| DEE & DEE OF 14TH STREE | | | $97,041 | | | | | $97,041 |
| DUCKWALL STORES INC | | $3,923 | $2,658 | | | | | $6,581 |
| FACTORY WHOLESALES INC | $933 | | $223 | | | | | $1,156 |
| FAMILEY DOLLAR STRS INC | $21,642 | $195,313 | | | | | | $216,955 |
| FEDCO INC | | $3,134 | | | | | | $3,134 |
| FISHERS BIG WHEEL INC | | $44,132 | | | | | | $44,132 |
| FLAUMS JERSEY CORP | | $16,731 | | | | | | $16,731 |
| GOLD CIRCLE DIV GEDERAT | $16,146 | $16,919 | | | | | | $33,065 |
| GRAHAM JOHN WHLSE INC | $16,350 | $10,657 | | | | | | $27,006 |
| GRAND CENTRAL INC | | $247,910 | | | | | | $247,910 |
| HARRIS DAVID SONS CO IN | $5,448 | | | | | | | $5,448 |
| HART STORES INC | $35,965 | $24,469 | | | | | | $60,434 |
| HECKS INC TRI-STATE DIS | | | $109 | | | | | $109 |
| HIGHWAY TEXTILE | $1,233 | $4,426 | $2,022 | | | | | $7,681 |
| HOWARD BROS DISCOUNT ST | $7,944 | $44,492 | $72,764 | | | | | $125,200 |
| JAMESWAY CORP | $8,990 | $201,260 | $1,263 | | | | | $211,514 |
| KDT INDUSTRIES INC | $1,502 | $1,494 | $4,868 | | | | | $7,864 |
| KLITHS INC | | $2,111 | | | | | | $2,111 |
| KESSLER H & CO | $738 | | | | | | | $738 |
| KLINCK WHLSE DRUG CO IN | $864 | | | | | | | $864 |
| KUHNS-BIG K STORES CORP | | | $73,656 | | | | | $73,656 |
| MACKS STORES INC SANFOR | | $1,681 | $13,621 | | | | | $15,302 |
| MARBURN STORES INC | $834 | $7,771 | $7,203 | $5,580 | | | | $21,388 |
| MARCADE GROUP | $7,985 | $10,400 | | | | | | $18,385 |
| NEW ENGLAND TRADING COR | | $151,732 | | | | | | $151,732 |
| NEWTON BUYING CORP | $74,150 | | | | | | | $74,150 |
| PENN-DANIELS SUPPLY CO | $1,330 | $1,562 | | | | | | $2,892 |
| RAEMART STORES INC | | $17,158 | | | | | | $17,158 |
| RICHWAY ACCTS PAYABLE | | $8,155 | | | | | | $8,155 |
| ROSES STORES INC | | $68,569 | $56,871 | | | | | $125,440 |
| SALISBURY SALES CORP | | | $4,636 | | | | | $4,636 |
| SHOPRO STORES INC | | $2,034 | $1,456 | | | | | $3,490 |
| STERLING STRS CO INC | $92,679 | | | $12,885 | | | | $105,564 |
| THRIFTY BROS STORES INC | $10,674 | $743,663 | | | | | | $754,337 |
| TOWELS INC TOWEL CITY D | $9,570 | | | | | | | $9,570 |
| TWIN FAIR INC | $29,646 | | | | | | | $29,646 |
| VAL CORP | | $279 | $2,070 | | | | | $2,348 |
| VORNADO INC GARFIELD | $26,856 | $29,334 | | | | | | $56,190 |
| WAL-MART STORES INC | $3,116 | | | | | | | $3,116 |
| TOTAL TRADE CLASS | $463,947 | $2,101,341 | $344,532 | $18,465 | | | | $2,928,285 |
| BILLING QUOTA | | $1,225,000 | $1,285,000 | ,000 | ,000 | ,000 | ,000 | $2,510,000 |
| TOTAL DIVISION | $463,947 | $2,101,341 | $344,532 | $18,465 | | | | $2,928,285 |
| DIV. QUOTA 43 | | $1,225,000 | $1,285,000 | ,000 | ,000 | ,000 | ,000 | $2,510,000 |

Figure 4–3. Reprinted by permission. Richard A. Grimley, Vice President, Consumer Product Sales, Cannon Mills, Co.

## CANNON MILLS INC.

REPORT NO. 242          [X] ORDERS BOOKED          [ ] BILLINGS          PAGE 210   DATE SEPTEMBER 3, 1981

| CUSTOMER CODE | SUFFIX | SALES-MAN | MILL | STATE / SALESMAN — CITY / CUSTOMER | DEPT | TRADE CLASS | YARN TYPE | AMOUNT CURRENT MONTH | | AMOUNT YEAR TO-DATE | |
|---|---|---|---|---|---|---|---|---|---|---|---|
| | | | | MINIMUM MARKUP DIV. MINIMUM MARK-UP | 43 | | | PRODUCT % BY BRAND | | | |
| 105 | | 788 | | A B C DISTRIBUTING CORP | 43 | | | | | | |
| | | | | CANNON TOWELS | | | | 24 | 30% | 1 | 705 |
| | | | | MONTICELLO TOWELS | | | | 75 | 70% | 5 | 311 |
| | | | | * TOTAL TOWELS * | | | | | | 7 | 016 * |
| | | | | NO-IRON MUSLIN | | | | 88 | 00% | 8 | 162 |
| | | | | N-I MUSLIN-PROM | | | | 12 | 00% | 1 | 113 |
| | | | | * TOTAL SHEETS * | | | | | | 9 | 275 * |
| 126 | | 560 | | AARONSON BROS STRS CORP | 43 | | | | | | |
| | | | | IRREGS. & CLOSEOUTS | | | | 100 | % | 16 | 344 |
| | | | | * TOTAL TOWELS * | | | | | | 16 | 344 * |
| | | | | NO-IRON MUSLIN | | | | 100 | % | 39 | 499 |
| | | | | * TOTAL SHEETS * | | | | | | 39 | 499 * |
| 923 | | 624 | | ALBRECHT FRED W GROCERY | 43 | | | | | | |
| | | | | CANNON TOWELS | | | | 40 | 64% | 20 | 830 |
| | | | | MONTICELLO TOWELS | | | | 42 | 16% | 21 | 609 |
| | | | | PROMOTIONAL TOWELS | | | | 17 | 21% | 8 | 820 |
| | | | | * TOTAL TOWELS * | | | | | | 51 | 259 * |
| | | | | NO-IRON MUSLIN | | | | 93 | 96% | 53 | 485 |
| | | | | NO-IRON PERCALE | | | | 2 | 72% | 1 | 546 |
| | | | | N-I PERCALE-PROM | | | | 3 | 33% | 1 | 895 |
| | | | | * TOTAL SHEETS * | | | | | | 56 | 926 * |
| 1299 | | 138 | | ALMOS HADDONFIELD INC | 43 | | | | | | |
| | | | | CANNON TOWELS | | | | 100 | % | 3 | 771 |
| | | | | * TOTAL TOWELS * | | | | | | 3 | 771 * |
| 2120 | | 549 | | ANN & HOPE INC | 43 | | | | | | |
| | | | | CANNON TOWELS | | | | 5 | 85% | 6 | 763 |
| | | | | MONTICELLO TOWELS | | | | 10 | 75% | 12 | 437 |
| | | | | PROMOTIONAL TOWELS | | | | 65 | 61% | 75 | 912 |
| | | | | IRREGS. & CLOSEOUTS | | | | 17 | 79% | 20 | 585 |
| | | | | * TOTAL TOWELS * | | | | | | 115 | 697 * |
| | | | | N-I MUSLIN-PROM | | | | 100 | % | 3 | 876 |
| | | | | * TOTAL SHEETS * | | | | | | 3 | 876 * |
| 2120 | 3 | 721 | | ANN & HOPE INC | 43 | | | | | | |
| | | | | KITCHEN TOWELS | | | | 100 | % | 3 | 330 |
| | | | | * TOTAL TOWELS * | | | | | | 3 | 330 * |
| 3323 | | 076 | | AYR-WAY STORES INC | 43 | | | | | | |
| | | | | CANNON TOWELS | | | | 6 | 18% | 16 | 877 |
| | | | | KITCHEN TOWELS | | | | 4 | 95% | 13 | 522 |
| | | | | MONTICELLO TOWELS | | | | 88 | 87% | 242 | 760 |

Figure 4-4. Reprinted by permission. Richard A. Grimley, Vice President, Consumer Product Sales, Cannon Mills Co.

Figure 4-7 presents the "Margin Index Billings Summary." This is a weekly report of orders shipped by sheet product category within customer within region within trade class 43. The annual dollar target for each customer is listed. The dollar goal for the current period is three percent of the annual quota and the actual dollars shipped for the current period is shown next to the goal. The report is as of August 31, 1981 so that the year-to-date dollar goal represents two thirds of the annual goal. Here again, the actual dollars shipped through August 31, 1981 are presented next to the dollar goal and the percentage of actual goal dollars is calculated. For example, actual shipments to Economy Dry Goods Co. Inc. are only 42% of the dollar goal, while billings to Twin Fair Inc. are 211% of the dollar goal. The report also contains information on the profitability of sales in each product category. This is represented by comparing an index goal to an index actual. It may be seen, for example, that year-to-date sales of no-iron comfort sheets to Century 21 Inc. gen-

PREV YTD AND CURRENT YTD COMPARED  
MR.R.A.GRIMLEY    SELECTED TC  
C.M.INC.   NEW YORK OFFICE    A

CANNON MILLS INC  
KANNAPOLIS, NC.

| | SALES 04 PERIODS 1981 | SALES 04 PERIODS 1980 | COMPARISON INCREASE (DECREASE) | PERCENTAGE % |
|---|---|---|---|---|
| MINIMUM MARK-UP DIV. TOWELS | $9,010,382 | $8,100,213 | $910,169 | 11.24% |
| FOOD & DRUG DIV TOWELS | | | | |
|   FOOD | $410,922 | $406,723 | $4,199 | 1.03% |
|   DRUG | 264,771 | 599,772 | ( 335,001) | (55.85%) |
|   TOTAL | $675,693 | $1,006,495 | ($330,802) | (32.87%) |
| TOWEL TOTAL MINIMUM MARK-UP AND FOOD & DRUG DIVS. | $9,686,075 | $9,106,708 | $579,367 | 6.36% |
| MINIMUM MARK-UP DIV. SHEETS | $3,639,691 | $5,949,953 | ($2,310,262) | (38.83%) |
| FOOD & DRUG DIV SHEETS | | | | |
|   FOOD | $72,342 | $83,927 | ($11,585) | (13.80%) |
|   DRUG | | 64,732 | ( 64,732) | (100.00%) |
|   TOTAL | $72,342 | $148,659 | ($76,317) | (51.34%) |
| SHEET TOTAL MINIMUM MARK-UP AND FOOD & DRUG DIVS. | $3,712,033 | $6,098,612 | ($2,383,579) | (39.13%) |

Figure 4-5. Reprinted by permission. Richard A. Grimley, Vice President, Consumer Product Sales, Cannon Mills Co.

## CANNON MILLS, INC.

REPORT NO. 754    ☐ ORDERS BOOKED    ☒ BILLINGS    DATE DECEMBER 31, 1972

| SALES-MAN | M L L | STATE CITY CUSTOMER | D E P T | TRADE CLASS | AMOUNT CURRENT YEAR TO-DATE | AMOUNT PREVIOUS YEAR TO-DATE | INCREASE OR DECREASE (−) |
|---|---|---|---|---|---|---|---|
| | | MINIMUM MARK-UP | | 43 | | | |
| | | A B C DISTRIBUTING CORP | | 43 | 4 702 | 1 451 | 3 251 |
| | | | 4 | 43 | 17 184 | 22 252 | 5 068− |
| | | | 14 | 43 | 32 756 | 30 355 | 2 401 |
| | | | 21 | 43 | 17 | | 17 |
| | | | | | 54 659 * | 54 058 * | 601 * |
| | | ALFREDS DEPT STR INC | 14 | 43 | 2 137 | 2 104 | 33 |
| | | | | | 2 137 * | 2 104 * | 33 * |
| | | ALLENS OF HASTINGS INC | 4 | 43 | 1 495 | 2 282 | 787− |
| | | | 14 | 43 | 3 705 | 3 611 | 94 |
| | | | | | 5 200 * | 5 893 * | 693−* |
| | | ALMOS HADDONFIELD INC | 14 | 43 | 9 769 | 19 745 | 9 976− |
| | | | 21 | 43 | 745 | 2 496 | 1 751− |
| | | | | | 10 514 * | 22 241 * | 11 727−* |
| | | ALMART − J B HUNTER | 4 | 43 | 3 147 | | 3 147− |
| | | | 30 | 43 | 3 471 | | 3 471 |
| | | | | | 3 471 * | 3 147 * | 324 * |
| | | ANN & HOPE FACTORY OUTL | 4 | 43 | 121 860 | 149 236 | 27 376− |
| | | | 14 | 43 | 46 798 | 137 522 | 90 724− |
| | | | 21 | 43 | 2 545 | 6 423 | 3 878− |
| | | | 30 | 43 | 12 129 | 6 675 | 5 454 |
| | | | | | 183 332 * | 229 856 * | 116 524−* |
| | | AYR-WAY DIV ASSOCIATED | 4 | 43 | 203 754 | 159 258 | 44 496 |
| | | | 14 | 43 | 552 867 | 532 889 | 19 978 |
| | | | 21 | 43 | 511 | 11 544 | 11 033− |
| | | | 30 | 43 | 4 397 | 2 267 | 2 130 |
| | | | | | 761 529 * | 705 958 * | 55 571 * |
| | | BARAM JOSEPH CO | 4 | 43 | | 3 531 | 3 531− |
| | | | 14 | 43 | | 2 088 | 2 088− |
| | | | | | | 5 619 * | 5 619−* |
| | | BARGAIN TOWN U S A INC | 4 | 43 | 13 301 | 30 261 | 16 960− |
| | | | 14 | 43 | 17 845 | 11 177 | 6 668 |
| | | | 21 | 43 | 5 005 | 720 | 4 285 |
| | | | 30 | 43 | 4 373 | 2 420 | 1 953 |
| | | | | | 40 524 * | 44 578 * | 4 054−* |
| | | MARKERS FRANKLIN STRS C | 4 | 43 | 52 872 | 26 929 | 25 943 |
| | | | 14 | 43 | 138 313 | 62 892 | 75 421 |
| | | | 21 | 43 | 16 566 | 24 293 | 7 727− |
| | | | 30 | 43 | 8 005 | 806 | 7 199 |
| | | | | | 215 756 * | 114 920 * | 100 836 * |
| | | BERKOWITZ BENJAMIN & SO | 4 | 43 | 15 929 | 17 101 | 1 172− |

Figure 4-6. Reprinted by permission. Richard A. Grimley, Vice President, Consumer Product Sales, Cannon Mills Co.

PRODUCT   TRCLS   REGION

SHEETS   43   EASTERN

PERIOD ENDING AUGUST

| Account / Product | <-- CURRENT PERIOD --> $ GOAL | $ ACTUAL | INDEX GOAL | INDEX ACTUAL | CURR YEAR $ GOAL | <-- YEAR TO DATE --> $ GOAL | $ ACTUAL | $ IDX | INDEX GOAL | INDEX ACTUAL |
|---|---|---|---|---|---|---|---|---|---|---|
| N-I PERCALE-PRO | 0 | 0 | 101.0 | .0 | | | 135,255 | | 101.0 | 91.2 |
| N-I MUSLIN-PROM | 0 | 0 | 101.0 | .0 | | | 357,623 | | 101.0 | 91.3 |
| IRREGS. & CLOSE | 0 | 0 | 101.0 | .0 | | | 109- | | 101.0 | 107.4 |
| NO-IRON MUSLIN | 0 | 0 | 101.0 | .0 | | | 15,030 | | 101.0 | 98.2 |
| KINGS DEPT STRS NEWTON   -> | 24,225 | 0 | 101.0 | .0 | 807,500 | 554,754 | 502,799 | 91 | 101.0 | 91.3 |
| NO-IRON PERCALE | 0 | 0 | 101.0 | .0 | | | 17- | | 101.0 | 93.6 |
| NO-IRON MUSLIN | 7,500 | 180,003 | 101.0 | 93.7 | 250,000 | 171,750 | 179,979 | | 101.0 | 93.6 |
| NEW ENGLAND TRADING CO   --> | 7,500 | 180,003 | 101.0 | 93.7 | 250,000 | 171,750 | 179,962 | 105 | 101.0 | 93.6 |
| D C BEHRENS   --> | 31,725 | 180,003 | 101.0 | 93.7 | 1,057,500 | 726,504 | 692,761 | 94 | 101.0 | 92.2 |
| N-I PERCALE-PRO | 0 | 0 | 101.0 | .0 | | | 5,100 | | 101.0 | 97.2 |
| NO-IRON COMFORT | 0 | 0 | 101.0 | .0 | | | 11,770 | | 101.0 | 107.0 |
| IRREGS. & CLOSE | 0 | 3,095 | 101.0 | 93.8 | | | 6,805 | · | 101.0 | 87.3 |
| NO-IRON PERCALE | 0 | 29,983 | 101.0 | 100.1 | | | 157 | | 101.0 | 98.1 |
| CENTURY 21 INC   -> | 1,050 | 33,978 | 100.5 | 99.5 | 35,000 | 24,045 | 23,832 | 99 | 101.0 | 98.1 |
| NO-IRON MUSLIN | 0 | 0 | 101.0 | .0 | | | 5,158 | | 101.0 | 93.8 |
| ECONOMY DRY GOODS CO I   -> | 540 | 0 | 101.0 | .0 | 18,000 | 12,366 | 5,158 | 42 | 101.0 | 93.8 |
| N-I PERCALE-PRO | 0 | 0 | 101.0 | .0 | | | 55,327 | | 101.0 | 94.3 |
| NO-IRON COMFORT | 0 | 0 | 101.0 | .0 | | | 30- | | 101.0 | 117.7 |
| N-I MUSLIN-PROM | 0 | 0 | 101.0 | .0 | | | 191,722 | | 101.0 | 93.7 |
| IRREGS. & CLOSE | 0 | 0 | 101.0 | .0 | | | 3,003 | | 101.0 | 94.1 |
| NO-IRON MUSLIN | 0 | 0 | 101.0 | .0 | | | 388,283 | | 101.0 | 99.2 |
| JAMESWAY CORP   -> | 30,600 | 0 | 101.0 | .0 | 1,020,000 | 700,740 | 638,205 | 91 | 101.0 | 96.7 |
| N-I MUSLIN-PROM | 0 | 0 | 101.0 | .0 | | | 24,608 | | 101.0 | 90.1 |
| IRREGS. & CLOSE | 0 | 0 | 101.0 | .0 | | | 319- | | 101.0 | .0 |
| NO-IRON MUSLIN | 0 | 0 | 101.0 | .0 | | | 48,280 | | 101.0 | 100.8 |
| TWIN FAIR INC   -> | 1,500 | 0 | 101.0 | .0 | 50,000 | 34,350 | 72,569 | 211 | 101.0 | 95.2 |
| N-I MUSLIN-PROM | 0 | 0 | 101.0 | .0 | | | 39,414 | | 101.0 | 101.3 |
| IRREGS. & CLOSE | 0 | 0 | 101.0 | .0 | | | 76,593 | | 101.0 | 98.6 |
| NO-IRON MUSLIN | 0 | 0 | 101.0 | .0 | | | 2,486 | | 101.0 | 107.1 |
| UNISHOPS INC   --> | 10,500 | 33,078 | 101.0 | 99.5 | 350,000 | 240,450 | 118,493 | 49 | 101.0 | 99.7 |
| J C BRAY   --> | 44,190 | 33,078 | 100.5 | 99.5 | 1,473,000 | 1,011,951 | 858,257 | 85 | 101.0 | 97.0 |
| N-I MUSLIN-PROM | 0 | 0 | 101.0 | .0 | | | 58,825 | | 101.0 | 96.0 |
| NO-IRON MUSLIN | 0 | 0 | 101.0 | .0 | | | 8,259 | | 101.0 | 92.5 |
| SCOA INDUSTIRES INC   --> | 1,350 | 13,286 | 101.0 | 95.6 | 45,000 | 30,915 | 67,084 | 217 | 101.0 | 95.3 |
| S B CALDER   --> | 1,350 | 13,286 | 101.0 | 95.6 | 45,000 | 30,915 | 67,094 | 217 | 101.0 | 95.3 |
| N-I MUSLIN-PROM | 0 | 0 | 101.0 | .0 | | | 4,245 | | 101.0 | 97.6 |

Figure 4-7. Reprinted by permission. Richard A. Grimley, Vice President, Consumer Product Sales, Cannon Mills Co.

erated an actual profit index of 107.0 as compared to a goal index of 101.0. Yet year-to-date sales of irregulars and closeouts to the same customer yielded an index of 87.8 as compared to a goal index of 101.0. By reviewing this report in conjunction with the daily "Sheet Sales Summary" previously described, our manager may pinpoint both the customers and the sheet product categories by customer where some immediate sales action is warranted.

In discussing the unshipped order report above, it was mentioned that the sales-marketing manager also has the responsibility of coordinating his activities with the production department. In order to properly fulfill this responsibility, the manager is in need of product information relating the products ordered to their availability for shipment. Among the reports Cannon Mills furnishes our divisional marketing manager is the "Weekly Stock and Sales" report presented in Figure 4–8. It may be seen that the finished goods warehouse contains 495 dozens of Style 8390 in excess of all unshipped orders. However, upon close inspection, the manager finds that orders exceed available stock in four colors of this style.

To cope with this situation, the manager then studies the report illustrated in Figure 4–9. Here he will find that while there are no unallocated orders on Style 8390, as he discovered from the previous report, the plant is actually planning to produce 119 dozen this week. He is thus in a position to contact the production manager to confirm whether the four oversold colors will be included in this week's production. He also learns from this report that the plant is not scheduled to produce any units of Style 8630 to fill the unallocated orders of 92 dozen, but will continue to produce Style 8890 to cover the 12,710 dozen unallocated orders of this style. With this knowledge, the manager can attempt to persuade his customers to accept an available substitute for Style 8630 and can advise his customers for Style 8890 when they can expect their orders to be shipped.

## EVALUATION OF THE SALES-MARKETING INFORMATION SYSTEM

The reports used by the divisional manager at Cannon Mills, Inc. illustrate the basic categories of information needed by all sales-marketing managers in order to perform their functions properly. The diversity of organizational requirements in our complex ecomony often calls for many other kinds of information outputs beyond the basic reports described above. For example, some firms may find their profitability threatened by an excessive volume of returns of merchandise from their customers. In these circumstances, an analysis of returns is called for. Why are customers returning goods in such quantities? Are certain sales representatives overstocking their customers' shelves in order to maximize their sales commissions? A breakdown of returns by sales representatives may confirm the validity of this suspicion. Are certain classes of customers more prone to return merchandise than other classes? The answer may be found in an analysis of returns by customer classification. A report of returns by product may reveal that a small number of product items are responsible for a high percentage of returns. The assignment of a reason for each return shipment and a subsequent summary report may perhaps reveal an unacceptable level of quality defects in certain products, the prevalence of duplicate shipments or the shipment of wrong merchandise. Thus the "Returns Analysis"

FORM. T-136 REV.

| = PUT UP CODES | |
|---|---|
| 1 - SPECIAL SIZE | 5 - SPECIAL PUT UP |
| 2 - BERMUDA (RUN OF LOOM) | |

## CANNON MILLS CO.

**REPORT 1701**  
WEEKLY TOWEL STOCK & SALES REPORT

PAGE 67 1

| UNIT CODE | |
|---|---|
| 1 - DOZENS | 3 - SINGLE UNITS |
| 2 - YARDS | 6 - POUNDS |

DATE 11/26/81    REGULAR

| STYLE # | U/N/T | COLOR | UNSPECIFIED | PAST DUE | NOV | DEC | JAN | AFTER | PACKED ON ORDER | PACKED IN SETS & ASS'TS | IN BINS | DOZENS IN CASES | SALES OR STOCK POSITION | SALES RATIO |
|---|---|---|---|---|---|---|---|---|---|---|---|---|---|---|
| 8590 | 1 | WH1 | | 2 | 86 | 443 | 24 | | 97 | 8 | 285 | 2500 | 2727 | 467 |
| | 1 | Y1 | | 3 | 138 | 380 | 1 | | 492 | | 215 | 750 | 943 | 2650 |
| | 1 | Y8 | | | | | | | | | 170 | 125 | 295 | |
| | 1 | BR7 | | | | | | | | | 108 | 375** | | 10 |
| | 1 | B9 | | | 2 | 48 | | | 13 | | 289 | 375** | | 24 |
| | 1 | L1 | | | 23 | | | | 17 | | 300 | 625** | | 4 |
| | 1 | RD10 | 24245 | 96 / 722 | 2055 | 3251 | 55 | | 4447 | 36 | 4778 | 14625 | 16244 | 17526 |
| 8390 | U | 1 AS | 369 | | | 269 | 100 | | | | | | | |
| | 1 | BLK1 | | | | | | | | | 7 | | 7 | 28 |
| | 1 | BR12 | | 1 | 31 | 7 | | | 25 | | 7 | 8 | 5 | 31 |
| | 1 | BR18 | | 1 | 13 | 2 | | | 14 | | 7 | 16 | 21 | 37 |
| | 1 | BR21 | | 1 | 11 | | | | 12 | | 12 | | 12 | 3 |
| | 1 | BR24 | | 1 | 12 | 2 | | | 1 | | 11 | | 13 | |
| | 1 | BR4 | | 1 | 12 | 17 | | | 14 | 16 | 38 | | 38 | 12 |
| | 1 | B17 | | 1 | 1 | 7 | | | 2 | | 13 | | 11 | 16 |
| | 1 | B4 | | 1 | 11 | 7 | | | 11 | | 5 | | 6 | |
| | 1 | GR10 | | 1 | 10 | | | | 11 | | 5 | | 45 | 1 |
| | 1 | GR2 | | 1 | 1 | 1 | | | | | 19 | 40 | 41 | 2 |
| | 1 | GR24 | | | | | | | 2 | 16 | 8 | | 35 | 22 |
| | 1 | GR9 | | 1 | | | | | 1 | | 10 | | 10 | |
| | 1 | PH4 | | | | | | | | | 14 | | 14 | 3 |
| | 1 | P2 | | 1 | 11 | 8 | | | 12 | 16 | 13 | 16 | 29 | 10 |
| | 1 | RD4 | | | 10 | | | | 10 | 8 | 14 | 8 | 14 | 16 |
| | 1 | RD8 | | 1 | 11 | 3 | | | 12 | 16 | 13 | 16 | 29 | 2 |
| | 1 | WH1 | | | | | | | | | 10 | | 7 | |
| | 1 | Y1 | | 1 | 11 | 7 | | | 1 | 40 | 14 | 40 | 119 | 18 |
| | 1 | Y8 | | | | 2 | | | 1 | 112 | 18 | 112 | 40 | 7 |
| | 1 | BR7 | | | | | | | | 24 | 16 | 24 | 32 | |
| | 1 | B9 | | | | 2 | | | | 16 | 16 | | | |
| | 1 | L1 | | | | 2 | | | | | 15 | | | 1- |
| | 1 | RD10 | 369 | 15 | 148 | 67 | | | 133 | | 12 | 16** | 495 | 217 |
| | | | | | | | | | | | 300 | 344 | | |
| 8891 | U | 1 AS | REX | | PS# 8890 | | 15 | | | | | | | |
| | | 30 | | 48 | 19 | 15 | | | 24 | | 31 | 112 | 75 | 154 |
| | 1 | BR12 | | 2 | 9 | 25 | | | 12 | | 23 | 240 | 255 | 95 |
| | 1 | BR13 | | 2 | 7 | 11 | | | 15 | | 15 | 304 | 319 | 94 |
| | 1 | BR18 | | | 1 | 12 | | | | | 23 | | 32 | 1 |
| | 1 | BR21 | | | 25 | 30 | | | | 96 | 26 | 96 | 95 | |
| | 5 | BR24 | | | 1 | | | | | | 27 | | 26 | 126 |
| | 1 | BR4 | | 2 | 25 | 27 | | | 25 | 128 | 34 | 128 | 128 | 69 |
| | 1 | B11 | | 2 | 13 | 14 | | | 14 | 144 | 34 | 144 | 163 | 5 |
| | 1 | B4 | | | 1 | 1 | | | 2 | | | | | |

Figure 4-8. Reprinted by permission. Richard A. Grimley, Vice President, Consumer Product Sales, Cannon Mills Co.

FORM - T136 REV.    DATE 11/26/81

**CANNON MILLS CO.**
REPORT 1701    WEEKLY TOWEL STOCK & SALES REPORT

= PUT UP CODES
1 = SPECIAL SIZE
2 = BERMUDA (Run or Loom)
5 = SPECIAL PUT UP

UNIT CODE
1 - DOZENS  3 - SINGLE UNITS
2 - YARDS   6 - POUNDS

| STYLE # | UNIT | COLOR | REGULAR UNSPECIFIED | PAST DUE | NOV | DEC | JAN | AFTER | PACKED ON ORDER | PACKED IN SETS & ASS'TS | IN BINS | DOZENS IN CASES | SALES OR STOCK POSITION | SALES RATIO |
|---|---|---|---|---|---|---|---|---|---|---|---|---|---|---|
| 8891 | 1 | B9 | | | | | | | | | 30 | | 253 | 1 |
| | 1 | GR10 | | | 1 | 1 | | | | | 37 | | 372 | 2 |
| | 1 | GR2 | | 2 | 12 | 18 | | | 3 | | 12 | | 33 | 1 |
| | 1 | GR24 | | 2 | 7 | 12 | | | | | 26 | | 1 | 81 |
| | 1 | P9 | | | 1 | | | | 12 | | 28 | | 81 | 66 |
| | 1 | RD4 | | | | | | | | | | 64 | 123 | 5 |
| | 1 | WH1 | | 2 | 6 | 37 | | | 36 | | 36 | 96 | 47 | 73 |
| | 1 | Y1 | | | | 13 | | | 14 | | 24 | 48 | 205 | 67 |
| | 1 | BR7 | | 2 | 1 | | | | 2 | | 15 | 176 | | 1 |
| | 1 | L1 | | 2 | | | | | 3 | | 23 | 64 | | 2 |
| | 1 | RD10 | | 2 | | | | | | | | | | |
| | 1 | RD8 | 30 | 70 | 123 | 201 | | | 167 | | 479 | 2032 | 2157 | 937 ✓ |
| 8691 | 1 U | AS | 65 | | | 58 | 8 | | 12 | | 60 | 450 | 53 | 76 |
| | 1 | BR12 | | 1 | 7 | 13 | | | 9 | | 82 | | 527 | 76 |
| | 1 | BR13 | | 1 | 4 | 6 | | | 8 | | 65 | | 33 | 76 |
| | 1 | BR18 | | | 5 | 24 | | | 24 | | 100 | | 299 | 76 |
| | 1 | BR21 | | | 1 | | | | | | 115 | 200 | 100 | |
| | 1 | BR24 | | | 9 | 11 | | | 10 | | 90 | 100 | 115 | 98 |
| | 1 | BR4 | | 1 | 1 | 1 | | | 7 | | 44 | 400 | 480 | 54 |
| | 1 | B11 | | 1 | 1 | 7 | | | 1 | | 32 | 50 | 31 | 4 |
| | 1 | B4 | | | | | | | | | 30 | | 350 | |
| | 1 | GR10 | | | | 1 | | | 2 | | 85 | 200 | 350 | 1 |
| | 1 | GR2 | | | 6 | 8 | | | 1 | | 50 | 205 | 205 | 75 |
| | 1 | GR24 | | 1 | | 1 | | | 1 | | 90 | 150 | 386 | 54 |
| | 1 | RD4 | | | | | | | | | 150 | 150 | 239 | 4 |
| | 1 | WH1 | | 1 | 6 | 25 | | | 24 | | 100 | 100 | 200 | 49 |
| | 1 | BR7 | | 1 | 4 | 5 | | | 7 | | 100 | 50 | 153 | 76 |
| | 1 | Y1 | | 1 | | | | | 1 | | 84 | 100 | 195 | 1 |
| | 1 | RD10 | | 1 | | 2 | | | 2 | | 90 | 50 | | |
| | 1 | RD8 | 65 | 11 | 44 | 113 | 15 | | 111 | | 85 113 1795 | 200 2650 | 721 ✓ | 3766 |
| 8591 | 1 U | AS | 130 | | 10 | 115 | | | 48 | | 54 | 100 | 67 | 100 |
| | 1 | BR12 | | 2 | | 25 | | | | | 26 | | 25 | 76 |
| | 1 | BR13 | | 2 | 12 | | | | 3 | | 240 | | 229 | 76 |
| | 1 | BR18 | | | | 24 | | | | | 62 | | 38 | 88 |
| | 1 | BR21 | | | | | | | | | 236 | | 340 | |
| | 1 | BR24 | | 2 | 25 | 25 | | | 24 | | 240 | | 210 | 173 |
| | 1 | BR4 | | 2 | 1 | 2 | | | 2 | | 165 | 100 | 156 | 64 |
| | 1 | B11 | | | | 1 | | | | | 75 | | 73 | 5 |
| | 1 | B4 | | | | | | | | | 240 | | 340 | |
| | 1 | GR10 | | 2 | 18 | 12 | | | 3 | | 180 | | 180 | |
| | 1 | GR2 | | | | | | | | | 166 | | 166 | |
| | 1 | GR24 | | | | | | | | | 94 | | 64 | 128 |

PS# 8690
PS# 8590

* DISC. COLOR

PAGE    68

Figure 4-8. (Cont.)

| STYLE VALENCIA | REMARKS | TOTAL ORDERS LESS STOCK | ACTUAL WEEKLY PRODUCTION | SCHEDULED WEEKLY PRODUCTION | ORDERS AT MILL | (WEEKS SOLD) TOTAL INCLUDING UNSPEC. BALANCE |
|---|---|---|---|---|---|---|
| REPORT 1710  11/26/81 | | | | | PAGE NO. 43 | |
| 8882 | SEE 8828 | | | | | |
| 8682 | SEE 8628 | | | | | |
| 8582 | SEE 8528 | | | | | |
| 8584  DISC. | | 2 DOZ | 0 DOZ | 0 DOZ | | |
| ECTASY | | | | | | |
| 8890 | | 12,710 DOZ | 4,699 DOZ | 2,956 DOZ | | 2.0 |
| 8830 | | | | | | |
| 8881 | | 377 | | | | |
| 8891 | TOTAL | 13,087 | | | | |
| 8690 | | 0 DOZ | 0 DOZ | 0 DOZ | SAO | |
| 8630 | | 92 | | | | |
| 8681 | | | | | | |
| 8691 | | | | | | |
| | TOTAL | 92 | | | | |
| 8590 | | 5,540 DOZ | 3,723 DOZ | 4,097 DOZ | | .2 |
| 8530 | | | | | | |
| 8581 | | | | | | |
| 8591 | TOTAL | 5,540 | | | | |
| 8390 | | 0 DOZ | 151 DOZ | 119 DOZ | SAO | |
| 8381 | | | | | | |
| 8391 | | | | | | |
| | TOTAL | 0 | | | | |
| REX | | | | | | |
| 8891 | SEE 8890 | | | | | |
| 8691 | SEE 8690 | | | | | |
| 8591 | SEE 8590 | | | | | |
| 8391 | SEE 8390 | | | | | |
| ECTASY II | | | | | | |
| 8892 | | 0 DOZ | 105 DOZ | 105 DOZ | SAO | |
| 8692 | | 0 DOZ | 179 DOZ | 168 DOZ | SAO | |
| 8592 | | 0 DOZ | 255 DOZ | 204 DOZ | SAO | |

Figure 4–9. Reprinted by permission. Richard A. Grimley, Vice President, Consumer Product Sales, Cannon Mills Co.

reports will pinpoint the source or sources of the problem and point the way to corrective action.

In many consumer product industries, cooperative advertising is a traditional form of joint promotion effort between the manufacturer or distributor and the retailer. A typical arrangement may call for the manufacturer to contribute a fixed percentage of his sales to the retailer in the form of a cooperative advertising allowance. Since these allowances are charged to the expense budget of the sales-marketing manager, it is the latter's responsibility to administer the cooperative advertising program. To aid in this task, it would be most useful to provide the manager with a cooperative advertising allowance report for each customer showing the sales volume for the period, the amount of the advertising allowance based on the sales volume, the amount of advertising dollars charged back by the customer, and the amount of the underage or overage calculated by comparing the allowance accrued to the amount charged back. Such a report may confront the manager with two types of problems. There may be customers who have charged back more than they are allowed. This reduces the profitability of doing business with these customers. The manager may attempt to increase shipments to these customers in order to restore the proper advertising ratio, or failing this, the manager may persuade the customers to withdraw some of their chargebacks. The report may also reveal a group of customers who have not taken full advantage of their advertising allowance. If it is true that advertising stimulates sales, this lack of advertising means that the company is losing sales volume. In this situation, the manager will try to persuade these customers to use the allowances to which they are entitled.

These are but two examples of the specialized kinds of information that may be required by sales-marketing managers in specific companies. One test of the effectiveness of a sales-marketing information system is to analyze the unique types of information needed by managers in specific situations and to determine whether the outputs provided by the system satisfy these needs. On a more general level, each element of the sales-marketing information system can be matched to major tasks of the manager listed at the beginning of this section. For each goal listed there should be one or more information outputs designed to assist in its achievement. The absence of an output to match a goal indicates a gap in the information system. The existence of an output which does not correspond to one of the goals denotes an unnecessary information overload. The effectiveness of the sales-marketing information system is thus dependent upon a one-to-one match between the goals of the marketing function and the elements of the system.

# 5
# Manufacturing Information System

## DESCRIPTION OF FUNCTION

The characteristic distinguishing modern, advanced societies from today's under-developed countries and from all prior human civilizations is industrial technology. Few would deny that the Industrial Revolution marked a major turning point in determining the nature of human existence on this planet. Since the end of the Second World War, the miracle of our manufacturing prowess became so taken for granted that business schools started downgrading or even eliminating programs in production management as our brightest students opted for programs in accounting, law, finance, market research or advertising. Only in recent years, as we have found ourselves unable to compete successfully in international markets, has there been a resurgence of interest in our basic production processes and a realization that we must upgrade the efficiency of our industrial plant if we are to solve our economic programs.

There is a symbiotic relationship between technology and information. To help us better understand this connection, we will review briefly the various stages in the development of the Industrial Revolution. We will observe how information requirements increased and became more critical with each succeeding step of technological development.

Study of the lifestyle of all societies during the fourteenth and fifteenth centuries reveals relatively little difference from the way people lived in ancient Rome, ancient Greece or ancient China. The great majority (well over 90%) of the population lived on farms and spent their lives trying to grow enough food to survive. A few more hardy souls congregated in towns and became involved in various individual service activities to their fellow townsmen in order to make a living. Thus in a typical town one would find an innkeeper, a blacksmith, a barber, a few shopkeepers, a milliner, a cobbler and some other tradesmen. For the purpose of our review, we shall use the shoemaker as an example.

Depending on the size of the town one or a small handful of shoemakers could supply all the shoes required by the local inhabitants. Due to the absence of adequate interurban roads and the lack of security from brigands operating on the roads that did exist, it was not economically feasible to sell shoes beyond the limits of the shoemaker's town. By the fourteenth century, the shoemakers in the various towns of a region had learned that they could increase both their earnings and their social status by restricting entry into the shoemaker's trade. Thus they joined into craft guilds and limited new memberships to their immediate families. Each shoe-maker guarded the secret of his skill from all but his sons or nephews.

The defining characteristic of this craft guild period was the complete identifi-cation of the tradesman with his product. The shoemaker purchased the raw ma-terials, fabricated each pair of shoes in its entirety and personally sold his production. When he went to church services on Sunday, he could identify each pair of his shoes worn by his fellow townsmen. There is no doubt that the successful shoemaker possessed a large amount of information relevant to his trade, from the quality and price of various raw materials, to the best production methods and tools, to the needs of the townspeople for new shoes. However, since he performed all these functions himself and wished to keep the skills of his trade secret, he kept all this information in his head.

With the passage of time the towns grew in population and the craft guilds ex-panded through the training of sons and grandsons to accommodate the increased demand. By the fifteenth century it was not uncommon to find ten shoemaking guild members earning their livelihood in the same town. Despite the advantages of his economic and social position, each shoemaker discovered that his potential for continued growth in income was limited by the number of pairs of shoes he could fashion with his own hands. There did not seem to be a way of breaking through this limitation until some unknown administrative genius (who was also undoubt-edly imbued by the profit motive or greed depending on one's point of view) figured out that more shoes could be produced if the shoemaker did not have to spend so much time arranging financing for his raw material purchases, buying the materials and then transporting and selling the finished product. Our unknown entrepreneur's calculations showed that if one shoemaker devoted himself exclusively to what we would call today these staff functions, the other nine shoemakers in the town, spending their full working day producing shoes, would more than make up the lost production of the staff man and thus increase everyone's income.

We can only surmise what powers of persuasion were needed by our innovator to convince the other shoemakers to go along with the plan, but history records that the plan was indeed implemented. Almost immediately the staff man encoun-tered difficulty in performing his functions. Each shoemaker worked in his own home and the homes were spread all over town. There was not enough time for the staff man to deliver the raw materials to each shoemaker in the morning and pick up the finished shoes in the evening and then sell them. The solution was to build a cottage at the edge of town and have all the producing shoemakers come to this central workplace. Thus the raw materials could be delivered to and the finished shoes could be picked up at the same central location. This development gave the name *cottage period* to this early stage of industrial development.

Other problems became apparent with the implementation of the cottage system. When he was working at home, the shoemaker set his own starting and ending time, determined the length of his lunch period, and produced as many pairs of shoes as were necessary to achieve his income goal. Under the cottage system however there was an equal distribution of income among the producing shoemakers and the staff man. Fairness required that each shoemaker work as many hours and produce as many pairs of shoes as his fellow shoemakers. To achieve this equity, there had to be a consensus that all the shoemakers would start and finish work at the same time, take the same amount of time for lunch, and produce the same quantity of shoes each day. The staff man was the logical person to oversee and control adherence to this agreement and his acceptance of this responsibility was the start of what we call today the *managerial function*. To keep the system fair, adjustments in the distribution of income had to be made for loss of production due to illness or other absences. Thus an attendance record had to be maintained, leading to the start of a primitive information system.

The cottage system represented a considerable advance over the craft guild period and it dominated the industrial scene for a couple of centuries. Then a descendant of our original innovator began to chafe at the income limitation inherent in the system and cast about for some way to overcome this limitation. The answer this new unknown genius came up with was truly creative and revolutionary and formed the basis of the subsequent Industrial Revolution. Our creative thinker observed that the production of a pair of shoes required perhaps nine labor operations. He reasoned that it was not reasonable to expect a shoemaker to become equally skilled in performing all these operations. On the other hand, if the shoemaker were asked to concentrate on, let us say, only three labor operations, he would certainly become more expert and produce a greater quantity of units than under the present system. To accommodate the new approach, he conceived of reorganizing the three-story cottage so that the three shoemakers on the top floor would be limited to making the soles of the shoes, the three on the second floor the upper part of the shoes, and the three on the ground floor would assemble the soles and the uppers into finished pairs of shoes.

The adoption of the principle of specialization or division of labor proved remarkably successful and forms to this very day the basis of our factory systems. There developed however unintended and undesirable consequences which still bedevil industrial societies. For the first time in human history the concept of the identification of the artisan with his product became severely traumatized. The progressive dehumanization of the workplace led to the alienation of the workers. It is only in recent years that attempts have been made to improve the quality of life at work. The most extreme negative effects of specialization caused by the constant repetition by the worker of the same routine labor operation (marvelously satirized by Charlie Chaplin some fifty years ago in his film *Modern Times*) are being mitigated by the formation of work groups which are given responsibility for either the total product or at least a meaningful part of the product. For example, in an auto plant a work group may be assigned the complete engine assembly. While this does not restore complete product identification, the workers may take pride in turning out high quality and defect-free engines.

A second unforeseen consequence of the specialization system affected the need for expanded information. When the staff man came to pick up the completed pairs of shoes from the assemblers, he found several pairs of soles without their corresponding upper parts. It became evident that the new system required coordination of the efforts of the shoemakers who were producing soles with those who were producing the uppers. Thus was created *production scheduling and control* with the detailed records required to implement the activity.

It should be noted that the introduction of the principle of division of labor drastically reduced work opportunities for skilled artisans such as the shoemakers of the craft guild period. These master journeymen were replaced by blue-collar workers who required less training and thus could be more easily replaced. At the same time, the increased need for coordination led to a closer scrutiny of the work organization and to the policing of the work force. It was also natural for the staff man to evolve into the individual who did the coordinating and the controlling and thus in effect manage the organization.

The factory system became entrenched as the dominant form of industrial organization. When machines arrived on the scene during the eighteenth century, they fit easily into the factory structure. The few skills still required of workers were now transferable to the machines. Factory owners found machines to be more convenient than workers since they did not have to be paid nor did they require lunch breaks or coffee breaks. However, they did represent a substantial investment to the owner which had to be protected by even more policing of the workers operating the machines. This led to a growing hostility between management and the workers. In addition machinery increased the complexity of organizational functioning. Whereas previously coordination was required among the materials, the workers, and the financing of the operation, the managerial equation now had to add machines and coordinating methods. The relatively primitive information system of the manual factory system had to be upgraded to function properly and this led to the introduction of scientific research into industrial processes.

The final development in the full flowering of the Industrial Revolution arrived in the nineteenth century with the concept of interchangeable parts. The ability to specify standards for materials enabled products to be mass produced for the first time and made possible the introduction of continuous belt and assembly line concepts. Imbued with the nineteenth century positivist philosophy which held that mankind was perfectible and that human beings could solve any problem if they used the correct scientific approach, innovative managers in industry set about the study and improvement of manufacturing processes. They embarked upon the scientific analysis, classification and development of the major elements of the factory system-materials, methods, machines, money and man. As techniques were refined, these managers proceeded to examine microscopically the worker, the job and the workplace.

Foremost among these creative managers was Frederick W. Taylor, known both as the father of industrial engineering and the founder of the theory of scientific management. His influence was so pervasive that we shall have occasion to refer to his work when we discuss human resource management information systems.

Taylor grew up in comfortable middle-class surroundings in Pennsylvania. He was planning to study medicine at Harvard University when he was afflicted with an eye ailment. His physician feared that he would endanger his sight if he kept straining his eyes in academic studies and recommended that he pursue instead a manual vocation. Thus, when he graduated from high school, Taylor took a job as a manual laborer in a steel mill. It should be remembered that the work force in the steel industry in post–Civil War America consisted primarily of uneducated, illiterate recent immigrants from various European countries. They could neither read nor speak English and in many cases were unable to understand the instructions of their foremen. In this environment, it is not surprising that Taylor, a bright young man, stood out from all his fellow workers and was promoted to foreman and then manager.

While he was still a manual laborer, Taylor had the enthusiasm and curiosity of a young scholar. He observed closely how the steel mill was organized and run. He noticed, for example, that the laborers were told what to do but not how to do it. When a new laborer was hired, an experienced worker was asked to show him the ropes. Thus if ten new men were hired to do the same job and were trained by ten veteran workers, they acquired ten sets of work habits. Taylor noticed that there was a wide range of output among the workers depending on their work habits. Since they were all paid at the same rate, the better workers soon came to the conclusion that there was no point in working hard since the less efficient laborers received the same wages. Thus the level of productivity was reduced to that of the least efficient workers.

Taylor felt that management was foregoing a significant amount of profit by allowing this situation to continue. He mused about how much the profits of the firm could be increased if all new hires were trained by the most efficient experienced worker so that ultimately all would be producing at the level of the best rather that the worst worker. Taylor then took another step in his thought processes. Based on his own experience in working side by side with the other laborers, he became convinced that it would be possible to produce far more than even the best worker if a scientific analysis were made of each job. For every step, element, or motion of a task, the question would be asked, Is this step necessary for the performance of the task? If the answer was no, the step was eliminated. If the answer was yes, it led to the second question of whether the step was being performed in the most efficient manner. Using this methodology, Taylor in his studies was able to eliminate a large number of wasted motions in the tasks that he analyzed. This procedure lies at the heart of the industrial engineering profession.

The fundamental premise of Taylor's approach was that there was one best way to do a job. This one best way could be discovered through scientific analysis. One could not expect the workmen to know how to conduct a proper scientific study since he lacked an adequate educational background and, as Taylor thought, intelligence. Thus it was management's responsibility to find the one best way to do the job and then train the worker to do the job in just this way. In order to motivate the workers to accept this training, Taylor felt strongly that an incentive pay system should replace the then prevailing day rates which rewarded workers equally regardless of level of productivity. The successful implementation of job studies and incentive pay plans required a considerable expansion of the manufacturing information system. Voluminous records had to be maintained of time and motion studies to back up the labor operation rate system. Furthermore under an incentive pay system, precise production records were needed to identify which workers had performed how many of which operations. In the next section we shall examine the development of this information system which still forms the basis of most manufacturing concerns to this day.

The scientific management approach entailed a detailed examination of the job, the worker and the work place. If implemented properly it almost always resulted in increased plant efficiency and therefore greater profits for the firm as well as the social benefit of lower prices for the consumer. Its success was so dramatic that, together with the principle of classical management which applied Taylor's philosophy to the managerial levels of the firm, it became the dominant management approach with which all newer approaches were compared. After the Second World War, various human relations theories became popular among managers and Taylor's reputation went into a period of decline. However, in recent years, as our economy has been struggling with problems of stagflation, unemployment, and a seeming inability to compete with West German and Japanese companies, there has been a revival of interest in Taylor's theory and philosophy. In a recent article reevaluating Taylor's ideas, the author concluded as follows:

> With respect to the issues of a scientific approach to management and the techniques of time and motion study, standardization, goal setting plus work measurement and feedback, money as a motivator, management's responsibility for training, scientific selection, the shortened work week, and rest pauses. Taylor's views not only were essentially correct but they have been well accepted by management. With respect to the issues of management-labor relations and individualized work, Talyor was only partially correct, and he has been only partially accepted. . . . .
>
> Considering that it has been over 65 years since Taylor's death and that a knowledge explosion has taken place during these years, Taylor's track record is remarkable. The point is not, as it often claimed, that he was "right in the context of his time" but is now outdated, but that *most of his insights are still valid today.*[1]

The article from which the above excerpt was taken is presented in its entirety at the end of this chapter.

To bring the story of industrial development to the present, we now come to the most recent stage, that of automation and technological rule. This stage is characterized by intermechanization where machines interact with other machines without human intervention. The principle of cybernetics or feedback underlies automated operations and the application of the principle has been made possible by technological advances principally in the areas of electronics, miniaturization and computer science. This technological progress has brought us into the Information Age or the Knowledge Age, to which this book is primarily devoted. However the same technology is also revolutionizing industrial processes.

Since the introduction of productive machinery in plant operations during the eighteenth century, the main functions of plant workers have been to receive unprocessed materials, position and feed these materials into the machine, maintain the operability of the machine, control the quantity and quality of the output, and pass the approved processed materials on to the next machine for further processing. The new technology enables other machines to take over all these hitherto manual functions.

*original author's italics.
[1]Edwin A. Locke, The ideas of Frederick W. Taylor: an evaluation, *The Academy of Management Review* 1 (Volume 7, January, 1982), pp. 14–24.

To understand how the feedback principle led to automated quality control, let us take a look at one of the simplest automated devices. Most readers are familiar with the thermostat. This is a simple mechanism attached to a boiler and consisting of a thermometer and a degree-setting device. The thermostat is designed to set the boiler in operation when the mercury level in the thermometer falls below the desired temperature and to shut off the boiler when the mercury level rises above the desired temperature. In terms of cybernetic theory the thermostat is feeding back to the boiler instructions on when to operate and when not to operate based on a predetermined standard. Once the desired temperature has been set there is no more need of human intervention. In terms of a plant operation, the predetermined standards are the specifications, with tolerances, of a processed component. If a small part is supposed to emerge from a machine with a diameter of one inch and a tolerance of 1/32nd of an inch, the control machine which houses the specifications automatically receives and measures each part as it is produced. If the part meets the specification, it is passed via material-handling equipment to the next machine operation. If the measurement reveals that the part does not meet the specification but may be reworked to become acceptable, it is passed on to a repair station. And if the part fails to meet the standard and cannot be salvaged, it is passed on to the scrap station. A simple counter adds up the units received at each of the three destinations to provide quantity control.

The remaining manual functions in the older factory of material handling and positioning started to give way years ago to single-purpose material-handling equipment. The new technology gave birth about ten years ago to the new industry of robotics. Robotics firms produce robots that can be reprogrammed to perform new tasks. Robots can be programmed to do processing as well as parts-handling tasks. The robotics industry has advanced so rapidly, especially in Japan, that the Japanese have already defined several different categories of robotics (Figure 5-1).

The new technology operates under the control of a computer. The new equipment described above would be inert pieces of metal without the guidance and control of the computer. The computer in other words serves as the brain of these modern systems. In the manufacturing sphere, the computer-directed processes are known as CAD/CAM (computer-aided design/computer-aided manufacturing) systems. The advertisement reproduced in Figure 5-2 gives an idea of the services offered by a firm that specializes in CAD/CAM systems.

Computer-aided design, now widely practiced, involves the design of new products on computer terminals instead of drafting boards. The technique combines several state of the art technologies (digitizing, plotting, simulation, database techniques, etc., which have been individually available for some time) into one comprehensive interactive package. Treating the computer terminal as a drawing board enables the system to optimize productivity by permitting simple and efficient design representation aided by automatic features such as scaling, zooming, mirroring, translation, duplication, and rotation. Components of CAD/CAM systems include:

- geometry generation
- geometry manipulation and regrouping
- family of parts facility

## How Japanese Industry Defines a Robot

Japan is the only country to officially define what a robot is. Two categories in the Japanese definition—manual manipulator and sequence robot—are not considered true robots in the United States and Europe.

**Classification by input information and teaching method**

| | |
|---|---|
| **Manual Manipulator** | A manipulator that is directly operated by a man |
| **Sequence robot** | A manipulator, the working step of which operates sequentially in compliance with pre-set procedures, conditions and positions. |
| **Fixed sequence robot** | A sequence robot as defined above, for which the pre-set information cannot be easily changed. |
| **Variable sequence robot** | A sequence robot as defined above, for which the pre-set information can be easily changed. |
| **Playback robot** | A manipulator that can repeat any operation after being instructed by a man. |
| **Numerically controlled robot** | A manipulator that can execute the commanded operation in compliance with the numerically loaded working information on e.g. position, sequence and conditions. |
| **Intelligent robot** | A robot that can determine its own actions through its sensing and recognitive abilities. |
| **Robot** | A robot is defined as a mechanical system which has flexible motion functions analogous to the motion functions of living organisms or combines such motion functions with intelligent functions, and which acts in response to the human will. In this context, intelligent functions mean the ability to perform at least one of the following: judgment, recognition, adaptation or learning. |

Source: Japanese Industrial Standards JIS B 0134-1979

Figure 5-1. Reprinted from the July 19, 1982 issue of *Business Week* by special permission, © 1982 by McGraw-Hill, Inc., New York, NY 10020. All rights reserved.

- view and scale manipulation
- mechanical drafting
- geometric analysis
- numerical control
- file management

CAD systems users find that they are from three to five times faster than purely manual design processes, are more accurate, provide error-free design and are reus-

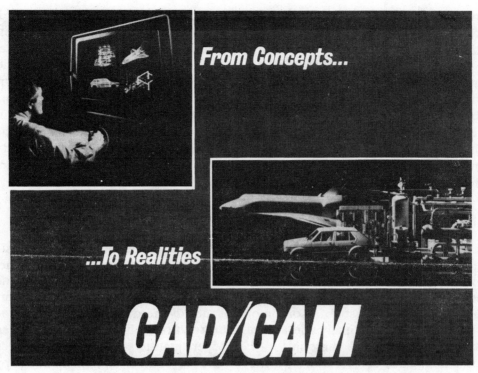
Figure 5-2. Illustration courtesy of Computervision Corporation.

able. In addition, designers are no longer required to do boring repetitive details, but are free to concentrate on creative aspects of design.

Computer-aided manufacturing (CAM) systems use the computer to design and run production lines. The typical plant structure for a CAM system requires a mix of workers, manually operated machines, machines programmed for one task such as a conveyor belt, or numerically controlled (N.C.) machines, and, now starting to come on stream in certain industries, robots that can be reprogrammed to perform new tasks. Some systems have a small microprocessor attached to and dedicated to controlling one machine. Others have a group of machines run by a central microprocessor. Research is presently begin done on finding ways of coordinating the operation of all the machines in a factory. Success thus far has been achieved only with the smallest operating unit in a plant, known as a work cell. A typical work cell may comprise a robot and its control system and machines or workers with which it works. The next step in building the plant control hierarchy is to develop the software to coordinate work cells with each other and with functions such as inspections, inventory control and purchasing. When the entire plant will be monitored by a central computer, we will have achieved computer-intergrated manufacturing (CIM) in a computer-integrated factory.

## MANAGEMENT INFORMATION REQUIREMENTS

The kinds of information needed by factory managers throughout the various stages of development described in the previous section did not change over time. Whether he was running a manual operation factory in seventeenth-century England, a sweatshop in Europe or the United States towards the end of the nineteenth century, or a completely automated factory in one of the advanced industrial nations today, the manager required timely and accurate information to help him insure the availability of incoming raw materials in the proper quantity and quality, the recruitment, training and control of his workforce, the provision of equipment and supplies at the various work stations, and a balanced flow of finished products to the market. What did change over the centuries was the quantity, complexity and sophistication of the required information and the techniques that were developed to accommodate the growing needs.

The format of the information used by operating managers became stabilized during the late nineteenth and early twentieth centuries. Before turning to an examination of this format, we wish to qualify the meaning and applicability of the term *manufacturing*. Historically, the Industrial Revolution involved the goods-producing sector of society. The information requirements we shall be discussing are treated within the context of a goods-producing operation. The reader may therefore infer that only those who are interested in or involved with manufacturing entities will find relevance in this discussion. Scholars who have applied the systems approach to organizational functioning have demonstrated that this is not the case. According to the systems approach every organism receives inputs from the outside environment and transforms these inputs, and the transformed inputs leave the organism as outputs, again to the outside environment. Thus the goods-producing organization receives raw materials from suppliers in the outside environment, molds, shapes, assembles, and otherwise transforms these inputs, and sends the results of its efforts in the form of finished products to the market in the outside environment. But the systems framework works equally well for the service industries which dominate our society today. For example, the university receives partially educated students, transforms them hopefully into more educated adults, and graduates them to be more productive citizens in the larger society. The hospital accepts sick people, transforms the patient by treating the illness, and, when successful, sends a healthy person back into the outside environment. Thus, if we understand manufacturing to be a specialized case of the transformation process, the following discussion should be useful to managers in service as well as goods-producing organizations.

We can distinguish ten major areas of responsibility for plant management, each with its own information requirements.*

### I Production Planning and Control

L. P. Alford, one of the pioneers in manufacturing management, formulated the following statement: "The highest efficiency in production is obtained by manufacturing the required quantity of product, of the required quality, at the required time, by the best and cheapest method."[2] There can be no clearer way of describing the objectives of the manager responsible for production planning and control. To fulfill this responsibility, the manager must have as complete information as possible in advance of production of the following factors which enter into the manufacturing procedure:

A. production material—including kind, grade, quality and quantity
B. availability of material—including balances on hand and time required for delivery when not stocked
C. standard of quality for each unit—expressed as limits and tolerances in machine work
D. operation method—the most efficient procedure for each operation on each unit of product
E. machine output or equipment capacity—expressed in units of work per hour capable of being handled by each machine or process
F. sequence of operations
G. operation time allowance for each operation on each unit
H. required completion dates
I. determination of economic lot sizes, in routine manufacturing situations

Availability of the above information enables the manager to formulate the production plan and put it into operation. There are other elements of information needed for implementation and control. These are known as operating procedures.

A. **Manufacturing or Production Orders.** The issuance of these orders is designed to:
   1. convey information as to customer and promised time of delivery;

---

*Much of the material in the following sections was drawn from the *Production Handbook,* edited by L. P. Alford and John R. Bangs, and published by the Ronald Press Company, New York, 1952. The authors believed that a description of the manufacturing process as it existed prior to the introduction of computers and automated equipment would facilitate the understanding of manufacturing information requirements and were able to discover a 30-year old text for this purpose.
[2]Ibid., p. 1385.

    2. serve as a nucleus for cost collection either for the order as a whole or for individual components and processes on components; and

    3. form a starting point for the control mechanism.

B. **Routing Procedure.** This procedure is based upon the product specifications received from the engineering department which include:

    1. list of parts and assembly

    2. blueprints of each part and assembly

    3. kind and quality of material for each part

    4. limits and tolerances on each part

    5. machine processes by which a part is to be made

    6. sequence in which these processes are to be done

    7. time allowances for each process

A *route sheet* serves as the history of the progress of a part through its cycle of operations. It is a control document which registers progress of the part from start to completion and delivery to stores or to assembly.

C. **Scheduling Procedure.** Scheduling involves the fitting in of specific jobs into a general timetable, so that each component may arrive at and enter into assembly on time, and each order may be completed and shipped to the customer within the time-frame requested by the sales department. One of the most comprehensive, condensed and effective means for maintaining control of production is by means of a *Gantt chart,* named after its developer, one of the early pioneers of scientific management. These charts, still widely used by companies that have not computerized their production control function, plot the item under consideration against the element of time. The status of each item is posted each day on the chart permitting a comparison with the required completion date also indicated on the chart. The manager is in a position to take corrective action if the progress of any item is falling behind schedule.

    Many firms today have computerized production planning and control information systems. Depending on the programmed level of sophistication, the system may track every component of every item at every stage of production and alert the manager immediately to any deviation from the plan.

D. **Dispatching Procedure.** Dispatching may be defined as the routine of setting productive activities in motion, through release of orders and instructions, and in accordance with previously planned times and sequences as embodied in route sheets and schedules. The principal activities included in dispatching are:

    1. movement of material from stores to first process, and from process to process

    2. issue of tool orders

    3. issue of job orders authorizing operations

    4. issue of time tickets, instruction cards, and drawings

    5. issue of inspection orders after each operation

    6. recording time of beginning and completing job

    7. forwarding time tickets to payroll department and job records to production control department

    8. recording idle time of machines and operators

The dispatching procedure is in effect the implementation stage of the production process. Each activity is initiated by information on a preprinted document which follows the work through each step of production so that the information needed for proper performance is available to all the participants in the process.

## II Purchasing and Materials Control

The two major inputs to the industrial process are materials and labor. This section deals with the types of information that can help the manager to acquire, consume efficiently and control materials.

Purchasing is a primary function. In most firms, materials represent a major investment of working capital. It is the responsibility of the purchasing executive to arrange purchases so as to insure receipt of proper materials when wanted in sufficient quantities to maintain production and on-time shipment, yet not to increase investment beyond that required to meet current needs and maintain a reasonable factor of safety. In well-run companies this objective is usually achieved through a purchase budget.

The purchase budget is the purchasing department's plan or schedule of operations. The function of the budget is to combine estimates of consumption requirements as submitted by the production department and the record of current materials inventory on hand with knowledge of market conditions, so as to form a workable plan for procurement of materials needed in time for production requirements, and at the least possible cost in inventory investment consistent with purchasing under favorable market condition.

An efficient purchasing procedure requires bringing materials of the proper quality, in the proper quantity and at the proper price. Adherence to quality standards is achieved by supplying the purchasing department with proper specifications. This may be done by specifying a brand or trade name, providing a blueprint, describing in detail the phsyical characteristics of the item to be purchased, description of purpose or use of the item to be purchased or submitting a sample of what is to be purchased. Determining the quantity to be purchased can be calculated mathematically through the application of an EOQ (Economic Order Quantity) model that will produce the level of purchasing that minimizes the sum of inventory carrying costs and out-of-stock costs. Purchasing at the best price is a function of the purchasing agent's expert knowledge of market conditions and trends. This expertise is acquired through experience and a constant flow of current information from the marketplace.

Since the purchasing procedure is fairly routine, preprinted forms and records will satisfy most information requirements. The most important of these are:

A. Forms
   1. **Purchase Requisition.** This is a formal request from the department needing the goods to the purchasing department. It should contain the quantity and date needed and a complete specification as described above.
   2. **Request for Quotation.** In order for the purchasing agent to decide with which vendor the order shall be placed he may solicit price quotations from

several suppliers. He will provide each vendor with the quantity to be ordered, the full specification of material, the delivery destination, the delivery time allowed and the date by which the quotation must be received.

3. **Purchase Order.** The purchase order is the most important of purchasing forms since it establishes a contractual relationship between the buyer and the vendor. It is the buyer's commitment to the vendor for the value of the goods ordered, and the vendor's authority to ship and charge for the goods specified.

4. **Receiving Document.** This document may be called variously a Receiving Report, a Receiving Voucher, or a Receiving Ticket. It records the receipt of goods ordered from vendors. If after inspection the goods are accepted, the task of the purchasing agent has been completed, and the goods become the responsibility of the manager at the next stage of the process.

B. Purchasing Department Records
1. Record of Material Specifications
2. Purchase Record (This record contains the history of the purchases of a particular item)
3. Contract Record (This is a record of purchase contract commitments)
4. Vendor Record
5. Price or Quotation Record

Computerized purchase order systems are in common use today and the purchasing department's records are stored in the computer's memory while the forms are generated by the system.

Once the ordered materials have been received, management has the responsibility of guarding this vital and expensive asset until it is consumed in production. There are two phases of material control:

A. physical—involves primarily the storage and materials and checking quantities by counting
B. clerical—involves primarily the determination of requirements, preparation of requisitions and keeping of records

The major investment in materials renders materials inventory control one of management's most important responsibilities. The materials manager must strive for maximum efficiency in the use of storage areas. Good storeroom management, coordinated with a well-organized stores record system, prevents the accumulation of excessive quantities of materials. Capital unnecessarily tied up in excess inventories cannot be used productively elsewhere. Wrong location of storerooms and wasteful use of storage space may interfere with good factory layout, cut down manufacturing efficiency, and tie up floor area needed for increased production. To avoid these problems, the manager when planning for storage should compile information on the items to be stored, available space, facilities for intraplant transportation, storeroom equipment and storage procedure with particular reference to stores control.

The materials control cycle calls for the implementation of firm procedures at all stages of the process that we have described in this section. Furthermore, there should be checks of quantities on hand through periodic physical inventories. Finally a good materials control program will be sensitive to the almost universal tendency to proliferation in the number of items and components. To offset this tendency, many firms set up a material standards committee charged with the responsibility for materials standardization and simplification. Typically, this committee crosses departmental lines and its membership includes representatives from engineering, production planning and control, purchasing, manufacturing, inspection and materials management.

## III Work Simplification

We now turn to labor, the second major input of the industrial process. To the degree that material and labor are the two major cost elements of most goods-producing organizations, profitability is a function of the efficient utilization of these two components. Labor productivity depends upon eliciting the maximum output in both quality and quantity from employees at the lowest cost, consistent with maintaining the human dignity of the worker and decent working conditions. In this section we shall deal with quantity output, leaving the treatment of quality to the next section.

Historically, the responsibility of upgrading labor efficiency has been assigned to the industrial engineer. We have previously related the contribution of Frederick W. Taylor, the father of the industrial engineering discipline. While most manufacturing managers are not engineers, it is important for the manager to understand what the industrial engineer does and in general how he does it. The industrial or methods engineer approaches his task by studying both the job and the worker doing the job. The purpose of studying the job is to develop the one best way of doing it and then to train all the workers assigned to the job to perform it this one best way. The underlying assumption of job standardization is that performance can be improved by the use of better methods and elimination of wasted energy and not by pushing the employee to work harder or faster. A task which results in the exhaustion of the worker has been wrongly set. The motto of the engineer is "Work smarter, not harder."

The engineer breaks down the job he is studying into its component tasks or operations and then looks at each task in detail. Operation analysis consists of a detailed study and analysis of each operation to determine whether the operation is necessary, and the best and quickest method of performing that operation with the best available tools, equipment, materials and working conditions. Once the optimum method for the operation has been developed, a time study is conducted to come up with a fair determination of the time required to do the task.

Taylor developed time studies in order to set standards for cost purposes, wage incentive plans and production standards. Two of his contemporaries, Frank and Lillian Gilbreth, were more interested in observing the motions of the worker performing the operation. They determined that all work can be subdivided into seventeen fundamental motions, or *therbligs* (Gilbreth spelled backwards, almost). Thus, they were able to break down the *operation,* which was Taylor's basic unit of work, into *elements* which they described as a series of motions in a work cycle which can be recognized, recorded and timed. They developed *motion study* which, combined with Taylor's *time study,* developed into *time and motion study,* the basic tool of the industrial engineer today.

Work simplification describes and embraces the fields of process analysis, simple motion study and micromotion study. These three fields represent degrees of refinement in the application of the analytic method to the problem of work simplification. The analysis always starts with a process analysis which expands the operation analysis to include the material movements attendant to the operation. These movements may comprise transportation, storage, inspection, and delay. What is in effect being studied is the flow of work joining adjacent operations. One result of the analysis is the preparation of an operation process chart and a material-flow process chart which describe in great detail how the procedure under investigation functions. Once the procedure has been thoroughly dissected through the process analysis, motion-time analysis is undertaken to weed out unnecessary motions and to set time standards for the remaining motions. The decision to perform a simple motion study or a micromotion study is a function of the economic payoff. Certain operations or motions within an operation may be performed millions of times a year and a time saving of a small fraction of a second may thus represent significant dollars. This situation would justify the greater expenditure of a micromotion study. Where the potential savings are small, a simple motion study would be adequate.

The key to successful work simplification is the willingness of the workers to accept and apply the results of the analysis. In most unionized operations, the workers have won the right through collective bargaining to question and negotiate the setting of rates. In firms where the workers are not unionized, management recognizes that their cooperation is essential for the work simplification program to be effective. In both cases, it is the manufacturing manager and not the engineer who deals with the workers or their representatives. Therefore, although the manager may not be an engineer, it is incumbent upon him to be familiar with and become skilled in interpreting the information on the engineering analysis and studies so that he may defend intelligently the essential fairness of a proposed rate structure.

## IV Inspection and Quality Control

The manufacturing manager has a staff relationship with the industrial engineering department that applies its specialized methodology to assist him in producing the desired quantity of output at least cost. He also has a staff relationship with the quality control department that provides him with specifications to help maintain a certain level of quality in production. However, quality control also includes an inspection function designed to insure that specifications have in fact been met. This adds a potentially controversial judgmental element to the relationship. The line manager is responsible for the quality as well as the quantity of production. In the case of a manager who is confident of his talent and ability, he looks forward to the report of an independent inspection team that will confirm to his superiors the high level of his performance. However, when a manager is insecure about his abilities, he tends to become defensive and resists accepting the validity of the inspection report, fearing that any criticism in the report will harm his reputation and potential for advancement.

Management should be sensitive to the delicate nature of this relationship and should strive to create an environment of trust and cooperation between the two functions. One way to accomplish this is for management to prove by its actions that it believes that the purpose of inspection reports is to cure troubles and not to find someone to blame. When a positive relationship exists, one of the greatest benefits of inspection service comes from its power to bring information promptly to the attention of management as to the true state of manufacturing operations so that faults and inefficiencies in processing may be corrected.

Production difficulties ordinarily appear in the form of too great losses in spoilage, or through slowing down of production at some operation, thus creating a bottleneck. The problem may be due to poor materials, inadequate or poorly maintained machinery and tools, careless set-up of work, untrained or incompetent workers, or ineffective supervision and control. The inspector is an unbiased observer who is excellently situated to locate manufacturing troubles, frequently to isolate their causes and sometimes to offer suggestions for their cures.

Inspections may take place at various stages of the process. When a new product is introduced, there will be a trial-run inspection, a first-piece inspection, and a pilot-piece inspection. During a full production run, various approaches may be adopted with the aim of achieving the highest quality at lowest cost. Thus one may find work-in-process inspected at various key operations, inspection performed on samples taken at random from lots of work, 100% or smaller percentage inspection, inspection performed on finished parts prior to going to assembly and finished product inspection. The latter category may include efficiency inspection to insure that the product performs as intended and destructive inspection to determine the ultimate resistance or effectiveness of the objects tested.

The results of an inspection are recorded on a document usually called an *inspection ticket* or an *inspection log*. Where statistical quality control techniques are employed, the form is somewhat more complex and is known as a *statistical quality control chart*. Regardless of format, the document indicates the number of units inspected, accepted, rejected and usually the percentage of rejections. Of those rejected, the report may list the number rejected because of material defects or labor defects. There is room at the bottom of the form for the inspector's remarks, where he may suggest possible causes for the problem or recommend corrective action. If accepted in a constructive manner, the report may provide invaluable information to the manager seeking to improve performance.

## V Plant Layout, Machinery and Equipment

One hundred years ago Taylor demonstrated that there was a direct relationship between efficiency and physical working conditions. If management was interested in increasing productivity, it had the responsibility of providing the worker with a workplace that would encourage or at least not hinder his efficient operation. Most organizations have accepted Taylor's prescription and have assigned to the manufacturing manager the responsibility for providing proper working conditions.

Proper plant layout is indispensable to productive efficiency. If the work does not flow smoothly from one operation to another, if the support services are not conveniently available when needed, there is no way to avoid incurring otherwise avoidable costs. In prior generations, attention was paid to plant layout mainly when the factory was being built. The layout chosen at that time lasted generally over the full span of the manager's tenure. In recent times however the more rapid introduction of new product lines requiring process changes and the coming on stream of new technologies every few years have called for moderate or radical revisions of plant layouts at periodic intervals. As with other professional areas, the manager calls upon the technical support of architects and plant layout specialists. It is the manager however who has the most intimate knowledge of his operation, and it is therefore he who must decide which recommendations of the specialists to accept. Furthermore, while many specialists are interested in enhancing their reputations among their fellow professionals by building a monument regardless of cost, it is the plant budget of the manager that is charged with the amortization costs during the life of the layout. Thus it behooves the manager to question the necessity for implementing each recommendation, and, if needed, to investigate whether a less costly approach is available to achieve the same end result.

Since the manager bears the ultimate responsibility for the effectiveness of the plant layout, he must learn something about the factors that determine the degree of effectiveness. For instance, if the layout is to be the expression of a purpose, it must be built around that purpose. In addition, the layout of the plant should be such as to facilitate the flow of material through it. The arrangement of machines (machine layout) must be such that work will flow smoothly from operation to operation without excessive delay. Where the product is not and cannot be standardized, or where the volume of like work produced is low, a layout according to the processes performed is required. Such a condition requires flexibility in the sequence of manufacturing which is readily obtainable with the process method of layout. On the other hand, product layout is the best adapted to mass production industries where there is a well-standardized product and large volumes of the same product.

Auxiliary factors to be considered by the manager in planning a proper layout include the relation of material-handling equipment to the proposed layout, handling deliveries and shipments with provision for truck or rail facilities, provisions for conveyor handling, elevators, floors, and power for machines and equipment. He must decide where to locate service departments, the general office, the factory office, receiving and shipping departments, storerooms, tool cribs and toolrooms, the powerhouse, locker rooms, washrooms, toilets, the dispensary, cafeterias, and the personnel and other support departments. The manager must become knowledgeable about the factors involved in good illumination, effective heating and cooling systems, the effect upon employee performance of the colors used to paint the walls and ceilings, providing proper sanitary facilities in general and appropriate facilities for women workers.

The information needed by the manager in these many areas is obtained by research which the manager does on his own and by contact with suppliers, contractors and specialists. Given the enormous demands upon the time of the manager, it is likely that the educational process will take place at the time a layout change is considered. Such a demand schedule is inappropriate when it comes to machinery and equipment. Machinery has a shorter productive life than plants, and in most firms some machinery is constantly being replaced. Thus the system required for proper management of machinery differs considerably from that of plant layout. The basic document for the system is a *machine equipment record*. A history is kept of every machine showing the date of acquisition, the cost, and the date, cost and nature of each service and repair. The tax laws permit firms to depreciate or write off the cost of machinery over a fixed period of years. In theory, the amount depreciated builds up a fund to enable a new machine to be purchased at the end of the depreciable period. The accounting profession has been struggling in vain for years to cope with the effects of inflation upon depreciation theory. During periods of inflation, a machine which was purchased for $10,000 may cost $20,000 to replace. Yet the writeoffs have provided only $10,000 towards the replacement, and the balance has to come from other sources.

The manufacturing manager cannot afford to be overly concerned with this accounting problem. If he is to remain cost competitive and provide his firm with the goods it needs to sell in the proper quantity and quality and at the proper cost, he must continually replace his obsolescent equipment with up-to-date more efficient machinery. Due to the large number of machines in operation, most progressive firms have found it beneficial to set up a planned machine replacement program. Based on a budgeted amount of funds allocated for the year, the firm may alternatively replace its oldest machines, its least efficient machines, or based on a cost-benefit comparison of each existing machine with its replacement model, replace those machines whose replacement will provide the company with the greatest return. For the replacement program to succeed, it is necessary for the manager to have accurate information about existing machines which should be available from his machine equipment records and about new machines which is obtainable from suppliers.

In many industries, the manager's responsibilities in this area also extend to tools, dies, jigs, and fixtures. These are small appliances which are either attached to machines to enable the machine to perform in a specific way or which hold materials so that machines or other tools may perform work on them. Tools generally are consumed more rapidly than machines in production and therefore have to be replaced more frequently. Certain tools are fabricated on the premises of the firm and others are purchased from outside suppliers. The tools owned by the company are stored in tool cribs and toolrooms. The control of the tool inventory involves records which govern procurement, quantities carried and disbursements to tool cribs from the toolroom. The inventory management procedure described above in the section on materials control is generally required also for tools because of the significant financial investment involved.

## VI Job Estimating

The job shop is one of the major forms of industrial organization together with mass production and process manufacturing. The job shop is distinguished from other forms of organization in that it accepts orders from customers to produce and deliver a custom-made item. A job shop in the furniture field, for example, will produce a table in any size and build with any material desired by the customer.

In this form of organization, job estimating becomes a major responsibility of the manufacturing manager. This type of business is complicated by two factors. The manager has no way of knowing in advance which or how many orders will be received, or what will be requested on the orders. Secondly, the customer will almost always send out requests for quotation to several companies, so that the manager is continually bidding for jobs in a highly competitive situation.

The successful manager in a job shop must be highly skilled in two areas. He requires intimate familiarity with the capabilities of his employees and his equipment. This expertise will enable him to juggle his people and his machines so as to accommodate the maximum number of orders at one time. In utilizing his resources to the maximum, he reduces the fixed costs charged to each job and thus becomes more competitive.

The second type of knowledge needed by the manager is the area of manufacturing costs. In addition to the costs of material and direct labor which will be incurred on the job, he must be able to assign costs to design time, drafting time, methods and time studies, set-up time, requirements for special patterns, tools, dies, jigs and fixtures, and various overhead items such as indirect labor, rent, light, heat, power, supplies, and so forth. The experienced manager will also keep in mind expected future rates of labor, material, and overhead. Costing is an art and the manager who is aware of different costing approaches will do a better job for his firm. All costing systems agree upon the inclusion of the direct costs of material and labor in the job estimate. It is in the technique used to allocate overhead that costing approaches differ. If the manager's firm is in a slack period or if the customer's order indicates a potential to be followed by many reorders for the same item, he may charge only a portion of the calculated overhead in estimating the job. By filling in slack capacity and by increasing the utilization of otherwise idle resources, the firm can spread its fixed costs over a greater number of jobs, resulting in a reduced fixed cost charge per job. With this knowledge, the manager has some flexibility in assigning overhead costs. By the same token, when the firm is in a very busy period or when the order calls for a process that no competitor can handle, the manager can basically charge as much as the traffic will bear.

The job estimate should be prepared as rapidly as possible after receipt of the order. The first task is to sketch out the job flow and list the material, labor, and equipment needed to fill the order. It is at this point that the information system comes into play. In the short run, most costs are constant. A well-designed labor cost estimate form, material cost estimate form and estimated cost summary form permit the manager to pull from the files the records of recently submitted estimates for jobs requiring the same materials, the same or similar labor operations, and the same or similar equipment. Using these completed estimates as a guide, the manager can prepare the new estimate quickly and then apply his mature judgment in coming up with a selling price.

## VII The Compensation System

One finds a wide range of practice in the amount of discretion granted the manufacturing manager in determining the compensation of his subordinates. Where the workforce is unionized, wage rates are negotiated during labor—management bargaining sessions. In many large organizations, compensation specialists in the personnel department will establish salary scales and ranges for the supervisors, salaried indirect workers, factory office clerks and staff employees who report to the manufacturing manager. In many small, privately-owned concerns, the principals exercise strict control over the salaries they will permit to be paid to the manager's subordinates. Finally, the "going market rate" places a strict limit on whatever authority remains to the manager to determine the salary of his employee.

Nevertheless, wage and salary administration, once the original wages and salaries have been decided, remains a major responsibility of the manufacturing manager. Even though he may have had little or nothing to do with establishing the wage and salary structure, it is the manager's job to defend and administer it. Where the wage rates have been set down in the contract between the union and management, the manager will find in that agreement a detailed procedure for wage administration and his best strategy is to adhere strictly to the procedural details. Many wage plans are far more complex than an hourly rate for a job category, so that it behooves the manager to learn all the intricacies of the wage plan adopted by his firm so that he may implement it efficiently and equitably.

Wage and salary differentials are based upon an evaluation of each job's worth to the firm. In theory, if the chief operating officer is earning twenty times as much as a maintenance man, it is or should be because he is contributing twenty times as much as the maintenance man to the achievement of the organization's goals. Methods have been developed for quantifying the worth of a job to the organization. The job must first be analyzed to determine its exact nature. The result of this analysis is embodied in a job description. The description is then reviewed to determine the level of skill, training, experience and education required to do the job properly. This information is listed on a job specification form which is used as a guide by personnel recruiters seeking to fill the position. The information is also used by job evaluators who assign predetermined weights to each of the qualifications needed. There are several widely-used job evaluation ranking and grading procedures. The predetermined weighting is a function of the procedure selected by the firm. An engineer is generally paid a higher salary than an office clerk. One of the reasons is that the engineer has a college degree while the clerk may require only a high school diploma. Thus, for the factor of education, the engineer would receive more points, i.e., be ranked higher, than the clerk.

The market impacts upon pay levels set through job evaluation procedures in two ways. A "normal" market serves as a check upon the individual firm's job evaluation procedures. In any given labor market, many firms applying approximately the same job evaluation criteria would arrive at the same level for a given job, and this becomes the going rate. On the other hand, the market is also a supply and demand mechanism. When supply and demand are not in balance, the market rate may diverge significantly from the true worth of the job. Thus the shortage of computer programmers has raised their market rate well above that calculated by a job evaluation procedure. During periods of high unemployment, hiring rates for unskilled labor are considerably lower than called for by job evaluation criteria, and would go even lower were it not for minimum wage laws. If the manufacturing manager wishes to handle his responsibility for compensation administration intelligently, he should familiarize himself with the details of his firm's job evaluation procedure.

Most manufacturing managers will become involved with performance appraisal systems. These systems are often related to merit rating plans, salary increases, promotions, transfers, bonuses, premiums, or other payment schemes. In the past when most jobs were more routine than they are today, it was relatively simple to appraise a worker's performance. The employee was given a daily quota of units to be produced. If he exceeded his quota, his performance was appraised favorably. If not, he was rated negatively. Today, with the growing complexity and interdependence of industrial operations, and with the increasing proportion of service, staff, administrative, professional and managerial employees to be evaluated, the appraisal function has become more difficult and delicate.

The appraisal problem revolves around the subjective and judgmental nature of the evaluation. In the past, the most hostile worker would not dispute the objective validity of the number of units or defects produced. For most present-day jobs, quantity, quality, and perhaps attendance are the only objective criteria used. They are complemented by such factors as industriousness, initiative, dependability, integrity, cooperation, judgment and value to the department. These factors are inherently subjective and qualitative in nature and fair-minded people can have honest disagreements about the validity of ratings.

Despite these shortcomings, rating scales are used widely because the fact is that for an organization to be effective employees have to perform well, and, to distinguish the good from the poor performers, employee performance must be appraised. These imperfect scales are still to be preferred over global judgments by superiors based only on their biases and intuition. Thus the manufacturing manager should learn to implement the performance appraisal system used in his firm as fairly as possible. Where the appraisal system is tied into the compensation system, the manager will have the opportunity to reward his more capable subordinates and withhold monetary rewards from subordinates whose performance is not up to expectations.

## VIII Plant Maintenance

The task of maintenance is to keep buildings and grounds, service equipment and production machinery in satisfactory condition according to standards set by management. Since an ounce of prevention is worth a pound of cure, a well-managed firm will implement a preventive maintenance program whose success depends upon adequate inspection procedures. A schedule of routine maintenance inspection will be prepared listing the hundreds of items to be inspected in order of frequency of inspection, i.e., daily, weekly, monthly, quarterly and semiannually.

The inspection program forms the basis of a planned maintenance program. The purpose of long-term planning is to provide a basis for a stabilized maintenance force and to arrange major jobs so that peak loads do not develop into emergencies. In planning the work load, provision should be made for emergency work and definitely known peak loads. In continuous process industries, much of the maintenance work can be done only when the plant is shut down. To minimize the need for emergency shutdowns, the occurrence of which is reported as front-page news in the case of nuclear plants, the maintenance program should provide for periodic planned shutdowns when major inspections and preventive maintenance procedures can be implemented.

Good workmanship, high production, sound personnel relations and quality of product are so clearly dependent on order, neatness and cleanliness in the plant that the manufacturing manager finds himself a leading crusader for good housekeeping. While department foremen are supposed to instruct and supervise their workers in keeping departments and workplaces orderly and clean, there are certain facilities and equipment that are not in direct personal use by individual workers and therefore no one is responsible for their care. Therefore the manager should institute a good housekeeping program tied in to the maintenance program to oversee the care of walls, windows, ceilings, aisles, exits, stairways, floors, sanitary facilities, locker rooms, showers, drinking fountains and beverage dispensers. The program should also include safety installations, fire-fighting equipment, unused tools and equipment, scrap removal, and rubbish and garbage removal.

As with the other areas of responsibility of the manufacturing manager, an efficient information and paperwork system is vital to the success of the maintenance program. The machinery equipment record, which was discussed above in the section on management of machinery and equipment, is also the key record for the maintenance program. Space is provided on this record to provide a complete history of repairs and maintenance service to each item of equipment. Since the maintenance program comprises such a wide variety of items, specialized forms may be required. For example, the type of maintenance required for motor vehicles differs from that of production equipment, so that a motor vehicle maintenance record is provided for this purpose. Different inspection report formats are prepared for various types of inspections (for example, electrical or mechanical) and for different categories of equipment. Thus the inspection report format for material-handling equipment is likely to differ from the format used for production equipment.

The operation of the maintenance system requires its own set of records. A planned program starts with the preparation of a *general maintenance schedule*. This may be in the form of a Gantt chart referred to previously. The schedule triggers the issuance of *maintenance work orders* for routine maintenance. A tickler file may be maintained to insure compliance with the frequency-of-service schedule. Provision must also be made for the issuance of work orders for emergency or rush tasks.

Maintenance, unfortunately, is a function which receives almost no recognition when performed properly, and is noticed, perversely enough, only in the effects of its absence. There are firms that will resist allocating adequate resources for proper maintenance on the grounds that these expenditures do not contribute directly to short-term profits. We have only to look at the condition of our nation's highways, bridges, and public transportation systems to recognize the folly of this approach. The long-term viability of both the firm and the manufacturing manager depends upon the implementation of an effective maintenance system.

## IX Manufacturing Budgets

All the activities of an organization are translatable ultimately into dollars and cents. The top management of an effectively organized firm will define its goals and objectives and formulate policy guidelines for its executives. The operating managers will then proceed to develop plans whose implementation will lead to the achievement of the firm's objectives. The expression of these plans in quantitative or financial terms is called a *budget*. The budget may thus be defined as a device that enables management to plan and control the activities of an enterprise so that its profit and service objectives may be realized. Budgets are devised by forecasting future business conditions and using the data to establish a basis for controlling present operations. This process ordinarily involves the preparation of estimates of future plant activities expressed in terms of physical units which are then translated into dollar equivalents.

The corporate or master budget for a manufacturing concern is a summary of many functional and departmental budgets. The effectiveness of the subsidiary budgets depends upon the reliability of the sales estimate for the budget period. Sales forecasting techniques were discussed in some detail in the previous chapter on the marketing information system. Once the manufacturing manager is advised of the approved sales estimate for the period, he is in a position to prepare the six subsidiary manufacturing budgets for which he will be held responsible.

**A. Production Budget.**   The production budget serves production management in planning and controlling manufacturing operations. It is prepared to show:

1. estimated volume of production for the budget period to meet:
   a. anticipated sales requirements, and
   b. desired inventory requirements;
2. productive capacity of plant facilities;
3. cost of operations.

The production budget is broken down into monthly and weekly periods for more effective use in leveling production. It is well known that by maintaining an even rate of production, management can realize lower unit costs, stabilized employment, and more efficient utilization of plant capacity. To the degree that sales fluctuate, level production may be maintained by varying the level of inventory to buffer sales demand. The production budget is the first of the manufacturing budgets to be prepared, and based upon its data the others may be established.

**B. Materials Budget.**   This budget shows the quantity and quality of each kind of direct material required to maintain the planned production schedule. Indirect materials are usually budgeted as a part of overhead. For most products it is best to translate planned production into materials requirements through the use of standard material requirements records. Thus if the bill of materials specifies three units of component A for each unit of product Z, and the production plan calls for manufacturing 200 units of product Z, the materials budget would provide for the supply of 600 units of component A to the plant. Whether these units are to be purchased or to be drawn from stock is a function of the level of inventory on hand. If the determination is made that they are to be purchased, the proper quantity of component A is then included in the purchase budget.

**C. Purchase Budget.**   The purchase budget portrays the specific purchases that must be made of raw materials, supplies, parts and equipment to coordinate with the materials and production budgets. Proper establishment of the purchase budget enables:

1. the purchasing department to have on hand the desired quantity and quality of materials at the time specified by the materials budget to provide for the needs of the production program;
2. the head of the financial organization to know the purchase requirements and plan for probable expenditures at the time the budgets are being prepared; and
3. the amount of investment in inventories to be kept at a minimum consistent with purchasing under favorable market conditions.

**D. Labor Budget.**   Labor costs of a manufacturing concern entail both salaries and wages paid executive, supervisory, clerical and operating employees. The labor budget usually includes only wages paid to workers engaged in primary productive activities, i.e., direct labor costs. Indirect labor costs are shown in the manufacturing expense budget. After the production and materials budgets are determined, it is necessary to estimate the direct labor costs on the basis of planned production. This is done through the labor budget to:

1. enable the employment department to provide the employees necessary to perform the tasks outlined by the production program;
2. provide management with an estimate of total direct labor costs for use in the planning of disbursements and preparation of an estimated statement of cost of goods manufactured and sold; and
3. provide data to assist management in stabilizing employment and minimizing labor turnover.

Preparation of the labor budget necessitates estimating labor requirements in terms of some physical factor such as man-hours or machine-hours and applying a wage rate to the physical unit. Much depends upon the wage payment method in use as well as upon the possible relationship of labor costs to some manufacturing factor. Thus if past experience has shown a consistent relationship between labor costs per ton or yard consumed and the production plan calls for the consumption of a certain number of tons or yards, it takes but a simple arithmetic calculation to determine estimated labor costs. Or if standard rates have been set for each labor operation in each production, and the product plan identifies the quantity of each product to be made, the determination of standard labor costs becomes once again a simple calculation.

**E. Manufacturing Expense Budget.** The purpose of the manufacturing expense budget is to establish an effective method for planning and controlling manufacturing expenses. Proper budgeting of manufacturing expenses can reduce costs by keeping these costs in line with changing volumes of production. Usually manufacturing expenses can be determined in advance with a fair degree of accuracy from a study of past records.

Whereas labor and material costs tend to vary with the volume of production and are therefore easy to calculate once the production volume has been decided, manufacturing expenses often have little relationship to actual volume. Some expenses which vary with production are termed *variable* or *semivariable* depending upon the degree of variability. Those expenses which remain constant, such as depreciation, insurance, taxes, rent, supervisory labor, etc., are called *fixed expenses*. To construct a useful manufacturing expense budget, it is necessary to classify each item of expense as variable, semivariable, or fixed. The amount of fixed expenses remains the same during each equal time period regardless of the volume of production. Those items that vary directly with production can be grouped and expressed as a percentage of production. To project semivariable expenses is somewhat more tricky. Careful examination of each semivariable expense item will usually reveal that it bears a fairly constant relationship with some element in the manufacturing process. Consumable machine parts and electricity, for example, may be found to vary directly with machine hours. Indirect labor may vary either with ranges of production activity or with number of direct employees. Experience may show that one indirect employee may have to be added for each ten direct employees. The eleventh indirect employee may thus be hired when the level of direct employees reaches 101, but the twelfth does not have to be hired until there are 111 direct employees. Thus each item of semivariable expense is matched to its appropriate factor of variability and the amount of expense calculated for the budget period. The total of variable, semivariable, and fixed expenses is then calculated for several possible levels of plant output. Under a flexible budget system, only the fixed-expense items are assigned a definite dollar amount. The allowable budget for variable and semivariable items are calculated for each period by applying the percentage or factor of variability technique just described.

**F. Plant and Equipment Budget.** This budget gives management accurate data to aid in planning and controlling expenditures for plant and equipment. The latter constitute the producing capacity of a company. The classes of expenditures included in this budget are:

1. maintenance and repairs
2. additions, renewals, and replacement of equipment
3. prolongation of equipment life which involves rebuilding old equipment.

The plant and equipment budget differs somewhat from the other manufacturing budgets. The operating budgets are primarily estimates of income and expenses of a department or a plant for a predetermined budget period. The plant and equipment budget is mainly concerned with the maintenance of machine, tools, and equipment, and additions or replacements to the plant. Consequently, the plant and equipment budget involves expenditures which affect production operations throughout the budget period and perhaps for a considerable time in the future. The budget system handles this situation by incorporating maintenance and repair expenses in the operating budget for the period and segregating expenses for additions, renewals, replacements and prolongation of equipment life into a separate document known as the *capital expenditures budget*. This type of budget will be discussed in the chapter on financial information systems.

Management theorists have identified the universal management functions as planning, organizing, staffing, directing and controlling. As a manager moves up in the organizational hierarchy, planning and controlling emerge as the key functions. The budget is the ideal information tool for planning and controlling and as such is indispensible to the manufacturing manager.

## X Plant Personnel

For many years the General Electric Company defined its image with the slogan, "People are our most important product." This slogan exemplifies the widely-held conviction that people are the most important resource in the organization. It is thus reasonable to expect that an information system designed to utilize this resource efficiently should be of extreme importance to the manufacturing manager. However, since the management of human resources applies to all managers in the organization, and since the subject is so vital to organizational success, we shall defer our discussion at this point and devote the entire following chapter to the human resources information system.

## SOURCES OF DATA

The broad scope of responsibilities described in the previous section indicates that the manufacturing manager serves as a focal point drawing information from a wide range of sources both in the external environment and within the organization. When he is involved with the purchase of materials or equipment, he must look to outside suppliers for his information. In dealing with plant layout problems, he must likewise consult with outside architects and plant layout professionals. However, to enable him to cope with the bulk of his responsibilities, the manufacturing manager must turn for information and guidance to many kinds of staff specialists within the organization.

Thus, the production planning and control manager will develop and implement the production control system. The materials control and standardization function is overseen by the trained purchasing agent. The industrial engineering department will conduct time and motion and work simplification studies. Quality control engineers will generate inspection and quality control records. Job estimating will likely be handled by a cost accountant. The firm's compensation system will be developed by specialists in the field of human resources. The budgetary control system will be under the staff direction of financial control specialists. There can be no clearer example of the high degree of interdependence in our economy than to observe the need of the manufacturing manager to interact cooperatively with so many professional colleagues in order to obtain the information he needs for effective decisionmaking.

## INFORMATION SYSTEM OUTPUTS

The scope of the manufacturing manager's responsibilities makes it impractical to illustrate all the outputs from a comprehensive manufacturing information system. To give the reader an idea of the wide range of outputs used by manufacturing managers, we are reproducing herewith a flyer produced by Prentice-Hall, Inc. to promote its *Handbook of Production Management Forms and Formats* (see Figures 5–3) This handbook presents samples of 435 different outputs.

On a much more restricted basis, we present samples of a few manufacturing reports made available by Standard Motor Products, Inc., a well-known producer

## *435 models explained and illustrated in the* Handbook of
# Production Management Forms and Formats

### FACILITY DESIGN AND CONSTRUCTION

#### *Facility Planning*
Quarterly Area Report. Area and Head Count Statistics by Major Site; by Organization. Facilities Engineering Request. Cost Estimate Summary Plant Engineering Job Data Sheet. Construction Project Data Sheet. Lease-Back Deal—Client Interview Checklist. Facilities Project Schedule. Project Status Report. Monthly Status Report—Example.

#### *Facility Design*
Design and Drafting Work Order; Request—Rush. Design Input Sheet. Drawing Index History Card. Map File Record Card. Construction Specification Cover Sheet. Specification Log. Design Jobs—Status. Drawings for Issue. Structural Drawings for Issue. Construction Drawing Release. Drawing Release—Internal Transmittal.

#### *Site Evaluation and Acquisition*
Plant Budget Item Monthly Report. Project Work Element Estimate and Work Order Cost Estimate—Acquisitions. Proposed Real Estate Lease Summary; Purchase Summary. Surplus Owned Property Summary. Permission to Survey. Industrial Building Inventory; Instructions for Field Investigator. Lease Rental Register; Abstract of Lease. Appraisal Data Sheet.

#### *Facility Construction*
Notice of Selected Subcontractor Award and Request for Insurance. Contractor's Daily Report and Labor Segregation. Contractor's Daily Report. Major Construction Projects Summary. Construction Engineering Field Report. Field Change Order. Construction Change Request. Notice of Completion—2 Versions. Builders Performance Report. Notice of Work Termination.

### FACILITY OPERATION

#### *Plant and Equipment Maintenance*
Preventative Maintenance Checklist. Lubrication Schedule. Maintenance Work Order, Maintenance

Request. Building Maintenance Section Work Request. Maintenance Work Order. Annual Overhead and Gantry Crane and Hoist Inspection Checkoff List. Report of Operating or Maintenance Error. Report of Mechanical Trouble. Request for Equipment Repair. Out-of-Service Tag. In-Service Tag. Maintenance Tag; Alternate. Maintenance Activity Schedule. Building Maintenance Report. Office Machines on Service Contract.

#### *Plant Equipment Control*
Furniture/Equipment Ledger. Plant Layout Inventory Sheet. Acquisition Report—Property. Apparatus Tag. Equipment Record Card—2 Versions. Utilization Log Checklist. Equipment Usage Memo. Equipment Available for Redeployment: Instructions. Plant Equipment Redeployment Request. Equipment Transfer.

#### *Methods Engineering and Work Measurement*
Job Improvement Request. Cost Improvement Proposal. Machine Analysis. Motion and Time Analysis Sheet. Methods Analysis Chart. Time Observation Sheet. Nonrepetitive Time Observation Sheet. Flow Process Chart. Flow Diagram Form. Work Measurement Time Study Record. Work Measurement Task Standards. Notice of Permanent Change. Routing and Tool Layout Change Notice.

### PROCUREMENT

#### *Material Codes, Lists and Catalogs*
Material Catalog Page—Example. Request for Material Code and/or Request to Establish Supply for Item. Material Code Assignment. Material System Data—Additions and Changes. Request for Material Code—Changes and Corrections Establish Emergency Stock Catalog Data. Bill of Material. Material Listing—Bill of Material. Approved Source List. Qualified Vendor List for Apparatus.

#### *Material/Service Requisitions*
Requisition. Purchase Requisition. Prefab Material Requisition. Daily Material Request. Field Order. Order Request. Nonproductive Material Requisition. Material Requisition.

#### *Vendor/Contractor Qualification*
Vendor/Contractor Prequalification. Performance Evaluation Report. Request for Treasurer's Department Financial Review. Vendor Information Questionnaire—8 pages. Technical Services Supplier Questionnaire—4 pages. Bulk Commodity Supplier Questionnaire— 4 pages. Subcontractor/Supplier Configuration Management Evaluation—7 pages. Vendor/Contractor Prequalification Status Log.

#### *Bids/Quotations*
Request for Quotation—2 Versions. Invitation to Quote. Quotation Request. Postcard—Acknowledgment of Receipt of Request for Quotation. Telephone Quotation Abstract. Tabulation of Bids. Evaluation and Recommendations—Bids. Bid Analysis Summary. Request for Approval of Proposed Bidder. Status Report for Major Commitments. Material Control Schedule. Notice of Award or Memorandum of Change.

#### *Purchasing*
Requistion Log. Major Project Purchase Order Numbers. Purchase Order—4 Versions. Purchase Order—Terms and Conditions. Purchase Order Attachment—Vendor Data Requirements. Blanket Purchase Order—Material. Authorization to Fabricate. Vendor Warehouse Release Request. Distribution Slip for Purchase Order Copies.

#### *Purchase Control*
Monthly Status Report of Annual Purchase Order. Blanket Purchase Order Status Summary. Purchase Order Control Sheet. Vendor's Disposition Request. Memorandum of Change. Change Notice (Purchase Order). Purchase Order Cancellation Notice.

#### *Purchase Expediting/Tracing*
Expediting Report; Alternate Version. Open Purchase Order Tracer. Material Tracer. Blanket Purchase Order Critical Item Report. Vendor Status Report. Material Status Report. Critical Material Status Report.

### MATERIAL MANAGEMENT

#### *Receiving*
Receiving Report. Parts Manifest/Receiving Log.

(continued on next page)

Figure 5-3. From the book *Handbook of Production Management Forms and Formats* by Robert D. Carlsen and James F. McHugh © 1978 by Prentice-Hall, Inc. Published by Prentice-Hall, Inc., Englewood Cliffs, NJ 07632.

# Handbook of Production Management Forms and Formats

### Continued:

Emergency Pickup and Delivery of Material. Tracer for Notice of Receipt. Notification and Acknowledgment of Job Site Delivery. Report of Receipt of Unsatisfactory Vendor Material Shipment. Material Returned to Shipper.

### Stores Control

Establish Inventory Control Data. Stock Control Card. Material Inventory Control and Order Card. Spare Parts Inventory. Spare Parts Record. Perpetual Inventory Record. Inventory Control Sheet. Annual Inventory Verification Report. Inventory Overage and Shortage Report. Termination Inventory List.

### Material Issues/Returns

Stores Requisition. Routing Ticket. Daily Material Request. Pick List. Material Wanted. Material Issued. Material Turned in to Store. Material Withdrawals and Returns. Material Returns.

### Shipping

Commercial Shipping Document. Packing List; Instructions. Dummy Packing Sheet. Straight Bill of Lading. Transportation or Service Request. Truck Dispatch Order. Daily Truck Dispatch Log.

### Salvage

Disposal Authorization—Property. Disposal Tag. Surplus Property Invitation Bid. Scrap Material from Material Review. Material and Equipment Sales Invoice. Salvage Returns, Adjustments or Transfer.

## PLANNING AND CONTROL

### Reviews and Planning Summaries

Producibility Review Plan of Action and Record. Producibility Recommendation. Producibility Information Sheet. Planning Instruction Sheet. Record of Planning Action. Cost Estimate Summary and Manpower Schedule by Task. Production Cost Target/Estimate Work Sheet—Summary.

### Schedules

Model Setback Work Sheet. Production Analysis Graph. Two-Month Work Schedule. Manufacturing Test and Operations Thirty-Day Schedule. Production Control Schedule.

### Manpower

Three-Year Manpower Input. Manpower Forecast Work Sheet. Manning Table/Manpower Budget Summary. Manpower Budget Revision.

### Budgets

Plant Budget Work Sheet. Function Budget Estimate. Explanation of Function Budget Increase/Decrease. Budget Source Document. Estimating Summary Sheet. Cost Estimating Work Sheet. Annual Cost Schedule. Analysis of Budget Performance.

### Project Planning and Control

Project Planning and Control Form. Objectives. Delivery/Milestone Schedule. Project Schedule. Staffing Work Sheet. Project Cost and Schedule Summary. Cost Comparison. Employee Weekly Activity Report. Subtask/Activity Control. Work Package Plan. Major Project Change Control—Analysis Summary. Weekly Task Leader Status Report. Project Monthly Report.

### Tool Design

Tool Concept Sheet. Tool Design Variance. Tooling Bar Chart. Tool Order List of Component Tools.

### Production and Process Orders and Instructions

Standard Methods Sheet. Material Processing

Procedure. General Work Order. Work Authorization. Internal Work Assignment. Interdepartment Order. Manufacturing Order; Alternate Version. Job Order Request and Instruction Sheet. Work Instruction; Alternate Version. Request for Work Instruction Change. Work Instruction Change Record. Operations Route Sheet. Operation Sheet. Operation Summary. Operation Change Summary. Parts Rework/Replacement. Parts/Duplicate Order. Operations Stop Work Order. Manufacturing Stop Order.

### Dispatching/Expediting/Status

Status and Document Routing Record. Dispatcher's Log Sheet. Work Instruction Location and Status Log. Production Priority Guide. Expedite Distribution. Work Order Status. Work Order Status Report and Priority Schedule.

## MANUFACTURING OPERATIONS

### Shop Reports

Daily Operating Report. Monday Morning Report. Daily Production Report. Production Progress. Monthly Activity. Productive Labor Ticket. Down-Time Log. Acute Shortage Report. Shortage Report. Operation Sign-Off Record. Completions. Support Shop Release.

### Shop Assignments

Incoming Work Assignment Monitor Log. Weekly Flexible Assignments. Work Schedule—Long Form. Working Schedule. Leadman's Work Sheet. Daily Job Log. Start-Up Night Orders.

### Timekeeping

Daily Time Sheet and Log. Time Sheet. Weekly Time Record. Bi-Weekly Time Report. Monthly Time Record. Labor Record. Production Labor Hours. Request and Authorization to Work Overtime. Departmental Overtime Submittal. Weekly Overtime Recap. Cumulative Time Record in Man-Hours.

### Blueprints/Documents

Blue-Line Distribution Request. Document Release Transmittal. Serialized Assembly Drawing List. Index List—Drawing Breakdown. Drawing List. Document Request. Phone Order Request for Prints. Request for Document. Drawing Control Card. Drawing Charge-Out Card. Document Log Card.

### Tools

Tool Request. Tool Operation Card. Tooling Material Requisition. Tooling Material Credit Card. Reconditioned Tool Repairs. Truck Tool List. Tooling Inspection Record. Tool Inspection Rejection Record. Tool Filing Record—Withdrawal and Return; Tool Rework Record. Tool Withdrawal Slip. Tool Crib Receipt. Temporary Tool Issues. Employee Request for Purchase of Tools. Employee Tool Requisition and Invoice. Tool Purchase Deduction Authorization. Employee's Company-Owned Tool Records. Tool/Equipment Record Card. Removal Pass

### Problems and Changes

Request for Contract Investigation. Standards Change Request. Standards Deviation Request. Supplier Process Change Request. Supplier's Action Request. Problem Analysis Report. Problem Follow-Up Record. Follow-Up Record. Engineering Summary Report. Specification Discrepancy Notice. Specification Change Notice; Alternate. Specification Change Log. Document Release and Approval Record. Engineering Change Proposal. Engineering Change Analysis; Instructions. Engineering Change Analysis—Class I Addendum; Instructions. Engineering Change Analysis—Cost and Flow-Time Estimate. Design Change Order. Engineering Change

Revision Notice. Engineering Change Log.

### Configuration Management

Change Board Summary; Instructions. Program Configuration Control Board Directive; Instructions. Master CEI/CI Configuration List. Change Control Action Notification. Program Configuration Control Board—Agenda. Document Change Record. Lost Document List. Specification Configuration Chart. End-Item Configuration Chart. Class II Engineering Change Summary Transmittal.

### Completions/Deliveries

Report of Completion—General Work Order. Report of Completed Work Orders. Delinquency Delivery Report; Alternate Version.

### Audits/Housekeeping Reports

Engineering Audit Checklist. Engineering Audit Report. Engineering Audit Deficiency Notice. Audit Deficiency Notice; Instructions. Housekeeping Survey. Crew Visitation Checklist—Example.

## QUALITY ASSURANCE

### Quality Assurance Procedures

Quality Assurance Procedure Status Log. Test Requirement Cross-Reference Index. Inspection Plan. Quality Assurance—Inspection Support Data.

### Q A Program—Supplier Audit

Request for Supplier Quality Evaluation; Report; Questionnaire. Prequalification/Evaluation of Suppliers' Quality Assurance Program—17 pages. Quality Assurance Audit Report.

### Equipment and Instrument Control

Instrument List. Quality Assurance Measurement and Test Equipment Control Record. Test Equipment Record. Calibration/Service Specification; Data Record. Instrument Calibration Data; Data Sheet. Metrology and Calibration Test Report. Test Equipment Calibration and Repair Status. Metrology Laboratory Data Report. Metrology and Calibration Certification.

### Source and Receiving Inspection

Weekly Schedule—Inspection and Expediting. Inspection Report. Source Inspection. Source Inspected. Material Inspection and Receiving Report. Receiving Inspection Report. Inspection Report. Nonconformance Report; Alternate Version. Supplier Quality Assurance Release. Corrective Action Request. Fabricator's Quality and Workmanship Report. Log of Discrepancy Reports.

### Inspection and Test

Machined Parts Inspection Instruction Sheet. Ultrasonic-Certified Report of Nondestructive Examination. Report of Nondestructive Inspection. X-Ray Inspection Verification Report. Quality Assurance Information Transmittal. Process Control Element Record. Quality Control Log. Squawk Sheet. Inspection Squawks; Card. Discrepancy Report. Corrective Action Request; Instructions. Inspection Follow-Up Sheet. Material Disposition Record. Material Review Disposition. Corrective Action Status Log. In Test—Tag. Test In Process—Notice. Quality Assurance Test Log. Test Report. System Test Test Data Record. Test Discrepancy Report. Manufacturing Test Record. Parts Removal Record. Retest Log. Notice of Certification.

### Final Inspection, Acceptance

Acceptance Test Report. Acceptance Test Record. Inspection Operation Acceptance Record. Accepted—Tag. Engineering Sign-Off Record. Certification of Inspection—First Article. Inspector's Final Documentation—Checklist. Comments and Conditions of Acceptance.

Figure 5-3. (Cont.)

and distributor of electrical and fuel system automotive replacement parts. The firm is well advanced in the development of a computerized manufacturing information system.

### Corporate Production Plan

The relationship of production and inventory to sales is of major concern to the management of a firm. A summary picture of this relationship by product line is provided to the manufacturing managers of Standard Motor Products, Inc. on a monthly basis. The sample report illustrated in Figure 5–4 was prepared on March 15, 1982. It presents the historical record for each month of the prior year and the completed months of the current year, as well as projections for each month of the next two quarters. The past history compares actual to projected sales, production, and inventory and computes the variance between the plan and actual performance. Thus the manufacturing manager is able to analyze from one concise report the degree of adherence to the corporate plan. He also has the opportunity of reviewing the production plan for the next two quarters to ascertain that he is prepared to meet the requirements of the plan.

### Material Requirements Planning

The following outputs are presented in the area of materials management.

**A. Time-Phased Material Plan.** The on-line computer system permits the manager to call on demand for a screen presentation of the inventory status of each raw material item. The screen depicted in Figure 5–5 shows that Item No. D3240 had an on-hand balance of 36,292 units at the beginning of the year. The production plan called for 13,209 units to be released to the factory on January 6th, leaving a balance of 23,083 units on hand. On January 18th, 19,793 units were received from a supplier covered by Purchase Order No. 749999 of December 22nd. This brought the level of stock on hand up to 42,876 units. In this way the history of each *in* and *out* transaction affecting this item is available for immediate inspection by the manager. He is able to evaluate the efficiency of the timing and quantity of his purchases and thus to refine his future purchasing activities.

**B. Open Purchase Order Report.** Figure 5–6 presents the quantities of expected deliveries of each part which is used to produce a battery cable. It may be seen that receipts of three components are past due and two others are expected before the end of the month. This information should trigger an investigation to determine whether there is adequate stock on hand of these five parts to satisfy production requirements as well as a telephone call to the suppliers to prod them to speed up delivery.

**C. Made-from Part List–Indented Explosion.** Material specifications are continually referred to by manufacturing personnel to ascertain that each item produced has the correct quantity of the proper parts. The Made-from Part List illustrated

## Corporate Production Plan          Product Line:  Valves          Revision Date  3/15/82          Page No.  21A

| MONTH | YEAR | FORECAST SALES | ACTUAL SALES | VARIANCE | PRODUCTION PLAN LIC | PRODUCTION PLAN KAN-PR | ACTUAL PRODUCTION LIC | ACTUAL PRODUCTION KAN-PR | VARIANCE LIC | VARIANCE KAN-PR | PROJECT INV. | ACTUAL INV. | VARIANCE | REMARKS |
|---|---|---|---|---|---|---|---|---|---|---|---|---|---|---|
| January | 81 | | 6000 | | 11.4 | | 11.0 | | − .4 | | | 31.0 | | Availability |
| February | 81 | | 6700 | | 7.0 | | 7.2 | | + .2 | | | 31.0 | | To = 3 months sales |
| March | 81 | | 6300 | | 5.5 | | 5.3 | | − .2 | | | 30.7 | | |
| April | 81 | | 7000 | | 5.8 | | 5.3 | | − .5 | | | 29.0 | | |
| May | 81 | | 6500 | | 5.0 | | 5.2 | | + .2 | | | 29.5 | | |
| June | 81 | | 7300 | | 5.5 | | 5.6 | | + .1 | | | 27.0 | | |
| July | 81 | 6600 | 7000 | + 400 | .6 | | .0 | | − .6 | | 20.9 | 20.3 | − .6 | |
| August | 81 | 6600 | 9000 | + 2400 | 6.0 | | 6.9 | | + .9 | | 19.7 | 19.0 | − .7 | |
| September | 81 | 6600 | 8200 | + 1600 | 7.7 | | 7.7 | | — | | 20.1 | 18.2 | − 1.9 | |
| October | 81 | 7200 | 7700 | + 500 | 7.4 | | 6.4 | | − 1.0 | | 18.4 | 17.8 | − .6 | Start to build up to |
| November | 81 | 7200 | 7900 | + 700 | 10.0 | | 10.0 | | — | | 20.6 | 20.6 | | 4 mos. inv. by 6/30/82 |
| December | 81 | 7200 | 6800 | − 400 | 8.1 | | 9.0 | | + .9 | | 21.5 | 23.5 | + 2.0 | |
| January | 82 | 6800 | 5400 | − 1400 | 7.3 | | 7.3 | | — | | 25.6 | 25 | − .2 | |
| February | 82 | 6800 | 6500 | − 300 | 7.4 | | 6.8 | | — | | 25.6 | 26.6 | + 1.0 | |
| March | 82 | 6800 | | | 7.3 | | | | | | 27.1 | | | |
| April | 82 | 6300 | | | 6.0 | | | | | | 26.8 | | | |
| May | 82 | 6300 | | | 6.6 | | | | | | 27.1 | | | |
| June | 82 | 6300 | | | 7.5 | | | | | | 28.3 | | | |
| July | 82 | 6300 | | | 2.7 | | | | | | 22.0 | | | |
| August | 82 | 6300 | | | 5.4 | | | | | | 21.1 | | | |
| September | 82 | 6300 | | | 5.7 | | | | | | 20.5 | | | |
| October | 82 | | | | | | | | | | | | | |
| November | 82 | | | | | | | | | | | | | |
| December | 82 | | | | | | | | | | | | | |

Figure 5-4.

```
P/N
FN:                         TIME PHASED MATERIAL PLAN                    PAGE:    1
ITEM NO: D3240                        CASE                           DATE: 04/28/82
ORDER NO:            ORD POL: A  CTL: 1  SAFETY STK:                  SHRINK:   0 %
-----                                                                        -----
DUE   ***** REQUIREMENTS *****  ********* O R D E R S *********** PROJECTED
DATE  TYPE QUANTITY     REF.   REL. TYPE S   NUMBER    F QUANTITY  BALANCE
----  --- ---------     ------------- --- - -------   - --------- --------

                                                      ON-HAND:      36,292
01/06 ALC  13,209                   PEG O  0756999    M              23,083
01/16             6500   12/22 M    O  0749999    M   19,793        42,876
01/25 ALC  22,709                   PEG O  0768999    M              20,167
02/01 ALC  12,138                   PEG O  0773999    M
02/01             7020   12/28 M    O  0751999    M   12,209        20,238
03/02 DEP  14,280                   PEG F  0793048    M
03/02             8140   01/28 M    O  0771048        14,042        20,000
03/22                    02/18 M    P  0785048        13,209        33,209
04/13                    03/11 M    P  0800049        18,209        46,418
04/21 DEP   6,200                   PEG F  0828999    M              40,218
04/28 IND     100                        F           M              40,119
05/04                    04/01M     P  0815049        13,209        53,327
05/06 DEP  39,627                   PEG F  0839999    M              13,700
----- RPAD40: ITEM IN NEED OF REPLANNING                                    -----
```

Figure 5–5.

OPEN PURCHASES AS OF 04/17/82                              PAGE    1

| MATERIAL COST/M | RECEIPTS MTD$$ | LTD | PAST DUE | ASAP/ CURR | MAY | JUN | JUL | AUG | OVER 6/MTHS | HFR |
|---|---|---|---|---|---|---|---|---|---|---|
| | | | | ---------- OPEN PURCHASES | | | COMMITTED $$ ---------------- | | | |
| 4110.0000 | | 17 | | | 20554 | 20554 | | | | |
| 593.1300 | | 17 | | | 593 | | | | | |
| 18.1900 | | 30 | | | | 9095 | | | | |
| 7.6000 | | 30 | | | | | 3300 | | | |
| 616.6500 | | 17 | | | 969 | 969 | | 969 | | |
| 6360.0000 | | 24 | | | | | | 6360 | 12721 | |
| 625.2100 | | 24 | | | | 625 | | | | |
| 647.1300 | | 24 | 62 | | | | | | | |
| 385.2400 | | 17 | | 1926 | | | | 1540 | 1540 | |
| 222.2500 | | | | | | | | | | |
| 3313.7000 | | 16 | | | 3313 | | | | | |
| 181.7100 | | 14 | | | 4542 | | | | | |
| 21.0000 | | 10 | 105 | | | | | | | |
| 603.9300 | | 17 | | | 9662 | 4831 | | | | |
| 84.5000 | | 16 | | | 2535 | 5915 | | | | |
| 65.3600 | | 14 | 2549 | | | | | | | |
| 110.0000 | | | | 110 | | | | | | |
| TOTAL | | | 2716 | 2036 | 42108 | 41989 | 3800 | 8869 | 14261 | |

Figure 5–6.

ALT-CD= N   PART-NO.=GK235    DESCRIPTION=CONDENSER    DEPT=03   DIV=S1   PART-TYP=    DND=    UM=PC   MPB=M   CL=02   GP=26

| L V | 1 2 3 4 5 6 7 8 9 10 | QTY/PER ASSBLY | UM | QTY/PER THOU | ALT LTR | DESCRIPTION | DEPT NO. | DIV | PART TYP | DND CD | UM | MPD CD | CL | GP |
|---|---|---|---|---|---|---|---|---|---|---|---|---|---|---|
| 01 | A1113 | 1 | PC | | E | COND TCP | 26 | S1 | A | | PC | M | 02 | 26 |
| 02 | A1113A | | LB | 1.210 | | POWDER | 00 | S1 | | | LB | B | 02 | 26 |
| 01 | A1676X | 1 | PC | | | WINDING | 11 | S1 | A | | PC | M | 02 | 26 |
| 02 | A1676x-1 | 1 | PC | | | WINDING | 11 | S1 | | | PC | M | 02 | 26 |
| 03 | A412A | | LB | 4.800 | | MYLAR | 00 | S1 | | | LB | B | 01 | 25 |
| 03 | A701A | | LB | 4.200 | | FOIL | 00 | S1 | | | LB | B | 01 | 26 |
| 02 | CPS529A | | LB | .450 | K | STIP | 00 | S1 | | | LB | B | 02 | 65 |
| 01 | BN1 | | PC | | | CARTON | 00 | S1 | | D | PC | B | 99 | 99 |
| 01 | CPS147A | | LB | 1.880 | | WAX | 00 | S1 | A | | LB | B | 02 | 26 |
| 01 | CPS446-35X | 1 | PC | | | SHELL | 13 | S1 | A | | PC | M | 99 | 99 |
| 02 | CPS446-35XPL | 1 | PC | | | PL SHELL | 41 | S1 | | | PC | M | 99 | 99 |
| 03 | CPS446-35X1 | 1 | PC | | | SHELL | 13 | S1 | | | PC | M | 99 | 99 |
| 04 | A402A | | LB | 15.200 | P | STEEL STRIP | 00 | S1 | | | LB | B | 01 | 65 |
| 04 | MH-PRESS 26 | | MH | .337 | | MAN HOURS | 13 | S1 | Z | D | MH | M | 99 | 99 |
| 05 | MH-PP | | MH | 1000.000 | | MAN HOURS | 00 | S1 | Z | D | MH | B | 99 | 99 |
| 01 | CPS536A | | FT | 52.500 | F | TUBING | 00 | S1 | A | | FT | B | 02 | 26 |
| 01 | CPS635A | | FT | 292.000 | V | WIRE | 00 | S1 | A | | FT | B | 02 | 26 |
| 01 | CPS644 | 1 | PC | | G | TUBE | 00 | S1 | A | | PC | M | 02 | 26 |
| 01 | CPS783 | 1 | PC | | D | SOLD PELLET | 03 | S1 | A | D | PC | B | 02 | 26 |
| 02 | CPS783A | | LB | .440 | B | SOLDER | 00 | S1 | | | LB | B | 99 | 99 |
| 02 | CPS790 | 1 | PC | | D | BRACKET | 13 | S1 | A | | PC | M | 99 | 99 |
| 02 | CPS790PL | 1 | PC | | | PLBRACKET | 41 | S1 | | | PC | M | 99 | 99 |
| 03 | CPS790-1 | 1 | PC | | | BRACKET | 13 | S1 | | | PC | M | 99 | 99 |
| 04 | CPS790A | | LB | 11.400 | T | STEEL STRIP | 00 | S1 | | | LB | B | 02 | 29 |
| 01 | CPS858A | 1 | PC | | | TERMINAL | 00 | S1 | A | | PC | B | 02 | 26 |
| 01 | SM125 | 1 | PC | | F | TERMINAL | 00 | S1 | A | | PC | B | 01 | 26 |
| 02 | 205UX-GK235 | 1 | PC | | | PRINTED BOX | 32 | S1 | | D | PC | M | 02 | 26 |
| 01 | 205UX-BLANK | 1 | PC | | | BOX | 00 | S1 | | D | PC | B | 02 | 67 |
| 01 | 5UX-GK235 | 1 | PC | | | PRINTED BOX | 32 | S1 | | D | PC | M | 02 | 26 |
| 02 | 5UX-BLANK | 1 | PC | | | BOX | 00 | S1 | | D | PC | B | 02 | 67 |

Figure 5-7.

in Figure 5–7 indicates that there are 14 component parts in a condenser and further that several of these components are made up of subcomponents which in certain instances are made up of other subcomponents. Thus the second component listed, A 1676X, is made up of two subcomponents, A 1676X-1 and CPS 529A. Subcomponent A 1676X-1 in turn is made up of A 412A and A 701A. The system of Standard Motor Products also incorporates machine utilization in its component listing. It may be seen that the shell of the condenser, for example, is processed on a power press (MH-PP) and then on a specialized press (MH-Press 26).

**D. BOM Used On List.**   Traditionally the bill of materials is a document which lists all the component parts used in a finished product. From the point of view of material requirements planning however it is often useful to know which finished products contain a given component. At Standard Motor Products, this output is known as the *BOM used on list* and is presented in Figure 5–8. It may be seen that twenty finished items and/or parts make use of MH-Press 25 which is treated as a component part.

## Work in Process

The computerized manufacturing information system at Standard Motor Products provides a comprehensive mix of screen formats and hard copy reports both to manufacturing managers and to shop floor supervisors and foremen. Figure 5–9 is a production and inventory planning document designed for the managerial level. For each product item in the line, it plots requirements against planned work order releases. This information is provided for four ranges of time periods: (a) daily requirements and releases for the ten working days immediately following the report date, (b) weekly requirements and releases for the ten weeks following, (c) biweekly requirements and releases for the subsequent three-month period, and (d) all ad-

```
ICNDA15      3 0 M  USED ON LIST                    COMPONENT PART MH-PRESS 25
PLANNER   PS. POWER PRESS         UM=MH  PT-TYP= Z     DND=5 ALT=   MAN HOURS
USED ON PARENT  QTY/PARENT     MP3 PL      USED ON PARENT  QTY/PARENT    MPH PL
S4144X-2                .114 MH   M       CA150LX-2               .199 MH   M
MP910                   .104 MH   M       A1601                   .101 MH   M
G60J7-1                 .138 MH   M
FM160-55A               .130 MH   M
D1804-1                 .099 MH   M
D1702                   .101 MH   M
D1557-1                 .249 MH   M
D1523-1                 .229 MH   M
D1157-1                 .221 MH   M
D1058-1                 .249 MH   M
C64-70F1                .138 MH   M
C64-215F2               .194 MH   M
CPA50C-1                .261 MH   M
CPA18C-1                .261 MH   M
CA935XP-2               .097 MH   M
CA483L                  .139 MH   M
CA456-1                 .124 MH   M
CA150RX-2               .177 MH   M
```

Figure 5–8.

**B2346          COMPONENT ASSM.**

```
GENERAL ITEM DATA  : U/M = EA   , ITEM TYPE = 1 ASSEMB , UNITCST = 582.150 , ORDRCST =   800 , CARRYCST =  0.100%
ORDER POLICY       : DSCRET QTY , ORDER QTY = 20       , ORD CUT DT= 01/02/79 , MINIMUM =   0 , MAXIMUM =   0 , MULTIPLE = 0
SUPPLY INFORMATION : PRODUCTION ,                        MIN DAYS=  0 , MAX DAYS= 0 , RUN TIME= 2685/48000
INVENTORY DATA     :              PUR LEAD = 120        , PRD LEAD = 120/ , S/U TIME= 3/ 480
                     ON HAND  = 120 , SAFETY = 0 , SHRINK = 0%
```

|              | PAST DUE | 06/01/79 | 06/04/79 | 06/05/79 | 06/06/79 | 06/07/79 | 06/08/79 | 06/11/79 | 06/12/79 | 06/13/79 |
|--------------|----------|----------|----------|----------|----------|----------|----------|----------|----------|----------|
| GROSS REQ.   |          |          |          |          |          |          |          |          |          |          |
| ON ORDER     |          |          |          |          |          |          |          |          |          |          |
| NET REQ.     |          |          |          |          |          |          |          |          |          |          |
| PLANNED REL. |          |          |          |          |          |          |          |          |          |          |

|              | 06/14/79 | 06/21/79 | 06/27/79 | 07/06/79 | 07/13/79 | 07/20/79 | 07/21/79 | 08/03/79 | 08/10/79 | 08/17/79 |
|--------------|----------|----------|----------|----------|----------|----------|----------|----------|----------|----------|
| GROSS REQ.   |          |          |          |          | 40       | 39       | 40       | 37       | 41       | 40       |
| ON ORDER     |          |          |          |          |          |          |          |          |          |          |
| NET REQ.     |          |          |          |          | 36       | 41       | 40       | 36       | 41       | 40       |
| PLANNED REL. |          |          |          |          |          |          |          | 38       | 80       | 37       |

|              | 08/24/79 | 09/10/79 | 09/24/79 | 10/08/79 | 10/22/79 | 11/05/79 | 11/19/79 | 12/05/79 | 12/19/79 | BEYOND |
|--------------|----------|----------|----------|----------|----------|----------|----------|----------|----------|--------|
| GROSS REQ.   | 118      | 77       | 80       | 75       | 81       | 78       | 78       | 78       | 39       | 972    |
| ON ORDER     |          |          |          |          |          |          |          |          |          |        |
| NET REQ.     | 118      | 77       | 80       | 75       | 81       | 78       | 78       | 78       | 39       | 972    |
| PLANNED REL. | 81       | 77       | 78       | 79       | 79       | 76       | 40       | 78       | 77       | 856    |

**A8796          PART ASSM.**

```
GENERAL ITEM DATA  : U/M = EA   , ITEM TYPE = 1 ASSEMB , UNITCST = 32.490 , ORDRCST = 6.100 , CARRYCST =  0.100%
ORDER POLICY       : FIXED OQ   , ORDER QTY = 200      , ORD CUT DT= 01/02/79 , MINIMUM = 200 , MAXIMUM = 200 , MULTIPLE = 200
SUPPLY INFORMATION : PRODUCTION ,                        MIN DAYS= 0 , MAX DAYS= 0 , RUN TIME= 2650/48000
INVENTORY DATA     :              PUR LEAD = 168        , PRD LEAD = 120/ , S/U TIME= 19/ 480
                     ON HAND  = 168 , SAFETY = 0 , SHRINK = 0%
```

|              | PAST DUE | 06/01/79 | 06/04/79 | 06/05/79 | 06/06/79 | 06/07/79 | 06/08/79 | 06/11/79 | 06/12/79 | 06/13/79 |
|--------------|----------|----------|----------|----------|----------|----------|----------|----------|----------|----------|
| GROSS REQ.   |          |          |          |          |          |          |          |          |          |          |
| ON ORDER     |          |          |          |          |          |          |          |          |          |          |
| NET REQ.     |          |          |          |          |          |          |          |          |          |          |
| PLANNED REL. |          |          |          |          |          |          |          |          |          |          |

|              | 06/14/79 | 06/21/79 | 06/27/79 | 07/06/79 | 07/13/79 | 07/20/79 | 07/21/79 | 08/03/79 | 08/10/79 | 08/17/79 |
|--------------|----------|----------|----------|----------|----------|----------|----------|----------|----------|----------|
| GROSS REQ.   |          |          |          |          | 36       | 41       | 40       | 38       | 80       | 37       |
| ON ORDER     |          |          |          |          |          |          |          | 67       |          |          |
| NET REQ.     |          |          |          |          |          |          |          |          |          |          |
| PLANNED REL. |          |          | 200      |          |          |          |          | 200      |          |          |

|              | 08/24/79 | 09/10/79 | 09/24/79 | 10/08/79 | 10/22/79 | 11/05/79 | 11/19/79 | 12/05/79 | 12/19/79 | BEYOND |
|--------------|----------|----------|----------|----------|----------|----------|----------|----------|----------|--------|
| GROSS REQ.   | 81       | 77       | 78       | 79       | 79       | 76       | 76       | 40       | 77       | 856    |
| ON ORDER     |          |          |          |          |          |          |          |          |          |        |
| NET REQ.     | 81       | 77       | 78       | 79       | 79       | 76       | 76       | 40       | 77       | 856    |
| PLANNED REL. | 200      |          | 200      |          | 200      |          | 200      |          | 200      | 800    |

Figure 5-9.

ditional requirements and releases. In addition there is a comprehensive header description furnishing the manager with information such as the unit of measure, unit cost, order cost, carrying cost, order quantity, minimum, maximum, multiple, date of order, lead times, run times, on hand quantity, safety stock level, and allowable shrinkage percentage. The comprehensive information for every item scheduled for production enables the manager to control his operation and follow up the status of any item about which a question may arise.

At the shop floor level, the system provides 23 screen formats and hard copy reports designed for factory shop order control. We present in Figure 5–10 a menu listing these 23 outputs. It may be seen that the supervisors and foremen have access to a computerized recordkeeping system that assists them in controlling shop activities and at the same time provides input data, as a by product, for higher-level managerial reports.

## Finished Goods Inventory Management

The purpose of the manufacturing function is to deliver to the finished goods warehouse the proper quantity and quality of finished product items to satisfy actual or

THE FOLLOWING IS A LIST OF SCREENS AND REPORTS FOR
FACTORY SHOP ORDER CONTROL:

```
1......SHOP ORDER RELEASE SCREEN
2......FIRST R.S.L.C. ENTRY
3......SECOND R.S.L.C. ENTRY
4......FIRST MANIFEST ENTRY
5......FIRST RETURN TO STOCK MANIFEST ENTRY
6......FOREMAN'S CLOSE OUT ENTRY SCREEN
7......HISTORY OF SHOP ORDERS BY SHOP ORDER NUMBER
8......SHOP ORDER HISTORY BY ITEM
9......CLEARING HOUSE CLOSE ENTRY
10.....RECEIPTS INTO STOCK ENTRY FOR O. STITT
```

HARD COPY REPORTS—FACTORY SHOP ORDER CONTROL:

```
1......HORIZON REPORT SEVEN MONTHS OUT
1A.....L.M.P.S. REPORT MANPOWER LOADING
2......WEEKLY HORIZON REPORT SEVEN WEEKS OUT
3......IN PROCESS SHOP ORDER PRIORITY REPORT
4......PAST-DUE SECOND ENTRY FOR RS/MF/RSLC
5......BATCH CARDS
6......COMPARISON OF FIRST AND SECOND ENTRY FOR RS/MF/RSLC
6A.....MAINTENANCE REPORT OF AND TO R.S.L.C.
7......WEEKLY FLOOR STOCK INVENTORY REPORT
```

CLEARING HOUSE FUNCTION

```
1......SHOP ORDER CLOSE OUT OF UNRESOLVED DISCREPENCIES
2......DAILY CLEARING HOUSE SHOP ORDER CLOSE OUT
       EXCEPTION REPORT
3......DELAYED SHOP ORDER CLOSE OUT DUE TO STOCK
       ROOM DELAY
4......MONTHLY SUMMARY SHOP ORDER CLOSE OUT REPORT
```

Figure 5–10.

projected sales demand. Thus it is reasonable for the manufacturing manager to take an active interest in the condition of the finished goods inventory. Four of the outputs in this area available to the managers at Standards Motor Products are herewith presented:

**A. Net Requirement Report.** This report, depicted in Figure 5–11, accumulates by product item and by time periods the total number of units required to be delivered to the finished goods warehouse. As seen on a previous report there are varied ranges of time periods, in this case, weekly cumulative totals for the eight weeks following the report date, and four-week cumulative totals for the twenty subsequent weeks.

**B. Finished Goods Inventory Analysis.** In the United States, Standard Motor Products fills its customers' orders from distribution centers in Long Island City, New York; Edwardsville, Kansas; Reno, Nevada; and Montgomery, Alabama. It is important that each center have on hand an adequate stock to satisfy anticipated demand. The *finished goods inventory analysis,* a sample page of which is reproduced in Figure 5–12, provides the information needed by the manager to properly balance his finished goods inventory. For each product group within each product class within each distribution center, a twelve-month average sales figure as well as last month's shipments are given. In addition, projected sales for this month and for each of the next three months are listed. Actual sales for this month-to-date are also shown. These sales figures are then compared to the *on hand plus in transit inventory* and to the effective *available inventory*. The available inventory is the on hand inventory less the quantity already allocated to fill orders but not yet shipped. Thus, for inventory management, the available inventory is the more important figure.

If we examine the position of the first product class/group shown in Figure 5–12, 03 33, we see that the Long Island City center has 134 units available to ship against projected sales of 1,265 units this month and 1,343 units next month. At the same time, the Reno center has almost a two-year supply available and the Kansas facility has a six to seven week supply based on projected sales. After checking the production schedule to determine how many units he may expect to receive from the plant, the manager at Long Island City knows from this report that he may cover any shortfall by calling in stock from the other two distribution centers.

**C. Inventory Availability Analysis.** The unit information on the previously-discussed report is presented in somewhat different form on the *corporate inventory availability analysis,* illlustrated in Figure 5–13. Here, the amount available to ship of each product item is shown, as are also the number of units on back order, the month-to-date and year-to-date sales. In addition the equivalent dollar values of the units are given. The information on this report identifies for the manager the specific product items within each product class and group that require attention.

**D. Status Summary for Planners.** The finished goods inventory at Standard Motor Products is divided into five classes, identified as A, B, C, D, and E. Product items

DCWBC30
AS OF 04/09/82   CLASS 02   GROUP 67   MP P   STANDARD MOTOR PRODUCTS   *LIC MFG*   PAGE 46

NET REQUIREMENT REPORT FOR STANDARD

| ABC CD | AV CD | SAFETY STOCK | 04/12 | 04/19 | 04/26 | 05/03 | 05/10 | 05/17 | 05/24 | 05/31 | 06/07 06/28 | 07/05 07/26 | 08/02 08/23 | 08/30 09/20 | 09/27 10/18 |
|---|---|---|---|---|---|---|---|---|---|---|---|---|---|---|---|
| A | T | 649 | | | | | | | | | 3571 | 7731 | 12074 | 16627 | 21480 |
| A | 1 | 2701 | | | | | | 160 | 3079 | 5983 | 17371 | 29424 | 42056 | 55386 | 69791 |
| A | 1 | 2728 | | | | | | 1094 | 4480 | 7813 | 21146 | 35098 | 49837 | 65331 | 82090 |
| A | 8 | 824 | | | | | | | 951 | 2228 | 7331 | 12707 | 18377 | 24355 | 30787 |
| A | 8 | 327 | | | | 109 | 685 | 1256 | 1834 | 2411 | 4786 | 7215 | 9814 | 12584 | 15572 |
| A | 1 | 2919 | | | | | | 746 | 3887 | 7019 | 19442 | 32608 | 46383 | 60912 | 76808 |
| A | 1 | 2851 | | | | | | | | | 12210 | 27655 | 43848 | 60962 | 79194 |
| A | 1 | 5171 | | | | | | 1179 | | 6377 | 25883 | 46715 | 67966 | 91080 | 115512 |
| A | 1 | 7405 | | | | | | | | 3089 | 55186 | 109402 | 166239 | 225827 | 289304 |
| A | 1 | 1907 | | | | | | | 1294 | 3743 | 13449 | 23691 | 34410 | 45698 | 57789 |
| A | 1 | 1281 | | | | | | 1503 | 3390 | 5209 | 12687 | 20514 | 28734 | 37421 | 46650 |
| A | 1 | 3994 | | | | | | | | | 15175 | 34130 | 54084 | 74413 | 96940 |
| A | 1 | 6726 | | | | | | | 6226 | 17956 | 64879 | 113534 | 164497 | 217683 | 274474 |
| A | 1 | 4304 | | | | | 2823 | 6840 | 10643 | 14706 | 29965 | 46149 | 62978 | 80423 | 99635 |
| A | 1 | 1415 | | | | | | 8 | 1601 | 3200 | 9557 | 16282 | 23325 | 30762 | 38897 |
| A | 1 | 3751 | | 288 | 3309 | 6619 | 9910 | 13204 | 16520 | 19845 | 32391 | 44545 | 57444 | 71570 | 86592 |
| B | 1 | 378 | | | | | | | 288 | 707 | 2908 | 5203 | 7577 | 10080 | 12843 |
| B | 1 | 496 | | | | | | | | | 67 | 2251 | 4484 | 6822 | 9600 |
| B | 1 | 329 | | | | | | | | | | | 1395 | 2883 | 4559 |
| C | 1 | 482 | | | | | | | | | | | | | 146 |
| C | 8 | 24 | | | 6 | 18 | 29 | 39 | 79 | 89 | 158 | 233 | 309 | 388 | 482 |
| C | | | | | | | | | | | | | | | |
| C | 1 | 209 | | | | | | | | | | | | 819 | 2372 |
| C | 1 | 436 | | | | | | | | | 510 | 2228 | 3960 | 5682 | 7552 |
| PER TOTALS | | | 0 | 288 | 3027 | 3431 | 6701 | 11403 | 30601 | 44934 | 248287 | 268643 | 282476 | 297917 | 321361 |

Figure 5-11.

AS OF 05/29/81

FINISHED GOODS INVENTORY ANALYSIS
BY CLASS AND GROUP

PAGE NO. 5

| PROD CL/GR | M CL | PCT TOTAL | LOC | DEMAND HIST 12 MO AVE | LAST MO | CURRENT DSA | CH+INTRAN | EFF AVL | SAL | PROJECTED SALES SAL+1 | SAL+2 | SAL+3 |
|---|---|---|---|---|---|---|---|---|---|---|---|---|
| 03 33 | M | | LIC | 1,372 | 763 | 684 | 1,166 | 134 | 1,265 | 1,343 | 855 | 864 |
| | | | REN | 35 | 42 | 25 | 829 | 829 | 50 | 50 | 25 | 33 |
| | | | KAN | 1,663 | 1,743 | 2,430 | 9,569 | 7,804 | 4,980 | 5,032 | 2,894 | 3,082 |
| | | | MTG | 535 | 1,694 | 678 | 213 | 840 | 738 | 738 | 738 | 738 |
| | | | CRP | 3,605 | 4,242 | 3,817 | 11,777 | 9,607 | 7,033 | 7,163 | 4,512 | 4,717 |
| 03 33 | P | | LIC | 439 | 309 | 306 | 2,740 | 2,533 | 531 | 397 | 339 | 355 |
| | | | REN | 82 | 61 | 51 | 260 | 251 | 99 | 56 | 51 | 51 |
| | | | KAN | 582 | 407 | 409 | 1,096 | 646 | 791 | 561 | 423 | 482 |
| | | | MTG | 230 | 481 | 461 | 542 | 395 | 502 | 502 | 502 | 502 |
| | | | CRP | 1,333 | 1,258 | 1,227 | 4,638 | 3,825 | 1,923 | 1,516 | 1,315 | 1,390 |
| 04 24 | M | .9 | LIC | 89,216 | 44,693 | 79,775 | 568,671 | 518,194 | 63,009 | 64,134 | 70,753 | 85,803 |
| | | | REN | 28,915 | 25,056 | 25,757 | 51,111 | 60,301 | 23,747 | 20,099 | 23,363 | 27,513 |
| | | | KAN | 42,224 | 39,777 | 35,856 | 84,982 | 86,424 | 31,426 | 30,300 | 30,325 | 38,597 |
| | | | MTG | 10,403 | 14,971 | 17,640 | 53,659 | 49,010 | 19,226 | 19,226 | 19,226 | 19,226 |
| | | | CRP | 170,758 | 124,497 | 159,028 | 758,423 | 713,929 | 137,408 | 133,759 | 143,667 | 171,139 |
| 05 14 | P | | LIC | 135 | 50 | 77 | 664 | 564 | 57 | 75 | 79 | 97 |
| | | | REN | 36 | 58 | 37 | 65 | 99 | 31 | 39 | 35 | 47 |
| | | | KAN | 79 | 49 | 77 | 190 | 190 | 64 | 80 | 75 | 97 |
| | | | MTG | 20 | 9 | 30 | 106 | 115 | 32 | 32 | 32 | 32 |
| | | | CRP | 270 | 166 | 221 | 1,025 | 968 | 184 | 226 | 221 | 273 |
| 05 15 | P | .7 | LIC | 59,054 | 48,919 | 49,704 | 333,921 | 277,561 | 47,339 | 41,730 | 43,099 | 47,296 |
| | | | REN | 14,075 | 13,748 | 12,770 | 24,548 | 25,128 | 12,169 | 11,200 | 11,309 | 12,666 |
| | | | KAN | 44,197 | 29,277 | 34,267 | 69,445 | 67,069 | 36,268 | 30,291 | 28,313 | 32,610 |
| | | | MTG | 13,255 | 20,169 | 22,164 | 41,409 | 43,952 | 24,153 | 24,153 | 24,153 | 24,153 |
| | | | CRP | 130,581 | 112,113 | 118,905 | 469,323 | 413,710 | 119,929 | 106,374 | 106,874 | 116,725 |
| 06 89 | P | .3 | LIC | 21,682 | 16,371 | 16,562 | 150,797 | 135,967 | 25,466 | 18,866 | 19,307 | 16,923 |
| | | | REN | 3,183 | 3,534 | 3,589 | 9,141 | 9,585 | 4,142 | 3,645 | 4,525 | 3,807 |
| | | | KAN | 22,858 | 24,865 | 20,115 | 52,576 | 48,173 | 34,405 | 24,166 | 22,326 | 20,547 |
| | | | MTG | 8,813 | 27,935 | 16,076 | 26,829 | 25,323 | 17,522 | 17,522 | 17,522 | 17,522 |
| | | | CRP | 56,536 | 72,705 | 56,342 | 239,343 | 219,048 | 81,535 | 64,199 | 63,680 | 58,799 |
| 06 90 | M | .8 | LIC | 51,003 | 31,464 | 33,767 | 306,973 | 252,798 | 30,066 | 27,266 | 30,124 | 36,492 |
| | | | REN | 27,743 | 25,815 | 24,504 | 50,349 | 57,145 | 21,332 | 18,413 | 22,031 | 24,748 |
| | | | KAN | 48,028 | 27,696 | 29,278 | 62,752 | 87,639 | 28,991 | 24,879 | 24,879 | 31,617 |
| | | | MTG | 13,974 | 23,051 | 21,618 | 52,132 | 60,599 | 23,553 | 23,553 | 23,553 | 23,553 |
| | | | CRP | 140,748 | 108,026 | 109,167 | 492,206 | 458,181 | 103,942 | 94,111 | 100,587 | 116,410 |
| 06 90 | P | .2 | LIC | 20,515 | 13,666 | 15,895 | 116,159 | 107,242 | 18,157 | 10,858 | 16,195 | 17,329 |
| | | | REN | 10,001 | 10,021 | 8,982 | 19,459 | 19,396 | 8,902 | 7,193 | 7,102 | 10,246 |
| | | | KAN | 12,326 | 8,196 | 7,424 | 22,936 | 18,859 | 9,424 | 5,333 | 7,211 | 8,097 |
| | | | MTG | 5,840 | 8,250 | 9,104 | 24,109 | 21,402 | 9,931 | 9,931 | 9,931 | 9,931 |
| | | | CRP | 50,682 | 40,133 | 41,405 | 182,663 | 166,899 | 46,414 | 33,315 | 40,439 | 45,603 |

**Figure 5-12.**

PCMBC05     HYGRADE CORPORATE INVENTORY AVAILABILITY ANALYSIS     PAGE 21
             AS OF 4/28/82 IN ITEM SEQUENCE

| PART-NO. | INV CLASS | UNITS AVAILIBLE | UNITS BACK ORD | UNITS MTD-SALES | UNITS YTD-SALES | DOLLARS AVAILABLE | DOLLARS BACK ORD | DOLLARS MTD-SALES | DOLLARS YTD-SALES |
|---|---|---|---|---|---|---|---|---|---|
| | A | 4,540 | | 3,860 | 15,420 | 29,011 | | 24,665 | 98,534 |
| | D | 466 | 2 | 72 | 247 | 1,906 | 8 | 294 | 1,010 |
| | D | 1 | | | | 7 | | | |
| | D | 572 | 1 | 66 | 389 | 3,604 | 6 | 416 | 2,451 |
| | E | 1,680 | 8 | 38 | 197 | 9,643 | 6 | 218 | 1,131 |
| | D | | 10 | | | | 57 | | |
| | A | 15,421 | 6 | 4,766 | 17,394 | 109,335 | 43 | 33,791 | 123,323 |
| | A | 1 | 1 | | | 6 | 6 | | |
| | E | 3,090 | | 73 | 1,241 | 39,459 | | 932 | 15,848 |
| | C | 1,292 | 1 | 54 | 207 | 6,189 | 5 | 259 | 992 |
| | D | | 16 | | | | 184 | | |
| | D | 1,993 | 7 | 208 | 816 | 35,774 | 23 | 3,734 | 14,647 |
| | B | 1,668 | 142 | 2,886 | 15,935 | 7,423 | 632 | 12,843 | 70,911 |
| | E | | 9 | | | | 9 | | |
| | C | 5,383 | 18 | 449 | 1,899 | 83,652 | 280 | 6,977 | 29,510 |
| | A | | 3 | | | | 11 | | |
| | E | 2 | 12 | | | 8 | 46 | | |
| | D | 62 | 1 | 4 | 7 | 298 | 6 | 19 | 34 |
| | E | 696 | | 37 | 124 | 4,440 | | 236 | 791 |
| | D | 959 | 2 | 35 | 182 | 6,742 | 14 | 246 | 1,279 |
| | D | 7,680 | 13 | 3,026 | 13,638 | 49,459 | 84 | 19,487 | 87,829 |
| | C | 1,125 | 1 | 489 | 1,700 | 14,366 | 13 | 6,245 | 21,709 |
| | B | | | | 1 | | | | 7 |
| | A | 7,528 | 1 | 3,504 | 15,206 | 56,084 | 7 | 26,105 | 113,285 |
| | C | 3,032 | | 1,215 | 5,328 | 20,618 | | 8,262 | 36,230 |
| | C | 3,110 | | 1,169 | 5,360 | 17,851 | | 6,710 | 30,766 |
| | B | | | | | 4 | | | |
| | B | 88- | 7 | 2,633 | 13,489 | 515- | 30 | 15,403 | 78,911 |
| | A | 10,549 | 52 | 303 | 303 | 61,712 | 304 | 1,733 | 1,733 |
| | C | | 54 | | | | 316 | | |
| | C | 2,956 | 1 | 616 | 2,549 | 22,022 | 7 | 4,589 | 18,990 |
| | B | | | | | | | | |
| | E | 10,237 | 88 | 4,765 | 22,040 | 70,226 | 604 | 32,688 | 151,194 |
| | A | 1 | | | 7 | 5 | | | 35 |
| | C | 2,467 | 1 | 335 | 1,646 | 15,789 | 6 | 2,144 | 10,534 |
| | D | 169 | 1 | 37 | 137 | 472 | 3 | 103 | 382 |
| | D | 7 | | | | 7 | | | |
| | E | | | | | | | | |

Figure 5-13.

within these classes may be at the proper inventory level or they may be under-stocked or overstocked. The *status summary for planners,* shown in Figure 5-14, summarizes the total number of active items of product group and then gives the number and percentage of items that are understocked as well as those that are overstocked. Thus the summary of bulk items indicates that, out of 1412 active items 226 or 16% are understocked whereas 38% of the items have excessive stock. Certainly, this is the kind of information the manager needs to alert him to the possible need for revising his production schedule.

As the table of contents from the *Handbook of Production Forms* revealed, these few sample reports from Standard Motor Products, Inc. are but a small fraction of the voluminous outputs used by manufacturing managers at this or any other manufacturing firm to help them do their jobs properly. Yet it is hoped that they will give the reader an idea of the importance of a well-designed manufacturing information system.

## EVALUATION OF SYSTEM OUTPUTS

From a corporate point of view, the efficiency of the manufacturing operation can be assessed by investigating two areas of organizational activity. The records of the customer service department will reveal the degree to which the firm's customers have their orders filled in terms of quantity, quality and timing. A gross profit variance analysis performed by the accounting or controller's department will in-form management of the cost effectiveness of the manufacturing operation. If these two studies produce satisfactory results, it can be safely assumed that the manu-facturing information system is providing accurate, relevant and timely information

```
STATUS SUMMARY FOR PLANNER     RT. RESALE - BULK

                               QTY     PERC

TOTAL ACTIVE ITEMS
            A ITEMS             75
            B ITEMS            101
            C ITEMS            459
            C ITEMS            702
            E ITEMS             75
            TOTAL             1412

LOW STOCK ITEMS
      LOW STOCK A               28       2
      LOW STOCK B               36       3
      LOW STOCK C               92       7
      LOW STOCK C               64       5
      LOW STOCK E                6       0
            TOTAL              226      16

EXCESSIVE STOCK - A              5       0
EXCESSIVE STOCK - B             16       1
EXCESSIVE STOCK - C            110       8
EXCESSIVE STOCK - D            352      25
EXCESSIVE STOCK - E             58       4
```

Figure 5-14.

to the managers in the manufacturing division. On the other hand, if shortcomings are brought to light by these two studies, it is a good bet that one of the problems that must be worked on is the lack of effectiveness of the manufacturing information system.

From an operational point of view, current computer technology dictates the conversion of manufacturing information systems to computerized systems. The outputs of Standard Motor Products, Inc. described in the previous section are a good example of a computerized manufacturing information system. The efficiency of a manufacturing information system cannot be evaluated positively if it does not take advantage of modern computer technology. For those firms that are still operating a manual system, and for those that have converted or are in the process of converting to a computerized system and wish to ascertain that they are on the right path, we are appending two brief articles at the end of this chapter explaining the role of computers in manufacturing management.

# The Ideas of Frederick W. Taylor: An Evaluation[1]

EDWIN A. LOCKE
University of Maryland

*The ideas and techniques of Frederick W. Taylor are examined with respect to their validity and their acceptance in modern management. With respect to the principle of scientific decision making and techniques such as time study, standardization, goal setting, money as a motivator, scientific selection, and rest pauses, Taylor's views were fundamentally correct and have been generally accepted. Most of the major criticisms that have been made of Taylor are unjustified. Taylor's genius has not been appreciated by many contemporary writers.*

Few management theorists have been more persistently criticized than has Frederick W. Taylor, the founder of scientific management, despite his being widely recognized as a key figure in the history of managment thought (Wren, 1979). Taylor and scientific management frequently were attacked in his own lifetime, prompting, among other responses, Gilbreth's *Primer* (Gilbreth, 1914/1973), and the criticisms have continued to this day.

The present author agrees with Drucker (1976), although not with all of his specific points, that Taylor has never been fully understood or appreciated by his critics. Many criticisms either have been invalid or have involved peripheral issues, and his major ideas and contributions often have gone unacknowledged.

Wren (1979) did a superb job of showing how Taylor's major ideas permeated the field of management both in the United States and abroad. However, Wren was not concerned primarily with

evaluating all of Taylor's techniques or the criticisms of his ideas. Boddewyn (1961), Drucker (1976), and Fry (1976) have made spirited defenses of Taylor, but more by way of broad overviews than in systematic detail. The present paper summarizes Taylor's major ideas and techniques and considers both their validity and their degree of acceptance in contemporary management. In addition, the major criticisms made of Taylor are systematically evaluated.

## Taylor's Philosophy of Management

An essential element of Taylor's philosophy of management, as the name of the movement implies, was a scientific approach to managerial decision making (Taylor, 1912/1970b; Sheldon, 1924/1976). The name was intended to contrast his approach with the unscientific approaches that characterized traditional management practices. By scientific, Taylor meant: based on proven fact (e.g., research and experimentation) rather than on tradition, rule of thumb, guesswork, precedent, personal opinion, or hearsay (Taylor, 1911/1967).

There can be no doubt that this element of Taylor's philosophy is accepted in modern management. This is not to say that all contemporary managers are fully rational decision makers. Clearly this is not the case. However, most would sub-

[1]This paper is based on the Annual Frederick J. Gaudet Memorial Lecture given at the Stevens Institute of Technology, Hoboken, N. J., on April 17, 1980. The author is greatly indebted to J. Myron Johnson of the Stevens Institute and Daniel Wren of the University of Oklahoma for their helpful comments on an earlier draft of this paper, as well as to Marvin Levine for his helpful input on the issue of labor management relations. The preparation of this paper was supported in part by Contract N00014-79-C-0680 between the University of Maryland and the Office of Naval Research.

Reprinted from ACADEMY OF MANAGEMENT REVIEW, Vol. 7, No. 1, January 1982, pp. 14–24 by permission.

scribe to the principle of scientific decision making and many actually practice it, at least with respect to some of their decisions. In most business schools there now is a specialized field called management science (which includes operations research), but the scientific approach is reflected in other areas of business as well (e.g., cost accounting). [See Kendall, (1924/1976) for a discussion of Taylor's early influence.] Taylor's goal was to forge a "mental revolution" in management, and in this aim he clearly succeeded. Drucker wrote that "Taylor was the first man in history who actually studied work seriously" (1976, p. 26).

A second element of Taylor's philosophy of management, and the other key aspect of the mental revolution that he advocated, concerned the relationship between management and labor. At the turn of the century, management-labor strife was widespread, violence was not uncommon, and a number of radical labor groups were advocating the violent overthrow of the capitalist system. Many believed that labor-management conflict was virtually inevitable.

Taylor argued that this view was false, that, at root, the interests of both parties were the same. Both would benefit, he argued, from higher production, lower costs, and higher wages, provided that management approached its job scientifically. Taylor believed that there would be no conflict over how to divide the pie as long as the pie were large enough (Taylor, 1912/1970b).

In logic, one cannot argue with Taylor's fundamental premise of a community of interest between management and labor. There were virtually no strikes in plants in which he applied scientific management (Taylor, 1911/1967; 1912/1970a). Wren (1979) argues that during the 1920s Taylor's hopes for union cooperation in introducing scientific management and in reducing waste were realized to a considerable extent in two industries. Unfortunately this attitude of cooperation ended in the 1930s when unions turned their attention to the passage of prolabor legislation.

In general, management-labor relations now are far more amicable than they were at the turn of the century, but all conflict has not been eliminated. One reason for this is that no matter how big the pie is, there still can be disagreements over how to divide it up. Taylor did not anticipate that as the pie got bigger, aspirations would rise accordingly.

## Taylor's Techniques

### Time and Motion Study

Before Taylor, there was no objective method for determining how fast a job should be done. Most managers simply used past experience as a guide. Taylor's solution was to break down the work task into its constituent elements or motions; to eliminate wasted motions so the work would be done in the *"one best way"* (Taylor, 1912/1970a, p. 85)—a principle even more strongly emphasized by Frank Gilbreth (1923/1970); and to time the remaining motions in order to arrive at an expected rate of production (a proper day's work).

Time study now is used routinely in industrialized countries. However, there has been no final solution to the problem of (partially) subjective elements in time study (e.g., fatigue allowances); nor has worker resistance to time study disappeared, although it should be noted that resistance is most likely when there is a lack of trust in management (Bartlem & Locke, 1981). Such lack of trust often is earned by practices such as rate-cutting—something that Taylor explicitly warned against.

### Standardized Tools and Procedures

Before scientific management, every workman had his own private tool box. This resulted in great inefficiencies because the proper tools were not always used or even owned. Taylor pushed strongly for standardization in the design and use of tools. The tools and procedures were standardized in accordance with what designs that experiments had shown to be most effective in a given context (e.g., the best size and shape for coal shovels).

Like time study, the principle of standardization is now well accepted. Combined with the principle of designing tools to fit people, the technique of standardization has evolved into the science of human engineering. Standardization also has been extended beyond the sphere of tool use to include other types of organizational procedures, especially in large firms.

### The Task

Taylor advocated that each worker be assigned a specific amount of work, of a certain quality, each day based on the results of time study. This assigned quota he called a "task" (Taylor, 1911/1967,

p. 120). The term task (which was not original to Taylor) is roughly equivalent to the term goal. Thus, the use of tasks was a forerunner of modern day goal-setting. It is worth noting that Wren's (1979) discussion of scientific management at DuPont and General Motors implies that there is an historical connection between it and the technique of management by objectives (MBO). Pierre DuPont adapted Taylor's cost control ideas in order to develop measures of organizational performance (such as "return on investment") for the DuPont Powder Company. One of his employees, Donaldson Brown, further developed the return on investment concept so that it could be used to compare the efficiency of various departments *within* Du-Pont. When Pierre DuPont became head of General Motors, he hired Brown and Alfred P. Sloan, who institutionalized Brown's ideas at General Motors. Thus, although the technique of MBO may have been an outgrowth of scientific management, it developed more directly from the concepts of feedback, performance measurement, and cost accounting than from the task concept. Taylor had introduced an interlocking cost and accounting system as early as 1893 (Copley, 1923, Vol. 1).

Drucker acknowledges that Sloan was one of the earliest users of the MBO technique, but the term evidently was coined by Drucker (1954) himself, based not just on his studies at GM but on his work at General Electric with Harold Smiddy (Greenwood, 1980). At GE, the technique of MBO came to mean objectives set jointly by the manager and his superior rather than simply assigned objectives and/or work measurement.

Another term used widely today is organizational behavior modification (OB Mod); most OB Mod studies merely involve goal-setting with feedback, described in behavioristic terminology (Locke, 1977). Virtually every contemporary theory of or approach to motivation now acknowledges the importance of goal setting either explicitly or implicitly (Locke, 1978).

The main effect of the post-Taylor research has been to support the validity of his practices. For example, it has been learned that specific challenging goals lead to better performance than do specific, easy goals or vague goals such as "do your best" or "no" goals (Locke, 1968; Locke, Shaw, Saari, & Latham, 1981). Taylor anticipated these results. The tasks his workers were assigned were, in fact,

both specific (quantitative) and challenging; they were set by time study to be reachable only by a trained, "first class" workman (Taylor, 1903/1970). Remarkably, Alfred P. Sloan himself said: "The guiding principle was to make our standards difficult to achieve, but possible to attain, which I believe is the most effective way of capitalizing on the initiative, resourcefulness, and capabilities of operating personnel" (Odiorne, 1978, p. 15).

Further, it now seems clear that feedback (knowledge of one's progress in relation to the task or goal) is esssential for goal setting to work (Locke et al., 1981), just as it is essential to have goals if feedback is to work (Locke et al., 1968). Again Taylor anticipated these findings. His workers were given feedback at least daily indicating whether or not they had attained their assigned task (Taylor, 1911/1967). A precursor of evaluative feedback for workers, developed a century before Taylor, was Robert Owen's "silent monitor" technique, described by Wren (1979, p. 72).

**The Money Bonus**

Taylor claimed that money was what the worker wanted most, and he argued that the worker should be paid from 30 percent to 100 percent higher wages in return for learning to do his job according to scientific management principles, that is, for *"carrying out orders"* (Boddewyn, 1961, p. 105), and for regularly attaining the assigned task.

Although money has been attacked frequently by social scientists from the time of the Hawthorne studies to the present, on the grounds that it is an inadequate motivator, Taylor's claim—that money is what the worker wants most—was not entirely misguided. A plethora of new incentive schemes have developed since Taylor's time, and new ones are still being tried (Latham & Dossett, 1978), not only for workers but for managers as well. Most labor-management conflicts still involve the issue of wages or issues related to wages, such as senority, rate setting, layoffs, and fringe benefits. New analyses of the Hawthorne studies indicate that their disparagement of money as a motivator was wrong (Carey, 1967; Franke & Kaul, 1978; Sykes, 1965; Lawler, 1975), and recent books and articles again are advocating the use of money to motivate workers (Lawler, 1971; Locke, 1975; Vough, 1975).

Pay has become a major issue even in the famous

Topeka experiment at General Foods, which was intended to stress job enrichment and participation (Walton, 1977), and it is a key element in the still popular Scanlon Plan (Frost, Wakeley & Ruh, 1974), long considered a human relations/organizational development technique. The pendulum now clearly seems to be swinging back toward Taylor's view (Locke, Feren, McCaleb, Shaw, & Denny, 1980). It is notable that one of the most outspoken contemporary advocates of money as a motivator is, like Taylor, an industrial engineer, Mitchell Fein. Fein has developed a new plant-wide incentive system called "Improshare" (Fein, 1977), which is coming into increasingly wide use.

### Individualized Work

Taylor was a staunch advocate of individual as opposed to group tasks, as well as individual rewards, because he believed that group work and rewards undermined individual productivity, due to such phenomena as "systematic soldiering." Taylor wrote, "Personal ambition always has been and will remain a more powerful incentive to exertion than a desire for the general welfare" (1912/1976, p. 17). In this respect, Taylor's views are in clear opposition to the trend of the past four to five decades, which has been toward group tasks.

Nevertheless, Taylor's warnings about the dangers of group work have proven to have some validity. For example, Janis (1972) has demonstrated that groups that become too cohesive are susceptible to groupthink, a cognitive disorder in which rational thinking is sacrificed in the name of unanimity. Latané, Williams and Harkins (1979) have documented a phenomenon called "social loafing," in which people working in a group put out less effort than when working alone even when they claim to be trying their hardest in both cases.

Studies of group decision making indicate that there is no universal superiority of groups over individuals or vice versa. Although a group might outperform the average individual member, the best group member is often superior to the group as a whole (Hall, 1971).

The current view seems to hold that although people may work less hard in groups (as Taylor claimed), the benefits in terms of cooperation, knowledge, and flexibility generally outweigh the costs. Overall, the evidence is not conclusive one way or the other. Most likely the final answer will depend on the nature of the task and other factors.

### Management Responsibility for Training

In line with his emphasis on a scientific approach to management, Taylor argued that employees should not learn their skills haphazardly from more experienced workers, who may not be using the "one best way," but from management experts who are thoroughly familiar with the job. There can be no doubt that most contemporary managers fully accept the notion that training new employees is their responsibility. Furthermore, the objective evaluation of training is becoming increasingly common.

### Scientific Selection

Taylor advocated selecting only "first class" (i.e., high aptitude) men for a given job because their productivity would be several times greater than that of the average man. Colleague Sanford E. Thompson's use of a measure of reaction time to select bicycle ball bearing inspectors (Taylor, 1911/1967) was one of the earliest efforts at objective selection.

Thompson's selection testing antedated the pioneering work of Hugo Munsterberg (1913) as well as the more systematic attempts at validation of selection tests conducted by American psychologists for the Army during World War I. Since that time, personnel selection has mushroomed enormously and has become a science in its own right. Wren (1979) notes that Taylor's emphasis on scientific selection was an impetus to the development of the fields of industrial psychology and personnel management.

### Shorter Working Hours and Rest Pauses

Taylor's experiments with pig iron handlers and ball bearing inspectors determined that fatigue would be reduced and more work would be accomplished if employees were given shorter working hours and/or rest pauses during the day in proportion to the difficulty of the work. The findings with respect to shorter work week were corroborated by the British experiments during World War I (Vernon, 1921) and are now fully accepted. Similarly, the beneficial effects of periodic rest pauses have been documented in numerous experiments. Ryan (1947) summarizes the evidence on both issues.

## Criticisms of Taylor

### View of Work Motivation

A number of criticisms have been made of Taylor and his ideas. Taylor is frequently criticized for having an oversimplified view of human motivation. Although he never claimed to have a complete view (Taylor, 1911/1967), he did claim that what the worker wanted most was money. Taylor believed that men would not work or follow directions unless they attained some permanent, personal benefit from it. This assumption is fully in accord with the tenets of expectancy theory (Vroom, 1964).

What is the evidence for the power of money as motivator? The present author and his students recently analyzed all available field studies that examined the effectiveness of four motivational techniques: money, goal setting, participation in decision making, and job enrichment (Locke et al., 1980). It was found that the median performance improvement resulting from individual incentive systems was 30 percent. This figure was far higher than that for any of the other incentives. The median figure for group or plantwide incentive schemes was 18 percent, still higher than for any nonmonetary technique. These findings (which were based mainly on studies of blue collar workers) coincide with the results of numerous recent studies which indicate that extrinsic incentives such as money are more important for blue collar than for white collar employees (Locke, 1976). This should not be taken to imply that money is unimportant to white collar and professional workers.

Taylor's other major motivational technique was goal setting, that is, assigning specific tasks. A critical incident study by White and Locke (in press) found that goal setting and its equivalents (e.g., deadlines, a heavy work load) were associated with high productivity (and absence of goal setting or goal blockage with low productivity) more frequently than were any other factors. In the Locke et al. (1980) analysis referred to above, goal setting was the second most effective motivational technique. The mean improvement in performance in studies in which workers were assigned specific, challenging goals was 16 percent.

If the effects of Taylor's two main motivators, money and goals—or the task and the bonus, as he called them—are combined, there is an expected or potential performance improvement of 46 percent.

The figure is very close to the figure of a 40 percent mean performance improvement obtained in studies of individual task and bonus systems (Locke et al., 1980). A survey of 453 companies (Fein, 1973) found that task and bonus systems combined yielded productivity increases even greater than 40 percent. This figure far exceeds the combined effect of two more recently promulgated motivational techniques, job enrichment and participation (Locke, et al., 1980). Although Taylor offered nothing approaching a complete theory of human motivation, one must be impressed by the effectiveness of his techniques and by the little that has been added, at least by way of effective techniques, since his time.

### Social Factors

The Hawthorne studies (Roethlisberger & Dickson, 1939/1956) were supposed to represent a great enlightenment. They allegedly "discovered" the influence of human relations or social factors on worker motivation. It has been noted that most of the conclusions that the Hawthorne researchers drew from their own data were probably wrong (Franke & Kaul, 1978). But, beyond this, much of what they said was not even original. Much has been made of the studies in the Bank Wiring Observation room, which found that workers developed informal norms that led to restriction of output. It has been claimed that this discovery refuted Taylor's alledged assumption that workers respond to incentives as isolated individuals. Actually Taylor made no such assumption. In fact, he had identified exactly the same phenomenon as the Hawthorne researchers several decades earlier. He called it "systematic soldiering." (See also comments by Boddewyn, 1961.) Not only did Taylor recognize restriction of output, but one of the chief goals of scientific management was to eliminate it! He viewed soldiering as wasteful and as contrary to the interests of both management and the worker. The main difference between Taylor and Mayo (director of the Hawthorne studies) was that Taylor viewed soldiering as a problem caused by poor management and one that could and should be eliminated by scientific management; Mayo saw it as a reflection of an ineradicable human need.

Nor was Taylor unaware of the effect of social comparisons on worker morale. Discussing the need for the worker to perceive incentive systems as fair, relative to what other workers were getting, he said, "sentiment plays an important part in all our lives; and sentiment is particularly strong in the workman when he believes a direct injustice is being done him" (Copley, 1923, Vol. 2, p. 133). Taylor also was aware of social factors at a deeper level. Scientific management itself involved a social revolution in that it advocated replacing management-labor conflict with cooperation.

### Authoritarianism

Authoritarianism means the belief in obedience to authority simply because it is authority—that is, obedience for the sake of obedience. Such a doctrine clearly was in total contradiction to everything Taylor stood for. First and foremost he stood for obedience to facts—to reason, to proof, to experimental findings. It was not the rule of authority that he advocated but the rule of knowledge. To quote Taylor biographer F. B. Copley, "there is only one master, one boss; namely, knowledge. This, at all events, was the state of things Taylor strove to bring about in industry. He there spent his strength trying to enthrone knowledge as king" (1923, Vol. 1, p. 291).

Taylor did not advocate participation in management matters by his uneducated, manual workers because they did not have the requisite knowledge to do their jobs in the one best way. For example, he shortened the working hours of ball bearing inspectors even when they opposed any such reduction (despite the promise of no loss in pay), because the evidence indicated that their work day was too long (Taylor, 1911/1967). The positive results vindicated his judgement. Similarly, most workers, when they first heard about the task and bonus system, wanted no part of it. But when Taylor (1903/1947) showed them how such a system would actually benefit them (sometimes, to be sure, accompanied by pressures) most embraced it enthusiastically and performed far better as a result. Taylor was not averse to suggestions from the workers. He wrote, "Every encouragement...- should be given to him to suggest improvements in methods and in implements" (1911/1967, p. 128). (See also Gilbreth, 1914/1973.) Fisher quotes Copley on this issue as follows: "If you could prove that yours was the best way, then he would adopt your way and feel very much obliged to you. Frequently he took humble doses of his own imperious medicine" (1925/1976, p. 172).

### Specialization of Labor

There is little doubt that Taylor emphasized maximum specialization, not only for workers but for foremen (e.g., functional foremanship) and managers as well. His argument was the traditional one, that specialization decreases learning time and increases competence and skill. To evaluate the criticism that Taylor overemphasized specialization one must ask: How much emphasis is overemphasis?

Advocates of job enrichment have argued with some validity that extreme specialization leads to boredom and low morale and lack of work motivation due to underutilized mental capacity. However, it should be noted that Taylor always argued for a matching of men to jobs in accordance with their capacities. People who do jobs that require very little mental capacity should be people who have very little mental capacity (Taylor, 1903/1947). Those with more capacity should have more complex tasks to perform (e.g., by being promoted when they master the simple tasks). See Gilbreth (1914/1973) and Taylor (1912/1970a). In this respect Taylor might very well approve of individualized job enrichment, although, as noted earlier, its effects on performance may be limited. The present author does not agree, however, with Drucker's (1976) claim that Taylor anticipated Herzberg's theory.

There is a potential benefit of job enrichment (e.g., multicrafting and modular working arrangements), however, that Taylor did not foresee. There are fewer and fewer jobs in existence today that stay unchanged for long periods of time. If such jobs exist, they eventually are automated. People are more versatile than machines precisely because of their greater flexibility and adaptability. In times of rapid technological change, such as the present, spending months training a worker for one narrow specialty would not be very cost-efficient. It is more practical to have each worker master several different jobs and to work each day or hour where they are most needed.

With respect to supervision, Taylor's concept of functional foremanship clearly has not been accepted and probably is not very practical.

### Men as Machines

The criticism that Taylor's system treated men as machines is related to the previous one. It usually refers to scientific management's requirement of complete uniformity for a given job with respect to the tools and motions used by the workmen (the one best way). As noted earlier, Taylor was not against the workers making suggestions for improvements, provided they first mastered the best known methods. Taylor's well-chosen example of this principle was that of training a surgeon: "he is quickly given the very best knowledge of his predecessors [then]. . . he is able to use his own originality and ingenuity to make *real additions to the world's knowledge, instead of reinventing things which are old"* (1911/1967, p. 126). The alternative to treating men as machines in the above sense was the prescientific method of management, which allowed men to choose tools and methods based on personal opinions and feelings rather than on knowledge.

It often is forgotten that standardization included the redesign of machines and equipment in order to enable men to become more skilled at the tasks they performed. Taylor applied this principle as much to himself as to others. His unique modifications of the tennis racket and the golf putter for his own use are cases in point. (Both items are on display at the Stevens Institute of Technology.) As noted earlier, he did not force people to fit existing equipment. He, and the Gilbreths, (re-)designed equipment to fit people. It might be more accurate to say that Taylor, rather than treating men as machines, helped to develop the science of integrating men with machines.

### Exploitation of the Workers

During Taylor's lifetime, socialist Upton Sinclair and others claimed that Taylor's system was exploitative because, although under scientific management the worker might improve his productivity by around 100 percent, his pay was generally increased by a lesser amount. In fairness, they argued, the pay increase should match the productivity increase.

Taylor easily refuted this argument (Fisher, 1925/1976; Copley, 1923, Vol. 1). He pointed out, for example, that the increase in productivity was not caused by the worker only, but also by management; it was management who discovered the better techniques and designed the new tools, at some cost to themselves. Thus they deserved some of the benefits as well (Taylor, 1911/1967).

Ironically, Lenin, the self-proclaimed enemy of so-called "capitalist exploitation," himself strongly advocated the application of scientific management to Russian industry in order to help build socialism. However, socialist inefficiency, hostility to capitalist ideas, and resistance to change prevented the application of virtually all scientific management techniques in Russia except for the Gantt chart (Wren, 1980). The Soviets, however, may have been influenced by the Polish manager and theorist Karol Adamiecki, who developed his own scientific management theory independently of Taylor (Wesolowski, 1978).

### Antiunionism

The criticism that Taylor was antiunion is true in only one sense. Taylor foresaw no need for unions once scientific management was properly established, especially because he saw the interests of management and labor as fundamentally the same (Copley, 1925/1976). It is worth noting in this respect that companies that are known for treating their employees well, such as IBM, do not have unions. The belief that unions were unnecessary under the proper type of management did not indicate lack of concern for employee welfare. The leaders of the scientific management movement, including Taylor, showed great concern about the effects of company policies on employee well-being (Sheldon, 1924/1976). For example, they were constantly preoccupied with eliminating or reducing fatigue. This benevolence, however, did not always characterize the followers of Taylor, who often tried to shortcut the introduction of his methods and engaged in rate-cutting and other deceptive practices.

### Dishonesty

The strongest condemnations of Taylor, specifically of Taylor's character, have come in two recent articles (Wrege & Perroni, 1974; Wrege & Stotka, 1978). The first asserts that Taylor lied about the conduct of the famous pig iron handling experiments at Bethlehem Steel, and the second claims that Taylor plagiarized most of his *Principles of Scientific Management* from a colleague, Morris L. Cooke.

As for the pig iron experiments, it seems clear from Wrege and Perroni (1974) that Taylor did stress different things in the three reports that appeared in his writings. However, these descriptions were *not* contradictory to one another; they differed only in terms of emphasis and in the amount of detail presented. This in itself does not constitute dishonesty. Taylor apparently was in error as to certain details (e.g., the amount of tonnage of iron involved), but this could have involved errors of memory rather than deliberate deception. Nor do these details change the thread of his arguments.

Wrege and Perroni also claim that Schmidt (actual name: Henry Knolle) was not selected scientifically for the job of pig iron handling as claimed, but was simply the only worker who stuck with the task from the beginning to the end of the introductory period. This claim would appear to be true unless James Gillespie and Hartley Wolle, who conducted most of the research, omitted pertinent information in their report. However, if one accepts the idea that by a "first class" workman Taylor meant one who was not just capable but also highly motivated, then the choice of Schmidt was not inconsistent with Taylor's philosophy.

In addition, Wrege and Perroni could find no evidence that local papers had opposed Taylor's experiments as he had claimed. However, it is possible that Taylor was referring to some other paper or papers. Wrege and Perroni do not indicate whether the papers they looked at were the only ones published in the Bethlehem area or surrounding areas at that time.

Werge and Perroni argue further that Taylor never acknowledged that his "laws of heavy laboring" were based on the work of "two extraordinary workers" (1974, p. 21). However in *Principles of Scientific Management,* Taylor clearly states that *"a first class laborer,* suited to such work as handling pig iron could be under load only 42 percent of the day and must be free from load 58 percent of the day" (1911/1967, p. 60, footnote 1; italics added). In short, these laws were specifically *for* extraordinary workers.

Wrege and Perroni claim that Taylor lied about giving the workers rest pauses, because all of the rest periods referred to involved only the return walk after loading the pig iron rather than an actual seated or motionless rest period. However, if one reads Taylor's *Principles* carefully, one notes that he specifically described his laws of heavy laboring in terms of how much of the time the worker can be "under load" (1911/1967, pp. 60-61, footnote 1).

This implies that the return walk was the part not under load. Furthermore, near the end of footnote 1, Taylor states, "Practically the men were made to take a rest, generally by sitting down, after loading ten to twenty pigs. *This rest was in addition to the time which it took them to walk back from the car to the pile"* (1911/1967, p. 61, italics added). No evidence in Wrege and Perroni's (1974) paper contradicts this assertion; nor do they even mention it.

As to the Wrege and Stotka (1978) claim that Taylor plagiarized most of his *Principles* from a manuscript written by a colleague, Morris Cooke, several facts should be noted. First, Cooke's manuscript was based on a talk written and presented by Taylor himself. Apparently Cooke added to it, but the source of the additional material is not actually known; it could have been from other talks by or discussions with Taylor. Cooke himself gave Taylor credit for this allegedly plagiarized material (Wrege & Stotka, 1978). Fry argues, "It is ludicrous to accuse Taylor of plagiarizing Cooke if in fact Cooke's material was based on Taylor's own talks" (1976, p. 128). Second, Taylor published *Principles* with Cooke's full knowledge and apparent consent. Third, Taylor offered Cooke all the royalties lest his book reduce the sales of a similar book Cooke planned to author himself. All of this is hardly consistent with Wrege and Stotka's implication that Taylor was a dishonest exploiter. Actually, the reasons why Cooke agreed to let Taylor be sole author of the manuscript are not known. At most Taylor can be accused of lack of graciousness due to his failure to acknowledge Cooke's editorial work. It also is puzzling why, if Cooke actually wrote most of *Principles,* Wrege, Perroni, and Stotka did not accuse Cooke as well as Taylor of dishonesty in reporting the pig iron experiments.

Wrege and Perroni (1974) also accuse Taylor of not giving credit to Gillespie and Wolle for their work on the Bethlehem studies. Although Taylor did not acknowledge in print every assistant who ever worked with him, in *Principles* he did acknowledge his indebtedness to many colleagues, including, Barth, Gilbreth, Gantt, and Thompson. He also used the term "we" when describing the Bethlehem experiments. Thus he was clearly not in the habit of taking all credit for himself, as Wrege and Stotka (1978) charge. Again, however, a footnote acknowledging the work of Gillespie and Wolle would have been appropriate.

In the present author's opinion, not only is the evidence that Taylor was dishonest far from conclusive, it is virtually nonexistent. On the grounds of practicality alone, it seems doubtful that Taylor, who worked and performed experiments with so many different people, would deliberately attempt to distort what was done or who did it and thus leave himself open to exposure by any one of them.

## Conclusion

With respect to the issues of a scientific approach to management and the techniques of time and motion study, standardization, goal setting plus work measurement and feedback, money as a motivator, management's responsibility for training, scientific selection, the shortened work week, and rest pauses, Taylor's views not only were essentially correct but they have been well accepted by manage-

ment. With respect to the issues of management-labor relations and individualized work, Taylor probably was only partially correct, and he has been only partially accepted. These issues are summarized in Table 1.

With respect to criticisms, the accusations regarding the following points are predominantly or wholly false: Taylor's inadequate model of worker motivation, his ignorance of social factors, his authoritarianism, his treatment of men as machines, his exploitation of workers, his antiunionism, and his personal dishonesty. Several of them verge on the preposterous. The accusation of overspecialization seems partly but not totally justified. See Table 2 for a summary of these points.

Considering that it has been over 65 years since Taylor's death and that a knowledge explosion has taken place during these years, Taylor's track record is remarkable. The point is not, as is often

### Table 1
### Status of Taylor's Ideas and Techniques in Contemporary Management

| | Valid? | Now Accepted? | Manifested in (outgrowths): |
|---|---|---|---|
| *Philosophy* | | | |
| Scientific decision making | Yes | Yes | Management science: operations research, cost accounting, etc. |
| Management-labor cooperation | Yes | Partly | Greater management-labor cooperation (but conflict not eliminated) |
| *Techniques* | | | |
| Time and motion study | Yes | Yes | Widespread use; standard times |
| Standardization | Yes | Yes | Standardized procedures in many spheres; human engineering |
| Task | Yes | Yes | Goal setting, MBO, feedback |
| Bonus | Yes | Increasingly | Proliferation of reward system, Scanlon Plan, Improshare, need to consider money in job enrichment/OD studies |
| Individualized work | Partly | Partly | Recognition of dangers of groups, groupthink, social loafing, contextual theories of group decision making, (but group jobs sometimes more efficient) |
| Management training | Yes | Yes | Management responsibility for employee training |
| Scientific selection | Yes | Yes | Development of fields of industrial psychology and personnel management |
| Shorter hours; rest pauses | Yes | Yes | 40 hour (or less) work week; common use of rest pauses |

### Table 2
### Validity of Criticisms of Taylor's Ideas

| Criticism | Valid? | Relevant facts |
|---|---|---|
| Inadequate theory of work motivation | Specious, because no complete theory offered | Money and goals are the most effective motivators |
| Ignored social factors | No | SM designed specifically to facilitate cooperation and to eliminated negative effects of social factors; awareness of sentiments |
| Authoritarianism | No | Stressed rule of knowledge (the essence of SM) |
| Overspecialization | Partly | Specialization maximized expertise; matched men to job requirements (but ignored possible benefits of multicrafting) |
| Treated man as machines | No | Methods based on knowledge, not feelings |
| Exploitation of workers | No | Management deserves some of the benefits of increased efficiency based on its contribution |
| Antiunionism | No | Unions not needed under good management |
| Dishonesty | No | Accusations based on incomplete or false information |

claimed, that he was "right in the context of his time" but is now outdated, but that *most of his insights are still valid today.* The present author agrees with those who consider Taylor a genius (Johnson, 1980). His achievements are all the more admirable because, although Taylor was highly intelligent, his discoveries were not made through sudden, brilliant insights but through sheer hard work. His metal-cutting experiments, for example, spanned a period of 26 years (Taylor, 1912/1970a)!

Drucker (1976) claims that Taylor had as much impact on the modern world as Karl Marx and Sigmund Freud. This may be true in that Taylor's influence was certainly worldwide and has endured long after his death (Wren, 1979). Of the three, however, the present author considers Taylor's ideas to be by far the most objectively valid. But the historical figure that Taylor most reminds one of is Thomas Edison (Runes, 1948)—in his systematic style of research, his dogged persistence, his emphasis on the useful, his thirst for knowledge, and in his dedication to truth.

# References

Bartlem, C. S., & Locke, E. A. The Coch and French study: A critique and reinterpretation. *Human Relations,* 1981. 34. 555-566.

Boddewyn, J. Frederick Winslow Taylor revisited. *Academy of Management Journal,* 1961, 4, 100-107

Carey, A. The Hawthorne studies: A radical criticism. *American Sociological Review,* 1967, 32, 403-416.

Copley, F. B. *Frederick W. Taylor: Father of scientific management* (2 Vols.). New York: Harper & Row, 1923,

Copley, F. B. Taylor and trade unions. In D. DelMar & R. D. Collins (Eds.), *Classics in scientific management.* University, Ala.: University of Alabama Press, 1976, 52-56. (Originally published, 1925.)

Drucker, P. F. *The practice of management.* New York: Harper, 1954.

Drucker, P. F. The coming rediscovery of scientific management. *Conference Board Record,* 1976, 13 (6), 23-27.

Fein, M. Work measurement and wage incentives, *Industrial Engineering,* 1973, 5, 49-51.

Fein, M. An alternative to traditional managing. Unpublished manuscript, 1977.

Fisher, I. Scientific management made clear. In D. DelMar & R. D. Collins (Eds.), *Classics in scientific management.* University, Ala.: University of Alabama Press, 1976, 154-193. (Originally published, 1925.)

Franke, R. H., & Kaul, J. D. The Hawthorne experiments: First statistical interpretation. *American Sociological Review,* 1978, 43, 623-643.

Frost, C. F., Wakeley, J. H., & Ruh, R. A. *The Scanlon plan for organization development: Identity, participation, and equity.* East Lansing: Michigan State University Press, 1974.

Fry, L. W. The maligned F. W. Taylor: A reply to his many critics. *Academy of Management Review,* 1976, 1 (30), 124-139.

Gilbreth, F. B. Science in management for the one best way to do work. In H. F. Merrill (Ed.), *Classics in managment.* New York: American Management Association, 1970, 217-263. (Originally published, 1923.)

Gilbreth, F. B. *Primer of scientific management.* Easton, Pa.: Hive Publishing Co., 1973. (Originally published, 1914.)

Greenwood, R. Management by objectives: As developed by Peter F. Drucker assisted by General Electric's management consultation services. Paper presented at the Academy of Management meetings, 1980, Detroit.

Hall, J. Decisions, decisions, decisions. *Psychology Today,* 1971, 5 (6), 51ff.

Janis, I. *Victims of groupthink.* Boston: Houghton Mifflin, 1972.

Johnson, M. J. Fred Taylor '83: Giant of non-repute. *Stevens Indicator,* 1980, 97 (2), 4-8.

Kendall, H. P. A decade's development in management trends and results of scientific management. In D. DelMar & R. D. Collins (Eds.), *Classics in scientific management.* University, Ala.: University of Alabama Press, 1976, 118-133. (Originally published, 1924.)

Latané, B., Williams, K., & Harkins, S. Social loafing. *Psychology Today,* 1979, 13 (4), 104ff.

Latham, G. P., & Dossett, D. L. Designing incentive plans for unionized employees: A comparison of continuous and variable ratio reinforcement schedules. *Personnel Psychology,* 1978, 31, 47-61.

Lawler, E. E. *Pay and organizational effectiveness: A psychological view.* New York: McGraw-Hill, 1971.

Lawler, E. E. Pay, participation and organization change. In E. L. Cass & F. G. Zimmer (Eds.), *Man and work in society.* New York: Van Nostrand Rienhold, 1975, 137-149.

Locke, E. A. Toward a theory of task motivation and incentives. *Organizational Behavior and Human Performance,* 1968, 3, 157-189.

Locke, E. A. Personnel attitudes and motivation. *Annual Review of Psychology,* 1975, 26, 457-480.

Locke, E. A. The nature and causes of job satisfaction. In M. D. Dunnette (Ed.), *Handbook of industrial and organizational psychology.* Chicago: Rand McNally, 1976, 1297-1349.

Locke, E. A. The myths of behavior mod in organizations. *Academy of Management Review,* 1977, 2, 543-553.

Locke, E. A. The ubiquity of the technique of goal setting in theories of and approaches to employee motivation. *Academy of Management Review,* 1978, 3, 594-601.

Locke, E. A., Cartledge, N., & Koeppel, J. Motivational effects of knowledge of results: A goal-setting phenomenon? *Psychological Bulletin,* 1968, 70, 474-485.

Locke, E. A., Shaw, K. N., Saari, L. M., & Latham, G. P. Goal setting and task performance: 1969-1980. *Psychological Bulletin,* 1981, 90, 125-152.

Locke, E. A., Feren, D. B., McCaleb, V. M., Shaw, K. M., & Denny, A. T. The relative effectiveness of four methods of motivating employee performance. In K. Duncan, M. Gruneberg, & D. Wallis (Eds.), *Changes in working life.* Chichester, England: Wiley, 1980, 363-387.

Munsterberg, H. *Psychology and industrial efficiency.* Boston: Houghton Mifflin, 1913.

Odiorne, G. S. MBO: A backward glance. *Business Horizons,* October 1978, 14-24.

Roethlisberger, F. J., & Dickson, W. J. *Management and the worker.* Cambridge, Mass.: Harvard University Press, 1956. (Originally published, 1939.)

Runes, D. D. (Ed.). *The diary and sundry observations of Thomas Alva Edison.* New York: Philosophical Library, 1948.

Ryan, T. A. *Work and effort.* New York: Ronald, 1947.

Sheldon, O. Taylor the creative leader. In D. DelMar & R. D. Collins (Eds.), *Classics in scientific management.* University, Ala.: University of Alabama Press, 1976, 35-51. (Originally published, 1924.)

Sykes, A. J. M. Economic interest and the Hawthorne researchers. *Human Relations,* 1965, 18, 253-263.

Taylor, F. W. *Shop management* (published as part of *Scientific management*). New York: Harper, 1947. (Originally published, 1903.)

Taylor, F. W. *The principles of scientific managment.* New York: Norton, 1967. (Originally published, 1911.)

Taylor, F. W. Time study, piece work, and the first-class man. In H. F. Merrill (Ed.), *Classics in management.* New York: American Management Association, 1970, 57-66. (Originally published, 1903.)

Taylor, F. W. The principles of scientific management. In H. F. Merrill (Ed.), *Classics in management.* New York: American Management Association, 1970a. (Originally published, 1912.)

Taylor, F. W. What is scientific management? In H. G. Merrill (Ed.), *Classics in management.* New York: American Management Association, 1970b, 67-71. (Original testimony given, 1912.)

Taylor, F. W. Profit sharing. In D. DelMar & R. D. Collins (Eds.), *Classics in scientific management.* University, Ala.: University of Alabama Press, 1976, 17-20. (Originally written, 1912.)

Vernon, H. N. *Industrial fatigue and efficiency.* New York: Dutton, 1921.

Vough, C. F. *Tapping the human resource.* New York: Wiley, 1964.

Vroom, V. *Work and motivation.* New York: Wiley, 1969.

Walton, R. E. Work innovations at Topeka: After six years. *Journal of Applied Behavioral Science,* 1977, 13 (3), 422-433.

Wesolowski, Z. P. The Polish contribution to the development of scientific management. *Proceedings of the Academy of Management,* 1978.

White, F., & Locke, E. A. Perceived determinants of high and low productivity in three occupational groups: A critical incident study. *Journal of Management Studies,* in press.

Wrege, C. D., & Perroni, A. G. Taylor's pig-tale: A historical analysis of Frederick W. Taylor's pig-iron experiments. *Academy of Management Journal,* 1974, 17, 6-27.

Wrege, C. D., & Stotka, A. M. Cooke creates a classic: The story behind F. W. Taylor's principles of scientific management. *Academy of Management Review,* 1978, 3, 736-749.

Wren, D. A. *The evolution of management thought* (2nd ed.). New York: Wiley, 1979.

Wren, D. A. Scientific management in the U.S.S.R., with particular reference to the contribution of Walter N. Polakov. *Academy of Management Review,* 1980, 5, 1-11.

*Edwin A. Locke is joint Professor of Business and Management and of Psychology at the University of Maryland, College Park.*

**Manufacturing Resource Planning is a way that marketing, manufacturing, engineering, and finance can work together.**

# TOOLS FOR PROFIT

### by Oliver W. Wight

Productivity is the current theme in manufacturing—as well it should be. Over the last decade, we have watched U.S. productivity go up 23% while Japanese productivity went up 89%. The impact on the American economy shows up as inflation, and as the importing of more and more products, from television sets to automobiles, from overseas. American manufacturing is at a crossroads, and the computer is one of the most powerful tools available to address this problem.

Yet, of the reams of literature written on the subject of productivity over the last few years, and particularly in the last six months, virtually no article has recognized the powerful role the computer can play in improving productivity. Articles discuss computer-aided manufacturing (CAM) and computer-aided design (CAD) and surely these have great and proven potential. But as usual, those people writing the articles either know little or nothing about how manufacturing *really* works, or if they are manufacturing people, they are standing too close to the problem. We have a penchant for concerning ourselves with the exotics while overlooking fundamentals.

In a country where 60% of the average foreman's time is spent expediting, looking for material, and in general, firefighting because of poor scheduling; where 60% of the average purchasing buyer's time is spent shuffling paper and doing last minute expediting; where the automobile industry alone spends over $100 million a year on premium airfreight primarily because of poor scheduling; there is an opportunity to improve productivity that is largely untapped, and for that matter, poorly understood.

If we're going to take advantage of the

ILLUSTRATIONS BY JANE STERRETT

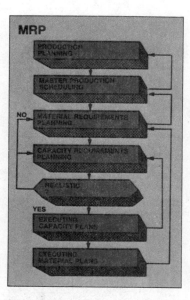

**MRP**

opportunity, the problem needs to be properly understood. The problem is very straightforward. Before computers, scheduling in a manufacturing company was simply out of the question. The typical company has hundreds or thousands of components to be scheduled. Many components go together to make assemblies. They are made from raw materials and often put into finished goods. There are branch warehouses in many companies that have to be scheduled properly.

The problem is monumental, and is made insurmountable by the constant change that is part of normal manufacturing. Forecasts aren't right, machines break down, vendors deliver late, there are engineering changes, tooling doesn't work, new products are introduced, and all of this is occurring simultaneously. The only constant in manufacturing is change, and the problem is making valid schedules so that people don't have to work to shortage lists and dissipate their efforts firefighting.

Before computers, all we could do was "order launch and expedite." The inventory control people ordered material and the

shortage list became the real schedule. For the first three decades we used the computer primarily for better "inventory management," really just better order launching. Even today, most people think MRP (Material Requirements Planning) is a better inventory control technique. And many companies would say that they have MRP installed—while they still *really* schedule to a shortage list.

A closed loop MRP system includes all of the elements shown in the figure on this page. It starts with a production plan that establishes the rate of production for product families in units. This is then broken down into a master production schedule that defines the specific items to be produced.

From this, the material requirements plan is developed, and this will be used to drive the dispatch lists down in the shop as a means of executing these material plans as well as giving purchasing valid schedules. The material requirements plan will also provide the input for capacity requirements planning to determine the man-hours required by the work center to produce the needed material. The capacity plans will be executed by fol-

lowing up to measure actual output against planned output in standard hours by the work center.

Closed loop MRP is a scheduling system that goes right down to the factory floor to produce daily schedules to tell manufacturing people what to work on. Properly managed—and this, of course, is the challenge—MRP can provide valid schedules and give factory management information well in advance so that it can be working on next month's "shortages" this month. It can provide the same type of information for purchasing. The result in improved productivity is not conjecture. When foremen have time to do the job that's in their job description, supervise and educate their people, install better methods, and foresee problems in advance, the result will show up in productivity.

For example, a manufacturer of electronic products reduced its overtime from 15,000 hours a week to 3,000 hours a month—and that translates directly into a productivity improvement. A pharmaceutical manufacturer improved customer service to 98% from 85%, reduces obsolescence 80%, improved inventory turns 69%, reduced distribution costs by 13%, while increasing productivity in the factory by 22%.

**BETTER USE OF TIME**  When customer service is improved, marketing and sales personnel can spend *their* time more productively getting new orders rather than defending why the customer hasn't received the orders that already exist. Reduced obsolescence translates directly into improved productivity, as does reduced distribution costs through better scheduling.

When purchasing people can spend their time working on negotiation, better sourcing, working with engineering on standardization, value analysis, and all the good

things that professional purchasing people know about rather than on firefighting, the typical cost reduction in purchasing for a company using a closed loop MRP system is approximately 5% of the annual purchased cost. A typical manufacturing company doing $50 million in sales would spend about $12.5 million on purchased material. This is usually *three times* what it spends on direct labor. So a 5% reduction in purchased cost translates into a 15% reduction in direct labor.

Today, MRP has gone beyond even the closed loop approach with material requirements planning at its core. MRP has developed into manufacturing resource planning, which ties in the financial numbers with the operating system. In a typical manufacturing company, for example, purchase commitment reports have a huge past-due quantity that everybody knows is unrealistic. Once again, the problem is fundamental. The formal system is the system that generates the numbers. When schedules are invalid and shortage lists are the real system, there will be a lot of past-due open purchase orders that simply aren't needed. When these are used as a basis for a purchase commitment report, the numbers simply won't be very meaningful.

Another excellent example of the problems that the financial people have because the operating system doesn't work is inventory shrinkage. Since the operating people are usually working primarily with shortage lists and expediting, they pay little attention to numbers and consider this mainly the concern of the "accountants." In the typical manufacturing company, there is an inventory shrinkage about once every four years because these numbers have gone awry. This shrinkage affects profits directly, and, of course, is a matter of great concern to every-

one in management. They spend 90 days trying to explain how this ever could have happened and why it will never happen again. And then the chief financial officer sets up an "inventory reserve" because he knows full well it probably *will* happen again.

Once again, the problem is fundamental. If the scheduling doesn't work well in a factory, if the people in the factory aren't using the numbers to run the business themselves, the financial numbers that result are

CHART BY CYNTHIA STODDARD

# Most companies approach MRP as a computer system rather than a people system made possible by the computer.

going to be highly suspect.

In a company using manufacturing resource planning—MRPII—the financial numbers are derived directly from the operating numbers. Obviously the prerequisite is that the operating numbers are correct and are used. One highly successful MRPII user had an inventory adjustment in total dollars last year of .0011%—enough to make any financial man happy.

Beyond that, manufacturing resource planning has become a company game plan, a way that marketing, manufacturing, engineering, and finance can work together. It is a virtual computer simulation of the business. Once again, this is not speculation or theory. Here is what George Bevis, former senior vice president of the Tennant Co., Minneapolis, had to say on that.

"Before long, MRP became more than a production and inventory control tool. It became a new way to run the business. It encompassed the whole business, not just manufacturing. We tied in finance, engineering, marketing. . . . In short, it became a company operating plan."

If this potential exists, why haven't more companies realized it? To be sure, many have improved inventory turnover and cus-

tomer service through the application of MRP. But few are really Class A MRP users who truly make it function as a scheduling system. Most of the users of MRP also use the shortage list and consequently have not taken the expediting burden off the foremen or the purchasing people. As a consequence, they have not seen the productivity improvements that can be attained when scheduling really works in a manufacturing company.

## MRP HAS FALLEN SHORT

The problem is not so much that MRP has *not* worked as that it has fallen short of its proven potential in most American companies today.

And the reasons are always the same:

1) Most companies approach MRP as a computer system rather than a people system made possible by the computer.

2) Having done this, they now wait for the data processing and systems people to somehow write some programs that will make a manufacturing company run differ-

ently, and, of course, this isn't going to happen.

3) Rather than recognize that MRP simply provides better tools for management to use to run the business, they somehow expect the tools to do the job. MRP is far from being a panacea. It simply shows people the problems sooner so that they can do what's necessary to lick them.

4) They don't do the necessary work to get the correct data to support an MRP system. This involves a major task of behavior modification in a manufacturing company. Foremen, for example, have had little interest in inventory record accuracy in the past because the shortage list did not require it. Bills of material didn't have to be correct to support a shortage list either. With MRP they must. And a common—almost prevalent—way to mismanage an MRP system is to overstate the master production schedule. This will destroy the credibility of the schedule faster than almost anything else.

5) And of course, they catch the old "computer virus" of making things so complicated that the users can't understand the system.

The thesis running through all of these reasons is the same: too many people think that the "system" does something, and if we just feed it the proper information and follow some instructions, wonderful things will happen. In a recent article* MRP was described as a system where the master scheduler has complete control and everybody else just runs around and follows instructions. Nobody who ever saw MRP work as a scheduling system in a factory would make a statement like that. It simply doesn't happen that way. The people in the factory and the purchasing people now have to work as hard to prevent the shortages as they once did to fix the shortages after they happened. And that requires plenty of personal effort, ingenuity, and cooperation.

The Japanese have done a fine job of showing us how to run a manufacturing economy more effectively. One of their strong suits is that they are culturally attuned to working as a team—whether or not they have a valid game plan.

*MRP—Who Needs It?, William S. Donelson II, DATAMATION, May 1979, p. 185.

In the U.S., it's one man, one vote. We are primarily function-oriented. Engineering, typically, doesn't work very well with manufacturing. Marketing and finance see each other as competitors. That must end if we are to get everybody working together to compete against the real competition.

The informal systems we have used encouraged finger-pointing. When the product didn't get shipped, the assembly foreman knew it wasn't his fault because he didn't have the parts. The marketing people knew it wasn't their fault because nobody worked to the forecast. The manufacturing people knew it wasn't their fault because the forecast was never right. . . .

A valid game plan is a prerequisite to operating effectively as a team. And perhaps, after all, that's the most important thing that MRP can provide: the opportunity for working together more effectively.

Data processing and systems professionals can provide a real service by spreading the word to manufacturing executives that the key to productivity is manufacturing resource planning. While it's important to install more productive equipment and to use better production methods, many companies have installed highly efficient expensive equipment only to make more of the wrong product at the wrong time on overtime. In manufacturing and distribution *scheduling* is fundamental. If the fundamentals are not done properly, much of the rest of what is done will fall far short of potential results.

And, most important, everybody in manufacturing needs to get the message that MRP is not *miracle* requirements planning. It does nothing but provide the tools: the tools to enable us to run our manufacturing businesses in our manufacturing economy at a much higher level of professionalism than has previously been possible.  ❋

## OLIVER W. WIGHT

Oliver Wight is president of Oliver Wight, Inc., a management counseling and MRP education firm. He is also president of Manufacturing Software Systems, a company that reviews and evaluates computer programs for use in manufacturing and distribution scheduling. He has authored several books, including two on production and inventory control and management, and his latest book, *MRP II: Manufacturing Resource Planning*, will be released this year.

# Infosystems Report

## Computers In Manufacturing

For more than a decade, US manufacturing productivity has lagged behind most of the Western World's industrial nations. The computer stands ready as the tool that can reverse the pattern.

# Top Management Involvement Needed

by John M. Lusa
Executive Editor

For years, the captains of American industry could point with pride to their production records and at the mass-produced volume of assembled goods coming out of the factories of the land. It was taken for granted that the pace would continue and that American industry would always be the world leader.

The growth pattern of American industry becomes more apparent when compared to the manufacturing productivity of other countries. According to US Department of Labor statistics, US manufacturing productivity growth during a recent 10-year period ranks at the bottom when compared to major free-world economies in Europe, Canada, the United Kingdom and Japan. At the top is Japan with a productivity growth rate that is four times greater than that of the US. Some disagree, though, with this viewpoint. One is economist Werner Chilton of Citibank. Writing in Citibank's *Monthly Economic Letter*, he said the US has been doing better in several areas than some critics indicate. He reports that US unit labor costs, or labor costs per unit output, rose by just 7.7 percent last year, compared with 26.2 percent and 19.7 percent for Japan and Germany, respectively, in dollar terms. Between 1970 and 1978, he added, the US posted the smallest rises in unit labor costs among practically all leading Western industrialized nations.

A knee-jerk reaction to the productivity problem by some businessmen might be to institute a cost reduction program. But just instituting a cost reduction, per se, can be equivalent to "shooting oneself in the foot." Short-term goals are reached, but a company is crippled for the long-term.

The problem of productivity is not a subject, though, that is being covered up and ignored. Top management, government, trade associations and educators are fully aware of the problem and are wrestling with solutions.

Just last month, two important conferences — one in Europe and one in Cambridge, MA — dealt with the "factory of the future" and "industrial technology innovation," respectively.

The Cambridge meeting was hosted by the Massachusetts Institute of Technology (MIT). Dr. J. Herbert Hollomon, director of the Center for

## Control System Must Be Flexible

Any computer system that tells you what to do and then functions as if you are going to do it, is not going to succeed. "People know more about your business than any dumb computer can ever know," asserted Eric Landau, a fellow of the American Production & Inventory Control Society (APICS). "The reasons you have for deviating from a plan are supposedly good and proper. If you don't want the system to lead you astray, then it is important to keep what the system thinks is happening in sync with what's really happening."

Claims abound that many computer systems can run the factory, Landau told a group of people attending a Scientific Time Sharing Corp. seminar on its "Comprehensive Manufacturing Control System" (CMCS). "In actuality, the computer is chugging away 'running the factory' while your people are doing things the computer never planned for," he said. "Your man on the floor is going to look around and see he doesn't have the materials on hand or the workers available and he is going to laugh at the system. Next time he'll ignore the system and, ultimately, it will fail."

This dreary scenario cannot materialize if the proper steps are taken to plan and implement a computer-controlled manufacturing system, Landau insisted. The first thing to do is identify the results being sought, he explained. In the manufacturing environment these are finished goods, produced on time, in the proper amount and at the least possible cost.

The idea is to set up a control system which ensures that production, procurement and material movement needed to meet the plan occur on schedule.

A computer system should not try to tell the foreman what jobs to do today. "The system should tell him how long the jobs will take, what materials are needed and where to get them," Landau said.

The foreman should be provided with a daily worksheet that is a priority list. This projected workload list should be flexible, though. "It should provide information to the floor personnel, but that information is primarily meant to be suggestive," Landau said. If there is a problem with personnel or materials, for instance, the foreman has to adapt to what is actually on hand. The worksheet serves as a turnaround document on which the department foreman can report progress. □

. . . continued on page 42

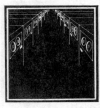

**Computers In Manufacturing**
*. . . continued*

Policy Alternatives at MIT's School of Engineering, said, "The Massachusetts Institute of Technology is sponsoring this symposium because of the importance of the information to be presented in helping to provide a sound basis for the development of US technology policy and for the management of innovation in industry."

Hollomon said, "In developing a national policy on innovation and industrial development, the United States must avoid the distrust for the new and the continued investment in the old that has characterized the actions of both firms and nations

faced by competition from new or cheaper products."

While the problems discussed at Cambridge are national or global in nature, the solutions are going to be applied to the factory floor and to the systems that control the factory floor. This was the subject of the "Factory of the Future" conference in Amsterdam, The Netherlands. It dealt with the computerization of the factory. Infotech International Ltd., a leading English consulting firm, sponsored the conference, as a means of highlighting the problems of exploiting advanced computer technology to help reduce costs and lead times.

The computerization of the factory has been receiving increasing attention lately. Industry has been a big user of computers, but the use by many has been limited to accounting and bookkeeping functions. The first big users of the computers on the factory floor were in the processing

industries—petrochemical, food and metals—where a continuous process could be electronically monitored and controlled. Other big users of computers have been the aerospace and automotive industries. Both are deeply involved in computer-aided design (CAD) and computer-aided manufacturing (CAM).

In spite of the gains in computer usage in these industries, the big steps are yet to come. As officials at Computer Aided Manufacturing-International Inc. (CAM-I) Arlington, TX, a not-for-profit organization made up of users and manufacturers from around the world, point out, "Less than 25 percent of the US industrial output is the result of mass production." According to CAM-I, "The rest is produced by batch manufacturing, a system plagued by long lead times, high in-process inventories, low machine utilization and very little automation."

. . . continued on page 46

# MRP—A Problem With Software?

by Darryl Landvater

If you're looking for a good excuse why material requirement planning (MRP) won't work for you, you can usually find it in the software.

MRP software has all kinds of problems. If you write your own software, something which is definitely not recommended, there is usually no end to the problems. If you use one of the older software packages, like IBM's PICS package for example, you have to work with software that is not well integrated, requires substantial functional modification to work as a complete MRP system, and is written in several different languages which makes it difficult to maintain. If you use one of the newer software packages, the system is bigger and more complex (more things to go wrong), is probably still being debugged, and in some cases, you may find yourself being part of the final phase of product development as you exercise the system in a way that no pre-release testing can do.

All this may not come as much of a surprise to you. But what may come as a surprise is that one of the most powerful weapons a company has in its arsenal for combating software

problems is its attitude.

Wanting something doesn't necessarily make it happen. There have been companies with a good attitude but it just wasn't enough to prevent serious delays. Yet, the odds are very definitely stacked in favor of those people with that overwhelming drive to obliterate technical bugs and glitches; those people who refuse to accept them as excuses.

One example of this was a company using a very complete, very popular software package. They said to me, "We've had a number of problems with the software, and it would have been easy to let that stop our progress. But our attitude is that we refuse to let the software stop our progress, and it hasn't."

Another example came from Ollie Wight. Ollie is associated with more successful MRP systems than anyone else. His question to me was, "Why is it that people using the old PICS package from IBM seem to have less trouble than those companies using the newer software packages?" My answer was that nearly any software package can be made to work, and nearly any package will have problems. The amount of difficulty a

company has with its software seems to be a function of two things: the problems with the software and its attitude toward solving them. People using PICS generally seem to have a good attitude since they are generally under no illusions about the software being either complete or easy-to-use. Some of the people using the newer software packages have the same attitude, but others don't. Without the right attitude, it is possible for the inevitable problems that crop up to turn into excuses and delays.

To put the whole thing in perspective, attitude counts. It's not the only thing, since people with a good attitude have had significant delays because of problems in the software, and people with lousy attitudes have put software in with little or no difficulty because the software was extraordinarily good. But generally, a good attitude means fewer delays, or no delays, in implementing MRP. □

*Editor's note:   Darryl Landvater is vice president, Manufacturing Software Systems Inc., Williston, VT. He is also an independent MRP consultant who has helped implement several successful Class A MRP systems.*

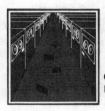

**Computers In Manufacturing**
*. . . continued*

As the productivity problems indicate, there is room for improvement. It appears a big part of the problem will be solved with the computer. That is easier said than done. There are many who are trying, but as Ollie Wight, Williston, VT, a leading consultant on the use of computers in manufacturing has pointed out, many are trying, but only a few have succeeded.

A few months ago, Booz-Allen & Hamilton Inc., a well-known and large management consulting firm, held an executive briefing in Chicago and took a business look at the manufacturing systems of tomorrow. Charles Allison, a Booz-Allen senior vice president and head of the firm's Chicago office, said at the start of the briefing that operations is probably the most extensively managed of all functions of an industrial corporation, but receives little strategic attention from the top.

John C. Reece, a Booz-Allen vice president specializing in information systems practice, in a later session outlined some approaches to the operations problem that have proved successful:

• The initial decision to proceed came from the top management and those executives have continued to involve themselves actively in accomplishing the development and use of manufacturing systems.

• Strategic objectives for the systems were established first, followed by selection of a systems design approach, and finally, decision-making on the hardware/software.

Top management did not view the implemented results as a magic, computerized placebo which would absolve it from running its manufacturing operation from day to day.

• Systems designs were matched to the organizational structures of the companies as well as to the capabilities of their manufacturing personnel to use them.

• Finally, the complexity of the development, implementation and on-going use of manufacturing systems was fully understood and compensated for through the use of multidisciplined approaches. These approaches embraced the full range of human and technical skills involved in designing and using the system from beginning to end.

Reece was, in effect, saying that successful users saw manufacturing systems as realistic tools requiring a great deal of top management time, planning and follow-through.

Another speaker, Dr. Joel D. Goldhar, the executive secretary of the National Research Council's committee on computer-aided manufacturing, was quick to point out that "the deeper you get into what's coming in manufacturing technology, the less sure you are about anything except the fact that what's coming is rapid change and a vast range of new capabilities, some of which are predictable and some of which really aren't." However, he explained, that "the electronic factory is not an unmanned factory."

According to Goldhar, for an organization to take advantage of this technology it will probably go through three stages. He said, "Stage one is to get new technology to perform existing tasks in established ways with more productivity. In stage two, the organization restructures itself to realize maximum economic advantages of the new capabilities." He said computers are introduced to the organization at this point. During the final stage, "the organization begins to offer new products and services not possible before the installation of the new technology."

The Booz-Allen executive seminar underscored the importance of the role of top management and the changes that will take place in the

Source data collection at a factory site is carried out with a unit from Mohawk Data Sciences.

factory. Now what's needed are some ideas to implement the "automated factory." These ideas are coming from all sources — Booz-Allen, CAM-I hardware vendors, software vendors, remote computing firms and even the users themselves. For instance, CAM-I is in the midst of an interesting project called the *Advanced Factory Management System.*

It's a serious attempt to pull together all the functional specifications for a factory management system. One of the functional goals for the system is the reduction of material flow time through the shop. This simplistic sounding goal touches practically every operational aspect of a batch-oriented manufacturing operation.

Another organization which does a considerable amount of work with computers in manufacturing is the American Production and Inventory Control Society, Inc. (APICS) Washington, DC. This large group spends a considerable amount of its effort in the study of the use of computers in manufacturing. This is greatly apparent at its annual conference and in its various publications. Materials requirements planning (MRP) receives intense attention by APICS.

It is possible to develop an MRP system in-house. But as Darryl Landvater, vice president, Manufacturing Software Systems, Inc., a firm that evaluates MRP software packages, points out, "Home-grown MRP packages don't have a good track record."

Most MRP packages are designed for IBM computers by software vendors. They have also developed packages for Digital Equipment, Hewlett Packard, Wang and Data General computers. The other mainframers — NCR, Honeywell, Univac and Burroughs — have developed programs for use on their own equipment. Leading software vendors and remote computing firms offering MRP and other manufacturing packages include Cincom Systems Inc., Cincinnati, OH; Software International Inc., Andover, MA; Martin-Marietta Data Systems, Towson, MD; American Software and Computer Co., Atlanta, GA; Resources Software International, Englewood Cliffs, NJ; University Computing, Dallas, TX; Control Data's Cybernet, Minneapolis, MN;

*. . . continued on page 48*

**Computers
In Manufacturing**
*. . . continued*

A.O. Smith, Milwaukee, WI, and Boeing Computer Services, Morristown, NJ.

The tools to improve the factory are available. It is now only a matter of resolve by top and information resource management to implement an effective information system. They must be made to fully understand that the most dynamic and unpredictable need in the manufacturing business is the need for information. They must nurture it as an asset and use it as a resource to gain effective control of the manufacturing function. □

# 6
# Human Resources Information System

**DESCRIPTION OF FUNCTION**

Historically, the formal function of human resources management appeared in organizations some two hundred fifty years after the primary functions of production, sales and finance. Due to the sociocultural conditions that existed during the early phases of the Industrial Revolution, labor was looked upon and treated as one of the cost factors of production, similar to land and capital. Managers, almost all of whom were entrepreneurs at the time, understood that the best way to maximize profits was to minimize costs. As far as labor costs were concerned, this meant paying workers as little as possible for as many hours of work as possible.

Thus we find that in the 1830s, workers in cotton factories were employed an average of seventy-eight hours per week in the United States at an average wage of ten shillings per week. These conditions compared favorably to those in Prussia where cotton plant workers toiled up to ninety-four hours per week for a wage of less than three shillings per week. It should be noted that twenty shillings were equal to one English pound. In an attempt to improve these subhuman conditions, Great Britain passed the British Factories Regulation Act in 1835 forbidding the employment of children under nine years of age in all textile mills except silk mills and restricting the working hours of employees between the ages of thirteen and eighteen to sixty-nine hours per week. This law did not help children, some as young as four or five years of age, who were working from fourteen to fifteen hours a day in English coal mines.

Given these circumstances, it is not surprising that working people would ultimately band together in an attempt to improve their wages and working conditions. Indeed, in 1786 a group of journeymen printers went out on strike in Philadelphia, the first recorded work stoppage in American history. During the following one hundred fifty years there were periodic outbursts of labor unrest and violence. It was not until the passage of the Wagner Act in 1935 that workers earned the right to organize and bargain collectively throughout the United States. Thus, in terms of historical development, collective bargaining was the first responsibility to be included within the personnel management function.

The introduction by Frederick W. Taylor of the scientific management movement during the last quarter of the nineteenth century provided the next areas of involvement for personnel specialists. Taylor proposed the substitution of a scientific method for the trial-and-error methods heretofore used in performing job tasks. His approach involved the systematic observation and analysis of job elements with the aim of simplifying the tasks to be done. This would be followed by the selection of people with the skills and ability to perform these tasks and training them to do the job properly. Taylor believed strongly that workers should be rewarded in proportion to their output and urged management to adopt an incentive pay plan to replace the then prevailing day-rate system. The technical aspect of Taylor's work led to the development of the industrial engineering discipline, with its emphasis upon plant methods and layout, time study of operations, and material-handling procedures. The managerial implications of Taylor's contributions involved the areas of job analysis and job design, selection, training, and compensation systems. These areas eventually fell under the domain of human resources management.

During the early part of the twentieth century, additional historical threads were being woven in ways which would converge upon the personnel management function. For example, the early industrial psychologists were interested in a better matching of workers' abilities with jobs. A well-known member of this profession, Hugo Munsterberg, reported in 1913 on the value of appropriate tests in the selection of telephone operators, streetcar motormen and ship's officers. His pioneering work laid the foundation for the development and extensive use of tests in the selection and promotion of employees. The acceptance of testing was also encouraged by the passage of the Pendleton Act in 1883 which established the Federal Civil Service Commission and mandated the administering of competitive examinations for admission into public service. While the primary purpose of the act was to eliminate the spoils system in government service, it served also to encourage the introduction of progressive personnel policies in business and industrial organizations.

After the United States Supreme Court in 1911 upheld the workmen's compensation laws of several states, many firms started to hire safety specialists whose responsibility it was to be concerned with the health and safety of the organization's employees on the job. The efforts of these safety specialists were supplemented by social secretaries or welfare secretaries who tried not only to improve conditions of employment on the job but to help and counsel employees whose off-the-job problems affected the quality of their work performance. These personal problems covered such diverse areas as health, education, housing and financial difficulties.

The historical events thus far described served to chip away at the idea inherited from the early Industrial Revolution that the working person was simply a factor of production and could be treated in the same way as land, capital, or machinery. The final blows to this concept were struck during the past half century. During the 1920s a team of researchers conducted experiments at the Hawthorne Works of the Western Electric Company in Chicago. The purpose of these studies was to test Taylor's predictions under his scientific management theory that improvement in the physical conditions of the workplace would lead to an improvement in worker productivity. When the predicted results did not materialize, the experiments were extended into the 1930s in an attempt to find an explanation for the findings. From these experiments there emerged a view of the industrial organization not only as a technical-economic system but also as a social system. The worker began to be seen as a human being who came to the job each day with attitudes, values and preconceptions. The employee was a social being who could be motivated by a feeling of belonging to the work group and being accepted as a member of the team.

The Hawthorne studies thus led to the development of the *human relations* theory of management whose credo may be summed up in the phrase "a happy worker is a productive worker." In order to learn how to make workers happy, organizations had to turn to experts in the social and biological sciences who concentrated on the study of human behavior. The disciplines of anthropology, economics, physiology, sociology, social psychology and psychology were included under the general heading of the behavioral sciences. Over the last two generations the educational background of personnel specialists has focused upon the behavioral sciences so that the manager will be equipped to deal with the human element in organizations.

The final step in the historical development of the personnel management function in organizations was the explosion of the civil rights movement during the 1960s. This led to the enactment of extensive social legislation during the 1960s and 1970s. Some of the major laws enacted during this period were the Equal Pay Act of 1963, the Civil Rights Act of 1964, the Age Discrimination in Employment Act of 1967, the Occupational Safety and Health Act of 1970, and the Employee Retirement Income Security Act of 1974. In addition, there were a large number of Presidential Executive Orders, administrative rulings and court decisions issued in these areas. Personnel management practices in today's organizations have been drastically influenced by these legislative, judicial and administrative actions.

As a result of the historical developments described above, the human resources management function in organizations has expanded to incorporate many different areas which are summarized in the following listing:

Job analysis and design
Recruitment
Selection and placement
Health and safety
Collective bargaining
Manpower planning
Career path planning
Employee motivation
Skill training and retraining
Reward systems
   Pay
   Benefits
   Incentive programs
Performance appraisal
Legal compliance-disabled, women, disadvantaged, minorities
Organization development
Employee privacy

The comprehensiveness and diversity of the above listing reveal the scope of knowledge and information which must be made available to the personnel specialist if these functions are to be performed properly. However it should be borne in mind that by definition a manager achieves his goals by coordinating the efforts and activities of his subordinates. Thus as we proceed to review the management information requirements of the human resources management function, we should remember that much of this information is used not only by the personnel specialist but by every operating manager in the organization.

## MANAGEMENT INFORMATION REQUIREMENTS

When, in the performance of his duties, the manager is concerned with human resources issues, he is in need of two broad categories of information. In dealing with longer-range issues such as manpower planning, information about the environment in which the organization operates is required. Political, economic, geographic, and sociocultural trends as well as anticipated actions of competitors must be identified so that the formulation of long-range plans will facilitate the organization's adaptation to environmental demands. These background information requirements are discussed in the chapter on information for strategic decisions.

However, due to growing governmental involvement in human rights areas since the 1930s and especially the explosion of social legislation over the last twenty years as described above, there is also a vital necessity for knowledge of environmental factors to assist managers in making operational decisions. Thus in the day-to-day administration of labor relations, the manager must be aware of currently valid statutes, NLRB rulings, and judicial interpretations. To insure that the organization is in compliance with requirements in the areas of discrimination by virtue of age, sex, religion, race, and, in certain communities, sexual preference, the manager must keep abreast of the various civil rights laws and the administrative and judicial regulations pertaining thereto. Knowledge of the thousands of rulings issued by federal, state and local regulatory bodies responsible for health, safety, environmental protection, transportation, job training, fringe benefit and retirement programs, and the like must be accessible to both the personnel specialist and the operating manager.

Another aspect of the background information needed by managers concerns internal organizational factors. In order for human resources policies to be effective, they must be consistent with the objectives and goals of the organization. The communication system within the organization must be geared to transmit these objectives and goals clearly and accurately to all managerial employees. Furthermore, human resources policies must be consonant with the value systems of managers, work groups within the firm, and the informal organization. In consequence, managers must be attuned to the organizational climate which reflects these values.

In addition to the background information requirements, there are specific human resources information requirements to support decisionmaking in the personnel area. Information about the job and the employee are the basic building blocks of the system. The key to the successful implementation of the human resources function is the effective matching of the person to the job. Traditionally, related tasks are grouped to form job positions. Job analysis techniques are utilized to develop accurate and usable job descriptions.

Reliable descriptions of all the jobs in the organization provide one-half of the information needed to match people to the jobs. Before discussing personnel data requirements however there is a bridging type of information needed which can be viewed either from the perspective of the job or the person on the job. The reference is to the value or worth of the job in monetary terms. There are many job evaluation techniques used in organizations to define the monetary value of jobs. These techniques are generally based upon a combination of the evaluation of the importance of the job in achieving the goals of the organization and the extent of education, training, and experience deemed necessary to perform the job properly. In our complex society these fairly objective evaluation techniques are limited and modified by real-world factors such as supply and demand, minimum wage laws, labor-management agreements, the company's profitability, and so forth. Thus, even in times of severe economic recession, it is likely that the demand for computer programmers will force organizations to offer high salaries to satisfy their personnel requirements in this area for the foreseeable future, regardless of the worth of these programming jobs as determined by the more objective job evaluation techniques.

The job description and the job evaluation for each position are the prerequisites for the job specification. As the term implies, the job specification details the educational background, training and experience needed by a candidate for the position. This leads us to the employee, the second major variable of the human resources information system. To make proper use of its human resources, the organization must not only match the employee to his starting position with the firm but also has to be capable of continuing to effectively match the same employee to successively higher position levels as the employee climbs the career ladder. An information system which provides this capability will enable the organization to retain the loyalty and services of its talented and ambitious younger employees and at the same time insure the satisfaction of the organization's future manpower needs.

To accomplish this goal, the information system should develop a profile of each employee. The profile starts with basic biographical data. Information such as marital status and number of children is of course needed to determine the amount of income tax to be withheld from the employee's salary. It is however also a significant input when the employee is being considered for transfer to another geographic, perhaps overseas, location. A record of the educational background of the employee will enable the firm to evaluate his eligibility for more advanced responsibilities which specify educational requirements. Similarly the history of previous jobs held and functions performed in other organizations may help in matching the employee to an available opening calling for familiarity with these functions.

Through transfers and promotions, employees tend to fill several positions in the organization. The employee profile contains such work history data, together with training and testing experiences gone through in preparation for such transfers and promotions. In most firms, employees are evaluated periodically and such evaluation data also form part of the employee record. The skills acquired by the employee throughout his education and work career are maintained in his profile. Thus the current assignment of a manager may not call for knowledge of a foreign language. But if the skills inventory contains this information, the manager may be tapped for a new job opening requiring such foreign language expertise. Finally, the employee profile is rounded off with compensation and benefit history containing a record of salary increments, bonuses, and the level of benefits coverage.

## SOURCES OF DATA

On the operational level, data for the human resources information system is generated primarily within the organization as a by-product of the day-to-day activities of the firm. Thus, as jobs are analyzed and evaluated, the organization prepares job descriptions, job evaluations and job specifications. These serve as the input database for information about the jobs in the firm. When an employee is hired, an application form is completed containing information about educational background and prior work experience, as well as indicating skills possessed by the employee. During the employee's work career with the organization, a record is maintained of the various positions held, evaluation of performance in these positions, training programs completed, new skills acquired, and pay and benefits history. A properly designed human resources information system thus compiles as input a record of each job and a history of each employee in the firm. Often the complete employee record is restricted to managerial personnel, with information on non-managerial employees limited to biographical and work history data.

## INFORMATION SYSTEM OUTPUTS

The Prudential Insurance Company of America, whose human resources model was presented in the chapter on strategic decisionmaking, operates a human resources information system designed to support the decisions of operating managers. This system is currently in the early stages of a consolidation and upgrading which, over a number of years and a series of developmental steps, will result in a comprehensive and integrated personnel system. The company has other computer systems which contain employee data but these are utilized for areas other than the human resources management function. Brief overviews of the major outputs of the system as they exist currently are herewith presented.

## PROFILE

This system has been in operation in all Regional Home Offices since 1971 and is the primary computer system used by the personnel department for recordkeeping and administration for all Home Office and Field Service employees. It contains basic identification data and education, salary and location history. In addition, Profile contains job analysis data, a skills inventory segment, test data and certain employee evaluation data. In 1972, Profile was tied to the Home Office/Field Service payroll system through a computer interface so that information on salary changes and other employee activity would pass from Profile to payroll. The Profile record is also the source used for most special reports on Home Office and Field Service employees. It is furthermore accessible for ad hoc report purposes. Figures 6-1 and 6-2 present a sample printout and a Profile format respectively.

```
DANCE               , JOAN        .          ORIG. APPT. DATE    08-01-81 AS 06   AT $      20.000     AUG 11, 1981
959-99-9999             J DA                 CURRENT APPT. DATE  08-01-81         APPT. STATUS U

                                             ADJ. SERVICE DATE   08-01-81         TERM CODE
SALARY  $      20.000  MAXIMUM SALARY  $      0.000
                                             SALARY CONSIDER. DATE 00-00-00       TERM DATE 00-00-00
CITY CLASS U3  W/L INDICATOR L  STATUS U  EMP.TYPE 3I
                                             DATE OF BIRTH       01-15-46
LEVEL 06   DATE OF CURR. LEVEL 08-01-81
                                                                                 CLU     NO       MAN DEV  NO
SAL CLASS  E        PREM PAY                                                      FLMI    NO       SSP      NO
                                                                                 FSA     NO
SEX        F        JOB GROUP 03
MARITAL    M        2
DISAB BEN  O              05                  COMP  RHO  SAT  DEPT  DIV                        SEC
                                             05    0    00   000   890-GIB LABS
WORK WEEK 00.00  DAYS WORKED 5.0  FIRST DAY-1  LAST DAY-5

TITLE  J090 -

JOB LEVEL 06        DATE OF DP  00-00-00              ED. SEG 00    SKILL SEG 00     HIST. SEG 01

                                       EDUCATION
         HIGH ED. LEVEL-   APPT ED. LEVEL-   HIGH SCHOOL-                 YEAR OF GRADUATION      00

                                   SALARY HISTORY
         LET                       JOB                          JOB                       SAL    LS
 DATE    NO. ACT        TITLE      GRP  CO RHO SAT   DIVISION   SEC NO.  LEV  STAT  SALARY  CLS    AMT
08-01-81 150 AP  J090-             03   05  0  00  890-GIB LABS          06   U     20.000  E
```

Figure 6-1.

# CAREER PROFILE

This subsystem of Profile was designed with the assistance of information Science Incorporated, an outside consultant, to store and display data relating to an employee's personal background and work experience. It is a well-designed and implemented system, which relies on the employee's voluntary response to a review and update of information on an annual basis. The basic content is the employee's concept of his work experience. A sample output of the career profile is illustrated in Figures 6-3A and 6-3B. The format of the master record in which career profile data are accumulated and stored is presented in Figures 6-4A, 6-4B, and 6-4C.

# EEO

The equal employment oportunity system (EEO) utilizes data from Profile and the agents index maintenance system (AIMS) to produce EEO compliance reports and management information. The system also has the ability to satisfy reporting requirements for utilization analyses, affirmative action plans (AAP), division action plans, and additional reports for monitoring progress. The basic EEO record is shown in Figure 6-5.

# APPLICANT RECORD SYSTEM

The applicant record system's main purpose is to provide basic data to aid in the internal analysis of applicants and satisfy EEO reporting requirements. The system is decentralized and handles all Home Office and Field Service applicants. Currently it is a stand-alone system with no computer ties to other systems. The system has been installed since 1976. Figure 6-6 lists the items of data that are gathered on each applicant.

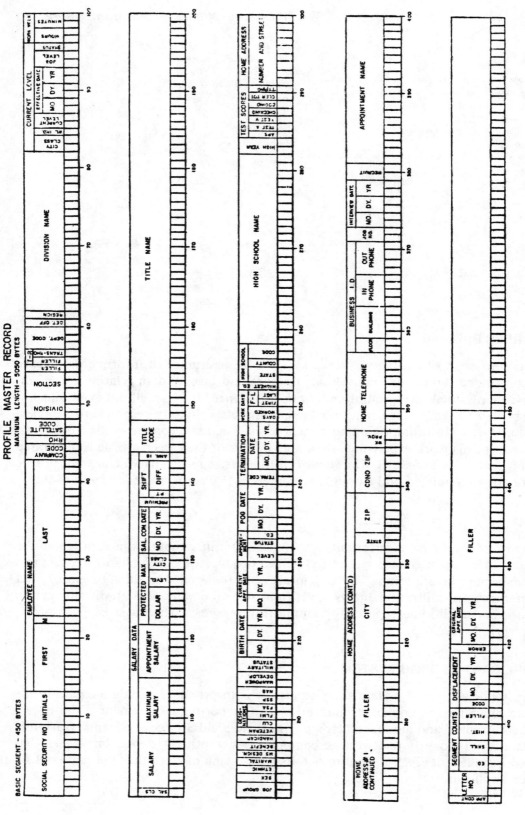

Figure 6-2.

278

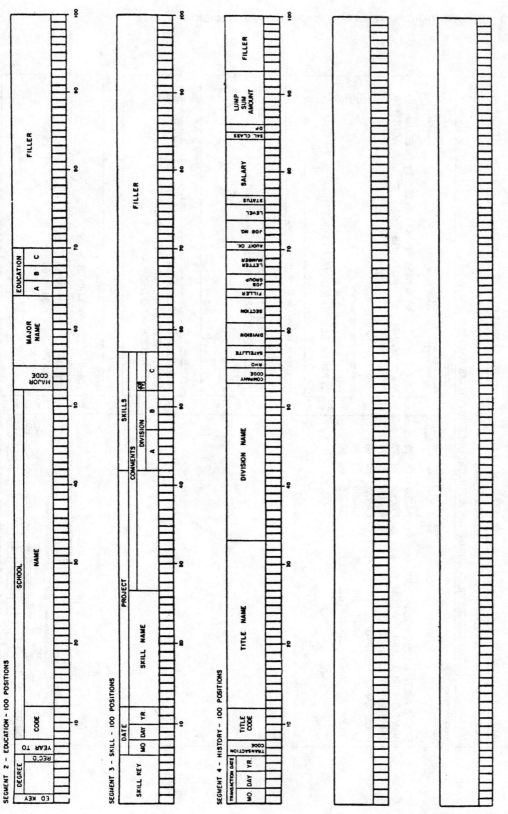

Figure 6-2. (Cont.)

279

SAMPLE
CAREER PROFILE

| Name | | | Identifying Number | | Date of Birth | Date of Service | Level | Date of Level | Date Printed | Last Updated |
|------|---|---|---|---|---|---|---|---|---|---|
| JACQUELIN B SNOW | | | 111223661 | JBSN | 06-12-38 | 06-22-63 | 20 | 11-71 | 07-28-75 | 07-07-74 |

| Nickname | HO or Sub | Location | Division/Department/Field Office | Title |
|----------|-----------|----------|----------------------------------|-------|
| JACKIE | SCHO | JACKSVILL | SYSTEMS & PROCEDURES | SYSTEMS ANALYST |

WORK EXPERIENCE

| Description | 20 300 | 23 Code | Yrs Exp | Last Year | 32 Action |
|-------------|--------|---------|---------|-----------|-----------|
| SYST & METH-LANGUAGES-COBOL | | PA250 | 05 | 73 | |
| HOME OFF./FLD. CLER. PAYROLL, GEN. | | PB695 | 04 | 73 | |
| CAREER PROFILE SYSTEM | | PB950 | 02 | 73 | |
| ACCEPTANCE TESTING | | PA970 | 04 | 69 | |
| EXPENSE ACCOUNT ANALYSIS | | GA205 | 03 | 66 | |
| PREPARATION OF ACCOUNTING SPECS. | | GA325 | 03 | 66 | |

EDUCATION

| | Degree or Professional Designation | Last Year | School | Major Field |
|---|---|---|---|---|
| 001 | BS | 61 | NEW YORK UNIVERSITY | ECON |
| 002 | MS (PART) | 67 | RUTGERS | ACCTG |
| 003 | FLMI (PART) | 73 | | |
| 004 | | | | |
| 005 | | | | |

OTHER EDUCATION AND TRAINING

| 311 | LOMA: PARTS 1, 2, 4, 6, 7 |
| 312 | SYSTEMS DESIGN & DEVELOPMENT, 1973 |
| 313 | |
| 314 | |

PROFESSIONAL, BUSINESS, OR COMMUNITY ACTIVITIES

| Code | Description |
|------|-------------|
| 321 | P VICE PRESIDENT, COMPUTER USERS OF SOUTHEAST |
| 322 | E SCHOOL BOARD MEMBER, JACKSONVILLE |
| 323 | |
| 324 | |
| 325 | |
| 326 | |

CAREER INTERESTS

| 331 | WOULD LIKE EXPOSURE TO LIFE INSURANCE OPERATIONS |
| 332 | (UNDERWRITING, CLAIM, ETC.) ADMINISTRATIVE |
| 333 | EXPERIENCE ALSO DESIRABLE. |
| 334 | |
| 335 | |

FAMILY

| | Spouse | Date of Birth |
|---|--------|---------------|
| 350 | JOHN | 12-01-36 |
| | Children | |
| 351 | ETHAN | 02-02-58 |
| 352 | SHARYN | 03-05-60 |
| 353 | | |
| 354 | | |
| 355 | | |
| 356 | | |

MANAGEMENT/SUPERVISORY EXPERIENCE
Largest Group Managed (more than 1 year)

| 0 | 1 to 10 | 11 to 40 | 41 to 100 | 101 to 500 | 501 + |
|---|---------|----------|-----------|-----------|-------|
| | | X | | | |

ORGANIZATIONAL EXPERIENCE
More than 1 year in

| CORP | RHO | FIELD | PRUPAC CORP | PRUPAC RSO | OTHER SUBS |
|------|-----|-------|-------------|------------|------------|
| X | X | | | | |

Comb 34919  Ed 5-77

Figure 6-3.

## SAMPLE

### CAREER PROFILE UPDATING FORM

**UPDATING OTHER PARTS OF CAREER PROFILE:** Use the following procedure to update or correct the information shown on your Career Profile for EDUCATION, OTHER EDUCATION AND TRAINING, PROFESSIONAL, BUSINESS OR COMMUNITY ACTIVITIES, CAREER INTERESTS, FAMILY, and INSURANCE. • Note the numbers of the lines on which the data to be changed in now shown on your Career Profile. • To *add* or *replace* a line of data, enter the new data below in the space designated by the line number involved. • To *delete* a line of data and leave the line blank, enter $\phi$ below next to the line number involved.

**IDENTIFYING NUMBER**

(COPY FROM FRONT OF FORM)

TODAY'S DATE — MO DAY YR 19

### WORK EXPERIENCE

Use the coding boxes below to *add* additional kinds of experience to your Career Profile. Refer to the Guide Book for the necessary codes. USE XX999 FOR EXPERIENCE NOT listed IN Guide Book ONLY. To *update* or *add* 1 year of experience to existing entries write U under Action on the front of this form. To *delete* entries write D under Action on the front of this form.

WORK EXP CODE | YRS LAST EXP YR | A C T

300
300
300
300
300
300
300
300 X X 9 9 9 A

### EDUCATION

| | DEGREE OR DESIG. | IF NOT RECEIVED ENTER (PART) BELOW | LAST YR OF STUDY | SCHOOL NAME | MAJOR SUBJECT |
|---|---|---|---|---|---|
| 001 | | | | | |
| 002 | | | | | |
| 003 | | | | | |
| 004 | | | | | |
| 005 | | | | | |

### OTHER EDUCATION AND TRAINING

311
312
313
314

### PROFESSIONAL, BUSINESS OR COMMUNITY ACTIVITIES

### CAREER INTERESTS

331
332
333
334
335

### MANAGEMENT

**SUPERVISORY EXPERIENCE**

If the largest group of employees supervised for 1 year or more has increased, check the appropriate box below.

341 | 0 to 10 | 1 to 11 | 11 to 40 | 41 to 100 | 101 to 500 | 500 to 501 | 501+

### ORGANIZATIONAL EXPERIENCE

If organizational experience has changed, check *all* of the types of offices where you have had more than 1 year of experience.

343 | CORP | RHO | FIELD CORP | PRUPAC CORP | RSO | PRO SUBS | OTHER SUBS

### FAMILY

| LINE NO | NAME | BIRTH DATE MO DAY YR |
|---|---|---|
| SPOUSE 350 | | |
| CHILDREN (ENTER LINE NO) | | |

### INSURANCE

| PERSONAL LIFE COVERAGE | |
|---|---|
| 345 | |

| PERSONAL INCOME PROTECTION COVERAGE AFTER 1 YEAR Mo Amount | Duration |
|---|---|
| 347 | |

NOTE: See Guide Book for examples of how to update your Career Profile. Contact Personnel to make any additions, changes or deletions on your Career Profile that are not covered by the conditions shown on this page.

After completing this form, please initial here _____

Figure 6-3. *(Cont.)*

CAREER PROFILE MASTER RECORD LAYOUT

Figure 6-4.

Page I

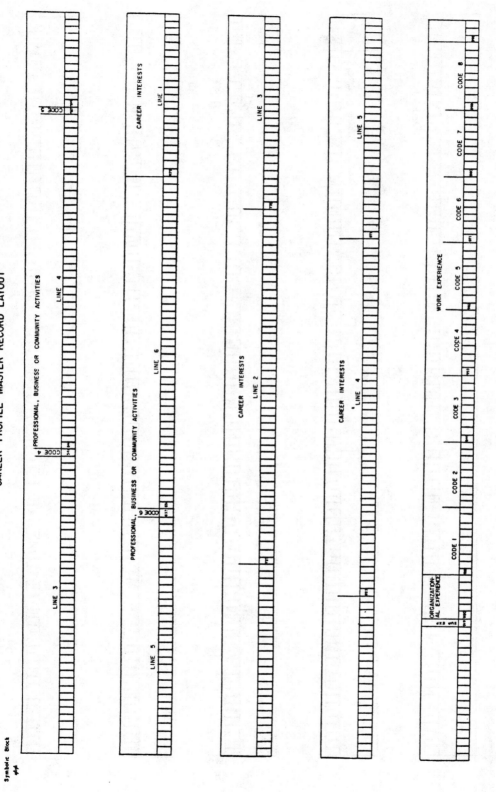

Figure 6–4. (Cont.)

Page 2

CAREER PROFILE MASTER RECORD LAYOUT

Figure 6-4. (*Cont.*)

# EEO MASTER RECORD

EEO CURR SS NO — X(9)

EEO CURR NAME FIRST — X(11)

EEO CURR NAME MI — X

EEO CURR NAME LAST — X(20)

FILLER — X(6)

EEO CURR SEX — X

EEO CURR ETHNIC — X

FILLER — XX

EEO CURR TITLE CODE — XXXX

EEO CURR STATUS — X

EEO CURR TERM CODE 1ST — X

EEO CURR TERM CODE 2ND — X

FILLER — X(4)

EEO CURR REPORT TYPE — XX

FILLER — X(22)

EEO CURR TERM MO — XX

EEO CURR TERM DA — XX

EEO CURR TERM YR — XX

FILLER — X(6)

EEO CURR SEX — X

EEO CURR ETHNIC — X

FILLER — X

Figure 6–5.

## EEO MASTER RECORD

FILLER

X(107)

EEO CMBR COMPANY

EEO CMBR COM 2 8

EEO CMBR TAPE YEAR

Figure 6-5. (Cont.)

## APPLICANT RECORD SYSTEM MASTER RECORD

| Field | Picture | Positions |
|---|---|---|
| APP SS 1 | X(4) | 1 2 3 4 |
| APP SS 2 | XX | 5 6 |
| APP SS 3 | XX | 7 8 |
| APP SS 4 | X | 9 |
| APP 1ST INIT | X | 10 |
| APP MID INIT | X | 11 |
| APP LAST NAME 2 | XX | 12 13 |
| APP LAST NAME BALANCE | X(18) | 14 15 16 17 18 19 20 21 22 23 24 25 26 27 28 29 30 31 |
| APP FIRST NAME 1 | X | 32 |
| APP FIRST NAME BALANCE | X(8) | 33 34 35 36 37 38 39 40 |
| APP MID INITIAL | X | 41 |
| APP ZIP | X(5) | 42 43 44 45 46 |
| APP COMPANY | XX | 47 48 |
| APP RHO | X | 49 |
| APP SATELLITE | XX | 50 |
| | | 51 |
| APP DIVISION | XXX | 52 53 54 |
| APP SECTION | XXX | 55 56 57 |
| APP OFFICE TYPE | X | 58 |
| APP POSITION TYPE | X | 59 |
| APP STATUS | X | 60 |
| APP CURRENT VACANCY | X | 61 |
| APP APPLICATION MO | XX | 62 63 |
| APP APPLICATION DAY | XX | 64 65 |
| APP APPLICATION YEAR | XX | 66 67 |
| APP EDUCATION CODE | X | 68 |
| FILLER | X | 69 |
| APP RECRUIT SOURCE | X | 70 |
| APP DIRECT RECRUIT | X | 71 |
| APP PROTECTED SOURCE | X | 72 |
| APP SEX | X | 73 |
| APP ETHNIC CODE | X | 74 |
| APP HANDICAPPED | X | 75 |
| APP VIET VET | X | 76 |
| APP TEST TYPE | X | 77 |
| APP A STANINE | X | 78 |
| APP V STANINE | X | 79 |
| APP APTITUDE INDEX | X | 80 |
| FILLER | X | 81 |
| I C TOTAL | X | 82 |
| I SPELLING | X | 83 |
| I TYPING | XX | 84 85 |
| I STENO | X | 86 |
| I STENO SCORE | XX | 87 88 |
| I APS | X | 89 |
| I FSET | X(6) | 90 91 92 93 94 95 |
| FILLER | X(6) | 96 97 98 99 100 |

Figure 6-6.

Figure 6-6. (Cont.)

DISABILITY SUMMARY REPORT

QUARTER ENDING - SEPTEMBER 1981

DIVISION 271 - PERSONNEL DATA SYSTS

| EMPLOYEE | BAND/ LEVEL | SAL CLASS | ASD DATE | 1/2 DAY | 1-1.5 DAYS | 2-2.5 DAYS | 3-3.5 DAYS | 4-4.5 DAYS | 5 DAYS OR MORE | 3RD QTR 81 DAYS | 3RD QTR 81 ABS | 2ND QTR 81 DAYS | 2ND QTR 81 ABS | 1ST QTR 81 DAYS | 1ST QTR 81 ABS | 4TH QTR 80 DAYS | 4TH QTR 80 ABS | 1981 YTD TOT DAYS | 1981 YTD TOT ABS |
|---|---|---|---|---|---|---|---|---|---|---|---|---|---|---|---|---|---|---|---|
| SECTION 001 | | | | | | | | | | | | | | | | | | | |
| | 07 | E | 08/22/66 | | 1 | | | | | 1.0 | 1 | | | | | 30.0* | 1# | 1.0 | 1 |
| | 09 | E | 06/25/79 | | | | | | | | | | | | | | | | |
| | 11 | E | 10/12/76 | | | 1 | | | | | | 2.0 | 1 | | | | | 2.0 | 1 |
| | 09 | E | 06/19/73 | | | | | | 1 | 7.0* | 1 | | | 1.0 | 1 | 1.0 | 1 | 9.0 | 3 |
| | 05 | E | 06/28/76 | | | | | | | | | | | | | | | | |
| | 60 | E | 06/17/57 | | | | | | | | | | | | | | | | |
| | 07 | A | 01/30/78 | | | | 1 | | | 3.0 | 1 | | | | | | | 3.0 | 1 |
| | 20 | E | 02/08/71 | | | | | | | | | | | | | | | | |
| | 07 | E | 07/30/79 | | | | 1 | | | | | | | 3.0 | 1 | | | 3.0 | 1 |
| | 09 | E | 05/07/73 | | | 1 | | | | 7.0* | 3 | 2.0 | 1 | | | | | 9.0 | 4 |
| | 09 | E | 04/12/76 | | | | | | | | | | | 1.0 | 1 | | | 2.0 | 2 |
| | 60 | E | 10/18/71 | | | | | | | | | 1.0 | 1 | | | 2.0 | 1 | 2.0 | 2 |
| | 09 | E | 06/24/68 | | 1 | | | | | 1.0 | 1 | 5.0* | 1 | 12.0* | 4 | 1.0 | 1 | 18.0 | 6 |
| | 11 | E | 06/16/58 | | | 1 | | | | 2.0 | 1 | | | | | | | 2.0 | 1 |
| DIVISION TOTALS | 14 | | | | 2 | 3 | 2 | 1 | | 21.0 | 8 | | | | | | | | |
| AVG. ABSENCE PER EMPLOYEE - DIV | | | | .000 | .143 | .214 | .143 | .071 | .000 | 1.500 | .571 | | | | | | | | |
| AVG. ABSENCE PER EMPLOYEE - RHO | | | | .015 | .215 | .082 | .025 | .062 | .015 | 1.823 | .415 | | | | | | | | |

THE TOTALS BELOW DO NOT INCLUDE LONG TERM DISABILITY ABSENCES GREATER THAN OR EQUAL TO 10 DAYS -

| | | | | 1/2 DAY | 1-1.5 DAYS | 2-2.5 DAYS | 3-3.5 DAYS | 4-4.5 DAYS | 5 DAYS OR MORE | 3RD QTR 81 DAYS | 3RD QTR 81 ABS |
|---|---|---|---|---|---|---|---|---|---|---|---|
| AVG. ABSENCE PER EMPLOYEE - DIV | | | | .000 | .143 | .214 | .143 | .071 | .000 | 1.500 | .571 |
| AVG. ABSENCE PER EMPLOYEE - RHO | | | | .015 | .215 | .082 | .025 | .062 | .015 | .670 | .376 |

* - INDICATES THE ABSENCE EXCEEDS THE PERSONNEL SUGGESTED AVERAGE (03.0 DAYS)

# - INDICATES THE EMPLOYEE HAS HAD AT LEAST ONE OCCURRENCE OF LONG TERM DISABILITY (10 DAYS OR MORE) DURING THE PERIOD

Figure 6-7.

## ATTENDANCE

The purpose of the attendance subsystem is to record employee disability absences and to provide absence information to the disability calculation program. Although the system was originally intended to record all types of absences, the initial installation was limited to disability absences in order to expedite its development. Other types of absences such as regular vacation and personal absence are to be included in future system enhancements. Figure 6-7 is a sample of an attendance system report.

## EMPLOYEE BENEFITS

This system was recently developed and is intended to serve as the nucleus of the future Prudential personnel systems. It is a database-oriented, on-line data entry system containing records for all Home Office, Field Service, Field Sales and Field Sales management employees as well as all retired employees. It contains all data required to administer the insurance employee benefits, i.e., Group Life, Supplemental Group, Survivor Benefits, Major Medical (or HMO), Dental, AD&D, Hazard Protection and Disability. The system is maintained by the employee benefits staff via CRT terminals. The database is interfaced with the payroll systems, passing EB data for deduction purposes and receiving personal data to maintain the database. Output products include notices of eligibility, confirmations of changes of coverage and enrollments, internally generated reminders, verification of coverages and inforce reports. Figures 6-8A and 6-8B are sample employee verification documents.

## CANDIDATE IDENTIFICATION

This system is a corporate-only system containing records of all employees in the company at the associate manager level and above. The system is fed by Profile and career profile as well as through manual maintenance. It contains personal, work experience, education, employee evaluation and test data. The database is accessed through use of a simple programming language which outlines criteria required for a position for which candidates are to be selected. A list of candidates is produced for each search which can be expanded or reduced by changing the criteria. When the list has an acceptable number of candidates, a printout of information about each candidate is produced for the final selection process. A sample of this printout is illustrated in Figures 6-9A, 6-9B, and 6-9C.

## SECOND PAYCHECK

Second paycheck is an individual benefits statement produced for all employees. The second paycheck uses data from all of the Payroll systems as well as Prudential investment plan and the retirement systems. The format for salaried employees is different from that used for sales employees. In the future, the document will be produced from the employee benefits system. Figures 6-10 are the components of a second paycheck.

The Prudential
Insurance Company
of America
Prudential Plaza
Newark New Jersey 07101

JUN 18, 1981

GROUP INSURANCE
NEWARK

ATTACHED IS INFORMATION THAT WE HAVE RECORDED RELATING TO YOUR
GROUP INSURANCE BENEFITS.  PLEASE REVIEW IT CAREFULLY TO VERIFY
THAT ALL OF THE INFORMATION IS CORRECT.

IF ANY OF THE INFORMATION THAT IS SHOWN IS INACCURATE,
CROSS IT OUT AND WRITE THE CORRECT INFORMATION ON THE
STATEMENT, SIGN AND DATE THE STATEMENT AND RETURN IT TO
ME.

SHOULD YOU WISH TO MAKE ANY CHANGES TO YOUR CURRENT COVERAGE,
PLEASE USE THE "EMPLOYEE'S REQUEST FOR CHANGE" FORM, ORD. 506.

IF YOU HAVE ANY QUESTIONS, PLEASE CALL ME ON EXT 7868.

EMPLOYEE BENEFITS EXAMINER
EMPLOYEE BENEFITS

Figure 6-8.

The Prudential
Insurance Company
of America
Prudential Plaza
Newark New Jersey 07101

*Prudential*

DATE OF BIRTH JUN 22, 1930 MARITAL STATUS   MARRIED

HOME ADDRESS ·

BASIC GROUP LIFE INSURANCE –
     BENEFICIARY DESIGNATION

SUPPLEMENTAL GROUP LIFE INSURANCE   –
                                    – AMT OF CONTRIBUTION $8.35
     BENEFICIARY DESIGNATION

SURVIVOR BENEFITS LIFE INSURANCE   –

                                   – EXTENT OF COVERAGE
                                   SPOUSE AND CHILD(REN)
                                   – AMT OF CONTRIBUTION $9.59

HEALTH CARE   MAJOR MEDICAL EXPENSE   – EXTENT OF COVERAGE
                                      EMPLOYEE, SPOUSE AND CHILD(REN)
                                         AMT OF CONTRIBUTION $2.70

DENTAL EXPENSE BENEFITS              – EXTENT OF COVERAGE
                                     EMPLOYEE, SPOUSE AND CHILD(REN)
                                        AMT OF CONTRIBUTION $2.00

         DEPENDENT/QUALIFIED FAMILY MEMBER INFORMATION

                (AN X INDICATES COVERAGE)

| NAME | DATE OF BIRTH | HEALTH CARE | DENTAL | SURVIVOR BENEFITS |
|------|---------------|-------------|--------|-------------------|
|  | JUN 28, 1929 | X | X | X |
|  | SEP 14, 1960 | X | X | X |

DATE _____        SIGNATURE _____

Figure 6–8. (*Cont.*)

A SAMPLE REQUEST OF THE CANDIDATE ID SYSTEM FOR ALL SCREENS ON
AN INDIVIDUAL EMPLOYEE

———▶ SSN                SHOWALL

---

ASSOCIATE DIR GRP INS

| DT CUR LVL | 063075 | | DT OF BIRTH | 090723 | |
|---|---|---|---|---|---|
| DATE APPT | 031247 | | SPOUSE NAME | | # CHILDREN    4 |

### EDUCATION

| DEGR | DECV | SCHOOL | MAJOR | YEAR | |
|---|---|---|---|---|---|
| MBA | | COLUMBIA UNIVERSITY NEW YORK | BUSINESS | 1950 | **1** |
| BS | | RUTGERS UNIVERSITY NEW JERSEY | ACCOUNTING | 1944 | |

---

### HISTORY OF ASSIGNMENTS

| YEAR | TITLE | DEPT/DIV/OFFICE | | RHO | |
|---|---|---|---|---|---|
| 1977 | ASSOC DIRECTOR GRP INS | 011 | 033 | 0 | |
| 1975 | ASSOC DIRECTOR GRP SYS | 055 | 056 | 0 | |
| 1971 | SR COMP SYS ANAL GRP INS | 055 | 056 | 0 | |
| 1969 | SR COMP SYS ANAL GRP INS | 099 | 056 | 3 | **2** |
| 1965 | COMP SYS ANAL GRP INS | 055 | 056 | 3 | |

---

| NAMED AS REPLACEMENT IN 1976 FOR | | IDENTIFIED ON LIST # 321 | |
|---|---|---|---|
| POS LVL | POSITION | YEAR QUAL | |
| 72 | DIRECTOR GRP INS | 1979 | **3** |

---

### SALARY HISTORY

| | CURRENT YEAR 070477 | PERIOD END 040477 | PERIOD END 052476 | PERIOD END 013176 | PERIOD END 040275 | |
|---|---|---|---|---|---|---|
| SALARY | $ 36,350 | $ 32,000 | $ 30,545 | $ 30,155 | $ 29,850 | |
| ANNUAL INCR | $ 4,350 | $ 0 | $ 0 | $ 0 | $ 1,500 | |
| INTERIM INC | $ 0 | $ 0 | $ 390 | $ 0 | $ 0 | |
| PROMOTE INC | $ 0 | $ 1,455 | $ 0 | $ 0 | $ 0 | |
| ONE TIM PAY | $ 0 | $ 0 | $ 0 | $ 305 | $ 0 | |
| SALARY ADJS | $ 0 | $ 0 | $ 0 | $ 0 | $ 0 | |
| | | | | | | |
| PRSONAL MAX | $ 38,000 | | | | | |
| PROPOSE MAX | $ 38,500 | | | | | |
| | | | | | | |
| SALARY RATE | | | | | | |
| | | | | | | |
| PERFRM RATE | | | | | | |
| DT MANGR RANK | 021669 | | | | | **4** |

---

EXECUTIVE RESOURCES VOLUME
CANDIDATE FOR POSITIONS AT          RANK                              **5**

---

Figure 6-9.

INDIVIDUAL DEVELOPMENT GUIDELINES

| HIGH LVL | YEAR DUE | FUNCTIONAL AREA | TYPE POS | 6 |
|---|---|---|---|---|

OTHER EDUCATION AND TRAINING

NATIONAL BUSINESSMEN'S AWARD MAY 1976
F.L.M.I.
CLU PARTS 1–2

| CODE | PROF BUSINESS OR COMMUNITY ACTIVITIES | |
|---|---|---|
| LOCAL ED | DREW COLLEGE DEVELOPMENT FUND | |
| OTHER AC | MADISON BOY SCOUT TROOP LEADER | |
| OTHER AC | MEMBER MADISON JAYCEES | |
| GOVERNME | VICE PRES MORRIS COUNTY REC DEPT. | 7 |

ORGANIZATIONAL EXPERIENCE

| CORP | RHO | FLD | PRU CORP | PAC RSO | OTH SUBS | MGT/SUPV EXP EMPL RESP FOR | RELOCATE |
|---|---|---|---|---|---|---|---|
| X | X | | | | | 50 | |

WORK PREFERENCE

CAREER INTEREST
5 YR GOAL    DIRECTOR OF RHO COMP SYST                    8

WORK EXPERIENCE

| CODE | YRS EXP | 1ST YR |
|---|---|---|
| KA105 | 01 | 1977 |
| JA537 | 09 | 1956 |
| EB907 | 04 | 1963 |
| AD103 | 13 | 1958 |
| AD105 | 13 | 1958 |
| AD220 | 10 | 1961 |
| EL231 | 07 | 1971 |
| EL234 | 04 | 1973 |

9

Figure 6–9. (*Cont.*)

## RETIREMENT

The Retirement system is a centralized system and is maintained and updated once a year including a computer feed from the Prudential investment plan system. The system contains identifying data, retirement earnings and benefit information for all active employees and terminated vested employes. In order to provide retirement estimates to employees, each personnel center is sent a copy of a portion of the retirement system record, and a calculation program to operate off these records to produce individual retirement estimates. This record and the calculation program are referred to as the current work system. When an employee retires, the retired life system produces the retired employee's monthly check. Figures 6–11A, 6–11B, and 6–11C represent the maintenance data that are prepared by the employee benefits area for the retirement system.

# YOUR

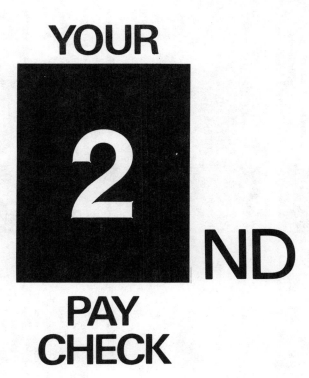

# ND

# PAY
# CHECK

You, the people of Prudential, make this Company great, and we point with pride to your creative zeal and enthusiastic commitment. We recognize the key role all of you play in our continuing success and try hard to provide an atmosphere in which you can pursue your personal goals. A key part of these efforts is Prudential's comprehensive benefits program, which can help free you from worry about the financial problems of illness, disability, death, or retirement.

This "Second Paycheck" is a personalized account of your benefits. Added to your earnings, these benefits help provide financial security for you and your family now and in the future.

The money the Company provides to back up this "Second Paycheck" is one of the best expenditures we make because it is actually an investment in the talents and dedication of the members of our Prudential family. We hope this information is useful to you in your long-range financial planning.

*Robert A Beck*

Figure 6–10.

# 1978 SECOND PAYCHECK

## MAJOR MEDICAL BENEFITS— UNLIMITED INDIVIDUAL LIFETIME MAXIMUM FOR YOU AND YOUR FAMILY.

| | |
|---|---|
| $5,000 | in full for eligible hospital expenses, then |
| 80% | of eligible hospital expenses in excess of $5,000, with no deductible. |
| 100% | of the Reasonable and Customary charge for surgical services as determined by the Company. |
| 80% | of eligible maternity expenses after a $100 pregnancy deductible. |
| $300 | supplemental accident benefit for certain charges made within 90 days of the accident. |
| $100 | for diagnostic x-ray and laboratory fees for each covered person in each calendar year. |
| 80% | of all other eligible expenses after a |
| $250 | deductible for 1978. |

*Above dollar amounts are maximums. Only actual expenses are covered.*

## DENTAL BENEFITS— FOR YOU AND YOUR FAMILY.

| | |
|---|---|
| 100% | of eligible charges for Basic Services after a $75 individual lifetime deductible. |
| 50% | of eligible charges for Major Services in a benefit year after satisfying a $75 individual annual deductible. |
| 50% | of eligible charges for orthodontic treatment provided for each covered dependent child under age 20, after satisfying a separate lifetime deductible of $75 per individual, up to a maximum lifetime benefit of $1,000 per individual. |

## DISABILITY BENEFITS

| | |
|---|---|
| 100% | If you are unable to work because of sickness or accident, you will receive Short Term Disability Benefits of: |
| $1,201 | of your weekly base salary of |
| 4 | less your normal deductions, including taxes—except Social Security, for an initial period for all disabilities commencing in each year of service of up to weeks. After initial period benefits are exhausted in a service |

## DEATH BENEFITS

| | |
|---|---|
| $125,000 | Basic Group Life Insurance |
| N/A | Supplemental Group Life Insurance |
| $255 | Social Security Death Benefit |
| $45,611 | Investment Plan Proceeds |
| $570 | RETIREMENT PLAN DEATH BENEFIT FOR DEATH OCCURRING BEFORE RETIREMENT. THIS IS THE AMOUNT OF YOUR CONTRIBUTIONS TO THE PLAN PLUS INTEREST. |
| $171,436 | Total Non-Accidental Death Benefit |
| $125,000 | Accidental Death Benefit |

### Survivor Benefits Life Insurance

| | |
|---|---|
| $1,041 | monthly spouse benefit, payable until the later of your spouse's age 65, and the 65th anniversary of your birth, but not beyond the death or remarriage of your spouse. |
| $520 | monthly child(ren) benefit, payable until your youngest child attains age 23. |

### Social Security Survivor Benefits

Social Security may provide the following estimated monthly survivor benefits:

| | |
|---|---|
| $326 | for each eligible child. |
| $326 | for your eligible spouse, regardless of age, with eligible children. |
| $311 | for your eligible spouse, age 60 or older. However, in no event will the combined Social Security monthly benefits exceed |
| $762 | (your estimated family maximum). |

## RETIREMENT BENEFITS— NEW PLAN

Retirement benefits are not vested until you have 10 years of "vesting service". As of January 1, 1978, **YOU ARE VESTED.**

The monthly pension you have earned up to January 1, 1978 is shown below. If you are vested, it will be payable to you at age 65 even if you terminate your employment.

**FIXED DOLLAR PENSION**

$1,925

Last year the cost to the Company of the employee benefits described in this statement was $192 million. For every $1,000 of cash compensation the Company paid an additional $190 for these benefits. The $190 figure is an average and does not apply to any one individual because of differences in ages, lengths of service, levels of earnings, dependent status, etc. Neither does it include many other fringe benefits not described in this "Second Paycheck".

$1,081 year, you will receive secondary period benefits of weekly, less your normal deductions, including taxes — except Social Security. This benefit represents

90% of your weekly base salary before deductions, and is payable

48 for a period of up to weeks.

*Benefits may be subject to reduction because of benefits from certain other sources.*

If you exhaust your Short Term Disability Benefits and are still disabled, *and at that time have completed 10 years of continuous service* you will receive monthly Long Term Disability Benefits of

$2,604 (reduced by any personal Social Security benefits and family Social Security Disability benefits), or your Early Retirement Amount (if any) — whichever is larger.

The benefit will be reduced:
1. Before age 65 — by 2/3 of earned income, if any, and by the amount of benefits from certain other sources.
2. On and after age 65 — by the retirement plan pension payment and by your personal Social Security retirement benefit.

$197 MONTHLY FOR 120 MONTHS FROM THE GROUP LIFE INSURANCE PLAN IF YOU ARE TOTALLY AND PERMANENTLY DISABLED. THESE PAYMENTS REDUCE THE AMOUNT OF YOUR BASIC GROUP LIFE INSURANCE.

**Social Security Disability Benefits**

After 5 months of disability, Social Security may provide the following estimated monthly disability benefits:

for you.
$435 for each eligible child.
$217 for your eligible spouse, regardless of age, with
$217 eligible child(ren), or
$163 for your eligible spouse, age 62 or older.

However, in no event will the combined Social Security monthly benefits exceed

$762 (your estimated family maximum).

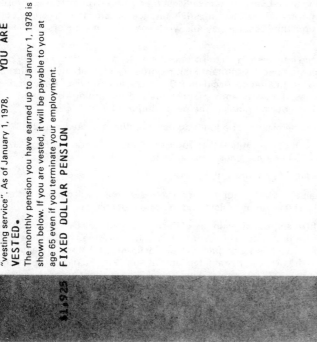
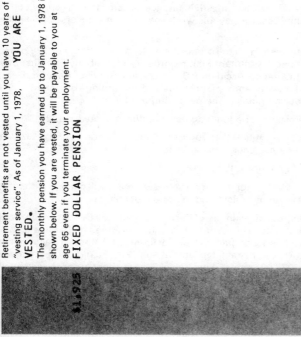

Figure 6-10. *(Cont.)*

## HOW YOUR BENEFITS REPORT WAS PREPARED

The information in this statement is subject to the terms and conditions of the Company's benefit plans. All benefit amounts shown (both Prudential and Social Security) are only estimates based on certain assumptions including earnings, length of service, marital status, age, and health insurance classification as shown on the Company's records. Actual benefits at the time they become payable will be based on the factors specified and applicable under each plan.

Three basic records were used to provide the information on the other side of the form – June 12, 1978 payroll records, 1977 year-end Retirement Plan records and Investment Plan records. Your Disability Benefits, Basic Group Life Insurance, Supplemental Group Life Insurance, Accidental Death Benefit, Survivor Benefits, Dental Benefits and Major Medical Benefits were based on your enrollment status and/or earnings on June 12, 1978. Your Major Medical deductible was based on your earnings at the beginning of 1978.

Short Term Disability Benefits are based on the assumption that you became disabled on June 12, 1978.

The Long Term Disability, if any, is based on the assumption that you became disabled on June 12, 1978 and remain disabled for one year, after which LTD benefits become payable.

Retirement Plan benefits are those accrued as of January 1, 1978.

If you retained Variable Annuity, the unit value of $1.4478 appearing on your statement will change with future investment results, but for purposes of this statement is considered to remain unchanged.

If you were eligible to retire on January 1, 1978, there is an estimate of the Retirement Plan Benefit which would have been payable had you retired early on that date. This estimated benefit assumes all service to have occurred in your present employee classification. It is accompanied by an estimate of the Social Security benefit which would be payable at age 65 (also the reduced benefit available at age 62 if you did not reach age 62 before January 1, 1978) assuming the January 1, 1978 retirement date. Social Security benefits are based on the computation method then in effect and consider only your earnings with the Company and/or its participating subsidiaries.

If a retirement estimate was prepared for you, and you are age 55 or more, and Company records indicate you are married, an estimated Spouse Income Benefit is also shown. This amount is based on the assumption that you retired on January 1, 1978, that your death occurs before age 65, that your spouse will be eligible to receive this benefit, and that no ERISA-mandated survivor annuity is payable. Details of the Spouse Income Benefit can be found in the booklet describing Group Life Insurance Benefits.

The amounts shown under the Retirement Benefits heading do not reflect any Options you have elected, or the possible effects of the Employee Retirement Income Security Act of 1974.

Investment Plan proceeds listed under Death Benefits assume no withdrawals since December 31, 1977.

## A SPECIAL NOTE ABOUT SOCIAL SECURITY SURVIVOR AND DISABILITY BENEFITS

Social Security Survivor and Disability benefits are displayed for you whether or not you presently have a spouse or children who might be eligible for these benefits. Furthermore, the benefit amounts shown do not take into account the actual ages of any potential beneficiaries.

The notation "N/A", meaning not applicable, appears where Company records indicate that you have not worked under the law for a period sufficient to ensure your right to these benefits.

These benefits are based on the computation method in effect on January 1, 1978 and consider only your earnings with the Company and/or its participating subsidiaries.

Figure 6-10. (*Cont.*)

PRUDENTIAL INSURANCE COMPANY
RETIREMENT PLANS INFORMATION BRIEF
FOR RETIREMENT, VESTED AND NON-VESTED TERMINATION AND DEATH IN SERVICE

☐ ACTUAL CALCULATION
☐ POST – RET CALCUALTION
☐ ESTIMATE CALCULATION

SOCIAL SECURITY NUMBER

1 2 3 4 5 6 7 8 9

DUPLICATE COLUMNS
1-9 ON ALL CARDS

**SPOUSE'S BENEFIT INFORMATION**

| SPOUSE'S DATE OF BIRTH | NON-QUALIFIED SPOUSE'S PENSION PROGRAM INFORMATION | | 60 MONTHS DOLLAR EQUIVALENT FACTOR AT TRANSACTION DATE | CARD # |
| | TRANSACTION DATE ANNUAL EARNINGS | GROUP LIFE INSURANCE | | |
| MO. DAY YR. | $ ¢ $ ONLY | $ ONLY | | 0 7 |

**PERIOD CERTAIN OPTION INFORMATION**

**CONTINGENT ANNUITANT INFORMATION**

| DATE OPTION ELECTED | ANNUITY AT ELECTION DATE | | CA DATE OF BIRTH | % TO CA | CA SEX | CARD # |
| | FIXED DOLLAR | VARIABLE UNITS | | | | |
| MONTHS OF PCO | $ ¢ | $ ¢ (2 DECIMAL PLACES) | MO. DAY YR. | | | 0 8 |
| MO. DAY YR. | | | | | | |

**MONTHLY DEDUCTIONS (DOLLARS AND CENTS)**

| #1 | #2 | #3 | #4 | #5 | #6 | #7 | #8 | #9 | #10 | | CARD # |
| Cd. Code AMOUNT | Cd. Code AMOUNT | Cd. Code AMOUNT | Cd. Code AMOUNT | Cd. Code AMOUNT | Cd. Code AMOUNT | Cd. Code AMOUNT | Cd. Code AMOUNT | Cd. Code AMOUNT | Cd. Code AMOUNT | | 0 9 |

**CHECKWRITING DEDUCTION CHANGE INFORMATION**

| #1 | #2 | #3 | #4 | #5 | #6 | #7 | #8 | #9 | #10 | CARD # |
| Chng. Code CHANGE DATE MO. YR. | Chng. Code CHANGE DATE MO. YR. | Chng. Code CHANGE DATE MO. YR. | Chng. Code CHANGE DATE MO. YR. | Chng. Code CHANGE DATE MO. YR. | Chng. Code CHANGE DATE MO. YR. | Chng. Code CHANGE DATE MO. YR. | Chng. Code CHANGE DATE MO. YR. | Chng. Code CHANGE DATE MO. YR. | Chng. Code CHANGE DATE MO. YR. | PAYROLL BUDGET EFFECTIVE DATE MO. YR. |
| | | | | | | | | | | 1 0 |

**TAX INFORMATION**

| TAX CDS. | FEDERAL | | STATE | | CARD # |
| | TAX CODE | WITHHOLD TAX AMOUNT | TAX CODE | WITHHOLD TAX AMOUNT | |
| FEDERAL STATE | | $ ONLY | | $ ONLY | 1 1 |

GP-3661   Ed. 12-77

Printed in U.S.A.

**PRUDENTIAL RETIREMENT PLANS**

Figure 6-11.

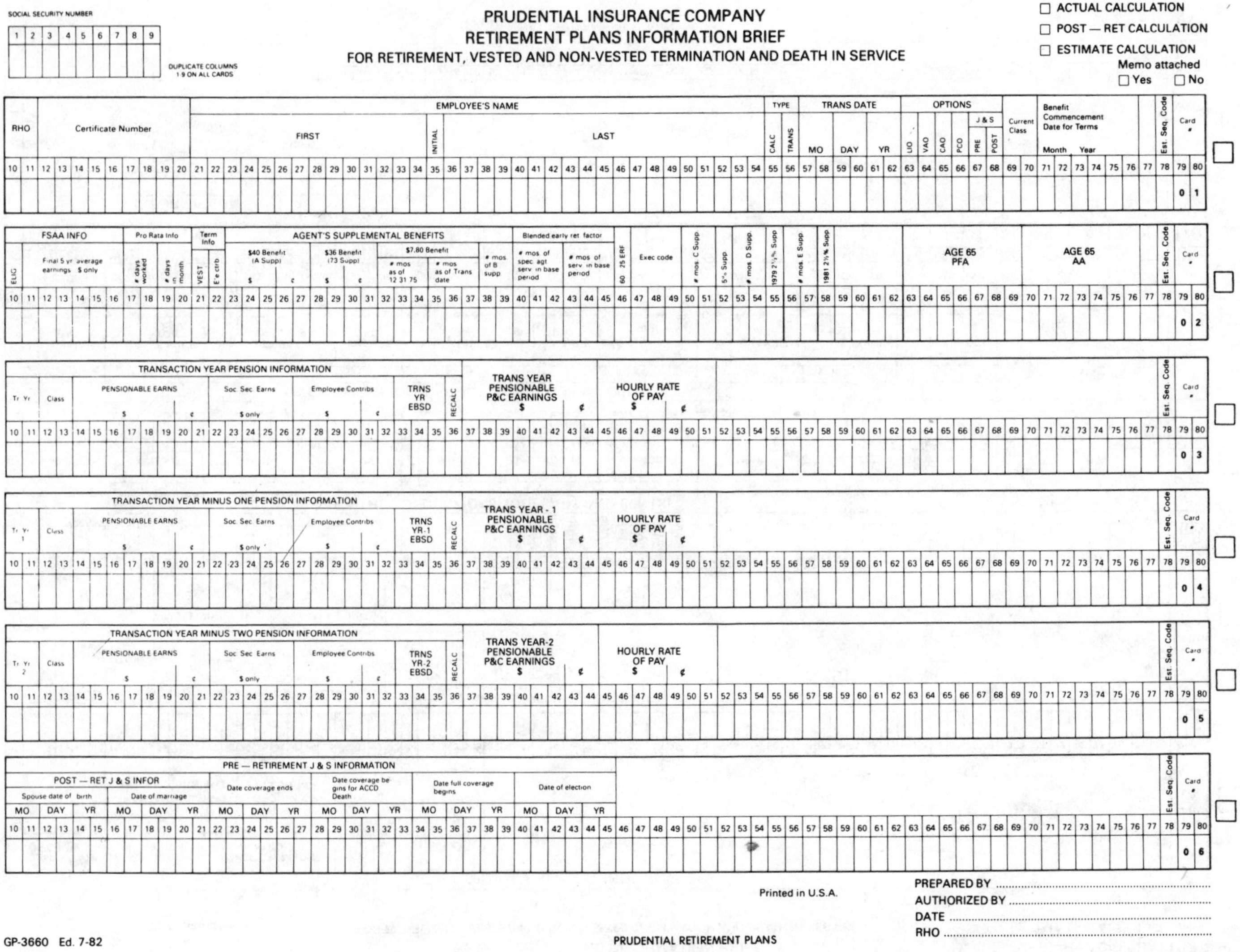

SOCIAL SECURITY NUMBER

1 2 3 4 5 6 7 8 9

DUPLICATE COLUMNS 1-9 ON ALL CARDS

PRUDENTIAL INSURANCE COMPANY
RETIREMENT PLANS INFORMATION BRIEF
FOR RETIREMENT, VESTED AND NON-VESTED TERMINATION AND DEATH IN SERVICE

☐ ACTUAL CALCULATION
☐ POST — RET CALCULATION
☐ ESTIMATE CALCULATION
Memo attached ☐ Yes ☐ No

RHO | Certificate Number | EMPLOYEE'S NAME: FIRST, INITIAL, LAST | TYPE: CALC, TRANS | TRANS DATE: MO, DAY, YR | OPTIONS: UO, VAO, CAO, PCO, J & S: PRE, POST | Current Class | Benefit Commencement Date for Terms: Month, Year | Est. Seq. Code | Card #

10–80 | Card 0 1

FSAA INFO: ELIG, Final 5 yr average earnings $ only | Pro Rata Info: # days worked, # days in month | Term Info: VEST, E'e ctrb | AGENT'S SUPPLEMENTAL BENEFITS: $40 Benefit (A Supp) $ ¢, $36 Benefit (73 Supp) $ ¢, $7.80 Benefit: # mos as of 12 31 75, # mos as of Trans date; # mos of B supp | Blended early ret factor: # mos of spec agt serv in base period, # mos of serv in base period | 60 25 ERF | Exec code | # mos. C Supp | 5% Supp | # mos D Supp | 1979 2½% Supp | # mos. E Supp | 1981 2½% Supp | AGE 65 PFA | AGE 65 AA | Est. Seq. Code | Card #

10–80 | Card 0 2

TRANSACTION YEAR PENSION INFORMATION: Tr Yr | Class | PENSIONABLE EARNS $ ¢ | Soc Sec Earns $ only | Employee Contribs $ ¢ | TRNS YR EBSD | RECALC | TRANS YEAR PENSIONABLE P&C EARNINGS $ ¢ | HOURLY RATE OF PAY $ ¢ | Est. Seq. Code | Card #

10–80 | Card 0 3

TRANSACTION YEAR MINUS ONE PENSION INFORMATION: Tr Yr 1 | Class | PENSIONABLE EARNS $ ¢ | Soc Sec Earns $ only | Employee Contribs $ ¢ | TRNS YR-1 EBSD | RECALC | TRANS YEAR - 1 PENSIONABLE P&C EARNINGS $ ¢ | HOURLY RATE OF PAY $ ¢ | Est. Seq. Code | Card #

10–80 | Card 0 4

TRANSACTION YEAR MINUS TWO PENSION INFORMATION: Tr Yr 2 | Class | PENSIONABLE EARNS $ ¢ | Soc Sec Earns $ only | Employee Contribs $ ¢ | TRNS YR-2 EBSD | RECALC | TRANS YEAR-2 PENSIONABLE P&C EARNINGS $ ¢ | HOURLY RATE OF PAY $ ¢ | Est. Seq. Code | Card #

10–80 | Card 0 5

POST — RET J & S INFOR: Spouse date of birth MO DAY YR | Date of marriage MO DAY YR | PRE — RETIREMENT J & S INFORMATION: Date coverage ends MO DAY YR | Date coverage begins for ACCD Death MO DAY YR | Date full coverage begins MO DAY YR | Date of election MO DAY YR | Est. Seq. Code | Card #

10–80 | Card 0 6

Printed in U.S.A.

PREPARED BY ........
AUTHORIZED BY ........
DATE ........
RHO ........

GP-3660 Ed. 7-82

PRUDENTIAL RETIREMENT PLANS

Figure 6-11 (Cont.)

PRUDENTIAL INSURANCE COMPANY
RETIREMENT PLANS INFORMATION BRIEF
FOR RETIREMENT, VESTED AND NON-VESTED TERMINATION AND DEATH IN SERVICE

☐ ACTUAL CALCULATION
☐ POST – RET CALCULATION

SOCIAL SECURITY NUMBER

DUPLICATE COLUMNS
1-9 ON ALL CARDS

Card #

HOME ADDRESS

LINE 1

LINE 2

12

HOME ADDRESS

LINE 3

LINE 4

HOME ZIP CODE

ST. CD.

PNA

Bank Code

Special Handle

13

BANK OR PAYEE NOT ANNUITANT

NAME

1ST. LINE OF ADDRESS

BANK OR PNA ZIP CODE

BK. OR PNA ST. CD.

14

BANK OR PAYEE NOT ANNUITANT

2ND. LINE OF ADDRESS

3RD. LINE OF ADDRESS

BANK ACCOUNT NUMBER

15

BENEFICIARY'S FIRST NAME

Middle Initial

BENEFICIARY'S LAST NAME

BENEFICIARY'S SOCIAL SECURITY NUMBER

16

PRUDENTIAL RETIREMENT PLANS

GP-3662    Ed. 12-77

Printed in U.S.A.

Figure 6-11. (Cont.)

## PERSONNEL EVALUATION

Management theory recommends continual feedback by superiors on the performance of subordinates. Effective managers practice such feedback on an ongoing, informal basis. Nevertheless, most organizations implement a formal evaluation program on a quarterly, semiannual or annual basis. Research has shown that when appraisal interviews are combined with salary reviews, the subordinate is most concerned with the salary issue and tends to neglect the substance of the performance evaluation. Thus, many firms now separate the salary review from the appraisal interview.

The only valid purpose of a discussion between superior and subordinate reviewing past performance is to help improve future performance. The appraisal process therefore leads naturally to discussion of the career and personal development of the subordinate. Separate meetings are conducted for the formal appraisal and the developmental discussion. This kind of procedure is explained in Exhibit 6-1. The exhibit also presents the appraisal portion of the process which is completed both by the superior and the subordinate.

## EVALUATION OF HUMAN RESOURCE SYSTEM OUTPUTS

Objective measurement of the effectiveness of a human resource information system is difficult to come by. As a decision support tool the information system is but one component, albeit a vital one, of the decisionmaking process. The successful organization utilizes and coordinates all the elements of managerial decisionmaking in the pursuit of its goals and objectives. Thus, it is not feasible to assign to one element the major responsibility for success or failure of corporate activities.

Nevertheless, it is possible to arrive at a reliable evaluation through indirect methods. The responsible executive can for example, seek answers to the following types of questions:

1. a. To what extent has the organization achieved its aims?
   b. How was goal attainment hindered by shortcomings in the human resources information system?
   c. Could these aims have been achieved without the information system?
2. a. Was the implementation of the long-range plans of the firm adversely affected by personnel shortages?
   b. If so, would a more effective information system have minimized this problem?
3. a. Do turnover and absentee rates reflect employee satisfaction or dissatisfaction?
   b. Do the promotion rates tie in to the career development plans?
4. Do successive EEO reports reflect company policy?

The ability to obtain responses to such questions and the nature of these responses will provide a fairly reliable indication of the effectiveness of the organization's human resources information system. In the final analysis, it may be stated that the information system, in the language of the scientist, is a necessary but not sufficient condition of organizational effectiveness.

Associate Manager Evaluation

Name_____ Title_____

Date of Level_____ Time in Current Assignment_____

Completed By_____ Date_____

The performance appraisal process is divided into two steps-the formal appraisal and the developmental discussion.  Part 1 of the process should provide accurate and specific feedback on how the individual is performing his/her job.  The developmental discussion will provide the opportunity to discuss plans to continue career and personal development.

Conducting the Evaluation

The individual's supervisor should complete Part 1 of the form by evaluating all dimensions that pertain to the individual's job.  All universal and personal dimensions must be evaluated.  (It is suggested that the individual separately complete a copy of Part I to prepare for discussion.)

Check the box that best represents the individual's typical performance on the dimension.  In the supporting comments section, examples of typical behavior that support your rating must be provided.  *These supporting comments should outline the manner in which the individual usually addresses the dimension as specified and should contain the essence of both the positive and negative aspects of the performance.

After completion of Part 1, the individual and his/her supervisor should meet to discuss its contents.  Following that discussion, the individual should complete Parts II & III of the form, outlining his/her development plans.  The individual and his/her supervisor should again meet to discuss the development plans, and documentation of this discussion should complete the process.

Exhibit 6-1.

Part I- Performance Appraisal

This section will provide evaluation of performance based on specific tasks and personal traits. Only those dimensions which apply to the individual's assignment should be evaluated; those dimensions that are most important should be so noted in the supporting comments.

I. Task Dimensions

A. Management

1. Managing Work: Planning and organizing resources to meet section/division goals. Monitoring activities of subordinates. Using subordinates effectively through delegation of work or responsibility.

   Poor                    Satisfactory                Superior
   [ ] [ ]                 [ ] [ ] [ ]                 [ ] [ ]

Supporting
Comments: 1. _____
             _____
          2. _____
             _____
             _____

2. Managing People: Obtaining the willing cooperation of subordinates. Motivating subordinates, resolving interpersonal problems and conflicts. Being sensitive to the needs, aspirations, and feelings of others.

   Poor                    Satisfactory                Superior
   [ ] [ ]                 [ ] [ ] [ ]                 [ ] [ ]

Supporting
Comments: 1. _____
             _____
          2. _____
             _____
             _____

3. Development of Subordinates: Increasing the skills and competencies of subordinates through developmental activities related to current and future jobs.

   Poor                    Satisfactory                Superior
   [ ] [ ]                 [ ] [ ] [ ]                 [ ] [ ]

Supporting
Comments: 1. _____
             _____
          2. _____
             _____
             _____

Exhibit 6-1. (*Cont.*)

B.   Communication

1.   Written Communication:  Clearly and concisely conveying
     information and instructions in writing so that the message
     accomplishes its purpose.

     Poor                    Satisfactory              Superior
     [ ] [ ]                 [ ] [ ] [ ]               [ ] [ ]


Supporting
Comments:   1. _____
               _____
               _____
            2. _____
               _____
               _____


2.   Oral Communication:  Making one's self understood in oral
     communication situations (e.g., meetings, interview, one-to-one
     conversations) and effectively listening to and understanding
     oral communication from others.

     Poor                    Satisfactory              Superior
     [ ] [ ]                 [ ] [ ] [ ]               [ ] [ ]


Supporting
Comments:   1. _____
               _____
            2. _____
               _____
               _____


3.   Influencing Others:  Effectiveness in getting others to accept
     one's ideas and take appropriate action.

     Poor                    Satisfactory              Superior
     [ ] [ ]                 [ ] [ ] [ ]               [ ] [ ]


Supporting
Comments:   1. _____
               _____
            2. _____
               _____
               _____


C.   Analysis and Research

1.   Analyzing Information:  This dimension has two components —
     verbal and quantitative.  Depending on the nature of the job,
     either or both may apply or one may be more important than the·
     other.

     a.   Quantitative - Identifying the correct analytical
          techniques and using them appropriately to draw conclusions

Exhibit 6-1. (*Cont.*)

from quantitative material (e.g., statistical analysis of data).

|       Poor       |       Satisfactory       |      Superior     |
| [ ]  [ ]         | [ ]   [ ]   [ ]          | [ ]   [ ]         |

Supporting
Comments:    1. _____
_____
2. _____
_____
_____

b.  <u>Verbal</u> - Quickly identifying and understanding essential verbal information contained in written material, oral presentations, or other media. Drawing appropriate conclusions from analysis of a problem or issue.

|       Poor       |       Satisfactory       |      Superior     |
| [ ]  [ ]         | [ ]   [ ]   [ ]          | [ ]   [ ]         |

Supporting
Comments:    1. _____
_____
2. _____
_____
_____

2.  Research and Auditing: Determining what information is needed and developing and/or applying effective means of obtaining that information (as in performing audits, designing surveys).

|       Poor       |       Satisfactory       |      Superior     |
| [ ]  [ ]         | [ ]   [ ]   [ ]          | [ ]   [ ]         |

Supporting
Comments:    1. _____
_____
2. _____
_____
_____

3.  Recordkeeping: Maintaining complete and accurate records which can be readily accessed when information is needed.

|       Poor       |       Satisfactory       |      Superior     |
| [ ]  [ ]         | [ ]   [ ]   [ ]          | [ ]   [ ]         |

Supporting
Comments:    1. _____
_____
2. _____
_____
_____

Exhibit 6-1. (*Cont.*)

D. Leadership

1. Coordinating Activities: Keeping informed of activities of individuals or groups and taking appropriate action at the proper time.

| Poor | Satisfactory | Superior |
|------|--------------|----------|
| [ ] [ ] | [ ] [ ] [ ] | [ ] [ ] |

Supporting
Comments:   1. _____
   _____
   2. _____
   _____
   _____

2. Decision Making: Appropriately applying rules and standards and using good judgement. Understanding where rules apply and where they do not apply.

| Poor | Satisfactory | Superior |
|------|--------------|----------|
| [ ] [ ] | [ ] [ ] [ ] | [ ] [ ] |

Supporting
Comments:   1. _____
   _____
   2. _____
   _____
   _____

II. Universal Job Dimensions

A. Interpersonal Relations: Dealing with supervision and management, co-workers, and others in a tactful, cooperative, and helpful manner. Reacting positively to suggestions from others or instructions from supervisors.

| Poor | Satisfactory | Superior |
|------|--------------|----------|
| [ ] [ ] | [ ] [ ] [ ] | [ ] [ ] |

Supporting
Comments:   1. _____
   _____
   2. _____
   _____
   _____

B. Work Habits: Demonstrated ability to organize and carry out duties with a minimum of direction. Includes setting priorities, following instructions, meeting deadlines, etc.

| Poor | Satisfactory | Superior |
|------|--------------|----------|
| [ ] [ ] | [ ] [ ] [ ] | [ ] [ ] |

Exhibit 6-1. (*Cont.*)

Supporting
Comments:    1. _____
                _____
             2. _____
                _____
                _____

C.  Work Motivation:  Taking an interest in the job, consistently
    working hard, taking action to improve performance, and
    striving to perform beyond the minimum requirements of the job.

    Poor                   Satisfactory              Superior
    [ ]  [ ]               [ ]  [ ]  [ ]             [ ]  [ ]

Supporting
Comments:    1. _____
                _____
             2. _____
                _____
                _____

D.  Job Knowledge:  Knowledge of the technical material, rules,
    procedures, or facts required to effectively perform the job,
    taking into account the person's experience and prior
    knowledge.

    Poor                   Satisfactory              Superior
    [ ]  [ ]               [ ]  [ ]  [ ]             [ ]  [ ]

Supporting
Comments:    1. _____
                _____
             2. _____
                _____
                _____

E.  Attendance:  The employee's overall record of absenteeism and
    tardiness.

    Poor                   Satisfactory              Superior
    [ ]  [ ]               [ ]  [ ]  [ ]             [ ]  [ ]

Supporting
Comments:    1. _____
                _____
             2. _____
                _____
                _____

III. Personal Dimensions

    A.  Adaptablility/Temperament:  Supporting higher level decisions
        and providing effort and cooperation; displaying ablility to
        react in a positive manner.  Using criticism constructively.

Exhibit 6-1. (*Cont.*)

```
        Poor                  Satisfactory              Superior
     [ ]  [ ]                 [ ]  [ ]  [ ]             [ ]  [ ]
```

Supporting
Comments:   1.  _____
            _____
        2.  _____
            _____
            _____

B.  Innovativeness:  Showing imagination in dealing with unusual
    problems.  Using previous experiences and applicable precedents
    to solve problems and draw conclusions.

```
        Poor                  Satisfactory              Superior
     [ ]  [ ]                 [ ]  [ ]  [ ]             [ ]  [ ]
```

Supporting
Comments:   1.  _____
            _____
        2.  _____
            _____
            _____

C.  Flexibility:  Effective transitioning to other assignments,
    sections, divisions; responding positively to new challenges.
    Demonstrating broad perspective as well as enthusiasm in job
    and company.

```
        Poor                  Satisfactory              Superior
     [ ]  [ ]                 [ ]  [ ]  [ ]             [ ]  [ ]
```

Supporting
Comments:   1.  _____
            _____
        2.  _____
            _____
            _____

D.  Promotability:  Demonstrating abilities/attitudes that provide
    certainty that positions at next level, and beyond, could be
    handled effectively.

```
        Poor                  Satisfactory              Superior
     [ ]  [ ]                 [ ]  [ ]  [ ]             [ ]  [ ]
```

Supporting
Comments:   1.  _____
            _____
        2.  _____
            _____
            _____

Exhibit 6–1. (*Cont.*)

IV.  Major Accomplishments

List below the major objectives, tasks or major responsibilities of this
person during the review period.  Rate the difficulty (average, below
average, above average) of the assignments and the person's performance and
indicate if these personal production items are in addition to the person's
normal assignment.


Task, Objectives, Resp.        Difficulty        Performance        Comments

Exhibit 6-1. (*Cont.*)

# 7
# Financial Information System

## DESCRIPTION OF FUNCTION

The financial function within an organization is in part unique to its own area of specialization but also serves to coordinate reports of all the other functions. As has been mentioned previously, all the activities of the firm are translatable ultimately into dollars and cents. It is the financial manager who has the responsibility for the translation procedure as well as the cash flows in and out and within the organization. We have also seen in the chapter on strategic information systems how the financial system overlaps both the strategic and operational levels of the firm. This overlap will appear again in this chapter as we present the outputs of the financial information system.

Financial management is concerned with two major areas of responsibility. In performing the *treasury function,* the financial manager has the obligation of satisfying the liquidity requirements of the firm. The goal of funds management is to insure that funds are available to meet the short-term cash needs of the operation. However, in meeting these needs, it is important that excess cash is not accumulated, since idle funds yield no return to the organization. As the cost of capital has soared during recent years, efficient working capital management has become crucial to the firm's viability. The treasury function is looked to also to provide long-term investment capital to insure the orderly growth and increased profitability of the firm.

The other major area of responsibility of the financial manager is the *controllership function.* As the term implies, the controller is responsible for overseeing the performance of the manufacturing, selling, financial, research and other functions within the company. According to management theory, control is one of the universal managerial functions, and each operating manager must control his own area of performance. However, for operating control to be effective it must be backed up by accounting control provided by the controller. Thus the controller is essentially a staff executive whose primary function is to gather and interpret data which will be of assistance to the other functional executives in the determination of sound policies and their successful execution.

The task of gathering and interpreting data leads naturally to the development of reports and reporting systems. Traditionally the job of developing and implementing reporting systems has fallen under the domain of the controller. However, as we have moved inexorably into the information age, a structural problem has arisen. The controller's area is part of the financial function. When computers started to come on stream, they were viewed as more advanced versions of bookkeeping machines. Historically, data processing departments were placed under the responsibility of the controller. Probably as a result of this relationship the first applications to be developed were in the accounting area.

As the technology developed and management started to become more familiar with the capabilities of the computer, other functional managers began to demand assistance from the computer in their areas. Competition arose among different departments for computer time. In most companies this competition was won by the financial department since the computer operation was under its control. Pressures from the frustrated managers of the other functions led to the establishment in many firms of an information department independent of and equal in level to the financial department. This development recognized that a corporate information system had to cut across functional lines and service all functions equitably.

At this stage, the controllership function was faced with a dilemma. Organizationally, it was responsible for the firm's reporting system, but the computer operation through which modern reporting systems are channeled had been removed from its domain. Technological advances may be providing the answer to this apparent contradiction. The development of the minicomputer and the microcomputer makes it economically feasible for each functional area to process information to service its functional needs on its own equipment. This holds true also for internal controllership needs. However, since this information must be summarized and consolidated for submission to corporate management, the controller can reassume the traditional responsibility of overseeing a coordinated reporting system.

To complete the description of the controller's functions, it may be noted that in many organizations there are tasks which fall between the cracks of the defined functions. These tasks are usually classified within general and administrative overhead and the controller is generally required to assume responsibility for their performance. Examples of such tasks are corporate insurance records and procedures, records retention procedures, and physical inventory procedures.

## MANAGEMENT INFORMATION REQUIREMENTS

The effective financial manager serves as the eyes and ears of top management providing information on the performance of every area within the firm. Accounting practice summarizes the activities and results of performance in terms of balance sheet and income statement categories. Our survey of financial management information requirements can be discussed conveniently in terms of these categories.

### Balance Sheet Categories

**A. Control of Cash.** One of the functions of the controller is to safeguard the assets of the business through the introduction of necessary records and controls. Cash is a particularly vulnerable type of property because it is easily concealed and readily negotiable. In addition to preventing the misappropriation of funds, cash control includes the following objectives:

1. establishment of accountability for cash receipts and sufficient safeguards until the moneys are placed in the depository;
2. establishment of controls to assure disbursements only for the legitimate liabilities of the company;
3. proper planning so that the requisite funds are on hand to meet the business needs—both short term and long range;
4. effective utilization at all times of the company funds.

With respect to the control of cash, a very close and cooperative relationship must exist between the controller and the treasurer. The latter is the custodian of cash funds and exercises supervision over the receipts and the disbursements. On the other hand, the procedures for cash receipts and disbursements are established and overseen by the controller. The close working relationship between the two functions may be observed also in the preparation and implementation of the cash budget. This budget is a working tool of the treasurer in securing funds and in making investments. Nevertheless, the cash budget is but one phase of the budgetary control program, for which the controller is responsible.

The cash budget is a projection or forecast of anticipated cash receipts and disbursements and the resulting cash balance within a specified period. The basic purpose behind the preparation of the cash budget is to plan so that the business will have the correct amount of cash available at the time it is needed. Further when excess cash is to be available, budget preparation offers a means of anticipating this opportunity for effective utilization. Aside from these general purposes, some specific uses to which a cash budget may be put are:

1. to point out peaks or seasonal fluctuations in business activity that make necessary larger investments in inventories and receivables;
2. to indicate the time and extent funds are needed to meet maturing obligations, tax payments, and dividend or interest payments;
3. to assist in planning the required funds for plant expansion;
4. to indicate well in advance of needs the extent and duration of funds required from outside sources and thus permit the securing of more advantageous loans;
5. to assist securing credit from banks, and improve the general credit position of the business;
6. to determine the extent and probable duration of funds available for investment;
7. to plan the reduction of bonded indebtedness or other loans;
8. to coordinate the financial needs of the subsidiaries and divisions of the company;
9. to permit the company to take advantage of cash discounts and forward purchasing, thereby increasing earnings.

The cash budget is generally dependent on other budgets—the sales forecast, the statement of estimated income and expense, and the various operating budgets. The comparison of actual cash performance to budget also serves as a check upon the entire budgetary program. If the operating budget goals are achieved, the results will be reflected in the cash position. Failure to achieve budgeted performance may result in the need to seek additional sources of cash.

For strategic planning purposes, cash forecasts may be prepared covering a multiyear period. These long-term forecasts are also prepared in connection with requests for capital budget project authorizations. However, on an operational level, cash requirement forecasts are prepared on an annual basis to coordinate with the operating budgets, and on a monthly and/or quarterly basis to guide day-to-day decisionmaking. Since cash budgeting is one of the most commonly found computer applications and is normally included in DSS financial models, it is possible for today's financial manager to exercise weekly, or, if desired, even daily control over cash receipts and disbursements.

**B. Control of Receivables.** Customers' accounts receivable are an important item on the balance sheets of most business concerns. Control of accounts receivable really begins before the agreement to ship the merchandise, continues through the preparation and issuance of the invoice, and ends with collection of all sums due. The procedure is closely related to cash receipts control on one hand and to inventory control on the other. The receivable is the link between the two. From the point of view of preventive management, there are three general control areas—points at which action can be taken to realize control of accounts receivable. These are:

1. **Granting of credit.** Credit policies must neither discourage sales of financially sound customers nor incur serious losses because of excessive bad debts.
2. **Making collections.** Once credit is granted and the merchandise shipped every effort must be made to secure payment in accordance with the terms of sale and within a reasonable time.
3. **Maintenance of proper internal control.** There must exist an adequate system of internal control to insure that every shipment is invoiced, that each invoice is accurate, and that the payment finds its way to the company's bank account.

In the accounts receivable area, the financial manager accepts the following responsibilities:

1. maintenance of accounts receivable records in a satisfactory condition to meet the needs of the treasurer, the credit manager and the controller,
2. installation and maintenance of the necessary internal control safeguards,
3. preparation of the required reports for management, the credit department, and others as to the condition of the receivables,
4. proper valuation of receivables on the balance sheet, including establishment of the necessary reserves.

The most important information requirement of a receivable system is to identify the status of every open and unpaid invoice as either current or past due, and, if past due, how long the invoice has been past due. This information is presented on a report known as an "Aging Analysis of Accounts Receivable." This report pinpoints for the financial manager those customers whose aging record calls for more or less urgent collection efforts depending on the length of time and the amount of dollars of past due items. Other reports from the receivable area which provide useful information to management include:

1. detail of accounts written off as bad debts, and reasons why,
2. percent of bad debt losses to credit sales, compared to prior periods,
3. historical monthly summary of average number of days of receivables outstanding,
4. analysis of bad debt losses by classes of customers,
5. comparison of actual and budgeted collections,
6. relationship of credit department costs to credit sales,
7. comparison of budgeted and actual credit and collection expense.

**C. Control of Inventories.** Inventory management was discussed previously in the chapter on manufacturing information systems. The coverage here will therefore be confined to the role played by the financial manager in inventory control.

Some of the specific techniques or means of achieving control are:

1. establishment of minimum and maximum inventory points
2. use of inventory turnover rates
3. budgetary control

With the information available to him from the sales and the manufacturing departments, the financial manager is well positioned to set standards and establish guidelines in these areas and then to report periodically on the extent of adherence to these guidelines. Other information which can be made available by the financial manager in report form includes:

1. a general summary of inventory by category
2. a comparison of budgeted and actual inventory
3. a summary of inventory activity, showing additions, withdrawals, and closing balances on hand
4. a summary of inventory aging, indicating slow moving or obsolete items
5. a report on turnover
6. a report on overages and shortages
7. a comparison of actual and maximum inventories

As indicated previously, the controller is responsible for establishing the physical inventory procedure. It is also his job to decide on the exact type of perpetual inventory records to be maintained. Finally, it is the financial manager who selects the basis of valuation which will most satisfactorily reflect income and presides over the inventory valuation.

**D. Control of Investments.** The authority to invest company funds in securities, or other types of investments, rests with the board of directors. Within the limits stipulated by the board, such authority is generally conferred on the financial manager. He usually has custody of the securities and supervises the analysis, purchase and sale of the investments. His responsibility involves:

1. maintaining all necessary records as to securities or investments;
2. determining that all investments are properly valued;
3. ascertaining that all directives of the board are followed as to investment of funds;
4. reporting on investments, as may be required.

A periodic summary report of the firm's investment position would list:

1. the name of the security or investment
2. cost
3. market value
4. effective yield or rate of return
5. dividend or interest received to date

**E. Control of Fixed Assets.**   In the chapter on manufacturing information systems, there was a discussion on the management of plant, machinery and equipment. However, as with inventory control, the financial manager also has responsibility for the control of fixed assets. A statement of his duties would include:

1. preparation of the financial budgets and forecasts to indicate available funds,
2. critical analysis of all requests for capital expenditures, including calculation of savings or potential earnings,
3. establishment of controls to keep expenditures within authorization limits,
4. design and maintenance of property records,
5. establishment of an adequate system of reporting including:
    a. comparison of actual and authorized costs,
    b. maintenance costs by type of equipment,
    c. idle hours of machinery,
6. development of a sound depreciation policy,
7. determination of the basis of accounting for fixed assets and the applicable reserves,
8. institution of auxiliary control procedures such as:
    a. identification of machinery and equipment,
    b. transfers,
    c. sales and retirements,
9. handling of matters related to taxes and insurance.

The fixed asset area is a clear example of the overlap between the strategic and operational levels referred to earlier. The capital budget covers multiyear projects and is a strategic information document. However, the operating budget contains a section on expenditures for fixed assets during the period which derives from the longer-term capital budget.

The amount of funds which should be invested in plant and equipment is a matter of management judgement. This judgment may be based on the general pattern of investment in fixed assets that is discernible in each industry. The financial manager can help the decision maker by furnishing useful guidelines such as:

1. the ratio of net worth to fixed assets
2. the ratio of sales to fixed assets
3. the ratio of cost of goods manufactured to fixed assets

**F. Control of Liabilities.** The major objectives of satisfactory accounting control of liabilities include:

1. a proper recording and disclosure of all financial obligations of the company
2. the maintenance of a sound financial structure through the proper relationship of borrowed and equity capital
3. procurement of borrowed capital on the most advantageous basis
4. restriction of commitments within well defined limits before they become actual liabilities

Liabilities are divided into two categories. There are those obligations which must be discharged within a one-year period and are referred to as current liabilities. These current obligations reduce the amount of working capital available to the firm. The major items found under current liabilities are listed below:

1. *Notes payable* are the sum of short-term borrowings from banks which must be repaid within one year.
2. *Accounts payable* represent the firm's obligation to pay for the purchase of materials, supplies, and services.
3. *Accrued expenses* represent costs which have been incurred during the accounting period but have not been recorded in the books of account. In order to implement the basic accounting principle of matching costs and revenues such expenses should be reflected on financial statements and the accrual mechanism serves this purpose.
4. *Accrued tax liabilities* are a subcategory of accrued expenses and are usually listed separately because of their significance.

The second category of liabilities is long-term indebtedness. Short-term notes should be issued only when capital is needed for current operations. If funds are needed to finance fixed assets or other permanent investments, the firm would resort to long-term securities in the form of either bonds or stock. In this situation, the financial manager would analyze the alternatives of debt or equity financing and make his recommendation to the board of directors. The factors he would consider are interest rates, tax consequences, and the effect of his recommendation upon the debt-equity ratio.

Several useful and informative reports may be prepared from accounts payable data such as:

1. accounts payable by due date to assist in planning cash disbursements
2. summary of outstanding commitments
3. cash discounts earned or lost
4. payables recorded since last period
5. listing of payables by vendor:
   a. for open items
   b. cumulative, to determine total amount of business done with each

### Income Statement Categories

The income statement is headed by a statement of revenues followed by a listing of prime costs incurred to achieve those revenues. Under a system of responsibility accounting, the responsibility for the revenue section of the income statement is delegated to the sales/marketing executive, while in a goods-producing firm the manufacturing executive is charged with the responsibility for the prime cost section of the income statement. In two previous chapters we have discussed the information requirements for these two executives, so there is no need to repeat them here. It should be kept in mind however that as a coordinating executive the financial manager has the obligation of establishing and implementing the company's budget procedures as well as designing and interpreting the reports which are prepared for management. Thus he must establish a close working relationship with the operating managers and provide assistance in a staff capacity in the performance of their duties. We shall therefore proceed with a discussion of those areas of the income statement which have not been previously covered.

**A. Control of Research and Development Costs.** Research is generally defined as the activities involved in discovering new products or processes. Development refers to the functions carried on to put the results of research on a commercial basis. In the present national and international competitive climate, firms grow and prosper by inventing or developing new products, by improving existing products, or by developing new processes which reduce the cost of production. This must be done over the long run to insure a reasonable return on investment.

Research and development costs cover a variety of expenses. Some may be short term in nature whereas others may extend over a period of years. In considering the application of budgetary control to research and development costs, it is evident that this activity is not directly related to either production or sales. Thus it is not feasible to establish a budgetary allowance per production man-hour or dollar of sales. Rather, an appropriation type budget is generally used, and the budget may be increased or decreased as anticipated business income, research requirements or other considerations make it desirable.

Despite the inherent difficulties of controlling R & D costs, there are certain techniques available to the financial manager for this purpose. For example, provision may be made for recording actual expenditures and then making certain that such outlays are kept within budget limitations. For many research and development activities, just as in production and distribution, standards can be established. In these cases, an effective control technique is to compare actual and standard performance and to take corrective action as found necessary. A third approach may be applied in the planning of R & D activities. Before a specific project is undertaken, an analysis should be made to estimate the probable savings resulting from a successful application in comparison with the estimated cost of research. When the project is completed, an analysis is made to determine whether or not the research expenditures actually were worth the effort or produced the estimated savings.

The kinds of reports that the financial manager may prepare for the guidance of the research director as well as other member of management can include:

1. comparison of actual and budgeted expenses by departmental responsibility;
2. statement of project costs, indicating actual expenditures, commitments, and unexpended balances;
3. comparative statement of research costs with savings or earnings;
4. selected statistical data, including:
   a. comparison of R & D salary with standard or past months;
   b. number of tests per man-day, including comparison with standard;
   c. relationship of research and development costs, by product and in total, to net sales.

## B. Control of Administrative and Financial Expense..

At the beginning of this chapter it was mentioned that the financial manager was a specialist in his own right as well as serving as a coordinator for the total organization. In his specialized role, the financial manager has the responsibility (similar to other functional managers) of running his operation efficiently. The budgetary control program that the financial manager has established for the various divisions and departments should apply to his own function as well. In the financial area some of the departments which may be logical budgetary control centers are:

General Accounting
Cost Accounting
Auditing
Tax
Budgets and Standards
Insurance
Office Services
Payroll
Data Processing

While standards were originally developed for and are generally associated with factory operations, office methods engineers have succeeded over the years in establishing measurable standards for administrative and clerical tasks. Thus standard units of measurement have been developed for such functions as order processing, mail handling, billing, check writing, posting, filing, data entry and typing. There exist unit cost standards for such areas as credit and collection, invoice preparation, accounts receivable processing, commission calculation, and a variety of posting tasks. Of course, as office operations have been computerized, many of these functions are performed as automatic by-products of original transaction entries. Nevertheless, for those office duties that remain as manual tasks, these standards can be applied to calculating objective budgetary allowances.

It was also mentioned previously that there are certain administrative functions that seem to fall in the cracks between the major functions of the firm, and that the responsibility for their administration falls generally to the financial manager. In terms of the account classifications in the general ledger, these areas include contributions, interest expense, legal and professional expenses, corporate expenses, executive compensation, fringe benefit program expenses, and other income and expenses. Here again the budgetary control system has proven to be the most effective control mechanism, and budget reports provide the most valuable information to management.

## SOURCES OF DATA

In fulfilling his responsibility for developing and implementing the firm's reporting system, the financial manager must work with the other functional executives to search for, acquire, analyze and interpret data from the external environment. Thus he must be familiar with sources of external data as described in the chapter on strategic information systems. The major requirement for external information in the financial and administrative area involves the treasury function. When excess cash is available for investment the financial manager must have an intimate knowledge of the securities and other financial markets. Most companies have business relationships with banks, investment and brokerage firms, and other financial institutions, and it is the specialists in these organizations who furnish the financial manager with the information needed to make intelligent investment decisions.

However, in fulfilling his responsibilities, the bulk of the information the financial manager will use is derived from sources within the organization. Interestingly enough, the adequacy of this information depends upon the financial manager himself. Since he is responsible for the records and the recordkeeping in the firm and since he has set up the reporting system, the value of the information flowing back to the financial manager for analysis and interpretation is a function of the effectiveness of these records and this reporting system. Thus the financial manager must look to his own performance if he finds any shortcomings in his firm's information system.

## INFORMATION SYSTEM OUTPUTS

It should be obvious by now that all the outputs illustrated in the previous chapters are in a sense jointly owned by the functional manager and the financial manager. Clearly no purpose would be served by repeating these samples, so we shall restrict our presentation to outputs in the financial area alone. However, even in the limited financial area, the range of outputs is so diverse and voluminous that the only feasible approach is to present selected samples from several sources to give the reader an idea of the nature of the information that may be made available to the financial manager.

### Budget Versus Actual Financial Reports

The variance from budget approach has been incorporated in many decision support system models. Illustrated here is a Budget/Variance Financial Model offered by Ferox Microsystems Inc., a software firm. The model contains a command file that prompts the user for the desired month on the variance report. The DSS automatically fills the correct budget and actual data into the variance model and calculates dollars and percent variance. The model may also be used to compare current actuals with prior actuals. A second command file may be used to produce "Percent of Sales" reports. The DSS first divides each report by the sales row and then multiplies by 100.

The following five sample reports have been selected from this model:

Figure 7-1A. Budget/Actual Variance Report for any given month
Figure 7-1B. Income Statement Budget
Figure 7-1C. Income Statement Actual
Figure 7-1D. Percent of Sales Report Budget
Figure 7-1E. Percent of Sales Report Actual

### Profit Planning

The Ogden Corporation is a multibillion dollar conglomerate with many subsidiaries. In order for top management to maintain adequate control of activities, a standardized reporting system has been established through which each operating unit submits to corporate management financial details in the formats of a profit and loss statement and a balance sheet to support the preparation of an annual corporate profit plan. The operating units also submit cash flow data to determine corporate cash requirements for the following year.

As may be seen from the accompanying sample outputs, figures are provided for a four-year period. Actual performance figures are given for the second year prior to the plan year. For the year prior to the plan year, forecast figures are shown and the variance from the original plan figures is calculated. Planned or budgeted profit and loss and balance sheet dollars are listed for the plan year and the variance from the prior year's forecast is shown. Finally a projection is given for the year subsequent to the plan year and the dollar difference from the plan year is indicated. In the sample outputs, 1982 is the plan year (Figures 7-2A to 7-2K).

Supporting schedules are also illustrated that provide twelve monthly summaries of the income statement details for the plan year. In the case of the balance sheet, the plan year is divided into quarters rather than months. Quarters are also the time periods used for the cash flow data as well as the comparison of actual and forecasted results.

DSS/F BUDGET EXAMPLE
BUDGET / ACTUAL VARIANCE REPORT
FOR THE REPORT PERIOD OF
JUNE 30, 1982
--------------

| | CURRENT MONTH ACTUAL | CURRENT MONTH BUDGET | VARIANCE | PERCENT VARIANCE | YEAR TO DATE ACTUAL | YEAR TO DATE BUDGET | VARIANCE | PERCENT VARIANCE |
|---|---|---|---|---|---|---|---|---|
| SALES | 1,279 | 1,276 | 3 | .2 % | 6,409 | 6,803 | (394) | (5.8) % |
| RETURNS | 27 | 25 | 2 | 8.0 % | 134 | 135 | (1) | (.7) % |
| NET SALES | 1,252 | 1,251 | 1 | .1 % | 6,275 | 6,668 | (393) | (5.9) % |
| COST OF GOODS SOLD | 307 | 319 | (12) | (3.8) % | 1,744 | 1,701 | 43 | 2.5 % |
| GROSS MARGIN | 945 | 932 | 13 | 1.4 % | 4,531 | 4,967 | (436) | (8.8) % |
| OPERATING EXPENSES: | | | | | | | | |
| VARIABLE: | | | | | | | | |
| LABOR | 251 | 255 | (4) | (1.6) % | 1,352 | 1,361 | (9) | (.7) % |
| OFFICE EQUIPMENT | 37 | 38 | (1) | (2.6) % | 197 | 204 | (7) | (3.4) % |
| TRANSPORTATION | 62 | 64 | (2) | (3.1) % | 333 | 341 | (8) | (2.3) % |
| OFFICE SUPPLIES | 12 | 13 | (1) | (7.7) % | 67 | 69 | (2) | (2.9) % |
| UTILITIES | 75 | 77 | (2) | (2.6) % | 443 | 408 | 35 | 8.6 % |
| OTHER VARIABLE | 9 | 6 | 3 | 50.0 % | 43 | 34 | 9 | 26.5 % |
| TOTAL VARIABLE | 446 | 453 | (7) | (1.5) % | 2,435 | 2,417 | 18 | .7 % |
| FIXED: | | | | | | | | |
| RENT | 40 | 40 | - | - | 240 | 240 | - | - |
| SALARIES | 25 | 15 | 10 | 66.7 % | 129 | 90 | 39 | 43.3 % |
| ADVERTISING | 10 | 10 | - | - | 45 | 60 | (15) | (25.0) % |
| DEPRECIATION | 23 | 20 | 3 | 15.0 % | 132 | 120 | 12 | 10.0 % |
| OTHER FIXED | 7 | 5 | 2 | 40.0 % | 28 | 30 | (2) | (6.7) % |
| TOTAL FIXED | 105 | 90 | 15 | 16.7 % | 574 | 540 | 34 | 6.3 % |
| TOTAL OPER. EXPENSES | 551 | 543 | 8 | 1.5 % | 3,009 | 2,957 | 52 | 1.8 % |
| NET OPERATING INCOME | 394 | 389 | 5 | 1.3 % | 1,522 | 2,010 | (488) | (24.3) % |
| INTEREST EXPENSE | 34 | 33 | 1 | 3.0 % | 193 | 198 | (5) | (2.5) % |
| NET INCOME BEFORE TAX | 360 | 356 | 4 | 1.1 % | 1,329 | 1,812 | (483) | (26.7) % |
| INCOME TAX EXPENSE | 166 | 164 | 2 | 1.1 % | 611 | 834 | (222) | (26.7) % |
| NET INCOME | 194 | 192 | 2 | 1.1 % | 718 | 978 | (261) | (26.7) % |

COPYRIGHT (C) 1982 FEROX MICROSYSTEMS INC.

Figure 7-1a. Copyright © 1982 Ferox Microsystems Inc., Arlington, Virginia

```
                                    DSS/F BUDGET EXAMPLE
                                 BUDGET / ACTUAL VARIANCE REPORT
                                    INCOME STATEMENT BUDGET
                                    -----------------------
```

| | JAN | FEB | MAR | APR | MAY | JUN | JUL | AUG | SEP | OCT | NOV | DEC | TOTAL |
|---|---|---|---|---|---|---|---|---|---|---|---|---|---|
| ALES | 1,000 | 1,050 | 1,103 | 1,158 | 1,216 | 1,276 | 1,340 | 1,407 | 1,477 | 1,551 | 1,629 | 1,710 | 15,917 |
| ETURNS | 20 | 21 | 22 | 23 | 24 | 25 | 26 | 27 | 28 | 29 | 30 | 31 | 306 |
| ET SALES | 980 | 1,029 | 1,081 | 1,135 | 1,192 | 1,251 | 1,314 | 1,380 | 1,449 | 1,522 | 1,599 | 1,679 | 15,611 |
| OST OF GOODS SOLD | 250 | 263 | 276 | 289 | 304 | 319 | 335 | 352 | 369 | 388 | 407 | 428 | 3,980 |
| ROSS MARGIN | 730 | 766 | 805 | 846 | 888 | 932 | 979 | 1,028 | 1,080 | 1,134 | 1,192 | 1,251 | 11,631 |
| PERATING EXPENSES: | | | | | | | | | | | | | |
| VARIABLE: | | | | | | | | | | | | | |
| LABOR | 200 | 210 | 221 | 232 | 243 | 255 | 268 | 281 | 295 | 310 | 326 | 342 | 3,183 |
| OFFICE EQUIPMENT | 30 | 32 | 33 | 35 | 36 | 38 | 40 | 42 | 44 | 47 | 49 | 51 | 477 |
| TRANSPORTATION | 50 | 53 | 55 | 58 | 61 | 64 | 67 | 70 | 74 | 78 | 81 | 86 | 797 |
| OFFICE SUPPLIES | 10 | 11 | 11 | 12 | 12 | 13 | 13 | 14 | 15 | 16 | 16 | 17 | 160 |
| UTILITIES | 60 | 63 | 66 | 69 | 73 | 77 | 80 | 84 | 89 | 93 | 98 | 103 | 955 |
| OTHER VARIABLE | 5 | 5 | 6 | 6 | 6 | 6 | 7 | 7 | 7 | 8 | 8 | 9 | 80 |
| TOTAL VARIABLE | 355 | 374 | 392 | 412 | 431 | 453 | 475 | 498 | 524 | 552 | 578 | 608 | 5,652 |
| FIXED: | | | | | | | | | | | | | |
| RENT | 40 | 40 | 40 | 40 | 40 | 40 | 40 | 40 | 40 | 40 | 40 | 40 | 480 |
| SALARIES | 15 | 15 | 15 | 15 | 15 | 15 | 15 | 15 | 15 | 15 | 15 | 15 | 180 |
| ADVERTISING | 10 | 10 | 10 | 10 | 10 | 10 | 10 | 10 | 10 | 10 | 10 | 10 | 120 |
| DEPRECIATION | 20 | 20 | 20 | 20 | 20 | 20 | 20 | 20 | 20 | 20 | 20 | 20 | 240 |
| OTHER FIXED | 5 | 5 | 5 | 5 | 5 | 5 | 5 | 5 | 5 | 5 | 5 | 5 | 60 |
| TOTAL FIXED | 90 | 90 | 90 | 90 | 90 | 90 | 90 | 90 | 90 | 90 | 90 | 90 | 1,080 |
| TAL OPER. EXPENSES | 445 | 464 | 482 | 502 | 521 | 543 | 565 | 588 | 614 | 642 | 668 | 698 | 6,732 |
| T OPERATING INCOME | 285 | 302 | 323 | 344 | 367 | 389 | 414 | 440 | 466 | 492 | 524 | 553 | 4,899 |
| NTEREST EXPENSE | 33 | 33 | 33 | 33 | 33 | 33 | 33 | 33 | 33 | 33 | 33 | 33 | 396 |
| T INCOME BEFORE TAX | 252 | 269 | 290 | 311 | 334 | 356 | 381 | 407 | 433 | 459 | 491 | 520 | 4,503 |
| NCOME TAX EXPENSE | 116 | 124 | 133 | 143 | 154 | 164 | 175 | 187 | 199 | 211 | 226 | 239 | 2,071 |
| T INCOME | 136 | 145 | 157 | 168 | 180 | 192 | 206 | 220 | 234 | 248 | 265 | 281 | 2,432 |

PYRIGHT (C) 1982 FEROX MICROSYSTEMS INC

Figure 7-1b. Copyright © 1982 Ferox Microsystems Inc., Arlington, Virginia.

DSS/F BUDGET EXAMPLE
BUDGET / ACTUAL VARIANCE REPORT
INCOME STATEMENT ACTUALS
-------------------------

|  | JAN | FEB | MAR | APR | MAY | JUN | JUL | AUG | SEP | OCT | NOV | DEC | TOTAL |
|---|---|---|---|---|---|---|---|---|---|---|---|---|---|
| SALES | 947 | 900 | 1,113 | 1,023 | 1,147 | 1,279 | 1,358 | 1,579 | 1,467 | 1,631 | 1,789 | ,913 | 16,24( |
| RETURNS | 15 | 18 | 23 | 25 | 26 | 27 | 29 | 23 | 23 | 26 | 29 | 30 | 29 |
| NET SALES | 932 | 882 | 1,090 | 998 | 1,121 | 1,252 | 1,329 | 1,556 | 1,445 | 1,605 | 1,760 | 1,383 | 15,35 |
| COST OF GOODS SOLD | 276 | 288 | 282 | 292 | 299 | 307 | 320 | 327 | 335 | 350 | 365 | 376 | ?,61? |
| GROSS MARGIN | 656 | 594 | 808 | 706 | 822 | 945 | 1,009 | 1,229 | 1,110 | 1,255 | 1,395 | 1,506 | 12,03? |
| OPERATING EXPENSES: | | | | | | | | | | | | | |
| VARIABLE: | | | | | | | | | | | | | |
| LABOR | 201 | 205 | 222 | 230 | 243 | 251 | 265 | 275 | 290 | 300 | 320 | 325 | 3,12? |
| OFFICE EQUIPMENT | 30 | 31 | 32 | 33 | 34 | 37 | 35 | 36 | 40 | 42 | 41 | 49 | 44( |
| TRANSPORTATION | 55 | 50 | 54 | 55 | 57 | 62 | 65 | 69 | 73 | 75 | 80 | 86 | 78? |
| OFFICE SUPPLIES | 9 | 8 | 11 | 13 | 14 | 12 | 15 | 16 | 17 | 15 | 16 | 14 | 16( |
| UTILITIES | 79 | 80 | 75 | 69 | 65 | 75 | 80 | 85 | 92 | 99 | 105 | 120 | 1,02( |
| OTHER VARIABLE | 8 | 8 | 5 | 6 | 7 | 9 | 3 | 4 | 5 | 6 | 7 | 7 | 7? |
| TOTAL VARIABLE | 382 | 382 | 399 | 406 | 420 | 446 | 463 | 485 | 517 | 537 | 569 | 601 | 5,60? |
| FIXED: | | | | | | | | | | | | | |
| RENT | 40 | 40 | 40 | 40 | 40 | 40 | 40 | 40 | 40 | 40 | 40 | 40 | 48( |
| SALARIES | 20 | 20 | 20 | 20 | 24 | 25 | 27 | 25 | 26 | 25 | 25 | 23 | 28( |
| ADVERTISING | 5 | 7 | 6 | 8 | 9 | 10 | 12 | 11 | 13 | 14 | 15 | 12 | 122 |
| DEPRECIATION | 20 | 22 | 22 | 22 | 23 | 23 | 24 | 24 | 25 | 25 | 25 | 26 | 28? |
| OTHER FIXED | 3 | 3 | 4 | 5 | 6 | 7 | 5 | 6 | 4 | 5 | 6 | 4 | 5? |
| TOTAL FIXED | 88 | 92 | 92 | 95 | 102 | 105 | 108 | 106 | 108 | 109 | 111 | 105 | 1,221 |
| TOTAL OPER. EXPENSES | 470 | 474 | 491 | 501 | 522 | 551 | 571 | 591 | 625 | 646 | 680 | 706 | 6,828 |
| NET OPERATING INCOME | 186 | 120 | 317 | 205 | 300 | 394 | 438 | 638 | 485 | 609 | 715 | 800 | 5,207 |
| INTEREST EXPENSE | 30 | 31 | 31 | 33 | 34 | 34 | 34 | 35 | 35 | 35 | 36 | 36 | 404 |
| NET INCOME BEFORE TAX | 156 | 89 | 286 | 172 | 266 | 360 | 404 | 603 | 450 | 574 | 679 | 764 | 4,80? |
| INCOME TAX EXPENSE | 72 | 41 | 132 | 79 | 122 | 166 | 186 | 277 | 207 | 264 | 313 | 351 | 2,20? |
| NET INCOME | 84 | 48 | 154 | 93 | 144 | 194 | 218 | 326 | 243 | 310 | 367 | 413 | 2,594 |

Figure 7-1c. Copyright © 1982 Ferox Microsystems Inc., Arlington, Virginia.

DSS/F BUDGET EXAMPLE
BUDGET / ACTUAL VARIANCE REPORT
INCOME STATEMENT BUDGET
% OF SALES
----------

| | JAN | FEB | MAR | APR | MAY | JUN | JUL | AUG | SEP | OCT | NOV | DEC | TOTAL |
|---|---|---|---|---|---|---|---|---|---|---|---|---|---|
| SALES | 100% | 100% | 100% | 100% | 100% | 100% | 100% | 100% | 100% | 100% | 100% | 100% | 100% |
| RETURNS | 2 | 2 | 2 | 2 | 2 | 2 | 2 | 2 | 2 | 2 | 2 | 2 | 2 |
| NET SALES | 98 | 98 | 98 | 98 | 98 | 98 | 98 | 98 | 98 | 98 | 98 | 98 | 98 |
| COST OF GODDS SOLD | 25 | 25 | 25 | 25 | 25 | 25 | 25 | 25 | 25 | 25 | 25 | 25 | 25 |
| GROSS MARGIN | 73 | 73 | 73 | 73 | 73 | 73 | 73 | 73 | 73 | 73 | 73 | 73 | 73 |
| OPERATING EXPENSES: | | | | | | | | | | | | | |
| VARIABLE: | | | | | | | | | | | | | |
| LABOR | 20 | 20 | 20 | 20 | 20 | 20 | 20 | 20 | 20 | 20 | 20 | 20 | 20 |
| OFFICE EQUIPMENT | 3 | 3 | 3 | 3 | 3 | 3 | 3 | 3 | 3 | 3 | 3 | 3 | 3 |
| TRANSPORTATION | 5 | 5 | 5 | 5 | 5 | 5 | 5 | 5 | 5 | 5 | 5 | 5 | 5 |
| OFFICE SUPPLIES | 1 | 1 | 1 | 1 | 1 | 1 | 1 | 1 | 1 | 1 | 1 | 1 | 1 |
| UTILITIES | 6 | 6 | 6 | 6 | 6 | 6 | 6 | 6 | 6 | 6 | 6 | 6 | 6 |
| OTHER VARIABLE | 1 | | 1 | 1 | | | 1 | | | 1 | | 1 | 1 |
| TOTAL VARIABLE | 36 | 36 | 36 | 36 | 35 | 36 | 35 | 35 | 35 | 36 | 35 | 36 | 36 |
| FIXED: | | | | | | | | | | | | | |
| RENT | 4 | 4 | 4 | 3 | 3 | 3 | 3 | 3 | 3 | 3 | 2 | 2 | 3 |
| SALARIES | 2 | 1 | 1 | 1 | 1 | 1 | 1 | 1 | 1 | 1 | 1 | 1 | 1 |
| ADVERTISING | 1 | 1 | 1 | 1 | 1 | 1 | 1 | 1 | 1 | 1 | 1 | 1 | 1 |
| DEPRECIATION | 2 | 2 | 2 | 2 | 2 | 2 | 1 | 1 | 1 | 1 | 1 | 1 | 2 |
| OTHER FIXED | 1 | | | | | | | | | | | | |
| TOTAL FIXED | 9 | 9 | 8 | 8 | 7 | 7 | 7 | 6 | 6 | 6 | 6 | 5 | 7 |
| TOTAL OPER. EXPENSES | 45 | 44 | 44 | 43 | 43 | 43 | 42 | 42 | 42 | 41 | 41 | 41 | 42 |
| NET OPERATING INCOME | 29 | 29 | 29 | 30 | 30 | 30 | 31 | 31 | 32 | 32 | 32 | 32 | 31 |
| INTEREST EXPENSE | 3 | 3 | 3 | 3 | 3 | 3 | 2 | 2 | 2 | 2 | 2 | 2 | 2 |
| NET INCOME BEFORE TAX | 25 | 26 | 26 | 27 | 27 | 28 | 28 | 29 | 29 | 30 | 30 | 30 | 28 |
| INCOME TAX EXPENSE | 12 | 12 | 12 | 12 | 13 | 13 | 13 | 13 | 13 | 14 | 14 | 14 | 13 |
| NET INCOME | 14 | 14 | 14 | 15 | 15 | 15 | 15 | 16 | 16 | 16 | 16 | 16 | 15 |

Figure 7-1d. Copyright © 1982 Ferox Microsystems Inc., Arlington, Virginia.

```
                        DSS/F BUDGET EXAMPLE
                    BUDGET / ACTUAL VARIANCE REPORT
                      INCOME STATEMENT ACTUALS
                           % OF SALES
                           ----------
```

| | JAN | FEB | MAR | APR | MAY | JUN | JUL | AUG | SEP | OCT | NOV | DEC | TOTAL |
|---|---|---|---|---|---|---|---|---|---|---|---|---|---|
| SALES | 100% | 100% | 100% | 100% | 100% | 100% | 100% | 100% | 100% | 100% | 100% | 100% | 100% |
| RETURNS | 2 | 2 | 2 | 2 | 2 | 2 | 2 | 1 | 1 | 2 | 2 | 2 | 2 |
| NET SALES | 98 | 98 | 98 | 98 | 98 | 98 | 98 | 99 | 99 | 98 | 98 | 98 | 98 |
| COST OF GOODS SOLD | 29 | 32 | 25 | 29 | 26 | 24 | 24 | 21 | 23 | 21 | 20 | 20 | 24 |
| GROSS MARGIN | 69 | 66 | 73 | 69 | 72 | 74 | 74 | 78 | 76 | 77 | 78 | 79 | 75 |
| **OPERATING EXPENSES:** | | | | | | | | | | | | | |
| **VARIABLE:** | | | | | | | | | | | | | |
| LABOR | 21 | 23 | 20 | 22 | 21 | 20 | 20 | 17 | 20 | 18 | 18 | 17 | 19 |
| OFFICE EQUIPMENT | 3 | 3 | 3 | 3 | 3 | 3 | 3 | 2 | 3 | 3 | 2 | 3 | 3 |
| TRANSPORTATION | 6 | 6 | 5 | 5 | 5 | 5 | 5 | 4 | 5 | 5 | 4 | 4 | 5 |
| OFFICE SUPPLIES | 1 | 1 | 1 | 1 | 1 | 1 | 1 | 1 | 1 | 1 | 1 | 1 | 1 |
| UTILITIES | 8 | 9 | 7 | 7 | 6 | 6 | 6 | 5 | 6 | 6 | 6 | 6 | 6 |
| OTHER VARIABLE | 1 | 1 | | | 1 | 1 | 1 | | | | | | |
| TOTAL VARIABLE | 40 | 42 | 36 | 40 | 37 | 35 | 34 | 31 | 35 | 33 | 32 | 31 | 35 |
| **FIXED:** | | | | | | | | | | | | | |
| RENT | 4 | 4 | 4 | 4 | 3 | 3 | 3 | 3 | 3 | 2 | 2 | 2 | 3 |
| SALARIES | 2 | 2 | 2 | 2 | 2 | 2 | 2 | 2 | 2 | 2 | 1 | 1 | 2 |
| ADVERTISING | 1 | 1 | 1 | 1 | 1 | 1 | 1 | 1 | 1 | 1 | 1 | 1 | 1 |
| DEPRECIATION | 2 | 2 | 2 | 2 | 2 | 2 | 2 | 2 | 2 | 2 | 1 | 1 | 2 |
| OTHER FIXED | | | | | 1 | 1 | | | | | | | |
| TOTAL FIXED | 9 | 10 | 8 | 9 | 9 | 8 | 8 | 7 | 7 | 7 | 6 | 5 | 8 |
| TOTAL OPER. EXPENSES | 50 | 53 | 44 | 49 | 46 | 43 | 42 | 37 | 43 | 40 | 38 | 37 | 42 |
| NET OPERATING INCOME | 20 | 13 | 28 | 20 | 26 | 31 | 32 | 40 | 33 | 37 | 40 | 42 | 32 |
| INTEREST EXPENSE | 3 | 3 | 3 | 3 | 3 | 3 | 3 | 2 | 2 | 2 | 2 | 2 | 3 |
| NET INCOME BEFORE TAX | 16 | 10 | 26 | 17 | 23 | 28 | 30 | 38 | 31 | 35 | 38 | 40 | 30 |
| INCOME TAX EXPENSE | 8 | 5 | 12 | 8 | 11 | 13 | 14 | 18 | 14 | 16 | 17 | 18 | 14 |
| NET INCOME | 9 | 5 | 14 | 9 | 13 | 15 | 16 | 21 | 17 | 19 | 20 | 22 | 16 |

COPYRIGHT (C) 1982 FEROX MICROSYSTEMS INC

Figure 7–1e. Copyright © 1982 Ferox Microsystems Inc., Arlington, Virginia.

SUBSIDIARY: _____

PROFIT AND LOSS STATEMENT

FOR THE YEARS ENDING DECEMBER 31, 1980 – 1983

($ in 000's)

| | 1980 Actual | 1981 Forecast Amount | 1981 Forecast Better/(Worse) Than Plan | 1982 Plan Amount | 1982 Plan Better/(Worse) Than 1981 Forecast | 1983 Projection Amount | 1983 Projection Better/(Worse) Than 1982 Plan |
|---|---|---|---|---|---|---|---|
| INCOME | $ | $ | $ | $ | $ | $ | $ |
| Net Sales | | | | | | | |
| Service Revenues | | | | | | | |
| Intercompany | | | | | | | |
| Total Sales & Rev. | | | | | | | |
| Other Income: | | | | | | | |
| Miscellaneous | | | | | | | |
| Sub-Total | | | | | | | |
| TOTAL INCOME | | | | | | | |
| COST OF SALES | | | | | | | |
| GROSS PROFIT | | | | | | | |
| SELLING, ADMIN. & GEN. EXP. | | | | | | | |
| OTHER DEDUCTIONS | | | | | | | |
| OPERATING PROFIT | | | | | | | |
| INTEREST INCOME/(EXP.) | | | | | | | |
| Income | | | | | | | |
| Expense | | | | | | | |
| Short-Term | | | | | | | |
| Long-Term | | | | | | | |
| Parent & Affiliates | | | | | | | |
| Net Int. Inc./(Exp.) | | | | | | | |
| INCOME (LOSS) BEFORE TAXES | | | | | | | |
| PROVISION FOR TAXES | | | | | | | |
| Federal | | | | | | | |
| Foreign | | | | | | | |
| Total Taxes | | | | | | | |
| NET INCOME/(LOSS) | $ | $ | $ | $ | $ | $ | $ |
| SUPPLEMENTAL DATA | | | | | | | |
| Depreciation | | | | | | | |
| Capital additions | | | | | | | |
| Est. Investment credit | | | | | | | |
| Ogden Central Mgt. | | | | | | | |
| Chg. Incl. | | | | | | | |

Figure 7-2a

SUBSIDIARY: _____

PROFIT AND LOSS STATEMENT

MONTHLY SUMMARY FOR 1982 PLAN
($ in 000's)

| | Jan. | Feb. | Mar. | Apr. | May | June | July | Aug. | Sept. | Oct. | Nov. | Dec. | Full Year |
|---|---|---|---|---|---|---|---|---|---|---|---|---|---|
| **INCOME** | | | | | | | | | | | | | |
| Net Sales | $ | $ | $ | $ | $ | | | $ | $ | $ | $ | $ | $ |
| Service Revenues | | | | | | | | | | | | | |
| Intercompany | | | | | | | | | | | | | |
| Total Sales & Rev. | | | | | | | | | | | | | |
| Other Income: | | | | | | | | | | | | | |
| Miscellaneous | | | | | | | | | | | | | |
| Sub-Total | | | | | | | | | | | | | |
| TOTAL INCOME | | | | | | | | | | | | | |
| COST OF SALES | | | | | | | | | | | | | |
| GROSS PROFIT | | | | | | | | | | | | | |
| SELLING, ADMIN. & GEN. EXP. | | | | | | | | | | | | | |
| OTHER DEDUCTIONS | | | | | | | | | | | | | |
| OPERATING PROFIT | | | | | | | | | | | | | |
| INTEREST INCOME/(EXP.) | | | | | | | | | | | | | |
| Income | | | | | | | | | | | | | |
| Expense | | | | | | | | | | | | | |
| Short-Term | | | | | | | | | | | | | |
| Long-Term | | | | | | | | | | | | | |
| Parent & Affiliates | | | | | | | | | | | | | |
| Net Int. Inc./(Exp.) | | | | | | | | | | | | | |
| INCOME (LOSS) BEFORE TAXES | | | | | | | | | | | | | |
| PROVISION FOR TAXES | | | | | | | | | | | | | |
| Federal | | | | | | | | | | | | | |
| Foreign | | | | | | | | | | | | | |
| Total Taxes | | | | | | | | | | | | | |
| NET INCOME/(LOSS) | $ | $ | $ | $ | $ | | | $ | $ | $ | $ | $ | $ |
| **SUPPLEMENTAL DATA** | | | | | | | | | | | | | |
| Depreciation | | | | | | | | | | | | | |
| Capital additions | | | | | | | | | | | | | |
| Est. Investment credit | | | | | | | | | | | | | |
| Ogden Central Mgt. | | | | | | | | | | | | | |
| Chg. Incl. | | | | | | | | | | | | | |

Figure 7-2b

SUBSIDIARY: _____

PROFIT AND LOSS STATEMENT

FOR THE YEARS ENDING DECEMBER 31, 1980 - 1983

($ in 000's)

| | 1980 Actual | 1981 Forecast | | 1982 Plan | | 1981 Projection | |
|---|---|---|---|---|---|---|---|
| | | Amount | Better/(Worse) Than Plan | Amount | Better/(Worse) Than 1981 Forecast | Amount | Better/(Worse) Than 1982 Plan |
| **COST OF SALES - DETAIL** | | | | | | | |
| Direct | | | | | | | |
| Material | $ | $ | $ | $ | $ | $ | $ |
| Supplies | | | | | | | |
| Labor | | | | | | | |
| Utilities | | | | | | | |
| Transportation | | | | | | | |
| Other* | | | | | | | |
| Total | $ | $ | $ | $ | $ | $ | $ |
| Indirect | | | | | | | |
| Supervision | $ | $ | $ | $ | $ | $ | $ |
| Depreciation | | | | | | | |
| Maint. & Repairs | | | | | | | |
| Rentals | | | | | | | |
| Research & Development (1) | | | | | | | |
| Other (2) | | | | | | | |
| Total | $ | $ | $ | $ | $ | $ | $ |
| Total Cost of Sales | $ | $ | $ | $ | $ | $ | $ |

(1) This category should not include start-up costs on capital projects.
(2) Major items should be defined.

Figure 7-2c

SUBSIDIARY: _____

PROFIT AND LOSS STATEMENT

MONTHLY SUMMARY FOR 1982 PLAN

($ in 000's)

| COST OF SALES - DETAIL | Jan. | Feb. | Mar. | Apr. | May | June | July | Aug. | Sept. | Oct. | Nov. | Dec. | Full Year |
|---|---|---|---|---|---|---|---|---|---|---|---|---|---|
| Direct | | | | | | | | | | | | | |
| Material | | | | | | | | | | | | | |
| Supplies | | | | | | | | | | | | | |
| Labor | | | | | | | | | | | | | |
| Utilities | | | | | | | | | | | | | |
| Transportation | | | | | | | | | | | | | |
| Other* | | | | | | | | | | | | | |
| Total | | | | | | | | | | | | | |
| | | | | | | | | | | | | | |
| Indirect | | | | | | | | | | | | | |
| Supervision | | | | | | | | | | | | | |
| Depreciation | | | | | | | | | | | | | |
| Maint. & Repairs | | | | | | | | | | | | | |
| Rentals | | | | | | | | | | | | | |
| Research & Development (1) | | | | | | | | | | | | | |
| Other (2) | | | | | | | | | | | | | |
| Total | | | | | | | | | | | | | |
| | | | | | | | | | | | | | |
| Total Cost of Sales | | | | | | | | | | | | | |

(1) This category should not include start-up costs on capital projects.
(2) Major items should be defined.

Figure 7-2d

SUBSIDIARY: _____

PROFIT AND LOSS STATEMENT

FOR THE YEARS ENDING DECEMBER 31, 1980 - 1983

($ in 000's)

| | 1980 Actual | 1981 Forecast Amount | 1981 Forecast Better/(Worse) Than Plan | 1982 Plan Amount | 1982 Plan Better/(Worse) Than 1981 Forecast | 1983 Projection Amount | 1983 Projection Better/(Worse) Than 1982 Plan |
|---|---|---|---|---|---|---|---|
| **S, A, & G - DETAIL** | | | | | | | |
| **Selling Expense*** | $ | $ | $ | $ | $ | $ | $ |
| Salaries | | | | | | | |
| Bonuses | | | | | | | |
| Commissions | | | | | | | |
| Advertising | | | | | | | |
| Travel & Entertainment | | | | | | | |
| Other** | | | | | | | |
| Total | $ | $ | $ | $ | $ | $ | $ |
| **Administrative & General*** | $ | $ | $ | $ | $ | $ | $ |
| Salaries | | | | | | | |
| Bonuses | | | | | | | |
| Travel & Entertainment | | | | | | | |
| Other** | | | | | | | |
| Total | $ | $ | $ | $ | $ | $ | $ |
| Total Selling, Admin. & General | $ | $ | $ | $ | $ | $ | $ |

*Note: Expenses should be split between Selling and G & A where possible. Otherwise, consolidated figures are acceptable.

** Major items should be defined.

Figure 7-2e

SUBSIDIARY: _____

PROFIT AND LOSS STATEMENT

MONTHLY SUMMARY FOR 1982 PLAN
($ in 000's)

| | Jan. | Feb. | Mar. | Apr. | May | June | July | Aug. | Sept. | Oct. | Nov. | Dec. | Full Year |
|---|---|---|---|---|---|---|---|---|---|---|---|---|---|
| **S, A, & G – DETAIL** | | | | | | | | | | | | | |
| Selling Expense* | $ | $ | $ | $ | $ | $ | $ | $ | $ | $ | $ | $ | $ |
| Salaries | | | | | | | | | | | | | |
| Bonuses | | | | | | | | | | | | | |
| Commissions | | | | | | | | | | | | | |
| Advertising | | | | | | | | | | | | | |
| Travel & Entertainment | | | | | | | | | | | | | |
| Other** | | | | | | | | | | | | | |
| Total | $ | $ | $ | $ | $ | $ | $ | $ | $ | $ | $ | $ | $ |
| **Administrative & General*** | $ | $ | $ | $ | $ | $ | $ | $ | $ | $ | $ | $ | $ |
| Salaries | | | | | | | | | | | | | |
| Bonuses | | | | | | | | | | | | | |
| Travel & Entertainment | | | | | | | | | | | | | |
| Other** | | | | | | | | | | | | | |
| Total | $ | $ | $ | $ | $ | $ | $ | $ | $ | $ | $ | $ | $ |
| Total Selling, Admin. & General | $ | $ | $ | $ | $ | $ | $ | $ | $ | $ | $ | $ | $ |

\* Note: Expenses should be split between Selling and G & A where possible. Otherwise, consolidated figures are acceptable.

\*\* Major items should be defined.

Figure 7-2f

SUBSIDIARY: _____

PROFIT AND LOSS STATEMENT

FOR THE YEARS ENDING DECEMBER 31, 1980 - 83

($ in 000's)

| | 1980 Actual | 1981 Forecast | | 1982 Plan | | 1983 Projection | |
|---|---|---|---|---|---|---|---|
| | | Amount | Better/(Worse) Than Plan | Amount | Better/(Worse) Than 1981 Forecast | Amount | Better/(Worse) Than 1982 Plan |
| OTHER INCOME - DETAIL | $ | $ | $ | $ | $ | $ | $ |
| Commissions | | | | | | | |
| Rentals | | | | | | | |
| Royalties | | | | | | | |
| Gain on Sales of Fixed Assets | | | | | | | |
| Other* | | | | | | | |
| Total | $ | $ | $ | $ | $ | $ | $ |
| OTHER DEDUCTIONS - DETAIL | $ | $ | $ | $ | $ | $ | $ |
| All items over 10% of balance | | | | | | | |
| Total | $ | $ | $ | $ | $ | $ | $ |

*Major items should be defined.

Figure 7-2g

SUBSIDIARY: _____

PROFIT AND LOSS STATEMENT

MONTHLY SUMMARY FOR 1982 PLAN
($ in 000's)

| | Jan. | Feb. | Mar. | Apr. | May | June | July | Aug. | Sept. | Oct. | Nov. | Dec. | Full Year |
|---|---|---|---|---|---|---|---|---|---|---|---|---|---|
| OTHER INCOME - DETAIL | $ | $ | $ | $ | $ | $ | $ | $ | $ | $ | $ | $ | $ |
| Commissions | | | | | | | | | | | | | |
| Rentals | | | | | | | | | | | | | |
| Royalties | | | | | | | | | | | | | |
| Gain on Sales of Fixed Assets | | | | | | | | | | | | | |
| Other* | | | | | | | | | | | | | |
| Total | $ | $ | $ | $ | $ | $ | $ | $ | $ | $ | $ | $ | $ |
| OTHER DEDUCTIONS - DETAIL | $ | $ | $ | $ | $ | $ | $ | $ | $ | $ | $ | $ | $ |
| All items over 10% of balance | | | | | | | | | | | | | |
| Total | $ | $ | $ | $ | $ | $ | $ | $ | $ | $ | $ | $ | $ |

*Major items should be defined.

Figure 7-2h

SUBSIDIARY: _____

BALANCE SHEET - ASSETS

FOR THE YEARS 1960 - 1983

($ in 000's)

| ASSETS | 1980 Actual December 31 | 1981 Forecast December 31 | 1982 Plan March 31 | 1982 Plan June 30 | 1982 Plan September 30 | December 31 | 1983 Projection December 31 |
|---|---|---|---|---|---|---|---|
| | $ | $ | $ | $ | $ | $ | $ |
| **CURRENT ASSETS** | | | | | | | |
| Cash | | | | | | | |
| Marketable securities - at cost | | | | | | | |
| Accounts, acceptances & notes receivable: | | | | | | | |
| Trade | | | | | | | |
| Advances to suppliers | | | | | | | |
| Other | | | | | | | |
| Allowance for doubtful accounts | | | | | | | |
| Net Receivables | | | | | | | |
| Inventories | | | | | | | |
| Finished Goods | | | | | | | |
| Raw Material, WIP, Supplies | | | | | | | |
| Other | | | | | | | |
| Total Inventories | | | | | | | |
| Contracts in progress & joint & other ventures | | | | | | | |
| Prepaid expenses, etc. | | | | | | | |
| Total Current Assets | | | | | | | |
| **INTERCOMPANY ACCOUNTS** | | | | | | | |
| Invest. in capital stock of consol. subsids. | | | | | | | |
| Accounts & notes receivable | | | | | | | |
| Total Intercompany Accounts | | | | | | | |
| **PROPERTY, PLANT & EQUIPMENT - At Cost** | | | | | | | |
| Land | | | | | | | |
| Buildings, machinery & equipment | | | | | | | |
| Vessels | | | | | | | |
| Less: Accumulated Depreciation | | | | | | | |
| Property, plant & equipment - Net | | | | | | | |
| **OTHER ASSETS** | | | | | | | |
| Investments: | | | | | | | |
| Foreign subsidiaries not consolidated | | | | | | | |
| (at equity in underlying net assets) | | | | | | | |
| Other (at cost or nominal value) | | | | | | | |
| Goodwill | | | | | | | |
| Miscellaneous | | | | | | | |
| Total other | | | | | | | |
| TOTAL | $ | $ | $ | $ | $ | $ | $ |

Figure 7-2i

SUBSIDIARY:

BALANCE SHEET - LIABILITIES AND EQUITY

FOR THE YEARS 1979 - 1983

($ in 000's)

| LIABILITIES & EQUITY | 1980 Actual December 31 | 1981 Forecast December 31 | 1982 Plan March 31 | June 30 | September 30 | December 31 | 1983 Projection December 31 |
|---|---|---|---|---|---|---|---|
| CURRENT LIABILITIES | $ | $ | $ | $ | $ | $ | $ |
| Notes payable | | | | | | | |
| Current portion of long-term debt | | | | | | | |
| Accounts payable | | | | | | | |
| Federal & foreign taxes on income | | | | | | | |
| Accrued payrolls, taxes, pension costs, etc. | | | | | | | |
| Contracts in progress - billings in excess of costs, etc. | | | | | | | |
| Total current liabilities | | | | | | | |
| INTERCOMPANY ACCOUNTS & NOTES PAYABLE (see attached) | | | | | | | |
| DEFERRED CREDITS, RESERVES, ETC. | | | | | | | |
| LONG-TERM DEBT (exclusive of amounts due within one year) | | | | | | | |
| MINORITY INTERESTS | | | | | | | |
| SHAREHOLDERS' EQUITY | | | | | | | |
| Common Stock | | | | | | | |
| Preferred Stock | | | | | | | |
| Capital Surplus | | | | | | | |
| Retained Earnings | | | | | | | |
| Total Shareholders' Equity | | | | | | | |
| TOTAL | $ | $ | $ | $ | $ | $ | $ |

Figure 7-2j

SUBSIDIARY: _____

CASH FLOW

FOR THE 1982 PLAN YEAR

($ in 000's)

|  | 1982 Plan (Non-Cumulative) | | | | | 1983 |
|  | First Quarter | Second Quarter | Third Quarter | Fourth Quarter | Full Year | Projection |
|---|---|---|---|---|---|---|
| CASH PROVIDED BY: |  |  |  |  |  |  |
| Net Income | $ | $ | $ | $ | $ | $ |
| Depreciation charge |  |  |  |  |  |  |
| Increase (decrease) in: |  |  |  |  |  |  |
| Short-term debt |  |  |  |  |  |  |
| Long-term debt |  |  |  |  |  |  |
| Accounts payable |  |  |  |  |  |  |
| Federal & foreign income taxes (A) |  |  |  |  |  |  |
| Accrued payrolls, taxes, pension costs, etc. |  |  |  |  |  |  |
| Contracts in progress - billings in excess of costs |  |  |  |  |  |  |
| Deferred credits, reserves, etc. |  |  |  |  |  |  |
| Minority interests retained |  |  |  |  |  |  |
| Accounts payable to affiliated companies other than Ogden American Corporation |  |  |  |  |  |  |
| Sales or retirement of fixed assets |  |  |  |  |  |  |
| TOTAL |  |  |  |  |  |  |
| CASH USED FOR: |  |  |  |  |  |  |
| Capital additions (to be agreed to in annual approved capital budget presentation) (B) |  |  |  |  |  |  |
| Cash Dividends Paid |  |  |  |  |  |  |
| Increase (decrease) in: |  |  |  |  |  |  |
| Marketable securities |  |  |  |  |  |  |
| Accounts, acceptances and note receivable: |  |  |  |  |  |  |
| Trade (net of reserve for bad debts) |  |  |  |  |  |  |
| Advances to suppliers |  |  |  |  |  |  |
| Other |  |  |  |  |  |  |
| Inventories |  |  |  |  |  |  |
| Contracts in progress and joint and other ventures |  |  |  |  |  |  |
| Prepaid expenses, etc. |  |  |  |  |  |  |
| Other investments |  |  |  |  |  |  |
| Miscellaneous other assets |  |  |  |  |  |  |
| Accounts receivable from affiliated companies other than Ogden, Ogden Management or Ogden American Corporation |  |  |  |  |  |  |
| Increase in cash account to comply with Loan Agreement Restrictions (if any) |  |  |  |  |  |  |
| Other Increase (decrease) in cash accounts |  |  |  |  |  |  |
| TOTAL |  |  |  |  |  |  |

BALANCE - Cash provided (deficit) to be used to (increase) decrease amounts due to Parent company.

NOTES: (A) Assume all taxes provided for period will be paid during period
(B) Do not include items to be leased

Figure 7-2k

## Capital Budgeting Procedure

Investments are the lifeblood of capital-intensive organizations and are vital to the growth of all firms. For this reason detailed capital budgeting information systems have been developed to control this important activity. Four segments of the capital budgeting system of Ogden Corporation are herewith presented.

Figures 7–3A through 7–3H are an example of the request form submitted by an Ogden operating unit requesting corporate approval of a capital expenditure project. Figure 7–4 presents a summary description of an operating unit's expenditure request prepared for presentation to corporate management. In the sample outputs shown, the project used is the same one illustrated in Figures 7–3A through 7–3H. Capital expenditure data submitted by each operating unit to support preparation of the annual corporate capital plan are shown in Figures 7–5A through 7–5F. Finally Figure 7–6 is an example a capital expenditure performance review used to assess the outcome of a previously approved project. This form is prepared jointly by the operating unit and the corporate staff.

## Samples of Computerized Accounting Applications

This concluding section of financial information system outputs marries one of the oldest organizational activities, namely, paying bills and paying employees, to one of the newest information techniques, namely, an interactive computer system. We are using as our example a "Payroll Package" and an "Accounts Payable Package" designed by Mini-Computer Systems, Inc., a software firm in Elmsford, New York.

**A. Payroll Package.** This application is controlled and operated via a series of menus as shown on Figure 7–7A. The operator calls up the main payroll menu which lists the ten individual function menus on the screen. The desired function menu is selected leading to the listing of the details of that menu. Finally the operator calls for that section of the menu that is to be worked on at which point the processing of that operation takes place. A brief description is given of each menu and some sample outputs are illustrated.

**1. Payroll Main Menu.** This is the main menu of the "Payroll Package." This menu provides access to all the subsidiary menus which are organized by function. To go from one subsidiary menu to another, the user must go through the main menu.

**2. Employer File Maintenance Menu #1.** This menu contains extremely critical functions including creation and purges of master files for corporations, payrolls, departments, and bank accounts. The system control file is also maintained from this menu.

**3. Employer File Maintenance Menu #2.** This menu contains file maintenance programs necessary to establish and maintain the 941a form codes, the employer state registration numbers, and the fixed tax code. This menu is logically part of the previous menu, but had to be established as a separate section because the master information needed about the employer exceeded a single screen capacity.

**4. Employee File Maintenance Menu.** This menu contains those functions needed to create and maintain the employee master file; to print employee records; to dis-

OGDEN CORPORATION

RECEIVED

Capital Expenditure Request Form    JAN 2 6 1981

| Capability Area | Company | Location | OPERATIONS & DEVELOPMENT | Date | CER No. |
|---|---|---|---|---|---|
| Ogden Food Products | Tillie Lewis Foods | Stockton | | 1-22-81 | 81-401 |

Project Name and Description

Savi-Magnuson Tomato Peeler

This equipment provides a non-caustic method of peeling tomatoes which results in a reduction in peeling yield losses while improving the quality of the peeled tomato pack. It represents new technology for U.S. canneries and an opportunity for significant reduction of product costs which will be so vital in improving our competitive position in the 1980s.

REASON FOR EXPENDITURE:

☐ Mandatory

☐ Replacement

☒ Economically Justified

☐ Discretionary

☐ Expansion Project

Project Life:  15 years

Depreciable Life:  15 years

Included in Approved Capital Budget

☐ Yes    ☒ No

| FINANCIAL REQUIREMENT | FINANCIAL SUMMARY | CASH EXPENDITURE | |
|---|---|---|---|
| Capital | | APPROVAL YEAR | AMOUNT |
| Fixed Assets $_____ | Average Annual Rate ____ % of Return | 1st Quarter | |
| Working Capital $_____ - | | 2nd Quarter | |
| Total $_____ | D.C.F. Rate of ____ % Return | 3rd Quarter | |
| Associated Expense $_____ | | 4th Quarter | |
| Less Expense | | Subsequent Years | |
| Per Year $_____ | Payback Period ____ Yrs. | TOTAL CAPITAL EXPENDITURE | $_____ |
| Total Lease Term $_____ | | | |

SECTIONS I through VIII MUST BE COMPLETED PRIOR TO SUBMISSION

| COMPANY APPROVALS | CAPABILITY APPROVALS | OGDEN APPROVALS |
|---|---|---|
| _James D. Summ_ 1/23/81 | _____ 1/23/81 | _____ 3/12/81 |
| Vice President Engineering   Date | Sr. Vice President Operations Date | Chief Operating Officer   Date |
| _David Mandell_ 1/23/81 | _____ 1/23/81 | |
| Sr. Vice President Finance   Date | President   Date | Chairman of the Board   Date |

☐ Board of Directors

Figure 7-3a/h.

SECTIONS I through VIII MUST BE ANSWERED.  ATTACH ADDITIONAL PAGES WHERE NECESSARY.

I.  Provide detailed description of the proposed project and explain the reason for its undertaking.

This Capital Expenditure Request is for the purchase and installation of a Savi-Magnuson tomato peeler. The main advantage of this peeler is that it uses a medium of hot water rather than the traditional hot caustic to prepare the tomato for peeling.

The reasons for undertaking this project is the tremendous potential for decreasing production costs. This cost efficiency will come by reducing the raw material loss at the peeler from 20% to 5%. Currently the peeler loss cannot be recovered because it is mixed with caustic.  The proposed system, however, will recover all of this loss, except the skin, and use it for tomato products.

The financial detail in Section VIII shows that by replacing one peeler in Plant I and operating it for a half season, we can expect a $         savings the first year.  If this equipment proves out at Plant I, which is very likely (see Risks Section VI), the greatest potential is in replacing the four peelers at Plant D. Four peelers at Plant D operating over the full season would have the potential of reducing production costs by over $   million per season.

The appearance of the tomato packed by this process appears to be superior based on the cutting which has been observed.  The reason for this is that the caustic cuts into the pectin layer of the tomato whereas the hot water system does not.  This leaves the tomato with an appealing velvety appearance.  (We have not attempted to quantify this.)

II.  Explain basic assumptions and probability of occurrence.

This project is based on the assumption that the equipment can be delivered and installed by August 15, 1981.  This can be done if we place the order by February 2, 1981.

The equipment is rated at    tons per hour; we used approximately    tons per hour in our calculations. This is a very reasonable capacity based on the performance of over 150 peelers which are already in operation in Europe and South America.

We have assumed that the raw material loss at the peeler can be reduced from 20% to 5%.  This is a conservative figure since all of the peeling loss will be recovered and sent through the press to separate the skins.  (None of the peeling loss can be recovered with current peelers because of the caustic mixture.)

III.  Provide relevant data on markets, products, competition, industry trends, etc.

This is the first year this peeler has been offered in the United States.  If the technology proves out to be as good as it appears, we will have at least a year's jump on any competitors who are not testing it.

Figure 7-3b

IV.  Detailed composition of the proposed investment expenditure.

Land                          $_____          Working Capital

Buildings                                           Cash              $_____

_____    _____          Receivables       _____

_____    _____          Inventories       _____

_____    _____          Other             _____

_____    _____

_____    _____                            _____

Equipment                                           Less:

Savi Tomato Peeler     _____          Trade Payables    _____

Conveyors              _____

Catwalks               _____                  TOTAL     $_____

Installation Labor     _____

Misc. Materials        _____

Contingency            _____

_____    _____

Leasehold Improvements

_____    _____

_____    _____

_____    _____

           Subtotal    _____

Working Capital        _____

             TOTAL     $_____

V.  Explain the benefits expected to result from this project and their impact on present operations.

See Section VIII Financial Justification.

Figure 7-3c

VI. Discuss risks associated with project.

As stated above, over 150 of these peelers are currently in use in Europe and South America. Therefore although the technology is new to the United States, it has been thoroughly tested. The equipment is made by Savi Antonio, an Italian firm, and is represented by Magnuson in the United States. Magnuson is one of the most respectable and dependable dealers in the United States. When Magnuson brings the basic equipment into the United States, they will install all of their own motors, wiring, etc. to assure compliance with all of the United States codes.

The contract which we would write with Magnuson will guarantee performance to our specifications or they will refund the purchase price. If the peeler failed to perform, our exposure would be in freight to and from Italy, removal and crating, and installation, all of which would be approximately $90,000.

Since we are going to install this unit at Plant I, we will not be jeopardizing the 1981 peel pack, since over 85% of the peeled pack is scheduled for Plant D.

VII. Alternatives considered and reasons for selecting recommended action.

Not applicable.

VIII. Financial Justification: Cash Flow, ROI, Payback, etc. (Attach worksheet calculations.)

The development of the following financial indicators is detailed in Exhibits I-IV attached.

| | | |
|---|---|---|
| PBT (5 year average) | = | $ |
| Average ROI | = | % |
| Payback | = | years |
| DCF ROI | = | % |
| NPV @ 30% | = | $ |

Figure 7-3d

EXHIBIT I

PBT SUMMARY

| Year | Production Savings | Inflation Factor @ 8% | Adjusted Production Savings | Fixed Overhead Savings | Depreciation | PBT |
|------|--------------------|-----------------------|-----------------------------|------------------------|--------------|-----|
| 1 | | 1.00 | | | | |
| 2 | | 1.08 | | | | |
| 3 | | 1.17 | | | | |
| 4 | | 1.26 | | | | |
| 5 | | 1.36 | | | | |
| 6 | | 1.47 | | | | |
| 7 | | 1.59 | | | | |
| 8 | | 1.71 | | | | |
| 9 | | 1.85 | | | | |
| 10 | | 2.00 | | | | |

AVERAGE INVESTMENT

| | Beginning Investment | Depreciation | I.T.C. | End Investment | Average Investment |
|---|----------------------|--------------|--------|----------------|--------------------|
| 1 | | | | | |
| 2 | | | - | | |
| 3 | | | - | | |
| 4 | | | - | | |
| 5 | | | - | | |

Average Annual Investment

FINANCIAL INDICATORS

PBT (5 Year Average) =        ÷  5  = $

Average ROI            =      ÷    =     %

1/22/81

Figure 7-3e

EXHIBIT II

## CASH FLOW SCHEDULE

| | Year 0 | Year 1 | Year 2 | Year 3 | Year 4 | Year 5 | Year 6 | Year 7 | Year 8 | Year 9 | Year 10 | Total |
|---|---|---|---|---|---|---|---|---|---|---|---|---|
| PBT | | | | | | | | | | | | |
| Tax Effect | | | | | | | | | | | | |
| Investment Tax Credit | | | | | | | | | | | | |
| PAT | | | | | | | | | | | | |
| Depreciation | | | | | | | | | | | | |
| Investment | | | | | | | | | | | | |
| Net Cash Flow | | | | | | | | | | | | |
| Accumulative Cash Flow | | | | | | | | | | | | |

## FINANCIAL INDICATORS

PAYBACK = _____ years
DCF ROI = _____ %
NPV @ 30% = _____ $

Figure 7-3f

1/22/81

EXHIBIT III

## HOT WATER TOMATO PEELER
### PLANT 1

ANTICIPATED SCHEDULE

CSS #10 SPAGHETTI SAUCE x 15.096 TONS FILL/1,000 CSS ÷ 0.7 DICER YIELD = _____ TONS
CSS HOMADE CHILI x 1.764 TONS FILL/1,000 CSS ÷ 0.7 DICER YIELD = _____ TONS
CSS 250 PROGRESSO PEARS x 14.256 TONS FILL/1,000 CSS = _____ TONS
_____ TONS
PEELED INTO CAN

SAVINGS
  CAUSTIC PEELER

    _____ TONS INTO CAN ÷ .768 CANNABILITY ÷ .8 PEELER YIELD = _____ TONS INTO PEELER
    _____ TONS INTO PEELER x .2 PEELING LOSS = _____ TONS PEEL LOSS

HOT WATER PEELER

    _____ TONS INTO CAN ÷ .813 CANNABILITY ÷ .95 PEELER YIELD = _____ TONS INTO PEELER
    _____ TONS INTO PEELER x .05 PEELING LOSS = _____ TONS PEEL LOSS
    _____ TONS PEEL LOSS CAUSTIC PEELER - 320.7 TONS PEEL LOSS HOT WATER PEELER = _____ SAVINGS
    _____ TONS SAVED x $66/TON TOMATOES DELIVERED = $_____ SAVINGS

CAUSTIC AND PEELING ADDITIVE

    _____ GAL. ACTUAL 1980 USAGE - 1,400 GAL. ESTIMATED USAGE C/U'S = _____ GAL. FOR PEELING

30 ESTIMATED PEELING DAYS 1981 = 1.154% INCREASE
26 ACTUAL PEELING DAYS 1980

    _____ GAL. CAUSTIC 1980 x 1.154% INCREASE = _____ GAL. ESTIMATED 1981 USAGE
    _____ GAL. CAUSTIC x 12.8#/GAL. x 1 TON x $200/TON = $_____
                                     2,000#
    # ACTUAL 1980 ADDITIVE USAGE x 1.154% INCREASE = _____ ESTIMATED 1981 USAGE
    # ESTIMATED 1981 USAGE x $0.47/POUND = $_____

TOTAL SAVINGS

$_____ PEEL SAVINGS + $_____ CAUSTIC + $_____ ADDITIVE = $_____ TOTAL SAVINGS

Figure 7-3g

1/16/81

EXHIBIT IV

FIXED OVERHEAD SAVINGS

| | FMC Leases | | | |
|---|---|---|---|---|
| Year | Lye Peelers | Peel Removers | Additional Maintenance | Total |
| 1 | - | - | - | - |
| 2 | - | | | |
| 3 | - | | | |
| 4 | | | | |
| 5 | | | | |
| 6 | | | | |
| 7 | | | | |
| 8 | | | | |
| 9 | | | | |
| 10 | | | | |

1/23/81

Figure 7–3h

TILLIE LEWIS FOODS
SAVI-MAGNUSON TOMATO PEELER


Tillie Lewis Foods is requesting approval of a $          capital
expenditure to purchase and install a Savi-Magnuson Tomato Peeler at
Plant #1 in Stockton, California.  This equipment utilizes a non-
caustic solution in peeling tomatoes which increases peeling yield and
improves product quality.  This peeler is manufactured in Italy by
Savi Antonio and is marketed in the U.S. by Magnuson.  Although over
150 of these units are in operation in Europe and in South America,
the equipment has not been available in the U.S. until this time.
This project represents an opprotunity for Tillie Lewis to improve its
profit margin.

The main advantage of the Savi-Magnuson Tomato Peeler is that it
uses a medium of hot water rather than the traditional hot caustic to
prepare the tomato for peeling.  In the existing machine, peeler loss
cannot be recovered because it is mixed with the caustic solution; the
proposed system would recover all the peeler loss, except the skin,
and use it for tomato products.  Additional savings will be generated
by the elimination of the caustic solution and, eventually, by avoiding
lease costs of the existing equipment.

Tillie Lewis expects the following five-year average savings from
this project:

- Product loss savings - the Savi-Magnuson Peeler                 $
  would reduce product loss from 20% to 5%.

- Caustic solution and peeling additive savings -
  solution and additives would be completely eliminated and replaced by water.

- Lease costs savings - the existing peeler system
  will be returned to the manufacturer upon the
  expiration of operating leases.

- Incremental maintenance costs.

- Incremental depreciation charge.
                        Total ,

Investment

   - Savi-Magnuson peeler                                         $
   - Conveyor, catwalk, and installation cost
   - Contingency (all prices are firm except
     for $          )
                  Total                                          $

Figure 7-4.

- 2 -

| Pro Forma | First Year | Five Year Average |
|---|---|---|
| - Pre-interest PBT | $ | $ |
| - Return on Investment | % | % |

The project is expected to achieve a discounted cash flow of
% and achieve payback in     years.

It should be noted that Magnuson has agreed to buy back the peeler
if Tillie Lewis is not satisfied with its performance for any reason.
This protection clause, which extends through October 1, 1981, includes
only the price paid to Savi Antonio for the peeler itself and would
leave Tillie Lewis with a potential exposure of $        for installa-
tion, removal and crating, and freight to and from Italy.

This project was not included in Tillie Lewis' 1981 capital budget.
Tillie Lewis will fund this project by cancelling a Cooker Recycle
System for $        , modifying Peach Line Conversion to reduce its
cost by $        , and purchasing a used rather than a new Pilot Sterilizer
for a savings of $        . We support this project based on its attractive
returns and recommend its approval.

Figure 7-4 *(Cont.)*

OGDEN CORPORATION AND SUBSIDIARIES
CAPITAL APPROPRIATIONS BUDGET SUMMARY
1982

Capability Area _____

Company: _____

| | Capital Appropriation | Associated Expense | Associated Write-Off | Working Capital Requirement | Total Commitment |
|---|---|---|---|---|---|
| A   Mandatory | | | | | |
| B   Replacement | | | | | |
| C   Economically Justified | | | | | |
| D   Discretionary | | | | | |
| Basic Budget* | | | | | |
| E   Expansion** | | | | | |
| Total 1982 Appropriation Budget | | | | | |
| "Approval Basis" Carry Forward | | | | | |
| Total | | | | | |

Depreciation
1980 Actual _____
1981 Est. _____
1982 Est. _____

* Basic Budget--Capital asset additions required by an Operating Unit
to maintain the current level of operating activity. These include
all mandatory elements due to environmental or other government
regulations, replacement of assets due to wear and tear, and
economically justified programs to the extent that they do not
result in a major expansion of productive capacity.

** Expansion Budget--Major growth oriented capital commitments which
will result in a demonstrable increase in business volume. These
include loop deals and internal expansion programs for new products
and market development.

Figure 7-5a/f.

OGDEN CORPORATION AND SUBSIDIARIES
CAPITAL APPROPRIATIONS BUDGET-DETAIL
1982

Capability Area: _____
Company: _____

Reason Code:
 A-Mandatory
 B-Replacement
 C-Economically Justified
 D-Discretionary
 E-Expansion

| Project Number | Project Title | Est. Completion Date | Reason Code | Capital Appropriation* | Associated Expense | Associated Write-Off | Working Capital Required | Total Commitment |
|---|---|---|---|---|---|---|---|---|
| | | | | | | | | |
| | | | | | | | | |

*Indicate "L" if to be leased

Figure 7-5b

OGDEN CORPORATION AND SUBSIDIARIES
Projects Eligible for "Approval Basis" Carry Forward
1982

Capability Area: _____
Company: _____

Reason Code:
   A-Mandatory
   B-Replacement
   C-Economically Justified
   D-Discretionary
   E-Expansion

| Project Number | Project Title | Est. Completion Date | Reason Code | Capital Appropriation* | Associated Expense | Associated Write-Off | Working Capital Required | Total Commitment |
|---|---|---|---|---|---|---|---|---|
| | "Approval Basis" Carry Forward | | | | | | | |

Total 1981 Capital Budget
Less: 1981 Appropriations
        Undercommitment

Figure 7-5c

*Indicate "L" if to be leased

OGDEN CORPORATION AND SUBSIDIARIES
CAPITAL BUDGET-CASH BASIS
1982

Capability Area: _____
Company: _____

| Project Title | Through 1981 | Cash Flow 1982 | | | | | 1983 | Beyond 1983 | Total Expenditure |
| --- | --- | --- | --- | --- | --- | --- | --- | --- | --- |
| | | 1st Q | 2nd Q | 3rd Q | 4th Q | Total 1982 | | | |
| -Approved Before 1982 | | | | | | | | | |
| -Regular 1982 Budget | | | | | | | | | |
| -"Approval Basis" Carry Forward | | | | | | | | | |
| Total Expenditures | | | | | | | | | |

Figure 7-5d

OGDEN CORPORATION AND SUBSIDIARIES
CAPITAL BUDGET–CASH BASIS
1982

Capability Area: _____
Company: _____

| Project Number | Project Title | Through 1981 | Cash Flow 1982 | | | | | 1983 | Beyond 1983 | Total Expenditure |
| --- | --- | --- | --- | --- | --- | --- | --- | --- | --- | --- |
| | | | 1st Q | 2nd Q | 3rd Q | 4th Q | Total 1982 | | | |
| | "Cash Basis" for approvals prior to 1982 | | | | | | | | | |
| | Total Carry Forward | | | | | | | | | |

Figure 7-5e

353

OGDEN CORPORATION AND SUBSIDIARIES
CAPITAL BUDGET-CASH BASIS
1982

Capability Area: _____
Company: _____

Cash Flow

| Project Number | Project Title | Through 1981 | 1982 | | | | | 1983 | Beyond 1983 | Total Expenditure |
|---|---|---|---|---|---|---|---|---|---|---|
| | | | 1st Q | 2nd Q | 3rd Q | 4th Q | Total 1982 | | | |
| **TO BE APPROVED IN 1982** | | | | | | | | | | |
| | Regular 1982 Budget | | | | | | | | | |
| | "Approval Basis" Carry Forward | | | | | | | | | |
| | Total | | | | | | | | | |

Figure 7-5f

SUBSIDIARY _____

Comparison of Actual and Forecasted Operating Results to Profit Plan

Month Ended _____ 19____

| | Y-T-D | | Next Quarter | | Full Year | |
|---|---|---|---|---|---|---|
| | Actual | B/(W) Than Plan | Forecast | B/(W) Than Plan | Forecast | B/(W) Than Plan |
| **Income:** | | | | | | |
| Net Sales | | | | | | |
| Service Revenues | | | | | | |
| Intercompany | $ | $ | $ | $ | $ | $ |
| Total Net Sales and Service Revenues | | | | | | |
| **Other Income** | | | | | | |
| Interest | | | | | | |
| Equity in net income of unconsolidated subsidiaries | | | | | | |
| Miscellaneous | | | | | | |
| Total Income | | | | | | |
| **Costs and Expenses:** | | | | | | |
| Cost of Sales | | | | | | |
| Selling, General and Administrative Expenses | | | | | | |
| Interest: | | | | | | |
| Short term debt | | | | | | |
| Long term debt | | | | | | |
| Parent and affiliated companies | | | | | | |
| Minority interests in net income of subsidiaries | | | | | | |
| Other deductions | | | | | | |
| Total Costs and Expenses | $ | $ | $ | $ | $ | $ |
| Income (Loss) before Federal and foreign taxes on income | | | | | | |
| Provision for federal and foreign taxes on income: | | | | | | |
| Federal | | | | | | |
| Foreign | | | | | | |
| Total | | | | | | |
| Net Income (Loss) | $ | $ | $ | $ | $ | $ |

(1) If you do not expect to meet your original profit plan for the coming quarter or the current year, complete the appropriate columns above. If you expect to meet your original plans, please sign the applicable statements below.

(A) We expect to meet our original profit plan for the coming quarter _____

(B) We expect to meet our original profit plan for the current year _____

Figure 7-6.

MCS PAYROLL PACKAGE

Menu Overview

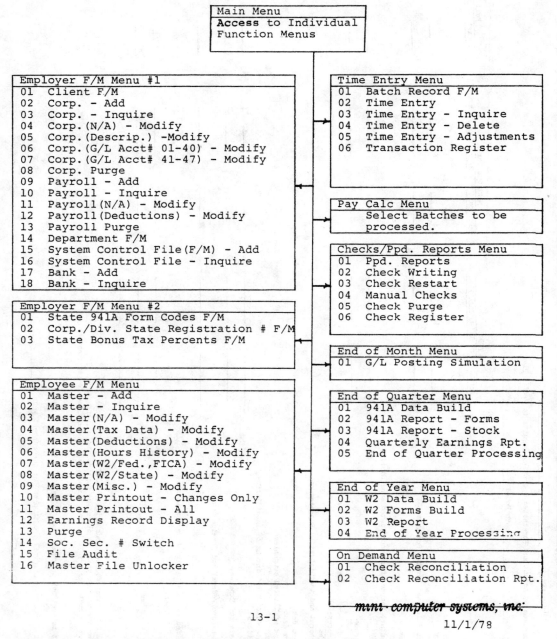

```
                        ┌─────────────────────────┐
                        │ Main Menu               │
                        │ Access to Individual    │
                        │ Function Menus          │
                        └─────────────────────────┘
```

**Employer F/M Menu #1**
01  Client F/M
02  Corp. - Add
03  Corp. - Inquire
04  Corp.(N/A) - Modify
05  Corp.(Descrip.) -Modify
06  Corp.(G/L Acct# 01-40) - Modify
07  Corp.(G/L Acct# 41-47) - Modify
08  Corp. Purge
09  Payroll - Add
10  Payroll - Inquire
11  Payroll(N/A) - Modify
12  Payroll(Deductions) - Modify
13  Payroll Purge
14  Department F/M
15  System Control File(F/M) - Add
16  System Control File - Inquire
17  Bank - Add
18  Bank - Inquire

**Employer F/M Menu #2**
01  State 941A Form Codes F/M
02  Corp./Div. State Registration # F/M
03  State Bonus Tax Percents F/M

**Employee F/M Menu**
01  Master - Add
02  Master - Inquire
03  Master(N/A) - Modify
04  Master(Tax Data) - Modify
05  Master(Deductions) - Modify
06  Master(Hours History) - Modify
07  Master(W2/Fed.,FICA) - Modify
08  Master(W2/State) - Modify
09  Master(Misc.) - Modify
10  Master Printout - Changes Only
11  Master Printout - All
12  Earnings Record Display
13  Purge
14  Soc. Sec. # Switch
15  File Audit
16  Master File Unlocker

**Time Entry Menu**
01  Batch Record F/M
02  Time Entry
03  Time Entry - Inquire
04  Time Entry - Delete
05  Time Entry - Adjustments
06  Transaction Register

**Pay Calc Menu**
    Select Batches to be
    processed.

**Checks/Ppd. Reports Menu**
01  Ppd. Reports
02  Check Writing
03  Check Restart
04  Manual Checks
05  Check Purge
06  Check Register

**End of Month Menu**
01  G/L Posting Simulation

**End of Quarter Menu**
01  941A Data Build
02  941A Report - Forms
03  941A Report - Stock
04  Quarterly Earnings Rpt.
05  End of Quarter Processing

**End of Year Menu**
01  W2 Data Build
02  W2 Forms Build
03  W2 Report
04  End of Year Processing

**On Demand Menu**
01  Check Reconciliation
02  Check Reconciliation Rpt.

*mini-computer systems, inc.*

13-1

11/1/78

Figure 7-7a. MCS payroll package; menu overview. Mini-Computer System, Inc., Elmsford, NY. Reprinted with permission.

MCS PAYROLL PACKAGE

Employee Master F/M - 1

```
X.PEM1XX     PAYROLL EMPLOYEE MASTER - PERSONNEL/SALARY DATA     MM/DD/YY

 1. CORP: 9999 2. DIV: 9999 3. SOCSECNO: BBBBBBBB  4. ID NO: 9999999999
 5. PAYROLL NO: 999    PAYPD: ___  6. HOME DEPT: XXXXXXXXXX
 7. STATUS CODE(A I S L D E): B   8. LAST NAME: XXXXXXXXXXXXXXX
 9. FIRST NAME: XXXXXXXXXXXXXXX   1Ø. MIDDLE : XXXXXXXXXXXXXXXX
11. ADDR1: XXXXXXXXXXXXXXXXXXXXXXXX 12. ADDR2: XXXXXXXXXXXXXXXXXXXXXXXX
13. CITY: XXXXXXXXXXXXXXXXXX 14. STATE: BB               15. ZIP: BBBBB
16. APT NO: XXXXXX 17. PHONE NO: 9999999999
18. SEX(M/F): B 19. MARITAL (S M D W H O): B 20. EEO: B
21. UNION NO: 999  22. INIT FEE PD(Y/N):B
23. EMPL TYPE(H N E O): B
24. PAYPD SALARY(N E O): 9999999.99 25. ANNUAL SALARY(N E O): 9999999.99
26. STD HRDAY: 99.99
27. REG SHIFT(1 2 3): B
28. REG RATE/SHIFT 1: 999.999 29. SHIFT DIFFERENTIAL (TYPE H) Y/N: B
3Ø. DIFFERENTIAL S/2: 999.999
31. DIFFERENTIAL S/3: 999.999
32. DATE LAST RAISE: 999999 33. AMT: 9999999.99 34. FOR PAYPD: BB
35. PENSION PLAN (Y/N)     : X 36. JOB SKILL: XXXXXX
```

Figure 7-7b. MCS payroll package; employee's master F/M—1 Mini-Computer Systems Inc., Elmsford, NY. Reprinted with permission.

```
EMPLOYEE MASTER LISTING                                          RUN DATE  8 / 18 / 77   PAGE  4

LAST NAME  ESPOSITO        SOC SEC NO   010 40 0000    STATUS      A      SALARY/PAY PD      0.00
FIRST      ROBERT          EMPLOYEE ID  010400000      SEX         M      SALARY/ANNUAL      0.00
MIDDLE     BARRY           CORPORATION  10             MARITAL     S      AMT LASTRAISE      2.00
ADDRESS 1  34 EL CAJON BLV.  DIVISION   10             JOB SKILL   FAIR   FOR PPD OF         WW
ADDRESS 2                   PAYROLL                    EEO CODE    1      SHIFT PREMIUM      A
CITY       SAN DIEGO        PAY PERIOD   WW            TERMCODE    0      SHIFT1 HRRATE      4.200
STATE      CA               HOME DEPT    16            EMPL TYPE   H      SHIFT2 DIFF        0.100
ZIP        10977            LOCATION     1             STDDAY/HR   7.00   SHIFT3 DIFF        0.200
HPT        6                UNION NUMER  0             REG SHIFT   1
TELEPHONE  678 346 7898     FEE PAID     N

HIRED  02/13/76   FICA TAX     Y   TAXABLE                     SS      0.00   BOND AMT    1.00   DBL/PPD/ 100%/TX   120.00
BIRTH  02/13/50   SUI/DBL TAX  Y   ADDL FICA                   0.00   FRAC/BAL    0.25   DBL/PPD/ 100%/NT     0.00
ELIG/HOL          STATE  04000     ADDL FED                    0.00   NMBR QTD    0      DBL/PPD/L100%/TX   100.00
ELIG/VAC          LOCAL1 00000     ADDL STATE                  0.00   NMBR YTD    0      DBL/PPD/L100%/NT     0.00
LAST WORKED       LOCAL2 00000     ADDL LOCAL1                 0.00   GARN/TOT    0.00   100% FOR N PPD       5
STARTED/DBL       SUI    04        ADDL LOCAL2                        GARN/PD     0.00   L100% FOR N PPD     10
TERMINATED        DBL    04        VAC/DUE              2      0.00   MISC1QTD    0.00   PPD PAID             0
LAST RAISE 04/12/76  FED/W4  1     SICKLV/DUE           1      0.00   MISC1YTD    0.25   DBL PAID(TX) YTD     0.00
PLANT SR          PERSONAL   1     SEVRNCE/DUE          0      0.00   MISC2YTD    0.00
DEPT SR           DEPENDENTS       SEVRNCE/PD           1      0.00

                  ADDITIONAL

                          DEDUCTIONS   FREQ   TYPE   RATE/AMOUNT            QTD      YTD
QTD HRS 01   40.00            26       1004    A        0.3000            0.00     0.00
        02    0.00            27       1004    R        0.0100            0.00     0.00
        03    0.00            28       0230    A        0.2500            0.25     0.25
        04    0.00            29       1004    A        1.2500            0.00     0.00
        05    0.00            30       0000    N        0.0000            0.00     0.00
        06    0.00            31       0000    N        0.0000            0.00     0.00
        07    0.00            32       1234    A        0.0000            0.00     0.00
        08    0.00            33       1004    A        0.2500            0.25     0.25
YTD HRS 01   40.00            34       1004    A        1.8300            0.00     0.00
        02    0.00            35       0000    N        0.0600            0.00     0.00
        03    0.00            36       0000    N        0.0000            0.00     0.00
        04    0.00            37       0000    N        0.0000            0.00     0.00
        05    0.00            38       0000    N        0.0000            0.00     0.00
        06    0.00            39       0000    N        0.0000           12.80    12.80
        07    0.00            40       0230    A        2.5000            2.50     2.50
        08    0.00

W2 HISTORY                TAXABLE GROSS              TAX WITHHELD
                          QTD       YTD              QTD      YTD
       FICA             170.50    170.50             9.97     9.97
    FEDERAL             170.50    170.50            18.75    18.75
      STATE             170.50    170.50             2.94     2.94
     LOCAL1             170.50    170.50             0.00     0.00
     LOCAL2             170.50    170.50             0.00     0.00
        SUI             170.50    170.50             0.00     0.00
        DBL             170.50    170.50             1.71     1.71

DOES PRIOR STATE RECORD EXIST ?   NO
```

Figure 7-7c. MCS payroll package; employee master listing. Mini-Computer Systems Inc., Elmsford, NY. Reprinted with permission.

```
                              TRANSACTICN REGISTER
                              PAYRCLL CC1 CCNTRCL 33      ENCING 04/07/78                           DATE C5/C2/78   PAGE    1
ELMSFORD TOCL ANC DIE         CCRP 1 CIV 1

                                        FYRL     EMP                                   EARNINGS
                                        TYPE ADJ TYPE                                    CCDE                  AMCLAT
EMPLOYEE #  EMPLOYEE NAME  CCST DEPTH   (RBA) (RC) (HNEO)  SHIFT  HRRATE  S/CIFF  F-CLRS
===========================================================================================================================

11111111    CCLLINS        1            R        H    1    6.CCC   C.CC    10.CC   C3  PREMIUM 2    12C.CC
11111111    CCLLINS        1            R        H    1    5.CCC   C.CC     5.CC   C2  PREMIUM 1    -37.5C
11111111    CCLLINS        1            R        H    1    5.CCC   C.CC    25.CC   C1  REGULAR     125.CC

22222222    BRINKLEY       1            R        E    1    C.CCC   C.CC     C.CC   1C                15.75
22222222    BRINKLEY       1            R        E    1    C.CCC   C.CC     C.CC   11               13C.CC

33333333    RCBINSCN       1            R        H    1    C.CCC   C.CC     C.CC   C9  SEVERANCE   15C.CC
33333333    RCBINSON       1            R        H    1    7.CCO   C.CC    20.CC   C8               14C.CC
```

Figure 7-7d. MCS payroll package; time entry menu. Mini-Computer Systems Inc., Elmsford, NY. Reprinted with permission.

```
                    P A Y R O L L   J O U R N A L                              PAGE:  001
                      ELMSFORD TOOL AND DIE                                     DATE: 04/21/82
            PAYROLL 001 CONTROL 26 PAY PERIOD ENDED 01/14/82                    TIME: 18:33:37
```

360

| SOC SEC NO. | EMPLOYEE NAME | REGULAR | O/T | OTHER | *GROSS PAY | FICA | FEDERAL | STATE | LOCAL | SUI/DBL | TOT DED. | ADDL. NET | *NET PAY |
|---|---|---|---|---|---|---|---|---|---|---|---|---|---|
| | | | | | | | ------ TAXES ------ | | | | | | |
| 090448372 | BLAKE | 1000.00 | | 31.12 | 1031.12 | 51.42 | 320.20 | 118.27 | 4.64 | 0.30 | 15.23 | | 521.06 |
| 124748830 | BRINKLEY | 1000.00 | | 120.00 | 1120.00 | 67.76 | 309.89 | 125.98 | | 0.30 | 15.23 | | 600.84 |
| 010293388 | COLLINS | 150.00 | 87.50 | | 237.50 | 14.37 | 41.58 | 10.23 | 4.09 | 0.30 | 15.23 | | 151.70 |
| DEPT 1 | TOTAL: | 2150.00 | 87.50 | 151.12 | 2388.62 | 133.55 | 671.67 | 254.48 | 8.73 | 0.90 | 45.69 | | 1273.60 |
| 013839271 | BEAUCARTER | 1000.00 | | | 1000.00 | 60.50 | 303.81 | 111.73 | | 0.30 | 15.23 | | 508.43 |
| DEPT 2 | TOTAL: | 1000.00 | | | 1000.00 | 60.50 | 303.81 | 111.73 | | 0.30 | 15.23 | | 508.43 |
| *** REPORT TOTALS *** | | 3150.00 | 87.50 | 151.12 | 3388.62 | 194.05 | 975.48 | 366.21 | 8.73 | 1.20 | 60.92 | | 1782.03 |

Figure 7-7e. MCS payroll package; payroll journal. Mini-Computer Systems Inc., Elmsford, NY. Reprinted with permission.

DEDUCTION REGISTER
PAYROLL 1 FOR PPD ENDING DATE 04/14/78
CORP 1 DIV 1
ELMSFORD TOOL AND DIF
RUN DATE: 05/24/78 PAGE: 1

| EMPLOYEE: SSN | NAME | (26) | (27) | (28) | (29) | (30) | (31) | (32) | (33) | (34) | (35) | (36) | (37) | (38) | (39) | (40) |
|---|---|---|---|---|---|---|---|---|---|---|---|---|---|---|---|---|
| DEPT: 1 | | | | | | | | | | | | | | | | |
| 444444444 | BLAKE | | | | | | | | | | | | | | | |
| 222222222 | BRINKLEY | | | | | | | | | 15.23 | | | | | | |
| DEPT: 2 | | | | | | | | | | | | | | | | |
| 121212121 | BEAUCARTER | 12.89 | | | | | | | | 15.23 | | | | | | |
| 123456789 | LINCOLN | | | | | | | | | 15.23 | | | | | | |
| PAYRCLL 1 PPD TOTAL: | | 12.89 | 0.00 | 0.00 | 0.00 | 0.00 | 0.00 | 0.00 | 0.00 | 60.92 | 0.00 | 0.00 | 0.00 | 0.00 | 0.00 | 0.00 |

Figure 7-7f. MCS payroll package; deduction register. Mini-Computer Systems Inc., Elmsford, NY. Reprinted with permission.

CHECK REGISTER
BANK ACCOUNT SEQUENCE NO.   10
RUN DATE .8 / 18 / 77 PAGE 1

| CHECK NO. | AMOUNT | EMPLOYEE NO. | LAST NAME | CHECK DATE | STATUS (NON/A) | CORP | PAYROLL | CONTROL | SUB-TOTAL |
|---|---|---|---|---|---|---|---|---|---|
| 1001 | 0.00 | | ** ALIGNMENT * | 08/19/77 | | 10 | 10 | 37 | |
| 1002 | 197.82 | 010300000 | DECKER | 08/19/77 | | 10 | 10 | 37 | |
| 1003 | 246.19 | 010100000 | DOE | 08/19/77 | | 10 | 10 | 37 | |
| 1004 | 124.53 | 010400000 | ESPOSITO | 08/19/77 | | 10 | 10 | 37 | |
| 1005 | 182.14 | 010200000 | SMITH | 08/19/77 | | 10 | 10 | 37 | 750.68 |

BANK ACCOUNT TOTALS:   NMBR OF CHECKS   5   NMBR OF VOIDS   1   TOTAL AMOUNT: 750.68

Figure 7-7g. MCS payroll package; check register. Mini-Computer Systems Inc., Elmsford, NY. Reprinted with permission.

CORP: 1    DIV: 1
ELMSFORD TOOL AND DIE
525 EXECUTIVE BLVD

ELMSFORD    NY   10503
FEDERAL REG #: 96508725

STOCK 941A REPORT    RUN DATE  5 / 24 / 82    PAGE  1

STATE    : NEW YORK
UIB $ LIMIT: 6000
FUTA$ LIMIT: 6000
UIB#    : 863489

| EMPLOYEE SOC SEC # | EMPLOYEE NAME LAST | FIRST | TAX.FICA QUARTERLY WAGES | TOTAL QUARTERLY WAGES | TOTAL Y-T-D WAGES | FUTA QUARTERLY TAX.WAGES | STATE UIB QUARTERLY TAX.WAGES | STATE Q-T-D WAGES | STATE Y-T-D WAGES | CS |
|---|---|---|---|---|---|---|---|---|---|---|
| 090 11 2468 | COLLINS | THOMAS | 507.50 | 507.50 | 2330.63 | 507.50 | 507.50 | 507.50 | 2330.63 | 31 |
| 121 29 2292 | BEAUCARTER | GEORGE | 2000.00 | 2000.00 | 9000.00 | 0.00 | 0.00 | 2000.00 | 9000.00 | 31 |
| 230 45 6980 | LINCOLN | STEVE | 1000.00 | 1000.00 | 1000.00 | 1000.00 | 1000.00 | 1000.00 | 1000.00 | 31 |
| 049 27 4482 | BRINKLEY | JAMES | 0.00 | 2145.75 | 23236.00 | 0.00 | 0.00 | 2145.75 | 23236.00 | 31 |
| 030 66 8290 | ROBINSON | GORDON | 500.00 | 500.00 | 8137.50 | 0.00 | 0.00 | 500.00 | 8137.50 | 31 |
| 480 42 0934 | BLAKE | SUSAN | 0.00 | 3300.00 | 25181.12 | 0.00 | 0.00 | 3300.00 | 25181.95 | 31 |
| 060 14 3571 | LOGGINS | ANDY | 1516.66 | 1516.66 | 11584.95 | 0.00 | 0.00 | 1516.66 | 11584.95 | 31 |
| 039 22 4331 | SAVITCH | JOHN | 1300.00 | 1300.00 | 10500.00 | 0.00 | 0.00 | 1300.00 | 10500.00 | 31 |
| 090 58 1930 | GREENE | JACOB | 1766.66 | 1766.66 | 13228.75 | 0.00 | 0.00 | 1766.66 | 13228.75 | 31 |

PAGE TOTALS:   NUMBER OF EMPLOYEES:   9     8590.82    14036.57   104198.95    1507.50    1507.50    14036.57   104198.95
STATE TOTALS:  NUMBER OF EMPLOYEES:   9     8590.82    14036.57   104198.95    1507.50    1507.50    14036.57   104198.95
CORP TOTALS:   NUMBER OF EMPLOYEES:   9     8590.82    14036.57   104190.95    1507.50    1507.50    14036.57   104198.95

Figure 7-7h. MCS payroll package; stock 941A report. Mini-Computer Systems Inc., Elmsford, NY. Reprinted with permission.

CORP: 1   DIV: 1   PAYROLL QUARTERLY EARNINGS   RUN DATE: 03/23/78   PAGE: 1

| DATE | GROSS WAGES | FEDERAL | FICA | STATE | SUI | DBL | LOC1 | LOC2 | ADD. NET | DEDUCTIONS | NET PAY |
|---|---|---|---|---|---|---|---|---|---|---|---|
| EMPLOYEE NAME: COLLINS THOMAS | | | | PAYROLL NO: 1 | | | | | | | |
| | | | | SSN: 111 11 1111 | | | | | | | |
| 010778 | 200.00 | 31.88 | 12.10 | 7.97 | 0.00 | 0.30 | 2.00 | 0.00 | 0.00 | 0.00 | 145.75 |
| 010773 | 212.50 | 34.88 | 12.86 | 8.71 | 0.00 | 0.30 | 3.56 | 0.00 | 0.00 | 15.23 | 136.96 |
| QTD | 412.50 | 66.76 | 24.96 | 16.68 | 0.00 | 0.60 | 5.56 | 0.00 | 0.00 | 15.23 | 282.71 |
| YTD | 412.50 | 66.76 | 24.96 | 16.68 | 0.00 | 0.60 | 5.56 | 0.00 | 0.00 | 15.23 | |
| EMPLOYEE NAME: BRINKLEY JAMES | | | | PAYROLL NO: 1 | | | | | | | |
| | | | | SSN: 222 22 2222 | | | | | | | |
| 022578 | 1000.00 | 266.69 | 60.50 | 107.98 | 0.00 | 0.30 | 0.00 | 0.00 | 0.00 | 15.23 | 549.30 |
| 021878 | 1000.00 | 266.69 | 60.50 | 107.98 | 0.00 | 0.30 | 0.00 | 0.00 | 0.00 | 15.23 | 549.30 |
| 021173 | 1000.00 | 266.69 | 60.50 | 107.98 | 0.00 | 0.30 | 0.00 | 0.00 | 0.00 | 15.23 | 549.30 |
| 020478 | 1000.00 | 266.69 | 60.50 | 107.98 | 0.00 | 0.30 | 0.00 | 0.00 | 0.00 | 15.23 | 549.30 |
| 012378 | 1000.00 | 266.69 | 60.50 | 107.98 | 0.00 | 0.30 | 0.00 | 0.00 | 0.00 | 15.23 | 549.30 |
| 012178 | 1000.00 | 266.69 | 60.50 | 107.98 | 0.00 | 0.30 | 0.00 | 0.00 | 0.00 | 15.23 | 549.30 |
| 011478 | 1000.00 | 266.69 | 60.50 | 107.98 | 0.00 | 0.30 | 0.00 | 0.00 | 0.00 | 15.23 | 549.30 |
| 010778 | 1000.00 | 266.69 | 60.50 | 107.98 | 0.00 | 0.30 | 0.00 | 0.00 | 0.00 | 15.23 | 549.30 |
| 010778 | 200.00 | 15.98 | 12.10 | 5.62 | 0.00 | 0.30 | 0.00 | 0.00 | 0.00 | 0.00 | 166.00 |
| QTD | 8200.00 | 2149.50 | 496.10 | 869.46 | 0.00 | 2.70 | 0.00 | 0.00 | 0.00 | 121.84 | 4560.40 |
| YTD | 8200.00 | 2149.50 | 496.10 | 869.46 | 0.00 | 2.70 | 0.00 | 0.00 | 0.00 | 121.84 | |
| EMPLOYEE NAME: ROBINSON SUGAR | | | | PAYROLL NO: 1 | | | | | | | |
| | | | | SSN: 333 33 3333 | | | | | | | |
| 022078 | 1000.00 | 500.00 | 60.50 | 400.00 | 0.00 | 0.30 | 39.20 | 0.00 | 0.00 | 0.00 | 0.00 |
| 021878 | 1000.00 | 42.00 | 60.50 | 43.00 | 0.00 | 0.30 | 44.00 | 0.00 | 0.00 | 0.00 | 810.20 |
| 021873 | 297.50 | 58.39 | 18.00 | 15.02 | 0.00 | 0.30 | 5.68 | 0.00 | 0.00 | 15.23 | 184.88 |
| 021178 | 297.50 | 58.39 | 18.00 | 15.02 | 0.00 | 0.30 | 5.68 | 0.00 | 0.00 | 15.23 | 184.88 |
| 021178 | 1000.00 | 309.00 | 60.50 | 113.60 | 0.00 | 0.30 | 34.19 | 0.00 | 0.00 | 0.00 | 482.41 |
| 020478 | 1000.00 | 0.00 | 18.00 | 20.00 | 0.00 | 0.30 | 0.00 | 0.00 | 0.00 | 0.00 | 919.20 |
| 020473 | 297.50 | 58.39 | 18.00 | 15.02 | 0.00 | 0.30 | 0.00 | 0.00 | 0.00 | 15.23 | 190.56 |
| 012878 | 297.50 | 58.39 | 18.00 | 15.02 | 0.00 | 0.30 | 0.00 | 0.00 | 0.00 | 15.23 | 190.56 |
| 012878 | 1000.00 | 200.00 | 60.50 | 113.60 | 0.00 | 0.30 | 0.00 | 0.00 | 0.00 | 0.00 | 625.60 |
| 012178 | 297.50 | 58.39 | 18.00 | 15.02 | 0.00 | 0.30 | 0.00 | 0.00 | 0.00 | 15.23 | 190.56 |
| 011478 | 1000.00 | 200.00 | 60.50 | 113.60 | 0.00 | 0.30 | 0.00 | 0.00 | 0.00 | 0.00 | 625.60 |
| QTD | 7487.50 | 1542.95 | 453.00 | 878.90 | 0.00 | 3.30 | 128.75 | 0.00 | 0.00 | 76.15 | 4404.45 |
| YTD | 7487.50 | 1000.95 | 453.00 | 435.90 | 0.00 | 3.30 | 45.55 | 0.00 | 0.00 | 76.15 | |
| EMPLOYEE NAME: BLAKE SUSAN | | | | PAYROLL NO: 1 | | | | | | | |
| | | | | SSN: 444 44 4444 | | | | | | | |
| 022578 | 1000.00 | 309.00 | 60.50 | 113.60 | 0.00 | 0.30 | 4.50 | 0.00 | 0.00 | 15.23 | 496.87 |
| 022078 | 1000.00 | 900.00 | 60.50 | 39.20 | 0.00 | 0.30 | 0.00 | 0.00 | 0.00 | 0.00 | 0.00 |
| 021873 | 1000.00 | 42.00 | 60.50 | 43.00 | 0.00 | 0.30 | 44.00 | 0.00 | 0.00 | 0.00 | 810.20 |
| 021878 | 500.00 | 129.00 | 30.25 | 38.67 | 0.00 | 0.30 | 2.16 | 0.00 | 0.00 | 15.23 | 284.39 |
| 021178 | 500.00 | 129.00 | 30.25 | 38.67 | 0.00 | 0.30 | 2.16 | 0.00 | 0.00 | 15.23 | 284.39 |
| 021178 | 1000.00 | 309.00 | 60.50 | 113.60 | 0.00 | 0.30 | 4.50 | 0.00 | 0.00 | 15.23 | 512.10 |
| 020479 | 1000.00 | 0.00 | 60.50 | 20.00 | 0.00 | 0.30 | 0.00 | 0.00 | 0.00 | 0.00 | 919.20 |
| 020478 | 500.00 | 129.00 | 30.25 | 38.67 | 0.00 | 0.30 | 0.00 | 0.00 | 0.00 | 15.23 | 286.55 |
| 012878 | 500.00 | 129.00 | 30.25 | 38.67 | 0.00 | 0.30 | 0.00 | 0.00 | 0.00 | 15.23 | 286.55 |
| 012878 | 1000.00 | 200.00 | 60.50 | 113.60 | 0.00 | 0.30 | 0.00 | 0.00 | 0.00 | 0.00 | 625.60 |
| 012173 | 500.00 | 129.00 | 30.25 | 38.67 | 0.00 | 0.30 | 0.00 | 0.00 | 0.00 | 15.23 | 286.55 |

Figure 7-7i. MCS payroll package; quarterly earnings report. Mini-Computer Systems Inc., Elmsford, NY. Reprinted with permission.

```
CHECK RECONCILIATION REPORT                                              RUN DATE  8 / 18 / 77   PAGE  1
BANK ACCOUNT SEQUENCE NUMBER -  10
```

| CHECK # | PAYROLL# | CONTROL# | CORP | DIV | EMPLOYEE# | LAST NAME | CHECK DATE | STATUS (O/A/V/C/M) | STATUS DATE | CHECK AMOUNT |
|---|---|---|---|---|---|---|---|---|---|---|
| 1001 | 010 | 37 | 10 | 10 | 010300000 | DECKER | 08/19/77 | A | 08/19/77 | 0.00 |
| 1002 | 010 | 37 | 10 | 10 | 010100000 | DOE | 08/19/77 | O | | 197.82 |
| 1003 | 010 | 37 | 10 | 10 | 010400000 | ESPOSITO | 08/19/77 | O | | 246.19 |
| 1004 | 010 | 37 | 10 | 10 | 010200000 | SMITH | 08/19/77 | O | | 124.53 |
| 1005 | 010 | 37 | 10 | 10 | | | 08/19/77 | O | | 182.14 |

```
* TOTALS FOR BANK ACCOUNT  -  10 *

FROM CHECK #     TO CHECK #

   1001             1005

TOTAL O (OUTSTANDING)    4      750.68
      V (VOID)           0        0.00
      C (CLEARED)        0        0.00
      M (MISSING)        0        0.00
      A (ALIGNMENT)      1        0.00
```

Figure 7-7j. MCS payroll package; check reconciliation report. Mini-Computer Systems Inc., Elmsford, NY. Reprinted with permission.

play employee earnings records; to purge the employee master file; and to audit the master and earnings file interrelationship for integrity. Figure 7–7B lists the 36 kinds of information the system records for each employee while Figure 7–7C displays an employee's master listing with all this information as well as payroll transaction data.

**5. Time Entry Menu.** This menu contains those functions relating to the entry of pay period transactions, adjustments, and related register report. A transaction register is presented in Figure 7–7D.

**6. Payroll Calculation (Pay Calc).** A separate menu is not required for Pay Calc since there is only one *response required* screen for this transaction. The user selects Pay Calc from the main menu when balanced payroll batches are ready for processing.

**7. Checks and PPd. Reports Menu.** This menu contains all of the functions relating to the processing of checks (except reconciliations) and the printing of pay period reports. Samples of two of these reports, the "Payroll Journal" and the "Deduction Register," are presented in Figures 7–7E and 7–7F, while the "Check Register" is shown in Figure 7–7G.

**8. End of Month Menu.** This menu is used only by customers who post their general ledger manually and who must therefore update the system control file by simulating automated posting.

**9. End of Quarter Menu.** This menu contains programs to produce the 941a reports(s) and initialize the quarter-to-date accumulators. Figure 7–7H illustrates a "Stock 941a" report, while a report of "Payroll Quarterly Earnings" is shown in Figure 7–7I.

**10. End of Year Menu.** This menu contains programs to produce the W2 forms and initialize the year-to-date accumulators.

**11. On Demand Menu.** This menu provides programs to alter the status of check reconciliation file records and print a formatted status report of that file, as shown in Figure 7–7J.

**B. Accounts Payable Package.**   The accounts payable main menu serves as the vehicle through which the specialized function menus are accesed. The access sequence to a particular program or function is always:

1. main menu
2. specialized menu
3. individual program or function

The sequence is reversed when a particular task is completed and another task must be initiated. The specialized menus of the "Accounts Payable" system are described briefly below.

**1. Vendor Menu.** This menu provides for vendor file maintenance and produces various master file lists. For example, Figure 7–8A is a listing of the vendor file in vendor code (numerical) sequence.

**2. Invoice Menu.** This menu contains all of the functions relating to the entry of vendor invoices. The output from this menu is the "Daily Purchase Journal," shown in Figure 7–8B.

VENDOR NUMERICAL LISTING

PAGE 0001
DATE 09/11/78
TIME 12:13:48

| VEND# | STCD | VT | VENDOR NAME | ADDRESS 1 | ADDRESS 2 | ADDRESS 3 | L T DATE |
|-------|------|----|-------------|-----------|-----------|-----------|----------|
| 111000 | JACK | P | JACKSON ELECTRICAL SUPPLI | ATTN: ACCOUNTS RECEIVABLE | 512 WEST 42ND ST. | NEW YORK, NY 22001 | 06/29/78 |
| 111111 | SANF | P | SANFORD TRANPORTATION | ATTN: ACCOUNTS RECEIVABLE | 56 WATER STREET | NEWBURG, NY 00678 | 06/29/78 |
| 222000 | FRED | P | FREDERICS PLUMBING | ATTN: ACCOUNTS RECEIVABLE | 45 WICKHAM AVENUE | MIDDLETOWN, NY 10940 | 06/29/78 |
| 222111 | KORM | P | KORMAN FURNITURE & FIXTUR | ATTN: ACCOUNTS RECEIVABLE | 456 BROADWAY | MONTICELLO, NY 45612 | 06/29/78 |
| 666000 | FERN | P | FERDINING UPHOLSTERY | 155 HOWARD DRIVE | SECAUCUS, NJ 05678 | | 06/30/78 |
| 666111 | ALBE | P | ALBERTS WAREHOUSES | ATTN: ACCOUNTS RECEIVABLE | 123 WEST 42ND ST | NEW YORK, NY 10566 | 09/13/78 |
| 777111 | HAST | P | HASTINGS REPAIRS | ATTN: ACCOUNTS RECEIVABLE | 55 MAPLE DRIVE | HASTINGS, NY 10566 | 09/13/78 |

Figure 7-8a. MCS A/P package; vendor numerical listing. Mini-Computer Systems Inc., Elmsford, NY. Reprinted with permission.

```
CORP: 11    MINI COMPUTER SYSTEMS              A/P  DAILY  PURCHASES JOURNAL                          PAGE:  1
                                                    AS OF: 02/28/82                                   DATE: 03/01/82
                                                                                                      TIME: 11:55:04
                                                                              ------- DEBITS -------  ------- CREDITS -------
VENDOR#  INVOICE#   INV DATE  DESCRIPTION           TERMS       AGE  CORP#  G/L ACCOUNT#    AMOUNT   G/L ACCOUNT#    AMOUNT
                    VENDOR NAME
=======  ========  =========  ====================  ==========  ===  =====  ============  =========  ============  =========
11000    1000-1    02/16/82   TRANSISTORS: X-PF100  2/10NET30    0    11        5060        234.89       2001        234.89
11000    1000-2    02/17/82   RETURNED CONECTORS    2/10NET30    0    22        5060        100.00-      2001        100.45-
                                                                      11        5060        100.45-
                                                                      22        2500        100.00-
                                                                      11        2500        100.00-
                                                                                             34.44
         ***  EASTCOAST SUPPLIERS      *  VENDOR TOTAL:

11111    11111-1   02/16/82   WAREHOUSE SHELVES     NET CASH     0    11        5000        789.33       2003        789.33
11111    11111-2   02/19/82   GHERKINS             2/10NET30     0    11        5080          6.89       2001        456.89
                                                                      11        5060        450.00
11111    11111-3   02/20/82   UNIFORMS              NET CASH     0    11        5080         20.00       2001        300.89
                                                                      11        5060        280.89
                                                                                           1547.11
         ***  PUTNAM UNIFORM           *  VENDOR TOTAL:

11222    11222-0   02/15/82   BOILERS              2/10NET30     0    11        5020       4500.67       2002       4500.67
                                                                                           4500.67
         ***  TUTTLE SUPPLY            *  VENDOR TOTAL:

                              *  CORPORATION TOTAL:  CURRENT                                6082.22                  6082.22
                              *  CORPORATION TOTAL:  FUTURES                                   0.00                     0.00
                              *  CORPORATION TOTAL:  BOTH                                   6082.22                  6082.22
```

Figure 7-8b. MCS A/P package; A/P daily purchases journal. Mini-Computer Systems Inc., Elmsford, NY. Reprinted with permission.

BANK NO : 1 CHASE MANHATTAN

A/P CHECK RECONCILIATION
FROM: 00000025 TO: 00000047

PAGE: 0001
RUN DATE: 04/15/82
TIME: 17:10:12

| CHECK NO. | CORP | VENDOR NO. | PAYEE NAME | CHECK DATE | TP | ST | CLEAR OR VD. DATE | VOID REASON | CHECK AMOUNT CLEAR | OUTSTANDING |
|===|===|===|===|===|===|===|===|===|===|===|
| 00000025 | 11 | 11000 | ALEXANDER'S | 02/17/82 | C | V | 02/20/82 | FFFFF | 25.98 | |
| 00000025 | 11 | 11000 | ALEXANDER'S | 02/17/82 | C | V | 02/20/82 | FFFFF | 25.98- | |
| 00000026 | 11 | 11111 | ALEXANDER'S | 02/17/82 | C | V | 02/20/82 | FFFFF | 1556.41 | |
| 00000026 | 11 | 11111 | ALEXANDER'S | 02/17/82 | C | V | 02/20/82 | FFFFF | 1556.41- | |
| 00000027 | 11 | 11222 | JACKSON ELECTRICAL SUPPL. | 02/17/82 | C | V | 02/17/82 | DFFFF | 778.88 | |
| 00000027 | 11 | 11222 | JACKSON ELECTRICAL SUPPL. | 02/17/82 | C | V | 02/17/82 | DFFFF | 778.88- | |
| 00000028 | 22 | 22000 | RICHARD DOPPINS & SON | 02/17/82 | C | V | 02/17/82 | CR/DR OFFS | 778.88- | |
| 00000029 | 11 | 11222 | JACKSON ELECTRICAL SUPPL. | 02/20/82 | C | V | 04/15/82 | JHJJJ | 776.88 | |
| 00000029 | 11 | 11222 | JACKSON ELECTRICAL SUPPL. | 02/20/82 | C | V | 04/15/82 | JHJJJ | 776.88- | |
| 00000030 | 11 | 11222 | JACKSON ELECTRICAL SUPPL. | 02/20/82 | C | V | 03/15/82 | GGFGG | 0.87 | |
| 00000030 | 11 | 11222 | JACKSON ELECTRICAL SUPPL. | 02/20/82 | C | V | 03/15/82 | GGFGG | 0.87- | |
| 00000031 | 11 | 11000 | ALEXANDER'S | 02/20/82 | C | V | 02/20/82 | CR/DR OFFS | 0.87- | |
| 00000032 | 22 | 22000 | RICHARD DOBBINS & SON | 02/20/82 | C | V | 04/15/82 | GHHGGH | 66967.40 | |
| 00000032 | 22 | 22000 | RICHARD DOBBINS & SON | 02/20/82 | C | V | 04/15/82 | GHHGGH | 66967.40- | |
| 00000033 | 11 | 11111 | FREDERICKS BOYS WEAR | 02/22/82 | M | V | 04/15/82 | GGGGG | 984.00 | |
| 00000033 | 11 | 11111 | FREDERICKS BOYS WEAR | 02/22/82 | M | V | 04/15/82 | GGGGG | 984.00- | |
| 00000034 | 11 | 11222 | JACKSON ELECTRICAL SUPPL. | 02/22/82 | M | V | 04/15/82 | HHHH | 555.34 | |
| 00000034 | 11 | 11222 | JACKSON ELECTRICAL SUPPL. | 02/22/82 | M | V | 04/15/82 | HHHH | 555.34- | |
| 00000035 | 11 | 11222 | JACKSON ELECTRICAL SUPPL. | 02/22/82 | M | V | 03/15/82 | CR/DR OFFS | 555.34- | |
| 00000036 | 22 | 22000 | RICHARD DOBBINS & SON | 03/15/82 | C | V | 04/15/82 | HGDSA | 5673.13 | |
| 00000036 | 22 | 22000 | RICHARD DOBBINS & SON | 03/15/82 | C | V | 04/15/82 | HGDSA | 5673.13- | |
| 00000037 | 22 | 22111 | THE GAMMA CORPORATION | 03/15/82 | C | V | 04/15/82 | GHDDD | 2625.41 | |
| 00000037 | 22 | 22111 | THE GAMMA CORPORATION | 03/15/82 | C | V | 04/15/82 | GHDDD | 2625.41- | |
| 00000038 | 11 | 11000 | ALEXANDER'S | 03/16/82 | C | V | 04/15/82 | KKKKK | 200.00 | |
| 00000038 | 11 | 11000 | ALEXANDER'S | 03/16/82 | C | V | 04/15/82 | KKKKK | 200.00- | |
| 00000039 | 11 | 11111 | ALEXANDER'S | 03/16/82 | C | V | 04/15/82 | KKLII | 1567.77 | |
| 00000039 | 11 | 11111 | ALEXANDER'S | 03/16/82 | C | V | 04/15/82 | KKLII | 1567.77- | |
| 00000040 | 11 | 11222 | JACKSON ELECTRICAL SUPPL. | 03/16/82 | C | V | 04/15/82 | JJJJJ | 13.91 | |
| 00000040 | 11 | 11222 | JACKSON ELECTRICAL SUPPL. | 03/16/82 | C | V | 04/15/82 | JJJJJ | 13.91- | |
| 00000041 | 11 | 11333 | ALFREDS' FURNITURE | 03/16/82 | C | V | 04/15/82 | HGDDS | 664.67 | |
| 00000041 | 11 | 11333 | ALFREDS' FURNITURE | 03/16/82 | C | V | 04/15/82 | HGDDS | 664.67- | |
| 00000042 | 11 | 11000 | ALEXANDER'S | 04/15/82 | C | O | | | | 200.00 |
| 00000043 | 11 | 11111 | ALEXANDER'S | 04/15/82 | C | O | | | | 2567.77 |
| 00000044 | 11 | 11222 | JACKSON ELECTRICAL SUPPL. | 04/15/82 | C | O | | | | 1357.46 |
| 00000045 | 11 | 11333 | ALFREDS FURNITURE | 04/15/82 | C | O | | | | 678.23 |
| 00000046 | 22 | 22000 | RICHARD DOBBINS & SON | 04/15/82 | C | O | | | | 72679.03 |
| 00000047 | 22 | 22111 | THE GAMMA CORPORATION | 04/15/82 | C | O | | | | 2678.99 |

BANK TOTALS: CHECKS: 37 CLEAR: 31 OUTSTANDING: 6 AMOUNTS: 0.00 80161.48

Figure 7-8c. MCS A/P package; A/P check reconciliation. Mini-Computer Systems, Inc., Elmsford, NY. Reprinted with permission.

BANK NO  1  CHASE MANHATTAN  
CORP:  11    MINI COMPUTER SYSTEMS

DAILY DISBURSEMENTS JOURNAL  
AS OF: 02/16/78

PAGE: 0001  
RUN DATE: 02/16/78  
TIME: 11:21:58

| CHECK NO. | CHECK DATE | TYPE VF | VOID DATE | VENDOR NO. | PAYEE NAME | INVOICE NO. | G/L ACCOUNT DEBITED | INVOICE AMT. DR. | DISCOUNT CR. | CASH CR. |
|---|---|---|---|---|---|---|---|---|---|---|
| 06000018 | 021678 | C | | 11111 | GOODMAN'S ELECTRONICS | 11111-1 | 2003 | 789.33 | 21.49 | 1061.31 |
| | | | | | | 11111-3 | 2001 | 300.89 | 7.42 | |
| 00000019 | 021678 | C | | 11222 | JACKSON ELECTRICAL SUPPL. | 11222-0 | 2002 | 4500.67 | 900.13 | 3600.54 |
| | | | | | | | BALANCES: | 5590.89 | 929.04 | 4461.85 |

CORPORATION TOTAL:        # CHECKS PD    AMOUNT PD    # CHECKS VD.    AMOUNT VD.  
                     4661.85        2      4661.85        0         0.00

Figure 7-8d. MCS A/P package; daily disbursements journal. Mini-Computer Systems Inc., Elmsford, NY. Reprinted with permission.

CORP: 11    MINI COMPUTER SYSTEMS

CASH REQUIREMENTS REPORT   PAY THRU DATE: 04/25/82  
SELECTIVITY CODE: 0  (0=DISC DT/1=DUE DT)

PAGE: 001  
RUN DATE: 02/16/82  
TIME: 10.55:32

| VENDOR# | VENDOR NAME | DATES | | | INVOICE# | AMOUNTS | | | CASH RECED (ROLLING) |
|---|---|---|---|---|---|---|---|---|---|
| | | DUE | DISC | INVOICE | | OPEN$ | DISCOUNT$ | PAYMENT$ | |
| 11030 | GOODMAN'S ELECTRONICS | 03/18/82 | 02/26/82 | 02/16/82 | 11000-1 | 234.89 | 4.70 | 230.19 * | 230.19 |
| | | 03/19/82 | 02/27/82 | 02/17/82 | 11000-2 | 200.45- | 4.01- | 196.44- * | 33.75 |
| 11111 | ALFRED GARMENT | 02/16/82 | 02/16/82 | 02/16/82 | 11111-1 | 789.33 | 21.49 | 767.84 * | 767.84 |
| | | 02/20/82 | 02/20/82 | 02/20/82 | 11111-0 | 300.89 | 7.42 | 298.47 * | 1061.31 |
| | | 03/21/82 | 02/01/82 | 02/19/82 | 11111-2 | 456.89 | 9.00 | 447.89 * | 1509.20 |
| 11222 | JACKSON ELECTRICAL SUPPL. | 03/17/82 | 02/25/82 | 02/15/82 | 11222-0 | 4500.67 | 900.13 | 3600.54 * | 3600.54 |
| | COMPANY TOTAL | *********** | | | | 6082.22 | 938.73 | 5143.49 | 5143.49 |

Figure 7-8e. MCS A/P package; cash requirements report. Mini-Computer Systems Inc., Elmsford, NY. Reprinted with permission.

CORP: 11     MINI COMPUTER SYSTEMS

A/P AGED OPEN ITEMS REPORT
AGED AS OF 02/16/78

PAGE: 0001
RUN DATE: 02/16/78
TIME: 11:25:12

| VENDOR | VENDOR NAME | INV DATE | INVOICE NO | CURRENT | 30 DAYS | 45 DAYS | 60 DAYS | 90 DAYS | OVER 120 |
|---|---|---|---|---|---|---|---|---|---|
| 11000 | GOODMAN'S ELECTRONICS | 02/16/78 | 11000-1 | 234.89 | | | | | |
| | | 02/17/78 | 11000-2 | 200.45- | | | | | |
| | VENDOR TOTAL: | | | 34.44 | 0.00 | 0.00 | 0.00 | 0.00 | 0.00 |
| 11111 | ALFRED GARMENT | 02/19/78 | 11111-2 | 456.89 | | | | | |
| | VENDOR TOTAL: | | | 456.89 | 0.00 | 0.00 | 0.00 | 0.00 | 0.00 |
| | CORPORATION TOTAL: | | | 491.33 | 0.00 | 0.00 | 0.00 | 0.00 | 0.00 |

Figure 7-8f. MCS A/P package; A/P aged open items report: detailed. Mini-Computer Systems Inc., Elmsford, NY. Reprinted with permission.

CORP: 11     MINI COMPUTER SYSTEMS

ACCOUNTS PAYABLE LEDGER
AS OF: 02/28/78

PAGE: 0001
RUN DATE: 02/16/78
TIME: 12:06:09

| VENDOR NO. | VENDOR NAME | OPENING BALANCE | TRANS. DATE | CHECK# | DEBITS PAYMENT$ | DISCOUNT$ | CREDITS INVOICE NO. | INVOICE $ | CLOSING BALANCE |
|---|---|---|---|---|---|---|---|---|---|
| 11000 | GOODMAN'S ELECTRONICS | 0.00 | | | | | | | |
| | | | 02/16/78 | | | | 11000-1 | 234.89 | 234.89 |
| | | | 02/16/78 | | | | 11000-2 | 200.45- | 34.44 |
| | TOTAL VENDOR: | | | | | | | 34.44 | 34.44 |
| 11111 | ALFRED GARMENT | 0.00 | | | | | | | |
| | | | 02/16/78 | | | | 11111-1 | 789.33 | 789.33 |
| | | | 02/16/78 | | | | 11111-2 | 456.89 | 1246.22 |
| | | | 02/16/78 | | | | 11111-3 | 300.89 | 1547.11 |
| | | | 02/16/78 | 18 | 1061.31 | 28.91 | | 1547.11 | 456.89 |
| | TOTAL VENDOR: | | | | 1061.31 | 28.91 | | | 456.89 |
| 11222 | JACKSON ELECTRICAL SUPPL. | 0.00 | | | | | | | |
| | | | 02/16/78 | 19 | 3600.54 | 900.13 | 11222-0 | 4500.67 | 4500.67 |
| | TOTAL VENDOR: | | | | 3600.54 | 900.13 | | 4500.67 | 0.00 |
| 11333 | JACK SMITH | 0.00 | | | | | | | |
| | TOTAL VENDOR: | | | | | | | | 0.00 |
| | TOTAL CORPORATION: | 0.00 | | | 4661.85 | 929.04 | | 6082.22 | 491.33 |

Figure 7-8g. MCS A/P package; accounts payable ledger. Mini-Computer Systems Inc., Elmsford, NY. Reprinted with permission.

| VENDOR# | INVOICE# | INV DATE VENDOR NAME | DESCRIPTION | TERMS | AGE | CORP# | ------ DEBITS ------ G/L ACCOUNT# | AMOUNT | ------ CREDITS ------ G/L ACCOUNT# | AMOUNT |
|---|---|---|---|---|---|---|---|---|---|---|
| 11000 | 1000-1 | 02/16/82 | TRANSISTORS: X-PF100 | 2/10NET30 | 0 | 11 | 5060 | 234.89 | 2001 | 234.89 |
| 11000 | 1000-2 | 02/17/82 | RETURNED CONECTORS | 2/10NET30 | 0 | 22 | 5060 | 100.00- | 2001 | 100.45- |
|  |  |  |  |  |  | 11 | 5060 | 100.45- |  |  |
|  |  |  |  |  |  | 22 | 2500 | 100.00- |  |  |
|  |  |  |  |  |  | 11 | 2500 | 34.44 |  |  |
| *** GOODMAN'S ELECTRONICS | * VENDOR TOTAL: |  |  |  |  |  |  |  |  |  |
| 11111 | 11111-1 | 02/16/82 | WAREHOUSE SHELVES | NET CASH | 0 | 11 | 5000 | 789.33 | 2003 | 789.33 |
| 11111 | 11111-2 | 02/19/82 | GHERKINS | 2/10NET30 | 0 | 11 | 5080 | 6.89 | 2001 | 456.89 |
|  |  |  |  |  |  | 11 | 5060 | 450.00 |  |  |
| 11111 | 11111-3 | 02/20/82 | UNIFORMS | NET CASH | 0 | 11 | 5080 | 20.00 | 2001 | 300.89 |
|  |  |  |  |  |  | 11 | 5060 | 280.89 |  |  |
|  |  |  |  |  |  |  |  | 1547.11 |  |  |
| *** ALFRED GARMENT | * VENDOR TOTAL: |  |  |  |  |  |  |  |  |  |
| 11222 | 11222-0 | 02/15/82 | BOILERS | 2/10NET30 | 0 | 11 | 5020 | 4500.67 | 2002 | 4500.67 |
| *** JACKSON ELECTRICAL SUPPL. | * VENDOR TOTAL: |  |  |  |  |  |  | 4500.67 |  |  |

|  |  |  |  |  |  |
|---|---|---|---|---|---|
| * | CORPORATION TOTAL: | CURRENT | 6082.22 |  | 6082.22 |
| ** | CORPORATION TOTAL: | FUTURES | 0.00 |  | 0.00 |
| * | CORPORATION TOTAL: | BOTH | 6082.22 |  | 6082.22 |

Figure 7-8h. MCS A/P Monthy purchases journal. package; A/P Mini-Computer Systems Inc., Elmsford, NY. Reprinted with permission.

BANK NO 1 CHASE MANHATTAN  
CORP: 11 MINI COMPUTER SYSTEMS  

MONTHLY DISBURSEMENTS JOURNAL  
AS OF: 02/28/78  

PAGE: 0001  
RUN DATE: 02/16/78  
TIME: 11:59:33  

| CHECK NO. | CHECK DATE | TYPE VF | VOID DATE | VENDOR NO. | PAYEE NAME | INVOICE NO. | G/L ACCOUNT DEBITED | INVOICE AMT. DR. | DISCOUNT CR. | CASH CR. |
|---|---|---|---|---|---|---|---|---|---|---|
| 00000018 | 021678 | C | | 11111 | GOODMAN'S ELECTRONICS | 11111-1 | 2003 | 789.33 | 21.49 | 1061.31 |
| | | | | | | 11111-3 | 2001 | 300.89 | 7.42 | |
| 00000019 | 021678 | C | | 11222 | JACKSON ELECTRICAL SUPPL. | 11222-0 | 2002 | 4500.67 | 900.13 | 3600.54 |
| CORPORATION TOTAL: | | | | | | | | 5590.89 | 929.04 | 4661.85 |

# CHECKS PD 2    # CHECKS VD 0    AMOUNT PD. 4661.85    AMOUNT VD. 0.00    BALANCES: 0.00

Figure 7-8i. MCS A/P package; monthly disbursements journal. Mini-Computer Systems Inc., Elmsford, NY. Reprinted with permission.

CORP: 11    MINI COMPUTER SYSTEMS  

A/P EXPENSE DISTRIBUTION REPORT  
AS OF: 02/28/78  

PAGE: 0001  
RUN DATE: 02/16/78  
TIME: 12:01:49  

| ACCOUNT# | ACCOUNT NAME | VENDOR# | VENDOR NAME | INVOICE# | EXPENSE DR AMOUNT | NON-EXPENSE DR. AMOUNT |
|---|---|---|---|---|---|---|
| 2500 | INTERCOMP MCS-ABC | 11000 | GOODMAN'S ELECTRONICS | 11000-2 | 0.00 | 100.00- |
| | | | | * ACCOUNT TOTAL * | 0.00 | 100.00- |
| 5000 | OFFICE SUPPLIES | 11111 | ALFRED GARMENT | 11111-1 | 789.33 | 0.00 |
| | | | | * ACCOUNT TOTAL * | 789.33 | 0.00 |
| 5020 | ELECTRIC COMPONENTS | 11222 | JACKSON ELECTRICAL SUPPL | 11222-0 | 4500.67 | 0.00 |
| | | | | * ACCOUNT TOTAL * | 4500.67 | 0.00 |
| 5060 | MISCELLANEOUS | 11000 | GOODMAN'S ELECTRONICS | 11000-1 | 234.89 | |
| | | 11000 | GOODMAN'S ELECTRONICS | 11000-2 | 100.45- | |
| | | 11111 | ALFRED GARMENT | 11111-2 | 450.00 | |
| | | 11111 | ALFRED GARMENT | 11111-3 | 280.89 | |
| | | | | * ACCOUNT TOTAL * | 865.33 | 0.00 |
| 5080 | FREIGHT | 11111 | ALFRED GARMENT | 11111-2 | 6.89 | |
| | | 11111 | ALFRED GARMENT | 11111-3 | 20.00 | |
| | | | | * ACCOUNT TOTAL * | 26.89 | 0.00 |
| | | | | *** CORP. TOTAL *** | 6182.22 | 100.00- |

Figure 7-8j. MCS A/P package; A/P expenses distribution report. Mini-Computer Systems Inc., Elmsford, NY. Reprinted with permission.

CORP: 11    MINI COMPUTER SYSTEMS      A/P VENDOR PAYMENT RECONCILIATION
AS OF: 02/28/78

PAGE: 0001
RUN DATE: 02/16/78
TIME: 12:09:25

| VENDOR NO. | VENDOR NAME | INVOICE NO. | INVOICE DATE | ORIGINAL INVOICE AMT. | CHECK NO. | VF | CHECK DATE | PAYMENT AMOUNT | DISCOUNT TAKEN | INVOICE BALANCE |
|---|---|---|---|---|---|---|---|---|---|---|
| 11111 | ALFRED GARMENT | 11111-1 | 02/16/78 | 789.33 | 18 | 0 | 02/16/78 | 767.84 | 21.49 | |
| | | 11111-3 | 02/20/78 | 300.89 | 18 | 0 | 02/16/78 | 293.47 | 7.42 | |
| | | VENDOR TOTALS: | | 1090.22 | | | | 1061.31 | 28.91 | 0.00 |
| 11222 | JACKSON ELECTRICAL SUPPL. | 11222-0 | 02/15/78 | 4500.67 | 19 | 0 | 02/16/78 | 3600.54 | 900.13 | |
| | | VENDOR TOTALS: | | 4500.67 | | | | 3600.54 | 900.13 | 0.00 |

Figure 7-8k. MCS A/P package; A/P vendor payment reconciliation. Mini-Computer Systems Inc., Elmsford, NY. Reprinted with permission.

CORP: 11    MINI COMPUTER SYSTEMS      A/P JOURNAL ENTRIES
PROOF LIST
AS OF: 02/28/78

PAGE: 0001
RUN DATE: 02/16/78
TIME: 12:11:52

| CORP. | BATCH-SOURCE # | ACCOUNT NO. | ACCOUNT NAME | DEBITS | CREDITS | BALANCE |
|---|---|---|---|---|---|---|
| 11 | AP11 CDCR | 1000 | CASH | 0.00 | 4661.85— | 4661.85— |
| | | 4002 | DISCOUNTS EARNED | 0.00 | 929.04— | 929.04— |
| 11 | AP11 CDDR | 2001 | ACCOUNTS PAYABLE | 300.89 | 0.00 | 300.89 |
| | | 2002 | A/P ELECTRICAL | 4500.67 | 0.00 | 4500.67 |
| | | 2003 | A/P OFFICE SUPPLIES | 789.33 | 0.00 | 789.33 |
| | | | BATCH TOTALS: | 5590.89 | 5590.89— | 0.00 |
| 11 | AP11 PJCR | 2001 | ACCOUNTS PAYABLE | 200.45 | 992.67— | 792.22— |
| | | 2002 | A/P ELECTRICAL | 0.00 | 4500.67— | 4500.67— |
| | | 2003 | A/P OFFICE SUPPLIES | 0.00 | 789.33— | 789.33— |
| 11 | AP11 PJDR | 2500 | INTERCOMP MCS-A3C | 0.00 | 100.00— | 100.00— |
| | | 5000 | OFFICE SUPPLIES | 789.33 | 0.00 | 789.33 |
| | | 5020 | ELECTRIC COMPONENTS | 4500.67 | 0.00 | 4500.67 |
| | | 5060 | MISCELLANEOUS | 965.78 | 100.45— | 865.33 |
| | | 5080 | FREIGHT | 26.89 | 0.00 | 26.89 |
| | | | BATCH TOTALS: | 6483.12 | 6483.12— | 0.00 |
| | | | CORP TOTALS: | 12074.01 | 12074.01— | 0.00 |

Figure 7-8l. MCS A/P package; A/P journal entries proof list. Mini-Computer Systems Inc., Elmsford, NY. Reprinted with permission.

**3. Payment Selection Menu.** This menu selects invoices for payment, alters payment status as desired, and produces a preliminary check trial run. The screen is used to put invoices into or release them from *Hold* status. The hold status prevents an invoice from being selected for payment except when it is selected on an individual basis.

**4. Check Menu.** The menu includes check writing and restarts, manual checks, check reconciliation entry and report, and the "Daily Disbursement Journal." Samples of the latter two outputs are presented in Figures 7–8C and 7–8D.

**5. On Demand Reports Menu.** This menu produces the "Cash Requirements" report (see Figure 7–8E) which lists by vendor all invoices payable through a desired date. By accessing the payment selection menu, described above, the user may instruct the system to pay all or some of the invoices printed on the "Cash Requirements" report. The on demand reports menu also produces an "Accounts Payable Open Items" report in two versions, either aged or not aged. In the aged report, invoices are listed by vendor under one of six possible time periods. The time period under which an invoice is listed is determined by the relationship of the invoice date to the user-selected "aged as of" date. All invoices less than thirty days old will list as "current." A sample of an "Aged Open Items" report is illustrated in Figure 7–8F.

**6. End of Month Menu.** This menu processes the monthly payable transactions for summarization, interfacing with the general ledger, and production of the following reports:

a. "Accounts Payable Vendor Ledger" (Figure 7–8G). This report is a detailed vendor ledger showing a month opening balance for the vendor account plus all transactions (debits and credits) for the month.

b. "Monthly Purchases Journal" (Figure 7–8H). This report lists all of the invoices entered during the month. Invoice details and expense distribution(s) are shown for every invoice.

c. "Monthly Disbursements Journal" (Figure 7–8I). This report lists all checks written during the month, including manual and void checks.

d. "Accounts Payable Expense Distribution Report" (Figure 7–8J). This is a monthly report which lists by general ledger account number all of the invoices entered during the report month.

e. "Accounts Payable Vendor Payment Reconciliation" (Figure 7–8K). This report provides an audit trail for vendor payments to aid the user in reconciling vendor inquiries. All payment history for an invoice will be listed if any payment or reversal occurs during the current month.

f. "Accounts Payable Entries Proof List" (Figure 7–8L). This report provides the basis for manual posting of accounts payable to the general ledger or in the case of automated posting provides a clear audit trail of the general ledger transaction records. The report prints the source folio from which the records are created.

## EVALUATION OF SYSTEM OUTPUTS

The primary specialized task of the financial manager is to insure the liquidity of the firm for day-to-day operations and to obtain the funds required for capital investment. It may be safely assumed that the manager who carries out these responsibilities successfully is working with an efficient cash management information system.

By the same token, a firm may feel confident that the financial manager has designed and implemented an effective reporting system if accurate and prompt information enables both top management and the functional managers to perform their responsibilities so that the objectives of the firm are realized.

# 8
# The Hardware and Software Decision

## INTRODUCTION

Achieving an effective information system is harder than ever, especially for the first-time user. But the problem is only slightly less acute for the experienced firm. There are many causes for this lack of computer success, and we have already mentioned some of them. One significant problem is rapid technological advancement. This improved technology leaves in its wake a demand for qualified people which schools and colleges do not seem to be able to fill. The more technology advances the more training is required and the larger the "knowledge gap" becomes. Technological improvement also means increased hardware capability (and usually at a lower price). This results in increased expectations by management and increased demands on the information processing department. The more technology improves, the wider the "performance gap" becomes. The third aspect of technology change which impacts on a firm's ability to master it in a cost effective manner is the proliferation of vendors and devices which are offered in the marketplace. The more devices which are offered the more knowledge is required and the more possibilities become apparent to management. Thus, these three aspects of the technology are intimately related and all three must be dealt with for a satisfactory solution.

Since the major purpose of this book is to assist the knowledgeable manager, we can address all three areas by helping managers to be better informed about the vast array of technology available to them today. To do this we will explain the implications of the hardware choice, the meaning of software and its critical position in the hardware choice and then give some guidelines for taking advantage of the situation in the best interests of effective information processing.

## THE SOFTWARE DILEMMA

Software is termed a dilemma since the software "problem" usually must be solved before management can address hardware issues. This is so because technology has virtually no limits in the machines and devices it can offer. Whatever function one wants a machine to perform can essentially be provided by the industry today. The

376

limiting factor is whether you can get this machine to work effectively and perhaps in concert with other machines you have acquired. In a word, the limiting factor is software—the instructions which "move" the machine. The only valid approach today for anyone seeking a machine solution to an information (or industrial) problem is to define the need, seek the software which will meet that need and then investigate the devices on which that software will operate. To do otherwise is more time consuming, more costly and may well result in failure to achieve the desired performance.

Such an approach was not always the recommended procedure. In the past, the array of hardware offerings was quite limited and there was a great deal of similarity between products. Most hardware was sold as a complete system and that system usually was produced by a single vendor. The jobs which the system was expected to perform were rather standard transaction-processing applications not often involving communications lines or interactions with other computers or geographic locations.

In this set of circumstances, hardware could be chosen first, the limiting factor being intangibles like the reputation of the vendor, the amount of "support" promised or the opportunity for expansion to accommodate the firm's growth. Sometimes the decision was made on price. Machine performance characteristics were so similar that they did not significantly discriminate between vendors. The applications software which would follow the hardware decision would most likely be developed completely by the firm's own programming staff using a workable but not very powerful language, yet one certainly adequate for producing the kinds of results management expected.

But we're getting ahead of our story. First we must understand what the term *software* means and through that explanation appreciate the dilemma software presents to the manager. Then solutions to the dilemma will be offered.

## Systems Software

Of the two basic types of software, *systems software and applications software,* systems software is the more complex, more difficult to produce, more complex to run and extremely difficult to modify. It is also a lesser concern for management than applications software. Management need be less concerned with systems software not because it is unimportant in the information system—quite the contrary. But management may give less attention to this type of software for the very practical reason that systems software evaluation does take a trained information systems professional and when such an evaluation is required the enlightened manager will acquire such professional talent.

Systems software is almost always purchased and then frequently from the hardware supplier. This means that the using organization is not concerned with the design of systems software, a most difficult task, but only with determining whether it performs those functions required for the firm's information processing, for systems software is a facilitator. Its job is to insure that the other applications or jobs running on the machine are executed properly and efficiently. And we determine the value of systems software by examining the results, i.e., through looking at how the jobs run. So for management systems software evaluation is done through examining how the applications software runs.

Of course, the professional who makes the technical evaluation of the proposed systems software has other things in mind. To understand what the analysis entails it is important to understand more of what systems software is all about. This is best done through a historical perspective.

Computers first became commercially available in the early 1950s and for the first ten years of their existence systems software was a very minor consideration. This was so because very little of it existed. When a firm acquired a computer it expected the supplier to provide some kind of programming language so that programs could be written in-house. Sometimes two languages were available, one oriented toward commercial data processing and one for scientific processing where extensive numerical manipulation was required. Beyond one or two languages the only other programming provided for the customer were some useful programs which performed common functions required in any data processing installation. These utility programs as they were called included, among others, programs which would sort data, some which would take data from cards or files and print it out, others which would copy tape or disk files or just make copies of card decks. The most important of these of course was the *sort* program, without which no information processing installation can be effective, since processing efficiency is a measure of how many different ways the same information can be displayed. And sorting is the key to that facility.

As computer installations matured, managers sought ways to make them more efficient. One of the inefficiencies they tried to eliminate was the delay between jobs. Often the machine time used in one eight-hour shift was only a small fraction of that period with the rest being taken up with setting up the jobs to be run. One solution was to let the computer help in running itself. Thus monitors or executive programs were developed which would aid this job transition process by keeping track of what job was running, recognizing when it was completed and initiating the next job, all with minimal human operator intervention. As machine capabilities increased to the point where there were many input and output devices on one system, this input/output management capability became a more essential part of systems software in order to operate these devices simultaneously to take full advantage of the speed of this hardware. Since such software was complex, difficult and expensive to write, and since the general capability was required by all users of similar systems, it fell to the hardware supplier to provide this software.

As disk drives became more prevalent, managers saw another way to make their operations more efficient. Rather than storing programs on cards with all their attendant disadvantages of bulk, vulnerability to loss, and slow speed of processing, they established files of programs or libraries on disk files. This had the advantages of insuring that the program was not inadvertently altered by cards being out of sequence or lost and making the process of reading the program in from disk quite rapid. To accomplish this program storage on disk, library programs were developed to put the programs on disk, provide a means for calling them into memory when they were to be used, and for deleting them from the file when they were obsolete or new versions were to be catalogued. Once again, the common need for these library programs by many users made their development logically another responsibility of the manufacturer.

Each of these developments complemented the others. As hardware got more capability, such as the ability to share its memory with two or more programs, or as computers were linked to each other or to terminals through communication facilities, the management of the computer operation demanded some sophisticated overall program to make sure it all ran smoothly and, when it didn't, to help to find out why. Today that overall program is the successor to the monitor or executive program and is called the *operating system*. It has all the parts that we have seen developed in our discussion (see Figure 8-1).The I/0 management system still controls the data flow to and from the program(s) to allow the I/0 devices to operate at their maximum speeds. Sort programs and other utilities are still required and along with the user's own application programs can be filed on disk through a series of library programs. The languages are also there, except that now there are often many to choose from, each with different capabilities. And the operating system itself even has its own language often called a Job Control Language or some similar term, which the operator uses to communicate with the operating system to select various options for the efficient running of the installation. And all these are integrated by the *resident supervisor*. Today, virtually all computers are provided with some sort of operating system. Some are very sophisticated and offer the user many options. Others may only have the essentials in a fixed format. Still others may only provide some of the facilities we have discussed. It is this facilities aspect of the operating system which the professional information systems person will evaluate. The evaluation will be based on how well the operating system allows the application programs to run. It is not management's job to evaluate an operating system, but to appreciate why a given operating system is effective or ineffective for the kind of processing required to meet the firm's information needs.

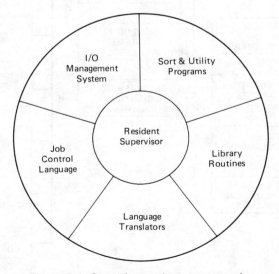

Figure 8-1. Operating system components.

### Applications Software

The second category of software and the one management is most concerned with is applications software. This includes all the programs which process the data into the various forms and reports needed by the organization. Quite often these specific application programs are written by programmers from the firm's own programming staff. But more frequently in recent times, application programs are purchased from other firms. The pros and cons of this purchased software approach is the subject of a subsequent section.

An in-house programming staff may report directly to the information systems manager or in larger installations may have its own manager who in turn reports to a director of information systems. Sometimes the programming manager also has responsibility for systems analysis and design but in the larger installations this function often has its own manager (see Figure 8–2). Thus the typical and most clearly defined organization has both a systems design (and analysis) manager and a programming manager each with his own specialized subordinates, both of whom report to the informations systems manager. Completing the organization structure is an operations manager who is responsible for all data entry and machine oper-

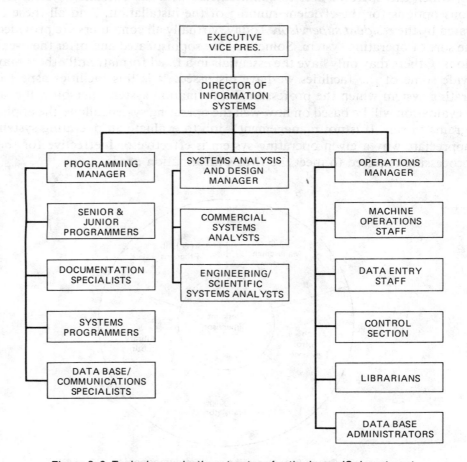

Figure 8–2. Typical organization structure for the larger IS department.

ation. (See Appendix A for detailed position descriptions and a discussion of computer career progression.) As described in Chapter 2, once the designer has an understanding of the information needs of the user, a set of detailed program specifications are prepared which in turn are reviewed by the user for accuracy. Once approved, these specifications are turned over to the programming manager and programming is begun. The programming process has many variations but the general approach is as follows.

Let us assume that management wants to automate the payroll function. Currently all payroll processing is done manually. The specifications include eight programs: Edit Program, Payroll Calculations, Payroll Register, Deduction Register, Pay Checks, 941A Tax Report, W-2 forms and a File Update program. The programming manager will probably divide the eight programs among various members of his staff. He will do this for a number of reasons. First, it may not be possible for one programmer to get all eight programs completed by the deadline date. Second, some programs may be extremely complex and the junior programmers may not have the proficiency to handle them. And last, there is some benefit derived from the team effort both in ideas for programming approaches and also in morale and motivation. If the group is large, a project leader may be chosen from among the programmers assigned to the payroll project who will be the coordinator of all payroll programming activities.

The first thing the assigned programmers do is read the specifications and meet with the analyst/designer to be sure of complete understanding. Though this is a major meeting and essential for project initiation, it is only the first of many that will take place between the analyst and the programmers as the programming continues. In effect this meeting is a structured walkthrough of the type described in Chapter 2.

The programmers then commence their coding of the programs and when they have reached a fairly high level of completion, programming walkthroughs are held where the other programmers review the coding and attempt to catch errors prior to testing the program on the computer. At the completion of the pre-test walkthrough, the program is tested and any further corrections which the testing process uncovers are made and the results are reviewed with the user to insure that the program output is what was requested. As additional programs in the payroll system are completed, they are run in concert with the others until all interact smoothly with each other. When the final total system test is satisfactory, the programming is deemed complete and the programs are turned over to the operating group. The operating group will in effect stage a walkthrough of its own, attempting to run the programs based on the operator instructions and other written documentation provided by the programming staff. If the walkthrough is unsatisfactory, the programming group will have to make sufficient changes to convince the operations department to take responsibility for running the programs. Once responsibility has shifted to the operations department the programming department has little to do with the payroll processing unless and until further bugs are uncovered from situations which arise in the actual operation which were not able to be tested fully in the programming stage. These must be corrected rather rapidly as the firm is now dependent on the computerized version of the payroll system and can no longer revert to manual operations. Other than overcoming bugs, the only other circumstances which will further involve the programming staff with the payroll programs will be additions and modifications as requested by management. These may arise due to the need for more management information, such as could be obtained from a labor distribution report, or through some tax law change, such as the imposition of a state income tax or even just a change in tax rates for an existing tax. These changes all come under the heading of maintenance programming and such tasks are major and continuing aspects of the programming function.

## The In-house Programming Staff

Among the personnel in the programming department there will be a variety of skills and skill levels (see Figure 8–2). Besides leadership skills among management and project leaders, there will be programmers who have expertise in certain languages, some who are particularly knowledgeable about disk files and database management systems, others who may be expert in communications lines and on-line processing, and one or more who may be relied upon to be responsible for the proper use and operation of the systems software provided by the supplier. Though extensive modifications are not usually made to systems software, someone on the staff must know how all the options work and select those that best meet the needs of this installation and be able to apply vendor updates. And among all of these programmers there will be varying experience levels. Perhaps the most senior programmers will also be performing some analysis functions and may eventually be expected to transfer fully to that (higher-level) skill. Some programmers, usually the most junior, will be assigned to the very difficult task of maintaining and modifying programs which were already written. This is most difficult since the programmer doing the modification is most likely not the original programmer. And since programming is much like any kind of authorship, in that each person has his own style, the maintenance programmer must first understand the original author's style before changes can be made. Not only is this quite time consuming, but it is also very unrewarding since the maintenance programmer gets less satisfaction from the "little" change that he has made than he would if he used the same amount of time to write an entire program. It is this unpleasant aspect of the maintenance function which causes it to get assigned to the juniors on the programming staff. Yet these are the people who are least qualified to perform the function. On the other hand, experienced programmers may elect to change employers rather than do maintenance. This maintenance problem is another reason for establishing programming standards which are reinforced by walkthroughs.

Another aspect of the in-house programming staff is the difficulty of obtaining qualified employees. There are more than a million computer systems installed in the United States today and that number is growing at an increasing rate. However, the supply of even adequately trained programmers has not kept pace with the demand created by the large number of computers installed. Some statistics predict that by 1990 the need for programmers could reach 1.5 million, more than triple the number working today. The demand for highly skilled software people is currently estimated to be 40% greater than the supply. Programmers, according to industry magazines,command among the highest salaries for recent college graduates and often can garner raises which outstrip other professionals. The result is that acquiring a competent staff can be very difficult and, if it can be done, that staff will be rather expensive. This may not only affect the cost/benefit analysis of the information systems function, but may also have broader policy implications across the organization if salary levels are inconsistent with other "similar" positions.

Some things which can be done to mitigate the shortage and expense of programmers are to train your own, use programming aids and, as suggested earlier, buy the programs from someone else. Training your own programmers has both advantages and disadvantages. In its favor it has the greatest advantage of taking a person who knows your own business and training him or her in computers. It is easier to train people about computers than it is to train them in how your own business works. This is so because computer knowledge is standardized, organized and developed into courses. Typically, training in a given business comes from one-on-one instruction which is very informal, has few training materials, and relies heavily on actually doing the job. Another good reason for training from within is that you will know the person. Thus, rather than hiring a programmer about whom you know very little, you will be training someone who has been punctual, reliable, steady, etc. for some years. In addition, you may be reasonably sure this person likes working for your firm and will continue to work for you after the training has ended. (You might even write a contract.) The disadvantages are that you may not find anyone in your firm who really has the aptitude, or when you do train them if you do not engender loyalty by salary adjustment and the like you may have simply trained a programmer for someone else to steal.

Programming aids fall into a number of categories and are too numerous to describe in detail here. There are languages and other software tools which allow inexperienced programmers to write more sophisticated programs than they would otherwise be capable of. And there are also aids that allow managers to generate their own programs and reports. Such software aids are called *query languages, nonprocedural languages* and *report generators,* among others. In some firms, the corporate database is constructed in such a way that all managers can be confident that any information they want is available to them. Then they are given access to computer terminals and with an English-like language they state what information they want on a report, what sequence it is to be in, what calculations should be made, what totals should be shown and the like. This in effect is writing the program for that report. When the request is completed, the "program" is run and if it is not satisfactory, the manager can modify his request repeatedly until he is satisfied. During the process, the computer is aiding the manager by asking questions and clarifying for the computer (and the manager himself) exactly what information is required and in what format. Such an approach does not eliminate the programmer entirely, since the programmer had to set up the system and the database, but for the manager to get his report, no programmer is really required.

## The Make or Buy Decision

Because of the difficulties of executing the creation of programs with an in-house programming staff, many firms today are considering the purchase of applications programs from other firms or software vendors. There are more issues to the make or buy decision than we have so far mentioned and they are shown in Figure 8-3. The first is one we have mentioned, however, *personnel cost,* and it is important because the prime element of the make or buy decision is the comparative cost of the approaches. These costs are weighed with their attendant benefits, and this becomes a part of the decision criteria. Software programs or packages purchased from outside are generally cheaper than those of in-house creation simply because the vendor can amortize the programming costs over a number of users. But this is only one element in the equation.

A second consideration in the make or buy decision is personnel availability. As mentioned above, even if the desire is to produce a program in-house, the scarcity of qualified programming personnel may force the decision in favor of going outside. If you have good people now, a third consideration is whether they can be retained until project completion. Turnover is high among data processing people of all types as their scarcity makes them the object of bidding wars between potential employers. This is a problem even after a project has been completed. You hope to retain the author of any major program so that changes and late-appearing bugs can be handled more easily. To do this, a bonus or new, more interesting projects may have to be offered. If turnover is a problem in your organization, going to a software vendor may minimize that risk.

A difficult parameter to measure is the value of the time delay in getting any program operational. Traditionally when jobs are requested from the information systems department the requestors claim they are needed immediately. In-house

PERSONNEL COST vs. PACKAGE COST

PERSONNEL AVAILABILITY

EMPLOYEE TURNOVER

TIME TO GET OPERATIONAL

REQUIRED TAILORING

CHANGE ACCEPTABILITY

INEVITABILITY OF PROGRAM BUGS

PROBABILITY OF INSTALLATION AND USE

COST: ACTUAL/HIDDEN

RESISTANCE FROM THE IS DEPARTMENT

Figure 8-3. Software make or buy issues.

software development cycles can be lengthy, often extending over a year or more. Packages can often be running much sooner. Actual package lead time is dependent on whether modifications are required. This required tailoring is the next point. A purchased package may not meet all the requestor's specifications. If the lesser capability of the package is not acceptable to the requestor the package will have to be modified. This may be done by the package vendor or by the in-house staff. Either way the modifications will take time and may also incur additional cost. However, even if we assume the in-house version is closer to what the requestor wants, it may be worth the difference in performance to get something going sooner through a package and for less money.

A corollary to the rule that getting something sooner and cheaper may be better than getting everything you want later and more expensively is a rule that says a more restrictive approach to the application may be better for the organization as a whole, particularly if the computer is new to the organization. For example, a firm may want a computer-supported budgetary accounting system. One reason for computerization is that there is an overall lack of discipline in the organization and the budget process itself is poorly managed. Among other problems, variances are not caught early enough nor are they analyzed thoroughly. Through the standard in-house systems design approach such a firm may consciously or otherwise build a computerized budgetary system reflecting these same lax approaches. In other words, it often happens that poor manual systems become poor automated systems. But a package from a vendor would more likely have stricter controls. It would have been designed to meet an objective set of budgetary accounting requirements. Perhaps the package would not meet all the firm's needs, but because of the way its operating rules are structured the use of it would bring a discipline to the organization which it sorely needs and could not provide for itself.

*Change acceptability* addresses the issues of whether all requested changes should be made, their impact as implementation nears, and how packages can sometimes help the situation. It is the IS manager's responsibility to be aware of the demand for changes, judge the necessity for the changes, and implement or defer them in the best interests of the organization. As described in chapter 2 the ability to change and the requirement to change are characteristic of any information system. Initially changes come about because of the user's unfamiliarity with the computer and the system professional's unfamiliarity with the information needs of the users. So systems are designed based on imperfect information. As each learns more, the needed changes become more apparent. The question here is how many changes are required and when are they discovered? Late changes can be costly whether to a package or an in-house program. Usually manpower is at a premium at the final stages of a project so overtime or other additional personnel costs may have to be incurred. Time pressure will create it own errors during the change process which will further delay the project and may be the cause of bad publicity should the project get off to a bad start. If the changes are not crucial perhaps they should be deferred. This is easier to do when purchasing a package than when preparing an in-house program. A purchased package could be used as an excuse not to accept last minute changes, if denying the changes is in the best interest of the firm at this time. Some packages cannot be modified due to legal or other limitations and it may be too late to find a substitute. Those which can be modified may incur additional expense or may delay the project if it is not possible to convince the vendor to rush the changes to meet your schedule.

Though the purpose of the IS organization is service, all requests must not be automatically fulfilled. These trade-offs, among many others, must be considered when weighing the relative value to the organization.

Problems or bugs will continue to surface long after programs are operational. No matter how carefully pre-installation testing is performed it is impossible to create or anticipate all the possible circumstances the program will encounter. The longer it takes the untested condition to appear the more effect it may have on the worth of the system. For example, if only at year-end closing is it discovered that an important balance sheet figure had not been accumulated each period, there could be serious consequences to closing the books on time. Some bugs may be relatively easy to fix while others may be impossible to fix, and in such cases it may be easier to rewrite the program. The question in this discussion is whether bugs are more of a problem with in-house software than with packages. Since bugs are found through program use the package would seem to be the more bug-free approach. The longer a package has been in use, the larger the number of users, and the history of changes or modifications already made are all important factors in favor of the package.

Many programs and entire applications never become operational no matter how vital they are to the information needs of the organization. Among the reasons for this are diversion of resources to projects of higher priority and loss of key personnel. On the other hand even if a project is programmed and tested it may never be implemented. This usually happens because the application outputs do not really meet the user needs. In both these problem areas the package has the advantage. The cost of the package is usually a known specific amount and can be protected against cutbacks. Perhaps a substantial down payment will be lost if the purchase is not followed through. Loss of key people is the vendor's problem, and if the package is popular and the firm substantial there should be sufficient knowledgeable employees to cover any temporary turnover. And finally, since a package is often a completed project when it is being evaluated, it is much easier to determine that its outputs are satisfactory. There should be no surprises in the results when the package runs live.

As mentioned in the previous section, purchased package costs can be known early and even with last minute changes are not likely to vary much from the original price. In-house costs however are not only difficult to control but in many cases impossible to measure for an individual program or application.

This is true because there are numerous hidden, intangible and indirect costs and these always pose an accounting problem when allocating expenses. For one example, how should machine time be charged to the programmers for testing? The whole area of computer charges is filled with philosophical differences and there is no satisfactory solution. Depending on which (unsatisfactory) method is chosen, a different project cost will be generated. But no matter what method is used for measuring in-house costs, the likelihood is that the same results can be achieved from a proven outside package for less.

In years past purchased packages were a last resort or at best an attempt to substitute for an inadequate or ill-prepared staff. To use a package was a reflection on
in-house capabilities and a sign of technical weakness. This established an air of
resistance to packages which is probably much diminished today. However, the enlightened manager when deciding to use a package should make sure the idea is
acceptable to the staff by emphasizing any economic advantages, schedule needs
and the like. There is also a learning experience for the staff through installing and
operating many of the very sophisticated packages now available. The staff should
welcome the opportunity.

If through the analysis of these make or buy issues the software decision weighs
heavily in favor of buying an outside package there are a number of questions or
issues which must be addressed in terms of dealing with the software vendor. These
package software decision issues are listed in Figure 8–4 and discussed in detail here.

The absolute sine qua non is the question of whether the package will run on
equipment available to the firm. This may be some already installed hardware, a
new system on order or even a system acquired specifically and exclusively for the
package. But initial compatibility is not enough. It is often useful to investigate how
transferable the package would be if there were a future equipment change. Additionally, its adaptability to processing enhancements not in the original planned
usage would be important, such as whether input could be converted from batch

HARDWARE COMPATABILITY

FIT TO SYSTEM SOFTWARE

SOURCE CODE AVAILABILITY

AMOUNT OF TAILORING PROVIDED

RESPONSIBILITY FOR MAINTENANCE

SIGN OFF DATE

BENCHMARK TEST

REPORT GENERATION MODULE

SUPPORT:   modification
           maintenance
           installation & conversion
           education
           documentation, etc.

CONTRACT TERMS

CURRENT USER CONTACTS

SECURITY/DISASTER RECOVERY

Figure 8–4. Package software decision issues.

to on-line, or the files incorporated into a database environment. Previous discussions about modification time and expense apply here too.

Similar caution is urged in examining the fit between the systems software on any current or future system on which the package will be expected to operate. The object is not simply to see if the package "works" or can be operated easily, although these are important to know. More important is whether the use of the package restricts or interferes with other features of the computer system and vice versa. For example, if the package is to run concurrently with other programs on your computer, the amount of memory the package uses or the way it operates may slow down or otherwise interfere with the way the other programs perform. Likewise the characteristics of the operating system or other software may degrade the package performance. Either of these conditions may require package modification.

On the subject of modification, one thing is certain. If the in-house staff is going to modify a package, you must have access to the source code. Programs come in two stages or versions. *Object code,* (sometimes called machine code) which is the state the program must be in when it is actually processing, is usually all the vendor provides. It is in effect the finished product. *Source code* is an intermediate stage. In it the program is set out in such a way that almost any programmer familiar with that programming language could understand the process being performed. Because of the greater ease and simplicity of source code, programmers work in that stage rather than at the object code level. Thus, if you plan to modify the package, the vendor must provide the source code. This necessarily implies providing new source code if new or updated versions of the package are issued. The source code must always reflect the current object code. Vendors may be reluctant to make source code available since it is a company asset and would be susceptible to easy copying and bootlegging if it got into unscrupulous hands. If the vendor is unwilling to provide the source code for legal or protective reasons then you will be forced to use the vendor to perform any desired modifications.

Another reason for requesting source code is the possible feeling that the vendor is unstable and may not remain in business. Such an eventuality could cause serious problems should package modification become necessary. One way to overcome this and solve the problem of the vendor's shaky business position is to deposit a copy of the source code in escrow to be available only under a specific set of circumstances. This can be done with a simple agreement.

The topic of tailoring has been discussed earlier in making the make or buy decision. The main questions are: (1) How much do you get for the basic package price both in terms of total man-hours and over what time period? (2) What is the cost when the free service ends? (3) How qualified is the vendor staff? and (4) How responsive is the vendor to your time requirements? This last question may require checking with other of the vendor's clients.

The topic of maintenance is really directed toward the specific question of to what extent the vendor takes responsibility for bugs in his programs. In theory, if ever at any future time some aspect of the program should not work, the vendor should make a fix. But this is too simple an approach. Can maintenance support really go on for twenty years? Can and should it remain free all that time? One bug may really be a specific problem only for one or a few users, while another may be a general problem to all. Should both these bugs be fixed on the same basis? In pricing the package, future maintenance costs are anticipated so maintenance is not really free. But the more that is built in at the beginning, the more it will add to the package cost. Another situation which muddies the maintenance issue is bugs which appear after the user has made some modification to the package. It is often difficult in these circumstances to decide whether the bug was caused by the user modification or whether the user modification simply uncovered another vendor bug. The problem is often unresolvable.

One solution to the maintenance problem is the issuance of revision levels or new versions. Many software vendors periodically issue revised versions of their packages which reflect corrections to bugs and often some improvements to the way the package runs. The user has the option of remaining with his current version (and possibly losing any further vendor maintenance support) or moving to the new version and retaining the support. Ordinarily the updated version of the package incurs a fee which is some small fraction of the original package price.

Any package agreement is going to have deadlines or sign-off dates. There will be times when payments are due or when free services terminate or some other criteria is to be met. Be sure both parties are absolutely clear on the conditions surrounding these deadlines. If the measure is not clear the result will be finger-pointing and disagreement. Using such general phases as "support could continue until the program is running satisfactorily" is not good enough. What is satisfactory to the vendor may not be the same to the user. The decision should be made on more objective criteria such as running sets of test data properly or meeting other specific benchmarks.

It is also essential to be careful of partial payments for partial performance. As in any contracting situation if your payments to the vendor exceed by far your value received to date you lack leverage and the vendor lacks motivation to complete the project. There is an adage about computer programming that says the first 80% of the program takes 80% of the time and effort and the remaining 20% takes another 80% of the time and effort. Don't be fooled into thinking there is just a litte more to do, and pay the balance due or accept the product. As the adage implies, much goes wrong in the final stages and performance must be proven before the job can really be considered done.

The best way to know that your job runs well under a vendor's package would seem to be to run the actual job. But this is not really "scientific" enough. A single job run does not necessarily contain all the options or conditions that might arise. Some aspects of any job are very intermittent and exceptions are often hard to predict. But it would be impractical to run a year's work or even a month's processing to test out a package. The solution is the careful construction of a benchmark test or series of tests to establish what and how the package should perform. When these are available they not only aid in evaluating the package and aid in sign-offs, as mentioned in the previous section, but they become communication aids between both user and vendor. The benchmarks really reflect the specifics of what is expected from the package.

Benchmark tests should contain a number of normal transactions, as many errors or exceptions as can be anticipated, expected outputs to match results against, controls to balance with and timings. The benchmark may be run both with and then without the exceptions. But the objective is to establish a standard measurement. It is important to decide in benchmark situations just how closely the test approximates the actual user operating environment. Things to consider are whether vendor assistance during the test biases the results, whether the test hardware and software are identical to that proposed for the firm, and when a true life environment cannot be simulated how some conclusion can be drawn from the test. Benchmark tests are also useful in comparing two or more packages or when selecting options within a package. They should also be used as a kind of diagnostic program to be run after any changes have been made to the package, to insure that only the desired modification has taken place.

Many packages offer as a standard feature or extra cost option a report generation module. This is a program which allows the user to define his own reports. Even though the package is designed to do a total application and contains its own sets of reports, invariably individual organizational approaches require something more or different. To make getting these reports easier for management, report generator programs were developed. What is required is that the manager tells what information the report should contain, in what sequence and with what totals and the like. The raw data is in files which have already been established for the package. The report generator finds the data, processes it according to the rules the manager set up and produces the report. The lengthy steps of the systems development life cycle need not be done. All that is required is a data file, knowledge of what is on that file, and the report generator. In many cases the generator is so easy to use that after a few hours of practice the manager does not even need the assistance of a programmer to state the problem definition and run the report.

If the manager is not satisfied with the generated report he can change the request and modify it. If he likes it he can make it a regular part of the processing or call for it only when the occasion demands. And quite importantly, the manager at his own pace can experiment with many different kinds of reports and information presentations establishing which are most useful in decisionmaking. It should be stated that the word *report* here is used in a most general sense and could include, in addition to hard copy paper output, report displays on CRT screens as well as charts and other graphic displays, often in color.

Support is a very general area and has already been discussed in terms of modification and maintenance. But there are other equally crucial areas where the vendor can be of assistance, and the level and quality of this support as well as its cost are important package selection considerations. Foremost among these is installation assistance. This may include converting the package programs from one medium to another, i.e., putting them on your own disk drives, selecting and activating any options chosen, creating or converting any required files and running the benchmark tests. If the vendor is also supplying equipment, its unpacking and set-up would also be a part of this process.

There are alternatives to how these functions can be performed and variations in who does them. They may all be done at the user's site by vendor personnel, all at the vendor's site by vendor's personnel or some combination in between. Each situation is different, but the more that takes place in the user location the better the control and the greater the user's understanding of the package.

Understanding and confidence are the keys to package success. And education is essential to fostering both. Not only does the in-house IS staff have to be trained in the package, but the ultimate user should be given as much knowledge as possible so that the greatest potential can be gotten from the package for the organization. If the user doesn't know the package has a particular feature, he may not ask for it. Just how much education is of the formal classroom type or informal training should be based on the situation. Some people may be more effectively trained at the user's site; others (particularly "interruptible" busy persons) may be a better audience at vendor site schools.

An integral part of education is written material and this is no less true of package support. Documentation must be provided to guide package installation, operation, modification and maintenance. In all DP installations, having adequate documentation is a perennial problem. So too vendor documentation must be examined and evaluated carefully to insure it is truly useful and complete.

Various arrangements will demand other kinds of support, but all of these should receive the same careful investigative treatment. Then the entire agreement with the vendor should be reduced to contractual form. Every promise, deadline, and performance criterion should be included. A lawyer should be used. Much is riding on the success of this package, and legal documents go a long way to insure high levels of performance. And if performance is not forthcoming legal documents may assist greatly in getting some form of compensation or indemnification. It should be noted that contract negotiation should start very early in the decision process. When you have already made up your mind to buy a particular package, the vendor is less likely to make concessions. But when you are still deciding between competing firms, the greater advantage is the buyer's. The first step is to get a copy of the standard agreement, and then determine through the elements listed in Figure 8-3 what changes would be in the firm's best interests.

Another insurance approach is to contact current users of the same package or other packages from the same vendor to get firsthand reports on product performance, support, responsiveness, user acceptance and other aspects of dealing with this vendor. The reference should be using similar equipment, using the package and features you are interested in, be in your industry, and have an organization structure similar to your own, if possible. Do not assume that the vendor's willingness to provide references is sufficient evidence of satisfactory performance. Reference checking often results in some interesting surprises. Such checks should be made in person wherever possible, rather than over the phone. This approach provides the opportunity to see a demonstration of the package as well as to allow for more candor and detail on the part of the reference.

Finally, although the performance aspects of the package have been a major decision factor there are certain aspects of any program or system which are essential over and above the specific job the application is to perform. These include provision for data file protection from accidental destruction, data security from unauthorized access and procedures for recovering from improperly run jobs or major systems disasters. There are numerous methods for accomplishing these protections. The initial recommendation in each area should come from the vendor, but once again the user has the responsibility to insure the result is adequate for the organization.

There are numerous sources for packages and a great range of stability and performance among vendors. Buying from a large firm whose primary business is not software can be risky as well. These companies look to offset their large in-house programming costs by reselling their programs. But in spite of the size and fine qualifications of their DP departments these firms have been rather unsuccessful. Two examples are Standard Oil (Indiana) and Westinghouse Electric Corp. both of which had major efforts in software sales and have either cut back sharply or ended their commercial software thrust. Those companies that seem most reliable are the specialists, the software houses, whose primary business is marketing packages they have written or ones licensed from the original user. Other sources include: (1) hardware manufacturers who offer programs to run on their equipment, (2) a moonlighting programmer who does free-lance work (perhaps based on his full-time job responsibilities), (3) consulting firms, which offer a software capability as part of their management services, (4) users groups—associations of users of similar hardware who share information and exchange programs (often sponsored by manufacturers), (5) software brokers who seek out "good" programs and bring buyer and seller together (but take no responsibility for the programs as a software house would), (6) system houses which provide hardware and packaged software and are usually quite willing to make customized modification or write entirely new software, (7) computer retail stores which sell mainly "as-is" or "off the shelf" packages with limited support, and (8) trade organizations which often share information much like user groups. A good place to start when looking for software is in the publications of several organizations which specialize in evaluating computer hardware, software and services. Among these are the *Datapro Directory of Software* (Datapro Research Corp., Delran, NJ), *ICP Directory* (International Computer Programs, Inc., Indianapolis, IN), and *Auerbach Data World* (Auerbach Publishing Co., Pennsauken, NJ).

In summary, the package purchase process has a procurement life cycle similar to and complementory with the applications program development life cycle (see Figure 8–5). Recognizing the need is still the starting point. The feasibility study still determines whether further steps should be taken. The analysis phase must still be undertaken to insure a proper understanding of the job to be done. Here the make or buy decision is made. Continuing in-house leads to the remaining steps of the applications program development life cycle. For package purchase the next step is identifying potential package sources. Then some sort of solicitation should be made, perhaps a brief requirements statement sent to various vendors. This should qualify the vendors who are interested and have a potential product. Then a formal "Request for Proposal" (RFP) may be issued to detail specific needs and establish performance criteria. Background information on each vendor is developed and an independent evaluation of the software is made from the literature while the vendor proposals are being prepared. Then follow vendor conferences, demonstrations of each package, reference checking, benchmark tests, and initial contract analysis and negotiation. During this time, need for modification and other issues of Figure 8–4 are raised. Some sort of rating is given to each of these elements and a score for each vendor is calculated. This is not an absolute score but those in the higher range will be the top contenders. Such a rating scale is shown in the Newpeck and Hal-

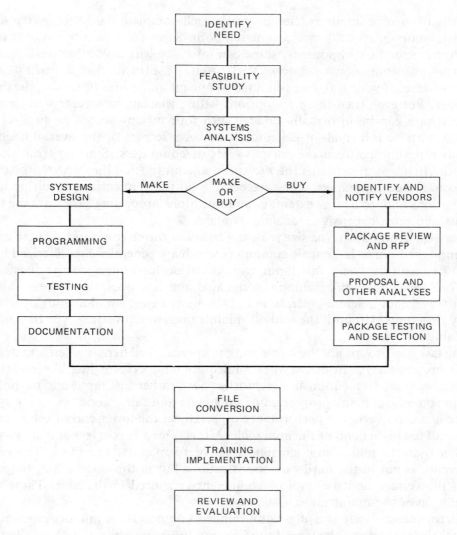

Figure 8–5. Applications development life cycle.

bauer article reprinted at the end of this chapter. It is often easy at this time to narrow the field to two or three firms. Formal contract negotiations take place next, and based on their outcome and all accumulated information, a selection is made. From this point the implementation portion of the applications software development life cycle takes over. (The RFP process is described in detail in Appendix B and guidelines for managing vendor relationships are discussed in Appendix C.)

## THE HARDWARE DILEMMA

Hardware is its own dilemma because of the enormous variety of products available. No longer are similar machines being offered by just a few vendors. Today there is a wide disparity in size, capability, price and market approach among the various vendors offering computers. Some vendors sell complete hardware systems, some sell just components or devices, some sell both. Some components can only operate with other specific components, some can interface with any other devices, and so on. The problem is how to choose. Very often the software decision will determine the hardware. If your software is limited to one manufacturer or model, the decision is easier. But even then there are options within that manufacturer's category.

Hardware can be informally divided into four groups according to size. These groups must be informal in their definition because part of the overall dilemma is the dividing line between the various sizes of computers. Starting from the large end, the first group contains the *monsters* which are found at NASA, the military and some large companies. They are being used for applications requiring massive calculations and, to a large extent, communications processing. They are the largest, fastest and most expensive machines available.

The next group down the size scale are the *mainframe* computers. These are your common medium to large scale computers which are generally characterized by large and fast memories, very fast input and output devices, large storage files on both tape and disk, many programming languages and fine operating systems which allow for efficient machine operation and, in many cases, simultaneous operation of many programs. Up until the mid-60s mainframes were the only type of computers available.

The last two groups are the *minis* and the *micros*. And here is where the definition problems get severe. In many ways minicomputers perform just like mainframes. They have small to medium size memories, have rather fast input and output units, and in some cases many programming languages and fairly good operating systems. There is much overlap in performance especially at the lower end of the mainframe scale and the higher end of the mini scale. Minis generally cost less and are physically smaller than the mainframe machines that perform equally to them. The practical difference is not in the hardware specifications but in the ease of use, the support from the vendor and the level of competence required in the user. These criteria usually favor the mainframes.

Microcomputers are the physically smallest computers. A microcomputer system has all the functional elements found in any larger computer. The smallest micro has its central processing unit (memory/logic/control) all on a single silicon chip. The basic business micros are stand-alone, single-user systems where the entire computer is handling only one job at a time. A video display unit, a keyboard and low speed printer complete the typical system. Magnetic tape cassettes and disks are also available. Their cost is lower than the minis, and many are in use in the home and the classroom as well.

### The Evolution of the Minicomputer[1]

History is repeating itself. Microprocessors are having an impact on the information processing arena much the same way that minicomputers did some ten years ago. But there are differences, and they have great significance for the potential user.

[1]This and the following section are excerpted from "Micros—Personal Computers with Power" by Ernest A. Kallman and James C. Krok, published in the October/December 1982 issue of *Business*, pp. 2–9.

An understanding of how minis emerged from the factory and laboratory to supplant low-end mainframe processors in the area of commercial data processing helps one to realize where microcomputers are now and where they may be heading in the commercial marketplace.

The original development of the minicomputer is generally attributed to the Digital Equipment Corporation (DEC) of Maynard, Massachusetts. That company's Programmed Data Processor (PDP), introduced in the mid-1960s, was the first of a series of machines. The original PDP-8 was a desktop unit selling for around $80,000. This was an impressive breakthrough. Both the reduction in the physical size of the machine, and the reduction in its price catapulted the minicomputer into a newly awakened market. Hundreds of applications that were ideal candidates for computerization could not previously be justified because of the high price of suitable machines. The thought of devoting an entire computer system to the control of a single industrial process or to the collection of experimental data in a laboratory had been quite unrealistic when computer prices were quoted in six-figure numbers. Likewise, the thought of providing the individual scientist or engineer with his or her own computer was completely alien to the computer mentality of the time.

Clearly, the place of the minicomputer was initially seen to be limited to industrial control and laboratory data-gathering. The user of such a computer was to be the scientist or engineer, and the programmable computer was seen as a cost-effective substitute for the expensive and custom-built (mechanical) systems in use at the time. The programmable nature of the machine gives it the flexibility to adapt to varied applications without the need for extensive and expensive hardware rework.

Part of what was unknown about the future of the minicomputer was the array of barriers to the growth of applications for it. The critical ingredient in every computer application is the programming that directs the actions of the machine. Unfortunately, the early days of the industry were spent enhancing hardware performance and reducing costs, with little attention paid to the problem of creating the software systems that would drive the new minimachines. Perhaps this was due to the established discipline surrounding electrical engineering, where technicians and engineers were accustomed to dealing with circuits which could be analyzed and studied and probed with instruments, while software was left to the unshaven, sneaker-shod magician who could never actually demonstrate what it was he was working on. No one could measure the software with a meter, or watch it on an oscilloscope.

The lack of established software standards, and of any common pool of proven software to draw upon, severely restricted the new applications for minicomputers. Every scientist or engineer who sat down at the computer was required to "re-invent" even the most elemental software routines. Designing that software, given the primitive nature of the new machines, was a challenge for the user. Actually translating those designs into working machine programs was a challenge to patience. Taken together, those elements operated to divert attention from the problem at hand (controlling the industrial process or automating a laboratory experiment) and created a host of new ancillary problems where there was no previous body of experience to fall back on for solutions.

While advances in electronic technology were reducing the cost of the computing element, no corresponding developments were affecting the size and cost of the input/output devices. Card readers, line printers, and mass-storage devices were still priced well above the minicomputer itself.

To maintain the relationship between the cost of the computer and the cost of the peripheral devices, the minicomputers were usually assigned to applications where all-electronic peripherals could take advantage of falling prices. However, those kinds of peripherals are limited to data collection and industrial control applications using analog-to-digital, digital-to-analog devices which convert measurements to signals the computer can process.

It was not until the early 1970s that small companies began to aggressively scale-down mainframe-type peripherals, and bring their prices down to a level where they were proportionate to the minicomputer and also provide operating systems and software development tools specifically for commercial applications.

**The Microcomputer Challenge.**   Now in the 1980s the progression continues as the microcomputer, or computer on-a-chip, rivals the capabilities of the traditional mini as it too moves out of the process control and laboratory arena and into commercial data processing.

But the emergence of the microcomputer as a force in the commercial application marketplace is and will be different from the minicomputer story. For one, the small business computer industry, if not mature, has over ten years' experience to draw upon. This experience base will mean that the "micro revolution" will not exhibit as random or haphazard a pattern of growth as did the commercial use of minis. The requirements for success are well known, and they are being developed rapidly. Many micros already have sophisticated operating systems; many well-known languages are available, and a variety of peripherals can be attached to some systems. The conclusion is that the race to provide inexpensive processing power is on, and small business will be the prime market in the next decade.

Though there is much value in the use of micros in computerizing the small business, a significant opportunity for the microprocessor is in the medium to large scale processing application. Though the major micro use runs from laboratory automation at one end to single-user desktop computers of minimal horsepower at the other end, microcomputers do have potential for challenging the upper end of the processing spectrum and can provide economical processing power equal to these systems. They can do this best through the use of multiple processors, adding power when and where it is needed. Rather than having a single CPU in which each added function reduces the ability of that uniprocessor to respond, micro based systems under this concept will add processors with each new function thereby boosting the machine's capability with each expansion.

Admittedly the micros are more ready for commercial processing at the low end. For the kinds of systems needed to challenge the mainframes some special problems must be solved. The hardware is there; the technology exists. But, as with the early minis, what is required is the software to bring this all together into a workable system. This implies a powerful operating system and compatibility between computer products offered by different manufacturers. This compatibility is emerging, and it is appropriate to anticipate that adequate software will follow.

The essence of the microcomputer is the single silicon chip not more than one quarter inch on a side which contains a highly complex central processing unit. The first such chip was introduced in production quantities at low cost by the Intel Corporation of Santa Clara, California, in 1971. The technological influence of that company is represented by the recent actions of several major corporations. The Xerox Corporation, IBM Corporation, and Tandy Corporation have all announced that major new products bearing their trademarks will incorporate microprocessors designed and manufactured by Intel. Thus, Intel has established itself as the leader in microcomputer technology, and its specifications have been adopted by leaders in the computer industry. This is one form of emerging compatability.

Another Intel standard, the MULTIBUS, has also recently been formally adopted by an industry association as a standard. The MULTIBUS is a physical and electrical specification for the common interconnection of all the elements of a computer system. With no such specification previously available, each computer manufacturer adopted its own internal interconnection scheme, with the result that subsystems from different vendors were completely incompatible with one another, thus complicating the hardware dilemma. The MULTIBUS specification defines the interconnection scheme so unambiguously that is is now possible for different vendors to produce computer subsystems that are compatible. The Institute of Electrical and Electronic Engineers (IEEE) has recently adopted the full MULTIBUS specification (version 3, 1981) as an industry standard, known as IEEE-796. This should go a long way toward the building of systems with components from many manufacturers.

The impact on the hardware dilemma of standardization through microprocessor chips and the MULTIBUS is both bad and good. The bad result is that the dilemma gets harder to solve as the user's options expand, but the good effect is that the system ultimately developed has a significantly higher probability of better meeting the user's needs. By being able to freely intermix CPUs and peripheral devices, a single computer system can be adopted to an enormous range of applications from industrial automation to business data processing to office automations and telecommunication. The burden is on the information systems technicians to be informed, imaginative and competent. The closed approach fostered by proprietary computer design architecture is fast disappearing. The opportunity for choosing specialized computer systems from the largest number of possible options to meet any processing need in the organization is here and can be described in one word: *open-ended*.

What this open-endedness means to the business user is that a machine and its software can be configured to handle any application mix in the firm. As additional resources are required, more microprocessor modules are added. In fact micros, minis and mainframes can all be intermixed. No longer will performance be constrained by machine limitations. The age of the truly custom system is arriving.

One major change in the marketplace however is how the smaller computer will reach the user. Like mainframes, early minicomputers were sold by a direct sales force calling on potential buyers and demonstrating the features and benefits that a computer offered the organization. Elaborate sales presentations, much travel, and long lead times before a sale was closed, were the rule. With the price of a system well over $100,000, such selling costs are acceptable viewed against the profit margin built into the sale.

However, with the price of a desktop microcomputer at $2,500, such direct selling carries far too high an expense to be considered. Two alternative approaches are generally used, depending on the operating margins required:

1. Where a substantial amount of added-value is possible, distributors purchase machines from the manufacturer and sell to the ultimate user. In the process, the distributor adds custom applications software, provides installation and support, and services machine breakdowns. For this service, the distributor is able to add sufficient margin to his cost to provide this individualized service.
2. Where such extensive hand-holding by distributors is precluded due to expense considerations, then retailing is the appropriate approach. As with any other form of retailing, computer retailing requires that the potential customer come to the seller with some idea of his requirements. The retailer is strictly a sales agent, whose only added-value is in stocking the machines, and providing a local outlet for them. With his lower operating margins, the retailer is unable to offer custom services at the basic computer price. Retailing, then, depends upon the knowledge of the consumer in selecting an appropriate machine and in providing his own programming. As a natural accessory to the computer hardware, the retailer is able to offer "soft" goods such as packaged programs, educational materials, and computer supplies such as paper and diskettes. A full-service retailer will offer, at extra cost, courses in programming and after-sale assistance in the use of the computer. He may also offer installation and service.

Retailing has succeeded in bringing a knowledge of computing to masses of people. That this is a legitimate computer distribution method is demonstrated by the fact that IBM has chosen to retail its line of personal computers through Sears, Roebuck and Company business machine stores as well as through its company-owned retail outlets.

Of course, there will be a whole spectrum of distribution approaches between the extremes of the full service mainframe direct sales approach and the retail store. But those of the distributor and the retail store will be among the most popular, and both add to the user's hardware and software dilemma. It is becoming increasingly more important to become a smart buyer.

The management responsibility for meeting the organization's information needs is clear. And there are many tools available today to assist in that effort. These tools are more effective, more powerful and in many cases, less expensive than their less useful predecessors. But improvements expected in the next few years portend to be far more dramatic than those experienced to date. The alert manager will anticipate these changes and be ready to take advantage of them when they appear. The next chapter surveys the future of information processing and other advances in technology which will impact the information area.

## REFERENCES

Alker, P. L. 1981. Distributed intelligence vs. centralized logic. *Mini-Micro Systems* (May): 103, 106, 108, 111, 115.

Discusses the proliferation of small computers vs. one large, centralized computer. Explains distributed data processing and shows cost performance comparisons between processing alternatives.

*The Computer Buyer's Checklist.* Chicago: Nixdorf Computers, Inc.

A useful guide to the computer evaluation process. One of several similar instruments offered by computer manufacturers. May be obtained by contacting local sales offices.

*Computer Salary Survey.* 1982. Northfield, IL: Source EDP.

A compendium of computer job descriptions, salary ranges and career information. Major portions are reprinted herein on pp. 430–443.

Couger, J. D. and R. A. Zawacki. 1978. What motivates DP professionals? *Datamation* **24** (9): 116–123.

An introduction to managing and motivating data processing people. Some good advice is offered on how to keep them happy on the job and increase their productivity.

Hemenway, J. 1980. Microcomputer operating system comes of age. *Mini-Micro Systems* (October: 97–8, 103–112, 114, 119.

An explanation of the power of the operating systems now available for microcomputers. Also includes a table of suppliers and the characteristics and price of their products.

Kallman, E. A. and L. Reinharth. 1982. Buying a computer: 12 rules to follow. *Business* **32** (1): 45–47.

A basic guide to dealing with any vendor and maintaining control of the situation. Reprinted herein on pp. 467–468.

Mandell, S. L. 1981. *Principles of Data Processing.* St. Paul, MN: West Publishing Co.

An elementary explanation of computer hardware, software and usage for the nontechnical person. One of many introductory books in the field.

Newpeck, F. F. and R. C. Hallbauer. 1981. Some advice for the small business considering computer acquisition. *Journal of Small Business Management* (July): 17–23.

As the title suggests, a step-by-step approach to making the computer selection decision is presented. Also deals with software as an element in the evaluation. Reprinted herein on pp. 400–406.

Sanders, D. H. 1981. *Computers in Society.* 3rd ed. New York: McGraw-Hill.

A unique kind of introductory text in that it has in addition to explanations of hardware and software capability, extensive explanations of the kinds of applications the computer can perform as well as the impact these have on business and society.

Seaman, J. 1981. Microcomputers invade the executive suite. *Computer Decisions* (February): 68–74, 158–160, 165–6, 168, 172, 174.

A detailed look at how some managers are using their "personal" computers to enhance the executive function.

Shaw, D. R. 1981. *Your Small Business Computer: Evaluating, Selecting, Financing, Installing and Operating the Hardware and Software that Fits.* New York: Van Nostrand Reinhold.

A layman's guide to every aspect of the small business computer selection decision. Many good checklists and charts. Chapter 12 is reprinted herein on pp. 444–466.

# SOME ADVICE FOR THE SMALL BUSINESS CONSIDERING COMPUTER ACQUISITION

*by Frederick F. Newpeck and Rosalie C. Hallbauer*

Small businesses now are able to afford computers to help them in many different areas of their operations. To make the best decisions regarding the acquisition and subsequent use of a computer, the advice of the internal accounting staff, a CPA firm, or an outside consultant should be sought.

However, the small business manager considering computerization ought not to leave the process of computerization totally to "the experts." A working knowledge of types of computers and of feasibility study components is necessary to manage the process of computerization. To that end, after a brief look at the type of computer system a small business might use and the items that make up its cost, this article will discuss some of the factors that should be considered in a feasibility study and some practical points to be considered in the acquisition process.

## THE COMPUTER AND SYSTEM-RELATED COSTS

Figure 1 depicts a typical small business computer hardware system.

Dr. Newpeck is a consultant with Nolan, Norton and Company, Lexington, Massachusetts. He is active in the Association for Computing Machinery and the Society for Management Information Systems and has served as a consultant for small business and local and federal government agencies. He has also authored numerous articles and papers on management science and information system topics.

Dr. Hallbauer is associate professor of accounting at Florida International University. She is a member of the following professional organizations: National Association of Accountants, American Institute of CPAs, American Accounting Association, American Management Association and American Women's Society of CPAs. In addition, she has published several articles in various accounting journals.

The cost of such systems has decreased mainly because of the declining cost of their microelectronic components. Because of the ability to automate the manufacture of these increasingly complex elements, the price of electronic parts of a computer system has declined at a rate of 30 percent per annum for the past 10 years. However, because electromechanical devices such as printers and disk drives still require a significant amount of manual labor, the cost of which is increasing, the total cost of a computer hardware system can be expected to decline at a rate of only 10 to 20 percent per annum through 1985.

In contrast to the hardware costs, the manufacturer's cost of developing computer software has increased to the extent that, at present, it equals or exceeds that of the hardware. Figure 2 portrays the relationship between these cost components. Once a software package is acquired by a user, its programs may need modification to meet the firm's unique needs—an additional cost to the business that increases its software cost three to four times over the acquisition cost. However, custom software is more expensive to develop and more difficult to maintain because it is one-of-a-kind.

After the system is acquired, several related operating costs are incurred, including clerical and other labor-related costs, insurance, taxes, main-

[1] R. M. Noyce, "Microelectronics," *Scientific American,* Vol. 237, No. 3 (September 1977), pp. 63-69.

Reprinted from the *Journal of Small Business Management,* July, 1981, pp. 17–23.

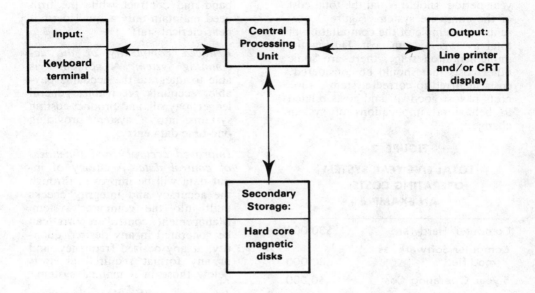

# FIGURE 1
## TYPICAL SMALL BUSINESS COMPUTER SYSTEM CONFIGURATION

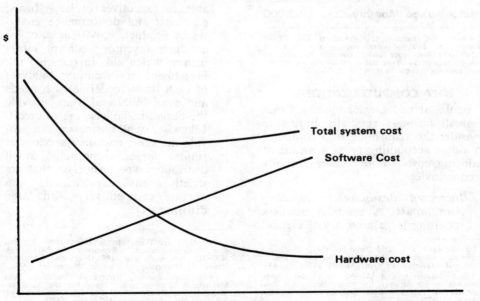

# FIGURE 2
## COMPUTER SYSTEM COST EXPERIENCE

tenance, paper forms, office space, and special fireproof storage for backup data. A rule of thumb is that operating costs, when summed over a five-year period, should equal the total cost of the complete system. Figure 3 presents an example of the computation of total average system cost. During the implementation stage, there are some other costs that should be considered: costs incurred to correct system errors, costs of lost goodwill and costs related to behavioral implications of system change.[2]

### FIGURE 3

### TOTAL FIVE YEAR SYSTEM
### OPERATING COSTS:
### AN EXAMPLE

| | |
|---|---|
| Computer Hardware | $30,000 |
| Computer Software, as modified* | 30,000 |
| 5-year Operating Cost | 60,000 |
| Salvage Value— End of Year 5 | —0— |
| Total 5-Year Cost | $120,000 |
| Total Average Monthly Cost | $2,000 |

*Software, for example, cost the seller $100,000 to develop, test and document; base price to buyer is $7,500 (the low price being possible because the package is sold to many users). Modifications of the basic package brings the cost up to $30,000.

### WHY COMPUTERIZATION?

Benbasat and Dexter indicated that a small business generally begins to consider the acquisition of a computer to aid in accounting or as a means of reducing costs.[3] Four reasons usually predominate:

1. *Increased flexibility in handling data inputs.* A seasonal business requiring large amounts of clerical work for short periods of time may automate its accounting procedures so that the business and, thus, the volume of data inputs can expand and contract while the firm need maintain only a small permanent clerical staff.

2. *Reduced complexity of the accounting system.* A computer is able to integrate the accounts payable, accounts receivable, general ledger, payroll, and product costing systems into a system providing one-time data entry.

3. *Improved accuracy and timeliness of control data.* Accuracy of input data will be improved through the accuracy and integrity checks built into the computer system. Management control reports can be generated in any desired quantity, at any desired frequency, and in any format required at costs below those in a manual system.[4]

4. *Improved competitive advantages.* Small business managers can receive many of the same types of sophisticated information available to executives of large firms, e.g., cost and performance analyses by product, activity area, or individual; inventory control information which aids in reducing the investment in inventory; analyses of cash flows to define cash needs and availability and, thus, provide the basis for the wise use of credit. Likewise, small businesses can provide the same customer services as similar larger firms, e.g., small distributor-type businesses that are strictly customer-oriented can operate competitively with large distributors.[5]

[2] J. Edward Kitz and John Walker, "Software Packages: Should a Firm Make or Buy Them?" *Cost and Management* (July-August 1978), p. 43.

[3] Isak Benbasat and Albert S. Dexter, "Approaches to IS Analysis In Small Business," *Proceedings of the American Institute for Decision Sciences* (1977), p. 571.

[4] Frederic G. Withington, "Information Systems and Computerization," *Economic Leaflets*, Vol. XXXIII, No. 9, Bureau of Business and Economic Research, University of Florida (November 1974).

[5] See, for example, Robert H. Goldstein and Stephen B. Zimmerman, "Help for the Small-to-Medium Size Distributors," *The CPA Journal*, Vol. XLVIII, No. 10 (October 1978), pp. 21-25.

An additional reason for studying the feasibility of computerization relates to the need to regain control over a business whose data base size has outgrown its one-person entrepreneurial management.[6] The purpose of information flow automation is to increase the efficiency and effectiveness of the interorganizational communication channels so that the firm can react to its environment as a single entity.

Any size business confronted with any of the situations, problems, or needs mentioned above should consider the automation of its information flows.[7] If the CPA, in the course of working for the company, sees any of these conditions developing, he or she should suggest the possibility of computerization to the client. The same holds true for the internal accounting staff or any member of top management.

### MANAGEMENT'S ROLE

A computer is not a panacea for all business problems. A firm has to be well-structured. Its market and competitive strengths and weaknesses should be analyzed and five- to ten-year forecasts developed. Such analyses and planning should be documented. Once this has been done and a structure is set up to help achieve the plans, the information needs of the firm can be analyzed, either by the firm or by a CPA or outside consultant in conjunction with the firm's management.

Analysis of the information needs starts with the operational day-to-day

6 Several articles have appeared suggesting that some decentralization of the information flow automation is occurring in large firms since the advent of the minicomputer, e.g., Laurence Richman, "Firms of All Sizes Convert to Minis," *Datamation* (October 1978), pp. 94-100; "Large Corporations, Small Computers," *Small Business Computers Magazine*, Vol. 2, No. 9 (November/December 1978), pp. 10-13.

7 For example, see Layton McCartney, "Small Business Systems: They're Everywhere," *Datamation* (October 1978), pp. 91-93 and Douglas C. Curling and James O. Hicks, Jr., "Minicomputer Feasibility in the Small Business Environment," *Cost and Management* (March-April 1979), pp. 4-8.

mainline information flow. In a manufacturing firm it is the data flow pertaining to men, materials and machines —all data related to movement of product and development of its inventory value as it proceeds through the production process. It is composed mainly of documents generated as production is carried out, e.g., raw material purchase orders, production schedules, material requisitions, time cards. A mainline flow exists for any type of business, although its components will differ depending on the type of business. The importance of this flow for the purposes of this discussion is that, in theory, it can be automated.

Independent subsystems in the mainline flow—frequently separate departments such as shipping and receiving—should be identified and ranked in order of their importance. Some of these subsystems are critical to operations and should, if possible, be automated first. Better management in these areas can lead to improved functioning of the firm. These critical subsystems of the mainline flow form the basis of the functional specifications to be given to the vendor.

The top management and the accountant, in particular, need to be involved at each stage of the analysis. Because the bulk of the mainline information flow also makes up inputs to the accounting system, the accountant is in the best position to help in the information flow analysis. Lack of support from line and staff people at any stage of computerization—acquisition, implementation, operation—can lead to the achievement of suboptimal results or failure.

Some firms make the mistake of giving a single outside technician total responsibility for analyzing the information flow as well as placing it on the computer. The developing and managing of a system containing the firm's valuable, irreplaceable data resources should not be delegated without proper management control and supervision. Precautions in this area have to be included in the firm's system of internal control.[8]

## THE CRITICAL ISSUE

Software is the critical issue—it determines whether or not the computer system will be successful and accepted by people in the firm using its information product. Frequently small businesses have unique procedures to which the employees have become accustomed; to help in the acceptance of the computer, the software package should result in minimum disturbance to such procedures.[9] To help ensure this, the firm's accounting staff, working with someone knowledgeable in computer software, should be involved in any program modifications.

The software package also determines whether the information needs of the firm will be met. One profitable construction firm showed a $250,000 loss the year it acquired its computer because it could not access the data in the cost estimating system. Profitability returned with a return to the manual system. Similarly, a manufacturing firm automated its accounting functions and later was unable to access its accounting data for government auditors. The result was a delay in payment for the government contracts and a substantial investment of the company president's time. Both of these problems might have been avoided had someone questioned whether the software could provide the necessary information.

In general, a small business should not write its own software.[10] There are several practical reasons for this: 1) lack of expertise, 2) lack of financial resources needed to write and document a system, 3) lack of flexibility in terms of the hardware—the software would be designed for a specific machine, and 4) tying the firm to the developer(s) of the software, a major problem if the system is not properly documented. Standard software, with modifications, avoids these pitfalls.

## ACQUISITION GUIDELINES

The ideal situation would be for the firm to have a computer-wise manager, but a consultant knowledgeable in the small computer field may be made use of to advise in the acquisition. Such a person also can serve as an intermediary between the firm's management and the vendor.[11] However, the final decision regarding the equipment is the responsiblity of the firm's management, since an incorrect decision could cost more than the hardware itself.

The following procedures can minimize the possibility of a loss. They should be explained to, and discussed with, the firm's personnel.

1.  Hire a consultant if there is no computer expert in the firm. He or she should have appropriate educational background and real-world experience and be a expert in the automation of business systems.

2.  Generate functional specifications for the firm, including: a) system objective, b) brief description of what is to be automated, e.g., the

---

[8] For a discussion of security problems in a computer installation, see Stuart E. Madnick, "Management Policies and Procedures Needed for Effective Computer Security," *Sloan Management Review*, Vol. 20, No. 1 (Fall 1978), pp. 66-74.

[9] *The International Computer Programs Software Directory* (1119 Keystone Way, Carmel, Indiana 46032) lists software packages available for small business computer systems.

[10] Kitz and Walker, pp. 43-46, weigh the advantages and disadvantages of internally and externally developed software packages. For another viewpoint, see Ted Cary, "Custom Programming/Analysis in the Small Business Environment," *Computer* (September 1976), pp. 16-22.

[11] There are several different ways in which small business systems are marketed. The major methods are described by Louis B. Marienthal in "Selling Small Business Systems," *Datamation* (October 1978), pp. 87-90.

## FIGURE 4
## RATING MATRIX

| Criteria | Value | Vendor A Weight | Vendor A Score | Vendor B Weight | Vendor B Score |
|----------|-------|-----------------|----------------|-----------------|----------------|
| Modular | 10 | 6 | 60 | 5 | 50 |
| Upward compatible | 10 | 7 | 70 | 5 | 50 |
| Reliable | 30 | 8 | 240 | 9 | 270 |
| Maintenance | 30 | 5 | 150 | 2 | 60 |
| Vendor support | 30 | 5 | 150 | 1 | 30 |
| Training courses | 20 | 2 | 40 | 1 | 20 |
| Cost | 20 | 1 | 20 | 5 | 100 |
| Total | | | 730 | | 600 |

mainline information flow, and c) parameters of the business, such as number of customers, inventory items, and orders.

3. Ask each prospective vendor for information on similar systems it has installed, its maintenance capability, and the warranties and terms of purchase or lease.

4. Narrow vendors down to three to five bidders using, for example, a matrix presentation of vendors versus product attributes weighted by their importance (see figure 4).

5. Visit similar operating systems installed by prospective vendors and ask users questions on: customer satisfaction, installation delays, length of installation operations, major difficulties during installation, system reliablity, service level, system modification, and system scope and complexity.

6. Disregard claims by salespeople when selecting a vendor; rely instead on facts from information gathered, vendor's past performance, and evaluation of competence of people with whom the firm will work in system development.

7. Other items:

   a) Specify a terminal-oriented system; cards are costly and unwieldy for small systems.

   b) Never purchase a cassette-based system; it does not provide for random access. A floppy disk, while allowing random access, cannot handle large quantities of data. The more expensive hard core disk provides both random access and substantial opportunities for growth.

   c) Concentrate on availability of software to meet the firm's needs.

8. Carry out a cost analysis comparing costs of existing manual system to costs of the various computer systems under consideration.[12]

9. Once the vendor has been chosen and the standard contract obtained, a lawyer familiar with computer systems should write any necessary addendum covering spe-

[12] Further discussion of the types of costs to be considered in a feasibility study may be found in the article by Curling and Hicks, pp. 7-8.

cific areas of concern to the business.[13]

## CONCLUSIONS

There is no way to guarantee that the computer system, once installed, will not fail. All that can be done is to suggest ways of lessening this possibility. If, after the analysis of the business, its plans, forecasts, and mainline information flow is completed, the business decides computer acquisition still is not feasible, the work done up to this point will not be wasted. The company will have a better grasp of its plans and objectives, will have studied its information flow in such a way that it can be improved and streamlined even in the manual system, and will be better structured.

[13] Robert A. Bucci, "Beware the Standard Lease," *Datamation* (March 1973), pp. 75-76. The Auerback *Data Processing Manual* contains model contracts for computer equipment. Access to this document may be through a local university library or a large corporation, university, or city data processing department. See, also, Dick H. Brandon and Sidney Segelstein, *Data Processing Contracts—Structure, Contents and Negotiation* (New York: Van Nostrand Reinhold Co., 1976). In addition, International Computer Negotiations, Inc., Winter Park, Florida, may be of assistance in contract development.

# 9
# The Future

## THE CURRENT AND CONTINUING CHALLENGE

Through the preceding chapters and the examples of real life information use in this book the major theme has been the importance of information to the organization. To be successful the modern manager must gain control of the information needed to support his function and use it effectively to make better decisions. When this takes place at all levels in the organization, that organization will truly have an information system and will be in the best possible position to meet its objectives. Admittedly this "total" information system is difficult to achieve, and perhaps no organization has yet achieved it. But there are patterns and pathways to follow, and the enlightened firm will follow them and allocate the resources to move through the stages of EDP growth (see chapter 1) to reach the maturity stage and the rewards it offers.

Fortunately these procedures and guides for the manager who is leading his firm to the "ultimate" information system are well tested. For instance, the steps of the systems development life cycle (see chapter 2) are clearly defined and when followed closely result in well-planned, smooth-running, effective applications. This is especially true when there is an overall plan for the information systems function and that information systems plan is a subset of the overall corporate plan. On the other hand when the information systems function must stand alone, when the leadership of the information systems function must develop systems without knowing the organization's ultimate objectives and goals, then it is quite likely that the priorities of the information system will not match those of the organization, and the result will often be suboptimal use of the information resource. The strong IS manager will insist on a corporate planning process within which to develop his own plan, and will work throughout the organization to convince management of the value of planning. The result can only be better, more rational decisionmaking, a clear idea of the consequences of alternative actions, and an organization where responsibility is well defined and performance is objectively measured against meaningful standards.

To have an effective information system function however requires talented people. These people are in scarce supply and command high salaries. The main reason for this scarcity is the technical complexity of the skills which IS people must master: systems analysis, systems design, programming, testing, and system operation as well as people management among others. But no matter which of these the IS professional specializes in, the skill which distinguishes the exceptional IS professional is communications ability. The more effective the IS professional is in communicating with users and with each other, the more effective the resultant information system will be. The key to effective communication between the IS professional and the nontechnical user is keeping the conversation focused on results rather than procedures, machines or techniques. The best communicators are often IS people from departments where the IS mission is defined as servicing the organization's information needs. This attitude creates a climate in which user satisfaction comes before technical efficiency and in which the end product is measured in terms of the value of the results to the organization and not in the amount and kind of technology installed in the computer room.

Top management can insure information systems success by using some tested methods of control and leadership. The first and most important of these is establishing the proper organization for supporting the information systems effort. Planning or advisory committees should be appointed representing all aspects of the organization. Then the IS department itself should be established with clear lines of responsibility and authority and with access to top management.

To insure that the information system reflects the corporate need, one of the various analysis tecbniques described in chapter 2 can be used to examine the organization and its information structure. Through modern communication and design aids such as structured walkthroughs, management can insure that the information systems effort is controlled, organized, on schedule and meeting objectives.

Together with these challenges, management must face up to the dilemmas of which software to use and what hardware to run it on. The software decision goes beyond the basic question of what applications the organization needs. It also includes the decision of whether to make the software in- house, to buy packages or to use some combination of each. The hardware options in today's marketplace are so extensive that it is almost impossible to evaluate all that is available. In fact the variety of functions, speeds and capacities found in the hardware offerings today allow almost any combination of machine features to be assembled into a workable system often using components from different manufacturers. The only limitation on this hybrid system approach is the availability of software to run on that combination of machines. But such systems are technically feasible, and many custom built systems are currently in operation.

Another aspect of the hardware decision is which of the various distribution channels to use. If the hardware is obtained directly from a manufacturer, usually certain support services are available. But when computers are purchased from retail outlets there is often no support at all. The amount of support varies within these extremes, and it is up to the buyer to know how much assistance he needs beyond the hardware. Such decisions are not easy now and will not get easier in the future. In subsequent sections of this chapter the various aspects of the information system (software, people, hardware, applications, distribution) will be examined and the trends for these areas discussed. This is important because as difficult and critical as it is to control the information systems function today, the changes anticipated will make it even more so in the months and years ahead. But first it is necessary to discuss one aspect of information systems which is intensifying the rapidity of change and making much of that change possible: data communications.

## DATA COMMUNICATIONS

Data communications, sometimes called telecommunications or teleprocessing, is simply the ability to send or receive data or information from one location to another. For our purposes a computer is part of the communications process. The "remote" location might be a room adjacent to the computer facility or a location half way around the world. Distance does not alter the definition, only, perhaps, the method of transmission used.

Data communications have been available for some time, even before the advent of computers. Railroads used teletype machines for many years to report freight cars on given trains and to keep track of train movements. Motor carriers too were large users of telephone and telegraph services long before computers became popular in that industry. The difference now is that the communications are controlled by computer; the sending station and receiving station are usually both computers or parts of a computer, and the communications facility is an integral part of the organization's information system and thus subject to the same need for management involvement and control as any other IS function. And another difference today is that present communications facilities are much more reliable. Not only are there wires or lines, but microwave facilities and satellite networks. There is much less weather interference, and when problems arise alternate routing is often available. And due to competition and government action the price is coming into a range where such facilities are a practical reality for most firms.

The major objectives of a communications system are quick response and accuracy. These two elements are the major advantages of and reasons for the concept of distributed data processing (DDP), which was only made possible by the practicality of data communications facilities. In a DDP system, information is entered into the system at the source where the transaction takes place. This insures better accuracy than there would be if documents had to be brought to some central location because reference material is immediately accessible and questions can be answered before mistakes are made. Information at the source is entered in a more timely fashion as well since there is no need to wait until a batch is assembled as is the case at the central location. Often there is a computer at the remote site as part of the data entry system. If so, local processing can be run locally, once again gaining the advantages of timeliness and accuracy as well as lack of dependence on the central facility. The information that is transmitted to the central computer facility is combined with information from other remote locations into corporate reports or made available in some other fashion to management. Without inexpensive and reliable communications facilities, this would not be a practical approach. However, in all such systems, the organization is dependent on the communications link, and when that fails it must be prepared to use another means or do without until service is restored.

The future of information systems will center around communications. New techniques like fiber optics and laser channels will decrease costs even more and increase the reliability and availability of communications transmissions. And the impact will not only be on business. TV sets will become communications terminals in the home as home information services like videotex are developed turning the home into an *electronic cottage*. Through communications, people at home will be able to work, shop and provide for many of their needs much as these activities were centered in the home in times past.

## VIDEOTEX

Videotex is the generic name for home information retrieval systems. Through modified television sets, people at home will have access to large data banks which will provide them with services like world and local news, financial market reports, classified ads, airline timetables, and weather reports as well as announcements of local sporting and entertainment events. And there will also be "active" aspects to videotex. Bills will be paid, deposits switched between accounts, merchandise ordered from "electronic" catalogs, and games played for both fun and profit. Already many home videotex experiments are taking place in this country and abroad, and the question is one of arriving at a standardized approach to videotex rather than the technology or practicality of the concept. (For a discussion of foreign videotex approaches see Haeckel's article reprinted at the end of this chapter.)

The implications of such a system for retailing and many other aspects of how we do business and live our lives are vast. Newspapers will feel the impact both in news reporting and advertising. Banks and other financial institutions will be among the first to change and will welcome videotex. Such aspects as checkless bill paying will reduce bank costs and complement such concepts as *electronic funds transfer systems* (EFTS) which the banks have been advocating for years. The leaders in providing services will be financial institutions, then retailers led by the major stores like Sears and J. C. Penney, then airlines, news wire services and finally publishers like the *New York Times, Time, Reader's Digest,* Mc-Graw Hill and Dow Jones who will be mainly information providers.

Videotex systems will be operated by a variety of companies, but they will usually have a communications or information base. Of course, American Telephone & Telegraph (AT&T) can be expected to have a major position due to its extensive communications facilities. Cable companies like Warner Amex Cable Communications will also have a natural growth path into this area. Broadcasters such as CBS and NBC are also obvious entrants. And finally, as a competitive necessity publishers and information suppliers will be shifting resources to this media as traditional income sources shrink. Though modified TV sets will allow for videotex usage, there will be a market for specialized terminals specifically designed for the system, and such familiar names as Apple, Atari, and Western Electric will be producing these units.

Though Videotex originally had the consumer or home user in mind, to date the major users of the services already established have been business organizations. Though a comprehensive videotex approach is still in development, there are over 800 unique on-line services of the videotex type which can be subscribed to. Among the services being used are such well-known databases as the New York Times Information Bank and the Dow Jones News Retrieval Service as well as specialized services offering stock quotations, commodity futures and patent information. And business demand for this electronically stored information continues to grow.

One indirect effect for business management from the emergence of videotex is that with it will come a tremendous increase in computer literacy among the general population. This will mean that firms can expect their customers and employees to feel more comfortable with computers, and there should be less resistance to computer interaction on the job and in the marketplace.

## SOFTWARE FUTURE

The future of software development especially applications software will be heavily impacted by the continuing scarcity of experienced programmers. And as less qualified persons are hired to meet this scarcity the level of competence of the average programmer will drop. This will mean that in-house software development will cost more and take more time. The situation is compounded by the fact that the kinds of systems which will be designed and programmed in the future will be more complex than those being installed today. These systems are likely to include communications capabilities, database systems, distributed processors and other features which will require programmers to have more than just routine ability.

Four possible scenarios can mitigate this software development dilemma. First, manufacturers will enhance old languages to take advantage of structured techniques. This will build on the knowledge and experience of present programmers allowing them to quickly master these techniques and increase their productivity. Second, new languages will be developed to aid nonprogrammers and new programmers. These will be interactive languages in that the "programmer" will be in direct communication with the computer through a display terminal and will describe the problem to be solved. The computer will then lead the programmer through the program steps with a series of prompting questions. This approach will aid in the development of new programmers as well as provide the opportunity for nontechnical people to write programs for their own functional area with little or no assistance from the information systems department.

A third solution, and one which according to market forecasts will be extremely popular, is purchasing software, either as packages or as custom designed. The software vendors will be able to attract and keep the very best programmers since they can pay them well and can offer them a broad range of experience and programming diversity. Thus their program products will be of good quality and the purchasers will get good value for their price.

Last, hardware advancements may contribute to the software solution in two ways. In terms of applications software, it may be easier to add more hardware than wrestle with complex programming problems. For example, it may be easier and cheaper to add another processor and construct two simple programs than to expend the effort to develop a more complex "double program" to run in one processor. Second, the hardware solution also has an advantage in system software development in the ability to use *firmware,* or circuit elements, which perform like software. When multiple users can use the same software, as in operating systems, firmware programs can be developed and "mass produced" more cheaply than software programs. These firmware programs then become "part of the hardware", freeing up not only programmer time but machine memory and perhaps running time. But even with these solutions, there is no doubt that software is the major potential bottleneck to future information systems success.

## HARDWARE FUTURE

There is no reason to believe that hardware development will slacken, but whether the trend of decreasing cost for increasing power can be sustained is questionable. The price/performance advancements that have brought down the price of so many products from pocket calculators to video games to computers themselves have been advancements in electronics. As the price of the electronic component has shrunk, it has therefore become a smaller percentage of the total cost of the machine. For example, in a typical intelligent workstation the electronic components (memory, logic, display) compose only about 40% of the total cost. The printer, power supply, cabinetry and labor make up the other 60%.[1] This latter group is not affected by the kind of technological enhancements that drop prices so dramatically. In fact, this group is subject to rising costs for materials and labor. Thus, any drop in the electronics category will at least be partially offset by increases in the other components. At some point the electronics price reduction will be less than other cost increases and product cost will begin to rise. As this happens, new applications will be harder to justify and IS growth may slow somewhat.

Other hardware trends will include a decline in the use of punched cards. Cards will continue to be a substantial method of data input for some time until older systems are phased out. Newer systems will use CRTs for keyed input and where possible optical character readers, and ultimately speech recognition devices.

Color graphics will be used for displaying much management information aiding interpretation and analysis while eliminating difficult to use and costly to produce paper reports. Salespersons and similar mobile employees will make increasing use of portable data entry devices, carrying distributed entry to almost its ultimate limit. Based on the availability of communications facilities there will be increased use of point of sale (POS) terminals in retail merchandising, teller terminals in banking and intelligent terminals in business. This intelligent terminal use will further the trend to distributed data processing and away from large mainframe central computers. Whereas mainframes make up about 60% of the market share today, some forecasters indicate this will drop to around 35% by 1985. The slack will be taken up by a slight rise in demand for minicomputers but mainly by greater use of word processors and significant increases in microcomputer installations.

Another way to view the trends in both hardware and software is through the mix of costs for the three major elements in distributed systems: software, central computer and terminals. Presently the central computer accounts for about 65% of the total cost, terminals about 25% and software 10%. Future systems will see the emphasis shift to 40% for central computer, 35% for terminals and 25% for soft-

---

[1]U. Weil, *IBM: Its Future Impact on the EDP Industry* (New York: Morgan Stanley & Co., 1979) p. 14.

ware. This means more and powerful (intelligent) terminals will be used and more software will be needed to support the network.[2]

## DISTRIBUTION AND SERVICE FUTURE

As the price of hardware decreases and the use of mainframes diminishes, new methods of marketing and service will emerge. We have already seen the advent of the computer retail stores such as Computerland and Radio Shack. Major retailers like Sears, Montgomery Ward and J. C. Penney offer computers, and manufacturers themselves (e.g. DEC and IBM) have their own stores or product centers. Computers can also be bought from office equipment dealers, consumer electronic stores and through the mail. This is a dramatic change from the traditional approach where a sales representative took responsibility for a customer and provided technical support people, education, repair service and general "hand holding" to insure an effective installation. The latest concept leaves much more responsibility in the hands of the user organization. The larger mainframe systems will still need considerable vendor support. But as mentioned above, their number as a percentage of the market is declining. For the smaller system user some of these services will be available from the vendor for a price. Others may have to be obtained from a third party. Though all kinds of support services are available from third party firms, machine repair service will become an increasingly important third party offering as more smaller manufacturing firms enter the market. These firms will not be able to support their own service network and will rely on service firms to support their products, particularly outside major metropolitan areas.

The major firms may offer the alternative of remote diagnostic capabilities. When a user has a machine failure, the vendor is notified and phone contact is established between the vendor's diagnostic equipment and the faulty system. The user will have spare parts on the premises and under the direction of the diagnostician will substitute parts. The defective component will then be returned to the manufacturer for repair or replacement.

For the very smallest computers, the only cost effective way to obtain service may be to take the machine to a repair center much as the householder does with small appliances. The impracticality and time-consuming nature of this approach should be a major consideration in purchasing a system of this type. In fact, though we have isolated software as a major bottleneck to system development, support services, particularly repair services, are a close seond to software in their potential to undermine a system if not properly acquired.

A lot of the potential problems in acquiring and servicing a computer in the '80s depends on the quality of the vendor or dealer. This entire area will be greatly influenced by the entry of Japanese firms into the computer market. The strength of the current domestic computer firms is in their marketing approach and the loyalty developed in the user through this intimate and continuing contact. Once the distribution pattern shifts greatly to the impersonal "retail" approach, this advan-

---

[2]Ibid., p. 7

tage will be diminished and the competition with the Japanese will be on a more equal footing. At that time even more firms will enter the market forcing management to be even more diligent it its evaluation and choice of information systems and services.

## APPLICATION FUTURE

The scarcity of well-trained information systems professionals has been discussed above. But the proliferation of computers will have other impacts on users and the population at large. The general public will continue to gain familiarity with computer-based products as more of them are installed in supermarkets, banks, factories and offices. This will advance opportunities for even more computer use as resistance to the unknown lessens.

There will also continue to be a changing occupation mix as jobs shift away from agriculture and industry and continue to increase in service industries and what is being termed *information occupations*. The article by Haeckel at the end of this chapter explores this in more detail.

Computer uses will change as all these other areas change. The home computer will still be a hobbiest's diversion but will also aid in home accounting chores and will be able to be a terminal in a videotex system. Specialized applications will be developed or expanded such as the area of telemedicine where distant medical specialists will participate in diagnosis and treatment through computer facilities. Home feedback applications will also be expanded. Like the currently operating QUBE network, these systems allow the user not only to receive TV and cable programs but to express opinions or vote on issues.

In the commercial area, office automation and the institution of electronic mail will bring major productivity advancements. Energy conservation will continue to be enhanced as computer controlled systems are increasingly installed in both plant and office and begin to move into homes and apartments. Utilities will develop and implement automatic meter reading applications. The potential in the financial area will be in the extension of the electronic funds transfer system (EFTS). Already many institutions offer debit cards which in effect substitute for cash and checks, in effect drawing directly on one's bank account. Current debit cards have a magnetic strip with account identifying information on it. But experiments are now being performed on a new type of debit card which has a computer chip embedded in the plastic card with the capacity to hold much more information than account number making the card valuable for other applications. Some suggested uses for this *smart card* are as a general identification card, i.e., as a library card, driver's license, debit card, credit card and the like. It could also contain medical history and other identifying information such as next of kin in case of emergency. Some predict that eventually every person would have just two cards. One would be a *commercial card* and would contain credit information and personal data such as the emergency information suggested above. The other would be a *government-issued card* and would be used for "official" purposes such as a driver's license, passport, social security claims, unemployment benefits and other government services. Whether such a smart card system and the cashless society it offers will ever come about is more of a social question than a technical problem. The cards have been developed, and the processing capability is available. But it remains to be seen whether fears of invaded privacy and other psychological objections will delay or even prevent such a system from being implemented.

In the factory great potential exists for the automation of the production process with attendant increases in productivity. Such systems will be particularly effective in processes requiring short production runs. Automation should help reduce set-up time and allow for specification changes to be made rapidly. This will reduce costs and encourage product modification and differentiation, creating a situation exactly opposite to the "common" or identical output which resulted from early plant automation and mass production. Now we have the potential for specialized production on as large or small a scale as is necessary. Aiding this plant automation thrust are the computer-aided design (CAD) and computer-aided manufacturing (CAM) systems described in chapter 5. But the ultimate in factory automation will be through robots.

Related to the concepts of automated manufacturing and robots is that of artificial intelligence (AI). This is a catch phrase for a number of approaches at making the computer "think" like a human being. What this means is that computers will be able to reason and make judgments and perhaps even learn. The implications of this are vast both in terms of the impact on individuals and on society in general. New jobs will be created, some jobs will disappear,others will be radically changed and greatly improved. Even now, early forms of AI have been developed and are being used successfully. In one application it is being used to aid a computer manufacturer select components to create least-cost custom systems for clients from thousands of individual parts and combinations. In another use, computers are providing business facts and figures in answer to managers' English language queries which require no special format or structure. Also devices are being developed which react to sights and sounds. This is where the possibilities with robots become quite dramatic.

AI is another area where the Japanese are very involved. In fact there is a government-announced program to create the "fifth generation" computer which will be aimed specifically at AI applications. There will be technological advances that will enable these machines to store vast amounts of information and to link the information together in "thought patterns" much like human brain linkages. It is even anticipated that user-computer interaction will be simply through normal speech. The expected voice vocabulary will exceed 10,000 words. One of their biggest uses will be as consultants. With their resevoirs of knowledge they can be asked for advice and information over a broad range of areas and subjects. These "expert programs" will differ from simple data processing information hookups in that the software will allow for some interpretation or modification of the question by the computer, for partial answers and for substitutes or alternate solutions. In effect expert programs offer heuristic know-how or rule-of-thumb decisionmaking in addition to factual information.

Of all the issues raised, that of job displacement is the most critical if only because it is the most visible. If computers (robots) can think and act like humans there will be a strong desire on the part of business managers to substitute these standardized, well-engineered, thoroughly tested, precisely programmed robots for the unreliable, imprecise, potentially-ill, somewhat uncooperative and unevenly skilled humans. The effect, it is predicted, will take place particularly in blue collar jobs. For instance, one forecaster predicts the advent of driverless trucks. Such computer-guided vehicles will mean thousands of lost jobs for truck drivers. One solution to such unemployment is retraining these people for the vast number of new information systems jobs. This would be feasible because where previously people in this and similar blue collar categories did not have the background for IS positions, advances in hardware and software will reduce the skill levels necessary for these IS jobs and thus allow these people the new opportunities. Whether there will be sufficient opportunities for all those displaced is the essential question. No one really knows the answer. But if the displaced do not find productive means of employment, then there will be no one to buy the mountains of goods that the automated factories will be producing. So the problem must be solved.

The significance of AI and the other future applications for the manager is this: the present opportunities for computer assistance in aiding the manager have hardly been recognized let alone taken, and the future is already here. The enlightened manager will prepare for these future opportunties by building the best system that today's technology allows and modifying that as rapidly as new advances take place.

## CONCLUSION

Whether this progress is all worthwhile is a debatable issue. Certainly where there are productivity gains, they are to be applauded. Robots and computer-assisted manufacturing allow more individuality in the products produced and this should contribute to a higher standard of living. Other benefits like shorter work weeks and more leisure time also seem desirable. On the other hand there is the fear that computers will rule our lives, that their dominance in society will depersonalize and dehumanize our day-to-day activities. It is felt individuals will lack control over their affairs and will certainly have less privacy than they have now. Finally there is sure to be a loss of jobs or at best a shift of occupations, especially in the plant and other labor intensive occupations.

So the challenge of the present and the future remains for the manager. There is no lack of opinion about what lies ahead. The general consensus is that there will be more distributed processing and increased use of communications facilities. IS budgets will reflect a move away from central site hardware which in turn will mean more of a reliance on communications. Salaries, software, services and supplies will also be increased expense areas, but not with the same percentage growth as communications.

Making the transition and taking advantage of the opportunities will not be easy. There are many tangible and intangible obstacles to IS success. Figure 9–1 shows the results of a Booz Allen survey of executives as to their perceptions of what stands in the way of their IS achievements. Tied for the lead were not linking IS plans to corporate plans and not having experienced employees in-house. Close behind was the incomplete, inadequate or inefficient state of current hardware and software. Next came user resistance, then not expanding the role of systems to serve all aspects

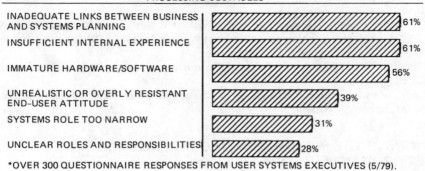

USERS PERCEPTIONS* OF INFORMATION
PROCESSING OBSTACLES

INADEQUATE LINKS BETWEEN BUSINESS AND SYSTEMS PLANNING — 61%

INSUFFICIENT INTERNAL EXPERIENCE — 61%

IMMATURE HARDWARE/SOFTWARE — 56%

UNREALISTIC OR OVERLY RESISTANT END–USER ATTITUDE — 39%

SYSTEMS ROLE TOO NARROW — 31%

UNCLEAR ROLES AND RESPONSIBILITIES — 28%

*OVER 300 QUESTIONNAIRE RESPONSES FROM USER SYSTEMS EXECUTIVES (5/79).

Figure 9-1.

Source: Booz, Allen & Hamilton Inc.

of the organization. The final obstacle is the danger of unclear roles and responsibilities.

We have addressed these issues and others in our attempt to give the manager both the direction and the tools to take advantage of what the information age has to offer. Hopefully this guidance will lead to greater IS success.

## REFERENCES

Artificial intelligence. *Business Week* (March 8, 1982): 66–69, 72, 75.
A detailed account of the present state of the art. Provides a good background for the layman who meets up with the emerging technology.

Asimov, I. 1978. And it will serve us right. *People's Computers* 7 (1): 16–20.
An essay on the mythology of robots. A "must" primer for the newly initiated robot addict. Asimov's theme involves the relationship between the creator and the created. When faced with the ultimate question of how we can prevent being taken over by the computer, Asimov answers, "If ever a species needed to be replaced for the good of the planet, we do."

Graziano, L. 1978. Robots in literature and life. *People's Computers* 7 (1): 13–15.
Reviews the treatment of robots in literature and poses some interesting questions on human-robot relations: Is the human in control because he can always pull the plug? Can the machine "come up with an idea" that is not the direct response of having been programmed to do so? What qualities do we want our machines to have?

Haeckel, S. 1982. Marketing in the eighties: a decade of transition. Armonk, NY: IBM Corporation.
An overview of where technology is leading society. Discusses videotex and other anticipated changes from the perspective of their impact on marketing. Reprinted herein on pp. 418–427.

The home information revolution. *Business Week* (June 29, 1981): 74–77, 80, 83.
Reviews videotex's present and future capabilities. Good descriptions of the services and advantages.

Jastrow, R. 1978. Post-human intelligence. *People's Computers* 7 (1): 21–23.
Speculates on where evolution will lead in terms of the human brain and machine intelligence. Jastrow believes that the brain is no longer expanding and that its development is almost complete. He assumes that further evolution will be manifested in new and higher forms of life.

Japan's strategy for the '80s. *Business Week* (December 14, 1981): 39–120.
Full report on Japan's government-supported drive into the computer industry. Among others, specific areas covered are semiconductors, information processing, AI, robots and communications.

The speedup in automation. *Business Week* (August 3, 1981): 58–63, 66–67.

A discussion of factory and office automation techniques and impacts. Excellent section on job displacement.

Weil, U. 1979. *IBM: Its Future Impact on the EDP Industry.* New York: Morgan Stanley & Co.

A review of IBM's industry position as well as many projections of EDP trends in hardware and software expenditures, occupations and prices.

Zachmann, W. F. 1982. Planning and designing a communications system: a practical guide. *Computerworld* **16** (11a): 41–47.

A thorough and somewhat technical explanation of how to take advantage of this increasingly essential element of information processing.

## TRANSITIONS IN THE INFORMATION TECHNOLOGY INDUSTRY
## A MARKETING REVIEW

Stephan H. Haeckel

Reprinted by permission: Stephen H. Haeckel, IBM Corporation, 1982.

### RELATING TO THE ENVIRONMENT

Professor Ray Corey of Harvard University describes marketing as the process by which an organization relates itself productively to its environment. This definition brings into sharp focus the appropriate orientation of marketing: to the environment.

It suggests that an attempt to determine the marketing issues of the eighties should be built on an assessment of how the environment will change during this decade. Once we have a handle on that, the issues involved in responding to, managing, and exploiting these changes can be identified.

### THE CENTRALITY OF INFORMATION

The environmental changes in store for us in the 1980s are not trivial. According to Daniel Bell, the Harvard sociologist, they add up to nothing less than a new era in history—which he calls the Post-Industrial Era. Post-Industrial Society is predominantly a service economy, and its essential charac-

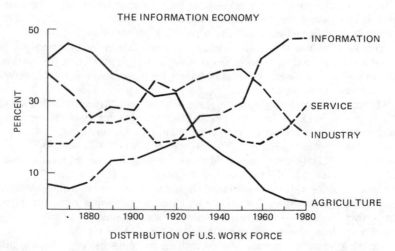

Figure 1

teristic is that *codified information and knowledge replace capital and energy as the primary resources by which other resources are transformed.*

The new *centrality of codified information* is a powerful concept. As a premise, it is analogous to the law of gravity: once you accept it, you have a pretty good idea of the direction things will ultimately take.

Bell's formulation goes a long way toward making concrete the fuzzy concept of "the information age." In fact, there is quantitative support for the assertion that we have already become an information-centered, Post-Industrial Society. (Figure 1.)

## TWO FUNDAMENTAL MOTIVATIONS

From this chart we can see that, prior to 1900, the U.S. was predominantly an agricultural economy; between 1900 and 1960 we were an industrial society; and since 1960 have been a service and information society—at least in terms of work force distribution.

The productivity implications of this distribution are important: 4% of the work force is feeding the United States and a goodly portion of western Siberia. 24% are blue collar workers. Bell projects that by the year 2000, blue collar workers will represent 10% of the work force and contribute over 50% of the GNP. The white collar work force represents more than 2/3 of the work force. Their productivity was estimated in 1976 to be less than 2/3 that of their blue collar brethren.

There is a high correlation between productivity and the amount of capital investment behind each class of worker. Estimates vary, but typically, the average agricultural worker is said to have around $75,000 of capital investment behind him; the industrial worker around $35,000–$45,000; and the white collar worker only $2,000–$2,500.

Now, to economists, that may sound like a problem. But to marketers, it's clearly an opportunity—an opportunity to sell capital goods to service and information workers which will "industrialize" their activity. Office systems, point of sale terminals, teller machines, computer aided instruction systems—all these products represent a "capitalization" of manpower intensive services.

According to some observers, this trend,—which Professor T. Levitt termed "the industrialization of service"—has been accelerating over the past five to ten years and is beginning to pay off. The Hudson Institute, for one, has undertaken studies which indicate that segments of the service industry are making substantial gains in productivity—gains largely masked by current measurement techniques.

Some industry analysts have projected that, by 1990, as much as 60% of the U.S. white collar work force will be direct users of terminals, personal computers, keyboards, and workstations costing less than $10,000. That class of equipment will probably represent more than 40% of the shipments of the industry by 1990—which suggests strongly that, sometime in the *next* decade, individuals will become the predominant factor in acquisition decisions for our industry's products. This implies a substantial shift in the character and quantity of the decision-makers with whom we deal.

We have now identified two primary motivations: the need of individuals for information; and the need for service/information worker productivity. The question now becomes, "What will happen in the 1980s to turn these motivations into demand?"

## TECHNOLOGY: ENABLER OF MANY FUTURES; DETERMINANT OF NONE

According to its manufacturer, the programmable calculator which I keep in my upper left hand desk drawer, has half the main memory, adds ten times as fast, and multiplies four times as fast as the IBM 650 on which I learned to program. (Figure 2.) The IBM 650 cost around 200,000 1955 dollars, the programmable calculator around 200 1980 dollars.

That works out to an improvement of four orders-of-magnitude in the efficiency of processing information, the primary transforming resource of the Post-Industrial Era. Comparing that to the two orders-of-magnitude improvement in the efficiency of converting energy from one form to an-

| | IBM 650 COMPUTER | T1-59 CALCULATOR |
|---|---|---|
| COMPONENTS | 2,000 TUBES | 166,500 TRANS. EQUIV'TS |
| POWER, KVA | 17.7 | 0.00018 |
| VOLUME, CU. FT. | 270 | 0.017 |
| WEIGHT, LBS. | 5,650 | 0.67 |
| AIR CONDITIONING | 5 TO 10 TONS | NONE |
| MEM. CAPACITY • PRIMARY • SECONDARY | 3,000 BITS 100,000 BITS | 7,680 BITS 40,000 BITS |
| EXECUTION TIME, MILLISECONDS ADD MULTIPLY | 0.75 20.0 | 0.070 4.0 |
| PRICE | $200,000 (1955 DOLLARS) | $200 (1979 DOLLARS) |

Source: Texas Instruments

Figure 2

other—which sparked the Industrial Revolution 200 years ago—lends credence to the argument of Professor Bell that the forces at work are indeed of a magnitude which can effect historic change.

The impact of this steady improvement, expected to continue at about the same rate for at least the next ten years, can be described in very personal terms. The four function electronic calculator which my wife bought me for $125 in December of 1973, cost only $95 in January of 1974. In the 18 months subsequent to breaking the $100 barrier, the annualized volumes for that calculator rose by a factor of 10; the market changed from "producer-push" to "consumer pull;" the channels of distribution changed; the potential for the product went from one to several per household; and, most importantly, the purchase criterion changed from "investment" to "discretionary."

The same phenomenon occurred subsequently with the personal computer. For the past two years, I have had a computer in my home which is more powerful than the 1401 IBM hired me to install in the early 1960s. Our personal computer was a discretionary purchase in the sense that it was not financially justified. It is used for entertainment, family finances, and education.

The growth in demand for personal computers has consistently exceeded projections. A recent forecast suggested that there would be almost ten million personal computers installed in the U.S. by 1985, roughly two thirds of them in homes. Should this occur, personal computers will have reached roughly the level of household penetration at which black and white—and later color—television set sales began to grow explosively, due to their potential as an advertising medium.

As more and more information technology becomes packaged at discretionary price levels, vendors in the information technology industry will face the prospect of a significant change in both the people who will be making the purchase decisions for their products, and the criteria by which those decisions will be made.

## THE INTEGRATION OF MULTIPLE MEDIA IN INFORMATION SYSTEMS

Not too long ago, the information technology industry was neatly segmented by medium. Computers did data processing, typewriters handled text, copiers dealt with images, and telephones with voice.

Over the past two decades, technology has made it economically attractive to transmit these media over communication lines as numerical codes. "Digitizing" makes pictures and the spoken word processable by digital computers, and has led to the intermixing of these four media in a variety of applications. (Figure 3.)

One industry consultant has projected that, by 1984, 100% of the data, 92% of the text, 25% of the image, and 40% of the voice information which is communicated among commercial establishments in the U.S. will be in digital form.

Different combinations of media have resulted in a wide variety of new products: "intelligent" copiers, videoconferencing systems, shared logic office systems, etc. New combinations of media result in new offerings, with new users and new usages. Our industry is experiencing significant growth in demand for these different ways of packaging essentially the same technology.

The trend of integrating digitized information has spawned at least one new industry: the so called "electronic publishing" industry, which furnishes multi-media information over communication or broadcasting facilities for a fee. Early experiments with these offerings have highlighted a significant public policy issue: which, if any, of the regulations/statutes/federal agency jurisdictions that were established for the individual medium are applicable to services which combine them electronically? The uncertainties arising from this question have not inhibited widespread trials of a variety of offerings; they may well, however, delay large scale commercial implementation of public offerings.

Intra-enterprise integrated information systems are the heart of the so-called "office of the future." They are directly aimed at improving the productivity of the white collar worker. The potential payoffs are so great that industry projections of demand for office systems range between $35–45 billion by 1990.

But precisely what executives, management, and professionals will *do* with this capability, once they have it, is unclear...almost as unclear as the major applications of the digital computer were thirty years ago.

Just as was the case then, the first efforts at answering the question are being directed at discovering which parts of existing activities can be automated. But this is just the tip of the iceberg. If we recall the central importance of information, it seems clear that the very act of placing an executive or

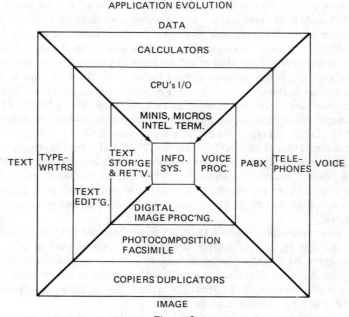

Figure 3

professional "on-line" to information that he needs, but previously did not have, will change the nature of his job and the way he organizes his work.

One study of white collar work concluded that we office workers spend over 90% of our time collecting, distilling, reorganizing, and communicating information; and less than 4% analyzing and exploiting it. To the extent that relevant information is made available, not only to the specific individual, but to his peers, subordinates, and superiors, his job will *have* to change—from collecting, distilling, and communicating information, to exploiting it.

Therefore, as a marketer, I conclude that it is less important for us to understand what part of existing jobs can be automated, than it is to learn "what is the information of greatest usefulness to each class of users?" The answers to that question are important to all of us, because changes in people's jobs will affect their needs for other-than-information products and services, as well.

As we did in the 1960s, we will work with our customers to find these answers. Only this time, instead of identifying the major applications by *industry,* we will be focusing on the information of greatest usefulness by *occupation.*

# INFORMATION INFRASTRUCTURE: THE POTENTIAL OF VIDEOTEX

VIDEOTEX is a form of electronic publishing which turns a television set into a terminal, giving its user access to an information network. Its contribution is primarily the very easy-to-use nature of its implementation, making an "on-line tree-structured data base data communications system" appear as an advanced function television set.

Because virtually everyone is familiar with, and comfortable with, a television set, the prospect of achieving rapid penetration of homes with a set which has been modified to handle VIDEOTEX is good. Current costs for the electronics to modify a TV set for VIDEOTEX range from $150 to $1500, but this cost is coming down fast, and some TV manufacturers are building the capability into their newer models in anticipation of public offerings in the U.S.

VIDEOTEX was originally developed in the United Kingdom, and is currently available there as a public offering under the name PRESTEL. Although it was intended for the home market, almost 90% of its current subscribers are business users. From this, some conclude that there is no demand for electronic consumer information services. But these people, again, fail to take into account the "centrality of information." Because, if one looks at the nature of the information available on PRESTEL, one finds it is predominantly the kind of information of interest to someone in the office (reservations, financial reports, travel schedules, etc.) rather than the type that is selling personal computers to home owners in the U.S. (Adventure, PAC-MAN, Backgammon, Chess, etc.).

Accordingly, there has been increasing demand by businesses for private PRESTEL systems which run on their own computers, because the ease-of-use characteristics and the relatively inexpensive cost of TV sets makes VIDEOTEX an attractive offering for certain classes of "casual use" applications.

In France, the implementation of VIDEOTEX is called TELETEL. It is the centerpiece of the French Government's "Telematique" program—one of whose objectives is to place a 960 character display with alphanumeric keyboard in over 30 million French homes, free of charge, by the early 1990s. The implications of this objective are profound: if successful, the French will have established an information infrastructure in their society which parallels the communications infrastructure represented by the telephone system.

In Germany, the government sponsored VIDEOTEX system is called BILDSCHIRMTEXT. In Canada it's called TELIDON; in Japan CAPTAINS. But in the U.S., due to the lack of a central authority to dictate standards, there are literally dozens of independent, incompatible implementations of this kind of capability. This diversity will certainly retard the rate at which information providers, equipment manufacturers, and users invest in VIDEOTEX in the U.S.—although, as mentioned previously, it doesn't seem to be retarding experimentation.

VIDEOTEX is important because of its potential for creating an information infrastructure. It is currently developing more coherently in other countries than it is in the United States.

# INHIBITORS

VIDEOTEX and the "office of the future" are but two of many areas of opportunity for information technology providers, and for the providers of information and transaction systems. The discovery, definition and implementation of new information services may well be the focus of an era of entrepreneurial and innovative activity which will make the supporting technological innovation—impressive as it is—secondary.

But this promise cannot be realized without coming to grips with some intractable realities which will determine the rate at which the potential of technology is realized. To mention a few:

## Complexity

The complexity—in a systems sense—of information infrastructures which are composed of multiple, hierarchial networks, is truly mindboggling. Much more than physical connection of multiple computers and terminals to a communications network is involved, though this is complicated enough. Multiple data representations, device characteristics, formats, protocols, software systems, applications, etc., etc., etc., must be accommodated. A wide range of security, reliability, auditability, privacy, and performance trade-offs must be permitted. "User friendliness" or "ease of use"—whatever they mean (and they mean different things to different users in different environments)—must be sufficient. A wide range of physical media, each with greatly differing cost/performance/function characteristics, (cable, copper wire, optical fibre, satellite, microwave, cellular radio, etc.) must be supported. Indeed, our ability to manage complexity will likely be the ultimate determinant of the extent to which the information society is realized.

## Productivity

White collar productivity, as we have seen, is a primary motivation behind Post Industrial Society. But we do not know how to measure it. What is the value of a new technology, process, or procedure? Until we understand the metrics of productivity, justification for investments in information systems will be less rapid than otherwise.

## Regulation

Because access to public information is a "right," and control of information represents power, a degree of regulation is certain. Much less certain is the extent to which regulation, legislation, and the promulgation of standards will add up to a coherent body of public policy.

## Valuation

As Professor Bell has pointed out, there exists no economic value theory for information. What then will be the metric by which investment in information and information technology is justified and prioritized? The most likely answer is that information will be valued in terms of the net amount of other resources which are conserved when the "right" information is made available under the "right" circumstances. This is basically the method by which data processing equipment has been rationalized for the past three decades. It has the merit of being conservative, but the disadvantage of any substitute measurement: certain dimensions of value are simply not counted.

For example, a study of the economics of videotex home banking concluded that the videotex solution

- reduced the cost to the consumer of paying a bill by 50%,
- reduced the cost to the biller of managing accounts receivables by 50%,
- enabled the bank—by charging for each transaction—to realize a net surplus, instead of the current deficit, per transaction.

It can be seen that the cost of stamps, envelopes, checks, bricks, mortar, teller cages, teller salaries, etc., represent an expenditure of resources which can be avoided if the right information is available at the right time via an electronic information delivery system. But what about the fact that the service itself is enhanced? Banking can be done at 3:00 a.m.; budget and tax reports can be produced as a by-product; better control of financial assets is possible, etc.

## Social Impacts

There are at least two profound implications associated with automation and information infrastructures.

The first is the fact that in redistributing information and knowledge, power is also redistributed. Redistributions of power are not often accomplished without tension and conflict. These must be recognized and managed.

The second is the oft-heard concern that automation will "throw people out of work." Actually, that doesn't happen, of course. Precisely the reverse occurs: automation "throws work out of people." The distinction is much more than semantic. The first formulation conjures up unemployment; the second the need for re-training and re-deployment of human resource to activities of higher added value. Recognizing the need to retrain and redeploy people at the outset can be the difference between success and disaster in the implementation of information systems.

## MARKETING IN THE 1980s

In the face of the profound environmental changes which accompany the introduction of the Post-Industrial Era, what changes will the marketing profession experience?

Everything and nothing.

"Nothing," in the sense that there will be no change in the basic function of marketing: relating the organizations' products and services to its environment. The marketing process of identifying customer needs and demonstrating how they are satisfied by vendor offerings is a constant.

"Everything," in the sense that the nature of the needs and the offerings will be substantially different.

These changes will not occur overnight, of course. They will be evolutionary, and the rate and extent of change will vary industry by industry. Accordingly, we have the option of dealing with them as evolutionary transitions over the next several years, or as planning discontinuities at the end of that period.

## Customers

I heard an executive of one of the largest banks in the country say that his bank's plans call for 90% of their transactions to be carried out electronically by 1990, versus 3% in 1980. If that comes to pass, this bank will be a different institution at the end of the decade: with new services, new skills, new support requirements, and a new structure.

More recently, I had a discussion with the vice president for corporate development of a large retail chain. By the end of the afternoon he was making notes to himself to charter market research to identify the characteristics of products which will continue to be sold through stores, and those which will be more efficiently and competitively marketed through a combination of a few large automated warehouses, overnight delivery services, and a shop-at-home information service.

That led him to consider whether or not his company had a sufficiently generic definition of the business they were really in: was it the business of managing retail stores, or the business of placing manufacturers' products in the hands of consumers? If the latter, where would reside the primary economic "added value"—in the management of the assets, the physical distribution system, or the information service?

In manufacturing companies, the introduction of robots and microprocessors will dramatically change the economics of short production runs, and permit much greater tailoring of products to individual customer needs.

The list goes on and on. And it is not restricted to large companies. Technology has brought the cost of information processing tools down to the point that the smallest company or entrepreneur is a prospect for systems of startling sophistication. There is increasing capability for individual designers, composers, authors, editors, lawyers, tax accountants, etc., etc., to perform their work on terminals or personal computers much more productively; and to transform their services into more complete and competitive offerings in the process.

It is diverting—and a temptation to which many have succumbed—to fill pages and volumes with fantasies on "a day in the life of an electronic cottage." But an objective observer will note that there is not a raging consumer demand for these services at present. It therefore seems to me unlikely that the consumer will dictate what we will see as commercial offerings—at least initially. It will be the institutions with the economic incentive to make their services available electronically that will undertake the considerable investment necessary to make it attractive for the consumer. Attractive enough that he will change his life-style for it—as he did for the television set, the car, and the supermarket.

How a given company and its customers will be affected depends upon the degree to which their businesses are information intensive. It also depends on the premises of information availability that are implicit in the current structure and objectives of the enterprise. The nature of this kind of assessment is exemplified by a quote attributed to the CEO of a large aircraft manufacturing company: "We are in the *knowledge* business . . . it just so happens that airplanes come off the end of our assembly lines."

## Products

The products of information technology vendors will change as new combinations of voice, data, text, and image are developed. A greater premium will be placed on the completeness and useability of offerings that are combinations of hardware, software, and services. Architectural coherence will be of paramount importance in providing a reliable, secure, and cost effective path between information providers and information users.

The integration of electronic chips in telephones, credit/debit cards, cars, dishwashers, television sets, and a host of other devices will modify their cost, function, service, and use characteristics.

And services will be enhanced, integrated, and delivered in different ways.

## Competition

Existing competitors will change, and new competitors will emerge. Banks, broadcasters, newspapers, publishers, communication companies, computer companies, and others are currently prototyping new services which bring them into competition with one another—in many cases for the first time.

Entrepreneurs are arising who package multiple services into a coherent product line in order to attract end users at home and in the office.

Existing firms have the advantage of being a going concern with an established customer base, distribution system, and structure. Newcomers have the advantage of greater flexibility, fewer "locked-in" investments, and therefore, tend to be faster on their feet in establishing their claim on "new-turf" opportunities.

## Channels of Distribution

As the cost of information technology products continues to fall, and as individuals become the primary acquirers of them, non-sales force channels assume greater importance. In many cases the sophistication of these products require greater knowledge and different skills at the point of sale than currently exists.

Substituting better and more timely information for other resources may substantially change the economics of distribution. The distribution channel for electronic bank-at-home systems, for example, will be cables, telephone wires, satellites, or microwave, which have vastly different capital and operating costs than branch banks. At a recent seminar on the future of the financial services industry one speaker speculated—only half in jest—that the big winners in that industry ten years from now may be the computing services firms who manage the distribution of information, not the funds.

## STRATEGIC TRANSITIONS

For those involved in the management of information and information technology, the decade of the 1980's promises to be one of major transition—transition in the sense that the answers to several strategic questions will be different in the 1990's than they were in the 1970's. (Figure 4.)

- The resource of primary economic value will evolve from hardware (capital) via software (service) to information.
- End-user departments and individuals will replace the data processing executive as the primary acquirer of information technology and services. The DP executive will have the responsiblity for creating and managing the information system infrastructure, and will be held accountable, to an increasing extent, for the husbanding of an enterprise's information resource in a manner analogous to the way a CFO is held accountable for "control" of the capital resource.
- Information services revenues (software, maintenance, computing services) will grow faster than information equipment revenues.
- Selection of network and database architectures which integrate voice, text, image and data into an information infrastructure will become a more strategic decision than the selection of computer processor architecture.

### SEVEN STRATEGIC TRANSITIONS

|  | 1970's | 1990's |
|---|---|---|
| COMPONENT OF PRIMARY ECONOMIC VALUE | • HARDWARE | • INFORMATION |
| PRIMARY ACQUIRER | • DP EXEC | • END-USER |
| PRIMARY DISTINCTION AMONG VENDORS | • PRODUCT | • OFFERINGS |
| STRATEGIC ARCHITECTURE | • DP HARDWARE | • NETWORK, DATA BASE |
| PRIMARY SOURCE OF INDUSTRY GROWTH | • EQUIPMENT • BUSINESS | • SERVICES • INDIVIDUAL (BUSINESS AND CONSUMER) |
| PRIMARY SOURCE OF "FUTURE" DEMAND FOR CAPACITY | • ON-LINE DATA BASE APPLICATIONS | • NON-CODED INFORMATION APPLICATIONS |
| PRIMARY INHIBITORS TO GROWTH | • COST OF EQUIPMENT • COST OF COMMUNICATIONS • COMPLEXITY | • USEABILITY • REGULATION • STANDARDS • INFRASTRUCTURE CHANGES • COMPLEXITY |

Figure 4

- Vendors will, to an increasing degree, distinguish themselves by the quality and completeness of information offerings, rather than products. These offerings will be combinations of hardware, software, and services packaged to provide information of high value to important classes of individuals.
- Ten years hence, in articles describing the source of industry growth for decade to come, th focus will be on "non- coded" information applications (e.g., voice and image). For the 1980's, on-line access to coded information (data and text) will prevail.

Both vendors and users will be devising business strategies to address a new set of inhibitors of the realization of the "information age."

## CONCLUSION

The technology is, for all intents and purposes, available. The infrastructures are evolving.

It remains for the entrepreneurs to discover, create, package, price and market those information offerings which will induce us to change the way we work and live. These will be the entrepreneurs of the Information Age—of Post-Industrial Society.

# APPENDICES

The following section contains selected reprints which provide detailed explanations in four general areas. They are included as a ready reference for the manager when a particular need arises.

**APPENDIX A: SOURCE EDP COMPUTER CAREER PLANNING GUIDE**

A guide to information system careers including job descriptions, career development strategies and a career planning case study.

# The Career Planning Cycle

Career planning is not unlike developing long-term plans to solve any other business problem. Essentially, one must establish objectives, develop a strategy to meet these objectives, monitor actual versus planned progress and take corrective action if needed. There are, however, several aspects which make career planning unique. First, career planning is highly complex in nature because the structure under which one works may be broad or expanding and can shift unexpectedly. Second, much of the information that can directly affect career planning — such as salary structures or opportunities for promotion — is shrouded in a veil of confidentiality and not available for general knowledge. Finally, long-term career planning is a continuous activity made up of a series of intermediate steps, each of which, must be executed for the total plan to meet with success. We would like to review these steps, briefly, in this section.

The Career Planning Cycle, presented graphically in Exhibit 1 (see opposite page), involves the following steps:

## 1
### Know the Structure

A realistic long-term career goal can be established only after the structure of the computing profession is well known and understood. This includes a thorough knowledge of the various levels of responsibility within the field, the makeup of experience and training required for each position within these levels and the logical alternative career paths that exist within the profession.

## 2
### Establish Goals

Given knowledge of the structure of the computing profession, the next step involves establishing a long-term career objective which is both realistic

in terms of the professional environment and consistent with personal ambition. A series of intermediate goals may then be established which, if achieved, will logically lead to fulfillment of the long-term objective.

## 3
### Assess Current Position

It is necessary to evaluate exactly where one stands currently in relation to his or her long-term goal. As we will review later in detail, experience gained and responsibility level achieved to date in relation to current compensation is a crucial factor in long-term career planning. In this step, as well as the next, it is important that objectivity not be obscured as a result of personal bias in self-appraisal.

## 4
### Assess Needed Exposure

A sharp focus must now be placed upon defining the exact elements of new experience needed to progress along a chosen career path. As we will discuss, areas of new exposure are not restricted solely to development of technical computing disciplines but include others as well. An accurate appraisal in this step is essential if career progress is to be optimized.

## 5
### Develop a Plan of Action

Once needed areas of new exposure are defined, the next step is to develop a plan of action that will result in providing such exposure. There are a number of strategies in career planning. They may or may not involve a change in employment, a redirection of career path, an industry shift, etc. Once a plan is developed, it must be *acted* upon in a reasonable time frame, or, as we will discuss, career progress may be seriously impeded.

## 6
### Evaluate the Results

Whatever career planning strategy executed, it is necessary periodically to evaluate and measure the results achieved compared to those planned. Is the new exposure sought actually being gained? Has responsibility level been improved? Is the current working environment conducive to taking a further step along the planned career path?

## 7
### Take Corrective Action

If, for any reason actual exposure has not measured up to planned exposure, it is necessary to "recycle" the career plan beginning at step 1.

Reprinted by permission. The report is published annually. For a complete copy of the current Computer Salary Survey and Career Planning Guide, call a Source EDP office near you.

Exhibit 1
The Career Planning Cycle

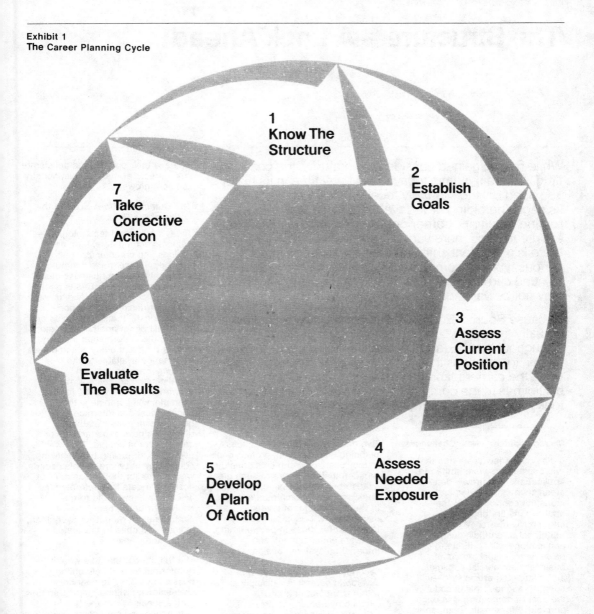

1
Know The
Structure

2
Establish
Goals

3
Assess
Current
Position

4
Assess
Needed
Exposure

5
Develop
A Plan
Of Action

6
Evaluate
The Results

7
Take
Corrective
Action

# The Structure—A Look Ahead

While having gained considerable maturity, the computer field is more dynamic today than at any time in its history. You need only to scan any recent trade journal to find its pages heralding new developments in technology with routine regularity. Career opportunities in the industry are greater and more varied than ever before. Moreover, there is a constant shift and expansion in demand for various types of computer skills. What may have been a sound career planning strategy only a year or two ago may not be valid today.

Because Source Edp is in regular and close contact with virtually the entire computer employment community throughout the U.S. and Canada, we are in a unique position to monitor trends as they develop, and interpret their impact upon the career planning strategy for each of the many disciplines in the computer field. Some of the things we look for in the months and years ahead are outlined below.

### Microcomputers—New Challenges

It was only a few years ago that microcomputers were limited to applications in narrowly defined areas such as scientific and industrial control. Today, the applications are becoming enormously diverse. While the traditional scientific/industrial control applications will continue to grow, newer areas—such as small business/commercial applications and distributed processing—will boom throughout this decade. While the cost of computing was once prohibitive for smaller companies, today the impact of sophisticated computing power is being realized by even the smallest business establishment. It is now economically practical for such organizations to use computers to process not only their traditional routine accounting functions but also to apply computing technology to their more complex decision making processes.

Two major implications for career planning emerge. First, professionals in the "user" environments should broaden their exposure to such areas as distributed processing, networking and communications in order to stay in the mainstream of career development. This is particularly important for those in programming, software enhancement, and information systems design.

Second, new opportunities will develop in several key disciplines within manufacturers of microcomputers in the areas of software development, commercial and scientific systems development, programming, marketing, and marketing support; and within service organizations that support manufacturers' systems by providing timesharing, turnkey applications, consulting services, and more. Of course, those who associate directly with a microcomputer vendor will have a unique opportunity to increase their options and accelerate their careers at the rate this industry segment grows.

### The Communications Era and the Office of the Future

Today's advanced technologies — mini/microcomputers, terminal devices and communications networks—have made computer decentralization in business much more commonplace. This is another factor which will magnify demand for computer design and support professionals. It also places us on the threshold of another explosion, labeled the "Information Industry." This is the technology which makes information available to the consumer sector, through sophisticated computer-driven networks. Home TV sets, for example, will combine with communications interface units to become terminals capable of displaying newspaper articles or catalogs for shopping. They will be used also for paying bills, banking, educating, and more. In this decade, we can predict that the amount of accessible data in electronic files will expand seven-fold to the equivalent of fourteen full-size dictionaries of output for every man, woman and child in the United States and Canada.

The full impact that this wealth of information and networking possibilities bring to bear on professionals will be major. Certainly, professionals with expertise in networking and data communications will be called upon to develop new approaches to information handling and management. The professional who understands the software technology needed to convey information from computer to consumer will be at the cutting edge of this rapidly growing technology.

Similarly, automation in offices— such as the networking of computer systems and word processing systems—will also create significant new opportunities for computer professionals who understand these "Office of the Future" concepts and can offer sophisticated human-factor solutions.

### The Shift to Automation

Perhaps the newest and among the most exciting career opportunities today are within the emerging sphere of industrial automation. Production-intensive larger factories and smaller plants alike are finding that computer controlled systems produce unprecedented gains in productivity. Known generally as Computer Aided Manufacturing (CAM) systems, these sophisticated computer controlled devices are reducing waste and improving efficiencies in myriad production environments. Yet, the shift to automation is only in its infancy.

Coincidentally, the application of computers to the design of complex industrial products and systems has also created an explosion in Computer Aided Design (CAD). Here, engineers and scientists with the aid of powerful computer driven simulation aids and graphics technology are able to dramatically improve the efficiency and speed of the design process.

We expect that the future of revolutionary automated design and production systems will provide many exciting career opportunities for the astute professional. Not only will CAD/CAM systems designers and programmers be in substantial demand, but the need for new automation specialists—systems sales representatives, technicians, graphics specialists, and system implementors—will grow in quantum leaps. The professional who develops sales and/or marketing skills in addition to preparing technically will be in a better position to meet tomorrow's demand.

In summary, we see constant change ahead and new trends in job positions will emerge. These position definitions and trends are as follows:

# 1

### Commercial Programmers and Programmer Analysts

**Responsibilities:** Perform detailed program design, coding, testing, debugging, documentation and implementation of commercially oriented information systems. May also be responsible for overall systems specification and design. In larger facilities, typically assigned to one or more of the various sub-sets making up a total systems development project.

**Trends:** Will continue to be in exceptionally high demand. More alternatives open to Commercial Programmers and Programmer Analysts than any other group. Wide diversity or new openings exist in type of industry, application, hardware/software and specific responsibility. Continuing trend within user organizations to combine programming and systems functions into a single group provides excellent learning environment. Most opportunities for those with a minimum of one year COBOL programming. Those in greatest demand will also have direct exposure to some of the following: large operating systems, job control languages, data base management and direct access techniques, remote processing, virtual systems, CRT drivers and data base handlers. Structured systems design, programming and distributed processing techniques becoming more important. Conversational programming and time-sharing experience are also valuable. The demand for Programmers and

Programmer Analysts experienced in Basic, RPG II and Pascal on small commercial systems will remain very strong as the mini/micro explosion continues. A degree in Business, Management Information Systems or Accounting preferred but type and depth of experience much more important.

# 2

### Engineering/Scientific Programmers and Programmer Analysts

**Responsibilities:** Perform detailed program design, coding, testing, debugging, documentation and implementation of scientific and/or engineering computer applications and certain commercial applications that are mathematical in nature. May also assist in overall systems specification and design.

**Trends:** Demand increasing significantly for people with specific specialties such as teleprocessing, graphics and real-time control systems. Requirements include one year minimum with FORTRAN, Pascal, Assembler or C Programming languages. Exposure to the use and integration of microprocessors also valuable. One segment of the market will depend heavily upon level of federal spending and degree of industry commitment to projects in design automation, aerospace, graphics, numerical control, quantitative methods, etc. Increased activity expected, however, from computer oriented companies,

# The Structure (cont'd)

particularly those involved in time-sharing and mini/micro computers. On the user side, greatest demand will be in the area of sensor based computer control systems made more practical by the improvement of mini/micro processors. Again, usual requirements include minimum of one year FORTRAN and/or Assembly language experience and undergraduate engineering or math degree (physical sciences usually acceptable). M.S., large scale or mini/micro hardware exposure and systems (software) programming experience desired.

## 3
### Mini/Microcomputer Programmers and Programmer Analysts

**Responsibilities:** Perform detailed program design, coding, testing, debugging, documentation and implementation of real-time or interactive systems typically using dedicated mini/micro hardware. Program design may consist of application modules or support specific subfunctions such as communications, graphics, data base or operating systems interface.

**Trends:** Demand increasing as hardware continues to decrease in price and as software improves in reliability and flexibility. For the technically oriented professional, most opportunities will require minimum of one year experience with a high level structured language (Pascal, Basic, FORTRAN). Those in greatest demand will also have direct exposure to real-time programming, operating systems, I/O drivers and data base handlers. The mini/micro explosion will provide unique

opportunities for Assembly Language Programmers in vendor companies and specialized firms promoting turnkey systems. Continuing trend to decentralization will create an excellent learning environment. The interactive nature of the typical mini/micro system will facilitate conversational programming thus promoting a return to a close man/machine relationship. One newer trend is increased demand for people knowledgeable in the "office of the future" technologies such as teleprocessing, word processing, electronic mail and the integration of office automation and data processing functions.

## 4
### Systems (Software) Programmers

**Responsibilities:** Create and/or maintain operating systems, monitors, data base packages, compilers, assemblers, utility programs, etc. Within users, typically support applications programming, provide hardware/software planning and evaluation, modify existing and create new software for specific company needs, maintain and modify vendor software packages, develop programming standards, oversee technical education, and insure systems efficiency and integrity.

**Trends:** High level of demand will continue, providing excellent career path for the technically oriented professional. Strong demand exists across a broad front, including computer and peripherals manufacturers, computer service organizations, management consulting firms as well as user organizations. Significant market acceptance of minicomputers and recent emphasis on

distributed processing systems has created a strong demand for Systems Programmers knowledgeable in data communications, network planning and analysis, data base concepts, terminal systems and vendor evaluation. Those seeking to enter the systems programming field should have at least one year of Assembly language programming or B.S. in Computer Science. Current Systems Programmers in greatest demand will have direct exposure to interfacing and/or modifying communications or data·base software.

## 5
### Data Base Specialists

**Responsibilities:** Design and control the use of an organization's data resources. Analyzes the interrelationships of data usage and defines physical data structures and logical views of data sets. Utilizes the facilities of the Data Base Management System (DBMS) and Data Dictionary software packages to control the data usage. Responsible for procedures to insure data security, data base backup and recovery, and to eliminate data redundancy.

**Trends:** Demand is increasing for Data Base Specialists due to the projected growth in number of DBMS installations nationally. Needs exist for persons with technical knowledge of programming and systems methodologies to design data base oriented application systems. Background in systems software is also valuable for persons moving into planning of physical data base structures and implementation of security and recovery tactics. Career path within the data base specialty leads to Corporate Data Base Administrator, a management level position responsible for control of the entire data resource. Data Base Specialists are also needed by software consulting firms who are often engaged by clients to support major sophisticated data base systems development. Current Data Base Specialists in greatest demand will have exposure to a major CODASYL or hierarchical data base package, a knowledge of communications or distributive systems, and Relational Data Bases.

# 6
## Data Communications Programmers and Programmer Analysts

**Responsibilities:** Perform detailed program design, coding, testing, debugging, documentation and implementation of data communications software. Within user environment will evaluate communications hardware/software, modify vendor software for individual company needs, maintain existing software and function as technical advisor to Application Programmers. Within vendor environment will work in group responsible for new communications software development.

**Trends:** Demand will continue to grow providing excellent career opportunities for technically oriented professionals. The industry is showing strong movement toward more data communications with centralized mainframes communicating to remote locations through large networks, distributed data processing and large terminal systems. New concepts such as electronic mail and the "cashless" society seem to indicate a move away from paper communication to electronic communication. Current technologies will emphasize microwave and satellite data transmission. This will be one of the most exciting areas of new development within the industry. The impact on our society will be significant. B.S. in Electrical Engineering or Computer Science and at least one year Assembly language are highly desirable.

# 7
## Documentation Specialists

**Responsibilities:** Document programs and systems as well as user manuals, marketing brochures and other documentation required to properly utilize computing systems. Requires interface not only with systems and programming staff to determine system functions, but also with users and/or customers to assure understanding of the proper utilization of the systems. May also participate in systems specification and design.

**Trends:** Demand will grow due to the increased use of time-sharing and distributive processing systems. Positions will require increased knowledge of sophisticated documentation techniques as well as increased technical knowledge of hardware, applications, or programming languages. Awareness of various advertising techniques will be an asset to companies marketing data processing services or hardware.

# 8
## EDP Auditors

**Responsibilities:** Perform detailed evaluation of existing and proposed systems and operational procedures. Report findings to upper level management along with specific recommendations to insure systems and procedural integrity and accuracy.

**Trends:** Growth in size and complexity of data processing systems has resulted in a strong need for EDP Auditors. Professionals with a broad programming and systems background and exposure to many different computer systems, programming languages, and financial, distribution or manufacturing application areas are in greatest demand. Leading CPA firms as well as computer users are finding it essential to evaulate continually the efficiency, accuracy and security of systems and software as well as computer production. The EDP Auditor will often work for a CPA firm or for the finance or audit organization within a corporation. This offers the Senior Programmer or Analyst the

# The Structure (cont'd)

opportunity to broaden professional direction by moving toward a consulting or corporate management career path. Minimum requirements usually include two years design and programming of business systems and excellent communications skills. College degree highly preferred. MBA or CPA desired.

## 9
### Senior Analyst, Project Leaders and Consultants

**Responsibilities:** Typically responsible for user liaison, systems specification, systems design and project control. May also supervise Analysts and Programmers through implementation phase and occasionally assist in programming effort. Provide key link between ultimate user and computing resource.

**Trends:** Demand to continue at very high levels across a broad front. Those in greatest demand will possess in-depth, advanced industry knowledge in manufacturing, insurance, banking, distribution, etc., and actual information systems implementation experience involving data base/data communications. Typical user assignments range from responsibility for development of stand-alone systems to high level staff assignments in hardware/software evaluation, data base administration, long-range planning, etc. Because of intimate company and industry knowledge gained, more organizations than ever before providing persons at this level promotion to line operating functions. As the data bases increase in size and complexity and as access to this information is distributed more broadly through remote job entry and time-sharing, security problems are

expanding beyond the capability of existing control and security procedures. This has led to the need for skilled, innovative computer specialists who can develop and apply new ideas in the control of information access and integrity. Also in demand are experts who can provide the quality assurance necessary through audit and evaluation of functional technology and procedures. Continued growth of management consulting firms and computer services organizations (including facilities management) offer additional opportunities to gain diverse exposure and function in the mainstream of a business environment. Likewise, high demand will continue within computer manufacturers (including micros and minis) for systems professionals to move into marketing support roles. Importance of this position level dictates unique blend of technical, business and interpersonal skills as well as maturity and sound judgment. Minimum requirements usually include two years systems design experience and prior programming with some specialized industry experience desired. College degree highly preferred. MBA or some graduate study desired.

## 10
### Technical Services Managers

**Responsibilities:** Direct the technical staff responsible for operating system software, telecommunications and data base system support, maintenance of packages and hardware/software planning and evaluation. Often has additional responsibility for computer operations and/or internal technical education.

**Trends:** Growth of teleprocessing and data base management have greatly increased the complexity and

sophistication of the technical support function and therefore the size of the technical support group. This has resulted in a marked increase in level of responsibility of this position within medium and large user organizations as well as in the creation of new openings as smaller installations grow. Typical experience includes five years systems programming background with demonstrated experience or potential for leadership and an in-depth awareness of current computer technology.

## 11
### Systems and Programming Managers

**Responsibilities:** In larger organizations, responsible for information systems development and implementation within a major functional area or areas; in smaller organizations, usually direct efforts of all Analysts and Applications Programmers.

**Trends:** Continued emphasis on successful systems implementation, advanced industry knowledge, awareness of current computer technology, intimate understanding of user operations and problems and proven management ability. Opportunities to use this position as an avenue to general management. Minimum requirements: five years significant systems development experience along with project management.

## 12
### Data Center Operations Managers

**Responsibilities:** Direct all computer and peripheral machine operations, data entry, data control, scheduling and quality control. Responsibility for systems (software) programming, software maintenance and/or applications maintenance programming sometimes included.

**Trends:** Continued upgrading of position level due to increased hardware/software complexity. As the production resource responsible for providing user departments with computer output, essential to interface well at all levels of management and to structure an effective and responsive production control and end product distribution function. Minimum requirements: supervisory operations experience and good knowledge of installed hardware, software and operating systems. Increased emphasis on distributed processing places premium on those with exposure in large-scale, data base/communications-oriented environment. Degree will be required more frequently in large installations.

## 13
### Information Systems Directors

**Responsibilities:** Major executive who devotes bulk of energies to overall management and direction of all information systems and data processing efforts.

**Trends:** Position level more frequently reports to chief executive officer or general executive as importance of information systems is enhanced. Demand will remain relatively high as intermediate and smaller organizations continue to upgrade. Profit, loss and budget responsibilities are more important as companies expand or establish independent profit centers. Prime candidates hold systems management positions in larger organizations. Increasing numbers of smaller organizations installing first computer systems offer opportunities for current Systems Analysts, Project Leaders and Programming Managers to move up. Such organizations must look to the outside for direction, providing opportunities for younger

professionals to gain their first management experience and/or assume total responsibility for all computing activities. Larger organizations require a minimum of two years heavy management experience, advanced industry knowledge, preference for MBA degree and all technical professional and business skills.

## 14
### Computing Industry Marketing Representatives

**Responsibilities:** Sell computer mainframes, mini/micro systems, special purpose systems, supplies and peripherals and/or services.

**Trends:** Demand to remain at extremely high level across the board with mini/micro computer systems, communications interface, time-sharing and proprietary software packages (both systems and applications) firms providing significant stimulus. Proven track record of quota accomplishment highly desirable, but some organizations willing to consider Analysts, technical professionals and Managers interested in marketing. This particularly includes engineers in the minicomputer and communications interface areas.

## 15
### Computing Industry Marketing Managers

**Responsibilities:** Responsible for management and administration of marketing representatives. May also have territory or key account direct marketing duties.

**Trends:** High demand for proven marketing management experience will continue across a broad front. Geographic expansion of computing industry provides opportunities for current Marketing Representatives ready to assume first management responsibility.

## 16
### Marketing Technical Support Representatives

**Responsibilities:** Provide technical support in the marketing of hardware and software products and services. Duties include both pre- and post-sales support, system studies, feasibility studies, demonstrations and technical presentations. Requires good oral and written communication skills and the ability to interface with clients and to understand their requirements.

**Trends:** Demand is increasing as the number of products in the marketplace increases, particularly in the areas of data base management systems, mini and micro systems, visual display units, specialty software and custom systems. Requires the ability to assimilate new product specifications and capabilities rapidly and to relate it to customer requirements. Technical depth in software, hardware or applications needed. Career path usually leads to marketing, technical services management or consulting.

# Strategy for Career Development

For the past twenty years, Source Edp has been in a highly unique position enabling us to witness computer professionals as they have developed their careers. There have been those who have stretched their abilities and experience to the utmost achieving extremely high levels of responsibility in the field. Unfortunately, there have been others who, for one reason or another, were unable to fulfill their true potential. Out of this experience, we have formed some definite conclusions regarding the strategies and planning techniques successful computer professionals have employed to enhance their long-term career development. Some of these conclusions are presented in this section.

## A Case Study

As a vehicle for discussion, we will concentrate on a single career path within the computing field — that of the one leading to MIS Director. *All* computer professionals are encouraged to read this material carefully, however, since the *concepts* presented here are equally valid and applicable in career planning for achieving success in other areas such as software, technical services, operations, operations research, management consulting, marketing, etc.

## The Six Steps to MIS Director

In most computer facilities, there are a multitude of grades, levels, job titles, etc. Upon close examination, however, information systems professionals in a user environment may typically be separated into six basic functional areas, each having a progressively higher level of responsibility. Although these groups may overlap to some degree, each has its own unique set of skills which, if mastered properly, will yield maximum career development. Exhibit 2 graphically depicts these six functional steps of progression and the relative population found in each group.

# 1
## Programming and Programming Analysis

Programmers and programmer analysts represent the initial functional level of responsibility. Specific duties at this level have been previously defined.

# 2
## Systems Analysis and Senior Programming Analysis

The second level of responsibility includes senior programmer analysts and systems analysts. In addition to performing the duties previously described, individuals in this group typically provide technical guidance and assistance to junior level professionals and will begin to participate in feasibility studies and cost justifications. A favorable reputation will be gained as a result of successfully completing project assignments on time with a minimum of supervision.

# 3
## Project Leadership

The third level of responsibility includes Senior Analysts and Project Leaders. In addition to performing the duties previously described, persons at this level will have the capability of preparing oral and written management presentations and assuming responsibility for supervising the efforts of other professionals. This level represents a key in career development as it is the point at which an individual begins to develop and exercise the supervisory and leadership skills essential to qualify for succeeding levels.

# Strategy (cont'd)

**Exhibit 2**
**The Career Path Leading to MIS Director**

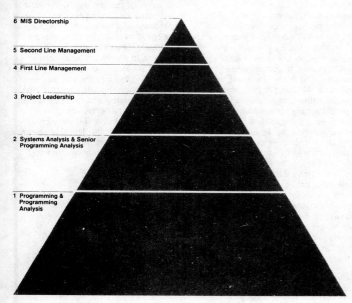

6 MIS Directorship

5 Second Line Management

4 First Line Management

3 Project Leadership

2 Systems Analysis & Senior Programming Analysis

1 Programming & Programming Analysis

## 4
### First Line Management

The fourth level of responsibility represents first line management, and typically includes such position titles as project manager, programming supervisor, systems supervisor, etc. As a group, these individuals typically assume direct responsibility for implementing major functional systems projects to meet the overall computing objectives established by higher levels of management. Management ability is a dominant characteristic of success at this level. Management responsibilities are both functional and administrative (including hiring and firing, manpower planning, salary administration and review, budgeting, etc.).

## 5
### Second Line Management

The fifth level of responsibility represents second line management, and typically includes such position titles as systems director, manager of programming services, etc. As a group, these individuals are responsible for directing the systems and programming efforts to insure compatibility and integration of all functional application areas (e.g. manufacturing, finance, administration, marketing, etc.). In addition to the general management duties defined in level four, this group typically participates in the establishment of corporate information systems objectives, including long-range planning and hardware/software selection.

# 6

## MIS Directorship

The sixth and final level of responsibility is represented by the individual who assumes total responsibility for the profitable utilization of the computing resource within an organization. In addition to direct involvement with the information systems function, he or she will participate with other key company line and staff executives in shaping overall organizational policy and plans.

## A Critical Shift in Career Emphasis

At levels one and two, individual career success is almost exclusively dependent upon the degree of technical competence mastered and exhibited. These two levels provide the basic training and exposure needed to understand fully the capabilities of the computer as a control tool. The computer professional will begin, at level three, to be evaluated not only by technical competence, but also by his or her ability to communicate and to organize, motivate and direct the efforts of other professionals. Development of these supervisory and managerial skills is of crucial importance to advancement beyond level three. But this alone is not enough.

At level three, a basic shift in career emphasis *must* occur in order for a computer professional to achieve maximum personal development. The computer professional must begin to relate his or her computer expertise to the "needs of the business." As a career develops from levels three through six, this factor assumes increasing, and finally dominant, importance. At these higher levels, the computer professional is charged with the responsibility for insuring maximum utilization and profitability from the computing resource. To accomplish this goal, he or she must gain a thorough knowledge and understanding of the organization's objectives, plans, operations, problems, competition, etc., in addition to remaining abreast of information systems technology. In short, the computer professional becomes at these higher levels a "management generalist" as opposed to a "computer technician."

It is apparent in reviewing Exhibit 2 that only a select few will reach the top levels of the six step pyramid. *It is our contention, however, that those individuals who do reach the top do so as a result of planning their careers effectively. Sheer ability alone is not sufficient to achieve this objective.* Further, while we do not propose that every individual has the interest and/or talent to reach the MIS Director level, it is our experience that most computer professionals have the ability to achieve levels beyond their current status (along with the financial rewards that such advancement provides) by establishing proper career planning techniques.

# Career Planning Case Study

We believe that those persons who achieve the highest position and compensation levels within the computing field are those professionals who recognize that there are unique points in a career—a certain level of compensation relative to time and experience—when the transition to the next responsibility level is needed. That is, there are transitional "windows" through which an individual must pass at a given point in time in order to achieve career success. Let us elaborate on the keys to successful passage—and what to watch for—on the way to the top.

Exhibit 3, the Career Planning Chart, on the right, graphically illustrates this relationship between compensation level and years of experience in the field. Also depicted are the points in time, the transitional "windows," at which a successful individual typically passes from one responsibility level to the next. The key to career advancement is to recognize when the proper time has arrived to move through the next transitional "window." Once the specific skills of a particular level have been mastered, it is vital to move ahead to the next responsibility level. To do so prematurely or too late can result in career retardation.

### The Development of Five Careers

The shaded area on the Career Planning Chart represents the ideal relationships between experience level and compensation. Those persons fitting into this area are in the mainstream of career development. The further one strays from this area, the more difficulty he or she will have in achieving optimum career success. Line A on the Career Development Chart depicts the career of an individual who has passed through

each transitional "window" at exactly the proper moment in time. This person has successfully prepared for each succeeding step and then has taken the necessary action to achieve a move to the next level of responsibility. In contrast to the effective job of career planning demonstrated by this individual, lines B, C, D and E represent persons who have made career planning errors typical of many computer professionals.

Cases B and C depict individuals who have achieved an income level in excess of their marketable skills. Individual B began to deviate early in his or her career, and in fact never reached the first transitional "window." Individual C, on the other hand, did not begin to deviate significantly until well into the senior levels. Although entering the level of Project Leadership, this person is now at an income level prohibitive of future management career development. In both cases, the individuals involved *at this point in time* are worth more to their present employers than they are in the external marketplace. It is difficult, and in some cases impossible, for persons such as B and C to correct their situations, since to do so involves at best a lateral salary move,

and usually a salary cut. Since most people are unwilling, or unable (as a result of their standard of living) to accept a reduction in pay and most good companies are reluctant to offer even a lateral salary move, the result can mean dead-ending a career at what can be a very early age.

Typically, such situations occur as a result of overspecialization, and usually happen when a company recognizes the critical skills of a professional at a particular point in time and compensates accordingly, or when an individual is "bought" by another company for the same set of unique skills.

Individuals B and C should have recognized the threat of overspecialization and taken the proper steps to balance their exposure. While it may seem important to be the "expert" in any one or more professional skills, once a certain level of proficiency has been achieved, it may be wise to seek more broadening experience at a time when salary level permits a selection of alternative position opportunities.

The compensation of B and C may be considered to consist of several elements:

- *"Intrinsic Value,"* which is roughly equivalent to the compensation available externally on the open market for their specific skills;

- *"Specific Value,"* which is the additional value they have to their organizations as a result of certain knowledge they have gained of their specific company environments;

- *"Insurance Money,"* which volatile companies pay to attract and keep people who would not otherwise stay in their typically insecure environments; and,

- *"Golden Handcuffs,"* where companies pay a special premium to highly valuable employees whom they feel they cannot afford to lose.

**Exhibit 3**

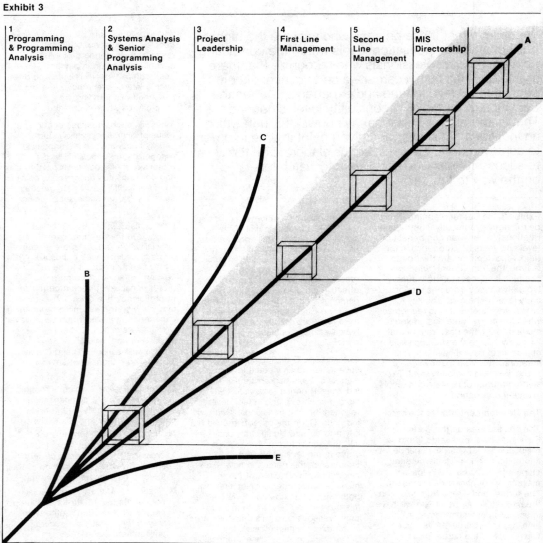

| 1 Programming & Programming Analysis | 2 Systems Analysis & Senior Programming Analysis | 3 Project Leadership | 4 First Line Management | 5 Second Line Management | 6 MIS Directorship |

Years of Experience

# Career Planning Case Study (cont'd)

Generally, it is the latter two elements that are responsible for taking a computer professional away from the mainstream of career development.

Cases D and E depict individuals who have allowed themselves to stagnate. In both cases, the persons involved have repeated the same experience in non-critical areas many times over — that is, they received one year of experience three or four times over, rather than three or four years of diverse and broadening exposure. Individual E has continued coding long past the time he or she should have moved into systems analysis responsibilities, and consequently never reached the first "window." The classic example of this is people who allow themselves to become involved in maintenance programming 100% of the time. Certainly maintenance programming is an important function and must be done by many professionals, but as a full time activity it will stifle career development. Unfortunately, many professionals become enamored with the computer as an end in itself, and, as a result, fail to gain the other knowledge necessary to continue their professional development. Because these people never become fully rounded professionals, they are evaluated as dead-ended by their managements.

Individual D, though moving well through the first two levels, has not received the necessary project control and supervisory skills to qualify for a first line management position. Cases D and E typically occur when an individual

overstays a current position and results when a person mistakenly feels that job security is dependent upon years of service with a single company, or is generally apathetic to career development.

The classic example of this is the person who remains with an organization that has leveled in growth or is actually declining. Such an environment generally creates "limited headroom" since there is rarely a position created to which he or she may be promoted. A similar situation can result when a computer professional is passed over in promotion. Since management is never infallible, promoting the wrong person may mean a wait of many months or even years before the mistake may be rectified, and during this delay, valuable exposure is lost. Closely parallel to this is the case of a change in the organization's top information systems management. In some cases, a new person from the outside will bring along several former key assistants who fill positions which are logical next promotion steps for existing professionals.

Situations D and E are more easily correctable than B and C, but nevertheless, if not addressed at an early point in a career, will lead to total stagnation.

Finally, one additional hazard faces those professionals not in the mainstream of career development during times of general economic recession — the threat of layoff. The critical skills possessed by B and C suddenly become in much greater supply on the open market and at a much lower cost. Their employers need no longer pay "insurance" or "golden handcuffs" compensation premiums. Likewise, since D and E have demonstrated either disinterest in their careers or the inability to

progress, their duties may be temporarily assumed by others in the organization who are more in the career mainstream and upon whom the company may build as economic conditions recover.

*In summary,* a computer professional must strive to remain in the mainstream of career development and advancement in relation to his or her compensation and experience to insure maximum long-term growth. This is true regardless of whether a professional aspires to attain the ultimate level of MIS Directorship or some level beneath it. It is also worth noting that in career planning, it is essential to understand and interpret the six levels of responsibility in light of position function — not position title. Titles will vary from one company to the next and in some instances an organization may offer a "title promotion" with no meaningful increase in level of responsibility.

**Natural Career Progress**

*It is our experience that the natural career development within one company over a period of time will often deviate from the ideal.* This is true because the maximum learning curve will usually be one to three years at each responsibility level. It may happen that a position enabling a professional to pass through the next transitional "window" will become available within a current employer at precisely the right time. However, it is rare to expect the company to sustain a growth rate that would continually meet the needs of the individual at the proper point in time throughout the course of an entire career. The thoughtful professional will, therefore, continually monitor his or her personal development and take the action necessary to insure that he or she is in the mainstream of career development. "Where am I on the Career Planning Chart?" is a question that each computer professional must address on a periodic and frequent basis.

**APPENDIX B: THE RFP (REQUEST FOR PROPOSAL)**

A step by step approach to the preparation, distribution, and analysis of this most important document.

# The RFP (Request For Proposal)

Having established a presumed need for data processing, a solid cost base from which to measure its effects and the broad outlines of the desired new system, you are now ready to do something about it. Generally speaking, the wrong thing to do is to begin entertaining vendor sales presentations and proposals. If initiated and controlled by the vendors, these importunings are bound to confuse both you and the issues. The vendor representatives go to school to learn how to get orders, not perform objective analyses. It is best that the user take control of the situation, rigidly legislating the rules by which the game will be played, if he is to have any hope of coming up with an unbiased decision.

There are at least 2,000 mini- and microcomputer systems vendors in the U.S. as of this writing and an equal number of service bureaus. Yet, according to an International Data Corporation study published in *Fortune,* most small businessmen in the market for a computer contact two competing vendors, and the average contact only three. The survey found that "Generally it takes a salesman 5–6 visits to close a sale. . . ."[1]

Other surveys and the author's experience confirm that few buyers perform any kind of systematic comparison of one vendor's offering to another, and few perform a financial analysis to determine if automation is even warranted in the first place.

And, as this author asserted in another computer industry publication, the user "frequently makes no provision whatever to protect himself against the failure of the software supplier to adequately maintain the system in the future by (a) analyzing the financial soundness and survival potential of the vendor in the first place and (b) protecting himself physically and contractually so he can take

[1]International Data Corporation, "Computing for Business Into the 80's," *Fortune* (advertising supplement, 5 June 1978).

control of the software in the event of bankruptcy, default or nonresponsiveness of the supplier.''[2]

This chapter presents a methodology whereby the relevant issues cannot escape attention and, to the greatest practical extent, can be evaluated objectively, alternative by alternative, vendor by vendor, with the goal of arriving at sound conclusions and minimum risk.

## RATIONALE FOR THE RFP

A Request For Proposal, or RFP, as it is customarily called, is nothing more than a written statement from the prospective buyer telling prospective sellers what is wanted, under what conditions the buyer intends to do business, and what information the buyer requires of the vendor in order to make an intelligent decision. It has to be in writing because that way each vendor gets the same message and can at leisure and in detail study the requirements fully and develop a thoughtful reply.

Although a formal, written RFP sounds like overkill—something more appropriate for the federal government or a multibillion-dollar corporation—it is the only way to achieve comparability between proposals. Each vendor sells toward his strengths and away from his weaknesses and limitations. Left to himself, he will propose what he thinks has the best chance of getting him the order, not what does the job the the way you want it done or in the same way other vendors will propose.

The vendor must be *told* what to propose, so his offering can be compared on an ''apples-to-apples'' basis with others. If he then wants to go on to propose alternate approaches which do not conform to the exact requirements of the RFP, he may do so in a separate document; but the burden of justifying the deviation is his. He must explain how his proposed system accomplishes the equivalent result. In other words, the RFP is a proclamation in which the user says loudly and clearly: ''Here is the kind of system I want. Here's what it has to do for me, in what volumes, over what space of time. Here's a list of questions I want you to anwer. Fill in the blanks. Your answers will help me determine how well your products and services fill the bill.''

[2]D. R. Shaw, ''Who Needs a Formal Software RFP? You Do!'' *Interface: Mini-Small Business Systems* (Fall, 1978): 6–7, 12.

And, perhaps, the proclamation may go on to say: "If you take serious exception to what is demanded, then you may separately propose alternatives; but remember that proving your method is better than mine is an uphill battle. I may choose to ignore your suggestions altogether."

### Conserving Time and Energy

By taking the lead and spelling out exactly what is needed, the user avoids having each bidder "traipsing" around his place of business, making independent studies, interviewing the same people and asking of them the same questions that two or six or a dozen other vendors have done or will shortly do.

It is unquestionably a great deal of work to prepare an RFP. And, no matter how well executed, an RFP will still leave unanswered questions in the minds of prospective bidders which will have to be answered, briefly, by phone, letter or in person. Yet, all of this represents but a fraction of the time that might be spent, in total, considering all the people involved, in assisting each vendor separately in the development of his proposal. To escape this problem, users typically compromise either by arbitrarily limiting the number of vendors to be considered or by giving vendors short shrift, hurrying them through the process, providing vague statements of what is wanted, thereby not only permitting but positively encouraging a slipshod job. The former runs the risk of bypassing a truly outstanding solution simply for not having considered a broad enough range of possibilities. The latter results in a babel of incomparable, inadequate proposals from which it is impossible to objectively select a winner and which sets the stage for increasingly uncomfortable and expensive surprises as the detailed design and implementation of the winning system unfolds (which may cost more time than would have been invested in a proper RFP at the outset).

In general, then, your time and that of your staff will be conserved by doing a proper analysis and RFP up front, rather than dealing piecemeal through time with numerous vendors, entertaining proposals that miss the mark and choosing one that appears reasonable but, through faulty communication between the parties, ends up wide of the target after the action is underway.

## Comparability

A well-structured RFP asks questions of each vendor in a format and sequence that facilitates comparing one to another. Left to themselves, bidders will choose their own styles, scattering facts and fancies in a wide profusion of material. They will carefully avoid stating damaging information. They will paint other factors with an unnaturally positive and seductive glow. Some will compose original literary works. Some will create a brief cover letter to which is appended "boiler plate," that is, brochures, stock paragraphs and other prefabricated material. Some will attach operator's guides, user's manuals and other technical references. Some even mass-produce proposals via computer by inserting a few user-specific parameters into a generalized program that prints out a customlike proposal on a high-speed line printer.

The only practical way of picking out the relevant facts, rating them and comparing them across all the various alternatives is to demand that the vendors answer each question fully, in writing and in the prescribed sequence.

Suppose, for example, you are interviewing aspiring copywriters for your cosmetics advertising department. The race is between William Shakespeare and say, Harold Robbins. Not an easy or obvious choice, since both have their strengths, though in different genres. It might be well to ask questions about experience specifically related to selling beauty aids, request samples of their work and, perhaps, ask each to write an essay in 25 words or less on "How I can 'crank up' the effectiveness of your current ad campaign."

Less facetiously, how would you go about comparing two offerings, the first from a "Fortune 500" computer giant and the second from a local 15-man turnkey house doing under $1 million per year in sales? If you considered only the giant's reputation and stability versus the local firm's flexibility and eagerness you still wouldn't have a basis for comparison, and the decision would likely be an emotional one. On the other hand, if you reduce the evaluation to a point-for-point comparison, giving each contender a fair and honest score on many factors, including the ones mentioned above, and assuming you have attached the proper weight and emphasis to each factor, then at least you have some chance of making an objective choice.

### Specificity

Computer salesmen are justly famous for implying much, committing little and falling noticeably short even of *that* when it comes to delivery. As a breed, they prefer to talk reassuringly about users' legitimate concerns rather than to make pledges, commitments and guarantees in writing. If a miscalculation or, shall we say, overly optimistic representation has been made, it's those made in writing that can come back to haunt, to embarrass, to get one in "hot water" with the home office, even to generate legal action, which is sure to bring headquarters to a boil. Written commitments are second only to being below sales quota in the lexicon of sins to be avoided by computer salesmen.

The written response to a well-conceived RFP is the first step toward putting the vendor's "feet in the fire," getting him to be specific about the issues about which he'd rather verbalize and "arm wave." The RFP should leave little or nothing to chance or good faith when it comes to specifying what is to be done, with how much equipment or service, at what price, how long it should take and what the vendor must do about it if the requirements aren't met.

Put that way, the user leaves no doubt about what he wants in terms of specific information and binding commitments. This has the effect of warning off any computer "con artists" and putting the rest on notice that they'd better be scrupulously accurate and, perhaps, even a little conservative in their claims making. Just to narrow the field a bit and put a little extra pallor and teeth clenching into the otherwise glamorous and glossy sales routine, you might include a notification in the RFP of your intention to incorporate the winning vendor's response to it in the contract you and he will eventually sign. That's a little like etching glass or metal with an acid bath. Only the pattern that's fully covered survives; the rest washes away quickly. Some vendors' slates may come up completely blank under such circumstances.

The specificity angle works both ways. Not only does the RFP demand it of the vendor, but it helps the vendor immeasurably by being specific about what the buyer wants. Too often, selling is a guessing game in which the vendor tries to estimate on the basis of a brief and inadequate investigation. This is necessarily so, because the prospective vendor cannot afford to make as thorough a study of your requirements as *you* can, just on the faint hope of getting an order. So he crosses his fingers and guesses what will do the job and at the same time will look good enough and low enough in cost to get the business.

Most vendors prefer to work on the facts rather than these rough estimates. If you provide them with solid data, they are much more likely to propose the right solution and to feel confident about it. That confidence, in turn, can manifest itself in a lower price (less hedging against the unknown) and in firmer commitments and performance guarantees than would otherwise be the case. And that, in turn, bolsters *your* confidence and pocketbook and reduces risk.

## ANATOMY OF AN RFP

There is no set formula for constructing an RFP. A great deal depends upon how complex your particular situation is, to what level of detail you've analyzed it, and how far you've gone toward constructing a detailed design of the desired solution. The wording and format depend on what you think will communicate the best in your situation. However, there are some categories of information that should be included and, probably, in the suggested sequence, unless you can think of a better one.

### Introduction

A little background on your company or institution and its previous experiences with manual, mechanical and electronic systems will be helpful to the bidder. Size, number of employees, type of business, organization structure, past history and future projections of business growth and diversification will be very useful in proposing a system with sufficient expansion potential.

It wouldn't hurt to state why you think you need automation and what you hope to gain from it. The bidders may honestly aver that some of your expectations are unrealistic. If so, you should know about it.

Finally, the introduction should state the "rules" under which bids will be accepted.

· To whom questions are to be directed and when.
· To whom proposals are to be submitted and what the final deadline is.
· When you plan to make a decision.
· When contract negotiations will begin and end.
· When you intend to install the system.
· If detailed specifications are required, apart from the proposal, (which is normally the case), when they are expected.
· What portions of the RFP response and/or the specifications are to be appended to the contract.
· What the basic contractual arrangements are under which you intend to do business; for example, if you require performance guarantees and penalties, say so. Why waste time with vendors who can't or won't conform?
· And, as a matter of information and courtesy, you might explain to bidders how you intend to evaluate proposals and go about reaching a decision.

### Description of the Present System

The buyer should define in as much detail as is reasonable, along the lines discussed in Chapter 9, what is being done *now,* how, and, if you're willing to be totally open with the vendors, how much it's costing. An open approach helps the vendor make better judgments about what to propose because he can understand the related cost trade-offs.

Copies of the forms in use, flowcharts of procedures, volumes and file sizes concerned with the present system aren't absolutely necessary if the new system is fully specified later in the RFP, but such information can't hurt, and it might help. No vendor will ever be offended or put off by receiving too much information about your job.

### System Requirements

The statement of your requirements can take many forms, ranging from a narrative describing what is wanted in concept, to a listing of desired functions and features of each application, to an elaborate quasi-design document that spells out the new system in quite a bit of detail.

In any case, tell all you know or are reasonably sure of. Most RFP's classify wants into "must-have" and "nice-to-have" classifications. That way the vendors know what features they absolutely have to propose, the lack of which will either disqualify them or put them at a serious disadvantage in the bidding. A vendor who can also incorporate many of the "nice-to-have" options without unduly complicating or cost-escalating his proposal will do so, thereby increasing his chances of getting the order.

It's hard to conceive of too much information in this section of the RFP. Especially important are input, file and output descriptions. If you already know the approximate formats of key documents and reports, by all means include them. One common means of depicting such requirements is shown in Figure 12-1. The 132-column layout forms for this purpose are abundantly available from computer vendors, forms companies and consultants throughout the industry. Table 12-1 shows a sample file description. Listing each field with its composition—alphabetic, numeric or mixed, right or

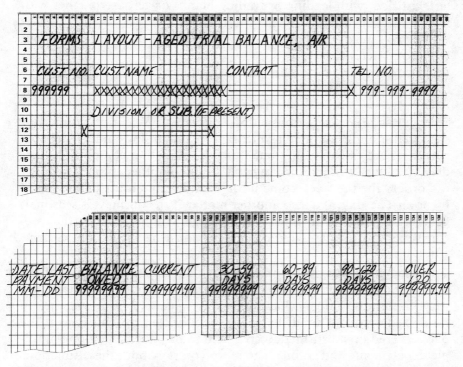

Figure 12-1. Sample Document Format Using Standard 132-Column Computer Layout Forms.

**Table 12-1. Sample File Description Showing Composition of a Hypothetical Accounts Receivable Master File.**

Accounts Receivable Master File (One occurrence per active customer account)

| FIELD | SIZE AND TYPE | COMMENT |
|---|---|---|
| Indentifier | 2 Numeric | Record type code 06 = A/R Master |
| Account number | 6 Numeric | Sort and access key |
| Customer name | 21 Alphanumeric | Company name |
| Division or subsidiary | 21 Alphanumeric | Used only if applicable |
| Street address | 22 Alphanumeric | |
| City | 15 Alphabetic | Standard abbreviations if necessary |
| State | 2 Alphabetic | Standard state code |
| Zip code | 9 Numeric | New postal code |
| Contact name | 21 Alphabetic | Used only if applicable |
| Telephone number | 10 Numeric | Format: xxx/xxx/xxxx for area, exchange and number |
| Date of last activity | 6 Numeric | Format: xx/xx/xx for month/day/year |

left justified, with leading or trailing blanks or zeros—together with its size, if you know all these specifics, will be helpful. If not, the vendor will make assumptions about the details and check them out with you later.

There are four other items essential, or at least highly desirable, in this segment of the RFP.

**Volumes.** File sizes, transaction counts and exception counts for each major application area with expected high, low and average occurrences are essential. It's one thing to know that company X handles 20 orders a day on average. It's quite another thing if 90% of the orders for the week come in on Monday and must be processed by noon Tuesday. It's also another matter if the business is seasonal, generating, say, four times the average volume during the pre-Christmas rush. These volume vagaries must be spelled out clearly.

**Processing rules.** Decision rules (or "algorithms" as some of the unrepentant vendors up from the scientific leagues call them) are very important. Under what conditions, precisely, is a customer to be denied credit, a small balance to be written off, an item to be backordered or substituted, a cost item to be allocated among multiple departments and so on? The more you say about these functions the better the vendor can determine which of his systems is capable of performing the desired functions and how much programming or adjustment is required to match your need.

A serious mistake here could have a profound impact on the appropriateness of a packaged software approach versus a custom system. If the vendor assumes, in the absence of fine detail, that the package fits, and it later turns out not to, then trouble is in store for all concerned. Considerable redesigning and added cost may ensue. Or, the user may have to give up certain important features in order to avoid excessive tailoring of the package. At worst, he may decide to give up altogether and begin again with a whole new procurement. (Of course, if the user has signed a contract without specification approval rights or has approved specifications without being aware of the short-fall, then it's too late for anything but raising one's heel in a swift arc from the rear and upward, making sharp contact with the corresponding hemisphere of the gluteus maximus. This form of exercise, though regarded as harmful by some authorities, seems to be gaining steadily in popularity and frequency among computer buyers. Perhaps this book may, in some small measure, help reverse the tide, channeling buyers into more acceptable forms of recreation.)

**Critical timing considerations.** If there are sharp cutoff times pertaining to certain input, processing and output, these must be put forth. Not only do such constraints influence volume and speed determinations, but also the fundamental design of the applications and whether such important systems functions as multiprogramming will be required.

For example, if monthly financial statements must be in the hands of management by the seventh working day after month-end, but branch receivables cannot be closed until after the tenth day because of local processing plus mailing-time requirements, this tells the systems designer two important facts: (1) some subsidiary ledgers have to remain open after regular closing, and (2) the system must accommodate accrual entries that are subsequently adjusted.

Or, if parts-requirements processing can be deferred until day-end in a manufacturing-control environment when the entire computer can be given over to it, rather than at a time when other processes such as order entry or production reporting must proceed in parallel, the size of the computer, its memory and the complexity of the operating system needed may be reduced considerably.

At this point you should be able to clarify to the vendor which applications, such as payroll, can be processed in batch rather than a transaction at a time and which files are subject to unscheduled inquiry and/or reporting. This information will tell the vendor what files must remain on-line at all times and whether some kind of ad hoc data base reporting system is warranted.

**Archival records.** If period history from prior years, for example, is to be retained, it's a good idea to specify what, how much and how it's going to be used. These requirements could suggest the addition of a magnetic tape storage facility to an otherwise all-disk system. Subsequent manipulation of the data might require a distinctly different complement of numbers, speeds and size devices, depending on what you intend to do with the information.

## Mandatory Information

The RFP will include a list of questions to be answered and information to be supplied by each bidder. Make it clear that every question or issue must be succinctly addressed in writing and in sequence with the item numbers and headings provided. This is going to make analysis and evaluation of responses very much easier.

Some of the issues you may want addressed are:

### Hardware.

- Configuration proposed. Description of each component, including quantity, speed, capacity and special features.
- Maximum size, quantity and capacity to which each of the above may be expanded.
- Other devices. Detailed description of other separate items required such as data-entry devices, remote terminals, communication lines and equipment, along with their maximum expansion potential.
- Environmental requirements. Complete description of site, power, air conditioning and other requirements.
- Reliability and maintenance. Repair manning, spare parts stocking and response time policies. Details of various contract maintenance plans. Historic, factual data on average mean time between failure (MTBF)

and mean time to repair (MTTR) for similar equipment in similar applications.
· Costs. Prices, under whatever purchase, lease and rental plans are available for each element of the above, including additional equipment for future expansion.

### Applications software.

· Specifications and features. A reasonably detailed list of features and functions of the proposed applications software, showing point for point how it matches the requirements set forth in the RFP.
· Other features. Additional functions not asked for, which could be beneficial.
· Sample inputs and outputs. Illustrations supporting the claimed features and functions.
· File design. A complete layout of each file in the system showing content and format.
· Running time estimates for the major applicational procedures (which the vendor is willing to guarantee).
· Prices under various plans for the above.
· Maintenance. A discussion of application program architecture, language, parametric control, if any, and other features bearing on future maintainability. Description of program documentation. Determination of ongoing rights, responsibilities, recourse, prices and guarantees with respect to future correction and enhancement.

### Systems software.

· Description of each element of systems software proposed, including operating system, language processors, data base and communication management systems, query and report generators and utility programs. Listing of features and functions.
· Any limitations of the above with respect to memory size, number of concurrent activities, number of terminals, and so on, indicating minimums, maximums and level proposed (if not maximum).
· Description of documentation to be supplied.
· Prices and terms for the above. Description of cost versus performance trade-offs, upgrade potential and costs thereof.
· Maintenance provisions for all systems software proposed.

### Support.

· Responsibilities of each member of the bidder's organization who will directly support the buyer.

· Organization chart and brief resumés of key individuals.
· List of all the other accounts for whom these individuals play similar roles.
· Training facilities, methods and materials, with samples and training class schedule.
· Identification of all the costs associated with support: systems analysis, design, programming, consultation, training, start-up and ongoing problem solving and enhancement.

### Contractual obligations.

· Sample contract and other agreements.
· Description of how sales proposals and written specifications are incorporated into equipment and/or service agreements.
· Position with respect to performance guarantees and remedies covering hardware, systems software, applications software and remedial maintenance.
· Buyer's options in the event of seller default through each stage of development, test, delivery, acceptance and ongoing operation.

### Acceptance tests.

· Description of the location, duration and nature of demonstrations, tests and formal acceptance procedures to which the system will be subjected.
· Statement indicating whether formal written specifications are a part of the overall acceptance procedure and where they fit.
· Relationship of all payments, deposits, progress payments and payment of the balance to the specification and acceptance process.

### Financial responsibility.

· Audited financial reports showing current and historical performance of the bidder's business.
· Credit and bank references.
· If private or closely held firm, background and financial status information regarding principals.

### Record of success.

· Names of (number) customers whose systems have been installed for at least one year.
· Names of (number) customers in this locality.

· Names of (number) customers in buyer's type of business.
· Name, address and phone number of decision makers in above roster.
· Other evidence of expertise, customer satisfaction and seller's willing-
  ness to perform.

**Integration.** If more than one organization will be involved in developing or supporting the proposed system:

· Description of each one and its role.
· Statement of how coordination is to be effected and precisely how control is to be exercised and by whom.
· Full financial, organizational and background information on each
  company participating.

**Implementation plan.**
· Proposed plan of action leading from vendor selection through final
  acceptance and full implementation of the system, showing each step,
  with the individual or organization responsible in a timetable or Gantt
  chart arrangement.

## WHO SHOULD BID?

Finding the right vendors and the optimum number of them is a very
difficult problem. Certainly no less than three bidders for a given approach to the problem should be considered: that is, three service
bureaus, three hardware manufacturers, three turnkey systems
houses, and so forth. If the user is already certain of the type of vendor he wants to do business with, then he may not go to the trouble
of soliciting bids from other categories of companies. But this may
turn out be a mistake. How can the user be really certain that the service bureau, or the in-house mini or the off-the-shelf micro is the
right approach until he's had the opportunity of comparing each side
by side on the basis of common bid specifications?

If the buyer has gone to the trouble of preparing a more or less
formal RFP, then it doesn't cost much more to consider a broader
range of alternatives. After all, the work of proposal preparation
from this point on is mostly the vendor's. If the vendor thinks he has
something special to offer, why not let him have his say? The pros
and cons can then be weighed not only within but also between each
alternative approach.

Assuming, then, that the buyer wants to consider at least three potential suppliers of each acceptable approach, the question remains as to where to find qualified bidders; or, if the company is fairly large and visible, how to select which ones from among a host of aspirants of each type to allow to bid seriously. Among 100 manufacturers, 2,000 or more systems houses and 2,000 or so service bureaus there are bound to be more contenders than can possibly be considered. In general, you might wish to include on your selected-bidders list vendors who meet one or more of the following criteria:

· The current supplier of manual or semiautomated equipment or outside services if he
  (a) has done a good job
  (b) appears to have something to offer in a more advanced system
  (c) has some special knowledge of your needs, based on past exposure
· A vendor who has been calling regularly and
  (a) has made a good impression and
  (b) has picked up some understanding of your requirements in the process
· A vendor with a particularly notable reputation in your industry, field or geographic locality; someone who is known to be doing lots of business with organizations like yours, or in the same neighborhood
· Suppliers recommended by friends, business acquaintances, bankers, accountants and/or consultants
· Companies that have come to notice based on advertising, trade shows, direct mail promotion or general reputation

A rather concentrated exposure to a broad range of companies representing a cross-section of different approaches can be obtained by attending a computer industry trade show. Annual affairs like the National Computer Conference, Western Electronics Show and Convention, Data Processing Management Association Conference, National Mini-Micro Computer Conference and many, many others can be quite useful in this regard.

Watching the ads, product announcements and news stories in one or two popular computer industry publications can be a source of information about potential vendors and will provide details and dates of upcoming computer conferences in your area. It's very difficult to single out a few of the many excellent magazines and newspapers devoted to data processing, but the two with the greatest circulation are

*Datamation,* a controlled-circulation monthly magazine from Tecnnical Publishing Co., (circulation department) 35 Mason St., Greenwich, CT 06830. And *Computerworld,* a weekly newspaper published by Computerworld Inc. 797 Washington Street, Newton, MA 02160.

Research reports published by professional industry watchers can be a rich source of inspiration, ideas and specific information about vendors. The two most prominent such sources are Auerbach Publishers Inc., 6560 North Park Drive, Pennsauken, NJ 08109; and Datapro Research Corporation, 1805 Underwood Boulevard, Delran, NJ 08075.

Seminars on subjects related to small business data processing are a regular feature of today's landscape. The American Management Associations, various universities, trade associations, accounting and consulting firms and, of course, the vendors themselves are constant sources of user education for a fee and, in some cases, for free. The no-charge sessions are subject to suspicion that the hosts hope to achieve some direct or indirect benefit for themselves. Nevertheless, the prospect well fortified with caution and totally immunized against infectious sales contagion is probably safe in exposing himself to "free" educational sessions now and then. It is wise, however, to leave your checkbook and the corporate seal at home when attending such conferences.

## EVALUATING PROPOSALS

The most important principle in evaluating vendor proposals in response to an RFP is to break the process down into small enough segments so that each component can be judged pretty much independently and on merit. It's impossible to read through a dozen thick proposals and objectively answer the question: "Which one is the best deal?" However, by putting a microscope on specific elements, one at a time, it's fairly easy to figure out which one has the closest service facility, or to rank the vendors in order from most to least on the basis of how many computer installations are claimed in a particular line of business.

By separating the evaluation into a number of clearly defined subevaluations, one escapes the well-known "halo effect" which asserts an overall emotional tone to most rating methods if the categories are too few, too broad and nonspecific. Then, by reassembling the subcomponents into an overall score, a much more meaningful, objective and sometimes surprising result is achieved.

Things like the neatness, readability and professionalism exhibited in the proposal itself are factors but not decisive ones. By measuring and rating such items separately, and combining them into the overall scoring formula on the basis of the weight they deserve, they become just some many criteria, each in proper proportion to the others.

## The Framework for Rating

The RFP itself spells out the basic framework for a proposal rating scheme. Under each of the major topical headings are a list of important questions and information requirements. Some of these may need still further analysis to be useful, but the outline is already established. For example, under the heading of Hardware, you may already have the data on maximum growth potential for the proposed system in terms of maximum memory size, auxiliary storage capacity, number of terminals supported, and so on. It would be a simple matter to rate each offering on a scale of 1–5 on the strength of this factor by assigning the value 5 to the system with the greatest expansibility, 1 to the lowest, and all the others proportionally in between. But cost of expansion may vary, too, so you may decide to calculate the cost, from the prices supplied, of some arbitrary amount of growth such as: doubling the size of memory, adding the next increment of disk storage closest to 20 million bytes and adding four more CRT's. Now you have a new list, ranging from high to low. This time assign the value 5 to the *lowest* vendor and 1 to the highest.

By the time you have rated all the factors you will have constructed a spread sheet similar to the one shown in Table 12–2. By assigning weights to the individual factors, or at least to groupings of them, the rest is simple arithmetic. Multiply the ratings times the weight and then sum down the columns to arrive at an overall score for each vendor. In Table 12–2, a greatly simplified version, you see that vendor C won by a narrow margin, mainly on the strength of price. If some other factor, such as customer support, had been more heavily weighted by giving it a 40% weight instead of 30%, then the results would have favored vendor A. Thus, you see how easy it is to manipulate the results: but establishing the rating scheme and the weights *in advance, objectively,* is not manipulation—it's good business. It allows you to judge what's important to you out of the atmosphere of an emotion-charged, high-powered sales presentation. There's no law against choosing a vendor other than the best scoring one, but the score itself should be unbiased.

The example in Table 12-2 is an unrealistically simple one compared with an actual situation. A real evaluation would, first of all, probably encompass more than three vendors and, frequently, several separate offerings from each of some of those vendors. In other words, vendor A may propose a system that conforms closely to the specifications and also propose a different, perhaps less expensive, alternative which conforms less closely but which the vendor contends will do the job. Both alternatives would be set up as separate entities in the evaluation table, as if they had come from different companies. (Of course, some of the factors would be rated in common, such as nearness of service, quality of proposal, vendor's reputation and financial stability.)

Secondly, there are many more factors to consider, rate and score than the handful illustrated. The example shown doesn't separate hardware from software, systems software from applications software, the various applications from each other, and doesn't touch on such vital aspects as ease of use, reliability, the vendor's experience and track record in the industry or the geographic area involved, detailed examination of specifications, acceptance testing, contracting procedures and so on.

The weighting factors will be much more finely distributed in a real-life situation, too. Perhaps "functionality" in the applications sense *is* worth 30% in a given instance; but, of that, inventory control might be several times as important as accounts payable to a manufacturer, for example. So the multiplier factor for payables might be 1% as compared to 15% for inventory. In an insurance agency, however, the exact reverse may be true; payables (and/or accounts current) might be of overriding importance whereas inventory control may not even be under consideration.

In general, the more precise the breakdown and the more powerful the microscope put to the minute factors, the more accurate and unbiased the result. But the result is still just a number, a numeric

**Table 12-2. Sample Simplified Vendor Rating Sheet.**

| Factor | Weight | Vendor A Rating | Vendor A Weighted Score | Vendor B Rating | Vendor B Weighted Score | Vendor C Rating | Vendor C Weighted Score |
|---|---|---|---|---|---|---|---|
| (1) Ability to perform specified functions | 30% | | | | | | |
| (a) Conformance to mandatory features | | 5 | 150 | 1 | 30 | 4 | 120 |
| (b) Conformance to additional features | | 4 | 120 | 3 | 90 | 3 | 90 |
| (c) Guaranteed timings | | 4 | 120 | 5 | 150 | 5 | 150 |
| (2) Customer support | 30% | | | | | | |
| (a) Nearness of sales and service | | 4 | 120 | 1 | 30 | 5 | 150 |
| (b) Commitment to ongoing software maintenance | | 5 | 150 | 1 | 30 | 1 | 30 |
| (c) Quality of training and documentation | | 5 | 150 | 4 | 120 | 3 | 90 |
| (3) Cost | 40% | | | | | | |
| (a) Initial price | | 1 | 40 | 2 | 80 | 5 | 200 |
| (b) Estimated operating costs | | 4 | 160 | 1 | 40 | 4 | 160 |
| (c) Cost of future expansion | | 3 | 120 | 2 | 80 | 5 | 200 |
| TOTAL | 100% | | 1130 | | 650 | | 1190 |

score. The process of picking the winner isn't quite as mechanical as that.

## SELECTING A WINNER

The numeric scoring system described above will bring the prospective buyer of a computer or computer-based services as close to an accurate, unemotional decision as possible, yet much work and thought may remain to be done. For one thing, the factors that have been evaluated are those contained in the proposals in accordance with the instructions contained in the RFP. There are others. Also, there may be some very important last-minute "jockeying" among vendors that goes on after the proposals have been rated and the leading contender(s) identified.

### Tentative Selection

Typically, all but one, two or three leading contenders are effectively eliminated by the time the user is able to distill proposals down to the level of numeric scoring. Some fall by the wayside because they haven't responded fully and honestly to the questions raised in the RFP. Others may exhibit lack of interest. Others may be priced out of line with the leaders. Others may exhibit a take-it-or-leave-it, iron-bound attitude toward contract terms, specifications and acceptance testing. Others may simply score consistently low overall compared to the leaders.

At any rate, with a handful of contestants left in the race, it is then practical to (1) check references and (2) engage in preliminary negotiations. The quicker the pack can be reduced to a few front runners, the sooner can this next important phase of selection begin.

### References

Not only will vendors freely provide names, addresses and phone numbers of satisfied customers, they will, apparently unknowingly, supply the names of a few restive, doubtful and sometimes dissatisfied ones, too. Unless the vendors take very special pains to "check the temperature" of each account periodically and to "reference their references" themselves, perhaps by posing on the telephone as a prospective buyer, they really never know what a user will say to a prospective one at a given point in time. The author's experience suggests that users are much more candid in their assessments than vendors would like them to be, and quite often a customer touted as a major "success" may with little provocation tell some damning tales about the vendor which would chill the very soul of the salesman who provided the reference and dim the enthusiasm of even the most ardently convinced prospective buyer.

Why does this happen? First of all, almost every vendor who has been in the business for any length of time and has done any significant number of installations has undoubtedly left a few "clinkers" along the way. Secondly, small businessmen, as a breed, tend to be rather open with each other about their successes and failures and their likes and dislikes compared to their counterparts in larger businesses. Fortune 500 companies may be very hard on vendors privately but refuse to "wash linen" publicly. However, most small businesses feel no obligation to coddle, educate and protect vendors, particulary those who have done less than the promised or expected job. They know what their customers expect of them and what happens if they don't deliver. They give the same as they get.

Point one, therefore, in checking references is not to be put off by a few negatives. Practically every vendor has a few skeletons in his closet. If fact, if you check a half dozen references and still haven't heard a single discouraging word, something may be wrong. You may, indeed, be in possession of one of those rare, up-to-date "purified" lists from which all but the most complimentary customers have been eliminated. It would be best for you to do some further checking by asking some of the originally listed customers for the names of others they may have heard about who are not so satisfied.

Second, don't just exchange bland and superficial generalities: probe! Ask questions about areas of crucial importance like what was delivered compared to what was promised, whether the vendor lived up to his support commitments, how the reliability of the products or services stack up against expectations, how smoothly the conversion was effected, whether hidden costs and unexpected operating expenses have surfaced, whether the system has been kept up to date with changing needs, how the vendor has handled problems, bugs, power outages, mechanical breakdowns, human error, and so forth. What about quality of vendor personnel, turnover, training and continuity with the user through time? How much longer did development, conversion and break-in take than originally planned? Why?

Like any good investigator you should zero in on key issues in your questioning, coming back at suspected weak points again and again from different angles. When you finish with an interview—face to face whenever possible and at length by phone, if not—you should know a great deal about the vendor's actual performance on the account in question, what went wrong and, perhaps, what steps might be taken in dealing with that vendor to guard against similar mistakes in your company. After sifting through the details, it should not be difficult to develop a simple rating scheme that yields another numeric score reflecting the degree of customer satisfaction and vendor performance evidenced by the reference visits or calls.

## Preliminary Negotiations

During the reference-checking process, or immediately upon its conclusion, the buyer will probably begin "serious" discussions with one or more likely winners with respect to contract terms and price. It may even make sense to negotiate in parallel with the finalists so that the moment a decision is made an agreement can be signed. Certainly, if there are any significant concessions vendors have been quietly holding back for the "end game," now is the time to draw them out. You should know just how far each contestant is prepared to go on the key items of price, guarantees, specifications and contractual obligations so that if the winner begins to back away from his prior promises during final contract negotiations, you can quickly transfer the winner's crown to the runner-up with only a momentary flicker of embarrassment.

There is a very great reservation to be stated with respect to price negotiation. Some companies simply will *not* negotiate price. Some will who shouldn't. One has to be a good enough practical psychologist and business strategist to recognize when concessions are either not going to be forthcoming or will be counterproductive if they do. For example, the degree to which a vendor is willing to make price and contract concessions is roughly proportional to his desperation for business. Too much flexibility in this respect may denote actual or incipient instability on the part of the vendor. Furthermore, negotiating him into a position of negligible profitability on your deal runs two risks. First, this one could push him over the edge, so to speak, into a precarious business situation if he's new, small, weakly capitalized, or all of the above. Second, even a solid company gets quickly fatigued answering distress calls from a marginal or unprofitable account. Your sharp negotiating talents could push the vendor into a corner from which his only profitable escape is to shortchange you later. The "no free lunch" theory says that a deal that looks too good is too bad for somebody—either the buyer or the seller. And either way, you could be the loser.

On the other hand, let's not get overly solicitous for the vendors. Most of them do have some extra negotiating room in whatever they propose, saving a few aces and trumps for the last few tricks of the game. And most will not walk away from a sure sale just to uphold ceremony, policy or the sanctity of "fair trade" pricing. How far you go is a matter of judgment.

## SUMMARY

An RFP and associated numerical rating scheme is essential if a large number of different vendors and/or alternatives are going to be considered. Such consideration cannot be applied without analyzing and objectifying the decision-making process.

- Take the lead in specifying what is wanted, both from the system and in the proposal.
- Demand precise, written answers to an exhaustive list of questions and information requests.
- Break down the evaluation process into a large number of factors that can be rated independently.
- Assign weights or emphasis multipliers to the factors roughly proportional to their importance.
- Sum up the weighted scores for each offering.
- Zero in on a few finalists and for these few check references and conduct tentative negotiations.
- Don't just check—*probe* references. Get behind the banalities.
- Tighten the "iron boot" a little on the finalists during the final selection stages, but don't cripple the winning contestant: he has to remain at least ambulatory to do your job properly.

## APPENDIX C: BUYING A COMPUTER: 12 RULES TO FOLLOW

A basic guide to dealing with any vendor so as to maintain the initiative and control.

# Buying a Computer: 12 Rules to Follow

Ernest A. Kallman and
Leon Reinharth

Louis Armstrong was as much philosophical as he was musical when he entertained us in the 1940s with the song "'Tain't What You Do (It's the Way That Cha Do It)." This truth could be applied to business life hundreds of times a day. If we had remembered its warning, how differently would we have handled that employee reprimand, how smoothly would we have responded to that customer complaint, and how effectively would we have concluded that contract negotiation?

There is a "way that cha do it" for every business situation. Even though business dealings today are more complex, happen faster, and carry more risk, certain fundamental approaches will guide management even in unfamiliar areas. And using these approaches helps ensure a quality outcome.

As an example, more and more companies are acquiring computers. For many, this is the first time they have made such a purchase. The first-time computer buyer runs a high risk that the wrong machine will be ordered or that the right machine will be ordered but will not perform as expected when installed. How does the buyer who lacks computer expertise protect a firm against these failures? The answer is to negotiate with the computer vendor according to proven, fundamental rules for dealing with any vendor. Twelve guidelines for achieving good vendor relations are discussed here, and although they use a computer acquisition as the model, such rules are useful in any vendor situation.

*1. Make it clear to the vendor that you are the key contact.* It is important that the vendor realize that you are the key contact for the hardware and/or software and other related items needed by your firm. Even if you report to a vice-president or other executive, you can be the key contact as long as you have a firm declaration from upper management that you are the person who should interface with the vendor. While you may not be the ultimate decision maker, you should be the one who makes strong recommendations to those who will make the final decision. Anyone other than the key contact should not be dealing with the vendor.

At all costs you must prevent the vendor from going over your head to higher levels of management. The easiest way to do this is to have your management committed to the concept of a single vendor contract within the firm and then have them refuse to see any vendors, referring them all back to you. However, getting management to adhere to this idea may be difficult because salespeople are trained to seek the highest level of contact, and the executive may be "seduced" into granting an interview to a vendor. For instance, the salesperson may flatter the executive into an interview, or request an interview on some other pretext, only to give a complete sales pitch.

At a large private eastern university a similar circumstance happened. In a multivendor competition, one of the major computer manufacturers grew impatient with the screening process and, working through a vice-president of his company, got an appointment with the university president to talk about a grant to the institution by the vendor. The grant was a ploy and at best would have been dependent on the university acquiring the firm's hardware. The result was a confused university president, alienation of the data-processing manager by the vendor because the manager was circumvented, and the forestalling of any decision on a new computer for almost three years.

So if the vendor is allowed to go directly to top management, he or she will confuse things by presenting arguments in a manner favorable to the product rather than your presenting the options to management in an orderly and objective fashion, using terms that are relevant to your firm. Then too, if all potential vendors go to higher management, your superiors will have little time for anything else. If management allows this, then you do not have their confidence. If you allow it, you are not doing your job. You must make sure you have your own management's backing; then tell all vendors that you are their highest contact level and that it will be a measure of their performance and cooperation to see how they follow this approach. In other words, if they do not respect your chain of command, it may disqualify them as a potential vendor in this situation.

*2. Vendors should make appointments.* This may seem like a simple and obvious rule, or in today's casual world perhaps an unnecessary one, but it represents a very subtle point. If vendors

> **Purchasing complex equipment for the first time can be nerve-racking. These fundamental guidelines will minimize the trauma.**

can come and go as they choose then, in a sense, they have control over you. But if vendor visits are at your initiation or with your permission, you retain control. If you are always expected to be available when a vendor drops in, then the vendor has what salespeople call "account control." If a vendor has to wait for you once in a while and is told, "Gee I'm sorry, if I had known you were coming, I could have been available earlier," the individual will soon take the hint and phone ahead. Remember, if the vendor has account control, you do not. It's all a matter of respect. Familiarity does breed contempt. The vendor should follow any and all of the firm's security procedures (signing in, wearing a badge, and so forth) and conform to those actions demanded by custom and courtesy.

*3. Present the needs, not just the problem.* Too often the vendor is presented only with the general problems and not with the required solutions. Many times managers will say, "I need more sales information" or "more accounts receivable information," when they should be saying that they want to know which of their salespeople are doing the most business by product type, which customers are buying which products, and what the paying habits are of the present and future customers. In

**Dr. Kallman** *is Professor of Computer Information Systems at Bentley College, Waltham, Massachusetts.* **Dr. Reinharth** *is Associate Professor of Management at Baruch College, City University of New York, New York City.*

fact, much more information is really required before any vendor could possibly suggest hardware and software to satisfy management's needs. Such a statement of specific requirements takes a great deal of time and effort on the part of management and should include in as much detail as possible what is required from the computer and what management and others are going to do with it.

The more detailed the specifications, the more easily the computer's performance can be measured. This is what a survey or feasibility study is all about—developing the specifications for an information system. The specifications become the basis for a document called a Request for Proposal (RFP) which is then presented to all potential vendors.

The RFP ensures that all vendors have the same idea of what your needs are. They will be more likely to respond in some fashion that makes comparison between proposals easier. If they each determine on their own what problems they are solving, there will be as many solutions as there are perceptions of the problem. If vendors want to propose a system that is outside the scope of the RFP, they may do so—but at their own risk. The vendor knows that it is an exception and may not be considered in the final decision making.

*4. Set deadlines and enforce them.* It is up to the user to set the deadlines. The RFP should state when the proposal is expected. When equipment is ordered, there will be an expected delivery date. On-time performance is a key indicator of vendor worth. You should not take missed deadlines lightly and neither should the vendor. If there are extenuating circumstances, you may make an exception, but the exception should definitely be justified before it is granted.

*5. Provide the vendor with access to you and your people.* In order to respond to your RFP and also to serve you in many other ways, the vendor will need much of your time and that of your people. As detailed as the RFP is, it will not answer all the questions or cover all the points. Most organizations convene a vendor meeting about two weeks after sending out the RFPs. At this meeting all vendors have the opportunity to ask questions and all receive the same answers. Then, once a vendor is selected to provide all or part of an information system, that vendor's people will have to interact with those in your organization most closely related to the function being automated. This time must be freely given. The better information the vendor gets, the better the ultimate system is for your firm.

> ## "If vendors can come and go as they choose then, in a sense, they have control over you."

*6. Seek the vendor's advice.* We do not want to make the vendor into a villain. Used properly, a vendor can be of great value to your firm. Often vendor personnel have had wide experience in other firms in your industry or in firms which have had similar needs. And even if the vendor is new to your firm and industry, sometimes just the independent perspective of a newcomer can uncover ideas and solutions that might not otherwise occur to you. Also, the vendor may be able to arrange visits to firms that have successful systems or to put you in touch with people who have gone through similar development situations.

*7. Cooperate with vendors and establish mutual confidence.* The user/vendor relationship should not be an adversary one. Each needs the other and the objective of these rules is to ensure that each gets from the other what is rightly theirs. You can both succeed. Your success is the vendor's success. Once you have decided to go with a particular vendor, let that person know that he or she is the one you are relying on. Remove the anxiety of the competitive situation. Simply ask the individual to perform as he or she has proposed and make assurances that you will assist and support in any way you can.

*8. Reassure yourself of the vendor's experience and that of his or her staff.* Even before the proposal is accepted, you should review the vendor's qualifications as to technical competence and ability to perform as promised. If other support personnel are to be provided, interview the people involved before allowing interaction with your people. Make sure you have the right of refusal if you feel someone is not of the caliber promised. New computer installations often serve as training assignments for new hires. You should not be the training site for the vendor's people.

*9. Get things in writing.* This means that whatever takes place in a user/vendor relationship should be documented. Write letters to confirm phone conversations; write memos to the file when you make decisions or things happen for which a letter is not appropriate; keep a diary of meetings and other events. If you do this you will be unique, because most people do not write anything down. This will give you great

credibility when your word is challenged. It will also support your position in those inevitable conflicts when deadlines are missed, instructions are misunderstood, or other evidence of nonperformance becomes apparent.

*10. Meet the vendor's management.* At some time before you sign the final agreement, make sure that you have met someone else in the organization besides the salesperson. This should definitely include the salesperson's boss, but should perhaps also include the service manager and managers of any other support services you will receive. You might meet them individually or as a group but what you want to do is verify that the promises the salesperson made are committed to by management. The questions you should ask include who will provide service when the salesperson is unavailable, whom should you call late at night, and the like. If handled properly, such a session with management can be a boost for the salesperson, a chance to show off a new and supportive customer.

*11. Make sure you are aware of all the vendor's services.* All vendors offer more than just their main product. Many have free services which you find out about only if you ask. Some services have fees attached, but the cost may be more reasonable than if you tried to perform the service yourself, such as training new programmers.

*12. Do not allow or force the vendor to assume your responsibilities.* This is really what the other eleven rules are saying. It may appear that it is to your advantage to have the vendor write some programs for you. But when you find they are poorly documented, and you cannot easily make changes the following year, it may prove to have been a poor move. On the other hand, in many areas the vendor has superior knowledge and resources. Let the vendor do the education and use the vendor's people for system analysis and design.

Following these rules will be the best course for you and the vendor. The vendor wants you to have all the services and benefits you are entitled to. But the vendor also wants you to know when your requests are outside reasonable limits.

At best, users of new systems should be prepared to endure delays, cost overruns, and installation headaches. However, the user who is aware of the knowledge that must be available in order to select and install a system and has established a proper relationship with the vendor, will have gone a long way in reducing unrealistic expectations about the process and thus minimized the inevitable aggravations.□

## APPENDIX D: UNDERSTANDING DISTRIBUTED DATA PROCESSING

A primer on the advantages and disadvantages of centralized vs. decentralized computer power.

# Understanding distributed data processing

*What managers need to know to make the most of the coming developments in information processing*

*Jack R. Buchanan and Richard G. Linowes*

Declining hardware costs, increasing self-confidence of users, and developing technologies have provided compelling reasons in the minds of many managers to bring distributed data processing (DDP) into their organizations. Rather than let it spread almost randomly, managers who recognize the strengths as well as the pitfalls of DDP are seeking to establish coherent policies and procedures. The authors define DDP in terms of responsibilities for managing all phases of information processing. They also provide a framework companies can use to evaluate alternatives and to develop a DDP strategy that both matches their organizational structure and enables their business plan.

Mr. Buchanan is associate professor at the Harvard Business School, where he specializes in computer-based management systems. Formerly he was director of the federal court automation project (Courtran project) at the Federal Judicial Center in Washington, D.C. and on the faculty at Carnegie-Mellon University. Mr. Linowes is a doctoral candidate at Harvard Business School specializing in distributed data processing. He spent several years in U.S. and Japanese industry designing and installing computerized information systems.

The data processing profession has generated a new set of buzzwords that purportedly describe the next generation of information systems. A new development, referred to as "distributed data processing," or "DDP," will figure in major expansion plans both now and throughout the 1980s. Managers in many organizations are eager to bring some of this state-of-the-art technical capability into their own operations, for distributed data processing, as they see it, is an opportunity to distribute computing facilities and allow access to a machine in a way that was never possible before.

Is distributed data processing just a new technological fad or does it represent a new concept that will enable organizations to make more effective use of their data processing resources? If DDP entails the spread of computing around an organization, what are the hazards of such proliferation? Is there some systematic way for managers to plan and monitor the introduction of DDP into their organizations? In this, the first of two articles, we shall attempt to answer these questions by developing a framework that enables managers to understand DDP and to identify opportunities for its use.

DDP is a concept that has only recently come of age. Technological, economic, and educational developments now allow us to design information systems that may achieve the objectives of matching the organizational structure, supporting the business strategy, and, in general, providing a more natural use of information processing. In essence, DDP involves the exciting prospect of assigning responsibility for DP-related activities so that both business and technical knowledge can be applied more readily to the achievement of an organization's goals.

# Underlying developments

The move to distributed data processing is possible today in large part because of the drop in cost of computer hardware. Minicomputers and now microcomputers are becoming so inexpensive that it is quite reasonable for a company to buy three or four small computers to do the work previously performed by one central computer or to automate activities previously performed manually. Whereas, in the past, economies of scale may have driven a company to use one large data processing center to perform a wide variety of services, a company now might employ several different computers in different locations to provide more specialized services. Management can now arrange data processing facilities with much less concern for hardware costs.

Technical developments are also responsible for the recent practicality of distributed data processing. Major innovations, primarily from the areas of telecommunications and data base systems, have ushered in many new capabilities. Improvements in both equipment and software have made possible the building of very sophisticated computer networks, and direct links from computer to computer are becoming more common. Tasks that have been handled in large centers may now be partitioned into subtasks, and these in turn may be farmed out to remote sites.

When information systems are designed in this fashion, a whole network of computers often becomes involved in carrying out an operation. Such systems represent prototypes for the distributed data processing of the future; they show how technical developments, perhaps for the first time, permit the decentralization of many data processing activities.

The DP manager has traditionally been responsible for cost center management, capacity planning, systems administration, and adaptation of new technology. Since DDP will increase direct access to the system by the end user, the administrative process of the user must be reflected in system design, and information systems must focus on business tasks.

The DP manager will participate with end users in more joint enterprises and consequently will have to be more concerned with how the user defines productivity. Where computer operations are decentralized, the manager must establish charge-out methods that are understandable to the user and that measure service to the organization. For example, the DP manager should translate from kilocore seconds, computer resource units (CRUs), or other technical terms into measures such as number of transactions processed and reports produced so that both user and top management can make practical use of them. If a user group manager is to have any control over the computer resource, he or she must have this type of information as well as the means to effect change.

Finally, the exposure that most managers have to computerized information systems grows all the time, and their increasing familiarity with data processing leads them to make better use of the systems they have and to demand more from their systems. Thus many of these managers can be expected to set up some kind of data processing activities in their own departments and to become involved in delivering some of their own data processing services.

Declining hardware costs, improving communications and data base capabilities, and the growing data processing experience of users are prime factors behind our projection that distributed data processing, including the extensive use of data bases,[1] will be the hallmarks of the computer era.

# Common pitfalls

To take advantage of the power of DDP, managers need a clear conception of the complexities of using and managing the computer resource. Yet managers at all levels too often find themselves in difficulty because of their overly simplistic understanding of data processing, which they see chiefly as a collection of machines and technical issues; and oddly enough, DP managers sometimes are the worst culprits. This narrow view has led to a number of common fallacies.

One manufacturing manager recently pulled us aside to show us a new microcomputer hidden away in his office. He said proudly that it permitted him to do a few small applications unencumbered by the red tape and priority system of the corporate data center, where such applications officially should be done. He was delighted with the department's new toy, and he was eager to expand his operation and bring all his data processing activity in-house. "After all," he argued, "we already have one machine operating successfully. And there is a young engineer upstairs who took some computer courses in school, so we're all set."

In another company, a division general manager was perturbed at the high data processing charges

---

1. Richard L. Nolan, "Computer Data Bases: The Future Is Now," HBR September-October 1973, p. 98.

appearing in his monthly income statement, charges that supposedly reflected his actual use of the corporate data center. He felt particularly disgruntled when he stumbled onto an advertisement for a new minicomputer that seemed capable of performing all the processing his division required yet whose monthly fee was significantly less than the figure he was paying. At the next quarterly meeting he complained, "For what we are paying for the data center, we could have our own minicomputer system and control our own priorities."

In a highly diversified conglomerate that has grown by the acquisition of other companies, the corporate controller was concerned about the alarming increase in data processing expenditures by the divisions. He appointed a corporate systems planner to investigate the problem. The planner returned with a suggestion: take data processing away from the divisions and place it in regional centers under corporate direction. The plan was rejected out of hand by the controller, who knew that the design would be unacceptable to division managers in the company because they would not give up data processing to a corporate group. The corporate controller exclaimed, "I don't want to *manage* data processing, I just want to *control* it."

Finally, in the federal courts, administrators were planning how computers should be distributed around the country to provide computer support for various administrative functions of the courts. The design of the new system could take any form because there was no existing data processing activity with which to conform. The leadership and development of the project were centered in Washington, and systems analysis and implementation were carried out jointly with district and appellate court administrators. The study team was considering two possible arrangements of data processing facilities: local court minicomputers or regional centers.

Proponents of regional data centers argued that the configuration they favored would permit more responsive systems and more effective control by the courts. Those favoring local minicomputers, on the other hand, felt it was *their* configuration that offered these benefits, primarily because they saw that physical custody of the machines established effective control of the information processing resource: "How could a court have more control over its information processing at regional centers than it would within its own four walls?"

In all four of these examples, the managers' positions regarding use of computer systems appeared quite reasonable at the time. Only later did the problems or unrealistic features of their stands emerge. As we shall see, their arguments rested on the conventional image of data processing and its role in an organization, a view too limited for data processing planning in the 1980s.

## Acquiring a broad view

How can a manager avoid the pitfalls of the narrow view and systematically plan the placement of DP responsibilities? Primarily, he or she should recognize and work with two fundamental assumptions: (1) information systems should match a company's structure and strategy; and (2) activities that support information systems are wide ranging and separable. These basic notions are not only a good general way to understand the data processing resource, but they also allow us to construct a framework for describing and planning distributed data processing systems.

To most technicians, DDP simply means the spread of computer hardware and data to multiple sites around an organization. This definition is deficient, however, because it overlooks a wide range of activities that help make information systems work, and furthermore it neglects the linkage of information systems to strategy and structure. In effect, its technical orientation leaves general managers out of discussions about the design of DDP systems.

A broader definition acknowledges that data processing is an organizational resource consisting of many areas of activity, each of which may be executed or controlled by various individuals. These activities, or areas of responsibility, can be spread across an organization in a variety of ways, and a manager should carefully consider the appropriate degree of decentralization for each of them. Assignment of responsibilities by default seldom works.

To facilitate a systematic approach to organizing data processing, one should identify the areas of responsibility that may be operationally assigned in an organization. *Exhibit I* shows suggested areas of activity, grouped rather loosely into the major categories of control and execution, with execution further divided into development and operations. The content of each area may be intuitively clear. Given this division of responsibilities, the major challenges of DDP planning lie, then, in determining the extent to which each should be decentralized, in understanding the interdependencies among them, and in assuring that the appropriate degree of

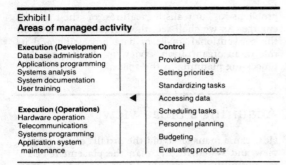

Exhibit I
**Areas of managed activity**

| Execution (Development) | Control |
|---|---|
| Data base administration | Providing security |
| Applications programming | Setting priorities |
| Systems analysis | Standardizing tasks |
| System documentation | Accessing data |
| User training | Scheduling tasks |
| **Execution (Operations)** | Personnel planning |
| Hardware operation | Budgeting |
| Telecommunications | Evaluating products |
| Systems programming | |
| Application system maintenance | |

authority and necessary level of competence coexist at the designated locations in the organization.

The areas of execution are the easily identifiable kinds of activities that are commonly associated with data processing. In most companies, technically trained persons, such as programmers, systems analysts, and computer operators, have responsibility for delivering the data processing product or service. The areas of control activity regulate the delivery of data processing in terms of dollars, people, time, quality assurance, and access to data, but they do not require a detailed level of technical knowledge of computers.

To describe the data processing in an organization as "distributed" is to say that authority over one or more of the areas of responsibility shown in *Exhibit I* has been vertically or horizontally decentralized; that is, authority may be delegated downward or assigned laterally. This definition is more inclusive than the definition commonly used. It can imply the spreading out not only of hardware and data but of the whole array of activities associated with managing information processing.

Before describing decentralization of activities within these areas in greater detail, we first consider the forces that shape the design of distributed information systems.

# Roots of decentralization

What causes an organization to decentralize? We have identified three general motivations that might lead a company to decentralize or distribute its data processing. These are the pressures for differentiation and the resulting needs for selective integration, the desire for direct control, and the wish to reallocate or lend support to authority. Heterogeneity or variability in task, function, or local situation leads

to a state of differentiation, which, according to Paul R. Lawrence and Jay W. Lorsch,[2] means that organizational units will differ in goals, time perspectives, interpersonal relationships, and structure. Such differentiation creates the need for various integrative devices. Information systems are common integrative tools which are often used to coordinate operations that span functions, products, divisions, and geographic locations.

Also, uncertainty about such aspects of centralized control as setting of priorities might motivate user group managers to seek control over all system services they see as critical to their operations. When volume permits suitable economies of scale, managers who feel sufficiently competent will have strong motivation to control and even to run their own data processing groups.

Finally, because power to make decisions tends to rest at the level where the necessary information is accumulated[3] and because information support is one of the necessary conditions for effective power,[4] managers can use distributed information systems strategically to bolster the authority of system users in the organization.

## Strategy, structure & information systems

Since Alfred D. Chandler's landmark book, *Strategy and Structure*, describing the history of America's first great corporations,[5] writers have noted how organizations alter their formal structure to facilitate achievement of goals. But the relationship between structure and business plan has many dimensions. The key to a good design for an organization is not only the match between strategy and structure but the more complex match involving strategy, structure, and other administrative systems. Today many of these administrative systems are embodied in computerized information systems, which assist management in controlling and coordinating most of the activities of modern, large-scale organizations —tying together the efforts of diverse departments that pursue different but complementary ends.

Yet computer applications in general have been so specialized that many organizations—the data processing profession along with them—have overlooked potential, and more general, roles for in-

2. Paul R. Lawrence and Jay W. Lorsch, *Organization and Environment*, Chapter 2 (Homewood, IL: Richard D. Irwin, 1967).

3. Ibid., Chapter 3.

4. Rosabeth Moss Kanter, "Power Failure in Management Circuits," HBR July-August 1979, p. 65.

5. Alfred D. Chandler, Jr., *Strategy and Structure* (Cambridge, MA: MIT Press, 1962).

Exhibit II
**Tendency toward distributing data processing in relation to product diversification and corporate structure**

Increasing tendency for data processing distribution

Rows (top to bottom): Unrelated products, Related products, Dominant products, Single product

Columns (left to right): Functional | Functional with vertical integration | Functional with geographic spread | Divisional with strong dependencies – transfer pricing – facility sharing – corporate coordination | Divisional with coordinated management control system – budget – performance at same location | Divisional with coordinated management control system and geographic spread | Holding company (completely autonomous "divisions")

formation systems. Information systems are not simply labor-saving devices that support the activities of people in one or more departments. Rather, they are control and coordination devices that should fit an organization's formal structure and facilitate achievement of its business goals.

Most information systems are designed to play such roles, and it is worthwhile to reexamine them in that light. Consider the following typical situations:

□ Production managers must maintain control over inventory levels to ensure that operations are not interrupted by sudden depletion of parts. They often establish this control by use of a computerized inventory control system, which, when coupled with formal procedures for requisitioning parts from storage, signals when inventory levels are low and in some cases even orders new parts automatically.

□ Managers must coordinate the activities of sales with production, so that when a large influx of

orders comes in from the field, production levels will rise to meet the demand. Managers often achieve such coordination by using an automated order entry system that processes sales orders in the field and then, to fill these orders, simultaneously updates the production schedule.

In the first case a computerized information system is used to *control* an important facet of operations, whereas in the second a system is used to *coordinate* different activities. In both cases the information systems fit the structural and strategic features of the organization.

In general, information systems can *support* the organizational structure by providing the information necessary to carry out the assigned responsibility. They can also *make* the structure more elaborate by providing project-based information in a functional organization or function-based information across divisions. Ideally, systems offer managers ac-

**Exhibit III**
**Responsibility spectra**

Increasing user responsibility ▶

**Hardware operation**

| | | | | |
|---|---|---|---|---|
| Prepare source documents | Manage data entry | Operate satellite processor without data base | Operate satellite processor with data base | Manage independent facility |

**Telecommunications**

| | | | | |
|---|---|---|---|---|
| Specify communications needs | Design network configuration | Specify interface protocols | Implement network | Maintain network |

**Systems programming**

| | | | |
|---|---|---|---|
| Use operating system, compilers, and utilities | Interface application programs to systems software | Maintain updates to systems software | Develop & modify systems software |

**Application systems maintenance**

| | | |
|---|---|---|
| Document system errors | Diagnose system errors | Correct system errors |

**Data base administration**

| | | | | | |
|---|---|---|---|---|---|
| Control source documents | Determine data requirements & conventions | Carry out logical data base design | Carry out physical data base design | Set & enforce conventions for data access | Manage all data bases |

**Application programming**

| | | | |
|---|---|---|---|
| Communicate needs to programmers | Participate on programming team | Supervise development | Select & develop system-building tools |

**Systems analysis**

| | | | | |
|---|---|---|---|---|
| Conduct preautomation analysis & procedure revisions | Define user data & functional specifications | Evaluate system relative to functional specifications | Participate in high-level system design | Carry out program-level system design |

**System documentation**

| | | | |
|---|---|---|---|
| Write functional specifications | Write user's manual | Write program design specifications | Write detailed description of all data structures & routine |

**User training**

Conduct preautomation interviews — Prepare user training materials — Conduct user training — Maintain adequate user competence

**Providing security**

Comply with security procedures — Devise security measures — Authorize security procedures — Manage security facilities

**Setting priorities**

Accept imposed priorities — Identify needs for system services — Rank alternatives — Authorize commitment of resources

**Standardizing tasks**

Carry out standards — Propose standards — Devise standards — Authorize standards — Enforce standards

**Accessing data**

Identify available data — Specify data needs — Authorize data collection & distribution privileges — Enforce data collection & distribution privileges

**Scheduling tasks**

Specify tasks — Determine feasibility of tasks — Sequence tasks — Allocate time to tasks — Approve schedule

**Personnel planning**

Determine system's impact on user staffing — Designate liaison staff for development & operation — Administer personnel assignments — Evaluate personnel performance

**Budgeting**

Specify needs in nonfinancial terms — Set upper bounds on system expenditures — Prepare detailed budget — Monitor complete budget

**Evaluating products**

Collect performance data — Define performance requirements — Monitor performance — Determine appropriate response cess to information that can help them fulfill their roles in the formal organizational structure.

What happens if the systems do not fit exactly? What occurs when the design of an information system no longer matches strategy and structure? Of even greater concern, how elastic is the fit of current systems to ever-changing organizations?

The elasticity of an information system may be explored by studying its ability to meet the reporting requirements placed on it. The typical evolution of a system might be: (1) at the outset, the new information system meets the needs of users; (2) changes occur in information requirements, and informal information channels develop as a result; (3) difficulties arise when analysts attempt to modify the system to match current needs—and the system thus becomes distorted, subverted, and inappropriately used, a situation marked by "information overkill"; and (4) eventually the system is replaced, with varying degrees of disruption.

Let us see how this evolution occurs in an example from an actual company that manufactures a variety of products in several plants. The central data processing department developed an information system for plant managers, and most users were happy with the reports they received. Later, top managers formulated a more comprehensive marketing strategy, creating new product lines that grouped products from different plants. Then they appointed new corporate-level product-line managers to monitor both the manufacture and the marketing of each product line.

The information needs of this new group of managers overlapped those of the plant managers to some extent, so they made minor changes in the plant managers' reports, using informal communication channels to meet their remaining needs. As time went on, unrelated additional products were added, so that the old information system became unsatisfactory even for the plant managers. Yet, ironically, nearly all managers clung to the system because they knew it so well and felt they had to have the same data they had always received. These people never stopped to realize that the system had become an encumbrance to rather than an enabler of the business strategy.

Information systems that do not fit the organization they were designed to serve are not uncommon. But with DDP, companies can organize their data processing support groups to better use the competence that exists and to better serve the formal structure. Systems so designed and operated will be less likely to suffer problems such as those just recounted.

Given the ideal that information systems should match an organization's strategy and structure, we can expect that companies with diversified interests and with greater autonomy among their operating units will find DDP particularly useful. DDP will offer them new opportunities for formal control and coordination.

The general influence of corporate structures [6] and product diversification [7] on decentralization of information systems is shown in *Exhibit II*. The exhibit suggests that the motivation to distribute computer resources will be felt most keenly in highly diversified conglomerates but will be less important to single-product companies that are organized according to function. Though other factors, of course, will be important in deciding how and when DDP is appropriate, *Exhibit II* reminds us that efficient information systems are inexorably linked to the strategy and structure of a company.

# Framework for analysis

To match information systems with the organization they serve, careful attention must go into planning the arrangement of the data processing resources that develop and operate information systems. All of the different activities appearing in *Exhibit I* are assigned to different groups in the organization, and it is useful to analyze systematically who has what responsibilities. We shall develop here a multidimensional framework that we can use to evaluate the way a company locates its data processing resources.

The purpose of such a framework, in general, is to divide the overall problem into interrelated subproblems so that each can be solved separately while it contributes to an overall solution. A framework may also be used to provide a system of measures by which to compare organizations or assess the impact of organizational change. The spectra in *Exhibit III* achieve both these ends.

For each of the areas listed in *Exhibit I*, we develop a spectrum of feasible positions, shown in *Exhibit III*, representing the variety of alternative arrange-

6. Richard P. Rumelt, *Strategy, Structure, and Economic Performance* (Boston: Division of Research, Harvard Business School, 1974), p. 33.

7. Leonard Wrigley, "Divisional Autonomy and Diversification," (Ph.D. diss., Harvard Business School, 1970).

8. Jack R. Buchanan, Rob Gerritsen, and David Root, "Automated Data Base Programming," to appear in *Communications of the Association for Computing Machinery*.

ments of activity ranging from complete centralization in a data processing unit to complete decentralization to user groups. Each spectrum shows an increasing and cumulative level of responsibility for the user group manager as the line is traversed from left to right. The ordering of the specific functions is normative, in that if a user participates in some way in a given function as described by a single point along a continuum, he or she will probably participate in all functions shown to the left along that continuum (though some mechanism may be employed to coordinate a shared responsibility). The functions to the right of a given user's position may be carried out by the company's data processing groups or be shared as well.

For example, if the user has technical people who perform data base administration activities up to and including the physical design of the data base, then, according to the fifth spectrum in *Exhibit III*, he or she is most likely responsible for logical data base design, the determination of data requirements and conventions, and the control of source documents. Similarly, the DP manager at some data center performs the remaining tasks, setting and enforcing conventions for data access based in part on the design and, in general, managing all data bases.

The spectra for controlling activities shown in *Exhibit III* are designed to be applicable to either operational or developmental activities under different interpretations. The dual interpretation of the control spectra is a useful feature of the framework. Using the same set of lines, we can analyze control of system development work and control of operations. In most situations, however, control of these two groups of activities is handled in such different manners that it makes sense to discuss them separately.

For example, "accessing data" as a developmental activity represents managements' desires and restrictions on the kinds of data that will be collected within a system. As an operational activity, it is a statement of policy defining authorized access to information within the organization.

The area of "providing security" addresses the engineering (during development) and enforcing (during operation) of mechanisms that prevent unauthorized access. Finally "tasks standardizing" is a control area whose purpose is to coordinate, without direct supervision, a control role that is relevant to all stages of the system's life cycle. It is usually a staff activity designed to magnify the efforts of the line managers and may apply to tasks ranging from defining the phases of system development, includ-

ing authorization protocols, to developing programming conventions.

One should recognize that management can control and coordinate activities not only by direct supervision but also by establishing comprehensive guidelines or standard operating procedures. The technical concerns of data base administrators, for example, are commonly controlled in this fashion. Their responsibilities can be either centralized in an individual or a group, decentralized but constrained by centrally designed standards,[8] or decentralized with virtual independence. In the future, the second approach, that is, decentralizing the data base administration activity while using centrally established standards, will probably become increasingly important. In this way, the DP manager can define comprehensive standards that can be enforced by top managers or a highly placed steering committee and that can be used in a decentralized organization to protect the data processing department from excessive control by the user.

Given this introduction to the spectra of data processing responsibilities, consider how the spectra can be applied to a typical application. *Exhibit IV* describes the inventory control system of a medium-sized manufacturing company that currently plays a critical role in production operations. The system is run at the corporate computer center located at headquarters, and the records are kept up to date via terminals located in the plants.

A team of programmers and analysts who came from both the user departments and the centralized systems development group originally developed the system. *Exhibit IV* shows how responsibilities for this system have been and are now distributed across the organization. Note that the control spectra appear twice, once for operations and once for development, because the nature and arrangement of control activities changed significantly when the inventory control system became operational.

In general, user group managers will select the level of responsibility they want for their information processing activities as they traverse the spectra from left to right. This decision is analogous to a company's decision about how far back from the market it wants to be vertically integrated. DP managers, in turn, will determine how much of each user's operation they want to be responsible for. The general manager must then arbitrate between the DP manager and the end user. The general manager must understand the issues well enough to allocate responsibility so as to best achieve the organization's objectives.

Exhibit IV
**Assigned responsibilities for a typical application: a manufacturing company's inventory control system**

## Execution (Operations)

**Hardware operation**
The user prepares source documents and manages data entry through terminals to DP center.

**Telecommunications**
The user specifies his volume and scheduling requirements for communications through his configuration of terminals.

**Systems programming**
The user only uses the DP center's operating system, compilers, and utilities.

**Application system maintenance**
The user both documents and assists in diagnosing system errors.

## Control (Operations)

**Providing security**
The user simply complies with security procedures.

**Setting priorities**
The user identifies his needs for system services.

**Standardizing tasks**
The user proposes operating procedures and performance standards.

**Accessing data**
The user authorizes data collection and report distribution.

**Scheduling tasks**
The user participates in sequencing the tasks.

**Personnel planning**
The user manages only his own data entry personnel.

**Budgeting**
The user controls his expenditures by limiting DP use.

**Evaluating products**
The user defines his performance requirements.

## Execution (Development)

**Data base administration**
The user determines his data requirements and develops a logical data base design.

**Applications programming**
The user assigns some internal personnel to participate in the programming team.

**Systems analysis**
The user is quite involved in most analysis work, including some program-level system design.

**System documentation**
The user develops his own manuals and shares in writing program design specifications.

**User training**
The user alone is responsible for all internal training activities.

## Control (Development)

**Providing security**
The user devises and authorizes security procedures.

**Setting priorities**
The user ranks alternative designs for his system.

**Standardizing tasks**
The user proposes standards and participates in an authorizing steering committee.

**Accessing data**
The user authorizes data collection and access privileges.

**Scheduling tasks**
The user participates in approving the schedule.

**Personnel planning**
The user jointly administers and evaluates all personnel.

**Budgeting**
The user jointly prepares and monitors the total budget.

**Evaluating products**
The user decides whether to use the system.

Distributed

Centralized

## How much decentralization?

The framework just described equips us to look inside our own organizations to see to what extent each area of data processing activity is decentralized. By examining the complete set of activities, we see that decentralization of some tasks—be they technical or managerial—is a common occurrence and that even classic types of information systems, such as inventory control applications run on centralized computers, are supported in part by a variety of decentralized, or user, activities. Thus we can say that even these classic information system applications represent a distribution of information processing responsibility.

As we have seen, DDP has implications that go beyond conventional approaches of applying computers to business. Although on the surface it appears to concern itself solely with the arrangement of computer hardware and data around an organization, at a deeper level it involves the management of a wide array of activities that go into the development and operation of computerized information systems.

Managers can organize these activities in many ways, and the choice they make should reflect the strategic and structural decisions they have made before. Thus, even if their information system design leaves hardware at some central site while assigning a few data processing tasks to users, their system is in some sense distributed.

According to this more general definition, nearly all computer applications are distributed. And, indeed, to ensure that information systems fit an organization, data processing *should* be distributed. Managers should concern themselves now with the question of how they can best distribute data processing for the information systems they require.

The next article in this series will provide tools for managers to help them in this undertaking. For now, however, let us summarize the implications this article has for the role of DDP in organizations:

☐ Data processing involves distinct types of technical activities and managerial or control activities. Managers can assign responsibility for these activities to different groups in the organization; usually they divide the responsibilities between a data processing manager and a user manager.

☐ Managers' assignment of data processing responsibilities should create a DP-support organization that can efficiently develop and operate information systems well suited to the organization. Assignment of data processing responsibilities thus may involve considerations more critical than those relating to cost alone.

☐ Organizations will face competing forces that push for and against decentralization. User groups may argue for more independence to design and operate their own systems, to escape what they see as the uncertainties posed by completely centralized operations, or to bolster their own power in the organization. Central data processing groups may counter with arguments for an arrangement that offers economies of scale, ensures a higher level of technical competence, and permits corporate managers closer scrutiny of data processing activities. Both arguments sound compelling.

☐ Although it is sometimes advantageous to assign control responsibility along with execution responsibility, separation of control activities from execution activities can in fact resolve the dilemma between competing forces. Controls may be distributed throughout an organization to provide checks and balances on activities performed by other groups, to share responsibility between cooperating units, or to assure that the behavior of various units is consistent with organizational objectives and guidelines.

The pitfalls described earlier came about because decision makers were unaware of these crucial considerations. They had only a limited understanding of data processing and so were unprepared to grapple with the problems inherent in the expanded role of computers in their organizations. Managers should seek to understand distributed data processing because, now that it has come of age, they have much to gain by using it to improve the inner workings of their organizations.▽

# Author Index

# Subject Index